TABLE OF CONTENTS

CHAPTER 1

CHARACTERS

A LITTLE HISTORY

Kingdom Hearts 358/2 Days is the fourth installment of the blockbuster video game series co-created by Disney and Square-Enix. Although the main protagonist of the series is Sora, *358/2 Days* follows the story of Roxas, Sora's double or "Nobody." Roxas slowly comes to grips with his inexplicable existence and life in Organization XIII during the days Sora is asleep, trying to recover his lost memories. Although this is the fourth game, the events take place after *Kingdom Hearts*, during *Chain of Memories and Reverse/Rebirth*, and prior to what occurs in *Kingdom Hearts II*.

Being the fourth *Kingdom Hearts* game, there's a lot to catch up on! This chapter attempts to introduce new and veteran players to the story thus far, as well as all the characters appearing in the game.

KINGDOM HEARTS

On the night his island home is besieged by a mysterious storm, Sora is separated from his two closest friends, Riku and Kairi. The storm scatters the three to different and unknown worlds.

Sora is whisked away to a world called Traverse Town. There he meets Court Wizard Donald and Captain Goofy from Disney Castle. Donald and Goofy are surprised to learn that Sora can wield the Keyblade, a mysterious weapon they thought only King Mickey could use. They set off to look for the missing King Mickey and Sora joins them to search for his lost friends Riku and Kairi.

The three are told of ominous creatures known as the Heartless—beings without hearts derived from an unknown dimension. It is said that they are the ones responsible for the storm that separated Sora from his friends. The Heartless are drawn to Sora's Keyblade, which is the only weapon capable of destroying them and sealing worlds against their spread.

The Disney villains, enticed by the power of darkness, manipulated the Heartless to help them gather the Princesses of Heart, who are needed to open the door to darkness. Unknown to anyone, Kairi is one of the princesses.

On the heels of this revelation, Sora learned that his friend Riku embraced darkness, thinking it would give him the power to save Kairi. Instead, the mysterious Ansem possessed Riku. Ansem revealed that Kairi's heart had been trapped inside Sora all along. Wielding a Dark Keyblade, the possessed Riku attacked Sora. The two battled over Kairi's heart and Sora won.

To save Kairi, Sora turned the Dark Keyblade weapon on himself and removed his own heart, freeing hers as well. The process transformed him into a Heartless—also creating his Nobody, Roxas. Revived, Kairi used her heart to restore Sora to human form.

Pursuing Ansem to a wasteland called "End of the World," Sora, Donald, and Goofy confronted and defeated him. The villain believed darkness to be the true strength of the heart. He sought Kingdom Hearts, the power source of all hearts. Believing he would find ultimate darkness there, he opened the door to find that Kingdom Hearts was not really darkness, but light. The light consumed Ansem.

Beyond the open door, Sora and friends found Riku and the King at last. But to save all worlds, Sora had to use his Keyblade to close the door to darkness, even though Riku and the King were on the other side.

Believing the King's parting words—that there will always be a door to the light—Sora locked the door. Then he, Donald, and Goofy set out on a new journey.

KINGDOM HEARTS CHAIN OF MEMORIES

Sora, Donald, and Goofy traveled down a long road that meandered through endless fields, eventually coming to a crossroads. As Sora stood in the crossroads, he gazed up at the night sky and thought of his lost friends.

Just then, a mysterious man approached. "Ahead lies something you need," he says, "but to claim it, you must lose something dear." The man vanished, reshaping the crossroads into a single path leading to a castle that eerily resembled a girl's drawing...

Within that place, called Castle Oblivion, Sora, Donald, and Goofy searched for clues to their friends' whereabouts. But as they journeyed deeper inside, bit by bit the three began to lose their memories. Eventually they met Naminé, a mysterious girl who somehow existed in all of Sora's memories.

Naminé was a young witch capable of rearranging the links in someone's chain of memories. She was following orders from the mysterious Organization XIII, whose goal was to capture Sora. However, a shift in loyalty among the Organization XIII members led Axel to betray his comrades.

Organization member Marluxia, the lord of Castle Oblivion, along with Larxene intended to use Sora to overthrow the rest of the Organization. After Sora defeated Larxene, Naminé apologized for her actions. She promised that if Sora, Donald, and Goofy reached the thirteenth floor of Castle Oblivion, she would restore their memories.

Although they barely remembered each other anymore, Sora, Donald, and Goofy fought together and defeated Marluxia. Naminé met them on the thirteenth floor and explained that they would need to sleep for almost a year to restore their memories. However, they wouldn't remember her, nor the events at Castle Oblivion. Promising he would always remember Naminé, Sora stepped into the memory chamber...

Meanwhile, Riku awoke in light and heard a voice offering him a choice. He decided to leave the light and found himself inside Castle Oblivion. There, the voice told him that his heart was empty save for darkness. Riku decided to shed darkness and destroy all those who embrace it.

But this was not as easy as he thought. Riku encountered Ansem, who had taken possession of Riku before. Ansem tried to force Riku to succumb to darkness when King Mickey intervened. Leaving, Ansem granted Riku the ability to call upon darkness at will.

Continuing to ascend from the basement of Castle Oblivion, Riku encountered Lexaeus, Vexen, and Zexion of Organization XIII. Riku assumed they served Ansem, but Vexen explained that the person Riku thought was Ansem was not really Ansem.

When later King Mickey gave him a card that took him to Twilight Town, Riku encountered the figure of Ansem once again. However, the person revealed his true form and called himself DiZ. This mysterious man admitted that he'd been guiding Riku all along, to help him face his darkness. He recommended that Riku meet with Naminé.

Naminé explained the choice Sora made to recover his memories. Rather than follow Sora's example, Riku chose to face Ansem and the darkness within. Entering the world of darkness with the help of King Mickey and DiZ, Riku defeated Ansem. Reuniting with King Mickey afterward, the two donned the robes of Organization XIII members and set out for the crossroads...

KINGDOM HEARTS 358/2 DAYS

*In **Kingdom Hearts**, Sora turned the Keyblade on himself to release Kairi's heart, but his heart was also released in the process. This brought about the creation of Roxas, Sora's Nobody.*

Unlike most Nobodies, Roxas has no memories of his past as a real person. He joins Organization XIII and slowly begins to discover the truth behind his existence and the Organization itself. Days later, several members head off to Castle Oblivion...

He meets and befriends the fourteenth member of the Organization, who also has no recollection of her past. What will Roxas see during his time in the Organization? What is the connection between him, Sora, and the fourteenth member? And what's to become of them?

ORGANIZATION XIII

The members of Organization XIII are all Nobodies, created when the students of Ansem the Wise—ruler of Hollow Bastion in Radiant Garden—removed their own hearts. Since then additional members have joined by unknown means. Each derived their Organization names by rearranging the letters of their old name and adding an "X." The group now resides in The Castle That Never Was. The members disguise their identities by wearing dark cloaks with hoods. They seek to reclaim their hearts and become whole again. Until then, they have no emotions, although they sometimes pretend as much.

Each member bears a rank in the form of a Roman numeral assigned in the order in which they joined. The rank does not determine who is in charge. For example, although Xemnas is number I and the leader, Saïx is number VII and second-in-command. All Organization XIII members can summon dark corridors that allow them to fold space and travel between worlds. Roxas and Xion are the newest members. Unlike the others, it seems as though they may experience emotions.

ROXAS

XIII

Weapon: Keyblade

A boy created from Sora, newly aware. Awakened by Xemnas, the leader of Organization XIII, he joins the group to learn about himself. He uses the Keyblade to perform a broad variety of missions and further their shadowy agenda. His light shines as bright and brief as the setting sun.

CHARACTER STATS

LEVEL	MAX HP	STRENGTH	MAGIC POWER	DEFENSE POWER	CRITICAL %	CRIT. BONUS
1	62	9	34	7	5	6
2	65	10	35	8	5	7
3	68	11	36	9	5	7
4	71	11	39	11	5	7
5	74	12	40	12	5	7
6	77	13	42	14	5	8
7	80	14	44	15	5	8
8	83	14	46	16	5	8
9	86	15	47	18	5	8
10	89	16	50	19	5	9
11	92	17	51	20	5	9
12	95	17	53	22	5	9
13	98	18	54	23	5	9
14	101	19	57	24	5	10
15	104	20	58	26	5	10
16	107	20	60	27	5	10
17	110	21	62	28	5	10
18	113	22	64	30	5	11
19	116	23	65	31	5	11
20	119	23	68	32	5	11
21	122	24	69	34	5	11
22	125	25	71	35	5	12
23	128	26	72	36	5	12
24	131	26	75	38	5	12
25	134	27	76	39	5	12
26	137	28	78	41	5	13
27	140	29	80	42	5	13
28	143	29	82	43	5	13
29	146	30	83	45	5	13
30	149	31	86	46	5	14
31	152	32	87	47	5	14
32	155	32	89	49	5	14
33	158	33	90	50	5	14
34	161	34	93	51	5	15
35	164	35	94	53	5	15
36	167	35	96	54	5	15
37	170	36	98	55	5	15
38	173	37	100	57	5	16
39	176	38	101	58	5	16
40	179	38	104	59	5	16
41	182	39	105	61	5	16
42	185	40	107	62	5	17
43	188	41	108	63	5	17
44	191	41	111	65	5	17
45	194	42	112	66	5	17
46	197	43	114	68	5	18
47	200	44	116	69	5	18
48	203	44	118	70	5	18
49	206	45	119	72	5	18
50	209	46	122	73	5	19
51	212	47	123	74	5	19
52	215	47	125	76	5	19
53	218	48	126	77	5	19
54	221	49	129	78	5	20
55	224	50	130	80	5	20
56	227	50	132	81	5	20
57	230	51	134	82	5	20
58	233	52	136	84	5	21
59	236	53	137	85	5	21
60	239	53	140	86	5	21
61	242	54	141	88	5	21
62	245	55	143	89	5	22
63	248	56	144	90	5	22
64	251	56	147	92	5	22
65	254	57	148	93	5	22
66	257	58	150	95	5	23
67	260	59	152	96	5	23
68	263	59	154	97	5	23
69	266	60	155	99	5	23
70	269	61	158	100	5	24
71	272	62	159	101	5	24
72	275	62	161	103	5	24
73	278	63	162	104	5	24
74	281	64	165	105	5	25
75	284	65	166	107	5	25
76	287	65	168	108	5	25
77	290	66	170	109	5	25
78	293	67	172	111	5	26
79	296	68	173	112	5	26
80	299	68	176	113	5	26
81	302	69	177	115	5	26
82	305	70	179	116	5	27
83	308	71	180	117	5	27
84	311	71	183	119	5	27
85	314	72	184	120	5	27
86	317	73	186	122	5	28
87	320	74	188	123	5	28
88	323	74	190	124	5	28
89	326	75	191	126	5	28
90	329	76	194	127	5	29
91	332	77	195	128	5	29
92	335	77	197	130	5	29
93	338	78	198	131	5	29
94	341	79	201	132	5	30
95	344	80	202	134	5	30
96	347	80	204	135	5	30
97	350	81	206	136	5	30
98	353	82	208	138	5	31
99	356	83	209	139	5	31
100	359	83	212	140	5	31

** Numbers in grey indicate when that number cannot go any higher than the previous number.*

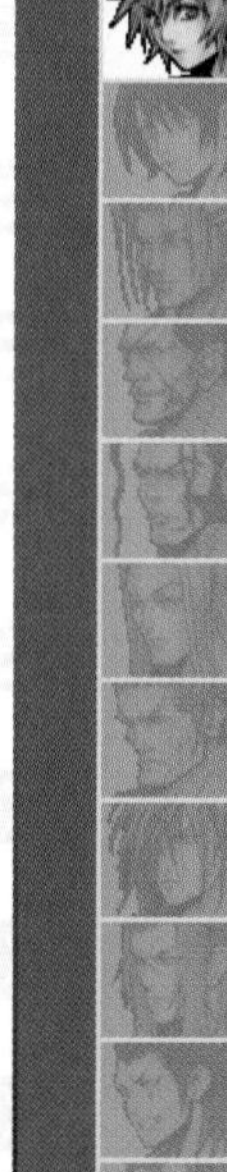

WEAPON LIST & STATS

Weapon	Gear Panel	Strength Add	Strength Unit	Magic Add	Magic Unit	Defense Add	Defense Unit	Crit. % Add	Crit. % Unit	Crit. Bonus Add	Crit. Bonus Unit
Kingdom Key	NA (No Panel)	15	—	0	—	0	—	0	—	2	—
Missing Ache	Skill Gear	20	—	0	—	0	—	3	—	2	—
Missing Ache+	Skill Gear+②	22	+1	0	+1	0	+1	4	+1	2	+1
Ominous Blight	Technical Gear③	45	+1	0	+1	0	+1	6	+2	3	+1
Ominous Blight+	Technical Gear+③	50	+1	0	+1	0	+1	8	+2	4	+1
Abaddon Plasma	Duel Gear④	71	+1	0	+1	0	+1	12	+2	8	+1
Abaddon Plasma+	Duel Gear+④	76	+1	0	+1	0	+1	9	+2	6	+1
Abaddon Plasma++	Duel Gear++⑤	62	+1	0	+1	0	+1	12	+5	7	+0
Pain of Solitude	Loaded Gear	24	—	12	—	0	—	2	—	3	—
Pain of Solitude+	Loaded Gear+②	55	+1	15	+1	0	+1	2	+1	5	+1
Sign of Innocence	Chrono Gear③	60	+1	18	+2	0	+1	4	+1	4	+1
Sign of Innocence+	Chrono Gear+③	62	+1	25	+2	0	+1	4	+1	6	+1
Crown of Guilt	Phantom Gear④	67	+1	29	+1	0	+2	6	+1	6	+1
Crown of Guilt+	Phantom Gear+④	73	+1	36	+1	0	+2	6	+1	9	+1
Crown of Guilt++	Phantom Gear++⑤	76	+1	39	+5	0	+1	8	+1	11	+1
Abyssal Tide	Lift Gear③	55	+1	0	+1	0	+1	4	+1	4	+2
Abyssal Tide+	Lift Gear+③	60	+1	0	+1	0	+1	4	+1	3	+2
Leviathan	Nimble Gear④	54	+1	0	+1	0	+1	6	+1	4	+2
Leviathan+	Nimble Gear+④	70	+1	0	+1	0	+1	6	+1	4	+2
True Light's Flight	Wild Gear③	55	+1	0	+1	4	+2	2	+1	3	+1
True Light's Flight+	Wild Gear+③	65	+1	0	+1	4	+2	2	+1	4	+1
Rejection of Fate	Ominous Gear④	52	+1	0	+1	6	+2	3	+1	6	+1
Rejection of Fate+	Ominous Gear+④	70	+1	0	+1	6	+2	3	+1	5	+1
Midnight Roar	Valor Gear②	70	+1	0	+1	1	+1	2	+1	5	+1
Midnight Roar+	Valor Gear+②	75	+1	0	+1	1	+1	0	+1	6	+1
Glimpse of Darkness	Fearless Gear③	70	+2	0	+1	2	+1	4	+1	6	+1
Glimpse of Darkness+	Fearless Gear+③	78	+2	0	+1	2	+1	0	+1	6	+1
Total Eclipse	Prestige Gear④	65	+2	0	+1	3	+1	0	+1	10	+1
Total Eclipse+	Prestige Gear+④	70	+2	0	+1	3	+1	6	+1	11	+1
Silent Dirge	Crisis Gear⑤	64	+3	23	+3	4	+1	8	+1	9	+1
Silent Dirge+	Crisis Gear+⑤	70	+3	28	+3	4	+1	0	+1	10	+1
Lunar Eclipse	Omega Gear⑥	100	+3	31	+3	5	+1	0	+1	14	+1
Lunar Eclipse+	Omega Gear+⑥	110	+3	34	+3	5	+1	10	+1	15	+1
Darker Than Dark	Hazard Gear⑤	75	+1	37	+3	8	+3	4	+1	10	+1
Darker Than Dark+	Hazard Gear+⑤	100	+1	45	+3	8	+3	4	+1	12	+1
Astral Blast	Rage Gear⑤	88	+1	0	+1	0	+1	10	+3	8	+3
Astral Blast+	Rage Gear+⑤	93	+1	0	+1	0	+1	10	+3	9	+3
Maverick Flare	Champion Gear⑤	80	+3	0	+1	2	+1	12	+3	11	+1
Maverick Flare+	Champion Gear+⑤	100	+3	0	+1	2	+1	16	+3	11	+1
Twilight Blaze	Ultimate Gear⑥	120	+3	0	+1	3	+1	20	+3	14	+1
Twilight Blaze+	Ultimate Gear+⑥	125	+3	0	+1	3	+1	15	+3	16	+1
Omega Weapon	Pandora's Gear⑤	90	+5	30	+5	0	+5	10	+5	11	+5
Omega Weapon+	Pandora's Gear+⑤	95	+1	34	+1	0	+1	10	+1	12	+1
Kingdom Key+	Zero Gear⑤	124	+4	30	+4	0	+4	10	+4	19	+4
Oathkeeper	Zero Gear⑤	100	+4	30	+4	0	+4	10	+4	13	+4
Two Become One	Zero Gear⑤	110	+4	30	+4	0	+4	10	+4	24	+4
Oathkeeper/ Oblivion	Zero Gear⑤	108	+4	34	+4	3	+4	15	+4	16	+4
Umbrella	Casual Gear②	40	+1	0	+1	0	+1	0	+1	4	+1
Aubade	Mystery Gear③	80	+1	0	+1	0	+1	4	+5	9	+5

WEAPON ABILITIES

Weapon	Abilities gained with units: 1 Unit	2 Units	3 Units	Act. Spd.	Atk. Move Land	Atk. Move Air	Combo Land	Combo Air
Kingdom Key	—	—	—	1.0	1.0	1.0	3	3
Missing Ache	—	—	—	1.2	1.13	1.0	4	2
Missing Ache+	Combo Boost	—	—	1.2	1.13	1.0	5	2
Ominous Blight	Combo Boost	Combo-Jump	—	1.2	1.19	1.0	7	2
Ominous Blight+	Chain Power	Chain Time	—	1.2	1.19	1.0	7	2
Abaddon Plasma	Chain Power	Chain Time	Heart Bonus	1.3	1.13	1.0	6	2
Abaddon Plasma+	Combo Boost	Combo-Jump	Critical Boost	1.3	1.13	1.0	6	2
Abaddon Plasma++	Combo Boost	Combo-Jump	Critical Boost	1.3	1.13	1.0	8	2
Pain of Solitude	—	—	—	1.0	1.0	1.0	3	2
Pain of Solitude+	Fire Finish	—	—	1.0	1.0	1.0	3	2
Sign of Innocence	Thunder Finish	Magic Bracer	—	1.0	1.0	1.0	3	2
Sign of Innocence+	Blizzard Finish	Magic Bracer	—	1.0	1.0	1.0	3	2
Crown of Guilt	Fire Finish	Magic Bracer	Magic Finale	1.0	1.0	1.0	4	3
Crown of Guilt+	Thunder Finish	Magic Bracer	Magic Finale	1.0	1.0	1.0	4	3
Crown of Guilt++	Magic Bracer	Magic Finale	Magical Strike	1.0	1.0	1.0	4	3
Abyssal Tide	Combo Boost	Combo-Jump	—	1.0	1.0	1.13	4	3
Abyssal Tide+	Chain Power	Combo-Jump	—	1.0	1.0	1.13	4	3
Leviathan	Chain Power	Combo-Jump	Combo-Air Slide	1.0	1.0	1.19	4	5
Leviathan+	Combo Boost	Combo-Jump	Combo-Air Slide	1.0	1.0	1.19	4	5
True Light's Flight	Offensive Block	Defender	—	1.0	1.0	1.0	3	3
True Light's Flight+	Offensive Block	Defender	—	1.0	1.0	1.0	3	3
Rejection of Fate	Offensive Block	Defender	Second Chance	1.0	1.13	1.0	6	3
Rejection of Fate+	Offensive Block	Defender	Damage Control	1.0	1.13	1.0	5	3
Midnight Roar	Defender	—	—	1.0	1.0	1.0	3	2
Midnight Roar+	Striker	—	—	1.0	1.0	1.0	3	2
Glimpse of Darkness	Defender	Striker	—	1.0	1.0	1.0	4	2
Glimpse of Darkness+	Defender	Striker	—	1.0	1.0	1.0	4	2
Total Eclipse	Defender	Striker	Combo-Block	1.0	1.0	1.0	3	3
Total Eclipse+	Defender	Striker	Brick Wall	1.0	1.0	1.0	3	3
Silent Dirge	Defender	Combo-Block	Brick Wall	1.0	1.0	1.0	5	3
Silent Dirge+	Striker	Combo-Block	Brick Wall	1.0	1.0	1.0	5	3
Lunar Eclipse	Striker	Grand Slam	Damage Control	1.0	1.0	1.0	5	3
Lunar Eclipse+	Magic Bracer	Brick Wall	Vitality Barrier	1.0	1.0	1.0	5	3
Darker Than Dark	Magic Bracer	Vitality Barrier	Damage Control	1.0	1.18	1.0	4	3
Darker Than Dark+	Fire Finish	Thunder Finish	Blizzard Finish	1.0	1.18	1.0	4	3
Astral Blast	Chain Power	Combo-Jump	Combo-Air Slide	1.0	1.25	1.25	6	4
Astral Blast+	Combo Boost	Combo-Jump	Combo-Air Slide	1.0	1.25	1.25	6	4
Maverick Flare	Combo Boost	Combo-Jump	Critical Boost	1.0	1.0	1.0	5	2
Maverick Flare+	Chain Power	Chain Time	Heart Bonus	1.0	1.0	1.0	5	2
Twilight Blaze	Combo-Jump	Combo-Block	Critical Boost	1.0	1.13	1.0	5	2
Twilight Blaze+	Combo Boost	Chain Power	Chain Time	1.0	1.13	1.0	5	2
Omega Weapon	Vitality Surge	Vitality Barrier	Alive 'n' Kicking	1.2	1.19	1.19	4	4
Omega Weapon+	Vitality Surge	Vitality Barrier	Alive 'n' Kicking	1.1	1.19	1.19	4	4
Kingdom Key+	Defender	Damage Control	Second Chance	1.3	1.19	1.19	4	2
Oathkeeper	Defender	—	—	1.0	1.19	1.19	5	2
Two Become One	Defender	Damage Control	—	1.2	1.19	1.19	5	2
Oathkeeper/ Oblivion	Defender	Damage Control	Second Chance	1.0	1.13	1.13	7	5
Umbrella	Offensive Block	—	—	1.3	1.0	1.0	3	2
Aubade	Striker	Grand Slam	—	1.4	1.19	1.0	4	3

XION

XIV

Weapon: Keyblade

The fourteenth member of Organization XIII. As a fellow Keyblade wielder, she soon grows close to Roxas and (through him) Axel, forming a friendly trio. After the events of one fateful mission, she begins to question the very nature of her existence.

Unlocking Xion:

Reach Story Mode Day 117.

CHARACTER STATS

LEVEL	MAX HP	STRENGTH	MAGIC POWER	DEFENSE POWER	CRITICAL %	CRIT. BONUS
1	62	9	34	7	5	6
2	65	10	35	8	5	7
3	68	11	36	9	5	7
4	71	11	39	11	5	7
5	74	12	40	12	5	7
6	77	13	42	14	5	8
7	80	14	44	15	5	8
8	83	14	46	16	5	8
9	86	15	47	18	5	8
10	89	16	50	19	5	9
11	92	17	51	20	5	9
12	95	17	53	22	5	9
13	98	18	54	23	5	9
14	101	19	57	24	5	10
15	104	20	58	26	5	10
16	107	20	60	27	5	10
17	110	21	62	28	5	10
18	113	22	64	30	5	11
19	116	23	65	31	5	11
20	119	23	68	32	5	11
21	122	24	69	34	5	11
22	125	25	71	35	5	12
23	128	26	72	36	5	12
24	131	26	75	38	5	12
25	134	27	76	39	5	12
26	137	28	78	41	5	13
27	140	29	80	42	5	13
28	143	29	82	43	5	13
29	146	30	83	45	5	13
30	149	31	86	46	5	14
31	152	32	87	47	5	14
32	155	32	89	49	5	14
33	158	33	90	50	5	14
34	161	34	93	51	5	15
35	164	35	94	53	5	15
36	167	35	96	54	5	15
37	170	36	98	55	5	15
38	173	37	100	57	5	16
39	176	38	101	58	5	16
40	179	38	104	59	5	16
41	182	39	105	61	5	16
42	185	40	107	62	5	17
43	188	41	108	63	5	17
44	191	41	111	65	5	17
45	194	42	112	66	5	17
46	197	43	114	68	5	18
47	200	44	116	69	5	18
48	203	44	118	70	5	18
49	206	45	119	72	5	18
50	209	46	122	73	5	19
51	212	47	123	74	5	19
52	215	47	125	76	5	19
53	218	48	126	77	5	19
54	221	49	129	78	5	20
55	224	50	130	80	5	20
56	227	50	132	81	5	20
57	230	51	134	82	5	20
58	233	52	136	84	5	21
59	236	53	137	85	5	21
60	239	53	140	86	5	21
61	242	54	141	88	5	21
62	245	55	143	89	5	22
63	248	56	144	90	5	22
64	251	56	147	92	5	22
65	254	57	148	93	5	22
66	257	58	150	95	5	23
67	260	59	152	96	5	23
68	263	59	154	97	5	23
69	266	60	155	99	5	23
70	269	61	158	100	5	24
71	272	62	159	101	5	24
72	275	62	161	103	5	24
73	278	63	162	104	5	24
74	281	64	165	105	5	25
75	284	65	166	107	5	25
76	287	65	168	108	5	25
77	290	66	170	109	5	25
78	293	67	172	111	5	26
79	296	68	173	112	5	26
80	299	68	176	113	5	26
81	302	69	177	115	5	26
82	305	70	179	116	5	27
83	308	71	180	117	5	27
84	311	71	183	119	5	27
85	314	72	184	120	5	27
86	317	73	186	122	5	28
87	320	74	188	123	5	28
88	323	74	190	124	5	28
89	326	75	191	126	5	28
90	329	76	194	127	5	29
91	332	77	195	128	5	29
92	335	77	197	130	5	29
93	338	78	198	131	5	29
94	341	79	201	132	5	30
95	344	80	202	134	5	30
96	347	80	204	135	5	30
97	350	81	206	136	5	30
98	353	82	208	138	5	31
99	356	83	209	139	5	31
100	359	83	212	140	5	31

** Numbers in grey indicate when that number cannot go any higher than the previous number.*

WEAPON LIST & STATS

Weapon	Gear Panel	Strength Add	Strength Unit	Magic Add	Magic Unit	Defense Add	Defense Unit	Crit. % Add	Crit. % Unit	Crit. Bonus Add	Crit. Bonus Unit
Kingdom Key	NA (No Panel)	15	—	0	—	0	—	0	—	2	—
Missing Ache	Skill Gear	20	—	0	—	0	—	3	—	2	—
Missing Ache+	Skill Gear+②	22	+1	0	+1	0	+1	4	+1	2	+1
Ominous Blight	Technical Gear③	45	+1	0	+1	0	+1	6	+2	3	+1
Ominous Blight+	Technical Gear+ ③	50	+1	0	+1	0	+1	8	+2	4	+1
Abaddon Plasma	Duel Gear④	71	+1	0	+1	0	+1	12	+2	8	+1
Abaddon Plasma+	Duel Gear+④	76	+1	0	+1	0	+1	9	+2	6	+1
Abaddon Plasma++	Duel Gear++⑤	62	+1	0	+1	0	+1	12	+5	7	+0
Pain of Solitude	Loaded Gear	24	—	12	—	0	—	2	—	3	—
Pain of Solitude+	Loaded Gear+②	55	+1	15	+1	0	+1	2	+1	5	+1
Sign of Innocence	Chrono Gear③	60	+1	18	+2	0	+1	4	+1	4	+1
Sign of Innocence+	Chrono Gear+③	62	+1	25	+2	0	+1	4	+1	6	+1
Crown of Guilt	Phantom Gear④	67	+1	29	+1	0	+2	6	+1	6	+1
Crown of Guilt+	Phantom Gear+④	73	+1	36	+1	0	+2	6	+1	9	+1
Crown of Guilt++	Phantom Gear++⑤	76	+1	39	+5	0	+1	8	+1	11	+1
Abyssal Tide	Lift Gear③	55	+1	0	+1	0	+1	4	+1	4	+2
Abyssal Tide+	Lift Gear+③	60	+1	0	+1	0	+1	4	+1	3	+2
Leviathan	Nimble Gear④	54	+1	0	+1	0	+1	6	+1	4	+2
Leviathan+	Nimble Gear+④	70	+1	0	+1	0	+1	6	+1	4	+2
True Light's Flight	Wild Gear③	55	+1	0	+1	4	+2	2	+1	3	+1
True Light's Flight+	Wild Gear+③	65	+1	0	+1	4	+2	2	+1	4	+1
Rejection of Fate	Ominous Gear④	52	+1	0	+1	6	+2	3	+1	6	+1
Rejection of Fate+	Ominous Gear+④	70	+1	0	+1	6	+2	3	+1	5	+1
Midnight Roar	Valor Gear②	70	+1	0	+1	1	+1	2	+1	5	+1
Midnight Roar+	Valor Gear+②	75	+1	0	+1	1	+1	0	+1	6	+1
Glimpse of Darkness	Fearless Gear③	70	+2	0	+1	2	+1	4	+1	6	+1
Glimpse of Darkness+	Fearless Gear+③	78	+2	0	+1	2	+1	0	+1	6	+1
Total Eclipse	Prestige Gear④	65	+2	0	+1	3	+1	0	+1	10	+1
Total Eclipse+	Prestige Gear+④	70	+2	0	+1	3	+1	6	+1	11	+1
Silent Dirge	Crisis Gear⑤	64	+3	23	+3	4	+1	8	+1	9	+1
Silent Dirge+	Crisis Gear+⑤	70	+3	28	+3	4	+1	0	+1	10	+1
Lunar Eclipse	Omega Gear⑥	100	+3	31	+3	5	+1	0	+1	14	+1
Lunar Eclipse+	Omega Gear+⑥	110	+3	34	+3	5	+1	10	+1	15	+1
Darker Than Dark	Hazard Gear⑤	75	+1	37	+3	8	+3	4	+1	10	+1
Darker Than Dark+	Hazard Gear+⑤	100	+1	45	+3	8	+3	4	+1	12	+1
Astral Blast	Rage Gear⑤	88	+1	0	+1	0	+1	10	+3	8	+3
Astral Blast+	Rage Gear+⑤	93	+1	0	+1	0	+1	10	+3	9	+3
Maverick Flare	Champion Gear⑤	80	+3	0	+1	2	+1	12	+3	11	+1
Maverick Flare+	Champion Gear+⑤	100	+3	0	+1	2	+1	16	+3	11	+1
Twilight Blaze	Ultimate Gear⑥	120	+3	0	+1	3	+1	20	+3	14	+1
Twilight Blaze+	Ultimate Gear+⑥	125	+3	0	+1	3	+1	15	+3	16	+1
Omega Weapon	Pandora's Gear⑤	90	+5	30	+5	0	+5	10	+5	11	+5
Omega Weapon+	Pandora's Gear+⑤	95	+1	34	+1	0	+1	10	+1	12	+1
Kingdom Key+	Zero Gear⑤	124	+4	30	+4	0	+4	10	+4	19	+4
Oathkeeper	Zero Gear⑤	100	+4	30	+4	0	+4	10	+4	13	+4
Two Become One	Zero Gear⑤	110	+4	30	+4	0	+4	10	+4	24	+4
Umbrella	Casual Gear②	40	+1	0	+1	0	+1	0	+1	4	+1
Aubade	Mystery Gear③	80	+1	0	+1	0	+1	4	+5	9	+5

WEAPON ABILITIES

Weapon	Abilities gained with units: 1 Unit	2 Units	3 Units	Act. Spd.	Attack Move: Land	Attack Move: Air	Combo: Land	Combo: Air
Kingdom Key	—	—	—	1.0	1.0	1.0	3	3
Missing Ache	—	—	—	1.2	1.13	1.0	4	2
Missing Ache+	Combo Boost	—	—	1.2	1.13	1.0	5	2
Ominous Blight	Combo Boost	Combo-Jump	—	1.2	1.19	1.0	7	2
Ominous Blight+	Chain Power	Chain Time	—	1.2	1.19	1.0	7	2
Abaddon Plasma	Chain Power	Chain Time	Heart Bonus	1.3	1.13	1.0	6	2
Abaddon Plasma+	Combo Boost	Combo-Jump	Critical Boost	1.3	1.13	1.0	6	2
Abaddon Plasma++	Combo Boost	Combo-Jump	Critical Boost	1.3	1.13	1.0	8	2
Pain of Solitude	—	—	—	1.0	1.0	1.0	3	2
Pain of Solitude+	Fire Finish	—	—	1.0	1.0	1.0	3	2
Sign of Innocence	Thunder Finish	Magic Bracer	—	1.0	1.0	1.0	3	2
Sign of Innocence+	Blizzard Finish	Magic Bracer	—	1.0	1.0	1.0	3	2
Crown of Guilt	Fire Finish	Magic Bracer	Magic Finale	1.0	1.0	1.0	4	3
Crown of Guilt+	Thunder Finish	Magic Bracer	Magic Finale	1.0	1.0	1.0	4	3
Crown of Guilt++	Magic Bracer	Magic Finale	Magical Strike	1.0	1.0	1.0	4	3
Abyssal Tide	Combo Boost	Combo-Jump	—	1.0	1.0	1.13	4	3
Abyssal Tide+	Chain Power	Combo-Jump	—	1.0	1.0	1.13	4	3
Leviathan	Chain Power	Combo-Jump	Combo-Air Slide	1.0	1.0	1.19	4	5
Leviathan+	Combo Boost	Combo-Jump	Combo-Air Slide	1.0	1.0	1.19	4	5
True Light's Flight	Offensive Block	Defender	—	1.0	1.0	1.0	3	3
True Light's Flight+	Offensive Block	Defender	—	1.0	1.0	1.0	3	3
Rejection of Fate	Offensive Block	Defender	Second Chance	1.0	1.13	1.0	6	3
Rejection of Fate+	Offensive Block	Defender	Damage Control	1.0	1.13	1.0	5	3
Midnight Roar	Defender	—	—	1.0	1.0	1.0	3	2
Midnight Roar+	Striker	—	—	1.0	1.0	1.0	3	2
Glimpse of Darkness	Defender	Striker	—	1.0	1.0	1.0	4	2
Glimpse of Darkness+	Defender	Striker	—	1.0	1.0	1.0	4	2
Total Eclipse	Defender	Striker	Combo-Block	1.0	1.0	1.0	3	3
Total Eclipse+	Defender	Striker	Brick Wall	1.0	1.0	1.0	3	3
Silent Dirge	Defender	Combo-Block	Brick Wall	1.0	1.0	1.0	5	3
Silent Dirge+	Striker	Combo-Block	Brick Wall	1.0	1.0	1.0	5	3
Lunar Eclipse	Striker	Grand Slam	Damage Control	1.0	1.0	1.0	5	3
Lunar Eclipse+	Magic Bracer	Brick Wall	Vitality Barrier	1.0	1.0	1.0	5	3
Darker Than Dark	Magic Bracer	Vitality Barrier	Damage Control	1.0	1.18	1.0	4	3
Darker Than Dark+	Fire Finish	Thunder Finish	Blizzard Finish	1.0	1.18	1.0	4	3
Astral Blast	Chain Power	Combo-Jump	Combo-Air Slide	1.0	1.25	1.25	6	4
Astral Blast+	Combo Boost	Combo-Jump	Combo-Air Slide	1.0	1.25	1.25	6	4
Maverick Flare	Combo Boost	Combo-Jump	Critical Boost	1.0	1.0	1.0	5	2
Maverick Flare+	Chain Power	Chain Time	Heart Bonus	1.0	1.0	1.0	5	2
Twilight Blaze	Combo-Jump	Combo-Block	Critical Boost	1.0	1.13	1.0	5	2
Twilight Blaze+	Combo Boost	Chain Power	Chain Time	1.0	1.13	1.0	5	2
Omega Weapon	Vitality Surge	Vitality Barrier	Alive 'n' Kicking	1.2	1.19	1.19	4	4
Omega Weapon+	Vitality Surge	Vitality Barrier	Alive 'n' Kicking	1.1	1.19	1.19	4	4
Kingdom Key+	Defender	Damage Control	Second Chance	1.3	1.19	1.19	4	2
Oathkeeper	Defender	—	—	1.0	1.19	1.19	5	2
Two Become One	Defender	Damage Control	—	1.2	1.19	1.19	5	2
Umbrella	Offensive Block	—	—	1.3	1.0	1.0	3	2
Aubade	Striker	Grand Slam	—	1.4	1.19	1.0	4	3

XEMNAS

I

Weapon: Ethereal Blades

Organization XIII's leader. Through power over nothing, he seeks power over everything.

LEVEL	MAX HP	STRENGTH	MAGIC POWER	DEFENSE POWER	CRITICAL %	CRIT. BONUS
1	62	10	38	6	3	6
2	65	10	43	8	3	7
3	68	11	43	9	3	7
4	71	13	45	10	3	7
5	74	13	48	11	3	7
6	77	14	49	13	3	8
7	80	15	51	14	3	8
8	83	16	53	15	3	8
9	86	17	54	17	3	8
10	89	17	56	18	3	9
11	92	18	59	19	3	9
12	95	19	60	20	3	9
13	98	19	63	22	3	9
14	101	21	65	23	3	10
15	104	22	66	24	3	10
16	107	22	68	26	3	10
17	110	23	71	27	3	10
18	113	24	71	28	3	11
19	116	24	74	29	3	11
20	119	26	75	31	3	11
21	122	27	78	32	3	11
22	125	27	80	33	3	12
23	128	28	81	35	3	12
24	131	29	83	36	3	12
25	134	29	86	37	3	12
26	137	31	87	38	3	13
27	140	32	90	40	3	13
28	143	32	92	41	3	13
29	146	33	93	42	3	13
30	149	33	95	44	3	14
31	152	34	98	45	3	14
32	155	36	99	46	3	14
33	158	36	101	47	3	14
34	161	37	104	49	3	15
35	164	38	105	50	3	15
36	167	39	107	51	3	15
37	170	39	110	53	3	15
38	173	41	111	54	3	16
39	176	41	113	55	3	16
40	179	42	114	56	3	16
41	182	43	117	58	3	16
42	185	44	119	59	3	17
43	188	44	120	60	3	17
44	191	46	123	62	3	17
45	194	46	125	63	3	17
46	197	47	126	64	3	18
47	200	48	129	65	3	18
48	203	49	131	67	3	18
49	206	50	132	68	3	18
50	209	50	135	69	3	19
51	212	51	137	71	3	19
52	215	52	138	72	3	19
53	218	52	141	73	3	19
54	221	54	143	74	3	20
55	224	55	144	76	3	20
56	227	55	147	77	3	20
57	230	56	149	78	3	20
58	233	57	150	80	3	21
59	236	57	153	81	3	21
60	239	59	154	82	3	21
61	242	60	156	83	3	21
62	245	60	159	85	3	22
63	248	61	160	86	3	22
64	251	62	162	87	3	22
65	254	62	165	89	3	22
66	257	64	166	90	3	23
67	260	65	168	91	3	23
68	263	65	171	92	3	23
69	266	66	172	94	3	23
70	269	66	174	95	3	24
71	272	67	177	96	3	24
72	275	69	178	98	3	24
73	278	69	180	99	3	24
74	281	70	183	100	3	25
75	284	71	184	101	3	25
76	287	72	186	103	3	25
77	290	72	189	104	3	25
78	293	74	190	105	3	26
79	296	74	192	107	3	26
80	299	75	193	108	3	26
81	302	76	196	109	3	26
82	305	77	198	110	3	27
83	308	77	199	112	3	27
84	311	79	202	113	3	27
85	314	79	204	114	3	27
86	317	80	205	116	3	28
87	320	81	208	117	3	28
88	323	82	210	118	3	28
89	326	83	211	119	3	28
90	329	83	214	121	3	29
91	332	84	216	122	3	29
92	335	85	217	123	3	29
93	338	85	220	125	3	29
94	341	87	222	126	3	30
95	344	88	223	127	3	30
96	347	88	226	128	3	30
97	350	89	228	130	3	30
98	353	90	229	131	3	31
99	356	90	232	132	3	31
100	359	92	233	134	3	31

** Numbers in grey indicate when that number cannot go any higher than the previous number.*

WEAPON LIST & STATS

Weapon	Gear Panel	Strength Add	Strength Unit	Magic Add	Magic Unit	Defense Add	Defense Unit	Crit. % Add	Crit. % Unit	Crit. Bonus Add	Crit. Bonus Unit
Malice	NA (No Panel)	15	—	0	—	0	—	0	—	2	—
Sanction	Skill Gear	20	—	0	—	0	—	2	—	2	—
Sanction+	Skill Gear+②	22	+1	0	+1	0	+1	2	+1	2	+1
Overlord	Technical Gear③	40	+1	0	+1	0	+1	4	+1	3	+2
Overlord+	Technical Gear+ ③	50	+1	0	+1	0	+1	4	+1	4	+2
Veneration	Duel Gear④	40	+1	0	+1	0	+1	6	+1	6	+2
Veneration+	Duel Gear+④	50	+1	0	+1	0	+1	8	+1	7	+2
Veneration++	Duel Gear++⑤	76	+1	0	+1	0	+1	6	+0	8	+5
Autocracy	Loaded Gear	24	—	12	—	0	—	2	—	3	—
Autocracy+	Loaded Gear+②	32	+1	15	+1	0	+1	2	+1	5	+1
Conquest	Chrono Gear③	50	+1	18	+2	0	+1	4	+1	4	+1
Conquest+	Chrono Gear+③	65	+1	25	+2	0	+1	4	+1	6	+1
Terminus	Phantom Gear④	60	+1	29	+2	0	+1	8	+1	11	+1
Terminus+	Phantom Gear+④	70	+1	36	+2	0	+1	6	+1	6	+1
Terminus++	Phantom Gear++⑤	80	+1	39	+5	0	+1	6	+1	9	+1
Judgement	Lift Gear③	48	+1	0	+1	0	+1	6	+2	4	+1
Judgement+	Lift Gear+③	30	+1	0	+1	0	+1	8	+2	3	+1
Discipline	Nimble Gear④	70	+1	0	+1	0	+1	9	+2	4	+1
Discipline+	Nimble Gear+④	54	+1	0	+1	0	+1	12	+2	4	+1
Aristocracy	Wild Gear③	48	+1	0	+1	4	+2	2	+1	3	+1
Aristocracy+	Wild Gear+③	30	+1	0	+1	4	+2	2	+1	4	+1
Superiority	Ominous Gear④	65	+1	0	+1	6	+2	3	+1	5	+1
Superiority+	Ominous Gear+④	68	+1	0	+1	6	+2	3	+1	6	+1
Aggression	Valor Gear②	44	+1	0	+1	1	+1	2	+1	5	+1
Aggression+	Valor Gear+②	46	+1	0	+1	1	+1	0	+1	6	+1
Fury	Fearless Gear③	52	+2	0	+1	2	+1	4	+1	6	+1
Fury+	Fearless Gear+③	57	+2	0	+1	2	+1	0	+1	6	+1
Despair	Prestige Gear④	70	+2	0	+1	3	+1	0	+1	10	+1
Despair+	Prestige Gear+④	80	+2	0	+1	3	+1	6	+1	11	+1
Triumph	Crisis Gear⑤	55	+1	31	+3	8	+3	4	+1	8	+1
Triumph+	Crisis Gear+⑤	62	+1	37	+3	8	+3	4	+1	9	+1
Ruination	Omega Gear⑥	73	+1	41	+3	0	+3	10	+1	13	+1
Ruination+	Omega Gear+⑥	103	+1	45	+3	0	+3	10	+1	12	+1
Domination	Hazard Gear⑤	97	+3	28	+3	4	+1	0	+1	14	+1
Domination+	Hazard Gear+⑤	109	+3	34	+3	4	+1	8	+1	11	+1
Annihilation	Rage Gear⑤	95	+3	0	+1	2	+1	16	+3	10	+1
Annihilation+	Rage Gear+⑤	105	+3	0	+1	2	+1	12	+3	10	+1
Tyrant	Champion Gear⑤	67	+1	0	+1	0	+1	10	+3	9	+3
Tyrant+	Champion Gear+⑤	80	+1	0	+1	0	+1	10	+3	9	+3
Magnificence	Ultimate Gear⑥	90	+1	0	+1	0	+1	10	+3	13	+3
Magnificence+	Ultimate Gear+⑥	94	+1	0	+1	0	+1	10	+3	12	+3
Infinity	Pandora's Gear⑤	92	+5	30	+5	0	+5	10	+5	11	+5
Infinity+	Pandora's Gear+⑤	125	+1	34	+1	0	+1	10	+1	12	+1
Interdiction	Zero Gear⑤	124	+4	30	+4	0	+4	10	+4	19	+4
Round Fan	Casual Gear②	36	+1	0	+1	0	+1	0	+1	4	+1
Absolute	Mystery Gear③	90	+1	0	+1	0	+1	0	+1	9	+1

WEAPON ABILITIES

Weapon	Abilities gained with units: 1 Unit	2 Units	3 Units	Act. Spd.	Attack Move: Land	Attack Move: Air	Combo: Land	Combo: Air
Malice	—	—	—	1.0	1.0	1.0	3	3
Sanction	—	—	—	1.0	1.0	1.0	3	3
Sanction+	Combo Boost	—	—	1.0	1.0	1.0	3	3
Overlord	Combo Boost	Chain Time	—	1.0	1.0	1.0	2	3
Overlord+	Chain Power	Chain Time	—	1.0	1.0	1.0	2	3
Veneration	Chain Power	Chain Time	Combo-Air Slide	1.0	1.0	1.0	2	4
Veneration+	Combo Boost	Chain Time	Combo-Air Slide	1.0	1.0	1.0	2	4
Veneration++	Combo Boost	Chain Power	Combo-Air Slide	1.0	1.0	1.0	3	4
Autocracy	—	—	—	1.0	1.0	1.0	3	1
Autocracy+	Magic Bracer	—	—	1.0	1.0	1.0	3	1
Conquest	Magic Bracer	Fire Finish	—	1.0	1.0	1.0	3	2
Conquest+	Blizzard Finish	Thunder Finish	—	1.0	1.0	1.0	3	2
Terminus	Magic Bracer	Aero Finish	Magic Finale	1.0	1.0	1.0	3	2
Terminus+	Magic Bracer	Blizzard Finish	Magic Finale	1.0	1.0	1.0	3	2
Terminus++	Magic Bracer	Magic Finale	Magical Strike	1.0	1.0	1.0	4	2
Judgement	Combo Boost	Chain Time	—	1.0	1.0	1.0	4	3
Judgement+	Chain Power	Chain Time	—	1.0	1.0	1.0	6	3
Discipline	Chain Power	Chain Time	Heart Bonus	1.1	1.0	1.0	4	3
Discipline+	Combo Boost	Chain Time	Heart Bonus	1.1	1.0	1.0	6	3
Aristocracy	Offensive Block	Chain Power	—	1.0	1.0	1.0	4	3
Aristocracy+	Offensive Block	Chain Time	—	1.0	1.0	1.0	6	3
Superiority	Offensive Block	Chain Power	Combo-Block	1.0	1.0	1.0	4	3
Superiority+	Offensive Block	Chain Time	Combo-Block	1.0	1.0	1.0	6	3
Aggression	Striker	—	—	1.0	1.0	1.0	2	2
Aggression+	Defender	—	—	1.0	1.0	1.0	2	2
Fury	Striker	Grand Slam	—	1.0	1.0	1.0	3	2
Fury+	Defender	Second Chance	—	1.0	1.0	1.0	3	2
Despair	Defender	Second Chance	Vitality Barrier	1.0	1.0	1.0	3	2
Despair+	Striker	Grand Slam	Vitality Surge	1.0	1.0	1.0	3	2
Triumph	Offensive Block	Fire Finish	Blizzard Finish	1.0	1.0	1.0	6	3
Triumph+	Offensive Block	Thunder Finish	Aero Finish	1.0	1.0	1.0	6	3
Ruination	Offensive Block	Blizzard Finish	Combo-Block	1.0	1.0	1.0	6	3
Ruination+	Offensive Block	Aero Finish	Combo-Block	1.0	1.0	1.0	6	3
Domination	Magic Bracer	Fire Finish	Blizzard Finish	1.0	1.0	1.0	3	2
Domination+	Magic Bracer	Thunder Finish	Aero Finish	1.0	1.0	1.0	3	2
Annihilation	Striker	Grand Slam	Critical Boost	1.1	1.0	1.0	6	3
Annihilation+	Combo Boost	Chain Power	Vitality Surge	1.1	1.0	1.0	6	3
Tyrant	Combo Boost	Combo-Jump	Combo-Air Slide	1.0	1.19	1.19	4	3
Tyrant+	Chain Power	Combo-Jump	Combo-Air Slide	1.0	1.19	1.19	4	3
Magnificence	Chain Time	Heart Bonus	Combo-Air Slide	1.2	1.25	1.25	4	3
Magnificence+	Chain Power	Chain Time	Combo-Jump	1.2	1.25	1.25	4	3
Infinity	Magic Finale	Grand Slam	Second Chance	1.2	1.13	1.13	3	3
Infinity+	Magic Finale	Grand Slam	Second Chance	1.1	1.13	1.13	3	3
Interdiction	Magic Bracer	Magic Finale	Combo-Air Slide	1.0	1.13	1.13	3	3
Round Fan	Aero Finish	—	—	1.0	1.0	1.0	3	3
Absolute	Aero Finish	Combo-Air Slide	—	1.1	1.0	1.0	3	3

XIGBAR

II

Weapon: Arrowguns

Founding member. He keeps an ear to the ground and a finger on the trigger. Manipulates space.

CHARACTER STATS

LEVEL	MAX HP	STRENGTH	MAGIC POWER	DEFENSE POWER	CRITICAL %	CRIT. BONUS
1	60	8	25	7	1	6
2	63	8	27	8	1	6
3	66	10	32	9	1	6
4	69	10	32	11	1	6
5	72	10	34	12	1	6
6	75	12	36	13	1	6
7	78	12	38	15	1	7
8	81	12	38	16	1	7
9	84	14	42	17	1	7
10	87	14	42	18	1	7
11	90	14	44	20	1	7
12	93	16	46	21	1	7
13	96	16	48	22	1	7
14	99	16	48	24	1	8
15	101	17	51	25	1	8
16	104	18	52	26	1	8
17	107	18	53	27	1	8
18	110	20	56	29	1	8
19	113	20	57	30	1	8
20	116	20	60	31	1	9
21	119	21	61	33	1	9
22	122	22	62	34	1	9
23	125	23	65	35	1	9
24	128	24	66	36	1	9
25	131	24	67	38	1	9
26	134	25	69	39	1	10
27	137	25	71	40	1	10
28	140	26	71	42	1	10
29	142	27	74	43	1	10
30	145	28	75	44	1	10
31	148	28	76	45	1	10
32	151	29	79	47	1	11
33	154	29	80	48	1	11
34	157	30	81	49	1	11
35	160	31	84	51	1	11
36	163	32	85	52	1	11
37	166	32	86	53	1	11
38	169	33	89	54	1	11
39	172	33	90	56	1	12
40	175	34	92	57	1	12
41	178	35	93	58	1	12
42	181	35	94	60	1	12
43	183	37	97	61	1	12
44	186	37	98	62	1	12
45	189	37	99	63	1	13
46	192	39	102	65	1	13
47	195	39	103	66	1	13
48	198	39	104	67	1	13
49	201	41	107	69	1	13
50	204	41	108	70	1	13
51	207	41	109	71	1	14
52	210	43	111	72	1	14
53	213	43	113	74	1	14
54	216	43	114	75	1	14
55	219	44	116	76	1	14
56	222	45	117	78	1	14
57	225	45	119	79	1	15
58	227	47	121	80	1	15
59	230	47	122	81	1	15
60	233	47	125	83	1	15
61	236	48	126	84	1	15
62	239	49	127	85	1	15
63	242	50	130	87	1	15
64	245	51	131	88	1	16
65	248	51	132	89	1	16
66	251	52	134	90	1	16
67	254	52	136	92	1	16
68	257	53	137	93	1	16
69	260	54	139	94	1	16
70	263	55	140	96	1	17
71	266	55	141	97	1	17
72	268	56	144	98	1	17
73	271	56	145	99	1	17
74	274	57	146	101	1	17
75	277	58	149	102	1	17
76	280	59	150	103	1	18
77	283	59	151	105	1	18
78	286	60	153	106	1	18
79	289	60	155	107	1	18
80	292	61	157	108	1	18
81	295	62	158	110	1	18
82	298	62	159	111	1	19
83	301	64	162	112	1	19
84	304	64	163	114	1	19
85	307	64	164	115	1	19
86	309	66	167	116	1	19
87	312	66	168	117	1	19
88	315	66	169	119	1	19
89	318	68	172	120	1	20
90	321	68	173	121	1	20
91	324	68	174	123	1	20
92	327	70	176	124	1	20
93	330	70	178	125	1	20
94	333	70	179	127	1	20
95	336	71	181	128	1	21
96	339	72	182	129	1	21
97	342	72	183	130	1	21
98	345	74	186	132	1	21
99	348	74	187	133	1	21
100	351	74	190	134	1	21

** Numbers in grey indicate when that number cannot go any higher than the previous number.*

WEAPON LIST & STATS

Weapon	Gear Panel	Strength		Magic		Defense		Crit. %		Crit. Bonus	
		Add	Unit	Add	Unit	Add	Unit	Add	Unit	Add	Unit
Stand-Alone	NA (No Panel)	15	—	0	—	0	—	0	—	2	—
Killer Bee	Skill Gear	20	—	0	—	0	—	3	—	2	—
Killer Bee+	Skill Gear+②	22	+1	0	+1	0	+1	4	+1	2	+1
Stingray	Technical Gear③	40	+1	0	+1	0	+1	6	+2	3	+1
Stingray+	Technical Gear+ ③	50	+1	0	+1	0	+1	8	+2	4	+1
Counterweight	Duel Gear④	40	+1	0	+1	0	+1	9	+2	6	+1
Counterweight+	Duel Gear+④	50	+1	0	+1	0	+1	12	+2	7	+1
Counterweight++	Duel Gear++⑤	76	+1	0	+1	0	+1	12	+5	8	+0
Precision	Loaded Gear	30	—	0	—	0	—	2	—	4	—
Precision+	Loaded Gear+②	35	+1	0	+1	0	+1	2	+1	5	+1
Dual Head	Chrono Gear③	57	+1	0	+1	4	+2	2	+1	7	+1
Dual Head+	Chrono Gear+③	60	+1	0	+1	4	+2	2	+1	5	+1
Bahamut	Phantom Gear④	90	+1	0	+1	6	+2	3	+1	10	+1
Bahamut+	Phantom Gear+④	65	+1	0	+1	0	+2	8	+1	13	+1
Bahamut++	Phantom Gear++⑤	80	+1	0	+1	6	+5	3	+1	7	+1
Gullwing	Lift Gear③	22	+1	0	+1	0	+1	4	+1	3	+2
Gullwing+	Lift Gear+③	48	+1	0	+1	0	+1	4	+1	4	+2
Blue Frame	Nimble Gear④	54	+1	0	+1	0	+1	6	+1	4	+2
Blue Frame+	Nimble Gear+④	70	+1	0	+1	0	+1	6	+1	4	+2
Star Shell	Wild Gear③	25	+1	14	+2	0	+1	4	+1	3	+1
Star Shell+	Wild Gear+③	40	+1	28	+2	0	+1	4	+1	3	+1
Sunrise	Ominous Gear④	55	+1	29	+2	0	+1	6	+1	4	+1
Sunrise+	Ominous Gear+④	71	+1	37	+2	0	+1	6	+1	5	+1

Weapon	Gear Panel	Strength		Magic		Defense		Crit. %		Crit. Bonus	
		Add	Unit	Add	Unit	Add	Unit	Add	Unit	Add	Unit
Ignition	Valor Gear②	44	+1	0	+1	1	+1	2	+1	5	+1
Ignition+	Valor Gear+②	46	+1	0	+1	1	+1	0	+1	6	+1
Armstrong	Fearless Gear③	45	+2	0	+1	2	+1	0	+1	6	+1
Armstrong+	Fearless Gear+③	50	+2	0	+1	2	+1	4	+1	6	+1
Hard-Boiled Heat	Prestige Gear④	69	+2	0	+1	3	+1	0	+1	10	+1
Hard-Boiled Heat+	Prestige Gear+④	90	+2	0	+1	3	+1	6	+1	11	+1
Diablo Eye	Crisis Gear⑤	66	+3	0	+1	2	+3	12	+1	9	+1
Diablo Eye+	Crisis Gear+⑤	73	+3	0	+1	2	+3	16	+1	11	+1
Double Tap	Omega Gear⑥	87	+3	0	+1	3	+1	15	+3	16	+1
Double Tap+	Omega Gear+⑥	125	+3	0	+1	3	+1	20	+3	14	+1
Stardust	Hazard Gear⑤	84	+1	37	+3	0	+1	8	+1	12	+3
Stardust+	Hazard Gear+⑤	96	+1	45	+3	0	+1	8	+1	10	+3
Energy Muzzle	Rage Gear⑤	95	+3	0	+1	0	+3	8	+1	10	+1
Energy Muzzle+	Rage Gear+⑤	105	+3	0	+1	0	+3	8	+1	10	+1
Crime & Punishment	Champion Gear⑤	64	+1	0	+1	0	+3	8	+1	9	+3
Crime & Punishment+	Champion Gear+⑤	67	+1	0	+1	0	+3	10	+1	9	+3
Cupid's Arrow	Ultimate Gear⑥	94	+1	0	+1	0	+3	10	+3	12	+1
Cupid's Arrow+	Ultimate Gear+⑥	90	+1	0	+1	0	+3	10	+3	13	+1
Final Weapon	Pandora's Gear⑤	92	+5	30	+5	0	+5	10	+5	11	+5
Final Weapon+	Pandora's Gear+⑤	125	+1	34	+1	0	+1	10	+1	12	+1
Sharpshooter	Zero Gear⑤	124	+4	30	+4	0	+4	10	+4	19	+4
Dryer	Casual Gear②	36	+1	0	+1	0	+1	0	+1	4	+1
Trumpet	Mystery Gear③	90	+1	0	+1	0	+1	0	+1	9	+1

WEAPON ABILITIES

Weapon	Abilities gained with units			Act. Spd.	Atk. Move		Combo		Am
	1 Unit	2 Units	3 Units		Land	Air	Land	Air	
Stand-Alone	—	—	—	1.0	1.0	1.0	3	2	12
Killer Bee	—	—	—	1.0	1.0	1.0	5	2	16
Killer Bee+	Combo Boost	—	—	1.0	1.0	1.0	5	2	16
Stingray	Combo Boost	Combo-Jump	—	1.0	1.0	1.0	2	2	36
Stingray+	Chain Power	Chain Time	—	1.0	1.0	1.0	2	2	36
Counterweight	Chain Power	Chain Time	Heart Bonus	1.0	1.0	1.0	2	2	36
Counterweight+	Combo Boost	Combo-Jump	Critical Boost	1.0	1.0	1.0	2	2	36
Counterweight++	Combo Boost	Combo-Jump	Critical Boost	1.0	1.0	1.0	2	2	48
Precision	—	—	—	1.0	1.0	1.0	3	2	16
Precision+	Defender	—	—	1.0	1.0	1.0	3	2	16
Dual Head	Defender	Combo-Block	—	1.0	1.0	1.0	3	2	9
Dual Head+	Vitality Barrier	Combo-Block	—	1.0	1.0	1.0	3	3	12
Bahamut	Defender	Combo-Block	Damage Control	1.0	1.0	1.0	3	2	9
Bahamut+	Vitality Barrier	Combo-Block	Second Chance	1.0	1.0	1.0	3	3	12
Bahamut++	Chain Power	Chain Time	Heart Bonus	1.0	1.0	1.0	3	3	24
Gullwing	Chain Power	Combo-Jump	—	1.0	1.0	1.0	2	2	24
Gullwing+	Combo Boost	Combo-Jump	—	1.0	1.0	1.0	2	2	24
Blue Frame	Chain Power	Combo-Jump	Combo-Air Slide	1.0	1.0	1.0	3	2	24
Blue Frame+	Combo Boost	Combo-Jump	Combo-Air Slide	1.0	1.0	1.0	3	2	24
Star Shell	Magic Bracer	Thunder Finish	—	1.0	1.0	1.0	2	3	12
Star Shell+	Magic Bracer	Fire Finish	—	1.0	1.0	1.0	2	3	12
Sunrise	Magic Bracer	Blizzard Finish	Magic Finale	1.0	1.0	1.0	2	3	12
Sunrise+	Magic Bracer	Aero Finish	Magic Finale	1.0	1.0	1.0	2	3	12
Ignition	Striker	—	—	1.0	1.0	1.0	3	2	16

Weapon	Abilities gained with units			Act. Spd.	Atk. Move		Combo		Am
	1 Unit	2 Units	3 Units		Land	Air	Land	Air	
Ignition+	Striker	—	—	1.0	1.0	1.0	3	2	16
Armstrong	Striker	Grand Slam	—	1.0	1.0	1.0	1	1	3
Armstrong+	Striker	Grand Slam	—	1.0	1.0	1.0	1	1	3
Hard-Boiled Heat	Striker	Grand Slam	Vitality Surge	1.0	1.0	1.0	3	1	12
Hard-Boiled Heat+	Striker	Grand Slam	Vitality Surge	1.0	1.0	1.0	3	1	12
Diablo Eye	Combo Boost	Grand Slam	Critical Boost	1.0	1.0	1.0	2	2	36
Diablo Eye+	Vitality Surge	Chain Time	Heart Bonus	1.0	1.0	1.0	2	2	36
Double Tap	Vitality Surge	Chain Time	Heart Bonus	1.0	1.0	1.0	2	2	36
Double Tap+	Striker	Grand Slam	Damage Control	1.0	1.0	1.0	2	2	36
Stardust	Aero Finish	Combo-Jump	Combo-Air Slide	1.0	1.0	1.0	3	2	24
Stardust+	Aero Finish	Combo Boost	Chain Power	1.0	1.0	1.0	3	2	24
Energy Muzzle	Vitality Surge	Vitality Barrier	Combo-Block	1.0	1.0	1.0	3	1	24
Energy Muzzle+	Defender	Striker	Damage Control	1.0	1.0	1.0	3	1	24
Crime & Punishment	Defender	Combo-Jump	Combo-Air Slide	1.0	1.0	1.0	3	2	12
Crime & Punishment+	Vitality Barrier	Combo-Jump	Combo-Air Slide	1.0	1.0	1.0	3	2	12
Cupid's Arrow	Vitality Barrier	Combo-Jump	Combo-Air Slide	1.0	1.0	1.0	3	2	12
Cupid's Arrow+	Defender	Combo-Jump	Combo-Air Slide	1.0	1.0	1.0	3	2	12
Final Weapon	Combo-Jump	Combo-Block	Combo-Air Slide	1.0	1.0	1.0	3	1	24
Final Weapon+	Combo-Jump	Combo-Block	Combo-Air Slide	1.0	1.0	1.0	3	1	12
Sharpshooter	Combo Boost	Chain Power	Chain Time	1.0	1.0	1.0	3	2	32
Dryer	Fire Finish	—	—	1.0	1.0	1.0	3	2	12
Trumpet	Aero Finish	Chain Time	—	1.0	1.0	1.0	3	2	12

XALDIN

III

Weapon: Lances

Founding member. A warrior with a silver tongue. He carries six lances and can harness the wind.

CHARACTER STATS

LEVEL	MAX HP	STRENGTH	MAGIC POWER	DEFENSE POWER	CRITICAL %	CRIT. BONUS
1	64	9	29	7	2	6
2	67	10	31	9	2	6
3	70	11	35	10	2	6
4	73	12	36	11	2	7
5	76	12	39	13	2	7
6	79	13	40	14	2	7
7	82	14	43	15	2	7
8	85	15	43	17	2	7
9	88	16	44	18	2	8
10	91	16	47	19	2	8
11	94	17	48	21	2	8
12	97	18	51	22	2	8
13	100	19	52	23	2	8
14	103	19	54	25	2	9
15	107	20	56	26	2	9
16	110	21	56	27	2	9
17	113	22	59	29	2	9
18	116	23	60	30	2	9
19	119	23	63	32	2	10
20	122	24	63	33	2	10
21	125	25	67	34	2	10
22	128	26	67	36	2	10
23	131	27	68	37	2	11
24	134	27	71	38	2	11
25	137	28	72	40	2	11
26	140	29	75	41	2	11
27	143	30	76	42	2	11
28	146	30	78	44	2	12
29	150	31	79	45	2	12
30	153	32	80	46	2	12
31	156	33	83	48	2	12
32	159	34	84	49	2	12
33	162	34	87	50	2	13
34	165	35	88	52	2	13
35	168	36	90	53	2	13
36	171	37	91	54	2	13
37	174	37	92	56	2	13
38	177	38	95	57	2	14
39	180	39	96	59	2	14
40	183	40	99	60	2	14
41	186	41	100	61	2	14
42	189	41	102	63	2	15
43	193	42	103	64	2	15
44	196	43	104	65	2	15
45	199	44	107	67	2	15
46	202	45	108	68	2	15
47	205	45	111	69	2	16
48	208	46	112	71	2	16
49	211	47	114	72	2	16
50	214	48	115	73	2	16
51	217	48	116	75	2	16
52	220	49	119	76	2	17
53	223	50	120	77	2	17
54	226	51	122	79	2	17
55	229	52	124	80	2	17
56	232	52	126	81	2	17
57	235	53	127	83	2	18
58	239	54	128	84	2	18
59	242	55	131	86	2	18
60	245	56	132	87	2	18
61	248	56	135	88	2	19
62	251	57	136	90	2	19
63	254	58	138	91	2	19
64	257	59	139	92	2	19
65	260	59	140	94	2	19
66	263	60	143	95	2	20
67	266	61	144	96	2	20
68	269	62	146	98	2	20
69	272	63	148	99	2	20
70	275	63	150	100	2	20
71	278	64	151	102	2	21
72	282	65	152	103	2	21
73	285	66	155	104	2	21
74	288	67	156	106	2	21
75	291	67	159	107	2	21
76	294	68	160	108	2	22
77	297	69	162	110	2	22
78	300	70	163	111	2	22
79	303	70	164	113	2	22
80	306	71	167	114	2	23
81	309	72	168	115	2	23
82	312	73	170	117	2	23
83	315	74	172	118	2	23
84	318	74	174	119	2	23
85	321	75	175	121	2	24
86	325	76	176	122	2	24
87	328	77	179	123	2	24
88	331	78	180	125	2	24
89	334	78	183	126	2	24
90	337	79	184	127	2	25
91	340	80	186	129	2	25
92	343	81	187	130	2	25
93	346	81	188	131	2	25
94	349	82	191	133	2	25
95	352	83	192	134	2	26
96	355	84	194	135	2	26
97	358	85	196	137	2	26
98	361	85	198	138	2	26
99	364	86	199	140	2	26
100	368	87	202	141	2	27

** Numbers in grey indicate when that number cannot go any higher than the previous number.*

WEAPON LIST & STATS

Weapon	Gear Panel	Strength		Magic		Defense		Crit. %		Crit. Bonus	
		Add	Unit	Add	Unit	Add	Unit	Add	Unit	Add	Unit
Zephyr	NA (No Panel)	15	—	0	—	0	—	0	—	2	—
Moonglade	Skill Gear	20	—	0	—	0	—	2	—	2	—
Moonglade+	Skill Gear+②	22	+1	0	+1	0	+1	2	+1	2	+1
Aer	Technical Gear③	40	+1	0	+1	0	+1	4	+1	3	+2
Aer+	Technical Gear+ ③	50	+1	0	+1	0	+1	4	+1	4	+2
Nescience	Duel Gear④	40	+1	0	+1	0	+1	6	+1	6	+2
Nescience+	Duel Gear+④	50	+1	0	+1	0	+1	8	+1	7	+2
Nescience++	Duel Gear++⑤	76	+1	0	+1	0	+1	6	+0	8	+5
Brume	Loaded Gear	30	—	0	—	0	—	2	—	4	—
Brume+	Loaded Gear+②	35	+1	0	+1	0	+1	2	+1	5	+1
Asura	Chrono Gear③	57	+1	0	+1	4	+2	2	+1	7	+1
Asura+	Chrono Gear+③	60	+1	0	+1	4	+2	2	+1	5	+1
Crux	Phantom Gear④	69	+1	0	+1	0	+2	8	+1	13	+1
Crux+	Phantom Gear+④	80	+1	0	+1	6	+2	3	+1	7	+1
Crux++	Phantom Gear++⑤	92	+1	0	+1	6	+5	3	+1	10	+1
Paladin	Lift Gear③	48	+2	0	+1	2	+1	0	+1	4	+1
Paladin+	Lift Gear+③	61	+2	0	+1	2	+1	4	+1	5	+1
Fellking	Nimble Gear④	68	+2	0	+1	3	+1	0	+1	5	+1
Fellking+	Nimble Gear+④	87	+2	0	+1	3	+1	6	+1	5	+1
Nightcloud	Wild Gear③	29	+1	0	+1	0	+1	8	+2	4	+1
Nightcloud+	Wild Gear+③	44	+1	0	+1	0	+1	6	+2	3	+1
Shimmer	Ominous Gear④	69	+1	0	+1	0	+1	9	+2	5	+1
Shimmer+	Ominous Gear+④	87	+1	0	+1	0	+1	12	+2	6	+1

Weapon	Gear Panel	Strength		Magic		Defense		Crit. %		Crit. Bonus	
		Add	Unit	Add	Unit	Add	Unit	Add	Unit	Add	Unit
Vortex	Valor Gear②	31	+1	17	+1	0	+1	2	+1	4	+1
Vortex+	Valor Gear+②	36	+1	19	+1	0	+1	2	+1	4	+1
Scission	Fearless Gear③	20	+1	25	+2	0	+1	4	+1	4	+1
Scission+	Fearless Gear+③	48	+1	29	+2	0	+1	4	+1	4	+1
Heavenfall	Prestige Gear④	31	+1	31	+2	0	+1	6	+1	7	+1
Heavenfall+	Prestige Gear+④	36	+1	39	+2	0	+1	6	+1	8	+1
Aether	Crisis Gear⑤	55	+1	31	+3	0	+1	8	+1	8	+3
Aether+	Crisis Gear+⑤	62	+1	37	+3	0	+1	8	+1	9	+3
Mazzaroth	Omega Gear⑥	73	+1	41	+3	0	+1	10	+1	13	+3
Mazzaroth+	Omega Gear+⑥	103	+1	45	+3	0	+1	10	+1	12	+3
Hegemon	Hazard Gear⑤	101	+3	0	+1	0	+3	8	+1	15	+1
Hegemon+	Hazard Gear+⑤	114	+3	0	+1	0	+3	8	+1	11	+1
Foxfire	Rage Gear⑤	88	+1	34	+3	0	+1	8	+3	8	+1
Foxfire+	Rage Gear+⑤	93	+1	37	+3	0	+1	8	+3	9	+1
Yaksha	Champion Gear⑤	64	+1	0	+1	0	+3	8	+1	9	+3
Yaksha+	Champion Gear+⑤	67	+1	0	+1	0	+3	8	+1	9	+3
Cynosura	Ultimate Gear⑥	90	+1	0	+1	0	+3	10	+1	13	+3
Cynosura+	Ultimate Gear+⑥	94	+1	0	+1	0	+3	10	+1	12	+3
Dragonreign	Pandora's Gear⑤	92	+5	30	+5	0	+5	10	+5	11	+5
Dragonreign+	Pandora's Gear+⑤	125	+1	34	+1	0	+1	10	+1	12	+1
Lindworm	Zero Gear⑤	124	+4	30	+4	0	+4	10	+4	19	+4
Broom	Casual Gear②	36	+1	0	+1	0	+1	0	+1	4	+1
Wyvern	Mystery Gear③	90	+1	0	+1	0	+1	0	+1	9	+1

WEAPON ABILITIES

Weapon	Abilities gained with units			Act. Spd.	Attack Move		Combo	
	1 Unit	2 Units	3 Units		Land	Air	Land	Air
Zephyr	—	—	—	1.0	1.0	1.0	3	3
Moonglade	—	—	—	1.0	1.0	1.0	4	2
Moonglade+	Combo-Jump	—	—	1.0	1.0	1.0	4	2
Aer	Combo-Jump	Combo Boost	—	1.0	1.0	1.0	3	3
Aer+	Combo-Jump	Chain Power	—	1.0	1.0	1.0	3	3
Nescience	Combo-Jump	Chain Power	Combo-Air Slide	1.0	1.0	1.0	3	3
Nescience+	Combo-Jump	Combo Boost	Combo-Air Slide	1.0	1.0	1.0	3	3
Nescience++	Combo-Jump	Combo-Air Slide	Aero Finish	1.0	1.0	1.0	3	3
Brume	—	—	—	1.0	1.0	1.0	3	2
Brume+	Defender	—	—	1.0	1.0	1.0	3	2
Asura	Defender	Offensive Block	—	1.0	1.0	1.0	4	2
Asura+	Vitality Barrier	Offensive Block	—	1.0	1.0	1.0	4	2
Crux	Defender	Offensive Block	Damage Control	1.0	1.0	1.0	5	2
Crux+	Defender	Offensive Block	Second Chance	1.0	1.0	1.0	5	2
Crux++	Defender	Offensive Block	Combo-Block	1.0	1.0	1.0	5	2
Paladin	Striker	Defender	—	1.0	1.0	1.0	4	2
Paladin+	Striker	Defender	—	1.0	1.0	1.0	4	2
Fellking	Defender	Vitality Barrier	Second Chance	1.0	1.0	1.0	4	2
Fellking+	Striker	Vitality Surge	Grand Slam	1.0	1.0	1.0	4	2
Nightcloud	Combo Boost	Chain Power	—	1.1	1.0	1.0	5	2
Nightcloud+	Chain Power	Chain Time	—	1.1	1.0	1.0	5	2
Shimmer	Chain Power	Chain Time	Heart Bonus	1.1	1.0	1.0	5	3
Shimmer+	Combo Boost	Chain Power	Critical Boost	1.1	1.0	1.0	5	3

Weapon	Abilities gained with units			Act. Spd.	Attack Move		Combo	
	1 Unit	2 Units	3 Units		Land	Air	Land	Air
Vortex	Magic Bracer	—	—	1.0	1.0	1.0	2	2
Vortex+	Magic Bracer	—	—	1.0	1.0	1.0	2	2
Scission	Magic Bracer	Aero Finish	—	1.0	1.0	1.0	3	3
Scission+	Magic Bracer	Aero Finish	—	1.0	1.0	1.0	3	3
Heavenfall	Magic Bracer	Aero Finish	Blizzard Finish	1.0	1.0	1.0	4	3
Heavenfall+	Magic Bracer	Aero Finish	Thunder Finish	1.0	1.0	1.0	4	3
Aether	Aero Finish	Combo-Jump	Combo-Air Slide	1.0	1.0	1.0	5	3
Aether+	Aero Finish	Magic Bracer	Magic Finale	1.0	1.0	1.0	5	3
Mazzaroth	Aero Finish	Magic Bracer	Magical Strike	1.0	1.0	1.0	5	3
Mazzaroth+	Aero Finish	Combo-Jump	Combo-Air Slide	1.0	1.0	1.0	5	3
Hegemon	Offensive Block	Grand Slam	Damage Control	1.0	1.0	1.0	4	2
Hegemon+	Offensive Block	Vitality Surge	Vitality Barrier	1.0	1.0	1.0	4	2
Foxfire	Aero Finish	Chain Time	Chain Time	1.2	1.0	1.0	5	3
Foxfire+	Aero Finish	Combo Boost	Critical Boost	1.2	1.0	1.0	5	3
Yaksha	Defender	Offensive Block	Combo-Jump	1.0	1.0	1.0	4	2
Yaksha+	Defender	Offensive Block	Combo-Air Slide	1.0	1.0	1.0	4	2
Cynosura	Chain Power	Offensive Block	Combo-Air Slide	1.0	1.0	1.0	4	2
Cynosura+	Combo Boost	Offensive Block	Combo-Jump	1.0	1.0	1.0	4	2
Dragonreign	Offensive Block	Combo-Block	Combo-Air Slide	1.0	1.0	1.0	5	2
Dragonreign+	Offensive Block	Combo-Block	Combo-Air Slide	1.0	1.0	1.0	5	2
Lindworm	Combo-Jump	Combo-Air Slide	Aero Finish	1.0	1.0	1.0	5	3
Broom	Aero Finish	—	—	1.0	1.0	1.0	4	2
Wyvern	Fire Finish	Combo-Air Slide	—	1.0	1.0	1.0	5	3

VEXEN

IV

Weapon: Shield

Founding member. A brilliant scientist with dominion over ice...and a personality to match.

CHARACTER STATS

LEVEL	MAX HP	STRENGTH	MAGIC POWER	DEFENSE POWER	CRITICAL %	CRIT. BONUS
1	60	7	38	6	6	6
2	63	7	43	8	6	6
3	66	9	43	9	6	6
4	69	9	45	10	6	6
5	72	9	48	12	6	6
6	75	11	49	13	6	6
7	78	11	51	14	6	7
8	81	12	53	15	6	7
9	84	13	54	17	6	7
10	87	13	56	18	6	7
11	90	14	59	19	6	7
12	93	15	60	21	6	7
13	96	15	63	22	6	7
14	99	16	65	23	6	8
15	101	17	66	24	6	8
16	104	17	68	26	6	8
17	107	18	71	27	6	8
18	110	19	71	28	6	8
19	113	19	74	30	6	8
20	116	20	75	31	6	9
21	119	21	78	32	6	9
22	122	21	80	33	6	9
23	125	22	81	35	6	9
24	128	23	83	36	6	9
25	131	23	86	37	6	9
26	134	24	87	39	6	10
27	137	25	90	40	6	10
28	140	25	92	41	6	10
29	142	26	93	42	6	10
30	145	27	95	44	6	10
31	148	27	98	45	6	10
32	151	28	99	46	6	11
33	154	29	101	48	6	11
34	157	29	104	49	6	11
35	160	30	105	50	6	11
36	163	31	107	51	6	11
37	166	31	110	53	6	11
38	169	32	111	54	6	11
39	172	33	113	55	6	12
40	175	34	114	57	6	12
41	178	34	117	58	6	12
42	181	35	119	59	6	12
43	183	36	120	60	6	12
44	186	36	123	62	6	12
45	189	37	125	63	6	13
46	192	38	126	64	6	13
47	195	38	129	66	6	13
48	198	39	131	67	6	13
49	201	40	132	68	6	13
50	204	40	135	69	6	13
51	207	41	137	71	6	14
52	210	42	138	72	6	14
53	213	42	141	73	6	14
54	216	43	143	75	6	14
55	219	44	144	76	6	14
56	222	44	147	77	6	14
57	225	45	149	78	6	15
58	227	46	150	80	6	15
59	230	46	153	81	6	15
60	233	47	154	82	6	15
61	236	48	156	84	6	15
62	239	48	159	85	6	15
63	242	49	160	86	6	15
64	245	50	162	87	6	16
65	248	50	165	89	6	16
66	251	51	166	90	6	16
67	254	52	168	91	6	16
68	257	52	171	93	6	16
69	260	53	172	94	6	16
70	263	54	174	95	6	17
71	266	54	177	97	6	17
72	268	55	178	98	6	17
73	271	56	180	99	6	17
74	274	56	183	100	6	17
75	277	57	184	102	6	17
76	280	58	186	103	6	18
77	283	58	189	104	6	18
78	286	59	190	106	6	18
79	289	60	192	107	6	18
80	292	61	193	108	6	18
81	295	61	196	109	6	18
82	298	62	198	111	6	19
83	301	63	199	112	6	19
84	304	63	202	113	6	19
85	307	64	204	115	6	19
86	309	65	205	116	6	19
87	312	65	208	117	6	19
88	315	66	210	118	6	19
89	318	67	211	120	6	20
90	321	67	214	121	6	20
91	324	68	216	122	6	20
92	327	69	217	124	6	20
93	330	69	220	125	6	20
94	333	70	222	126	6	20
95	336	71	223	127	6	21
96	339	71	226	129	6	21
97	342	72	228	130	6	21
98	345	73	229	131	6	21
99	348	73	232	133	6	21
100	351	74	233	134	6	21

** Numbers in grey indicate when that number cannot go any higher than the previous number.*

WEAPON LIST & STATS

Weapon	Gear Panel	Strength Add	Strength Unit	Magic Add	Magic Unit	Defense Add	Defense Unit	Crit. % Add	Crit. % Unit	Crit. Bonus Add	Crit. Bonus Unit
Tester Zero	NA (No Panel)	15	—	0	—	0	—	0	—	2	—
Product One	Skill Gear	18	—	11	—	0	—	2	—	2	—
Product One+	Skill Gear+②	20	+1	12	+1	0	+1	2	+1	2	+1
Deep Freeze	Technical Gear③	36	+1	14	+2	0	+1	4	+1	2	+1
Deep Freeze+	Technical Gear+ ③	44	+1	21	+2	0	+1	4	+1	4	+1
Cryolite Shield	Duel Gear④	35	+1	31	+2	0	+1	6	+1	5	+1
Cryolite Shield+	Duel Gear+④	45	+1	35	+2	0	+1	8	+1	6	+1
Cryolite Shield++	Duel Gear++⑤	68	+1	39	+5	0	+1	6	+1	7	+1
False Theory	Loaded Gear	30	—	0	—	0	—	2	—	4	—
False Theory+	Loaded Gear+②	35	+1	0	+1	0	+1	2	+1	5	+1
Glacier	Chrono Gear③	60	+1	0	+1	4	+2	2	+1	5	+1
Glacier+	Chrono Gear+③	68	+1	0	+1	4	+2	2	+1	7	+1
Absolute Zero	Phantom Gear④	69	+1	0	+1	0	+2	8	+1	13	+1
Absolute Zero+	Phantom Gear+④	80	+1	0	+1	6	+2	3	+1	7	+1
Absolute Zero++	Phantom Gear++⑤	92	+1	0	+1	6	+5	3	+1	10	+1
Gunz	Lift Gear③	22	+1	0	+1	0	+1	8	+2	3	+1
Gunz+	Lift Gear+③	48	+1	0	+1	0	+1	6	+2	4	+1
Mindel	Nimble Gear④	54	+1	0	+1	0	+1	12	+2	4	+1
Mindel+	Nimble Gear+④	70	+1	0	+1	0	+1	9	+2	4	+1
Snowslide	Wild Gear③	29	+1	0	+1	0	+1	4	+1	4	+2
Snowslide+	Wild Gear+③	44	+1	0	+1	0	+1	4	+1	3	+2
Iceberg	Ominous Gear④	65	+1	0	+1	0	+1	6	+1	5	+2
Iceberg+	Ominous Gear+④	78	+1	0	+1	0	+1	6	+1	6	+2
Inquisition	Valor Gear②	44	+1	0	+1	1	+1	2	+1	5	+1
Inquisition+	Valor Gear+②	46	+1	0	+1	1	+1	0	+1	6	+1
Scrutiny	Fearless Gear③	49	+2	0	+1	2	+1	0	+1	6	+1
Scrutiny+	Fearless Gear+③	58	+2	0	+1	2	+1	4	+1	6	+1
Empiricism	Prestige Gear④	69	+2	0	+1	3	+1	0	+1	10	+1
Empiricism+	Prestige Gear+④	85	+2	0	+1	3	+1	6	+1	11	+1
Edification	Crisis Gear⑤	64	+3	23	+3	4	+1	8	+1	9	+1
Edification+	Crisis Gear+⑤	70	+3	28	+3	4	+1	0	+1	10	+1
Contrivance	Omega Gear⑥	84	+3	31	+3	5	+1	10	+1	15	+1
Contrivance+	Omega Gear+⑥	120	+3	34	+3	5	+1	0	+1	14	+1
Würm	Hazard Gear⑤	84	+1	37	+3	0	+1	8	+3	12	+1
Würm+	Hazard Gear+⑤	96	+1	45	+3	0	+1	8	+3	10	+1
Subzero	Rage Gear⑤	78	+1	0	+1	0	+3	8	+1	8	+3
Subzero+	Rage Gear+⑤	88	+1	0	+1	0	+3	8	+1	9	+3
Cold Blood	Champion Gear⑤	64	+1	36	+3	0	+3	8	+1	9	+1
Cold Blood+	Champion Gear+⑤	67	+1	37	+3	0	+3	8	+1	9	+1
Diamond Shield	Ultimate Gear⑥	90	+1	36	+3	0	+3	10	+1	13	+1
Diamond Shield+	Ultimate Gear+⑥	94	+1	45	+3	0	+3	10	+1	12	+1
Aegis	Pandora's Gear⑤	92	+5	30	+5	0	+5	10	+5	11	+5
Aegis+	Pandora's Gear+⑤	125	+1	34	+1	0	+1	10	+1	12	+1
Frozen Pride	Zero Gear⑤	124	+4	30	+4	0	+4	10	+4	19	+4
Pot Lid	Casual Gear②	36	+1	0	+1	0	+1	0	+1	4	+1
Snowman	Mystery Gear③	90	+1	0	+1	0	+1	0	+1	9	+1

WEAPON ABILITIES

Weapon	Abilities gained with units: 1 Unit	2 Units	3 Units	Act. Spd.	Attack Move Land	Attack Move Air	Combo Land	Combo Air
Tester Zero	—	—	—	1.0	1.0	1.0	3	3
Product One	—	—	—	1.0	1.0	1.0	2	3
Product One+	Magic Bracer	—	—	1.0	1.0	1.0	2	3
Deep Freeze	Magic Bracer	Blizzard Finish	—	1.0	1.0	1.0	3	3
Deep Freeze+	Magic Bracer	Blizzard Finish	—	1.0	1.0	1.0	3	3
Cryolite Shield	Magic Bracer	Blizzard Finish	Magical Strike	1.0	1.0	1.0	3	3
Cryolite Shield+	Magic Bracer	Blizzard Finish	Magic Finale	1.0	1.0	1.0	3	3
Cryolite Shield++	Blizzard Finish	Magic Bracer	Magical Strike	1.0	1.0	1.0	3	3
False Theory	—	—	—	1.0	1.0	1.0	2	2
False Theory+	Offensive Block	—	—	1.0	1.0	1.0	2	2
Glacier	Offensive Block	Defender	—	1.0	1.0	1.0	3	2
Glacier+	Offensive Block	Combo-Block	—	1.0	1.0	1.0	3	2
Absolute Zero	Offensive Block	Defender	Vitality Barrier	1.0	1.0	1.0	3	3
Absolute Zero+	Offensive Block	Defender	Combo-Block	1.0	1.0	1.0	3	3
Absolute Zero++	Offensive Block	Vitality Barrier	Combo-Block	1.0	1.0	1.0	3	3
Gunz	Combo Boost	Combo-Block	—	1.1	1.0	1.0	3	3
Gunz+	Chain Power	Chain Time	—	1.1	1.0	1.0	3	3
Mindel	Chain Power	Chain Time	Heart Bonus	1.2	1.0	1.0	5	3
Mindel+	Combo Boost	Offensive Block	Combo-Block	1.2	1.0	1.0	5	3
Snowslide	Combo Boost	Combo-Jump	—	1.0	1.0	1.0	4	2
Snowslide+	Chain Power	Combo-Jump	—	1.0	1.0	1.0	4	2
Iceberg	Chain Power	Combo-Jump	Combo-Air Slide	1.0	1.0	1.0	4	2
Iceberg+	Combo Boost	Combo-Jump	Combo-Air Slide	1.0	1.0	1.0	4	2
Inquisition	Defender	—	—	1.0	1.0	1.0	4	2
Inquisition+	Defender	—	—	1.0	1.0	1.0	4	2
Scrutiny	Defender	Striker	—	1.0	1.0	1.0	4	2
Scrutiny+	Defender	Vitality Barrier	—	1.0	1.0	1.0	4	2
Empiricism	Defender	Vitality Barrier	Striker	1.1	1.0	1.0	5	2
Empiricism+	Defender	Striker	Vitality Source	1.1	1.0	1.0	5	2
Edification	Magic Bracer	Blizzard Finish	Brick Wall	1.0	1.0	1.0	4	2
Edification+	Magic Bracer	Blizzard Finish	Combo-Block	1.0	1.0	1.0	4	2
Contrivance	Magic Bracer	Blizzard Finish	Alive 'n' Kicking	1.0	1.0	1.0	4	3
Contrivance+	Magic Bracer	Blizzard Finish	Brick Wall	1.0	1.0	1.0	4	3
Würm	Combo Boost	Blizzard Finish	Combo-Block	1.2	1.0	1.0	5	3
Würm+	Combo Boost	Blizzard Finish	Magic Bracer	1.2	1.0	1.0	5	3
Subzero	Offensive Block	Combo-Air Slide	Vitality Barrier	1.0	1.0	1.0	3	5
Subzero+	Offensive Block	Combo-Jump	Vitality Barrier	1.0	1.0	1.0	3	5
Cold Blood	Offensive Block	Blizzard Finish	Magic Bracer	1.0	1.0	1.0	3	4
Cold Blood+	Offensive Block	Blizzard Finish	Combo-Block	1.0	1.0	1.0	3	4
Diamond Shield	Offensive Block	Blizzard Finish	Combo-Block	1.1	1.0	1.0	3	4
Diamond Shield+	Offensive Block	Blizzard Finish	Magic Bracer	1.1	1.0	1.0	3	4
Aegis	Magic Bracer	Offensive Block	Blizzard Finish	1.0	1.0	1.0	4	3
Aegis+	Magic Bracer	Offensive Block	Blizzard Finish	1.0	1.0	1.0	4	3
Frozen Pride	Blizzard Finish	Offensive Block	Combo-Block	1.0	1.0	1.0	3	3
Pot Lid	Offensive Block	—	—	1.0	1.0	1.0	4	2
Snowman	Blizzard Finish	Aero Finish	—	1.0	1.0	1.0	4	2

LEXAEUS

V

Weapon: **Axe Sword**

Founding member. Tremendously strong, but surprisingly quiet—stalwart as the earth itself.

LEVEL	MAX HP	STRENGTH	MAGIC POWER	DEFENSE POWER	CRITICAL %	CRIT. BONUS
1	67	10	25	8	3	7
2	71	11	27	10	3	7
3	74	11	29	12	3	8
4	77	13	32	13	3	8
5	80	14	34	15	3	8
6	84	15	34	16	3	9
7	87	15	35	18	3	9
8	90	16	38	19	3	9
9	93	17	39	21	3	10
10	97	18	40	23	3	10
11	100	19	41	24	3	10
12	103	20	44	26	3	11
13	106	21	45	27	3	11
14	110	22	46	29	3	11
15	113	22	47	30	3	12
16	116	23	50	32	3	12
17	119	24	51	34	3	12
18	123	25	52	35	3	13
19	126	26	53	37	3	13
20	129	27	56	38	3	13
21	132	28	57	40	3	14
22	136	29	58	41	3	14
23	139	29	59	43	3	14
24	142	30	62	45	3	15
25	145	31	63	46	3	15
26	149	32	64	48	3	15
27	152	33	65	49	3	16
28	155	34	68	51	3	16
29	158	35	69	52	3	16
30	162	36	70	54	3	17
31	165	36	71	56	3	17
32	168	37	74	57	3	17
33	171	38	75	59	3	18
34	175	39	76	60	3	18
35	178	40	77	62	3	19
36	181	41	80	63	3	19
37	184	42	81	65	3	19
38	188	43	82	67	3	20
39	191	43	83	68	3	20
40	194	44	86	70	3	20
41	197	45	87	71	3	21
42	201	46	88	73	3	21
43	204	47	89	75	3	21
44	207	48	92	76	3	22
45	210	49	93	78	3	22
46	214	50	94	79	3	22
47	217	50	95	81	3	23
48	220	51	98	82	3	23
49	223	52	99	84	3	23
50	227	53	100	86	3	24
51	230	54	102	87	3	24
52	233	55	104	89	3	24
53	236	56	105	90	3	25
54	240	57	106	92	3	25
55	243	57	108	93	3	25
56	246	58	110	95	3	26
57	249	59	111	97	3	26
58	253	60	112	98	3	26
59	256	61	114	100	3	27
60	259	62	116	101	3	27
61	262	63	117	103	3	27
62	266	64	118	104	3	28
63	269	64	120	106	3	28
64	272	65	122	108	3	28
65	275	66	123	109	3	29
66	279	67	124	111	3	29
67	282	68	126	112	3	29
68	285	69	128	114	3	30
69	288	70	129	115	3	30
70	292	71	130	117	3	30
71	295	71	132	119	3	31
72	298	72	134	120	3	31
73	301	73	135	122	3	31
74	305	74	136	123	3	32
75	308	75	138	125	3	32
76	311	76	140	126	3	32
77	314	77	141	128	3	33
78	318	78	142	130	3	33
79	321	78	144	131	3	33
80	324	79	146	133	3	34
81	327	80	147	134	3	34
82	331	81	148	136	3	34
83	334	82	150	138	3	35
84	337	83	152	139	3	35
85	340	84	153	141	3	36
86	344	85	154	142	3	36
87	347	85	156	144	3	36
88	350	86	158	145	3	37
89	353	87	159	147	3	37
90	357	88	160	149	3	37
91	360	89	162	150	3	38
92	363	90	164	152	3	38
93	366	91	165	153	3	38
94	370	92	166	155	3	39
95	373	92	168	156	3	39
96	376	93	170	158	3	39
97	379	94	171	160	3	40
98	383	95	172	161	3	40
99	386	96	174	163	3	40
100	389	97	176	164	3	41

** Numbers in grey indicate when that number cannot go any higher than the previous number.*

WEAPON LIST & STATS

Weapon	Gear Panel	Strength Add	Strength Unit	Magic Add	Magic Unit	Defense Add	Defense Unit	Crit. % Add	Crit. % Unit	Crit. Bonus Add	Crit. Bonus Unit
Reticence	NA (No Panel)	30	—	0	—	0	—	0	—	2	—
Goliath	Skill Gear	32	—	0	—	1	—	2	—	3	—
Goliath+	Skill Gear+②	37	+1	0	+1	1	+1	0	+1	3	+1
Copper Red	Technical Gear③	51	+2	0	+1	2	+1	4	+1	3	+1
Copper Red+	Technical Gear+ ③	62	+2	0	+1	2	+1	0	+1	5	+1
Daybreak	Duel Gear④	50	+2	0	+1	3	+1	6	+1	7	+1
Daybreak+	Duel Gear+④	63	+2	0	+1	0	+1	8	+1	8	+1
Daybreak++	Duel Gear++⑤	93	+5	0	+1	3	+1	0	+1	10	+1
Colossus	Loaded Gear	30	—	0	—	0	—	2	—	4	—
Colossus+	Loaded Gear+②	35	+1	0	+1	0	+1	2	+1	5	+1
Ursa Major	Chrono Gear③	57	+1	0	+1	4	+2	2	+1	7	+1
Ursa Major+	Chrono Gear+③	60	+1	0	+1	4	+2	2	+1	5	+1
Megacosm	Phantom Gear④	64	+1	0	+1	0	+2	8	+1	13	+1
Megacosm+	Phantom Gear+④	80	+1	0	+1	6	+2	3	+1	7	+1
Megacosm++	Phantom Gear++⑤	92	+1	0	+1	6	+5	3	+1	10	+1
Terrence	Lift Gear③	34	+1	14	+2	0	+1	4	+1	3	+1
Terrence+	Lift Gear+③	56	+1	16	+2	0	+1	4	+1	3	+1
Fuligin	Nimble Gear④	59	+1	25	+2	0	+1	6	+1	4	+1
Fuligin+	Nimble Gear+④	82	+1	31	+2	0	+1	6	+1	3	+1
Hard Winter	Wild Gear③	36	+1	0	+1	0	+1	4	+1	4	+2
Hard Winter+	Wild Gear+③	49	+1	0	+1	0	+1	4	+1	3	+2
Firefly	Ominous Gear④	60	+1	0	+1	0	+1	6	+1	5	+2
Firefly+	Ominous Gear+④	81	+1	0	+1	0	+1	6	+1	6	+2

Weapon	Gear Panel	Strength Add	Strength Unit	Magic Add	Magic Unit	Defense Add	Defense Unit	Crit. % Add	Crit. % Unit	Crit. Bonus Add	Crit. Bonus Unit
Harbinger	Valor Gear②	42	+1	0	+1	0	+1	3	+1	4	+1
Harbinger+	Valor Gear+②	45	+1	0	+1	0	+1	4	+1	5	+1
Redwood	Fearless Gear③	39	+1	0	+1	0	+1	6	+2	5	+1
Redwood+	Fearless Gear+③	42	+1	0	+1	0	+1	8	+2	5	+1
Sequoia	Prestige Gear④	40	+1	0	+1	0	+1	12	+2	8	+1
Sequoia+	Prestige Gear+④	45	+1	0	+1	0	+1	9	+2	9	+1
Iron Black	Crisis Gear⑤	78	+3	0	+1	0	+1	8	+3	9	+1
Iron Black+	Crisis Gear+⑤	85	+3	0	+1	0	+1	8	+3	11	+1
Earthshine	Omega Gear⑥	90	+3	0	+1	0	+1	10	+3	16	+1
Earthshine+	Omega Gear+⑥	125	+3	0	+1	0	+1	10	+3	14	+1
Octiron	Hazard Gear⑤	97	+3	28	+3	4	+1	0	+1	14	+1
Octiron+	Hazard Gear+⑤	109	+3	34	+3	4	+1	8	+1	11	+1
Hyperion	Rage Gear⑤	90	+1	0	+1	0	+1	8	+3	8	+3
Hyperion+	Rage Gear+⑤	92	+1	0	+1	0	+1	8	+3	9	+3
Clarity	Champion Gear⑤	76	+3	0	+1	0	+3	8	+1	11	+1
Clarity+	Champion Gear+⑤	80	+3	0	+1	0	+3	8	+1	11	+1
1001 Nights	Ultimate Gear⑥	111	+3	0	+1	0	+3	10	+1	16	+1
1001 Nights+	Ultimate Gear+⑥	116	+3	0	+1	0	+3	10	+1	14	+1
Cardinal Virtue	Pandora's Gear⑤	92	+5	30	+5	0	+5	10	+5	11	+5
Cardinal Virtue+	Pandora's Gear+⑤	125	+1	34	+1	0	+1	10	+1	12	+1
Skysplitter	Zero Gear⑤	124	+4	30	+4	0	+4	10	+4	19	+4
Bleep Bloop Bop	Casual Gear②	36	+1	0	+1	0	+1	0	+1	4	+1
Monolith	Mystery Gear③	90	+1	0	+1	0	+1	0	+1	9	+1

WEAPON ABILITIES

Weapon	Abilities gained with units: 1 Unit	2 Units	3 Units	Act. Spd.	Atk. Move Land	Atk. Move Air	Combo Land	Combo Air
Reticence	—	—	—	1.0	1.0	1.0	3	2
Goliath	—	—	—	1.0	1.0	1.0	3	2
Goliath+	Striker	—	—	1.0	1.0	1.0	3	2
Copper Red	Striker	Vitality Source	—	1.0	1.0	1.0	3	2
Copper Red+	Striker	Defender	—	1.0	1.0	1.0	3	2
Daybreak	Defender	Damage Control	Brick Wall	1.0	1.0	1.0	3	2
Daybreak+	Striker	Grand Slam	Brick Wall	1.0	1.0	1.0	3	2
Daybreak++	Striker	Vitality Source	Grand Slam	1.0	1.0	1.0	3	2
Colossus	—	—	—	1.0	1.0	1.0	3	2
Colossus+	Defender	—	—	1.0	1.0	1.0	3	2
Ursa Major	Defender	Offensive Block	—	1.0	1.0	1.0	3	1
Ursa Major+	Vitality Barrier	Offensive Block	—	1.0	1.0	1.0	3	1
Megacosm	Offensive Block	Damage Control	Brick Wall	1.0	1.0	1.0	4	1
Megacosm+	Offensive Block	Vitality Barrier	Combo-Block	1.0	1.0	1.0	4	1
Megacosm++	Defender	Vitality Barrier	Damage Control	1.0	1.0	1.0	5	1
Terrence	Fire Finish	Magic Bracer	—	1.0	1.0	1.0	4	1
Terrence+	Thunder Finish	Magic Bracer	—	1.0	1.0	1.0	4	1
Fuligin	Magic Bracer	Thunder Finish	Blizzard Finish	1.0	1.0	1.0	4	2
Fuligin+	Magic Bracer	Fire Finish	Aero Finish	1.0	1.0	1.0	4	2
Hard Winter	Chain Power	Combo-Jump	—	1.0	1.0	1.0	4	2
Hard Winter+	Chain Time	Combo-Jump	—	1.0	1.0	1.0	4	2
Firefly	Chain Time	Chain Power	Combo-Jump	1.0	1.0	1.0	5	2
Firefly+	Chain Power	Combo Boost	Combo-Jump	1.0	1.0	1.0	5	2

Weapon	Abilities gained with units: 1 Unit	2 Units	3 Units	Act. Spd.	Atk. Move Land	Atk. Move Air	Combo Land	Combo Air
Harbinger	Chain Power	—	—	1.0	1.0	1.0	3	2
Harbinger+	Chain Time	—	—	1.0	1.0	1.0	3	2
Redwood	Chain Power	Chain Time	—	1.0	1.0	1.0	5	2
Redwood+	Combo Boost	Chain Power	—	1.0	1.0	1.0	5	2
Sequoia	Combo Boost	Chain Power	Combo-Block	1.0	1.0	1.0	7	2
Sequoia+	Chain Power	Chain Time	Combo-Block	1.0	1.0	1.0	7	2
Iron Black	Combo Boost	Chain Power	Brick Wall	1.0	1.0	1.0	4	2
Iron Black+	Striker	Grand Slam	Critical Boost	1.0	1.0	1.0	4	2
Earthshine	Striker	Grand Slam	Critical Boost	1.0	1.0	1.0	7	2
Earthshine+	Combo Boost	Chain Power	Brick Wall	1.0	1.0	1.0	7	2
Octiron	Fire Finish	Aero Finish	Alive 'n' Kicking	1.0	1.0	1.0	4	3
Octiron+	Thunder Finish	Blizzard Finish	Alive 'n' Kicking	1.0	1.0	1.0	4	3
Hyperion	Chain Power	Chain Time	Combo-Jump	1.0	1.0	1.0	4	3
Hyperion+	Combo Boost	Chain Power	Combo-Jump	1.0	1.0	1.0	4	3
Clarity	Offensive Block	Damage Control	Combo-Block	1.0	1.0	1.0	4	3
Clarity+	Offensive Block	Brick Wall	Combo-Block	1.0	1.0	1.0	4	3
1001 Nights	Offensive Block	Brick Wall	Combo-Block	1.0	1.0	1.0	4	3
1001 Nights+	Offensive Block	Damage Control	Combo-Block	1.0	1.0	1.0	4	3
Cardinal Virtue	Vitality Source	Vitality Barrier	Alive 'n' Kicking	1.0	1.0	1.0	4	2
Cardinal Virtue+	Vitality Source	Vitality Barrier	Alive 'n' Kicking	1.0	1.0	1.0	4	2
Skysplitter	Grand Slam	Damage Control	Brick Wall	1.0	1.0	1.0	3	2
Bleep Bloop Bop	Heart Bonus	—	—	1.0	1.0	1.0	3	2
Monolith	Striker	Vitality Barrier	—	1.0	1.0	1.0	3	2

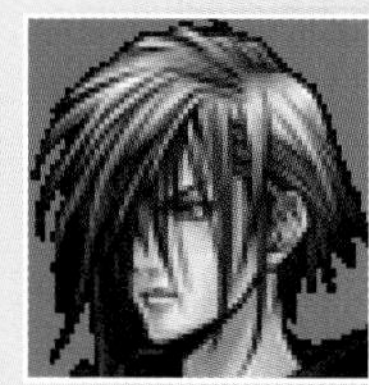

ZEXION

VI

Weapon: Lexicon

Founding member. An intellectual with no room for feelings. He can create illusions at will.

LEVEL	MAX HP	STRENGTH	MAGIC POWER	DEFENSE POWER	CRITICAL %	CRIT. BONUS
1	57	7	38	5	1	7
2	60	8	43	6	1	8
3	62	9	45	7	1	8
4	65	9	47	9	1	9
5	68	9	49	10	1	9
6	71	11	50	11	1	9
7	73	11	53	12	1	10
8	76	12	54	13	1	10
9	79	12	57	14	1	11
10	82	13	59	15	1	11
11	84	14	62	16	1	11
12	87	14	62	18	1	12
13	90	15	65	19	1	12
14	93	16	67	20	1	13
15	95	16	70	21	1	13
16	98	17	70	22	1	13
17	101	17	73	23	1	14
18	104	18	75	24	1	14
19	106	19	78	25	1	15
20	109	19	78	27	1	15
21	112	20	81	28	1	15
22	115	21	84	29	1	16
23	117	21	86	30	1	16
24	120	22	87	31	1	17
25	123	22	90	32	1	17
26	126	23	92	33	1	17
27	128	24	95	34	1	18
28	131	24	95	36	1	18
29	134	25	98	37	1	19
30	137	26	100	38	1	19
31	139	26	103	39	1	19
32	142	27	104	40	1	20
33	145	27	106	41	1	20
34	148	28	109	42	1	21
35	150	29	111	43	1	21
36	153	29	112	45	1	21
37	156	30	115	46	1	22
38	159	31	117	47	1	22
39	161	31	120	48	1	23
40	164	32	120	49	1	23
41	167	32	123	50	1	23
42	170	33	125	51	1	24
43	172	34	128	52	1	24
44	175	34	129	54	1	25
45	178	35	131	55	1	25
46	181	36	134	56	1	25
47	183	36	136	57	1	26
48	186	37	137	58	1	26
49	189	37	140	59	1	27
50	192	38	142	60	1	27
51	194	39	145	61	1	27
52	197	39	146	63	1	28
53	200	40	148	64	1	28
54	203	41	151	65	1	29
55	205	41	153	66	1	29
56	208	42	154	67	1	29
57	211	42	157	68	1	30
58	214	43	159	69	1	30
59	216	44	162	70	1	31
60	219	44	162	72	1	31
61	222	45	165	73	1	31
62	225	46	167	74	1	32
63	227	46	170	75	1	32
64	230	47	171	76	1	33
65	233	47	173	77	1	33
66	236	48	176	78	1	33
67	238	49	178	79	1	34
68	241	49	179	81	1	34
69	244	50	182	82	1	35
70	247	51	184	83	1	35
71	249	51	187	84	1	35
72	252	52	188	85	1	36
73	255	52	190	86	1	36
74	258	53	193	87	1	37
75	260	54	195	88	1	37
76	263	54	196	90	1	37
77	266	55	199	91	1	38
78	269	56	201	92	1	38
79	271	56	203	93	1	39
80	274	57	204	94	1	39
81	277	57	207	95	1	39
82	280	58	209	96	1	40
83	282	59	212	97	1	40
84	285	59	213	99	1	41
85	288	60	215	100	1	41
86	291	61	218	101	1	41
87	293	61	220	102	1	42
88	296	62	221	103	1	42
89	299	62	224	104	1	43
90	302	63	226	105	1	43
91	304	64	229	106	1	43
92	307	64	230	108	1	44
93	310	65	232	109	1	44
94	313	66	234	110	1	45
95	315	66	237	111	1	45
96	318	67	238	112	1	45
97	321	67	241	113	1	46
98	324	68	243	114	1	46
99	326	69	245	115	1	47
100	329	69	246	117	1	47

** Numbers in grey indicate when that number cannot go any higher than the previous number.*

WEAPON LIST & STATS

Weapon	Gear Panel	Strength Add	Strength Unit	Magic Add	Magic Unit	Defense Add	Defense Unit	Crit. % Add	Crit. % Unit	Crit. Bonus Add	Crit. Bonus Unit
Black Primer	NA (No Panel)	15	—	0	—	0	—	0	—	2	—
White Tome	Skill Gear	18	—	11	—	0	—	2	—	2	—
White Tome+	Skill Gear+②	20	+1	12	+1	0	+1	2	+1	2	+1
Illicit Research	Technical Gear③	36	+1	14	+2	0	+1	4	+1	2	+1
Illicit Research+	Technical Gear+ ③	44	+1	21	+2	0	+1	4	+1	4	+1
Buried Secrets	Duel Gear④	35	+1	31	+2	0	+1	6	+1	5	+1
Buried Secrets+	Duel Gear+④	45	+1	35	+2	0	+1	8	+1	6	+1
Buried Secrets++	Duel Gear++⑤	68	+1	39	+5	0	+1	6	+1	7	+1
Arcane Compendium	Loaded Gear	27	—	0	—	0	—	3	—	3	—
Arcane Compendium+	Loaded Gear+②	35	+1	0	+1	0	+1	4	+1	5	+1
Dissenter's Notes	Chrono Gear③	50	+1	0	+1	0	+1	6	+2	5	+1
Dissenter's Notes+	Chrono Gear+③	55	+1	0	+1	0	+1	8	+2	6	+1
Nefarious Codex	Phantom Gear④	53	+1	0	+1	0	+1	12	+2	13	+1
Nefarious Codex+	Phantom Gear+④	65	+1	0	+1	0	+1	9	+2	7	+1
Nefarious Codex++	Phantom Gear++⑤	86	+1	0	+1	0	+1	12	+5	10	+0
Mystic Album	Lift Gear③	50	+2	0	+1	2	+1	0	+1	4	+1
Mystic Album+	Lift Gear+③	61	+2	0	+1	2	+1	4	+1	5	+1
Cursed Manual	Nimble Gear④	75	+2	0	+1	3	+1	0	+1	5	+1
Cursed Manual+	Nimble Gear+④	87	+2	0	+1	3	+1	6	+1	5	+1
Taboo Text	Wild Gear③	29	+1	0	+1	0	+1	4	+1	4	+2
Taboo Text+	Wild Gear+③	44	+1	0	+1	0	+1	4	+1	3	+2
Eldritch Esoterica	Ominous Gear④	69	+1	0	+1	0	+1	6	+1	5	+2
Eldritch Esoterica+	Ominous Gear+④	87	+1	0	+1	0	+1	6	+1	6	+2
Freakish Bestiary	Valor Gear②	36	+1	0	+1	0	+1	2	+1	4	+1
Freakish Bestiary+	Valor Gear+②	39	+1	0	+1	0	+1	2	+1	5	+1
Madman's Vita	Fearless Gear③	24	+1	0	+1	4	+2	2	+1	5	+1
Madman's Vita+	Fearless Gear+③	30	+1	0	+1	4	+2	2	+1	5	+1
Untitled Writings	Prestige Gear④	37	+1	0	+1	6	+2	3	+1	9	+1
Untitled Writings+	Prestige Gear+④	41	+1	0	+1	6	+2	3	+1	9	+1
Abandoned Dogma	Crisis Gear⑤	60	+3	36	+3	0	+1	8	+1	8	+1
Abandoned Dogma+	Crisis Gear+⑤	67	+3	42	+3	0	+1	8	+1	9	+1
Atlas of Omens	Omega Gear⑥	73	+1	41	+1	0	+3	10	+3	13	+1
Atlas of Omens+	Omega Gear+⑥	103	+1	45	+1	0	+3	10	+3	12	+1
Revolting Scrapbook	Hazard Gear⑤	84	+1	5	+1	0	+3	8	+3	12	+1
Revolting Scrapbook+	Hazard Gear+⑤	96	+1	7	+1	0	+3	8	+3	10	+1
Lost Heterodoxy	Rage Gear⑤	98	+3	25	+3	4	+1	0	+1	10	+1
Lost Heterodoxy+	Rage Gear+⑤	100	+3	28	+3	4	+1	8	+1	10	+1
Otherworldly Tales	Champion Gear⑤	64	+1	36	+1	0	+3	8	+3	9	+1
Otherworldly Tales+	Champion Gear+⑤	67	+1	37	+1	0	+3	8	+3	9	+1
Indescribable Lore	Ultimate Gear⑥	90	+3	41	+3	0	+1	10	+1	13	+1
Indescribable Lore+	Ultimate Gear+⑥	94	+3	52	+3	0	+1	10	+1	12	+1
Radical Treatise	Pandora's Gear⑤	92	+5	30	+5	0	+5	10	+5	11	+5
Radical Treatise+	Pandora's Gear+⑤	125	+1	34	+1	0	+1	10	+1	12	+1
Book of Retribution	Zero Gear⑤	124	+4	30	+4	0	+4	10	+4	19	+4
Midnight Snack	Casual Gear②	36	+1	0	+1	0	+1	0	+1	4	+1
Dear Diary	Mystery Gear③	90	+1	0	+1	0	+1	0	+1	9	+1

WEAPON ABILITIES

Weapon	Abilities gained with units: 1 Unit	2 Units	3 Units	Act. Spd.	Atk. Move Land	Atk. Move Air	Combo Land	Combo Air
Black Primer	—	—	—	1.0	1.0	1.0	4	3
White Tome	—	—	—	1.0	1.0	1.0	4	3
White Tome+	Magic Bracer	—	—	1.0	1.0	1.0	4	3
Illicit Research	Magic Bracer	Fire Finish	—	1.0	1.0	1.0	3	3
Illicit Research+	Magic Bracer	Thunder Finish	—	1.0	1.0	1.0	3	3
Buried Secrets	Magic Bracer	Blizzard Finish	Magic Finale	1.0	1.0	1.0	3	3
Buried Secrets+	Magic Bracer	Aero Finish	Magic Finale	1.0	1.0	1.0	3	3
Buried Secrets++	Magic Bracer	Magic Finale	Magical Strike	1.0	1.0	1.0	3	3
Arcane Compendium	—	—	—	1.1	1.0	1.0	4	3
Arcane Compendium+	Combo Boost	—	—	1.1	1.0	1.0	4	3
Dissenter's Notes	Combo Boost	Chain Power	—	1.0	1.0	1.0	3	3
Dissenter's Notes+	Chain Power	Chain Time	—	1.0	1.0	1.0	3	3
Nefarious Codex	Combo Boost	Chain Power	Combo-Jump	1.1	1.0	1.0	3	3
Nefarious Codex+	Chain Power	Chain Time	Heart Bonus	1.1	1.0	1.0	3	3
Nefarious Codex++	Chain Power	Chain Time	Heart Bonus	1.1	1.0	1.0	3	3
Mystic Album	Striker	Vitality Source	—	1.0	1.0	1.0	4	3
Mystic Album+	Striker	Offensive Block	—	1.0	1.0	1.0	4	3
Cursed Manual	Defender	Second Chance	Combo-Block	1.0	1.0	1.0	4	3
Cursed Manual+	Striker	Vitality Source	Offensive Block	1.0	1.0	1.0	4	3
Taboo Text	Combo Boost	Combo-Jump	—	1.0	1.0	1.0	4	3
Taboo Text+	Chain Power	Combo-Jump	—	1.0	1.0	1.0	4	3
Eldritch Esoterica	Chain Power	Aero Finish	Combo-Air Slide	1.0	1.0	1.0	4	3
Eldritch Esoterica+	Combo Boost	Aero Finish	Combo-Jump	1.0	1.0	1.0	4	3
Freakish Bestiary	Defender	—	—	1.0	1.0	1.0	4	3
Freakish Bestiary+	Defender	—	—	1.0	1.0	1.0	4	3
Madman's Vita	Defender	Offensive Block	—	1.0	1.0	1.0	3	3
Madman's Vita+	Defender	Combo-Block	—	1.0	1.0	1.0	3	3
Untitled Writings	Defender	Chain Time	Combo-Block	1.0	1.0	1.0	3	2
Untitled Writings+	Defender	Chain Time	Offensive Block	1.0	1.0	1.0	3	2
Abandoned Dogma	Magic Bracer	Aero Finish	Alive 'n' Kicking	1.1	1.0	1.0	3	3
Abandoned Dogma+	Magic Bracer	Blizzard Finish	Alive 'n' Kicking	1.1	1.0	1.0	3	3
Atlas of Omens	Combo Boost	Chain Power	Offensive Block	1.1	1.0	1.0	3	3
Atlas of Omens+	Combo Boost	Chain Power	Combo-Block	1.1	1.0	1.0	3	3
Revolting Scrapbook	Combo Boost	Chain Power	Combo-Block	1.2	1.0	1.0	3	3
Revolting Scrapbook+	Combo Boost	Chain Power	Offensive Block	1.2	1.0	1.0	3	3
Lost Heterodoxy	Offensive Block	Thunder Finish	Blizzard Finish	1.0	1.0	1.0	4	3
Lost Heterodoxy+	Offensive Block	Fire Finish	Aero Finish	1.0	1.0	1.0	4	3
Otherworldly Tales	Chain Time	Offensive Block	Second Chance	1.0	1.0	1.0	3	2
Otherworldly Tales+	Chain Power	Combo-Block	Second Chance	1.0	1.0	1.0	3	2
Indescribable Lore	Aero Finish	Blizzard Finish	Alive 'n' Kicking	1.2	1.0	1.0	3	3
Indescribable Lore+	Magic Bracer	Magic Finale	Magical Strike	1.2	1.0	1.0	3	3
Radical Treatise	Chain Time	Vitality Barrier	Heart Bonus	1.1	1.0	1.0	4	2
Radical Treatise+	Chain Time	Vitality Barrier	Heart Bonus	1.0	1.0	1.0	4	2
Book of Retribution	Magic Bracer	Heart Bonus	Magical Strike	1.0	1.0	1.0	4	3
Midnight Snack	Heart Bonus	—	—	1.0	1.0	1.0	3	3
Dear Diary	Fire Finish	Thunder Finish	—	1.0	1.0	1.0	4	3

SAÏX

VII

Weapon: Claymore

Second in command who longs for the heart he does not have. Only the moon breaks his icy calm. He appears to have joined the Organization at the same time as Axel and the two may have known each other beforehand.

CHARACTER STATS

LEVEL	MAX HP	STRENGTH	MAGIC POWER	DEFENSE POWER	CRITICAL %	CRIT. BONUS
1	65	9	29	7	10	7
2	68	10	31	8	10	8
3	71	11	32	9	10	8
4	75	12	35	10	10	9
5	78	12	36	12	10	9
6	81	13	37	13	10	9
7	84	14	41	14	10	10
8	87	15	41	16	10	10
9	90	16	42	17	10	11
10	94	16	45	18	10	11
11	97	17	46	19	10	11
12	100	18	48	21	10	12
13	103	19	50	22	10	12
14	106	19	50	23	10	13
15	109	20	53	25	10	13
16	112	21	54	26	10	13
17	116	22	55	27	10	14
18	119	23	58	28	10	14
19	122	23	59	30	10	15
20	125	24	60	31	10	15
21	128	25	63	32	10	15
22	131	26	64	34	10	16
23	134	27	65	35	10	16
24	138	27	67	36	10	17
25	141	28	69	37	10	17
26	144	29	69	39	10	17
27	147	30	72	40	10	18
28	150	30	73	41	10	18
29	153	31	74	43	10	19
30	157	32	77	44	10	19
31	160	33	78	45	10	19
32	163	34	81	46	10	20
33	166	34	82	48	10	20
34	169	35	83	49	10	21
35	172	36	86	50	10	21
36	175	37	86	52	10	21
37	179	38	88	53	10	22
38	182	38	90	54	10	22
39	185	39	91	55	10	23
40	188	40	92	57	10	23
41	191	41	95	58	10	23
42	194	41	96	59	10	24
43	197	42	97	61	10	24
44	201	43	100	62	10	25
45	204	44	101	63	10	25
46	207	45	102	64	10	25
47	210	45	105	66	10	26
48	213	46	106	67	10	26
49	216	47	107	68	10	27
50	220	48	109	70	10	27
51	223	49	110	71	10	27
52	226	49	113	72	10	28
53	229	50	114	73	10	28
54	232	51	115	75	10	29
55	235	52	118	76	10	29
56	238	52	119	77	10	29
57	242	53	120	79	10	30
58	245	54	122	80	10	30
59	248	55	124	81	10	31
60	251	56	125	82	10	31
61	254	56	127	84	10	31
62	257	57	128	85	10	32
63	260	58	130	86	10	32
64	264	59	132	88	10	33
65	267	60	133	89	10	33
66	270	60	134	90	10	33
67	273	61	137	91	10	34
68	276	62	138	93	10	34
69	279	63	139	94	10	35
70	283	63	142	95	10	35
71	286	64	143	97	10	35
72	289	65	145	98	10	36
73	292	66	147	99	10	36
74	295	67	148	100	10	37
75	298	67	150	102	10	37
76	301	68	151	103	10	37
77	305	69	152	104	10	38
78	308	70	155	106	10	38
79	311	71	156	107	10	39
80	314	71	157	108	10	39
81	317	72	160	109	10	39
82	320	73	161	111	10	40
83	323	74	162	112	10	40
84	327	74	164	113	10	41
85	330	75	166	115	10	41
86	333	76	167	116	10	41
87	336	77	169	117	10	42
88	339	78	170	118	10	42
89	342	78	172	120	10	43
90	346	79	174	121	10	43
91	349	80	175	122	10	43
92	352	81	178	124	10	44
93	355	82	179	125	10	44
94	358	82	180	126	10	45
95	361	83	183	127	10	45
96	364	84	184	129	10	45
97	368	85	185	130	10	46
98	371	85	187	131	10	46
99	374	86	188	133	10	47
100	377	87	190	134	10	47

** Numbers in grey indicate when that number cannot go any higher than the previous number.*

WEAPON LIST & STATS

Weapon	Gear Panel	Strength Add	Strength Unit	Magic Add	Magic Unit	Defense Add	Defense Unit	Crit. % Add	Crit. % Unit	Crit. Bonus Add	Crit. Bonus Unit
New Moon NA	(No Panel)	15	—	0	—	0	—	0	—	2	—
Werewolf	Skill Gear	40	—	0	—	1	—	2	—	3	—
Werewolf+	Skill Gear+②	52	+1	0	+1	1	+1	0	+1	3	+1
Artemis	Technical Gear③	51	+2	0	+1	0	+1	4	+1	3	+1
Artemis+	Technical Gear+③	62	+2	0	+1	2	+1	0	+1	5	+1
Luminary	Duel Gear④	50	+2	0	+1	3	+1	6	+1	7	+1
Luminary+	Duel Gear+④	63	+2	0	+1	4	+1	8	+1	8	+1
Luminary++	Duel Gear++⑤	93	+5	0	+1	3	+1	0	+1	10	+1
Selene	Loaded Gear	27	—	0	—	0	—	3	—	3	—
Selene+	Loaded Gear+②	35	+1	0	+1	0	+1	4	+1	5	+1
Moonrise	Chrono Gear③	55	+1	0	+1	2	+1	6	+2	5	+1
Moonrise+	Chrono Gear+③	58	+1	0	+1	0	+1	8	+2	6	+1
Astrologia	Phantom Gear④	66	+1	0	+1	0	+1	12	+2	13	+1
Astrologia+	Phantom Gear+④	77	+1	0	+1	0	+1	9	+2	7	+1
Astrologia++	Phantom Gear++⑤	86	+1	0	+1	0	+1	12	+5	10	+0
Crater	Lift Gear③	19	+1	14	+2	0	+1	4	+1	3	+1
Crater+	Lift Gear+③	44	+1	16	+2	0	+1	4	+1	3	+1
Lunar Phase	Nimble Gear④	49	+1	25	+2	0	+1	6	+1	4	+1
Lunar Phase+	Nimble Gear+④	62	+1	31	+2	0	+1	6	+1	3	+1
Crescent	Wild Gear③	29	+1	0	+1	0	+1	4	+1	4	+2
Crescent+	Wild Gear+③	44	+1	0	+1	0	+1	4	+1	3	+2
Gibbous	Ominous Gear④	69	+1	0	+1	0	+1	6	+1	5	+2
Gibbous+	Ominous Gear+④	87	+1	0	+1	0	+1	6	+1	6	+2

Weapon	Gear Panel	Strength Add	Strength Unit	Magic Add	Magic Unit	Defense Add	Defense Unit	Crit. % Add	Crit. % Unit	Crit. Bonus Add	Crit. Bonus Unit
Berserker	Valor Gear②	36	+1	0	+1	2	+1	2	+1	4	+1
Berserker+	Valor Gear+②	39	+1	0	+1	2	+1	2	+1	5	+1
Twilight	Fearless Gear③	24	+1	0	+1	4	+2	2	+1	5	+1
Twilight+	Fearless Gear+③	33	+1	0	+1	4	+2	2	+1	5	+1
Queen of the Night	Prestige Gear④	37	+1	0	+1	6	+2	3	+1	9	+1
Queen of the Night+	Prestige Gear+④	41	+1	0	+1	6	+2	3	+1	9	+1
Balsamic Moon	Crisis Gear⑤	63	+3	36	+3	4	+1	8	+1	8	+1
Balsamic Moon+	Crisis Gear+⑤	72	+3	42	+3	4	+1	0	+1	9	+1
Orbit	Omega Gear⑥	78	+3	48	+3	5	+1	10	+1	13	+1
Orbit+	Omega Gear+⑥	108	+3	52	+3	5	+1	0	+1	12	+1
Light Year	Hazard Gear⑤	108	+3	0	+1	8	+3	0	+1	15	+1
Light Year+	Hazard Gear+⑤	114	+3	0	+1	8	+3	8	+1	11	+1
King of the Night	Rage Gear⑤	88	+1	0	+1	8	+3	8	+1	8	+3
King of the Night+	Rage Gear+⑤	90	+1	0	+1	8	+3	8	+1	9	+3
Moonset	Champion Gear⑤	71	+3	0	+1	4	+1	12	+3	11	+1
Moonset+	Champion Gear+⑤	76	+3	0	+1	4	+1	16	+3	11	+1
Horoscope	Ultimate Gear⑥	108	+3	0	+1	5	+1	15	+3	16	+1
Horoscope+	Ultimate Gear+⑥	112	+3	0	+1	5	+1	20	+3	14	+1
Dichotomy	Pandora's Gear⑤	92	+5	30	+5	0	+5	10	+5	11	+5
Dichotomy+	Pandora's Gear+⑤	125	+1	34	+1	0	+1	10	+1	12	+1
Lunatic	Zero Gear⑤	124	+4	30	+4	0	+4	10	+4	19	+4
Just Desserts	Casual Gear②	36	+1	0	+1	0	+1	0	+1	4	+1
Bunnymoon	Mystery Gear③	90	+1	0	+1	0	+1	0	+1	9	+1

WEAPON ABILITIES

Weapon	Abilities gained with units: 1 Unit	2 Units	3 Units	Act. Spd.	Atk. Move Land	Atk. Move Air	Combo Land	Combo Air
New Moon	—	—	—	1.0	1.0	1.0	3	3
Werewolf	—	—	—	1.0	1.0	1.0	2	3
Werewolf+	Striker	—	—	1.0	1.0	1.0	2	3
Artemis	Striker	Grand Slam	—	1.0	1.0	1.0	3	3
Artemis+	Striker	Vitality Source	—	1.0	1.0	1.0	3	3
Luminary	Striker	Vitality Barrier	Brick Wall	1.0	1.0	1.0	3	3
Luminary+	Striker	Vitality Source	Alive 'n' Kicking	1.0	1.0	1.0	3	3
Luminary++	Vitality Source	Vitality Barrier	Brick Wall	1.0	1.0	1.0	3	3
Selene	—	—	—	1.0	1.0	1.0	3	3
Selene+	Combo Boost	—	—	1.0	1.0	1.0	3	3
Moonrise	Combo Boost	Chain Power	—	1.0	1.0	1.0	4	3
Moonrise+	Chain Time	Combo-Jump	—	1.0	1.0	1.0	4	3
Astrologia	Combo Boost	Chain Power	Chain Time	1.1	1.0	1.0	5	3
Astrologia+	Chain Time	Combo-Jump	Critical Boost	1.1	1.0	1.0	5	3
Astrologia++	Combo Boost	Combo-Jump	Critical Boost	1.1	1.0	1.0	6	3
Crater	Fire Finish	Thunder Finish	—	1.0	1.0	1.0	3	2
Crater+	Aero Finish	Blizzard Finish	—	1.0	1.0	1.0	3	2
Lunar Phase	Thunder Finish	Aero Finish	Blizzard Finish	1.0	1.0	1.0	3	3
Lunar Phase+	Fire Finish	Thunder Finish	Aero Finish	1.0	1.0	1.0	3	3
Crescent	Chain Power	Chain Time	—	1.0	1.0	1.0	4	4
Crescent+	Combo-Jump	Combo-Air Slide	—	1.0	1.0	1.0	4	4
Gibbous	Combo-Jump	Combo-Air Slide	Critical Boost	1.0	1.0	1.0	5	4
Gibbous+	Chain Power	Chain Time	Critical Boost	1.0	1.0	1.0	5	4
Berserker	Defender	—	—	1.0	1.0	1.0	2	3

Weapon	Abilities gained with units: 1 Unit	2 Units	3 Units	Act. Spd.	Atk. Move Land	Atk. Move Air	Combo Land	Combo Air
Berserker+	Offensive Block	—	—	1.0	1.0	1.0	2	3
Twilight	Defender	Offensive Block	—	1.0	1.0	1.0	3	3
Twilight+	Defender	Offensive Block	—	1.0	1.0	1.0	3	3
Queen of the Night	Defender	Offensive Block	Chain Power	1.0	1.0	1.0	4	3
Queen of the Night+	Defender	Offensive Block	Combo Boost	1.0	1.0	1.0	4	3
Balsamic Moon	Vitality Source	Fire Finish	Aero Finish	1.0	1.0	1.0	4	2
Balsamic Moon+	Vitality Source	Thunder Finish	Blizzard Finish	1.0	1.0	1.0	4	2
Orbit	Aero Finish	Blizzard Finish	Alive 'n' Kicking	1.0	1.0	1.0	4	3
Orbit+	Fire Finish	Thunder Finish	Alive 'n' Kicking	1.0	1.0	1.0	4	3
Light Year	Offensive Block	Combo-Block	Vitality Barrier	1.0	1.0	1.0	3	4
Light Year+	Offensive Block	Combo-Block	Damage Control	1.0	1.0	1.0	3	4
King of the Night	Chain Power	Chain Time	Heart Bonus	1.0	1.0	1.0	3	4
King of the Night+	Offensive Block	Combo-Jump	Combo-Air Slide	1.0	1.0	1.0	3	4
Moonset	Combo-Jump	Striker	Vitality Source	1.0	1.0	1.0	5	2
Moonset+	Combo-Jump	Grand Slam	Critical Boost	1.0	1.0	1.0	5	2
Horoscope	Grand Slam	Critical Boost	Damage Control	1.2	1.0	1.0	5	3
Horoscope+	Chain Power	Combo-Jump	Combo-Block	1.2	1.0	1.0	5	3
Dichotomy	Chain Time	Heart Bonus	Vitality Source	1.0	1.0	1.0	4	3
Dichotomy+	Chain Time	Heart Bonus	Vitality Source	1.0	1.0	1.0	4	3
Lunatic	Combo Boost	Critical Boost	Brick Wall	1.1	1.0	1.0	3	3
Just Desserts	Heart Bonus	—	—	1.0	1.0	1.0	3	3
Bunnymoon	Fire Finish	Aero Finish	—	1.0	1.0	1.0	3	3

AXEL

VIII

Weapon: Chakrams

An assassin who puts his own agenda first and everything else on the back burner. Roxas's mentor within the Organization, he wields fire. Although he, like all Nobodies, lacks a heart, he appears to enjoy the time he spends with his protégé.

CHARACTER STATS

LEVEL	MAX HP	STRENGTH	MAGIC POWER	DEFENSE POWER	CRITICAL %	CRIT. BONUS
1	62	9	34	6	5	6
2	65	9	35	8	5	7
3	68	11	38	9	5	7
4	71	12	40	10	5	7
5	74	12	42	12	5	7
6	77	13	43	13	5	8
7	80	14	46	14	5	8
8	83	15	46	15	5	8
9	86	15	49	17	5	8
10	89	16	49	18	5	9
11	92	17	53	19	5	9
12	95	18	53	21	5	9
13	98	19	56	22	5	9
14	101	19	56	23	5	10
15	104	20	60	24	5	10
16	107	21	60	26	5	10
17	110	22	63	27	5	10
18	113	23	64	28	5	11
19	116	23	67	30	5	11
20	119	24	67	31	5	11
21	122	25	70	32	5	11
22	125	26	71	33	5	12
23	128	26	74	35	5	12
24	131	27	74	36	5	12
25	134	28	77	37	5	12
26	137	29	78	39	5	13
27	140	30	81	40	5	13
28	143	30	82	41	5	13
29	146	31	84	42	5	13
30	149	32	85	44	5	14
31	152	33	88	45	5	14
32	155	34	89	46	5	14
33	158	34	92	48	5	14
34	161	35	92	49	5	15
35	164	36	95	50	5	15
36	167	37	96	51	5	15
37	170	37	99	53	5	15
38	173	38	100	54	5	16
39	176	39	102	55	5	16
40	179	40	103	57	5	16
41	182	41	106	58	5	16
42	185	41	107	59	5	17
43	188	42	110	60	5	17
44	191	43	110	62	5	17
45	194	44	113	63	5	17
46	197	45	114	64	5	18
47	200	45	117	66	5	18
48	203	46	118	67	5	18
49	206	47	120	68	5	18
50	209	48	121	69	5	19
51	212	48	124	71	5	19
52	215	49	125	72	5	19
53	218	50	127	73	5	19
54	221	51	128	75	5	20
55	224	52	131	76	5	20
56	227	52	132	77	5	20
57	230	53	135	78	5	20
58	233	54	136	80	5	21
59	236	55	138	81	5	21
60	239	56	139	82	5	21
61	242	56	142	84	5	21
62	245	57	143	85	5	22
63	248	58	145	86	5	22
64	251	59	146	87	5	22
65	254	59	149	89	5	22
66	257	60	150	90	5	23
67	260	61	153	91	5	23
68	263	62	154	93	5	23
69	266	63	156	94	5	23
70	269	63	157	95	5	24
71	272	64	160	97	5	24
72	275	65	161	98	5	24
73	278	66	163	99	5	24
74	281	66	164	100	5	25
75	284	67	167	102	5	25
76	287	68	168	103	5	25
77	290	69	171	104	5	25
78	293	70	172	106	5	26
79	296	70	174	107	5	26
80	299	71	175	108	5	26
81	302	72	178	109	5	26
82	305	73	179	111	5	27
83	308	74	181	112	5	27
84	311	74	182	113	5	27
85	314	75	185	115	5	27
86	317	76	186	116	5	28
87	320	77	189	117	5	28
88	323	77	190	118	5	28
89	326	78	192	120	5	28
90	329	79	193	121	5	29
91	332	80	196	122	5	29
92	335	81	197	124	5	29
93	338	81	199	125	5	29
94	341	82	200	126	5	30
95	344	83	203	127	5	30
96	347	84	204	129	5	30
97	350	85	207	130	5	30
98	353	85	208	131	5	31
99	356	86	210	133	5	31
100	359	87	211	134	5	31

** Numbers in grey indicate when that number cannot go any higher than the previous number.*

WEAPON LIST & STATS

Weapon	Gear Panel	Strength		Magic		Defense		Crit. %		Crit. Bonus	
		Add	Unit	Add	Unit	Add	Unit	Add	Unit	Add	Unit
Ashes	NA (No Panel)	15	—	0	—	0	—	0	—	2	—
Doldrums	Skill Gear	18	—	11	—	0	—	2	—	2	—
Doldrums+	Skill Gear+②	20	+1	12	+1	0	+1	2	+1	2	+1
Delayed Action	Technical Gear③	36	+1	14	+2	0	+1	4	+1	2	+1
Delayed Action+	Technical Gear+ ③	44	+1	21	+2	0	+1	4	+1	4	+1
Dive-Bombers	Duel Gear④	35	+1	31	+2	0	+1	6	+1	7	+1
Dive-Bombers+	Duel Gear+④	45	+1	35	+2	0	+1	6	+1	5	+1
Dive-Bombers++	Duel Gear++⑤	68	+1	39	+5	0	+1	8	+1	6	+1
Combustion	Loaded Gear	27	—	0	—	0	—	3	—	3	—
Combustion+	Loaded Gear+②	35	+1	0	+1	0	+1	4	+1	5	+1
Moulin Rouge	Chrono Gear③	55	+1	0	+1	0	+1	6	+2	5	+1
Moulin Rouge+	Chrono Gear+③	58	+1	0	+1	0	+1	8	+2	6	+1
Blaze of Glory	Phantom Gear④	66	+1	0	+1	0	+1	12	+2	13	+1
Blaze of Glory+	Phantom Gear+④	77	+1	0	+1	0	+1	9	+2	7	+1
Blaze of Glory++	Phantom Gear++⑤	86	+1	0	+1	0	+1	12	+5	10	+1
Prometheus	Lift Gear③	22	+1	0	+1	4	+2	2	+1	3	+1
Prometheus+	Lift Gear+③	52	+1	0	+1	4	+2	2	+1	4	+1
Ifrit	Nimble Gear④	57	+1	0	+1	6	+2	3	+1	5	+1
Ifrit+	Nimble Gear+④	73	+1	0	+1	6	+2	3	+1	4	+1
Magma Ocean	Wild Gear③	44	+1	0	+1	0	+1	4	+1	3	+2
Magma Ocean+	Wild Gear+③	29	+1	0	+1	0	+1	4	+1	4	+2
Volcanics	Ominous Gear④	62	+1	0	+1	0	+1	6	+1	5	+2
Volcanics+	Ominous Gear+④	75	+1	0	+1	0	+1	6	+1	6	+2
Inferno	Valor Gear②	44	+1	0	+1	1	+1	2	+1	5	+1
Inferno+	Valor Gear+②	46	+1	0	+1	1	+1	0	+1	6	+1
Sizzling Edge	Fearless Gear③	55	+2	0	+1	2	+1	4	+1	6	+1
Sizzling Edge+	Fearless Gear+③	60	+2	0	+1	2	+1	0	+1	6	+1
Corona	Prestige Gear④	67	+2	0	+1	3	+1	0	+1	10	+1
Corona+	Prestige Gear+④	77	+2	0	+1	3	+1	6	+1	11	+1
Ferris Wheel	Crisis Gear⑤	55	+1	31	+3	0	+1	12	+3	8	+1
Ferris Wheel+	Crisis Gear+⑤	62	+1	37	+3	0	+1	16	+3	9	+1
Burnout	Omega Gear⑥	73	+1	41	+3	0	+1	15	+3	13	+1
Burnout+	Omega Gear+⑥	103	+1	45	+3	0	+1	20	+3	12	+1
Omega Trinity	Hazard Gear⑤	84	+1	0	+1	8	+3	6	+1	12	+3
Omega Trinity+	Hazard Gear+⑤	96	+1	0	+1	8	+3	6	+1	10	+3
Outbreak	Rage Gear⑤	88	+1	0	+1	0	+1	12	+3	8	+3
Outbreak+	Rage Gear+⑤	93	+1	0	+1	0	+1	10	+3	9	+3
Double Edge	Champion Gear⑤	72	+3	27	+3	4	+1	0	+1	11	+1
Double Edge+	Champion Gear+⑤	76	+3	28	+3	4	+1	8	+1	11	+1
Wildfire	Ultimate Gear⑥	107	+3	27	+3	5	+1	0	+1	13	+1
Wildfire+	Ultimate Gear+⑥	110	+3	34	+3	5	+1	10	+1	15	+1
Prominence	Pandora's Gear⑤	92	+5	30	+5	0	+5	10	+5	11	+5
Prominence+	Pandora's Gear+⑤	125	+1	34	+1	0	+1	10	+1	12	+1
Eternal Flames	Zero Gear⑤	124	+4	30	+4	0	+4	10	+4	19	+4
Pizza Cut	Casual Gear②	36	+1	0	+1	0	+1	0	+1	4	+1
Conformers	Mystery Gear③	90	+1	0	+1	0	+1	4	+8	9	+0

WEAPON ABILITIES

Weapon	Abilities gained with units			Act. Spd.	Atk. Move		Combo	
	1 Unit	2 Units	3 Units		Land	Air	Land	Air
Ashes	—	—	—	1.0	1.0	1.0	3	3
Doldrums	—	—	—	1.0	1.0	1.0	3	2
Doldrums+	Fire Finish	—	—	1.0	1.0	1.0	3	2
Delayed Action	Fire Finish	Magic Bracer	—	1.0	1.0	1.0	3	2
Delayed Action+	Fire Finish	Magic Finale	—	1.0	1.0	1.0	3	2
Dive-Bombers	Fire Finish	Magic Finale	Magical Strike	1.0	1.0	1.0	3	2
Dive-Bombers+	Fire Finish	Magic Bracer	Magic Finale	1.0	1.0	1.0	3	2
Dive-Bombers++	Fire Finish	Magic Finale	Magical Strike	1.0	1.0	1.0	3	2
Combustion	—	—	—	1.1	1.13	1.0	4	3
Combustion+	Combo Boost	—	—	1.1	1.13	1.0	4	3
Moulin Rouge	Combo Boost	Combo-Jump	—	1.1	1.0	1.0	5	3
Moulin Rouge+	Chain Boost	Combo-Jump	—	1.1	1.0	1.0	5	3
Blaze of Glory	Combo Boost	Chain Power	Chain Time	1.2	1.0	1.0	6	3
Blaze of Glory+	Combo Boost	Chain Power	Combo-Jump	1.2	1.0	1.0	6	3
Blaze of Glory++	Combo Boost	Chain Power	Combo-Jump	1.2	1.0	1.0	7	3
Prometheus	Offensive Block	Defender	—	1.0	1.13	1.0	3	2
Prometheus+	Offensive Block	Defender	—	1.0	1.13	1.0	3	2
Ifrit	Offensive Block	Defender	Chain Power	1.0	1.13	1.0	3	3
Ifrit+	Offensive Block	Defender	Chain Time	1.0	1.13	1.0	3	2
Magma Ocean	Combo Boost	Combo-Jump	—	1.0	1.0	1.13	3	4
Magma Ocean+	Chain Power	Combo-Jump	—	1.0	1.0	1.13	3	5
Volcanics	Chain Power	Combo-Jump	Combo-Air Slide	1.0	1.0	1.19	3	4
Volcanics+	Combo Boost	Combo-Jump	Combo-Air Slide	1.0	1.0	1.19	3	5
Inferno	Defender	—	—	1.0	1.0	1.0	2	1
Inferno+	Striker	—	—	1.0	1.0	1.0	2	1
Sizzling Edge	Defender	Striker	—	1.0	1.0	1.0	3	1
Sizzling Edge+	Defender	Striker	—	1.0	1.0	1.0	3	1
Corona	Defender	Striker	Grand Slam	1.0	1.0	1.0	4	1
Corona+	Defender	Striker	Damage Control	1.0	1.0	1.0	4	1
Ferris Wheel	Fire Finish	Combo Boost	Combo-Jump	1.2	1.0	1.0	7	3
Ferris Wheel+	Fire Finish	Magic Bracer	Combo-Jump	1.2	1.0	1.0	10	3
Burnout	Fire Finish	Magic Bracer	Magical Strike	1.3	1.25	1.0	7	3
Burnout+	Fire Finish	Combo Boost	Chain Power	1.3	1.25	1.0	10	3
Omega Trinity	Offensive Block	Chain Time	Combo-Jump	1.0	1.0	1.19	3	5
Omega Trinity+	Offensive Block	Chain Time	Combo-Air Slide	1.0	1.0	1.19	3	5
Outbreak	Combo Boost	Chain Power	Chain Time	1.0	1.13	1.19	3	5
Outbreak+	Combo Boost	Combo-Jump	Combo-Air Slide	1.0	1.13	1.19	3	5
Double Edge	Fire Finish	Magic Bracer	Brick Wall	1.0	1.0	1.0	4	2
Double Edge+	Fire Finish	Magic Finale	Grand Slam	1.0	1.0	1.0	4	2
Wildfire	Fire Finish	Magic Finale	Grand Slam	1.0	1.0	1.0	6	2
Wildfire+	Fire Finish	Magic Bracer	Brick Wall	1.0	1.0	1.0	6	2
Prominence	Fire Finish	Critical Boost	Alive 'n' Kicking	1.0	1.13	1.13	3	4
Prominence+	Fire Finish	Critical Boost	Grand Slam	1.0	1.13	1.13	3	4
Eternal Flames	Defender	Damage Control	Second Chance	1.0	1.13	1.13	3	3
Pizza Cut	Fire Finish	—	—	1.0	1.0	1.0	3	3
Conformers	Striker	Grand Slam	—	1.0	1.25	1.0	2	3

DEMYX

IX

Weapon: Sitar

Prefers to kick back with his sitar and leave the dirty work to the water under his command.

CHARACTER STATS

LEVEL	MAX HP	STRENGTH	MAGIC POWER	DEFENSE POWER	CRITICAL %	CRIT. BONUS
1	64	8	38	7	5	6
2	67	8	43	8	5	6
3	70	10	43	9	5	6
4	73	10	45	11	5	7
5	76	11	48	12	5	7
6	79	12	49	13	5	7
7	82	13	51	14	5	7
8	85	13	53	16	5	7
9	88	14	54	17	5	8
10	91	15	56	18	5	8
11	94	15	59	20	5	8
12	97	16	60	21	5	8
13	100	17	63	22	5	8
14	103	18	65	23	5	9
15	107	18	66	25	5	9
16	110	19	68	26	5	9
17	113	20	71	27	5	9
18	116	20	71	29	5	9
19	119	21	74	30	5	10
20	122	22	75	31	5	10
21	125	23	78	33	5	10
22	128	23	80	34	5	10
23	131	24	81	35	5	11
24	134	25	83	36	5	11
25	137	25	86	38	5	11
26	140	26	87	39	5	11
27	143	27	90	40	5	11
28	146	28	92	42	5	12
29	150	28	93	43	5	12
30	153	29	95	44	5	12
31	156	30	98	45	5	12
32	159	30	99	47	5	12
33	162	31	101	48	5	13
34	165	32	104	49	5	13
35	168	33	105	51	5	13
36	171	33	107	52	5	13
37	174	34	110	53	5	13
38	177	35	111	54	5	14
39	180	35	113	56	5	14
40	183	36	114	57	5	14
41	186	37	117	58	5	14
42	189	38	119	60	5	15
43	193	38	120	61	5	15
44	196	39	123	62	5	15
45	199	40	125	63	5	15
46	202	40	126	65	5	15
47	205	41	129	66	5	16
48	208	42	131	67	5	16
49	211	43	132	69	5	16
50	214	43	135	70	5	16
51	217	44	137	71	5	16
52	220	45	138	72	5	17
53	223	45	141	74	5	17
54	226	46	143	75	5	17
55	229	47	144	76	5	17
56	232	48	147	78	5	17
57	235	48	149	79	5	18
58	239	49	150	80	5	18
59	242	50	153	81	5	18
60	245	50	154	83	5	18
61	248	51	156	84	5	19
62	251	52	159	85	5	19
63	254	53	160	87	5	19
64	257	53	162	88	5	19
65	260	54	165	89	5	19
66	263	55	166	90	5	20
67	266	55	168	92	5	20
68	269	56	171	93	5	20
69	272	57	172	94	5	20
70	275	58	174	96	5	20
71	278	58	177	97	5	21
72	282	59	178	98	5	21
73	285	60	180	99	5	21
74	288	60	183	101	5	21
75	291	61	184	102	5	21
76	294	62	186	103	5	22
77	297	63	189	105	5	22
78	300	63	190	106	5	22
79	303	64	192	107	5	22
80	306	65	193	108	5	23
81	309	65	196	110	5	23
82	312	66	198	111	5	23
83	315	67	199	112	5	23
84	318	68	202	114	5	23
85	321	68	204	115	5	24
86	325	69	205	116	5	24
87	328	70	208	117	5	24
88	331	70	210	119	5	24
89	334	71	211	120	5	24
90	337	72	214	121	5	25
91	340	73	216	123	5	25
92	343	73	217	124	5	25
93	346	74	220	125	5	25
94	349	75	222	126	5	25
95	352	75	223	128	5	26
96	355	76	226	129	5	26
97	358	77	228	130	5	26
98	361	78	229	132	5	26
99	364	78	232	133	5	26
100	368	79	233	134	5	27

** Numbers in grey indicate when that number cannot go any higher than the previous number.*

WEAPON LIST & STATS

Weapon	Gear Panel	Strength		Magic		Defense		Crit. %		Crit. Bonus	
		Add	Unit	Add	Unit	Add	Unit	Add	Unit	Add	Unit
Basic Model	NA (No Panel)	15	—	0	—	0	—	0	—	2	—
Tune-Up	Skill Gear	18	—	11	—	0	—	2	—	2	—
Tune-Up+	Skill Gear+②	20	+1	12	+1	0	+1	2	+1	2	+1
Quartet	Technical Gear③	36	+1	14	+2	0	+1	4	+1	2	+1
Quartet+	Technical Gear+③	44	+1	21	+2	0	+1	4	+1	4	+1
Quintet	Duel Gear④	35	+1	31	+2	0	+1	6	+1	5	+1
Quintet+	Duel Gear+④	45	+1	35	+2	0	+1	8	+1	6	+1
Quintet++	Duel Gear++⑤	68	+1	39	+5	0	+1	6	+1	7	+1
Overture	Loaded Gear	27	—	0	—	0	—	3	—	3	—
Overture+	Loaded Gear+②	35	+1	0	+1	0	+1	4	+1	5	+1
Old Hand	Chrono Gear③	50	+1	0	+1	0	+1	6	+2	5	+1
Old Hand+	Chrono Gear+③	55	+1	0	+1	0	+1	8	+2	6	+1
Da Capo	Phantom Gear④	66	+1	0	+1	0	+1	12	+2	13	+1
Da Capo+	Phantom Gear+④	77	+1	0	+1	0	+1	9	+2	7	+1
Da Capo++	Phantom Gear++⑤	86	+1	0	+1	0	+1	12	+5	10	+1
Power Chord	Lift Gear③	61	+2	0	+1	2	+1	4	+1	5	+1
Power Chord+	Lift Gear+③	70	+2	0	+1	2	+1	0	+1	4	+1
Fermata	Nimble Gear④	68	+2	0	+1	3	+1	0	+1	5	+1
Fermata+	Nimble Gear+④	87	+2	0	+1	3	+1	6	+1	5	+1
Interlude	Wild Gear③	30	+1	0	+1	4	+2	2	+1	4	+1
Interlude+	Wild Gear+③	48	+1	0	+1	4	+2	2	+1	3	+1
Serenade	Ominous Gear④	72	+1	0	+1	6	+2	3	+1	5	+1
Serenade+	Ominous Gear+④	90	+1	0	+1	6	+2	3	+1	6	+1
Songbird	Valor Gear②	34	+1	0	+1	0	+1	2	+1	4	+1
Songbird+	Valor Gear+②	36	+1	0	+1	0	+1	2	+1	5	+1
Rise to Fame	Fearless Gear③	22	+1	0	+1	0	+1	4	+1	5	+2
Rise to Fame+	Fearless Gear+③	27	+1	0	+1	0	+1	4	+1	5	+2
Rock Star	Prestige Gear④	35	+1	0	+1	0	+1	6	+1	8	+2
Rock Star+	Prestige Gear+④	40	+1	0	+1	0	+1	6	+1	9	+2
Eight-Finger	Crisis Gear⑤	55	+1	31	+3	0	+1	8	+3	8	+1
Eight-Finger+	Crisis Gear+⑤	62	+1	37	+3	0	+1	8	+3	9	+1
Concerto	Omega Gear⑥	73	+1	41	+3	0	+1	10	+3	13	+1
Concerto+	Omega Gear+⑥	103	+1	45	+3	0	+1	10	+3	12	+1
Harmonics	Hazard Gear⑤	78	+1	37	+3	0	+3	8	+1	10	+1
Harmonics+	Hazard Gear+⑤	84	+1	45	+3	0	+3	8	+1	12	+1
Million Bucks	Rage Gear⑤	78	+1	0	+1	0	+1	10	+3	8	+3
Million Bucks+	Rage Gear+⑤	88	+1	0	+1	0	+1	10	+3	9	+3
Fortissimo	Champion Gear⑤	64	+1	6	+1	0	+3	8	+3	9	+1
Fortissimo+	Champion Gear+⑤	67	+1	7	+1	0	+3	8	+3	9	+1
Up to Eleven	Ultimate Gear⑥	90	+1	36	+1	0	+3	10	+3	13	+1
Up to Eleven+	Ultimate Gear+⑥	94	+1	45	+1	0	+3	10	+3	12	+1
Sanctuary	Pandora's Gear⑤	92	+5	30	+5	0	+5	10	+5	11	+5
Sanctuary+	Pandora's Gear+⑤	125	+1	34	+1	0	+1	10	+1	12	+1
Arpeggio	Zero Gear⑤	124	+4	30	+4	0	+4	10	+4	19	+4
Prince of Awesome	Casual Gear②	36	+1	0	+1	0	+1	0	+1	4	+1
After School	Mystery Gear③	90	+1	0	+1	0	+1	0	+1	9	+1

WEAPON ABILITIES

Weapon	Abilities gained with units			Act. Spd.	Attack Move		Combo	
	1 Unit	2 Units	3 Units		Land	Air	Land	Air
Basic Model	—	—	—	1.0	1.0	1.0	3	3
Tune-Up	—	—	—	1.0	1.0	1.0	4	3
Tune-Up+	Magic Bracer	—	—	1.0	1.0	1.0	4	3
Quartet	Magic Bracer	Aero Finish	—	1.0	1.0	1.0	3	3
Quartet+	Magic Bracer	Blizzard Finish	—	1.0	1.0	1.0	3	3
Quintet	Magic Bracer	Blizzard Finish	Magic Finale	1.0	1.0	1.0	3	3
Quintet+	Magic Bracer	Aero Finish	Magic Finale	1.0	1.0	1.0	3	3
Quintet++	Magic Bracer	Aero Finish	Blizzard Finish	1.0	1.0	1.0	3	3
Overture	—	—	—	1.1	1.0	1.0	3	3
Overture+	Chain Time	—	—	1.1	1.0	1.0	3	3
Old Hand	Chain Time	Chain Power	—	1.2	1.0	1.0	4	3
Old Hand+	Combo Boost	Combo-Jump	—	1.2	1.0	1.0	4	3
Da Capo	Chain Time	Chain Power	Heart Bonus	1.2	1.0	1.0	5	3
Da Capo+	Combo Boost	Combo-Jump	Heart Bonus	1.2	1.0	1.0	5	3
Da Capo++	Chain Time	Chain Power	Heart Bonus	1.3	1.0	1.0	6	3
Power Chord	Defender	Striker	—	1.0	1.0	1.0	3	2
Power Chord+	Striker	Vitality Source	—	1.0	1.0	1.0	3	2
Fermata	Striker	Vitality Source	Offensive Block	1.0	1.0	1.0	3	2
Fermata+	Defender	Striker	Offensive Block	1.0	1.0	1.0	3	2
Interlude	Defender	Offensive Block	—	1.0	1.0	1.0	4	2
Interlude+	Defender	Combo-Block	—	1.0	1.0	1.0	4	2
Serenade	Defender	Combo-Block	Heart Bonus	1.0	1.0	1.0	4	2
Serenade+	Defender	Offensive Block	Heart Bonus	1.0	1.0	1.0	4	2
Songbird	Combo-Jump	—	—	1.0	1.0	1.0	4	3
Songbird+	Combo-Jump	—	—	1.0	1.0	1.0	4	3
Rise to Fame	Combo-Jump	Chain Time	—	1.0	1.0	1.0	3	3
Rise to Fame+	Combo-Jump	Chain Power	—	1.0	1.0	1.0	3	3
Rock Star	Combo-Jump	Chain Power	Combo-Air Slide	1.0	1.0	1.0	3	3
Rock Star+	Combo-Jump	Chain Time	Combo-Air Slide	1.0	1.0	1.0	3	3
Eight-Finger	Chain Time	Chain Power	Aero Finish	1.2	1.0	1.0	4	3
Eight-Finger+	Chain Time	Chain Power	Blizzard Finish	1.2	1.0	1.0	4	3
Concerto	Chain Time	Heart Bonus	Blizzard Finish	1.2	1.0	1.0	5	3
Concerto+	Chain Time	Heart Bonus	Aero Finish	1.2	1.0	1.0	5	3
Harmonics	Magic Bracer	Offensive Block	Aero Finish	1.0	1.0	1.0	4	2
Harmonics+	Magic Bracer	Offensive Block	Blizzard Finish	1.0	1.0	1.0	4	2
Million Bucks	Chain Time	Combo-Jump	Combo-Air Slide	1.0	1.0	1.0	5	3
Million Bucks+	Chain Power	Combo-Jump	Combo-Air Slide	1.0	1.0	1.0	5	3
Fortissimo	Chain Time	Offensive Block	Combo-Jump	1.0	1.0	1.0	4	3
Fortissimo+	Chain Time	Offensive Block	Combo-Block	1.0	1.0	1.0	4	3
Up to Eleven	Chain Time	Offensive Block	Combo-Block	1.1	1.0	1.0	4	3
Up to Eleven+	Chain Time	Offensive Block	Combo-Jump	1.1	1.0	1.0	4	3
Sanctuary	Combo-Jump	Magic Bracer	Vitality Barrier	1.0	1.0	1.0	3	3
Sanctuary+	Combo-Jump	Magic Bracer	Vitality Barrier	1.0	1.0	1.0	3	3
Arpeggio	Chain Time	Heart Bonus	Magical Strike	1.0	1.0	1.0	4	3
Prince of Awesome	Offensive Block	—	—	1.0	1.0	1.0	4	3
After School	Offensive Block	Chain Time	—	1.0	1.0	1.0	3	3

LUXORD

X

Weapon: Cards

Life, to him, is just a game to be won… and he has all the time in the world to do it.

CHARACTER STATS

LEVEL	MAX HP	STRENGTH	MAGIC POWER	DEFENSE POWER	CRITICAL %	CRIT. BONUS
1	60	8	34	7	3	6
2	63	9	35	8	3	7
3	66	10	40	9	3	7
4	69	10	42	11	3	7
5	72	11	43	12	3	7
6	75	12	45	14	3	8
7	78	13	46	15	3	8
8	81	13	48	16	3	8
9	84	14	49	18	3	8
10	87	15	52	19	3	9
11	90	15	55	20	3	9
12	93	16	55	22	3	9
13	96	17	58	23	3	9
14	99	18	58	24	3	10
15	101	18	62	26	3	10
16	104	19	62	27	3	10
17	107	20	65	28	3	10
18	110	20	67	30	3	11
19	113	21	69	31	3	11
20	116	22	71	32	3	11
21	119	23	72	34	3	11
22	122	23	74	35	3	12
23	125	24	76	36	3	12
24	128	25	78	38	3	12
25	131	25	81	39	3	12
26	134	26	81	41	3	13
27	137	27	84	42	3	13
28	140	28	85	43	3	13
29	142	28	88	45	3	13
30	145	29	89	46	3	14
31	148	30	91	47	3	14
32	151	30	94	49	3	14
33	154	31	95	50	3	14
34	157	32	97	51	3	15
35	160	33	98	53	3	15
36	163	33	101	54	3	15
37	166	34	102	55	3	15
38	169	35	104	57	3	16
39	172	35	107	58	3	16
40	175	36	108	59	3	16
41	178	37	111	61	3	16
42	181	38	111	62	3	17
43	183	38	114	63	3	17
44	186	39	115	65	3	17
45	189	40	118	66	3	17
46	192	40	120	68	3	18
47	195	41	121	69	3	18
48	198	42	124	70	3	18
49	201	43	125	72	3	18
50	204	43	127	73	3	19
51	207	44	128	74	3	19
52	210	45	131	76	3	19
53	213	45	133	77	3	19
54	216	46	134	78	3	20
55	219	47	137	80	3	20
56	222	48	138	81	3	20
57	225	48	141	82	3	20
58	227	49	141	84	3	21
59	230	50	144	85	3	21
60	233	51	146	86	3	21
61	236	51	148	88	3	21
62	239	52	150	89	3	22
63	242	53	151	90	3	22
64	245	53	154	92	3	22
65	248	54	155	93	3	22
66	251	55	157	95	3	23
67	254	56	158	96	3	23
68	257	56	161	97	3	23
69	260	57	163	99	3	23
70	263	58	164	100	3	24
71	266	58	167	101	3	24
72	268	59	168	103	3	24
73	271	60	170	104	3	24
74	274	61	171	105	3	25
75	277	61	174	107	3	25
76	280	62	176	108	3	25
77	283	63	178	109	3	25
78	286	63	180	111	3	26
79	289	64	181	112	3	26
80	292	65	184	113	3	26
81	295	66	185	115	3	26
82	298	66	187	116	3	27
83	301	67	190	117	3	27
84	304	68	191	119	3	27
85	307	68	193	120	3	27
86	309	69	194	122	3	28
87	312	70	197	123	3	28
88	315	71	198	124	3	28
89	318	71	200	126	3	28
90	321	72	203	127	3	29
91	324	73	204	128	3	29
92	327	73	206	130	3	29
93	330	74	208	131	3	29
94	333	75	210	132	3	30
95	336	76	211	134	3	30
96	339	76	214	135	3	30
97	342	77	216	136	3	30
98	345	78	217	138	3	31
99	348	78	220	139	3	31
100	351	79	221	140	3	31

** Numbers in grey indicate when that number cannot go any higher than the previous number.*

WEAPON LIST & STATS

Weapon	Gear Panel	Strength		Magic		Defense		Crit. %		Crit. Bonus	
		Add	Unit	Add	Unit	Add	Unit	Add	Unit	Add	Unit
The Fool	NA (No Panel)	15	—	0	—	0	—	0	—	2	—
The Magician	Skill Gear	18	—	11	—	0	—	2	—	2	—
The Magician+	Skill Gear+②	20	+1	12	+1	0	+1	2	+1	2	+1
The Star	Technical Gear③	36	+1	14	+2	0	+1	4	+1	2	+1
The Star+	Technical Gear+ ③	44	+1	21	+2	0	+1	4	+1	4	+1
The Moon	Duel Gear④	35	+1	31	+2	0	+1	6	+1	5	+1
The Moon+	Duel Gear+④	45	+1	35	+2	0	+1	8	+1	6	+1
The Moon++	Duel Gear++⑤	68	+1	39	+5	0	+1	6	+1	7	+1
Justice	Loaded Gear	30	—	0	—	0	—	2	—	4	—
Justice+	Loaded Gear+②	35	+1	0	+1	0	+1	2	+1	5	+1
The Hierophant	Chrono Gear③	52	+1	0	+1	4	+2	2	+1	5	+1
The Hierophant+	Chrono Gear+③	57	+1	0	+1	4	+2	2	+1	7	+1
The World	Phantom Gear④	69	+1	0	+1	0	+2	8	+1	13	+1
The World+	Phantom Gear+④	80	+1	0	+1	6	+2	3	+1	7	+1
The World++	Phantom Gear++⑤	92	+1	0	+1	6	+5	3	+1	10	+1
Temperance	Lift Gear③	22	+1	0	+1	0	+1	8	+2	3	+1
Temperance+	Lift Gear+③	48	+1	0	+1	0	+1	6	+2	4	+1
The High Priestess	Nimble Gear④	54	+1	0	+1	0	+1	12	+2	4	+1
The High Priestess+	Nimble Gear+④	67	+1	0	+1	0	+1	9	+2	4	+1
The Tower	Wild Gear③	29	+1	0	+1	0	+1	4	+1	4	+2
The Tower+	Wild Gear+③	44	+1	0	+1	0	+1	4	+1	3	+2
The Hanged Man	Ominous Gear④	54	+1	0	+1	0	+1	6	+1	5	+2
The Hanged Man+	Ominous Gear+④	67	+1	0	+1	0	+1	6	+1	6	+2

Weapon	Gear Panel	Strength		Magic		Defense		Crit. %		Crit. Bonus	
		Add	Unit	Add	Unit	Add	Unit	Add	Unit	Add	Unit
Death	Valor Gear②	44	+1	0	+1	1	+1	2	+1	5	+1
Death+	Valor Gear+②	46	+1	0	+1	1	+1	0	+1	6	+1
The Hermit	Fearless Gear③	37	+2	0	+1	2	+1	0	+1	6	+1
The Hermit+	Fearless Gear+③	42	+2	0	+1	2	+1	4	+1	6	+1
Strength	Prestige Gear④	60	+2	0	+1	3	+1	6	+1	11	+1
Strength+	Prestige Gear+④	62	+2	0	+1	3	+1	0	+1	10	+1
The Lovers	Crisis Gear⑤	64	+3	23	+3	4	+1	8	+3	9	+1
The Lovers+	Crisis Gear+⑤	70	+3	28	+3	4	+1	0	+3	10	+1
The Chariot	Omega Gear⑥	84	+1	31	+3	0	+3	10	+1	14	+1
The Chariot+	Omega Gear+⑥	120	+1	34	+3	0	+3	10	+1	15	+1
The Sun	Hazard Gear⑤	84	+1	37	+3	0	+3	8	+1	12	+1
The Sun+	Hazard Gear+⑤	96	+1	45	+3	0	+3	8	+1	10	+1
The Devil	Rage Gear⑤	88	+1	4	+1	0	+3	8	+1	8	+1
The Devil+	Rage Gear+⑤	93	+1	7	+1	0	+3	8	+1	9	+1
The Empress	Champion Gear⑤	80	+3	0	+1	0	+3	8	+1	11	+1
The Empress+	Champion Gear+⑤	100	+3	0	+1	0	+3	8	+1	11	+1
The Emperor	Ultimate Gear⑥	112	+3	0	+1	0	+3	10	+1	14	+1
The Emperor+	Ultimate Gear+⑥	119	+3	0	+1	0	+3	10	+1	16	+1
The Joker	Pandora's Gear⑤	92	+5	30	+5	0	+5	10	+5	11	+5
The Joker+	Pandora's Gear+⑤	125	+1	34	+1	0	+1	10	+1	12	+1
Fair Game	Zero Gear⑤	124	+4	30	+4	0	+4	10	+4	19	+4
Finest Fantasy 13	Casual Gear②	36	+1	0	+1	0	+1	0	+1	4	+1
High Roller's Secret	Mystery Gear③	90	+1	0	+1	0	+1	0	+1	9	+1

WEAPON ABILITIES

Weapon	Abilities gained with units			Act. Spd.	Atk. Move		Combo	
	1 Unit	2 Units	3 Units		Land	Air	Land	Air
The Fool	—	—	—	1.0	1.0	1.0	3	2
The Magician	—	—	—	1.0	1.0	1.0	2	2
The Magician+	Fire Finish	—	—	1.0	1.0	1.0	2	2
The Star	Fire Finish	Thunder Finish	—	1.0	1.0	1.0	3	3
The Star+	Thunder Finish	Aero Finish	—	1.0	1.0	1.0	3	3
The Moon	Thunder Finish	Aero Finish	Blizzard Finish	1.0	1.0	1.0	4	3
The Moon+	Fire Finish	Thunder Finish	Aero Finish	1.0	1.0	1.0	4	3
The Moon++	Fire Finish	Blizzard Finish	Magic Finale	1.0	1.0	1.0	5	3
Justice	—	—	—	1.0	1.0	1.0	2	2
Justice+	Offensive Block	—	—	1.0	1.0	1.0	2	2
The Hierophant	Offensive Block	Combo Block	—	1.0	1.0	1.0	3	2
The Hierophant+	Chain Time	Combo Block	—	1.0	1.0	1.0	3	2
The World	Defender	Offensive Block	Combo-Block	1.0	1.0	1.0	3	2
The World+	Defender	Offensive Block	Vitality Barrier	1.0	1.0	1.0	3	2
The World++	Offensive Block	Damage Control	Combo-Block	1.0	1.0	1.0	3	2
Temperance	Chain Time	Chain Power	—	1.1	1.0	1.0	5	2
Temperance+	Combo Boost	Chain Power	—	1.1	1.0	1.0	5	2
The High Priestess	Combo Boost	Chain Power	Critical Boost	1.2	1.0	1.0	5	2
The High Priestess+	Chain Time	Chain Power	Critical Boost	1.2	1.0	1.0	5	2
The Tower	Combo Boost	Combo-Jump	—	1.0	1.0	1.0	4	5
The Tower+	Chain Power	Combo-Jump	—	1.0	1.0	1.0	4	5
The Hanged Man	Chain Power	Combo-Air Slide	Critical Boost	1.0	1.0	1.0	5	5

Weapon	Abilities gained with units			Act. Spd.	Atk. Move		Combo	
	1 Unit	2 Units	3 Units		Land	Air	Land	Air
The Hanged Man+	Combo Boost	Combo-Jump	Critical Boost	1.0	1.0	1.0	5	5
Death	Striker	—	—	1.0	1.0	1.0	2	2
Death+	Defender	—	—	1.0	1.0	1.0	2	2
The Hermit	Striker	Grand Slam	—	1.0	1.0	1.0	3	2
The Hermit+	Defender	Grand Slam	—	1.0	1.0	1.0	4	2
Strength	Defender	Striker	Grand Slam	1.0	1.0	1.0	3	2
Strength+	Striker	Grand Slam	Vitality Source	1.0	1.0	1.0	4	2
The Lovers	Fire Finish	Blizzard Finish	Alive 'n' Kicking	1.0	1.0	1.0	3	2
The Lovers+	Thunder Finish	Aero Finish	Alive 'n' Kicking	1.0	1.0	1.0	3	2
The Chariot	Thunder Finish	Aero Finish	Combo-Block	1.0	1.0	1.0	3	2
The Chariot+	Fire Finish	Blizzard Finish	Offensive Block	1.0	1.0	1.0	3	2
The Sun	Offensive Block	Fire Finish	Blizzard Finish	1.0	1.0	1.0	3	2
The Sun+	Offensive Block	Thunder Finish	Aero Finish	1.0	1.0	1.0	3	2
The Devil	Chain Time	Heart Bonus	Combo-Block	1.2	1.0	1.0	4	2
The Devil+	Combo Boost	Critical Boost	Combo-Block	1.2	1.0	1.0	4	2
The Empress	Offensive Block	Vitality Source	Vitality Barrier	1.0	1.0	1.0	3	2
The Empress+	Offensive Block	Grand Slam	Second Chance	1.0	1.0	1.0	3	2
The Emperor	Offensive Block	Grand Slam	Second Chance	1.0	1.0	1.0	4	2
The Emperor+	Offensive Block	Vitality Source	Vitality Barrier	1.0	1.0	1.0	4	2
The Joker	Grand Slam	Damage Control	Second Chance	1.0	1.0	1.0	3	3
The Joker+	Grand Slam	Damage Control	Second Chance	1.0	1.0	1.0	3	3
Fair Game	Grand Slam	Critical Boost	Fire Finish	1.0	1.0	1.0	3	2
Finest Fantasy 13	Chain Time	—	—	1.0	1.0	1.0	3	3
High Roller's Secret	Grand Slam	Heart Bonus	—	1.0	1.0	1.0	4	3

MARLUXIA

XI

Weapon: Scythe

In the arc of his scythe, flowers grow and all else perishes. His pretty face hides ugly motives.

LEVEL	MAX HP	STRENGTH	MAGIC POWER	DEFENSE POWER	CRITICAL %	CRIT. BONUS
1	64	10	34	5	8	7
2	67	11	35	6	8	7
3	70	11	40	8	8	7
4	73	13	42	9	8	7
5	76	14	43	10	8	8
6	79	14	45	11	8	8
7	82	15	46	12	8	8
8	85	16	48	14	8	9
9	88	17	49	15	8	9
10	91	18	52	16	8	9
11	94	19	55	17	8	9
12	97	19	55	19	8	10
13	100	20	58	20	8	10
14	103	21	58	21	8	10
15	107	22	62	22	8	11
16	110	23	62	23	8	11
17	113	24	65	25	8	11
18	116	24	67	26	8	12
19	119	25	69	27	8	12
20	122	26	71	28	8	12
21	125	27	72	29	8	12
22	128	28	74	31	8	13
23	131	28	76	32	8	13
24	134	29	78	33	8	13
25	137	30	81	34	8	14
26	140	31	81	36	8	14
27	143	32	84	37	8	14
28	146	33	85	38	8	14
29	150	33	88	39	8	15
30	153	34	89	40	8	15
31	156	35	91	42	8	15
32	159	36	94	43	8	16
33	162	37	95	44	8	16
34	165	38	97	45	8	16
35	168	38	98	46	8	16
36	171	39	101	48	8	17
37	174	40	102	49	8	17
38	177	41	104	50	8	17
39	180	42	107	51	8	18
40	183	42	108	53	8	18
41	186	43	111	54	8	18
42	189	44	111	55	8	18
43	193	44	114	56	8	19
44	196	46	115	57	8	19
45	199	47	118	59	8	19
46	202	47	120	60	8	20
47	205	48	121	61	8	20
48	208	49	124	62	8	20
49	211	50	125	63	8	21
50	214	51	127	65	8	21
51	217	52	128	66	8	21
52	220	52	131	67	8	21
53	223	53	133	68	8	22
54	226	54	134	70	8	22
55	229	55	137	71	8	22
56	232	56	138	72	8	23
57	235	57	141	73	8	23
58	239	57	141	74	8	23
59	242	58	144	76	8	23
60	245	59	146	77	8	24
61	248	60	148	78	8	24
62	251	61	150	79	8	24
63	254	61	151	81	8	25
64	257	62	154	82	8	25
65	260	63	155	83	8	25
66	263	64	157	84	8	25
67	266	65	158	85	8	26
68	269	66	161	87	8	26
69	272	66	163	88	8	26
70	275	67	164	89	8	27
71	278	68	167	90	8	27
72	282	69	168	91	8	27
73	285	70	170	93	8	27
74	288	71	171	94	8	28
75	291	71	174	95	8	28
76	294	72	176	96	8	28
77	297	73	178	98	8	29
78	300	74	180	99	8	29
79	303	75	181	100	8	29
80	306	75	184	101	8	30
81	309	76	185	102	8	30
82	312	77	187	104	8	30
83	315	77	190	105	8	30
84	318	79	191	106	8	31
85	321	80	193	107	8	31
86	325	80	194	108	8	31
87	328	81	197	110	8	32
88	331	82	198	111	8	32
89	334	83	200	112	8	32
90	337	84	203	113	8	32
91	340	85	204	115	8	33
92	343	85	206	116	8	33
93	346	86	208	117	8	33
94	349	87	210	118	8	34
95	352	88	211	119	8	34
96	355	89	214	121	8	34
97	358	90	216	122	8	34
98	361	90	217	123	8	35
99	364	91	220	124	8	35
100	368	92	221	125	8	35

* Numbers in grey indicate when that number cannot go any higher than the previous number.

WEAPON LIST & STATS

Weapon	Gear Panel	Strength		Magic		Defense		Crit. %		Crit. Bonus	
		Add	Unit	Add	Unit	Add	Unit	Add	Unit	Add	Unit
Fickle Erica	NA (No Panel)	15	—	0	—	0	—	0	—	2	—
Jilted Anemone	Skill Gear	18	—	11	—	0	—	2	—	2	—
Jilted Anemone+	Skill Gear+②	20	+1	12	+1	0	+1	2	+1	2	+1
Proud Amaryllis	Technical Gear③	36	+1	14	+2	0	+1	4	+1	2	+1
Proud Amaryllis+	Technical Gear+ ③	44	+1	21	+2	0	+1	4	+1	4	+1
Mad Safflower	Duel Gear④	35	+1	31	+2	0	+1	6	+1	5	+1
Mad Safflower+	Duel Gear+④	45	+1	35	+2	0	+1	8	+1	6	+1
Mad Safflower++	Duel Gear++⑤	68	+1	39	+5	0	+1	6	+1	7	+1
Poor Melissa	Loaded Gear	27	—	0	—	0	—	3	—	3	—
Poor Melissa+	Loaded Gear+②	35	+1	0	+1	0	+1	4	+1	5	+1
Tragic Allium	Chrono Gear③	55	+1	0	+1	0	+1	6	+2	5	+1
Tragic Allium+	Chrono Gear+③	57	+1	0	+1	0	+1	8	+2	6	+1
Mournful Cineraria	Phantom Gear④	66	+1	0	+1	0	+1	12	+2	13	+1
Mournful Cineraria+	Phantom Gear+④	77	+1	0	+1	0	+1	9	+2	7	+1
Mournful Cineraria++	Phantom Gear++⑤	86	+1	0	+1	0	+1	12	+5	10	+1
Pseudo Silene	Lift Gear③	61	+2	0	+1	2	+1	4	+1	5	+1
Pseudo Silene+	Lift Gear+③	68	+2	0	+1	2	+1	0	+1	4	+1
Faithless Digitalis	Nimble Gear④	68	+2	0	+1	3	+1	0	+1	5	+1
Faithless Digitalis+	Nimble Gear+④	87	+2	0	+1	3	+1	6	+1	5	+1
Grim Muscari	Wild Gear③	29	+1	0	+1	0	+1	4	+1	4	+2
Grim Muscari+	Wild Gear+③	44	+1	0	+1	0	+1	4	+1	3	+2
Docile Vallota	Ominous Gear④	69	+1	0	+1	0	+1	6	+1	5	+2
Docile Vallota+	Ominous Gear+④	87	+1	0	+1	0	+1	6	+1	6	+2
Quiet Belladonna	Valor Gear②	36	+1	0	+1	0	+1	2	+1	4	+1
Quiet Belladonna+	Valor Gear+②	39	+1	0	+1	0	+1	2	+1	5	+1
Parting Ipheion	Fearless Gear③	24	+1	0	+1	4	+2	2	+1	5	+1
Parting Ipheion+	Fearless Gear+③	35	+1	0	+1	4	+2	2	+1	5	+1
Lofty Gerbera	Prestige Gear④	37	+1	0	+1	6	+2	3	+1	9	+1
Lofty Gerbera+	Prestige Gear+④	41	+1	0	+1	6	+2	3	+1	9	+1
Gallant Achillea	Crisis Gear⑤	55	+1	31	+3	0	+1	8	+3	8	+1
Gallant Achillea+	Crisis Gear+⑤	62	+1	37	+3	0	+1	8	+3	9	+1
Noble Peony	Omega Gear⑥	73	+1	41	+3	0	+1	10	+3	13	+1
Noble Peony+	Omega Gear+⑥	103	+1	45	+3	0	+1	10	+3	12	+1
Fearsome Anise	Hazard Gear⑤	101	+3	0	+1	0	+3	8	+1	15	+1
Fearsome Anise+	Hazard Gear+⑤	114	+3	0	+1	0	+3	8	+1	11	+1
Vindictive Thistle	Rage Gear⑤	78	+1	0	+1	0	+1	8	+3	8	+3
Vindictive Thistle+	Rage Gear+⑤	88	+1	0	+1	0	+1	8	+3	9	+3
Fair Helianthus	Champion Gear⑤	64	+1	6	+1	0	+3	8	+3	9	+1
Fair Helianthus+	Champion Gear+⑤	67	+1	7	+1	0	+3	8	+3	9	+1
Solemn Magnolia	Ultimate Gear⑥	90	+1	36	+1	0	+3	10	+3	13	+1
Solemn Magnolia+	Ultimate Gear+⑥	94	+1	45	+1	0	+3	10	+3	12	+1
Hallowed Lotus	Pandora's Gear⑤	92	+5	30	+5	0	+5	10	+5	11	+5
Hallowed Lotus+	Pandora's Gear+⑤	125	+1	34	+1	0	+1	10	+1	12	+1
Graceful Dahlia	Zero Gear⑤	124	+4	30	+4	0	+4	10	+4	19	+4
Stirring Ladle	Casual Gear②	36	+1	0	+1	0	+1	0	+1	4	+1
Dainty Bellflowers	Mystery Gear③	90	+1	0	+1	0	+1	0	+1	9	+1

WEAPON ABILITIES

Weapon	Abilities gained with units			Act. Spd.	Atk. Move		Combo	
	1 Unit	2 Units	3 Units		Land	Air	Land	Air
Fickle Erica	—	—	—	1.0	1.0	1.0	5	2
Jilted Anemone	—	—	—	1.0	1.0	1.0	3	1
Jilted Anemone+	Magic Bracer	—	—	1.0	1.0	1.0	3	1
Proud Amaryllis	Magic Bracer	Aero Finish	—	1.0	1.0	1.0	3	2
Proud Amaryllis+	Magic Bracer	Thunder Finish	—	1.0	1.0	1.0	3	2
Mad Safflower	Magic Bracer	Blizzard Finish	Magic Finale	1.0	1.0	1.0	3	3
Mad Safflower+	Magic Bracer	Aero Finish	Magic Finale	1.0	1.0	1.0	3	3
Mad Safflower++	Magic Bracer	Aero Finish	Magic Finale	1.0	1.0	1.0	4	3
Poor Melissa	—	—	—	1.1	1.0	1.0	3	2
Poor Melissa+	Combo Boost	—	—	1.1	1.0	1.0	3	2
Tragic Allium	Combo Boost	Chain Power	—	1.1	1.0	1.0	5	2
Tragic Allium+	Chain Power	Chain Time	—	1.1	1.0	1.0	5	2
Mournful Cineraria	Combo Boost	Combo-Jump	Critical Boost	1.2	1.0	1.0	5	3
Mournful Cineraria+	Chain Power	Chain Time	Critical Boost	1.2	1.0	1.0	5	3
Mournful Cineraria++	Chain Power	Chain Time	Heart Bonus	1.3	1.0	1.0	7	3
Pseudo Silene	Striker	Vitality Source	—	1.0	1.0	1.0	4	1
Pseudo Silene+	Defender	Vitality Barrier	—	1.0	1.0	1.0	4	1
Faithless Digitalis	Defender	Vitality Barrier	Brick Wall	1.0	1.0	1.0	4	1
Faithless Digitalis+	Striker	Vitality Source	Grand Slam	1.0	1.0	1.0	4	1
Grim Muscari	Combo-Jump	Combo Boost	—	1.0	1.0	1.0	4	3
Grim Muscari+	Combo-Jump	Chain Power	—	1.0	1.0	1.0	4	3
Docile Vallota	Combo-Jump	Chain Power	Combo-Air Slide	1.0	1.0	1.0	4	5
Docile Vallota+	Combo-Jump	Combo Boost	Combo-Air Slide	1.0	1.0	1.0	4	5
Quiet Belladonna	Chain Time	—	—	1.0	1.0	1.0	3	3
Quiet Belladonna+	Chain Power	—	—	1.0	1.0	1.0	3	3
Parting Ipheion	Chain Time	Offensive Block	—	1.0	1.0	1.0	5	3
Parting Ipheion+	Chain Power	Offensive Block	—	1.0	1.0	1.0	5	3
Lofty Gerbera	Chain Power	Offensive Block	Second Chance	1.0	1.0	1.0	5	3
Lofty Gerbera+	Chain Time	Offensive Block	Second Chance	1.0	1.0	1.0	5	3
Gallant Achillea	Magic Bracer	Aero Finish	Critical Boost	1.0	1.0	1.0	6	3
Gallant Achillea+	Magic Bracer	Blizzard Finish	Critical Boost	1.0	1.0	1.0	6	3
Noble Peony	Magic Bracer	Blizzard Finish	Grand Slam	1.0	1.0	1.0	6	3
Noble Peony+	Magic Bracer	Aero Finish	Grand Slam	1.0	1.0	1.0	6	3
Fearsome Anise	Offensive Block	Vitality Source	Combo-Block	1.0	1.0	1.0	3	3
Fearsome Anise+	Offensive Block	Grand Slam	Combo-Block	1.0	1.0	1.0	3	3
Vindictive Thistle	Chain Power	Combo-Jump	Combo-Air Slide	1.0	1.0	1.0	5	4
Vindictive Thistle+	Combo Boost	Combo-Jump	Combo-Air Slide	1.0	1.0	1.0	5	4
Fair Helianthus	Offensive Block	Chain Time	Heart Bonus	1.0	1.0	1.0	5	3
Fair Helianthus+	Offensive Block	Combo-Jump	Combo-Block	1.0	1.0	1.0	5	3
Solemn Magnolia	Offensive Block	Combo-Jump	Combo-Block	1.1	1.0	1.0	5	3
Solemn Magnolia+	Offensive Block	Chain Time	Heart Bonus	1.2	1.0	1.0	5	3
Hallowed Lotus	Grand Slam	Critical Boost	Second Chance	1.0	1.0	1.0	5	4
Hallowed Lotus+	Grand Slam	Critical Boost	Second Chance	1.0	1.0	1.0	5	4
Graceful Dahlia	Combo Boost	Chain Power	Heart Bonus	1.0	1.0	1.0	5	2
Stirring Ladle	Offensive Block	—	—	1.0	1.0	1.0	2	3
Dainty Bellflowers	Heart Bonus	Second Chance	—	1.0	1.0	1.0	3	3

LARXENE

XII

Weapon: Knives

Wields sharp knives and a sharper tongue. Her lightning strikes as quick as her temper.

CHARACTER STATS

LEVEL	MAX HP	STRENGTH	MAGIC POWER	DEFENSE POWER	CRITICAL %	CRIT. BONUS
1	59	9	34	5	2	5
2	62	9	39	6	2	5
3	65	11	42	8	2	5
4	67	11	43	9	2	5
5	70	12	45	10	2	6
6	73	13	46	11	2	6
7	76	14	49	12	2	6
8	79	14	51	14	2	6
9	82	14	52	15	2	6
10	85	16	54	16	2	6
11	87	16	57	17	2	6
12	90	17	57	19	2	6
13	93	17	60	20	2	6
14	96	19	63	21	2	6
15	99	19	64	22	2	7
16	102	19	66	23	2	7
17	104	20	69	25	2	7
18	107	21	69	26	2	7
19	110	22	72	27	2	7
20	113	22	75	28	2	7
21	116	23	76	29	2	7
22	119	24	78	31	2	7
23	122	24	81	32	2	7
24	124	25	81	33	2	7
25	127	26	84	34	2	8
26	130	27	85	36	2	8
27	133	27	88	37	2	8
28	136	28	90	38	2	8
29	139	29	91	39	2	8
30	142	29	94	40	2	8
31	144	30	96	42	2	8
32	147	31	97	43	2	8
33	150	32	100	44	2	8
34	153	32	102	45	2	8
35	156	33	103	46	2	9
36	159	34	106	48	2	9
37	161	34	108	49	2	9
38	164	35	109	50	2	9
39	167	36	112	51	2	9
40	170	37	114	53	2	9
41	173	37	115	54	2	9
42	176	38	118	55	2	9
43	179	39	120	56	2	9
44	181	39	121	57	2	9
45	184	40	124	59	2	10
46	187	41	125	60	2	10
47	190	42	127	61	2	10
48	193	42	130	62	2	10
49	196	43	131	63	2	10
50	199	44	133	65	2	10
51	201	44	136	66	2	10
52	204	45	137	67	2	10
53	207	46	139	68	2	10
54	210	47	142	70	2	10
55	213	47	143	71	2	11
56	216	48	145	72	2	11
57	218	49	148	73	2	11
58	221	49	149	74	2	11
59	224	50	151	76	2	11
60	227	51	154	77	2	11
61	230	52	155	78	2	11
62	233	52	157	79	2	11
63	236	53	160	81	2	11
64	238	54	161	82	2	11
65	241	54	163	83	2	12
66	244	55	164	84	2	12
67	247	56	167	85	2	12
68	250	57	169	87	2	12
69	253	57	170	88	2	12
70	256	58	173	89	2	12
71	258	59	175	90	2	12
72	261	59	176	91	2	12
73	264	60	179	93	2	12
74	267	61	181	94	2	12
75	270	62	182	95	2	13
76	273	62	185	96	2	13
77	275	63	187	98	2	13
78	278	64	188	99	2	13
79	281	64	191	100	2	13
80	284	65	193	101	2	13
81	287	66	194	102	2	13
82	290	67	197	104	2	13
83	293	67	199	105	2	13
84	295	68	200	106	2	13
85	298	69	203	107	2	14
86	301	69	204	108	2	14
87	304	70	206	110	2	14
88	307	71	209	111	2	14
89	310	72	210	112	2	14
90	313	72	212	113	2	14
91	315	73	215	115	2	14
92	318	74	216	116	2	14
93	321	74	218	117	2	14
94	324	75	221	118	2	14
95	327	76	222	119	2	15
96	330	77	224	121	2	15
97	332	77	227	122	2	15
98	335	78	228	123	2	15
99	338	79	230	124	2	15
100	341	79	233	125	2	15

** Numbers in grey indicate when that number cannot go any higher than the previous number.*

WEAPON LIST & STATS

Weapon	Gear Panel	Strength		Magic		Defense		Crit. %		Crit. Bonus	
		Add	Unit	Add	Unit	Add	Unit	Add	Unit	Add	Unit
Trancheuse	NA (No Panel)	15	—	0	—	0	—	0	—	2	—
Orage	Skill Gear	20	—	0	—	0	—	3	—	2	—
Orage+	Skill Gear+②	22	+1	0	+1	0	+1	4	+1	2	+1
Tourbillon	Technical Gear③	40	+1	0	+1	0	+1	6	+2	3	+1
Tourbillon+	Technical Gear+ ③	50	+1	0	+1	0	+1	8	+2	4	+1
Tempête	Duel Gear④	40	+1	0	+1	0	+1	9	+2	6	+1
Tempête+	Duel Gear+④	50	+1	0	+1	0	+1	12	+2	7	+1
Tempête++	Duel Gear++⑤	76	+1	0	+1	0	+1	12	+5	8	+0
Carmin	Loaded Gear	24	—	12	—	0	—	2	—	3	—
Carmin+	Loaded Gear+②	32	+1	15	+1	0	+1	2	+1	5	+1
Météore	Chrono Gear③	41	+1	18	+2	0	+1	4	+1	4	+1
Météore+	Chrono Gear+③	48	+1	25	+2	0	+1	4	+1	6	+1
Etoile	Phantom Gear④	60	+1	29	+2	0	+1	8	+1	11	+1
Etoile+	Phantom Gear+④	70	+1	36	+2	0	+1	6	+1	6	+1
Etoile++	Phantom Gear++⑤	80	+1	39	+5	0	+1	6	+1	9	+1
Irrégulier	Lift Gear③	36	+2	0	+1	2	+1	4	+1	5	+1
Irrégulier+	Lift Gear+③	46	+2	0	+1	2	+1	0	+1	4	+1
Dissonance	Nimble Gear④	68	+2	0	+1	3	+1	0	+1	5	+1
Dissonance+	Nimble Gear+④	87	+2	0	+1	3	+1	6	+1	5	+1
Eruption	Wild Gear③	30	+1	0	+1	4	+2	2	+1	4	+1
Eruption+	Wild Gear+③	48	+1	0	+1	4	+2	2	+1	3	+1
Soleil Couchant	Ominous Gear④	72	+1	0	+1	6	+2	3	+1	5	+1
Soleil Couchant+	Ominous Gear+④	90	+1	0	+1	6	+2	3	+1	6	+1
Indigo	Valor Gear②	34	+1	0	+1	0	+1	2	+1	4	+1
Indigo+	Valor Gear+②	36	+1	0	+1	0	+1	2	+1	5	+1
Vague	Fearless Gear③	22	+1	0	+1	0	+1	4	+1	5	+2
Vague+	Fearless Gear+③	27	+1	0	+1	0	+1	4	+1	5	+2
Déluge	Prestige Gear④	35	+1	0	+1	0	+1	6	+1	8	+2
Déluge+	Prestige Gear+④	40	+1	0	+1	0	+1	6	+1	9	+2
Rafale	Crisis Gear⑤	55	+1	0	+1	0	+1	8	+3	8	+3
Rafale+	Crisis Gear+⑤	62	+1	0	+1	0	+1	8	+3	9	+3
Typhon	Omega Gear⑥	73	+1	0	+1	0	+1	10	+3	13	+3
Typhon+	Omega Gear+⑥	103	+1	0	+1	0	+1	10	+3	12	+3
Extirpeur	Hazard Gear⑤	84	+1	37	+3	0	+1	8	+1	12	+3
Extirpeur+	Hazard Gear+⑤	96	+1	45	+3	0	+1	8	+1	10	+3
Croix du Sud	Rage Gear⑤	88	+1	34	+3	0	+3	8	+1	8	+1
Croix du Sud+	Rage Gear+⑤	93	+1	37	+3	0	+3	8	+1	9	+1
Lumineuse	Champion Gear⑤	64	+1	6	+1	0	+3	8	+3	9	+1
Lumineuse+	Champion Gear+⑤	67	+1	7	+1	0	+3	8	+3	9	+1
Clair de Lune	Ultimate Gear⑥	90	+1	15	+1	0	+3	10	+3	13	+1
Clair de Lune+	Ultimate Gear+⑥	94	+1	16	+1	0	+3	10	+3	12	+1
Vol de Nuit	Pandora's Gear⑤	92	+5	30	+5	0	+5	10	+5	11	+5
Vol de Nuit+	Pandora's Gear+⑤	125	+1	34	+1	0	+1	10	+1	12	+1
Foudre	Zero Gear⑤	124	+4	30	+4	0	+4	10	+4	19	+4
Demoiselle	Casual Gear②	36	+1	0	+1	0	+1	0	+1	4	+1
Ampoule	Mystery Gear③	90	+1	0	+1	0	+1	0	+1	9	+1

WEAPON ABILITIES

Weapon	Abilities gained with units			Act. Spd.	Atk. Move		Combo	
	1 Unit	2 Units	3 Units		Land	Air	Land	Air
Trancheuse	—	—	—	1.0	1.0	1.0	3	3
Orage	—	—	—	1.1	1.0	1.0	3	3
Orage+	Combo-Jump	—	—	1.1	1.0	1.0	3	3
Tourbillon	Combo-Jump	Combo Boost	—	1.1	1.0	1.0	4	3
Tourbillon+	Combo-Jump	Chain Power	—	1.1	1.0	1.0	4	3
Tempête	Combo-Jump	Chain Power	Chain Time	1.2	1.0	1.0	4	3
Tempête+	Combo-Jump	Combo Boost	Critical Boost	1.2	1.0	1.0	4	3
Tempête++	Combo Boost	Chain Power	Combo-Jump	1.2	1.0	1.0	5	3
Carmin	—	—	—	1.0	1.0	1.0	3	2
Carmin+	Thunder Finish	—	—	1.0	1.0	1.0	3	2
Météore	Magic Bracer	Thunder Finish	—	1.0	1.0	1.0	4	2
Météore+	Thunder Finish	Fire Finish	—	1.0	1.0	1.0	4	2
Etoile	Magic Bracer	Thunder Finish	Magic Finale	1.0	1.0	1.0	4	3
Etoile+	Magic Bracer	Thunder Finish	Aero Finish	1.0	1.0	1.0	4	3
Etoile++	Magic Bracer	Thunder Finish	Magical Strike	1.0	1.0	1.0	4	3
Irrégulier	Striker	Combo Boost	—	1.0	1.0	1.0	3	3
Irrégulier+	Striker	Chain Power	—	1.0	1.0	1.0	3	3
Dissonance	Striker	Grand Slam	Combo-Block	1.0	1.0	1.0	3	3
Dissonance+	Combo Boost	Chain Power	Combo-Block	1.0	1.0	1.0	3	3
Eruption	Chain Power	Offensive Block	—	1.0	1.0	1.0	5	3
Eruption+	Chain Time	Offensive Block	—	1.0	1.0	1.0	6	3
Soleil Couchant	Defender	Chain Time	Offensive Block	1.0	1.0	1.0	7	3
Soleil Couchant+	Defender	Chain Power	Offensive Block	1.0	1.0	1.0	7	3
Indigo	Combo-Jump	—	—	1.0	1.0	1.0	4	2
Indigo+	Combo-Jump	—	—	1.0	1.0	1.0	4	2
Vague	Combo-Jump	Combo Boost	—	1.0	1.0	1.0	5	3
Vague+	Combo-Jump	Chain Power	—	1.0	1.0	1.0	5	3
Déluge	Combo-Jump	Chain Power	Combo-Air Slide	1.0	1.0	1.0	5	4
Déluge+	Combo-Jump	Combo Boost	Combo-Air Slide	1.0	1.0	1.0	5	4
Rafale	Combo-Jump	Combo-Air Slide	Combo Boost	1.0	1.0	1.0	5	3
Rafale+	Combo-Jump	Combo-Air Slide	Chain Power	1.0	1.0	1.0	5	3
Typhon	Combo-Jump	Combo-Air Slide	Critical Boost	1.0	1.0	1.0	5	4
Typhon+	Combo Boost	Chain Power	Critical Boost	1.0	1.0	1.0	5	4
Extirpeur	Combo-Jump	Thunder Finish	Aero Finish	1.0	1.0	1.0	4	3
Extirpeur+	Combo-Air Slide	Thunder Finish	Aero Finish	1.0	1.0	1.0	4	3
Croix du Sud	Magic Bracer	Thunder Finish	Aero Finish	1.0	1.0	1.0	3	3
Croix du Sud+	Magic Bracer	Thunder Finish	Fire Finish	1.0	1.0	1.0	3	3
Lumineuse	Combo-Jump	Chain Power	Chain Time	1.2	1.0	1.0	4	3
Lumineuse+	Offensive Block	Chain Power	Chain Time	1.2	1.0	1.0	4	3
Clair de Lune	Offensive Block	Chain Time	Heart Bonus	1.2	1.0	1.0	5	3
Clair de Lune+	Combo-Jump	Chain Time	Heart Bonus	1.2	1.0	1.0	5	3
Vol de Nuit	Combo Boost	Chain Power	Chain Time	1.0	1.0	1.0	4	3
Vol de Nuit+	Combo Boost	Chain Power	Chain Time	1.0	1.0	1.0	4	3
Foudre	Combo-Jump	Combo-Air Slide	Thunder Finish	1.0	1.0	1.0	3	3
Demoiselle	Combo-Air Slide	—	—	1.0	1.0	1.0	4	3
Ampoule	Thunder Finish	Fire Finish	—	1.0	1.0	1.0	4	3

The following characters become playable in Mission Mode when the player reaches certain days in Story Mode. Additionally, Xion is also unlocked on Day 117. All other playable characters are already unlocked and available in Mission Mode.

SORA

A fourteen-year-old boy and the hero. Chosen as the Keyblade master, he saved the worlds, but only at the cost of being separated from his friends.

Unlocking Sora:

View the Story Mode Ending having filled the Mission Gauge 100% in every mission and purchase Sora's Awakening item from the Moogle.

LEVEL	MAX HP	STRENGTH	MAGIC POWER	DEFENSE POWER	CRITICAL %	CRIT. BONUS
1	62	9	34	7	5	6
2	65	10	35	8	5	7
3	68	11	36	9	5	7
4	71	11	38	11	5	7
5	74	12	40	12	5	7
6	77	13	42	14	5	8
7	80	14	43	15	5	8
8	83	14	46	16	5	8
9	86	15	47	18	5	8
10	89	16	49	19	5	9
11	92	17	50	20	5	9
12	95	17	53	22	5	9
13	98	18	54	23	5	9
14	101	19	56	24	5	10
15	104	20	58	26	5	10
16	107	20	60	27	5	10
17	110	21	61	28	5	10
18	113	22	64	30	5	11
19	116	23	65	31	5	11
20	119	23	67	32	5	11
21	122	24	68	34	5	11
22	125	25	71	35	5	12
23	128	26	72	36	5	12
24	131	26	74	38	5	12
25	134	27	76	39	5	12
26	137	28	78	41	5	13
27	140	29	79	42	5	13
28	143	29	82	43	5	13
29	146	30	83	45	5	13
30	149	31	85	46	5	14
31	152	32	86	47	5	14
32	155	32	89	49	5	14
33	158	33	90	50	5	14
34	161	34	92	51	5	15
35	164	35	94	53	5	15
36	167	35	96	54	5	15
37	170	36	97	55	5	15
38	173	37	100	57	5	16
39	176	38	101	58	5	16
40	179	38	103	59	5	16
41	182	39	104	61	5	16
42	185	40	107	62	5	17
43	188	41	108	63	5	17
44	191	41	110	65	5	17
45	194	42	112	66	5	17
46	197	43	114	68	5	18
47	200	44	115	69	5	18
48	203	44	118	70	5	18
49	206	45	119	72	5	18
50	209	46	121	73	5	19
51	212	47	122	74	5	19
52	215	47	125	76	5	19
53	218	48	126	77	5	19
54	221	49	128	78	5	20
55	224	50	130	80	5	20
56	227	50	132	81	5	20
57	230	51	133	82	5	20
58	233	52	136	84	5	21
59	236	53	137	85	5	21
60	239	53	139	86	5	21
61	242	54	140	88	5	21
62	245	55	143	89	5	22
63	248	56	144	90	5	22
64	251	56	146	92	5	22
65	254	57	148	93	5	22
66	257	58	150	95	5	23
67	260	59	151	96	5	23
68	263	59	154	97	5	23
69	266	60	155	99	5	23
70	269	61	157	100	5	24
71	272	62	158	101	5	24
72	275	62	161	103	5	24
73	278	63	162	104	5	24
74	281	64	164	105	5	25
75	284	65	166	107	5	25
76	287	65	168	108	5	25
77	290	66	169	109	5	25
78	293	67	172	111	5	26
79	296	68	173	112	5	26
80	299	68	175	113	5	26
81	302	69	176	115	5	26
82	305	70	179	116	5	27
83	308	71	180	117	5	27
84	311	71	182	119	5	27
85	314	72	184	120	5	27
86	317	73	186	122	5	28
87	320	74	187	123	5	28
88	323	74	190	124	5	28
89	326	75	191	126	5	28
90	329	76	193	127	5	29
91	332	77	194	128	5	29
92	335	77	197	130	5	29
93	338	78	198	131	5	29
94	341	79	200	132	5	30
95	344	80	202	134	5	30
96	347	80	204	135	5	30
97	350	81	205	136	5	30
98	353	82	208	138	5	31
99	356	83	209	139	5	31
100	359	83	211	140	5	31

** Numbers in grey indicate when that number cannot go any higher than the previous number.*

WEAPON LIST & STATS

Weapon	Gear Panel	Strength		Magic		Defense		Crit. %		Crit. Bonus	
		Add	Unit	Add	Unit	Add	Unit	Add	Unit	Add	Unit
Kingdom Key	NA (No Panel)	100	—	0	—	0	—	7	—	7	—
Kingdom Key	Skill Gear	100	—	0	—	0	—	7	—	7	—
Kingdom Key	Skill Gear+②	100	+1	0	+1	0	+1	7	+1	7	+1
Kingdom Key	Technical Gear③	100	+2	0	+2	0	+2	7	+2	7	+2
Kingdom Key	Technical Gear+③	100	+2	0	+2	0	+2	7	+2	7	+2
Kingdom Key	Duel Gear④	100	+2	0	+2	0	+2	7	+2	7	+2
Kingdom Key	Duel Gear+④	100	+2	0	+2	0	+2	7	+2	7	+2
Kingdom Key+	Duel Gear++⑤	115	+3	25	+3	0	+3	10	+5	10	+3
Kingdom Key	Loaded Gear	100	—	0	—	0	—	7	—	7	—
Kingdom Key	Loaded Gear+②	100	+1	0	+1	0	+1	7	+1	7	+1
Kingdom Key	Chrono Gear③	100	+2	0	+2	0	+2	7	+2	7	+2
Kingdom Key	Chrono Gear+③	100	+2	0	+2	0	+2	7	+2	7	+2
Kingdom Key	Phantom Gear④	100	+2	0	+2	0	+2	7	+2	7	+2
Kingdom Key	Phantom Gear+④	100	+2	0	+2	0	+2	7	+2	7	+2
Kingdom Key	Phantom Gear++⑤	100	+3	0	+3	0	+3	7	+3	7	+3
Kingdom Key	Lift Gear③	100	+2	0	+2	0	+2	7	+2	7	+2
Kingdom Key	Lift Gear+③	100	+2	0	+2	0	+2	7	+2	7	+2
Kingdom Key	Nimble Gear④	100	+2	0	+2	0	+2	7	+2	7	+2
Kingdom Key	Nimble Gear+④	100	+2	0	+2	0	+2	7	+2	7	+2
Kingdom Key	Wild Gear③	100	+2	0	+2	0	+2	7	+2	7	+2
Kingdom Key	Wild Gear+③	100	+2	0	+2	0	+2	7	+2	7	+2
Kingdom Key	Ominous Gear④	100	+2	0	+2	0	+2	7	+2	7	+2
Kingdom Key	Ominous Gear+④	100	+2	0	+2	0	+2	7	+2	7	+2
Kingdom Key	Valor Gear②	100	+1	0	+1	0	+1	7	+1	7	+1
Kingdom Key	Valor Gear+②	100	+1	0	+1	0	+1	7	+1	7	+1
Kingdom Key	Fearless Gear③	100	+2	0	+2	0	+2	7	+2	7	+2
Kingdom Key	Fearless Gear+③	100	+2	0	+2	0	+2	7	+2	7	+2
Kingdom Key	Prestige Gear④	100	+2	0	+2	0	+2	7	+2	7	+2
Kingdom Key	Prestige Gear+④	100	+2	0	+2	0	+2	7	+2	7	+2
Kingdom Key+	Crisis Gear⑤	115	+3	25	+3	0	+3	10	+3	10	+3
Kingdom Key+	Crisis Gear+⑤	115	+3	25	+3	0	+3	10	+3	10	+3
Kingdom Key++	Omega Gear⑥	120	+3	30	+3	5	+3	12	+3	15	+3
Kingdom Key++	Omega Gear+⑥	120	+3	30	+3	5	+3	12	+3	15	+3
Kingdom Key	Hazard Gear⑤	100	+3	0	+3	0	+3	7	+3	7	+3
Kingdom Key	Hazard Gear+⑤	100	+3	0	+3	0	+3	7	+3	7	+3
Kingdom Key+	Rage Gear⑤	115	+3	25	+3	0	+3	10	+3	10	+3
Kingdom Key+	Rage Gear+⑤	115	+3	25	+3	0	+3	10	+3	10	+3
Kingdom Key++	Champion Gear⑤	120	+3	30	+3	5	+3	12	+3	15	+3
Kingdom Key++	Champion Gear+⑤	120	+3	30	+3	5	+3	12	+3	15	+3
Kingdom Key++	Ultimate Gear⑥	120	+3	30	+3	5	+3	12	+3	15	+3
Kingdom Key++	Ultimate Gear+⑥	120	+3	30	+3	5	+3	12	+3	15	+3
Bond of Flame	Pandora's Gear⑤	118	+5	28	+5	7	+5	15	+5	15	+5
Bond of Flame+	Pandora's Gear+⑤	125	+1	33	+1	7	+1	15	+1	15	+1
Dream Sword	Zero Gear⑤	124	+4	30	+4	7	+4	15	+4	19	+4
Kingdom Key	Casual Gear②	100	+1	0	+1	0	+1	7	+1	7	+1
Kingdom Key	Mystery Gear③	100	+2	0	+2	0	+2	7	+2	7	+2

WEAPON ABILITIES

Weapon	Abilities gained with units			Act. Spd.	Atk. Move		Combo	
	1 Unit	2 Units	3 Units		Land	Air	Land	Air
Kingdom Key	—	—	—	1.0	1.13	1.13	3	3
Kingdom Key	—	—	—	1.0	1.13	1.13	3	3
Kingdom Key	Defender	—	—	1.0	1.13	1.13	3	3
Kingdom Key	Defender	Damage Control	—	1.0	1.13	1.13	3	3
Kingdom Key	Defender	Damage Control	—	1.0	1.13	1.13	3	3
Kingdom Key	Defender	Damage Control	Second Chance	1.0	1.13	1.13	3	3
Kingdom Key	Defender	Damage Control	Second Chance	1.0	1.13	1.13	3	3
Kingdom Key+	Defender	Damage Control	Second Chance	1.0	1.13	1.13	3	3
Kingdom Key	—	—	—	1.0	1.13	1.13	3	3
Kingdom Key	Defender	—	—	1.0	1.13	1.13	3	3
Kingdom Key	Defender	Damage Control	—	1.0	1.13	1.13	3	3
Kingdom Key	Defender	Damage Control	—	1.0	1.13	1.13	3	3
Kingdom Key	Defender	Damage Control	Second Chance	1.0	1.13	1.13	3	3
Kingdom Key	Defender	Damage Control	Second Chance	1.0	1.13	1.13	3	3
Kingdom Key	Defender	Damage Control	Second Chance	1.0	1.13	1.13	3	3
Kingdom Key	Defender	Damage Control	—	1.0	1.13	1.13	3	3
Kingdom Key	Defender	Damage Control	—	1.0	1.13	1.13	3	3
Kingdom Key	Defender	Damage Control	Second Chance	1.0	1.13	1.13	3	3
Kingdom Key	Defender	Damage Control	Second Chance	1.0	1.13	1.13	3	3
Kingdom Key	Defender	Damage Control	—	1.0	1.13	1.13	3	3
Kingdom Key	Defender	Damage Control	—	1.0	1.13	1.13	3	3
Kingdom Key	Defender	Damage Control	Second Chance	1.0	1.13	1.13	3	3
Kingdom Key	Defender	Damage Control	Second Chance	1.0	1.13	1.13	3	3
Kingdom Key	Defender	—	—	1.0	1.13	1.13	3	3
Kingdom Key	Defender	—	—	1.0	1.13	1.13	3	3
Kingdom Key	Defender	Damage Control	—	1.0	1.13	1.13	3	3
Kingdom Key	Defender	Damage Control	—	1.0	1.13	1.13	3	3
Kingdom Key	Defender	Damage Control	Second Chance	1.0	1.13	1.13	3	3
Kingdom Key	Defender	Damage Control	Second Chance	1.0	1.13	1.13	3	3
Kingdom Key+	Defender	Damage Control	Second Chance	1.0	1.13	1.13	3	3
Kingdom Key+	Defender	Damage Control	Second Chance	1.0	1.13	1.13	3	3
Kingdom Key++	Defender	Damage Control	Second Chance	1.0	1.13	1.13	3	3
Kingdom Key++	Defender	Damage Control	Second Chance	1.0	1.13	1.13	3	3
Kingdom Key	Defender	Damage Control	Second Chance	1.0	1.13	1.13	3	3
Kingdom Key	Defender	Damage Control	Second Chance	1.0	1.13	1.13	3	3
Kingdom Key+	Defender	Damage Control	Second Chance	1.0	1.13	1.13	3	3
Kingdom Key+	Defender	Damage Control	Second Chance	1.0	1.13	1.13	3	3
Kingdom Key++	Defender	Damage Control	Second Chance	1.0	1.13	1.13	3	3
Kingdom Key++	Defender	Damage Control	Second Chance	1.0	1.13	1.13	3	3
Kingdom Key++	Defender	Damage Control	Second Chance	1.0	1.13	1.13	3	3
Kingdom Key++	Defender	Damage Control	Second Chance	1.0	1.13	1.13	3	3
Bond of Flame	Fire Finish	Magic Finale	Second Chance	1.0	1.13	1.13	5	6
Bond of Flame+	Fire Finish	Magic Finale	Second Chance	1.0	1.13	1.13	5	6
Dream Sword	Combo Boost	Chain Power	Striker	1.0	1.13	1.13	4	3
Kingdom Key	Defender	—	—	1.0	1.13	1.13	3	3
Kingdom Key	Defender	Damage Control	—	1.0	1.13	1.13	3	3

RIKU

A fifteen-year-old boy who is best friends with Sora and Kairi. Mature for his age, Riku is cool and collected. To save the worlds, he chose to remain in the realm of darkness.

Unlocking Riku:

Reach Story Mode Day 172.

LEVEL	MAX HP	STRENGTH	MAGIC POWER	DEFENSE POWER	CRITICAL %	CRIT. BONUS
1	64	9	29	7	6	7
2	67	9	31	8	6	7
3	70	11	32	9	6	8
4	73	11	35	11	6	8
5	76	12	37	12	6	8
6	79	13	39	14	6	9
7	82	14	41	15	6	9
8	85	14	41	16	6	9
9	88	15	44	18	6	10
10	91	16	45	19	6	10
11	94	17	46	20	6	10
12	97	17	48	22	6	11
13	100	18	50	23	6	11
14	103	19	50	24	6	11
15	107	20	53	26	6	12
16	110	20	54	27	6	12
17	113	21	55	28	6	12
18	116	22	58	30	6	13
19	119	23	59	31	6	13
20	122	23	60	32	6	13
21	125	24	63	34	6	14
22	128	25	64	35	6	14
23	131	26	65	36	6	14
24	134	26	67	38	6	15
25	137	27	69	39	6	15
26	140	28	71	41	6	15
27	143	29	72	42	6	16
28	146	29	73	43	6	16
29	150	30	76	45	6	16
30	153	31	77	46	6	17
31	156	32	78	47	6	17
32	159	32	81	49	6	17
33	162	33	82	50	6	18
34	165	34	83	51	6	18
35	168	35	86	53	6	19
36	171	35	86	54	6	19
37	174	36	88	55	6	19
38	177	37	90	57	6	20
39	180	38	91	58	6	20
40	183	38	92	59	6	20
41	186	39	95	61	6	21
42	189	40	96	62	6	21
43	193	41	97	63	6	21
44	196	41	100	65	6	22
45	199	42	101	66	6	22
46	202	43	103	68	6	22
47	205	44	105	69	6	23
48	208	44	106	70	6	23
49	211	45	108	72	6	23
50	214	46	109	73	6	24
51	217	47	110	74	6	24
52	220	47	113	76	6	24
53	223	48	114	77	6	25
54	226	49	115	78	6	25
55	229	50	118	80	6	25
56	232	50	119	81	6	26
57	235	51	120	82	6	26
58	239	52	122	84	6	26
59	242	53	124	85	6	27
60	245	53	125	86	6	27
61	248	54	127	88	6	27
62	251	55	128	89	6	28
63	254	56	130	90	6	28
64	257	56	132	92	6	28
65	260	57	133	93	6	29
66	263	58	136	95	6	29
67	266	59	137	96	6	29
68	269	59	138	97	6	30
69	272	60	141	99	6	30
70	275	61	142	100	6	30
71	278	62	143	101	6	31
72	282	62	145	103	6	31
73	285	63	147	104	6	31
74	288	64	148	105	6	32
75	291	65	150	107	6	32
76	294	65	151	108	6	32
77	297	66	152	109	6	33
78	300	67	155	111	6	33
79	303	68	156	112	6	33
80	306	68	157	113	6	34
81	309	69	160	115	6	34
82	312	70	161	116	6	34
83	315	71	162	117	6	35
84	318	71	164	119	6	35
85	321	72	166	120	6	36
86	325	73	168	122	6	36
87	328	74	169	123	6	36
88	331	74	170	124	6	37
89	334	75	173	126	6	37
90	337	76	174	127	6	37
91	340	77	175	128	6	38
92	343	77	178	130	6	38
93	346	78	179	131	6	38
94	349	79	180	132	6	39
95	352	80	183	134	6	39
96	355	80	184	135	6	39
97	358	81	185	136	6	40
98	361	82	187	138	6	40
99	364	83	188	139	6	40
100	368	83	190	140	6	41

* Numbers in grey indicate when that number cannot go any higher than the previous number.

WEAPON LIST & STATS

Weapon	Gear Panel	Strength		Magic		Defense		Crit. %		Crit. Bonus	
		Add	Unit	Add	Unit	Add	Unit	Add	Unit	Add	Unit
Soul Eater	NA (No Panel)	70	—	0	—	0	—	5	—	7	—
Soul Eater	Skill Gear	70	—	0	—	0	—	5	—	7	—
Soul Eater	Skill Gear+②	70	+1	0	+1	0	+1	5	+1	7	+1
Soul Eater	Technical Gear③	70	+2	0	+2	0	+2	5	+2	7	+2
Soul Eater	Technical Gear+③	70	+2	0	+2	0	+2	5	+2	7	+2
Soul Eater	Duel Gear④	70	+2	0	+2	0	+2	5	+2	7	+2
Soul Eater	Duel Gear+④	70	+2	0	+2	0	+2	5	+2	7	+2
Soul Eater+	Duel Gear++⑤	100	+3	15	+3	0	+3	7	+5	10	+3
Soul Eater	Loaded Gear	70	—	0	—	0	—	5	—	7	—
Soul Eater	Loaded Gear+②	70	+1	0	+1	0	+1	5	+1	7	+1
Soul Eater	Chrono Gear③	70	+2	0	+2	0	+2	5	+2	7	+2
Soul Eater	Chrono Gear+③	70	+2	0	+2	0	+2	5	+2	7	+2
Soul Eater	Phantom Gear④	70	+2	0	+2	0	+2	5	+2	7	+2
Soul Eater	Phantom Gear+④	70	+2	0	+2	0	+2	5	+2	7	+2
Soul Eater	Phantom Gear++⑤	70	+3	0	+3	0	+3	5	+3	7	+3
Soul Eater	Lift Gear③	70	+2	0	+2	0	+2	5	+2	7	+2
Soul Eater	Lift Gear+③	70	+2	0	+2	0	+2	5	+2	7	+2
Soul Eater	Nimble Gear④	70	+2	0	+2	0	+2	5	+2	7	+2
Soul Eater	Nimble Gear+④	70	+2	0	+2	0	+2	5	+2	7	+2
Soul Eater	Wild Gear③	70	+2	0	+2	0	+2	5	+2	7	+2
Soul Eater	Wild Gear+③	70	+2	0	+2	0	+2	5	+2	7	+2
Soul Eater	Ominous Gear④	70	+2	0	+2	0	+2	5	+2	7	+2
Soul Eater	Ominous Gear+④	70	+2	0	+2	0	+2	5	+2	7	+2

Weapon	Gear Panel	Strength		Magic		Defense		Crit. %		Crit. Bonus	
		Add	Unit	Add	Unit	Add	Unit	Add	Unit	Add	Unit
Soul Eater	Valor Gear②	70	+1	0	+1	0	+1	5	+1	7	+1
Soul Eater	Valor Gear+②	70	+1	0	+1	0	+1	5	+1	7	+1
Soul Eater	Fearless Gear③	70	+2	0	+2	0	+2	5	+2	7	+2
Soul Eater	Fearless Gear+③	70	+2	0	+2	0	+2	5	+2	7	+2
Soul Eater	Prestige Gear④	70	+2	0	+2	0	+2	5	+2	7	+2
Soul Eater	Prestige Gear+④	70	+2	0	+2	0	+2	5	+2	7	+2
Soul Eater+	Crisis Gear⑤	100	+3	15	+3	0	+3	7	+3	10	+3
Soul Eater+	Crisis Gear+⑤	100	+3	15	+3	0	+3	7	+3	10	+3
Soul Eater++	Omega Gear⑥	120	+3	25	+3	0	+3	12	+3	15	+3
Soul Eater++	Omega Gear+⑥	120	+3	25	+3	0	+3	12	+3	15	+3
Soul Eater	Hazard Gear⑤	70	+3	0	+3	0	+3	5	+3	7	+3
Soul Eater	Hazard Gear+⑤	70	+3	0	+3	0	+3	5	+3	7	+3
Soul Eater+	Rage Gear⑤	100	+3	15	+3	0	+3	7	+3	10	+3
Soul Eater+	Rage Gear+⑤	100	+3	15	+3	0	+3	7	+3	10	+3
Soul Eater++	Champion Gear⑤	120	+3	25	+3	0	+3	12	+3	15	+3
Soul Eater++	Champion Gear+⑤	120	+3	25	+3	0	+3	12	+3	15	+3
Soul Eater++	Ultimate Gear⑥	120	+3	25	+3	0	+3	12	+3	15	+3
Soul Eater++	Ultimate Gear+⑥	120	+3	25	+3	0	+3	12	+3	15	+3
Oblivion	Pandora's Gear⑤	110	+5	30	+5	0	+5	10	+5	20	+5
Oblivion+	Pandora's Gear+⑤	125	+1	30	+1	0	+1	10	+1	23	+1
Way to the Dawn	Zero Gear⑤	124	+4	30	+4	0	+4	10	+4	19	+4
Soul Eater	Casual Gear②	70	+1	0	+1	0	+1	5	+1	7	+1
Soul Eater	Mystery Gear③	70	+2	0	+2	0	+2	5	+2	7	+2

WEAPON ABILITIES

Weapon	Abilities gained with units			Act. Spd.	Atk. Move		Combo	
	1 Unit	2 Units	3 Units		Land	Air	Land	Air
Soul Eater	—	—	—	1.0	1.13	1.13	6	3
Soul Eater	—	—	—	1.0	1.13	1.13	6	3
Soul Eater	Striker	—	—	1.0	1.13	1.13	6	3
Soul Eater	Striker	Grand Slam	—	1.0	1.13	1.13	6	3
Soul Eater	Striker	Grand Slam	—	1.0	1.13	1.13	6	3
Soul Eater	Striker	Grand Slam	Critical Boost	1.0	1.13	1.13	6	3
Soul Eater	Striker	Grand Slam	Critical Boost	1.0	1.13	1.13	6	3
Soul Eater+	Striker	Grand Slam	Critical Boost	1.0	1.13	1.13	6	3
Soul Eater	—	—	—	1.0	1.13	1.13	6	3
Soul Eater	Striker	—	—	1.0	1.13	1.13	6	3
Soul Eater	Striker	Grand Slam	—	1.0	1.13	1.13	6	3
Soul Eater	Striker	Grand Slam	—	1.0	1.13	1.13	6	3
Soul Eater	Striker	Grand Slam	Critical Boost	1.0	1.13	1.13	6	3
Soul Eater	Striker	Grand Slam	Critical Boost	1.0	1.13	1.13	6	3
Soul Eater	Striker	Grand Slam	Critical Boost	1.0	1.13	1.13	6	3
Soul Eater	Striker	Grand Slam	—	1.0	1.13	1.13	6	3
Soul Eater	Striker	Grand Slam	—	1.0	1.13	1.13	6	3
Soul Eater	Striker	Grand Slam	Critical Boost	1.0	1.13	1.13	6	3
Soul Eater	Striker	Grand Slam	Critical Boost	1.0	1.13	1.13	6	3
Soul Eater	Striker	Grand Slam	—	1.0	1.13	1.13	6	3
Soul Eater	Striker	Grand Slam	—	1.0	1.13	1.13	6	3
Soul Eater	Striker	Grand Slam	Critical Boost	1.0	1.13	1.13	6	3
Soul Eater	Striker	Grand Slam	Critical Boost	1.0	1.13	1.13	6	3
Soul Eater	Striker	—	—	1.0	1.13	1.13	6	3

Weapon	Abilities gained with units			Act. Spd.	Atk. Move		Combo	
	1 Unit	2 Units	3 Units		Land	Air	Land	Air
Soul Eater	Striker	—	—	1.0	1.13	1.13	6	3
Soul Eater	Striker	Grand Slam	—	1.0	1.13	1.13	6	3
Soul Eater	Striker	Grand Slam	—	1.0	1.13	1.13	6	3
Soul Eater	Striker	Grand Slam	Critical Boost	1.0	1.13	1.13	6	3
Soul Eater	Striker	Grand Slam	Critical Boost	1.0	1.13	1.13	6	3
Soul Eater+	Striker	Grand Slam	Critical Boost	1.0	1.13	1.13	6	3
Soul Eater+	Striker	Grand Slam	Critical Boost	1.0	1.13	1.13	6	3
Soul Eater++	Striker	Grand Slam	Critical Boost	1.0	1.13	1.13	6	3
Soul Eater++	Striker	Grand Slam	Critical Boost	1.0	1.13	1.13	6	3
Soul Eater	Striker	Grand Slam	Critical Boost	1.0	1.13	1.13	6	3
Soul Eater	Striker	Grand Slam	Critical Boost	1.0	1.13	1.13	6	3
Soul Eater+	Striker	Grand Slam	Critical Boost	1.0	1.13	1.13	6	3
Soul Eater+	Striker	Grand Slam	Critical Boost	1.0	1.13	1.13	6	3
Soul Eater++	Striker	Grand Slam	Critical Boost	1.0	1.13	1.13	6	3
Soul Eater++	Striker	Grand Slam	Critical Boost	1.0	1.13	1.13	6	3
Soul Eater++	Striker	Grand Slam	Critical Boost	1.0	1.13	1.13	6	3
Soul Eater++	Striker	Grand Slam	Critical Boost	1.0	1.13	1.13	6	3
Oblivion	Defender	Damage Control	Second Chance	1.0	1.13	1.13	3	3
Oblivion+	Defender	Damage Control	Second Chance	1.0	1.13	1.13	3	3
Way to the Dawn	Vitality Source	Vitality Barrier	Alive 'n' Kicking	1.0	1.13	1.13	3	4
Soul Eater	Striker	—	—	1.0	1.13	1.13	6	3
Soul Eater	Striker	Grand Slam	—	1.0	1.13	1.13	6	3

KING MICKEY

The King of Disney Castle who realized what was happening in the world and went on a journey to investigate. He stayed behind in the world of darkness together with Riku and continues to journey apart from Sora and friends.

Unlocking Mickey:

*View the Story Mode Ending after completing every mission and purchase **The King's Return** item from the Moogle.*

CHARACTER STATS

LEVEL	MAX HP	STRENGTH	MAGIC POWER	DEFENSE POWER	CRITICAL %	CRIT. BONUS
1	59	9	38	6	8	7
2	62	9	43	8	8	7
3	65	11	43	9	8	7
4	67	11	45	10	8	7
5	70	12	48	11	8	8
6	73	13	49	13	8	8
7	76	14	51	14	8	8
8	79	14	53	15	8	9
9	82	15	54	17	8	9
10	85	16	56	18	8	9
11	87	17	59	19	8	9
12	90	17	60	20	8	10
13	93	18	63	22	8	10
14	96	19	65	23	8	10
15	99	20	66	24	8	11
16	102	20	68	26	8	11
17	104	21	71	27	8	11
18	107	22	71	28	8	12
19	110	23	74	29	8	12
20	113	23	75	31	8	12
21	116	24	78	32	8	12
22	119	25	80	33	8	13
23	122	26	81	35	8	13
24	124	26	83	36	8	13
25	127	27	86	37	8	14
26	130	28	87	38	8	14
27	133	29	90	40	8	14
28	136	29	92	41	8	14
29	139	30	93	42	8	15
30	142	31	95	44	8	15
31	144	32	98	45	8	15
32	147	32	99	46	8	16
33	150	33	101	47	8	16
34	153	34	104	49	8	16
35	156	35	105	50	8	16
36	159	35	107	51	8	17
37	161	36	110	53	8	17
38	164	37	111	54	8	17
39	167	38	113	55	8	18
40	170	38	114	56	8	18
41	173	39	117	58	8	18
42	176	40	119	59	8	18
43	179	41	120	60	8	19
44	181	41	123	62	8	19
45	184	42	125	63	8	19
46	187	43	126	64	8	20
47	190	44	129	65	8	20
48	193	44	131	67	8	20
49	196	45	132	68	8	21
50	199	46	135	69	8	21
51	201	47	137	71	8	21
52	204	47	138	72	8	21
53	207	48	141	73	8	22
54	210	49	143	74	8	22
55	213	50	144	76	8	22
56	216	50	147	77	8	23
57	218	51	149	78	8	23
58	221	52	150	80	8	23
59	224	53	153	81	8	23
60	227	53	154	82	8	24
61	230	54	156	83	8	24
62	233	55	159	85	8	24
63	236	56	160	86	8	25
64	238	56	162	87	8	25
65	241	57	165	89	8	25
66	244	58	166	90	8	25
67	247	59	168	91	8	26
68	250	59	171	92	8	26
69	253	60	172	94	8	26
70	256	61	174	95	8	27
71	258	62	177	96	8	27
72	261	62	178	98	8	27
73	264	63	180	99	8	27
74	267	64	183	100	8	28
75	270	65	184	101	8	28
76	273	65	186	103	8	28
77	275	66	189	104	8	29
78	278	67	190	105	8	29
79	281	68	192	107	8	29
80	284	68	193	108	8	30
81	287	69	196	109	8	30
82	290	70	198	110	8	30
83	293	71	199	112	8	30
84	295	71	202	113	8	31
85	298	72	204	114	8	31
86	301	73	205	116	8	31
87	304	74	208	117	8	32
88	307	74	210	118	8	32
89	310	75	211	119	8	32
90	313	76	214	121	8	32
91	315	77	216	122	8	33
92	318	77	217	123	8	33
93	321	78	220	125	8	33
94	324	79	222	126	8	34
95	327	80	223	127	8	34
96	330	80	226	128	8	34
97	332	81	228	130	8	34
98	335	82	229	131	8	35
99	338	83	232	132	8	35
100	341	83	233	134	8	35

** Numbers in grey indicate when that number cannot go any higher than the previous number.*

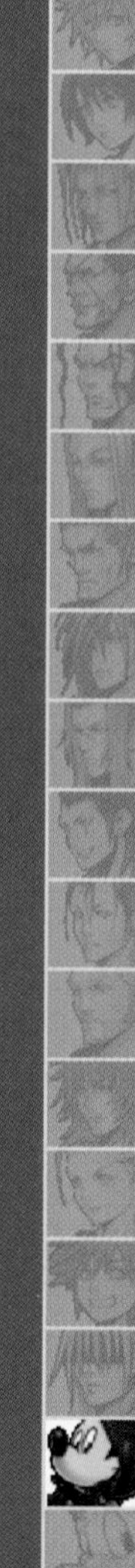

WEAPON LIST

Weapon		Gear Panel	Strength		Magic		Defense		Crit. %		Crit. Bonus	
			Add	Unit	Add	Unit	Add	Unit	Add	Unit	Add	Unit
Kingdom Key D	NA	(No Panel)	80	—	10	—	0	—	7	—	7	—
Kingdom Key D		Skill Gear	80	—	10	—	0	—	7	—	7	—
Kingdom Key D		Skill Gear+②	80	+1	10	+1	0	+1	7	+1	7	+1
Kingdom Key D		Technical Gear③	80	+2	10	+2	0	+2	7	+2	7	+2
Kingdom Key D		Technical Gear+ ③	80	+2	10	+2	0	+2	7	+2	7	+2
Kingdom Key D		Duel Gear④	80	+2	10	+2	0	+2	7	+2	7	+2
Kingdom Key D		Duel Gear+④	80	+2	10	+2	0	+2	7	+2	7	+2
Kingdom Key D+		Duel Gear++⑤	117	+3	25	+3	0	+3	10	+5	15	+3
Kingdom Key D		Loaded Gear	80	—	10	—	0	—	7	—	7	—
Kingdom Key D		Loaded Gear+②	80	+1	10	+1	0	+1	7	+1	7	+1
Kingdom Key D		Chrono Gear③	80	+2	10	+2	0	+2	7	+2	7	+2
Kingdom Key D		Chrono Gear+③	80	+2	10	+2	0	+2	7	+2	7	+2
Kingdom Key D		Phantom Gear④	80	+2	10	+2	0	+2	7	+2	7	+2
Kingdom Key D		Phantom Gear+④	80	+2	10	+2	0	+2	7	+2	7	+2
Kingdom Key D		Phantom Gear++⑤	80	+3	10	+3	0	+3	7	+3	7	+3
Kingdom Key D		Lift Gear③	80	+2	10	+2	0	+2	7	+2	7	+2
Kingdom Key D		Lift Gear+③	80	+2	10	+2	0	+2	7	+2	7	+2
Kingdom Key D		Nimble Gear④	80	+2	10	+2	0	+2	7	+2	7	+2
Kingdom Key D		Nimble Gear+④	80	+2	10	+2	0	+2	7	+2	7	+2
Kingdom Key D		Wild Gear③	80	+2	10	+2	0	+2	7	+2	7	+2
Kingdom Key D		Wild Gear+③	80	+2	10	+2	0	+2	7	+2	7	+2
Kingdom Key D		Ominous Gear④	80	+2	10	+2	0	+2	7	+2	7	+2
Kingdom Key D		Ominous Gear+④	80	+2	10	+2	0	+2	7	+2	7	+2
Kingdom Key D		Valor Gear②	80	+1	10	+1	0	+1	7	+1	7	+1
Kingdom Key D		Valor Gear+②	80	+1	10	+1	0	+1	7	+1	7	+1
Kingdom Key D		Fearless Gear③	80	+2	10	+2	0	+2	7	+2	7	+2
Kingdom Key D		Fearless Gear+③	80	+2	10	+2	0	+2	7	+2	7	+2
Kingdom Key D		Prestige Gear④	80	+2	10	+2	0	+2	7	+2	7	+2
Kingdom Key D		Prestige Gear+④	80	+2	10	+2	0	+2	7	+2	7	+2
Kingdom Key D+		Crisis Gear⑤	117	+3	25	+3	0	+3	10	+3	15	+3
Kingdom Key D+		Crisis Gear+⑤	117	+3	25	+3	0	+3	10	+3	15	+3
Kingdom Key D++		Omega Gear⑥	120	+3	34	+3	0	+3	10	+3	19	+3
Kingdom Key D++		Omega Gear+⑥	120	+3	34	+3	0	+3	10	+3	19	+3
Kingdom Key D		Hazard Gear⑤	80	+3	10	+3	0	+3	7	+3	7	+3
Kingdom Key D		Hazard Gear+⑤	80	+3	10	+3	0	+3	7	+3	7	+3
Kingdom Key D+		Rage Gear⑤	117	+3	25	+3	0	+3	10	+3	15	+3
Kingdom Key D+		Rage Gear+⑤	117	+3	25	+3	0	+3	10	+3	15	+3
Kingdom Key D++		Champion Gear⑤	120	+3	34	+3	0	+3	10	+3	19	+3
Kingdom Key D++		Champion Gear+⑤	120	+3	34	+3	0	+3	10	+3	19	+3
Kingdom Key D++		Ultimate Gear⑥	120	+3	34	+3	0	+3	10	+3	19	+3
Kingdom Key D++		Ultimate Gear+⑥	120	+3	34	+3	0	+3	10	+3	19	+3
Star Seeker		Pandora's Gear⑤	115	+5	30	+5	0	+5	10	+5	18	+5
Star Seeker+		Pandora's Gear+⑤	125	+1	35	+1	0	+1	10	+1	20	+1
Kingdom Key DΩ		Zero Gear⑤	125	+4	38	+4	0	+4	10	+4	20	+4
Kingdom Key D		Casual Gear②	80	+1	10	+1	0	+1	7	+1	7	+1
Kingdom Key D		Mystery Gear③	80	+2	10	+2	0	+2	7	+2	7	+2

WEAPON ABILITIES

Weapon	Abilities gained with units			Act. Spd.	Atk. Move		Combo	
	1 Unit	2 Units	3 Units		Land	Air	Land	Air
Kingdom Key D	—	—	—	1.0	1.13	1.13	3	3
Kingdom Key D	—	—	—	1.0	1.13	1.13	3	3
Kingdom Key D	Defender	—	—	1.0	1.13	1.13	3	3
Kingdom Key D	Defender	Damage Control	—	1.0	1.13	1.13	3	3
Kingdom Key D	Defender	Damage Control	—	1.0	1.13	1.13	3	3
Kingdom Key D	Defender	Damage Control	Second Chance	1.0	1.13	1.13	3	3
Kingdom Key D	Defender	Damage Control	Second Chance	1.0	1.13	1.13	3	3
Kingdom Key D+	Defender	Damage Control	Second Chance	1.0	1.13	1.13	3	3
Kingdom Key D	—	—	—	1.0	1.13	1.13	3	3
Kingdom Key D	Defender	—	—	1.0	1.13	1.13	3	3
Kingdom Key D	Defender	Damage Control	—	1.0	1.13	1.13	3	3
Kingdom Key D	Defender	Damage Control	—	1.0	1.13	1.13	3	3
Kingdom Key D	Defender	Damage Control	Second Chance	1.0	1.13	1.13	3	3
Kingdom Key D	Defender	Damage Control	Second Chance	1.0	1.13	1.13	3	3
Kingdom Key D	Defender	Damage Control	Second Chance	1.0	1.13	1.13	3	3
Kingdom Key D	Defender	Damage Control	—	1.0	1.13	1.13	3	3
Kingdom Key D	Defender	Damage Control	—	1.0	1.13	1.13	3	3
Kingdom Key D	Defender	Damage Control	Second Chance	1.0	1.13	1.13	3	3
Kingdom Key D	Defender	Damage Control	Second Chance	1.0	1.13	1.13	3	3
Kingdom Key D	Defender	Damage Control	—	1.0	1.13	1.13	3	3
Kingdom Key D	Defender	Damage Control	—	1.0	1.13	1.13	3	3
Kingdom Key D	Defender	Damage Control	Second Chance	1.0	1.13	1.13	3	3
Kingdom Key D	Defender	Damage Control	Second Chance	1.0	1.13	1.13	3	3
Kingdom Key D	Defender	—	—	1.0	1.13	1.13	3	3
Kingdom Key D	Defender	—	—	1.0	1.13	1.13	3	3
Kingdom Key D	Defender	Damage Control	—	1.0	1.13	1.13	3	3
Kingdom Key D	Defender	Damage Control	—	1.0	1.13	1.13	3	3
Kingdom Key D	Defender	Damage Control	Second Chance	1.0	1.13	1.13	3	3
Kingdom Key D	Defender	Damage Control	Second Chance	1.0	1.13	1.13	3	3
Kingdom Key D+	Defender	Damage Control	Second Chance	1.0	1.13	1.13	3	3
Kingdom Key D+	Defender	Damage Control	Second Chance	1.0	1.13	1.13	3	3
Kingdom Key D++	Defender	Damage Control	Second Chance	1.0	1.13	1.13	3	3
Kingdom Key D++	Defender	Damage Control	Second Chance	1.0	1.13	1.13	3	3
Kingdom Key D	Defender	Damage Control	Second Chance	1.0	1.13	1.13	3	3
Kingdom Key D	Defender	Damage Control	Second Chance	1.0	1.13	1.13	3	3
Kingdom Key D+	Defender	Damage Control	Second Chance	1.0	1.13	1.13	3	3
Kingdom Key D+	Defender	Damage Control	Second Chance	1.0	1.13	1.13	3	3
Kingdom Key D++	Defender	Damage Control	Second Chance	1.0	1.13	1.13	3	3
Kingdom Key D++	Defender	Damage Control	Second Chance	1.0	1.13	1.13	3	3
Kingdom Key D++	Defender	Damage Control	Second Chance	1.0	1.13	1.13	3	3
Kingdom Key D++	Defender	Damage Control	Second Chance	1.0	1.13	1.13	3	3
Star Seeker	Combo Boost	Combo-Jump	Combo-Air Slide	1.0	1.13	1.5	3	3
Star Seeker+	Combo Boost	Combo-Jump	Combo-Air Slide	1.0	1.13	1.5	3	3
Kingdom Key DΩ	Defender	Damage Control	Second Chance	1.0	1.13	1.13	3	3
Kingdom Key D	Defender	—	—	1.0	1.13	1.13	3	3
Kingdom Key D	Defender	Damage Control	—	1.0	1.13	1.13	3	3

DONALD

The court wizard who serves the King of Disney Castle. He is journeying with Sora and Goofy to find the King. Donald is talkative, moody, and a bit short-tempered.

Unlocking Donald:

Reach Story Mode Day 225.

CHARACTER STATS

LEVEL	MAX HP	STRENGTH	MAGIC POWER	DEFENSE POWER	CRITICAL %	CRIT. BONUS
1	57	7	38	6	5	6
2	60	7	43	7	5	6
3	62	8	45	8	5	6
4	65	9	47	9	5	7
5	68	9	49	10	5	7
6	71	10	50	11	5	7
7	73	10	53	12	5	7
8	76	12	54	14	5	7
9	79	12	57	15	5	8
10	82	13	59	16	5	8
11	84	13	62	17	5	8
12	87	14	62	18	5	8
13	90	15	65	19	5	8
14	93	15	67	20	5	9
15	95	15	70	21	5	9
16	98	17	70	23	5	9
17	101	17	73	24	5	9
18	104	18	75	25	5	9
19	106	18	78	26	5	10
20	109	19	78	27	5	10
21	112	20	81	28	5	10
22	115	20	84	29	5	10
23	117	21	86	30	5	11
24	120	22	87	32	5	11
25	123	22	90	33	5	11
26	126	23	92	34	5	11
27	128	23	95	35	5	11
28	131	24	95	36	5	12
29	134	25	98	37	5	12
30	137	25	100	38	5	12
31	139	26	103	39	5	12
32	142	27	104	41	5	12
33	145	27	106	42	5	13
34	148	28	109	43	5	13
35	150	28	111	44	5	13
36	153	29	112	45	5	13
37	156	30	115	46	5	13
38	159	30	117	47	5	14
39	161	31	120	48	5	14
40	164	32	120	50	5	14
41	167	32	123	51	5	14
42	170	33	125	52	5	15
43	172	33	128	53	5	15
44	175	34	129	54	5	15
45	178	35	131	55	5	15
46	181	35	134	56	5	15
47	183	36	136	57	5	16
48	186	37	137	59	5	16
49	189	37	140	60	5	16
50	192	38	142	61	5	16
51	194	38	145	62	5	16
52	197	39	146	63	5	17
53	200	40	148	64	5	17
54	203	40	151	65	5	17
55	205	41	153	66	5	17
56	208	42	154	68	5	17
57	211	42	157	69	5	18
58	214	43	159	70	5	18
59	216	43	162	71	5	18
60	219	44	162	72	5	18
61	222	45	165	73	5	19
62	225	45	167	74	5	19
63	227	46	170	75	5	19
64	230	47	171	77	5	19
65	233	47	173	78	5	19
66	236	48	176	79	5	20
67	238	48	178	80	5	20
68	241	49	179	81	5	20
69	244	50	182	82	5	20
70	247	50	184	83	5	20
71	249	51	187	84	5	21
72	252	52	188	86	5	21
73	255	52	190	87	5	21
74	258	53	193	88	5	21
75	260	53	195	89	5	21
76	263	54	196	90	5	22
77	266	55	199	91	5	22
78	269	55	201	92	5	22
79	271	56	203	93	5	22
80	274	57	204	95	5	23
81	277	57	207	96	5	23
82	280	58	209	97	5	23
83	282	58	212	98	5	23
84	285	59	213	99	5	23
85	288	60	215	100	5	24
86	291	60	218	101	5	24
87	293	61	220	102	5	24
88	296	62	221	104	5	24
89	299	62	224	105	5	24
90	302	63	226	106	5	25
91	304	63	229	107	5	25
92	307	64	230	108	5	25
93	310	65	232	109	5	25
94	313	65	234	110	5	25
95	315	66	237	111	5	26
96	318	67	238	113	5	26
97	321	67	241	114	5	26
98	324	68	243	115	5	26
99	326	68	245	116	5	26
100	329	69	246	117	5	27

** Numbers in grey indicate when that number cannot go any higher than the previous number.*

WEAPON LIST & STATS

Weapon	Gear Panel	Strength Add	Strength Unit	Magic Add	Magic Unit	Defense Add	Defense Unit	Crit. % Add	Crit. % Unit	Crit. Bonus Add	Crit. Bonus Unit
Mage's Staff	NA (No Panel)	60	—	30	—	0	—	5	—	8	—
Mage's Staff	Skill Gear	60	—	30	—	0	—	5	—	8	—
Mage's Staff	Skill Gear+②	60	+1	30	+1	0	+1	5	+1	8	+1
Mage's Staff	Technical Gear③	60	+2	30	+2	0	+2	5	+2	8	+2
Mage's Staff	Technical Gear+ ③	60	+2	30	+2	0	+2	5	+2	8	+2
Mage's Staff	Duel Gear④	60	+2	30	+2	0	+2	5	+2	8	+2
Mage's Staff	Duel Gear+④	60	+2	30	+2	0	+2	5	+2	8	+2
Mage's Staff+	Duel Gear++⑤	60	+3	35	+3	3	+3	8	+5	10	+3
Mage's Staff	Loaded Gear	60	—	30	—	0	—	5	—	8	—
Mage's Staff	Loaded Gear+②	60	+1	30	+1	0	+1	5	+1	8	+1
Mage's Staff	Chrono Gear③	60	+2	30	+2	0	+2	5	+2	8	+2
Mage's Staff	Chrono Gear+③	60	+2	30	+2	0	+2	5	+2	8	+2
Mage's Staff	Phantom Gear④	60	+2	30	+2	0	+2	5	+2	8	+2
Mage's Staff	Phantom Gear+④	60	+2	30	+2	0	+2	5	+2	8	+2
Mage's Staff	Phantom Gear++⑤	60	+3	30	+3	0	+3	5	+3	8	+3
Mage's Staff	Lift Gear③	60	+2	30	+2	0	+2	5	+2	8	+2
Mage's Staff	Lift Gear+③	60	+2	30	+2	0	+2	5	+2	8	+2
Mage's Staff	Nimble Gear④	60	+2	30	+2	0	+2	5	+2	8	+2
Mage's Staff	Nimble Gear+④	60	+2	30	+2	0	+2	5	+2	8	+2
Mage's Staff	Wild Gear③	60	+2	30	+2	0	+2	5	+2	8	+2
Mage's Staff	Wild Gear+③	60	+2	30	+2	0	+2	5	+2	8	+2
Mage's Staff	Ominous Gear④	60	+2	30	+2	0	+2	5	+2	8	+2
Mage's Staff	Ominous Gear+④	60	+2	30	+2	0	+2	5	+2	8	+2

Weapon	Gear Panel	Strength Add	Strength Unit	Magic Add	Magic Unit	Defense Add	Defense Unit	Crit. % Add	Crit. % Unit	Crit. Bonus Add	Crit. Bonus Unit
Mage's Staff	Valor Gear②	60	+1	30	+1	0	+1	5	+1	8	+1
Mage's Staff	Valor Gear+②	60	+1	30	+1	0	+1	5	+1	8	+1
Mage's Staff	Fearless Gear③	60	+2	30	+2	0	+2	5	+2	8	+2
Mage's Staff	Fearless Gear+③	60	+2	30	+2	0	+2	5	+2	8	+2
Mage's Staff	Prestige Gear④	60	+2	30	+2	0	+2	5	+2	8	+2
Mage's Staff	Prestige Gear+④	60	+2	30	+2	0	+2	5	+2	8	+2
Mage's Staff+	Crisis Gear⑤	80	+3	35	+3	3	+3	8	+3	10	+3
Mage's Staff+	Crisis Gear+⑤	80	+3	35	+3	3	+3	8	+3	10	+3
Mage's Staff++	Omega Gear⑥	85	+3	40	+3	5	+3	10	+3	13	+3
Mage's Staff++	Omega Gear+⑥	85	+3	40	+3	5	+3	10	+3	13	+3
Mage's Staff	Hazard Gear⑤	60	+3	30	+3	0	+3	5	+3	8	+3
Mage's Staff	Hazard Gear+⑤	60	+3	30	+3	0	+3	5	+3	8	+3
Mage's Staff+	Rage Gear⑤	80	+3	35	+3	3	+3	8	+3	10	+3
Mage's Staff+	Rage Gear+⑤	80	+3	35	+3	3	+3	8	+3	10	+3
Mage's Staff++	Champion Gear⑤	85	+3	40	+3	5	+3	10	+3	13	+3
Mage's Staff++	Champion Gear+⑤	85	+3	40	+3	5	+3	10	+3	13	+3
Mage's Staff++	Ultimate Gear⑥	85	+3	40	+3	5	+3	10	+3	13	+3
Mage's Staff++	Ultimate Gear+⑥	85	+3	40	+3	5	+3	10	+3	13	+3
Centurion	Pandora's Gear⑤	88	+5	32	+5	0	+5	12	+5	19	+5
Centurion+	Pandora's Gear+⑤	95	+1	32	+1	0	+1	12	+1	19	+1
Dream Rod	Zero Gear⑤	111	+4	50	+4	10	+4	10	+4	15	+4
Mage's Staff	Casual Gear②	60	+1	30	+1	0	+1	5	+1	8	+1
Mage's Staff	Mystery Gear③	60	+2	30	+2	0	+2	5	+2	8	+2

WEAPON ABILITIES

Weapon	Abilities gained with units: 1 Unit	2 Units	3 Units	Act. Spd.	Atk. Move Land	Atk. Move Air	Combo Land	Combo Air
Mage's Staff	—	—	—	1.0	1.13	1.13	2	3
Mage's Staff	—	—	—	1.0	1.13	1.13	2	3
Mage's Staff	Magic Bracer	—	—	1.0	1.13	1.13	2	3
Mage's Staff	Magic Bracer	Magic Finale	—	1.0	1.13	1.13	2	3
Mage's Staff	Magic Bracer	Magic Finale	—	1.0	1.13	1.13	2	3
Mage's Staff	Magic Bracer	Magic Finale	Magical Strike	1.0	1.13	1.13	2	3
Mage's Staff	Magic Bracer	Magic Finale	Magical Strike	1.0	1.13	1.13	2	3
Mage's Staff+	Magic Bracer	Magic Finale	Magical Strike	1.0	1.13	1.13	2	3
Mage's Staff	—	—	—	1.0	1.13	1.13	2	3
Mage's Staff	Magic Bracer	—	—	1.0	1.13	1.13	2	3
Mage's Staff	Magic Bracer	Magic Finale	—	1.0	1.13	1.13	2	3
Mage's Staff	Magic Bracer	Magic Finale	—	1.0	1.13	1.13	2	3
Mage's Staff	Magic Bracer	Magic Finale	Magical Strike	1.0	1.13	1.13	2	3
Mage's Staff	Magic Bracer	Magic Finale	Magical Strike	1.0	1.13	1.13	2	3
Mage's Staff	Magic Bracer	Magic Finale	Magical Strike	1.0	1.13	1.13	2	3
Mage's Staff	Magic Bracer	Magic Finale	—	1.0	1.13	1.13	2	3
Mage's Staff	Magic Bracer	Magic Finale	—	1.0	1.13	1.13	2	3
Mage's Staff	Magic Bracer	Magic Finale	Magical Strike	1.0	1.13	1.13	2	3
Mage's Staff	Magic Bracer	Magic Finale	Magical Strike	1.0	1.13	1.13	2	3
Mage's Staff	Magic Bracer	Magic Finale	—	1.0	1.13	1.13	2	3
Mage's Staff	Magic Bracer	Magic Finale	—	1.0	1.13	1.13	2	3
Mage's Staff	Magic Bracer	Magic Finale	Magical Strike	1.0	1.13	1.13	2	3
Mage's Staff	Magic Bracer	Magic Finale	Magical Strike	1.0	1.13	1.13	2	3

Weapon	Abilities gained with units: 1 Unit	2 Units	3 Units	Act. Spd.	Atk. Move Land	Atk. Move Air	Combo Land	Combo Air
Mage's Staff	Magic Bracer	—	—	1.0	1.13	1.13	2	3
Mage's Staff	Magic Bracer	—	—	1.0	1.13	1.13	2	3
Mage's Staff	Magic Bracer	Magic Finale	—	1.0	1.13	1.13	2	3
Mage's Staff	Magic Bracer	Magic Finale	—	1.0	1.13	1.13	2	3
Mage's Staff	Magic Bracer	Magic Finale	Magical Strike	1.0	1.13	1.13	2	3
Mage's Staff	Magic Bracer	Magic Finale	Magical Strike	1.0	1.13	1.13	2	3
Mage's Staff+	Magic Bracer	Magic Finale	Magical Strike	1.0	1.13	1.13	2	3
Mage's Staff+	Magic Bracer	Magic Finale	Magical Strike	1.0	1.13	1.13	2	3
Mage's Staff++	Magic Bracer	Magic Finale	Magical Strike	1.0	1.13	1.13	2	3
Mage's Staff++	Magic Bracer	Magic Finale	Magical Strike	1.0	1.13	1.13	2	3
Mage's Staff	Magic Bracer	Magic Finale	Magical Strike	1.0	1.13	1.13	2	3
Mage's Staff	Magic Bracer	Magic Finale	Magical Strike	1.0	1.13	1.13	2	3
Mage's Staff+	Magic Bracer	Magic Finale	Magical Strike	1.0	1.13	1.13	2	3
Mage's Staff+	Magic Bracer	Magic Finale	Magical Strike	1.0	1.13	1.13	2	3
Mage's Staff++	Magic Bracer	Magic Finale	Magical Strike	1.0	1.13	1.13	2	3
Mage's Staff++	Magic Bracer	Magic Finale	Magical Strike	1.0	1.13	1.13	2	3
Mage's Staff++	Magic Bracer	Magic Finale	Magical Strike	1.0	1.13	1.13	2	3
Mage's Staff++	Magic Bracer	Magic Finale	Magical Strike	1.0	1.13	1.13	2	3
Centurion	Damage Control	Brick Wall	Alive 'n' Kicking	1.0	1.0	1.0	2	3
Centurion+	Damage Control	Brick Wall	Alive 'n' Kicking	1.0	1.0	1.0	2	3
Dream Rod	Fire Finish	Thunder Finish	Blizzard Finish	1.0	1.13	1.13	2	2
Mage's Staff	Magic Bracer	—	—	1.0	1.13	1.13	2	3
Mage's Staff	Magic Bracer	Magic Finale	—	1.0	1.13	1.13	2	3

GOOFY

The clumsy but easygoing captain of the Disney Castle Royal Knights. Despite his position, Goofy dislikes weapons.

Unlocking Goofy:

Reach Story Mode Day 296.

CHARACTER STATS

LEVEL	MAX HP	STRENGTH	MAGIC POWER	DEFENSE POWER	CRITICAL %	CRIT. BONUS
1	64	9	25	7	3	6
2	67	9	31	9	3	7
3	70	11	32	10	3	7
4	73	11	32	12	3	7
5	76	12	34	13	3	7
6	79	13	36	15	3	8
7	82	14	38	16	3	8
8	85	14	38	18	3	8
9	88	15	39	19	3	8
10	91	16	42	21	3	9
11	94	17	44	22	3	9
12	97	17	44	24	3	9
13	100	18	45	25	3	9
14	103	19	48	27	3	10
15	107	20	49	28	3	10
16	110	20	50	30	3	10
17	113	21	51	31	3	10
18	116	22	54	33	3	11
19	119	23	55	34	3	11
20	122	23	56	36	3	11
21	125	24	57	37	3	11
22	128	25	60	39	3	12
23	131	26	61	40	3	12
24	134	26	62	42	3	12
25	137	27	63	43	3	12
26	140	28	66	45	3	13
27	143	29	67	46	3	13
28	146	29	68	48	3	13
29	150	30	69	49	3	13
30	153	31	72	50	3	14
31	156	32	73	52	3	14
32	159	32	74	53	3	14
33	162	33	75	55	3	14
34	165	34	78	56	3	15
35	168	35	79	58	3	15
36	171	35	80	59	3	15
37	174	36	81	61	3	15
38	177	37	84	62	3	16
39	180	38	85	64	3	16
40	183	38	86	65	3	16
41	186	39	87	67	3	16
42	189	40	90	68	3	17
43	193	41	91	70	3	17
44	196	41	92	71	3	17
45	199	42	93	73	3	17
46	202	43	96	74	3	18
47	205	44	97	76	3	18
48	208	44	98	77	3	18
49	211	45	99	79	3	18
50	214	46	102	80	3	19
51	217	47	103	82	3	19
52	220	47	104	83	3	19
53	223	48	105	85	3	19
54	226	49	108	86	3	20
55	229	50	109	88	3	20
56	232	50	110	89	3	20
57	235	51	111	91	3	20
58	239	52	114	92	3	21
59	242	53	115	94	3	21
60	245	53	116	95	3	21
61	248	54	117	97	3	21
62	251	55	120	98	3	22
63	254	56	121	99	3	22
64	257	56	122	101	3	22
65	260	57	123	102	3	22
66	263	58	126	104	3	23
67	266	59	127	105	3	23
68	269	59	128	107	3	23
69	272	60	129	108	3	23
70	275	61	132	110	3	24
71	278	62	133	111	3	24
72	282	62	134	113	3	24
73	285	63	135	114	3	24
74	288	64	138	116	3	25
75	291	65	139	117	3	25
76	294	65	140	119	3	25
77	297	66	141	120	3	25
78	300	67	144	122	3	26
79	303	68	145	123	3	26
80	306	68	146	125	3	26
81	309	69	147	126	3	26
82	312	70	150	128	3	27
83	315	71	151	129	3	27
84	318	71	152	131	3	27
85	321	72	153	132	3	27
86	325	73	156	134	3	28
87	328	74	157	135	3	28
88	331	74	158	137	3	28
89	334	75	159	138	3	28
90	337	76	162	140	3	29
91	340	77	163	141	3	29
92	343	77	164	143	3	29
93	346	78	165	144	3	29
94	349	79	168	146	3	30
95	352	80	169	147	3	30
96	355	80	170	149	3	30
97	358	81	171	150	3	30
98	361	82	174	151	3	31
99	364	83	175	153	3	31
100	368	83	176	154	3	31

* Numbers in grey indicate when that number cannot go any higher than the previous number.

WEAPON LIST

Weapon	Gear Panel	Strength Add	Strength Unit	Magic Add	Magic Unit	Defense Add	Defense Unit	Crit. % Add	Crit. % Unit	Crit. Bonus Add	Crit. Bonus Unit
Knight's Shield	NA (No Panel)	100	—	0	—	8	—	7	—	7	—
Knight's Shield	Skill Gear	100	—	0	—	8	—	7	—	7	—
Knight's Shield	Skill Gear+②	100	+1	0	+1	8	+1	7	+1	7	+1
Knight's Shield	Technical Gear③	100	+2	0	+2	8	+2	7	+2	7	+2
Knight's Shield	Technical Gear+ ③	100	+2	0	+2	8	+2	7	+2	7	+2
Knight's Shield	Duel Gear④	100	+2	0	+2	8	+2	7	+2	7	+2
Knight's Shield	Duel Gear+④	100	+2	0	+2	8	+2	7	+2	7	+2
Knight's Shield+	Duel Gear++⑤	105	+3	0	+3	10	+3	8	+5	10	+3
Knight's Shield	Loaded Gear	100	—	0	—	8	—	7	—	7	—
Knight's Shield	Loaded Gear+②	100	+1	0	+1	8	+1	7	+1	7	+1
Knight's Shield	Chrono Gear③	100	+2	0	+2	8	+2	7	+2	7	+2
Knight's Shield	Chrono Gear+③	100	+2	0	+2	8	+2	7	+2	7	+2
Knight's Shield	Phantom Gear④	100	+2	0	+2	8	+2	7	+2	7	+2
Knight's Shield	Phantom Gear+④	100	+2	0	+2	8	+2	7	+2	7	+2
Knight's Shield	Phantom Gear++⑤	100	+3	0	+3	8	+3	7	+3	7	+3
Knight's Shield	Lift Gear③	100	+2	0	+2	8	+2	7	+2	7	+2
Knight's Shield	Lift Gear+③	100	+2	0	+2	8	+2	7	+2	7	+2
Knight's Shield	Nimble Gear④	100	+2	0	+2	8	+2	7	+2	7	+2
Knight's Shield	Nimble Gear+④	100	+2	0	+2	8	+2	7	+2	7	+2
Knight's Shield	Wild Gear③	100	+2	0	+2	8	+2	7	+2	7	+2
Knight's Shield	Wild Gear+③	100	+2	0	+2	8	+2	7	+2	7	+2
Knight's Shield	Ominous Gear④	100	+2	0	+2	8	+2	7	+2	7	+2
Knight's Shield	Ominous Gear+④	100	+2	0	+2	8	+2	7	+2	7	+2

Weapon	Gear Panel	Strength Add	Strength Unit	Magic Add	Magic Unit	Defense Add	Defense Unit	Crit. % Add	Crit. % Unit	Crit. Bonus Add	Crit. Bonus Unit
Knight's Shield	Valor Gear②	100	+1	0	+1	8	+1	7	+1	7	+1
Knight's Shield	Valor Gear+②	100	+1	0	+1	8	+1	7	+1	7	+1
Knight's Shield	Fearless Gear③	100	+2	0	+2	8	+2	7	+2	7	+2
Knight's Shield	Fearless Gear+③	100	+2	0	+2	8	+2	7	+2	7	+2
Knight's Shield	Prestige Gear④	100	+2	0	+2	8	+2	7	+2	7	+2
Knight's Shield	Prestige Gear+④	100	+2	0	+2	8	+2	7	+2	7	+2
Knight's Shield+	Crisis Gear⑤	105	+3	0	+3	10	+3	8	+3	10	+3
Knight's Shield+	Crisis Gear+⑤	105	+3	0	+3	10	+3	8	+3	10	+3
Knight's Shield++	Omega Gear⑥	115	+3	0	+3	12	+3	10	+3	15	+3
Knight's Shield++	Omega Gear+⑥	115	+3	0	+3	12	+3	10	+3	15	+3
Knight's Shield	Hazard Gear⑤	100	+3	0	+3	8	+3	7	+3	7	+3
Knight's Shield	Hazard Gear+⑤	100	+3	0	+3	8	+3	7	+3	7	+3
Knight's Shield+	Rage Gear⑤	105	+3	0	+3	10	+3	8	+3	10	+3
Knight's Shield+	Rage Gear+⑤	105	+3	0	+3	10	+3	8	+3	10	+3
Knight's Shield++	Champion Gear⑤	115	+3	0	+3	12	+3	10	+3	15	+3
Knight's Shield++	Champion Gear+⑤	115	+3	0	+3	12	+3	10	+3	15	+3
Knight's Shield++	Ultimate Gear⑥	115	+3	0	+3	12	+3	10	+3	15	+3
Knight's Shield++	Ultimate Gear+⑥	115	+3	0	+3	12	+3	10	+3	15	+3
Frozen Pride	Pandora's Gear⑤	100	+5	25	+5	10	+5	15	+5	19	+5
Frozen Pride+	Pandora's Gear+⑤	125	+1	30	+1	10	+1	15	+1	19	+1
Dream Shield	Zero Gear⑤	124	+4	0	+4	10	+4	15	+4	19	+4
Knight's Shield	Casual Gear②	100	+1	0	+1	8	+1	7	+1	7	+1
Knight's Shield	Mystery Gear③	100	+2	0	+2	8	+2	7	+2	7	+2

WEAPON ABILITIES

Weapon	Abilities gained with units: 1 Unit	2 Units	3 Units	Act. Spd.	Atk. Move Land	Atk. Move Air	Combo Land	Combo Air
Knight's Shield	—	—	—	1.0	1.13	1.13	3	2
Knight's Shield	—	—	—	1.0	1.13	1.13	3	2
Knight's Shield	Offensive Block	—	—	1.0	1.13	1.13	3	2
Knight's Shield	Offensive Block	Defender	—	1.0	1.13	1.13	3	2
Knight's Shield	Offensive Block	Defender	—	1.0	1.13	1.13	3	2
Knight's Shield	Offensive Block	Defender	Combo-Block	1.0	1.13	1.13	3	2
Knight's Shield	Offensive Block	Defender	Combo-Block	1.0	1.13	1.13	3	2
Knight's Shield+	Offensive Block	Defender	Combo-Block	1.0	1.13	1.13	3	2
Knight's Shield	—	—	—	1.0	1.13	1.13	3	2
Knight's Shield	Offensive Block	—	—	1.0	1.13	1.13	3	2
Knight's Shield	Offensive Block	Defender	—	1.0	1.13	1.13	3	2
Knight's Shield	Offensive Block	Defender	—	1.0	1.13	1.13	3	2
Knight's Shield	Offensive Block	Defender	Combo-Block	1.0	1.13	1.13	3	2
Knight's Shield	Offensive Block	Defender	Combo-Block	1.0	1.13	1.13	3	2
Knight's Shield	Offensive Block	Defender	Combo-Block	1.0	1.13	1.13	3	2
Knight's Shield	Offensive Block	Defender	—	1.0	1.13	1.13	3	2
Knight's Shield	Offensive Block	Defender	—	1.0	1.13	1.13	3	2
Knight's Shield	Offensive Block	Defender	Combo-Block	1.0	1.13	1.13	3	2
Knight's Shield	Offensive Block	Defender	Combo-Block	1.0	1.13	1.13	3	2
Knight's Shield	Offensive Block	Defender	—	1.0	1.13	1.13	3	2
Knight's Shield	Offensive Block	Defender	—	1.0	1.13	1.13	3	2
Knight's Shield	Offensive Block	Defender	Combo-Block	1.0	1.13	1.13	3	2
Knight's Shield	Offensive Block	Defender	Combo-Block	1.0	1.13	1.13	3	2

Weapon	Abilities gained with units: 1 Unit	2 Units	3 Units	Act. Spd.	Atk. Move Land	Atk. Move Air	Combo Land	Combo Air
Knight's Shield	Offensive Block	—	—	1.0	1.13	1.13	3	2
Knight's Shield	Offensive Block	—	—	1.0	1.13	1.13	3	2
Knight's Shield	Offensive Block	Defender	—	1.0	1.13	1.13	3	2
Knight's Shield	Offensive Block	Defender	—	1.0	1.13	1.13	3	2
Knight's Shield	Offensive Block	Defender	Combo-Block	1.0	1.13	1.13	3	2
Knight's Shield	Offensive Block	Defender	Combo-Block	1.0	1.13	1.13	3	2
Knight's Shield+	Offensive Block	Defender	Combo-Block	1.0	1.13	1.13	3	2
Knight's Shield+	Offensive Block	Defender	Combo-Block	1.0	1.13	1.13	3	2
Knight's Shield++	Offensive Block	Defender	Combo-Block	1.0	1.13	1.13	3	2
Knight's Shield++	Offensive Block	Defender	Combo-Block	1.0	1.13	1.13	3	2
Knight's Shield	Offensive Block	Defender	Combo-Block	1.0	1.13	1.13	3	2
Knight's Shield	Offensive Block	Defender	Combo-Block	1.0	1.13	1.13	3	2
Knight's Shield+	Offensive Block	Defender	Combo-Block	1.0	1.13	1.13	3	2
Knight's Shield+	Offensive Block	Defender	Combo-Block	1.0	1.13	1.13	3	2
Knight's Shield++	Offensive Block	Defender	Combo-Block	1.0	1.13	1.13	3	2
Knight's Shield++	Offensive Block	Defender	Combo-Block	1.0	1.13	1.13	3	2
Knight's Shield++	Offensive Block	Defender	Combo-Block	1.0	1.13	1.13	3	2
Knight's Shield++	Offensive Block	Defender	Combo-Block	1.0	1.13	1.13	3	2
Frozen Pride	Offensive Block	Magic Bracer	Blizzard Finish	1.0	1.0	1.0	4	2
Frozen Pride+	Offensive Block	Magic Bracer	Blizzard Finish	1.0	1.0	1.0	4	2
Dream Shield	Offensive Block	Vitality Barrier	Brick Wall	1.0	1.13	1.13	10	2
Knight's Shield	Offensive Block	—	—	1.0	1.13	1.13	3	2
Knight's Shield	Offensive Block	Defender	—	1.0	1.13	1.13	3	2

HAYNER

A boy who lives in Twilight Town, he has a bit of an attitude problem. Once he gets an idea, he has to do it...always dragging along Pence and Olette for the ride. There's bad blood between Hayner and Seifer, the town's self-appointed "disciplinarian."

OLETTE

Olette is a responsible young lady who lives in Twilight Town with her friends Hayner and Pence. She enjoys shopping and always finishes her homework, even making the boys do theirs, too.

PENCE

Pence is a relatively laid-back young man who lives in Twilight Town with Olette and Hayner. When there's a problem, he takes his time and approaches the problem realistically.

ALADDIN

A young man living in the desert city of Agrabah. He fell in love with Princess Jasmine, despite his humble background. He found the legendary lamp and released the Genie, who is now his partner.

THE MAGIC CARPET

A magical flying carpet. Carpet is an old friend of the Genie's. Ever since Aladdin found him in the Cave of Wonders, Carpet will do anything to help him. Carpet can carry Aladdin across the vastness of the desert in the blink of an eye.

THE GENIE

The wacky spirit of the lamp. He spent centuries cooped up in the lamp until Aladdin found him. He must grant three wishes to whoever controls the lamp, even if they are evil.

ABU

Aladdin's faithful furry sidekick. Abu's size and ability make him valuable in tight spots. He has a weakness for jewels and treasure and when he's around them he can't think of anything else.

JASMINE

The strong-willed princess of Agrabah. Jasmine longs for the freedom of life outside the palace. She's in love with Aladdin, even though he isn't a real prince. She left the palace in pursuit of freedom, where she met Aladdin.

THE BEAST

A prince who was changed into a hideous beast because of his selfish heart. Belle has helped heal the loneliness he's suffered due to his ugliness.

BELLE

Tender-hearted, yet fearless, Belle is just the right young woman to transform a beast into a Prince.

COGSWORTH

The Beast's majordomo. He became a clock when an enchantress put a spell on the castle. Cogsworth is particular about order and punctuality. Maybe that's why he turned into a clock?

LUMIERE

The castle's maitre d'. He became a candlestick when an enchantress put a spell on the castle. Lumiere has a way with words and can be quite a charmer.

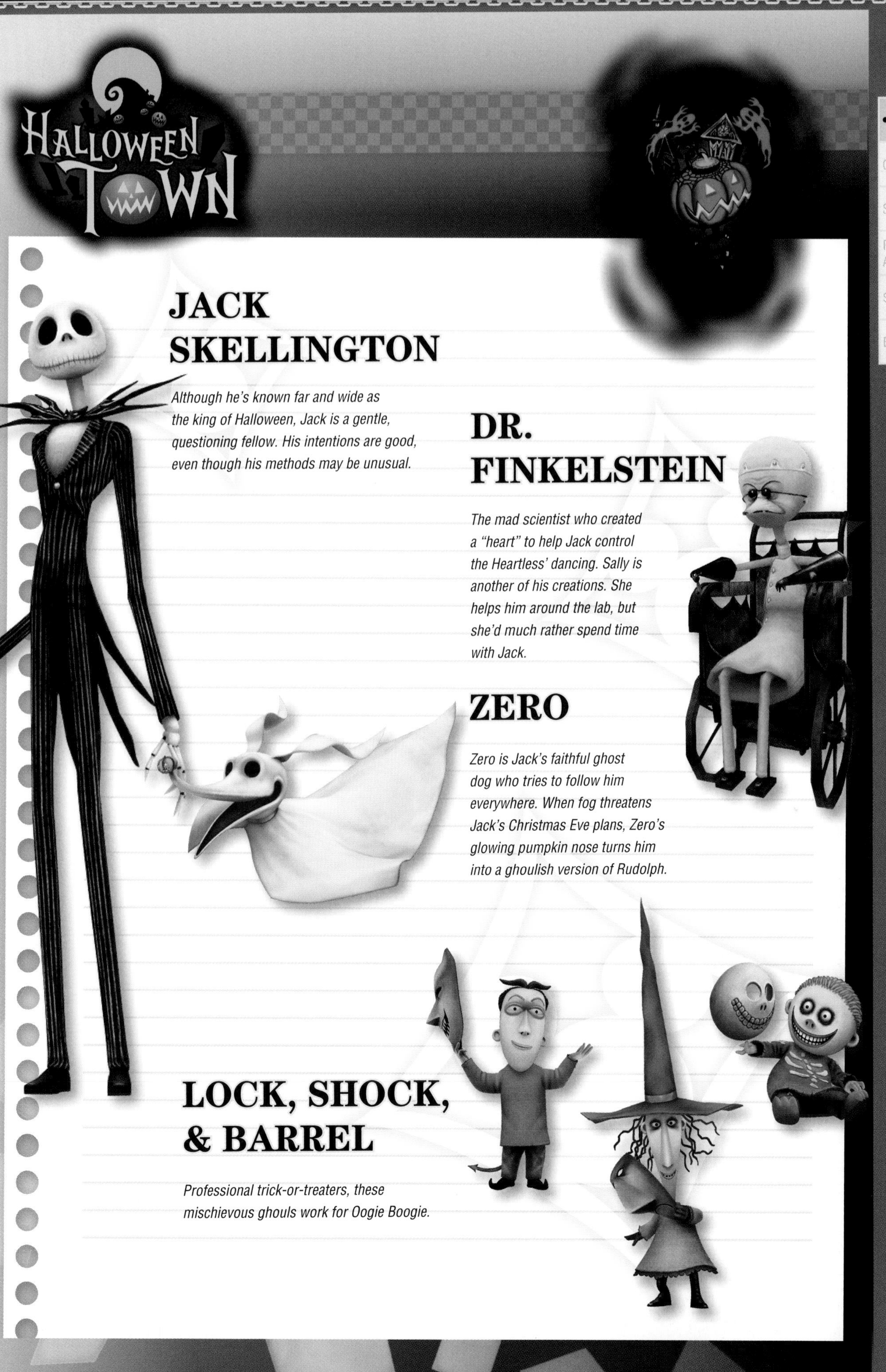

JACK SKELLINGTON

Although he's known far and wide as the king of Halloween, Jack is a gentle, questioning fellow. His intentions are good, even though his methods may be unusual.

DR. FINKELSTEIN

The mad scientist who created a "heart" to help Jack control the Heartless' dancing. Sally is another of his creations. She helps him around the lab, but she'd much rather spend time with Jack.

ZERO

Zero is Jack's faithful ghost dog who tries to follow him everywhere. When fog threatens Jack's Christmas Eve plans, Zero's glowing pumpkin nose turns him into a ghoulish version of Rudolph.

LOCK, SHOCK, & BARREL

Professional trick-or-treaters, these mischievous ghouls work for Oogie Boogie.

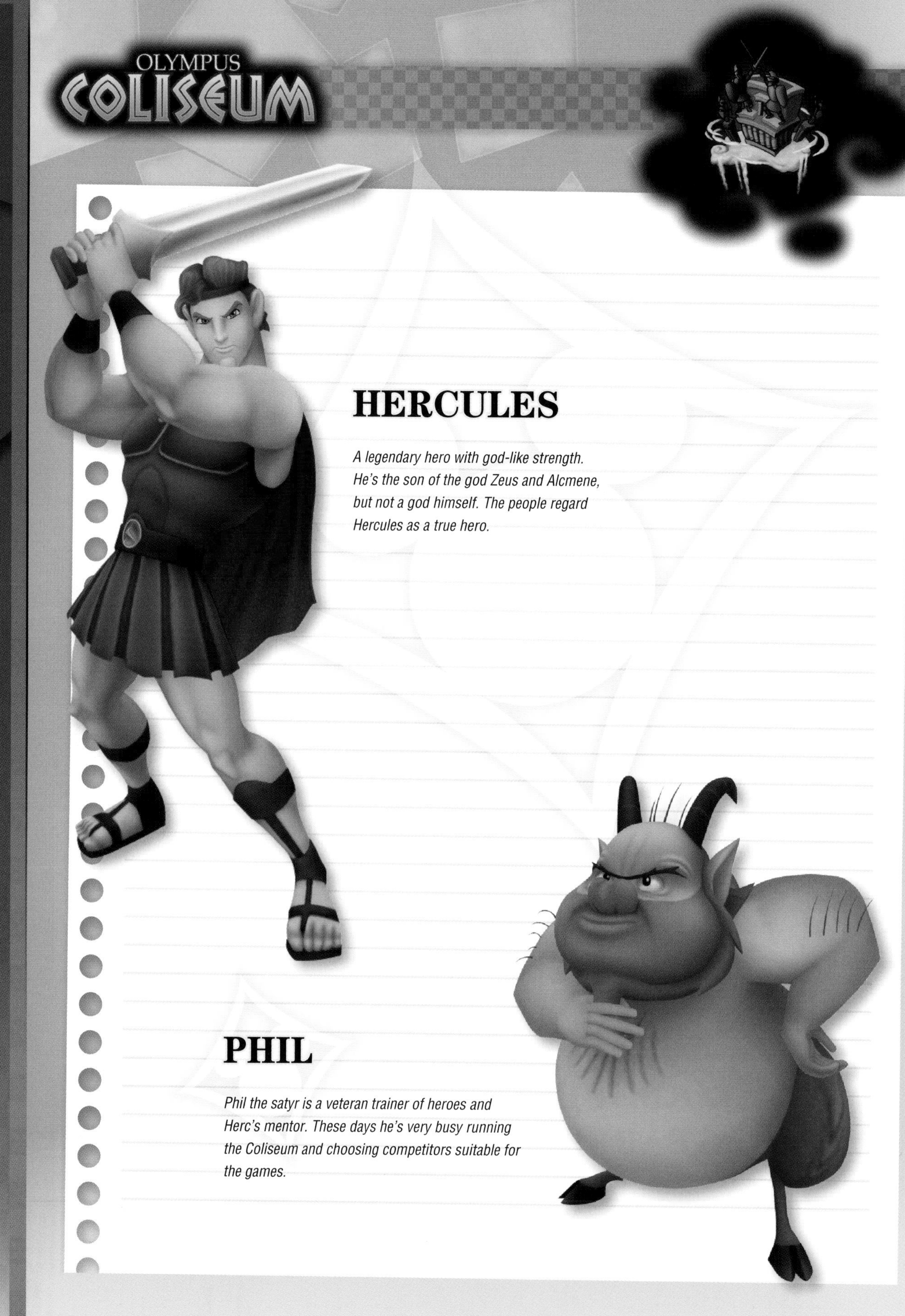

HERCULES

A legendary hero with god-like strength. He's the son of the god Zeus and Alcmene, but not a god himself. The people regard Hercules as a true hero.

PHIL

Phil the satyr is a veteran trainer of heroes and Herc's mentor. These days he's very busy running the Coliseum and choosing competitors suitable for the games.

THE QUEEN OF HEARTS

A queen of Wonderland who lives in a castle with decks and decks of card soldiers. Selfish and short-tempered, she beheads anyone who crosses her. She thinks Alice tried to steal her heart.

THE CHESHIRE CAT

A mysterious, grinning cat who talks in riddles and can appear and disappear at will. He loves to mislead and confuse.

CARD SOLDIERS

Guards in the service of the Queen of Hearts. They fear her temper and will do anything she orders.

THE WHITE RABBIT

A loyal retainer of the Queen of Hearts. He always carries out the Queen's orders no matter what they may be.

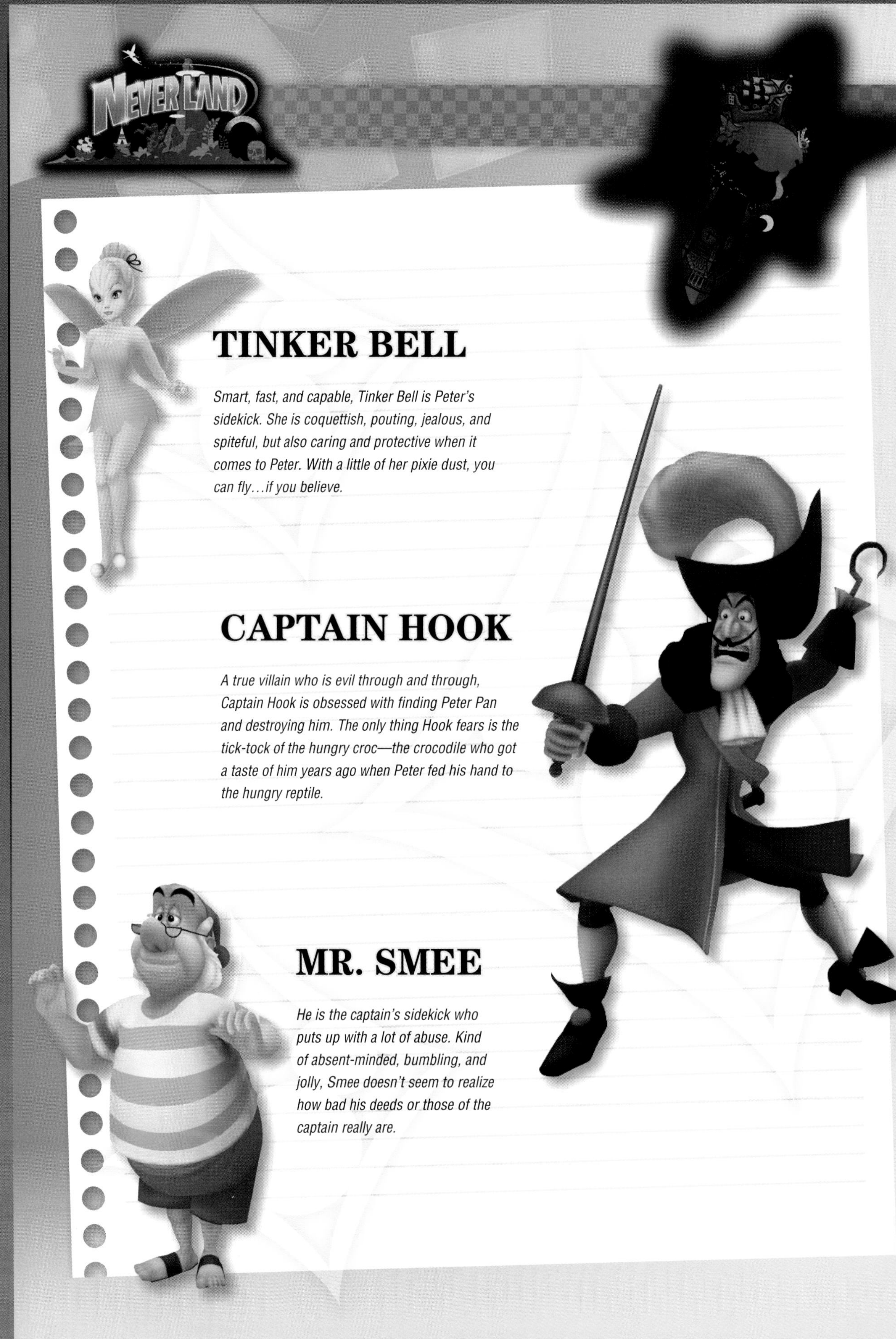

TINKER BELL

Smart, fast, and capable, Tinker Bell is Peter's sidekick. She is coquettish, pouting, jealous, and spiteful, but also caring and protective when it comes to Peter. With a little of her pixie dust, you can fly…if you believe.

CAPTAIN HOOK

A true villain who is evil through and through, Captain Hook is obsessed with finding Peter Pan and destroying him. The only thing Hook fears is the tick-tock of the hungry croc—the crocodile who got a taste of him years ago when Peter fed his hand to the hungry reptile.

MR. SMEE

He is the captain's sidekick who puts up with a lot of abuse. Kind of absent-minded, bumbling, and jolly, Smee doesn't seem to realize how bad his deeds or those of the captain really are.

OTHER CHARACTERS

PETE

A tough and mean former steamboat captain. Donald and Goofy know Pete well—he's so bad that King Mickey was forced to banish him to another dimension.

Maleficent found Pete there and helped him escape from exile. Since then, he's been traveling the worlds, assembling an army of Heartless for Maleficent. It's fairly certain that the two of them are planning to take over and rule all the worlds.

KAIRI

Riku and Sora's friend growing up. Kairi vanished when their home islands were devoured by darkness. Riku and Sora both journeyed to find her. Kairi was held captive by the Heartless, but thanks to Sora, she and the islands were saved. She waits there for Sora and Riku's return.

DIZ

An entity shrouded in mystery. Truly an enigma. DiZ appeared before Riku in the guise of Ansem, presenting him with choices regarding the darkness within his heart. It is said he and the King have met.

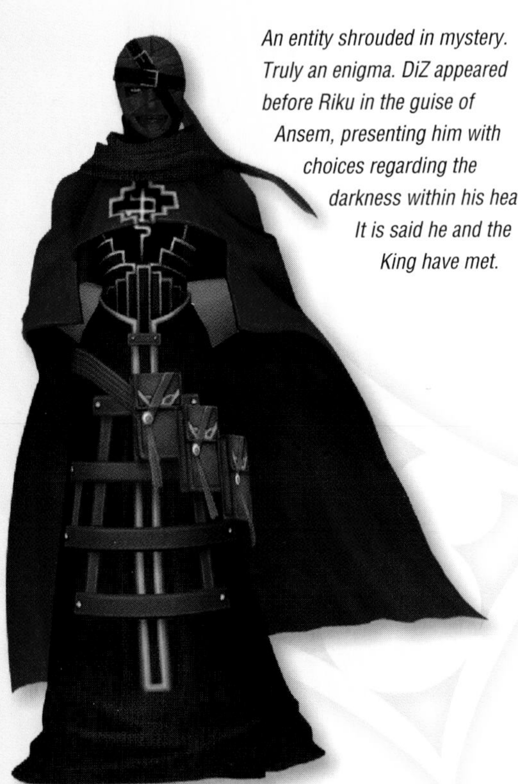

NAMINÉ

A young witch who—under orders from Marluxia—rewrote much of Sora's memory. Because Naminé based the false memories on Sora's feelings toward Kairi, Sora believed he and Naminé had been friends since childhood. But truth be told, the two had never met before Castle Oblivion.

Under orders from the Organization, Naminé shadowed Kairi and altered Sora's memory. But the forgiveness in Sora's heart moved her to disobey those orders. Now she watches over Sora until the reconstruction of his memories is complete.

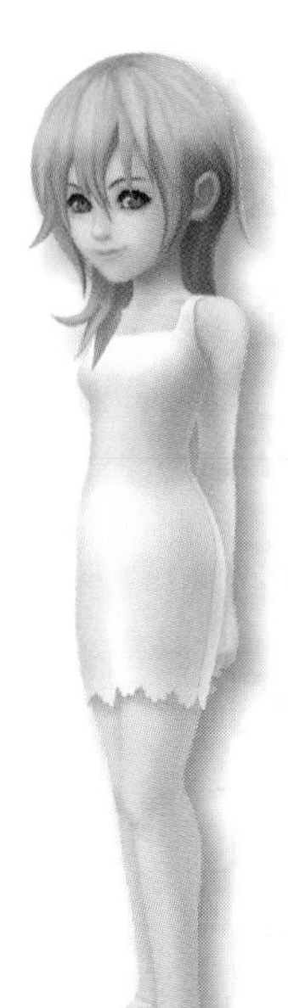

CHAPTER 2

GAME BASICS

If you find yourself confused about any game process or feature you read about in other chapters, refer to this section for better understanding. This section contains complete descriptions of all actions and menu functions in the game.

MODES

After starting *Kingdom Hearts 358/2 Days* on your Nintendo DS, the title screen appears. At first two modes are available: Story Mode and Mission Mode.

STORY MODE

Story Mode is the main, plot-driven mode of the game. You must start Story Mode and create a save game to play Mission Mode. As you progress in Story Mode, you'll unlock additional missions and earn rankings that allow you to play more missions in Mission Mode. Therefore, it is recommended that you play Story Mode first.

DIFFICULTY

After choosing to start a new Story Mode game, you'll then select a difficulty level. Choose a difficulty level that suits your preference and skill level. The following table illustrates the differences in the various difficulty modes. The multipliers shown are applied to every calculation in the game. Thus in Beginner Mode, Roxas sustains less damage and recovers more HP from HP prizes collected. In Proud Mode, Roxas sustains greater damage from every hit and recovers less HP by collecting prizes.

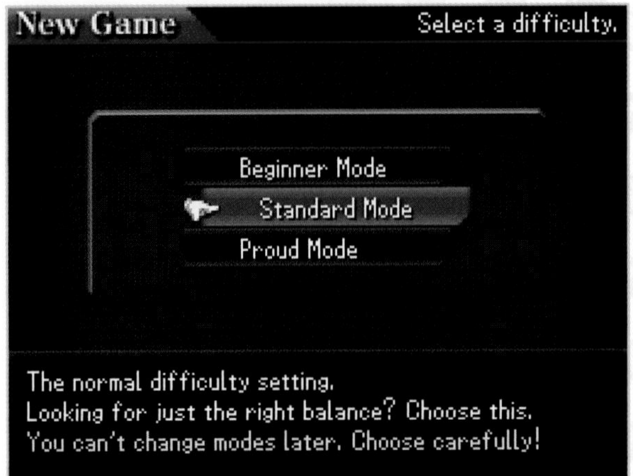

Although a warning appears near the bottom of the mode selection screen indicating that you'll be unable to change modes later, this isn't necessarily true. If the player chooses Standard Mode and Roxas loses all his HP too many times during a mission, the game offers the chance to decrease your difficulty level at the continue screen.

Difficulty Modes

Factor	Beginner	Standard	Proud
Damage sustained	x0.7	x1	x1.75
HP prize recovery	x2	x1	x0.7

MISSION MODE

Mission Mode allows you to replay missions unlocked in Story Mode where the player has obtained a special item called a "Unity Badge." Missions can be played in either Solo or Multiplayer mode through wireless DS communication with four players.

LOAD SAVE DATA

To begin Mission Mode, you must load a save game from Story Mode. Therefore, start Story Mode first, play the first few missions, and create a save file on the game card.

SELECT A CHARACTER

In Mission Mode you can play as any of the characters in Organization XIII. Each character utilizes unique weaponry as well as a unique combat style. Use the cursor to highlight a character and check the top screen to see the differences in the characters' stats per level. As you progress in Story Mode, more characters become available to play in Mission Mode.

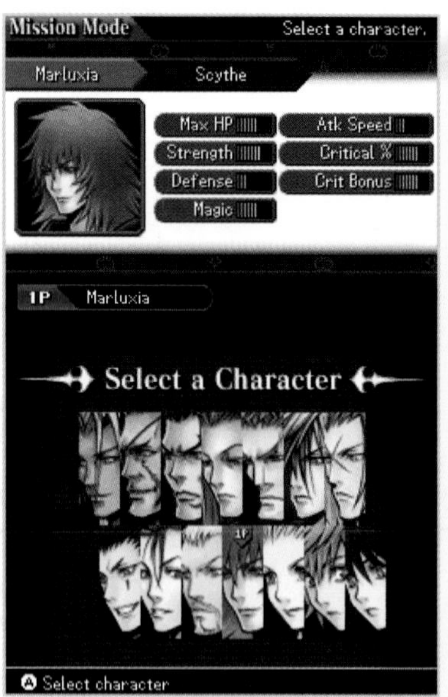

SELECT A MISSION

After selecting a character, the menu screen opens. Select a mission to begin from the Holo-Missions screen, or rearrange your panels, peruse the shop, change your character, adjust mission configuration settings, save your game, or return to the title screen.

The Holo-Missions screen is slightly different in Mission Mode. Missions are selected by the world in which they occur, not by the days they occur. Press the L and R buttons to select a different world. Eighty of the missions from Story Mode are playable in Mission Mode, along with a tutorial mission, Mission 00.

DIFFERENCES IN MISSION MODE

- ★ *Players receive Mission Crowns for completing missions in Mission Mode. The number received is based on the criteria stated on the Rewards page of the mission summary, usually one for completing the mission (Solo) or one for placing first (Multiplayer), plus bonus Crowns for completing the mission the first time, based on mission difficulty. Mission Crowns can be redeemed for prizes at the shop.*
- ★ *Mission Point prizes and breakable crates full of Mission Points appear on the maps. Collect Mission Points to place above other players in Multiplayer and receive more Mission Points. Only the player with the most Mission Points will be awarded Mission Crowns.*
- ★ *Players can damage one another, eliminating their competition from the mission. If you don't work together at least a bit however, all of the players will fail the mission. The entire group must share a small number of allowable defeats.*
- ★ *Certain doorways and exits are covered by circular halos called "Gathering Gates." All players must stand at the Gathering Gate before anyone can proceed to the next area. Other players cannot damage players standing near the Gathering Gate. Not every doorway has a Gathering Gate.*
- ★ *In Mission Mode, all enemies have three times more HP than in Story Mode. Therefore, it's best to work together to defeat enemies.*
- ★ *When the Mission Gauge is filled to the goal line, a countdown begins. When the countdown expires, the mission ends. Exit via the dark corridor before time expires to receive bonus Mission Points. This feature can be changed or deactivated in the Mission Config screen.*
- ★ *The Mission Config screen features additional pages of options allowing the user to adjust Universal Settings for all missions initiated, including whether players can use attack magic or recovery magic and items, adjustments to player and enemy strength, whether HP constantly drains, and more.*

THEATER MODE

Theater Mode is added to the title screen after the player completes Story Mode and saves his or her game. This mode allows for the viewing of all 28 movies that play between missions during Story Mode.

ON-SCREEN DISPLAY

The following image depicts the on-screen display typically seen when the player is engaged in a mission.

❶ **Heart Points:** *Hearts collected by defeating enemies known as "Emblem Heartless."*

❷ **Chain:** *Appears when the player eliminates two or more enemies in rapid succession, before the "chain ring" around other enemies expires.*

❸ **Item:** *Shows names of items collected or items that cannot be picked up because the backpack is full.*

❹ **Commands:** *Press A to perform the action listed. Press X to cycle through commands.*

❺ **Enemy Name/HP:** *Displayed when an enemy is targeted. The HP bar shows the enemies' remaining HP. Requires the Scan panel.*

❻ **Player:** *Shows which player you are playing as. In Story Mode and Solo Mission Mode, you are always 1P.*

❼ **Likeness:** *Drawing depicting the character's face.*

❽ **HP Bar:** *Shows life remaining; empties when damage is sustained. When fully depleted, the continue screen appears.*

❾ **Limit Gauge:** *When HP drops into the yellow portion of the HP bar, Limit Break becomes available.*

❿ **Information:** *Displays the current objective during the mission, or indicates that it is time to RTC (Return to the Castle).*

⓫ **Map:** *Depicts the world and the player's current area. Player location markers are color-coded for each player in the mission. Red doors on the map indicate points of entry/exit.*

⓬ **Parameter:** *The criteria required for completing the mission.*

⓭ **Chests:** *Shows the number of chests opened versus the total number.*

⓮ **Mission Gauge:** *Fills as the player achieves the criteria necessary to complete the mission. The grey X marks the "goal" line the player must reach in order to RTC.*

Kingdom Hearts 358/2 Days follows the daily life of Roxas between the events depicted in *Kingdom Hearts* and *Kingdom Hearts II*. As a member of the mysterious Organization XIII, Roxas's job is to get up every day and complete one mission. The day changes each time a mission is complete.

THE GREY AREA

On most days, Roxas begins his day by entering the Grey Area. This is where the other members of Organization XIII gather to receive their mission assignments from Saïx, the Organization's second-in-command.

FELLOW MEMBERS

Other members of Organization XIII sometimes convene in the Grey Area. Speak to them to learn about current events. Sometimes, other members hand over items or panels to use in your missions.

Occasionally, the other members challenge Roxas to fulfill some criteria, such as using Limit Breaks to defeat a certain number of enemies, equipping a specific panel configuration, or opening a certain number of item chests. Speak to these members again after fulfilling their criteria to receive an item. Sometimes, the member does not give Roxas an item, instead opting to add an additional mission to the roster.

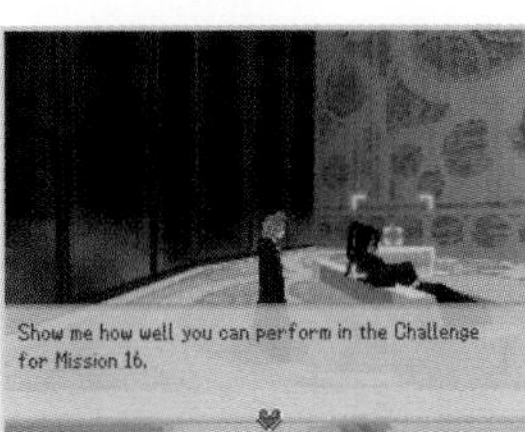

MOOGLE SHOP

Starting from Day 26, the Moogle appears in the Grey Area. Speak to the Moogle to purchase or sell items, synthesize panels, or redeem Mission Crowns and Challenge Sigils for prizes.

BUY

Purchasing panels requires heart points, gained by slaying certain enemies called Emblem Heartless. The Moogle's available inventory grows as Roxas achieves new ranks.

SELL

Sell panels to the Moogle for munny. Notice that buying panels requires heart points, but you can only sell them for munny. Therefore, it is impossible to reacquire spent heart points through the Moogle.

SYNTHESIZE

Synthesis allows for the creation of new panels out of two or more other panels. The Moogle charges certain amounts of munny for this service. New panels become available to synthesize as Roxas acquires new ranks or finds certain materials.

REDEEM

After completing challenges or missions in Mission Mode, use this option to redeem Challenge Sigils and Mission Crowns. The Moogle automatically gives you prizes when you enter the Redeem screen after acquiring a certain number of Sigils or Crowns.

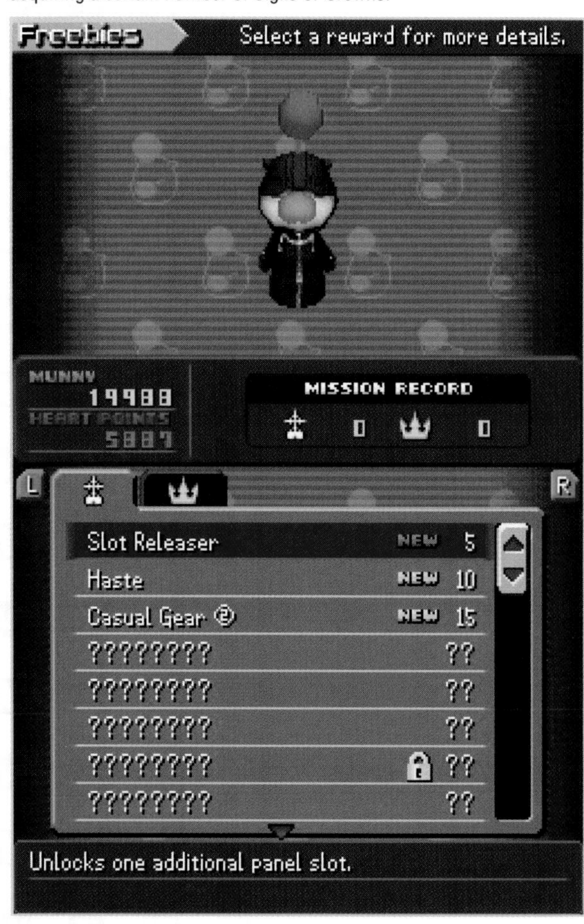

For instance, accumulate 5 Challenge Sigils by completing challenges and then speak to the Moogle and choose "Redeem." You'll automatically receive a Slot Releaser. Accumulate 5 more Challenge Sigils and speak to the Moogle to receive a Haste panel.

MENU

While in the Grey Area, press the START button to open the menu. The options on this screen allow you to customize Roxas's abilities, replay missions, view helpful files, review tutorial screens, change configuration settings, save your game, and quit. The various functions of each menu option are explained in further detail in the "Menu" section.

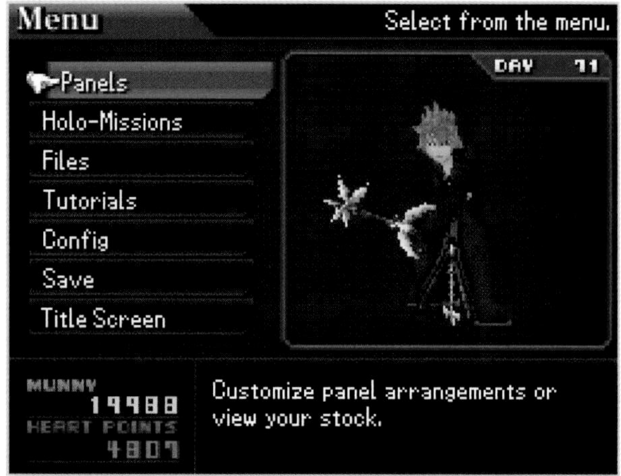

Press Y while in the Grey Area to open the Panel screen.

MISSIONS SCREEN

Speak to Saïx to receive your mission assignments. He's the blue-haired man standing at the top center of the area and is the Organization's second-in-command. After some words, Saïx opens the Missions screen, listing all the missions available for that day. Choose a mission to attempt to advance the calendar one day.

ADVANCE

Certain missions are marked with a Keyblade icon, indicating they are mandatory missions you must complete. When all mandatory missions are completed, the "Advance" option appears in the upper-left box on the lower screen. If you wish to skip the rest of the optional missions and advance to the next day, move the cursor up to Advance and press A.

Advancing Not Recommended

Because Roxas grows and benefits by completing all missions, skipping missions is not recommended. By skipping too many missions, further progression in the game may become more difficult with an under-powered Roxas. Furthermore, certain post-game bonuses only become available by completing all missions.

BONUS GAUGE

Completing missions fills the Bonus Gauge in the upper-right corner on the lower screen. The amount by which the mission fills the gauge is indicated prior to mission acceptance. When the Bonus Gauge fills past the x2 or x3 marks, completing subsequent missions rewards the player with double or triple the usual quantity of items! Thus, it's a wise idea to choose missions that will fill the Bonus Gauge to a greater extent, so that you start gaining bonus items by completing each subsequent mission.

MISSION DATA

Basic mission data displayed for each selection includes the mission number, world, overall objective or title, the number of chests available, and sometimes a Keyblade icon indicating whether the mission is mandatory or not. Move the cursor to select any mission and press A to view the mission summary.

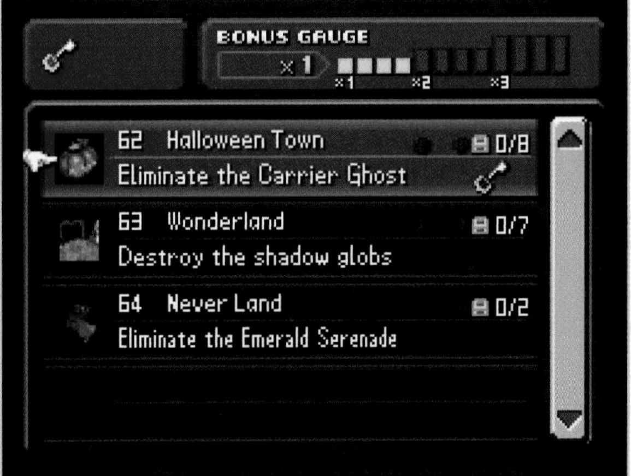

MISSION SUMMARY

Upon selecting a mission from the Missions screen, a three-page mission summary is displayed. Press left or right on the d-pad to read the various pages, and press up or down on the d-pad to scroll. Press A while viewing the mission summary to embark on a mission, or press B to return to the list of available missions.

Pay particular attention to the Summary page, which typically includes valuable "Intel." This information usually describes enemy situations or other dangers in the mission. Use this information to properly equip your panels before embarking.

RANK

On certain days, Saïx awards Roxas a new rank for doing well within the Organization. Achieving a new rank means that Roxas can participate in more missions in both Story Mode and Mission Mode. Additionally, new items become available in the Moogle shop.

In Multiplayer mode, all players who attempt to undertake a mission must have achieved the required rank. Players who have not achieved the required rank in Story Mode cannot participate in higher rank missions with other players in Multiplayer Mission Mode.

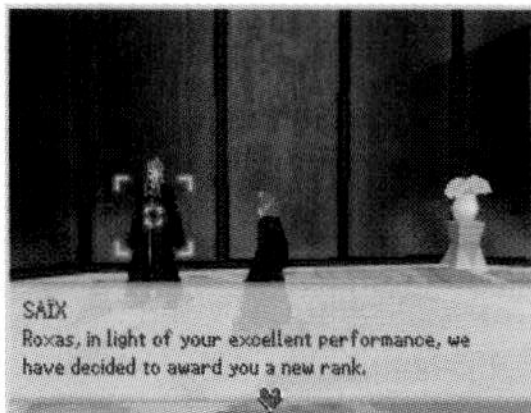

MENU

Press the START button while in the Grey Area to open the menu. This interface allows you to customize your character, replay missions, view important files, save your game, and many other functions described in this section. Press START or B to exit the menu.

PANELS

Panels raise your character's level and status and enable new abilities. Press Y or choose "Panels" from the menu to enter the Panels screen.

Here, you can equip panels from the collection on the right in your character's open slots on the left.

To sort the list on the right according to panel type, press the L or R buttons. If the slot deck on the left grows to more than one page, press Y to cycle through the pages. Collect "Slot Releaser" panels to make additional slots available in your deck.

PANEL PLACEMENT

Use the cursor to select a panel from the list on the right. Press A to grab the panel and then move the cursor to an open slot on the deck to the left. Press A again to set the panel in an open slot.

To remove a panel from a slot, place the cursor on it and press A to grab it. Then press B to put the panel away, back in the list to the right. In addition to using the cursor, the stylus can be utilized to drag panels from the inventory list to the slots on the left.

AUTO-LINK

After placing a panel that comprises two or more slots, point the cursor at an empty slot on the panel, also known as a "link slot." Press SELECT to auto-link an applicable panel to that slot. If a multi-slot panel has more than one open slot, pressing SELECT will fill all available slots with all available links.

Point the cursor at an open link slot on an equipped panel, then…

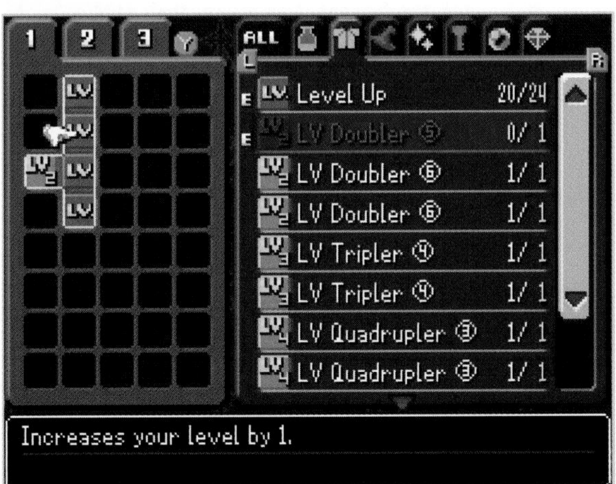

Press SELECT to auto-link every applicable panel.

For instance, set a LV Doubler⑤ panel and then point the cursor at an open link slot. Press SELECT to auto-link all available Level Up panels to every open slot on the LV Doubler⑤. Use this function to make panel placement faster.

VIEW ABILITIES

Each time a new type of panel is placed in a slot, the Abilities list is updated. Press X to view the Abilities list. While viewing the list, hold X and use the d-pad to scroll up or down the list of abilities. Ability descriptions appear while scrolling through, aiding in your understanding of how panels affect your character.

SUB-MENU

Press START while in the Panel screen to open the sub-menu. Options on this menu allow you to store your current deck for easy retrieval later. You can store up to three decks.

For instance, say you're about to start a mission that requires mainly Fire magic, but your current deck conveniently allows for a wide choice of spells. Store your current deck, then remove all magic and set nothing but Fire panels for the upcoming mission. When the mission's completed, enter the sub-menu and retrieve your preferred deck. The bottom option of the sub-menu allows you to clear all slots with one button press, saving time in rearranging your link panels.

HOLO-MISSIONS

The Holo-Missions option allows you to replay previously cleared missions, either normally or as challenges if you previously obtained an Ordeal Badge or Ordeal Blazon. Missions that were missed or skipped on earlier days also can be played using Holo-Missions.

NORMAL MISSIONS

Choose to replay a mission normally if you previously failed to fill the Mission Gauge 100%, or if you missed an item chest, or if you just want another crack at the job.

CHALLENGES

Collect Ordeal Badges and Ordeal Blazons during missions to trigger Challenge missions and Special Challenge missions, respectively. Challenges allow you to replay missions with added restrictions and additional criteria to acquire Challenge Sigils. Challenge Sigils can be redeemed at the Moogle's shop for prizes.

Challenge Sigils gained or remaining are displayed on-screen during Challenges.

FILES

The Files sub-menus contain journal entries and valuable data on enemies previously encountered.

ROXAS'S DIARY

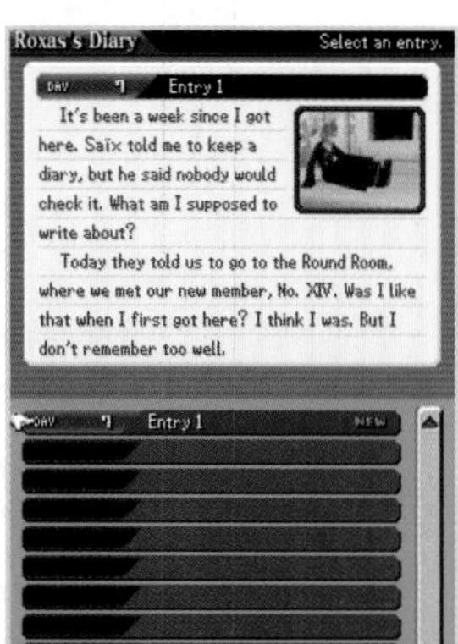

As each day or set of days passes, Roxas adds new entries to his diary. Review these files to remind yourself of previous events in the story.

UNLOCK SECRET REPORTS!

Complete the game to add Secret Reports to Roxas's Diary entries. Days with a Secret Report attached are marked with an A button icon. Press A to view the Secret Report attached to that day. Reading them one-by-one, you'll get a behind-the-scenes look into events from your compatriot's point of view. One Secret Report is available per day. To acquire the Secret Report for each day, fill the Mission Gauge 100%. If a Challenge Mission exists, obtain one or more Challenge Sigils.

ENEMY PROFILES

Defeated enemies appear in the Enemy Profiles. Here, you can review their descriptions and also read valuable strategies for defeating them. Press and hold A while viewing any enemy to view a list of items they've previously dropped. This information updates whenever an enemy drops a new item.

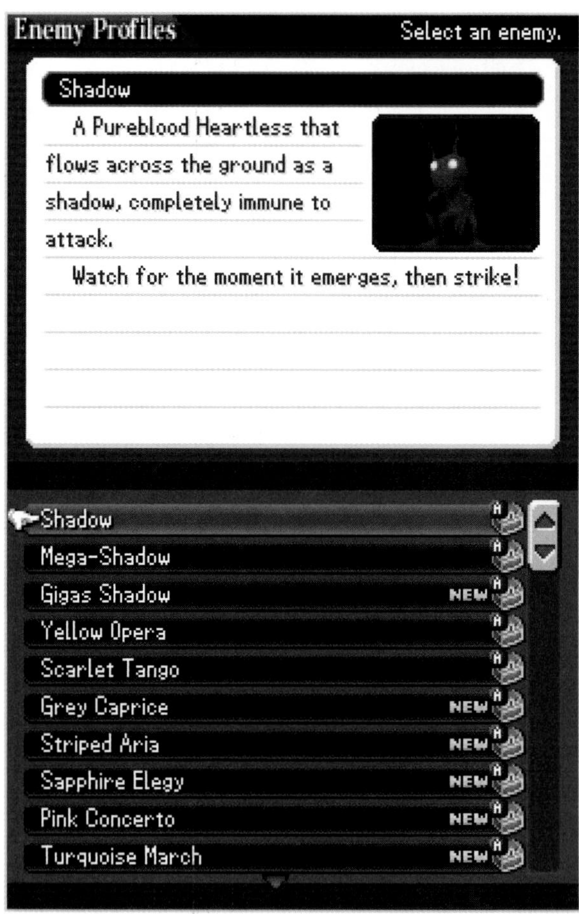

TUTORIALS

Review tutorial screens shown during certain missions of the game in the Tutorials sub-menu. L and R button icons appearing at the edges of the page signify that there are more than one screen to view. Press L or R to scroll through the screens. Tutorials provide helpful information on how to play the game.

CONFIG

The Config sub-menu allows you to adjust various settings regarding controls, camera controls, and combat partner behavior.

SAVE

Choose this menu option to save your progress between missions. You can create up to three saves. Save games from Story Mode can be opened in Mission Mode, then saved in Mission Mode and opened in Story Mode.

Each time you save the game, the background changes to show either Roxas, Xion, or Axel. However, Xion's face does not appear until Day 26. When the game is complete, the save data becomes marked with a crown.

TITLE SCREEN

Choose this option for a fast return to the title screen so that you can switch to Story Mode, Mission Mode, or Theater Mode. Unfortunately, this technique results in the loss of any unsaved progress.

SHOP

This option appears on the menu in Mission Mode, enabling access to the Moogle shop. The items available correspond to whatever rank the player has achieved.

CHARACTER

This option appears on the menu in Mission Mode, enabling the player to change characters between missions.

MISSION CONFIG

This option appears on the menu in Mission Mode. The Mission Config sub-menu has more options than the Config sub-menu from Story Mode. Partner controls are gone, getting replaced by several pages of universal settings that change the way missions are played in Mission Mode. You can set up Solo and Multiplayer matches that play more like challenges for extra resistance.

As previously described, the player progresses through the game by successfully completing missions in Story Mode. This section describes a few things to expect while in the field.

DARK CORRIDORS

Organization XIII members enter and exit worlds through dark corridors. Because of strict Organization rules, members cannot leave worlds until they have completed their mission. Therefore, the dark corridor remains unavailable as an exit until you complete the criteria required to fill the Mission Gauge to the goal line. When that occurs, an information message is displayed at the top of the screen, indicating that RTC is authorized.

"RTC" stands for Return to the Castle. To RTC, simply return to the area where the dark corridor is located. Move toward the dark corridor until a green target reticule appears over it and the top command in the Commands list changes to "Examine." Then press A and select the top option to RTC.

CHESTS

Gold-lined treasure chests are located in various places during certain missions. To open a chest, approach it until a green target reticule appears on it and the top command in the Commands list changes to "Examine." Then press A to open the chest. Roxas cannot open chests if his backpack is full. Discard or use items from the backpack to make room and then open the chest.

CRATES AND JARS

Attack small wooden crates and jars to break them open. When destroyed, these objects sometimes release HP prizes, munny, and Mission Points in Mission Mode. Approach crates and jars until a green reticule appears on it, then press A to attack the object and break it.

HP PRIZES

Small green balls sometimes appear when crates or jars are broken or when enemies are defeated. Touch these balls to collect them and replenish Roxas's HP. Equip the Treasure Magnet panel to collect HP prizes more easily and from farther away.

MUNNY

Small yellow balls sometimes appear when crates or jars are broken, or when enemies are defeated. Touch these balls to collect them, accumulating "munny" used to synthesize items in the shop. Equip the Treasure Magnet panel to collect munny more easily and from farther away.

PRIZE BOXES

Tiny treasure chests sometimes appear when enemies are defeated. These are referred to as "items dropped" and "prize boxes." Touch these boxes to collect them and receive an item.

Prize boxes cannot be collected if the backpack is full. Discard or use items in the backpack to make room. Equip the Treasure Magnet panel to collect prize boxes more easily and from farther away.

EMBLEMS AND BLAZONS

During certain missions, emblems hover in the air at certain locations. Emblems may hover at heights requiring additional abilities to reach, such as High Jump, Air Slide, or Glide. Touch these emblems to collect them for a variety of uses.

- ★ **Unity Badge:** *Red emblems that enable playing your current mission in Mission Mode to acquire Mission Crowns.*
- ★ **Ordeal Badge:** *Blue emblems that enable playing your current mission as a Challenge, with extra restrictions and requirements to acquire Challenge Sigils.*
- ★ **Ordeal Blazon:** *Blue emblems marked with "SP" that enable playing your current mission as a Special Challenge, with extra restrictions and requirements to acquire Challenge Sigils.*
- ★ **Organization Emblem:** *During certain missions, the player is required to collect these silver emblems. Touch them while a green ring emanates from the emblem to fill the Mission Gauge more.*

EXAMINE POINTS

When a yellow "?" icon appears over the character's head, it means a point of interest is nearby. Move closer to the area until a green reticule targets an object and the top command changes to "Examine." Press A to examine or interact with the object. Typical examine points include gate or door switches and "recon points," or points of examination that are crucial to find during recon missions.

MISSION GAUGE

The Mission Gauge at the bottom of the lower screen displays your progress toward achieving the overall objective of the mission. A small gray line in the Mission Gauge represents the "goal" line. Once the Mission Gauge is filled to the goal line, RTC is authorized. However, the Organization expects more from its members. By fulfilling additional criteria, the Mission Gauge can be filled 100%. Completing all missions 100% adds a new item to the Moogle shop, which can be purchased to make *Kingdom Hearts* series protagonist Sora playable in Mission Mode. Therefore, try to fill the Mission Gauge completely during all missions.

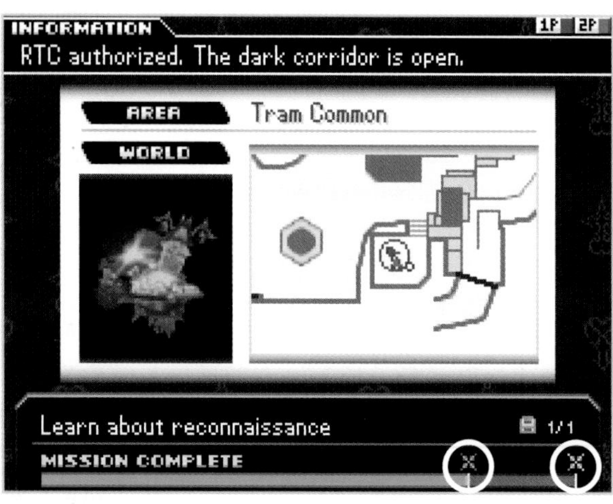

When enemies materialize, it's time to do battle! This section explains how combat works in *Kingdom Hearts 358/2 Days* and how to make the most of it.

COMMANDS

Enter commands to carry out combat. The Commands list is displayed in the lower-left corner of the upper screen. Press A to perform the selected command (Attack, by default), or press X to cycle through commands.

TALK/EXAMINE

When the top command changes to "Talk" or "Examine," the player cannot attack. This is because the character is standing next to a friendly person or a point of interest, respectively. Either select these commands to engage with the person or environment, or move away to change the top command back to "Attack."

ATTACK

This is the default top command during a mission. Press A while this command is selected to perform an attack with the character's equipped weapon. By pressing A repeatedly with the right timing, it is possible to launch a combo attack wherein each strike is different in form, function, and power depending on the weapon type and the gear panel equipped.

MAGIC

When magic panels are equipped, characters can cast magic spells. Each spell can be cast once per mission. To cast a spell multiple times, equip multiple spell panels or link spells to panels such as Doublecast④, Triplecast③, or Quadcast③, which enable multiple castings of each spell. To regain spell-casting ability after casting a spell, use items such as Ethers, Hi-Ethers, Mega-Ethers, Elixirs, or Megalixirs.

To use magic, press X to cycle down through the Commands list to "Magic" and press A to open the Magic sub-menu. Press X to cycle through the list of available spells, and press A to cast the desired spell. Spell-casting can be increased by assigning spells to the shortcut menu, as described later. Press B to cancel casting magic and close the sub-menu.

ITEMS

When item panels are equipped, characters can use items during missions. Each item can be used only once before it vanishes forever. Item panels include Potions, Hi-Potions, Ethers, Mega-Ethers, Elixirs, Panaceas, and others.

To use items, press X to cycle down through the Commands list to "Items" and press A to open the Items sub-menu. Press X to cycle through the list of available items, and press A to use the selection. Item use can be streamlined by assigning items to the shortcut menu as described later. Press B to cancel using an item and close the sub-menu.

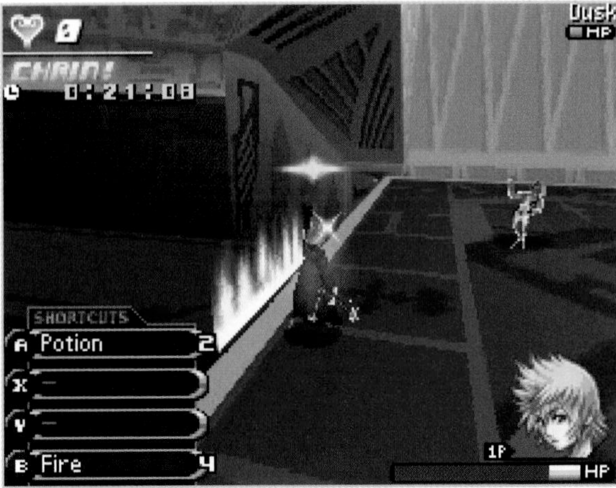

While cycling through the item menu, the first page displays items that are equipped as panels in slots on the character's deck. Continue pressing X to cycle to subsequent pages, which represent items in the backpack. Backpack items are ones that you pick up during your mission. The backpack can only hold a small number of items. Equipping a Backpack panel lets you carry two additional items in your backpack. Items in the backpack can be used or discarded; discarded items remain on the ground and can be picked up later.

Backpack items that appear in a yellow font represent items that were acquired by opening chests. If you discard these items, you won't get credit for opening the chest when you complete the mission. Backpack items that appear in a white font were dropped by enemies and can be discarded without mission consequences.

SHORTCUT MENU

Magic and recovery items can be set to a shortcut menu. Shortcuts make it easy to cast spells or recovery without cycling through the Items or Magic menus. To assign a shortcut, hold L while selecting an item or magic from their respective menus. Then press A, B, X, or Y to assign the item or spell to that button. Press B to close the item or magic sub-menu.

When you're ready to use a shortcut, hold L to view your shortcuts. Continue holding L and press A, B, X, or Y to use that shortcut. Items in the backpack cannot be assigned to shortcuts.

LOCK ON

Rapidly press R twice to lock on to an enemy; cycle to the next target by pressing R once. Rapidly press R twice to quit lock on. Use lock on to focus on eliminating a specific enemy and also to help control the game's camera better during combat.

CHAINS

Defeat enemies with attacks or magic to start a chain. While chaining, a ring of light appears around whichever enemy you lock on to. The ring shrinks over time and disappears. Keep hitting enemies to make it bigger, giving yourself longer to chain. Defeating enemies during a chain earns you bonus heart points.

Also, if you keep a chain going long enough, Roxas's heart counter begins flashing. Your chain becomes unbreakable during this time, providing a chance to collect tons of hearts.

LIMIT BREAK

When subsequent damage from enemies causes Roxas's HP to fall into the yellow range of the HP bar, press and hold A to activate Roxas's Limit Break. Your subsequent attacks deal massive damage until the white line reaches the left edge of his HP gauge.

Afterward, the yellow segment of the HP bar shrinks, meaning Roxas's HP must be reduced further to trigger Limit Break again. Reset your Limit Gauge to the full amount by using a Limit Recharge item.

STATUS EFFECTS

Many enemies are capable of attacks that can inflict status impairments on Roxas, reducing or negating his combat or movement abilities. All status effects subside after a brief time, or can be cured by using a Panacea.

- **Nulled Defense:** *Certain enemies can attack without regard to the character's defense. Certain rings protect against this.*
- **Shoe-glued:** *When a "1 ton" icon appears over the character's head, he or she becomes unable to jump or perform aerial combos.*
- **Air-tossed:** *When a green tornado appears over the character's head, he or she becomes incapable of action or recovery while in midair. The effect only lasts until the character lands on the ground. Typically caused by Aero magic.*
- **Frozen:** *When ice forms around a character's feet, he or she becomes incapable of action. Press A rapidly to break free of ice. Typically caused by Blizzard magic.*

★ **HP Halved:** *Certain enemies are capable of attacks that reduce a character's attacks by half his or her max HP. Specific rings protect against this.*

★ **Flip-footed:** *When question marks (??) appear over the character's head, movement controls become reversed.*

★ **Silenced:** *When three periods appear over the character's head, he or she becomes incapable of casting magic.*

★ **Ignited:** *When the character catches on fire, he or she continues to lose HP until the fire goes out. Typically caused by Fire magic.*

★ **Damage Drained:** *The ability of some enemies to continually draw HP out of a character, replenishing their own. Typically enacted by ghosts. Certain rings protect against this.*

★ **Rewound Defense:** *When a blue shield with "Lv.1" appears over the character's head, his or her defense is lowered for a short period of time.*

★ **Blinded:** *When sunglasses appear over a character's head, attacks attempted are more likely to miss. Typically caused by Dark magic.*

★ **Jolted:** *When a character is surrounded by electricity, he or she damages any allies he or she touches. Typically caused by Thunder magic.*

★ **Radar Zapped:** *The map displayed on the lower screen disappears for a short time. Typically caused by Light magic.*

CONTINUE

When a character's HP is reduced to zero, the continue screen appears. Choose to continue attempting the mission from your present point, or withdraw to quit the mission.

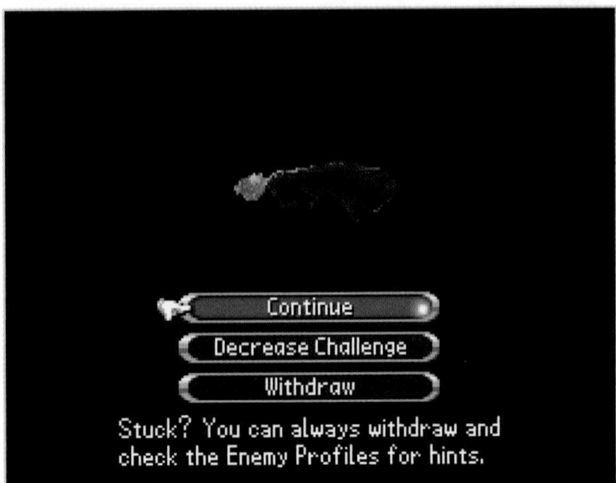

Continuing has good and bad points. The good news is your HP is reset to full and your Limit Gauge resets to its fullest. The bad news is that you don't regain items previously used. Also, any enemies still active in the area before you continued return with full HP.

If your HP is reduced to zero more than three times in Story Mode, an additional option allows you to decrease the challenge. This only occurs in Standard difficulty mode, and permanently reduces your difficulty level by one stage for the rest of the game. So if you're playing Standard, you'll switch to Beginner.

MISSION REVIEW

After completing a mission and returning to the castle, the Mission Review screen appears. The upper screen shows your final Mission Gauge, along with heart points and munny collected. Experience Points are awarded based on enemies defeated. When the EXP bar fills all the way, a new Level Up panel is obtained. Bonus amounts are applied to heart points, munny, and Experience as determined by the mission criteria as listed in **Chapter 3**.

The lower screen lists the items gained. Some "Rewards" are items acquired for completing the mission, or items randomly awarded each time. These items are also listed for each mission in **Chapter 3**. Items Collected lists the things you took from chests or picked up from defeated foes.

CHAPTER 3

STORY MODE WALKTHROUGH

This walkthrough of Story Mode covers Standard Mode difficulty. Each day and every mission that Roxas undertakes is covered herein. Each mission is presented with a complete map and walkthrough, along with certain data pertaining to mission enemies, bonuses, and rewards:

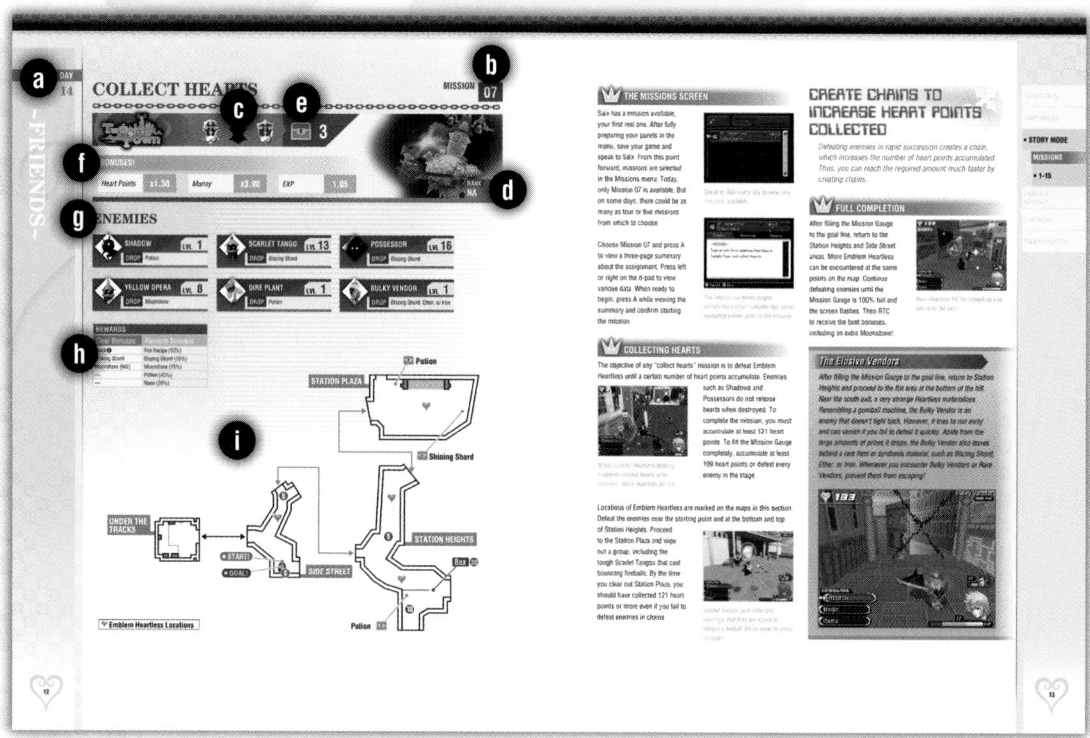

a Day: *The day or days during which the mission is available.*

b Mission number.

c Badges: *Indicate whether an Ordeal Badge, Ordeal Blazon, or Unity Badge can be found during this mission.*

d Rank: *Rank required to start a mission. In Story Mode, Saïx awards Roxas new ranks on certain days. In Mission Mode, all players must be the rank listed or higher in order to join the multiplayer mayhem. Thus, completion of Story Mode is essential for advancement.*

e Chests: *Total number of chests available during the mission.*

f Bonuses: *Shows the bonus multipliers applied to heart points, munny, and EXP at the end of a mission.*

g Enemies: *A list of enemies who appear during the mission, with information on their levels and items they might drop.*

h Rewards: *Items likely to be awarded after a mission along with the percentage chance of acquiring each item. "Clear Bonuses" are acquired when the mission is completed the first time. "Random Bonuses" can be acquired each time the mission is cleared in Story Mode. Items marked with a (MG) are only obtained by filling the Mission Gauge 100%.*

i Map: *Map of the interconnecting areas pertaining to the mission. Callouts include dark corridors, chests with item names, Heartless encounter locations, Unity and Ordeal Badge locations, Ordeal Blazon locations, and boss or target enemy locations. Special markings on a few maps indicate Organization emblem locations, Shadow Glob locations, recon points or treasure dig sites. Blue numbered circles indicate locations of freestanding (or floating) Mission Point crystals in Mission Mode.*

DAY 7

Speak to the other Organization XIII members in the Grey Area, which serves as the mission dispatch for the entire operation. When finished, speak to red-haired Axel and select the top option to proceed. That's it—call it a day!

Roxas is just starting to adjust to living with Organization XIII.

DAY 8

LEARN MISSION BASICS

MISSION 01

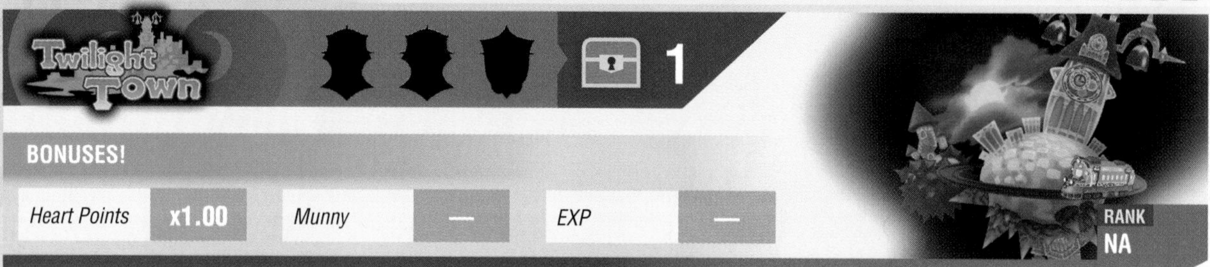

BONUSES!

Heart Points	x1.00	Munny	—	EXP	—

RANK NA

REWARDS	
Clear Bonuses	Random Bonuses
—	Fire Recipe (10%)
—	Blazing Shard (15%)
—	Moonstone (15%)
—	Potion (40%)
—	None (20%)

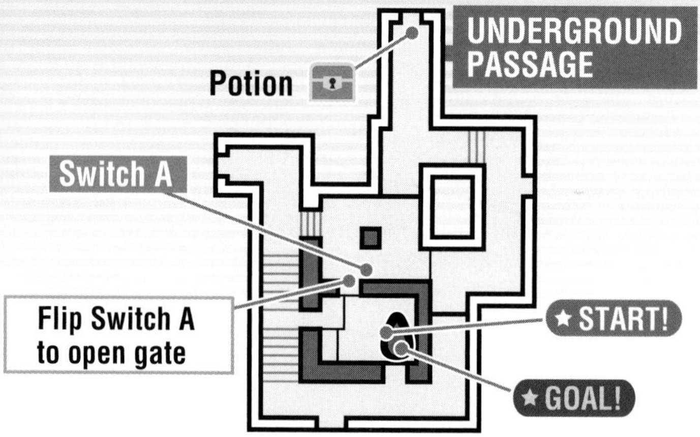

STARTING A MISSION

When ready to begin your first mission with Axel, speak to Saïx— the blue-haired man always standing in the back-center of the Grey Area.

Saïx is the guy with all the jobs.

JUMPING

Roxas and Axel use a dark corridor to enter Twilight Town's Underground Passage. Follow Axel over to the raised platforms. Press B to jump onto the lower platform or grab the edge of the higher platform. Then press up on the d-pad to make Roxas flip onto the ledge.

Press B to jump. Roxas grabs high ledges and hangs from them. Press up on the d-pad to flip onto the platform.

BREAKING OBJECTS

After the explanation of freelook, press SELECT and use the d-pad or the stylus on the lower screen to look around. Proceed into the corridor and head left down the stairs. Press A to smash the crates with Roxas's Keyblade, releasing munny and HP Prizes.

Break open crates, pots, and other objects in your path to release munny and HP Prizes.

Go back upstairs and past the room containing the dark corridor. Take the last right into another room with a breakable crate.

SWITCHES

When approaching switches or other areas of interest, a "?" icon appears above Roxas's head as shown.

Move to the glowing yellow switch on the wall. As you draw near, Roxas targets the switch and a "?" icon appears. Notice that the top command in the Commands window changes to "Examine." Press A to examine the switch. Roxas flips it, raising the nearby gate and creating a shortcut back to the dark corridor.

FIND THE CHEST...AND OPEN IT

Barriers sometime seal off areas of a world to keep you from wandering away from your mission objectives.

Continue past the switch and drop into the next corridor. Follow it until Axel stops to explain the barricades placed by Organization XIII to keep agents on track.

Afterwards, proceed up the passage until you reach the chest. Open the chest to obtain a **Potion** and complete the mission.

Move close to chests until Roxas's target reticule appears, then open it by pressing A and choosing the Examine command.

RTC

Return to the dark corridor in the room you originally entered. Approach the dark corridor until Roxas targets it, then examine it and choose the top option to RTC (Return to the castle).

After completing every mission, return to the dark corridor. Examine it and choose the top option to return to base.

DAY 9

LEARN THE BASICS OF COMBAT

MISSION 02

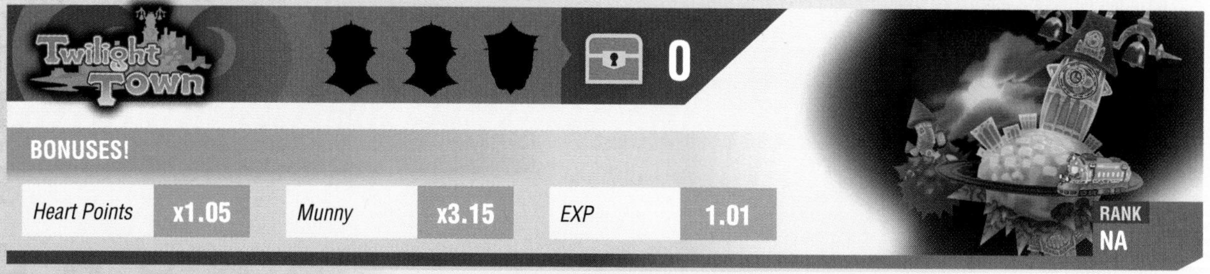

ENEMIES

SHADOW	LVL 1	DROP: Potion
YELLOW OPERA	LVL 1	DROP: Moonstone

REWARDS	
Clear Bonuses	Random Bonuses
—	Fire Recipe (10%)
—	Blazing Shard (15%)
—	Moonstone (15%)
—	Potion (40%)
—	None (20%)

COLLECTING HEARTS

This tutorial mission pairs Roxas with the scythe-wielding Marluxia. Speak to Saïx when you're ready to begin. Marluxia accompanies Roxas to the Sandlot in Twilight Town, this time to take on some Heartless.

Press A repeatedly to strike the Shadows with a combo of attacks. Continue bashing each one until they burst into a shower of munny, HP Prizes, and maybe Prize Boxes. Run around and pick up these items as they scatter before attacking the next target.

Collect prizes dropped by defeated enemies quickly, before they vanish.

When the Shadows are defeated, Marluxia explains that only "Emblem Heartless" release hearts. On cue, three Yellow Operas appear. When dealing with flying enemies such as Yellow Operas, double-tap the R button to lock on to a foe. Attack that foe until it is defeated and then lock onto another.

Quickly press R twice to lock on to a foe. Locking on simplifies dealing with airborne enemies.

AUTO JUMPS

Don't worry about jumping to attack flying enemies. Roxas automatically leaps to attack floating targets.

BUILDING A CHAIN

A much larger group of Yellow Operas appears. As explained on the tutorial screen, defeating enemies quickly is called a "chain." Enemies defeated during a chain release bonus heart points, as displayed in the upper-left corner of the screen. Try to defeat the Yellow Operas rapidly enough to make the display flash, signifying an unbreakable chain. After that, the only thing left to do is RTC.

Score bonus heart points by defeating additional enemies while the upper-left display flashes, before the ring surrounding each foe shrinks and vanishes.

DAY 10

LEARN ABOUT YOUR FIELD DUTIES

MISSION 03

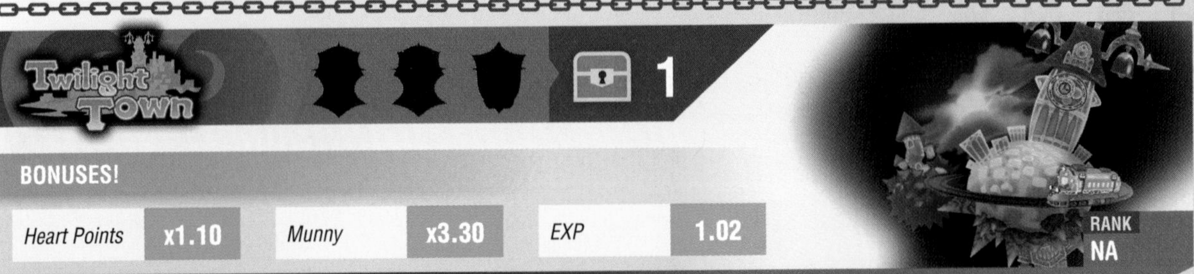

BONUSES!

Heart Points	x1.10	Munny	x3.30	EXP	1.02

RANK NA

ENEMIES

YELLOW OPERA LVL 1
DROP Moonstone

DIRE PLANT LVL 1
DROP Potion

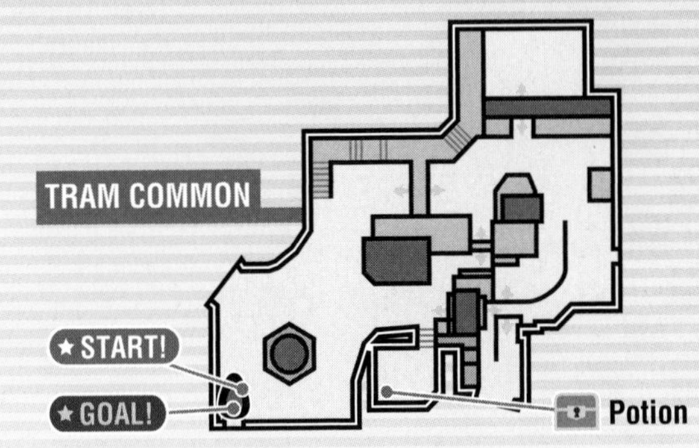

REWARDS	
Clear Bonuses	Random Bonuses
Fire	Fire Recipe (10%)
Fire	Blazing Shard (15%)
Fire (MG)	Moonstone (15%)
—	Potion (40%)
—	None (20%)

FILL THE GAUGE ALL THE WAY

Speak to Saïx to begin the mission, which pairs Roxas with Zexion. The two emerge from the dark corridor in the large Tram Common area of Twilight Town. Your first objective is to defeat seven Heartless foes. They appear as dots on the map on the lower screen. Most are spread so far apart that forming a chain is impossible, but don't sweat it.

Use the map on the lower screen to find enemies spread across the Tram Common.

When the seven are defeated, the mission is complete. However, Zexion explains that there are still Heartless in the area. The next tutorial screen explains the Mission Gauge at the bottom of the lower screen. Filling the gauge to the goal line means the mission is complete. However, completing extra objectives may fill the Mission Gauge even further, increasing the bonus heart points, munny, EXP, and Rewards gained in the Mission Review screen.

New dots appear on the lower screen map. Travel around the Tram Common area and fill the Mission Gauge by defeating six additional Heartless.

Continue defeating Heartless until the Mission Gauge fills completely and turns orange. That way, you gain full bonuses.

*Open the chest that contains a **Potion** in the enclosed area to the south.*

DAY 11

LEARN HOW TO USE MAGIC

MISSION 04

Twilight Town

3

BONUSES!

Heart Points	x1.15	Munny	x3.45	EXP	1.03

RANK NA

ENEMIES

YELLOW OPERA LVL 1
DROP Moonstone

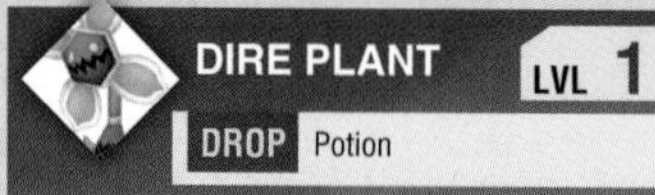

DIRE PLANT LVL 1
DROP Potion

REWARDS	
Clear Bonuses	Random Bonuses
Potion	Fire Recipe (10%)
Ether	Blazing Shard (15%)
Scan	Moonstone (15%)
—	Potion (40%)
—	None (20%)

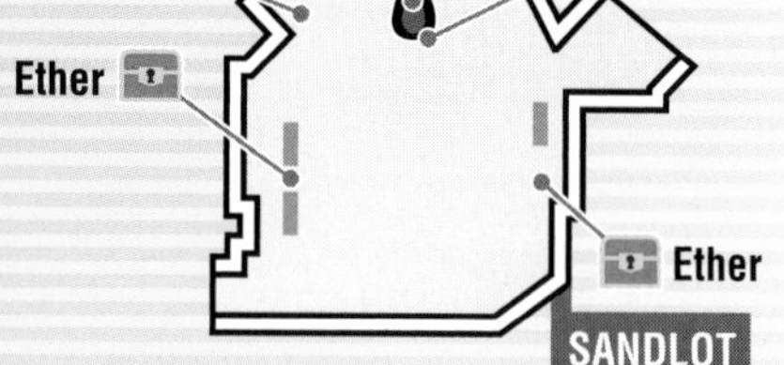

EQUIPPING PANELS

Saïx says that Roxas needs to use magic today. Prior to the mission, press START to enter the menu. Select "Panels" and press A. This opens the Panels screen, wherein you can install panels in Roxas's slots to gain new abilities or increase his status. Press A to grab a panel on the right and place it in a slot to the left. Place all the Fire panels gained from the previous mission, as well as every Potion Roxas holds.

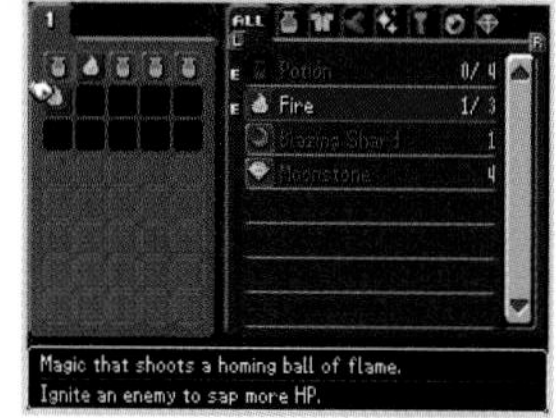

Grab panels from the right and place them in the slots to the left. This enables Roxas to use items and abilities during missions.

When done, press X to view Roxas's abilities. You can see that Roxas can now cast Fire LV1 three times and can use as many Potions as you equip. Also, save your game before exiting the menu.

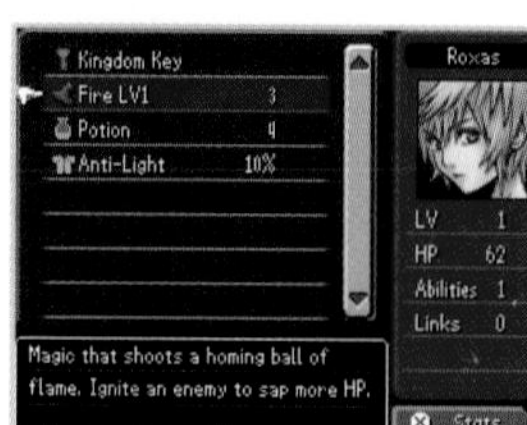

Press X to view abilities acquired by equipping panels. Hold X and use the d-pad to view descriptions of abilities.

CASTING MAGIC

Speak to Saïx to accept the mission with Larxene. When a Dire Plant appears, Larxene instructs Roxas to use magic to defeat it. Before doing that, move around the Sandlot and open the three treasure chests in the area to obtain three **Ethers**, which allow you to cast Fire again. To use your Fire spell, press X to select the "Magic" command, then press A. Fire will be your only spell, so press A to cast it on the Dire Plant. One casting should wipe it out. When the next set of enemies appears, Larxene says Roxas can use his Keyblade against them to complete the mission.

Press X during missions to scroll through commands in the lower-left corner of the screen.

Stationary Targets Die Fast

The tutorial explains how to select "Items" from the Commands window and also how to assign items and spells to the shortcut menu. However, assigning shortcuts while Heartless are nearby isn't a good idea; avoid doing anything during a mission that leaves Roxas exposed to harm. Always wait to customize your shortcuts or use items until the area is clear.

MIX A LITTLE MAGIC

The Yellow Operas should be easy to eliminate with the Keyblade. Cast Fire spells to take out the stronger Dire Plants more quickly. Otherwise, they'll work in concert with the Yellow Operas to try to defeat Roxas.

DAY 12

LEARN ABOUT RECONNAISSANCE

MISSION 05

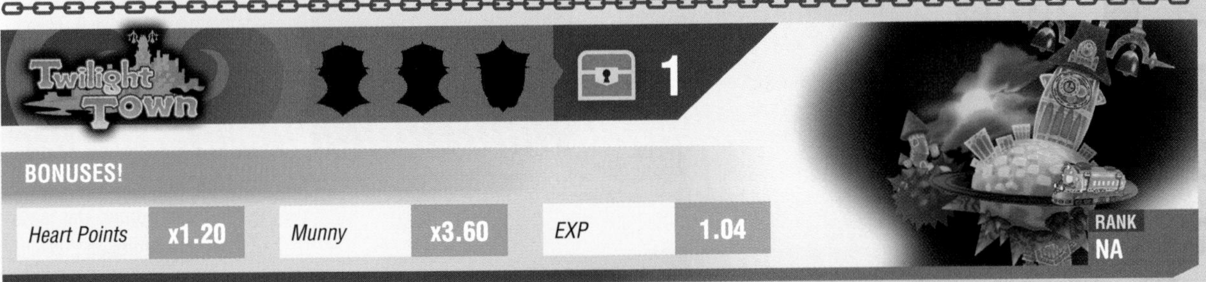

ENEMIES

REWARDS	
Clear Bonuses	Random Bonuses
Dodge Roll	Fire Recipe (10%)
Fire (MG)	Blazing Shard (15%)
—	Moonstone (15%)
—	Potion (40%)
—	None (20%)

TRAM COMMON
Blazing Shard
GOAL!
START!

CHECKMARKS

Checkmarks on the map are color-coded in sets for each breakthrough. Solid red checkmarks show recon points to check for the first breakthrough and solid blue checkmarks for the second. Find the two recon points with green checkmarks to fill the Mission Gauge. Hollow checkmarks are optional recon points; search there for extra dialog.

MAKE SHORTCUTS

In the menu, set new panels such as Ethers and the Scan ability gained from the previous mission before speaking to Saïx to begin the next mission. Once your panels are in place, set shortcuts to your Fire spells, Potions, and Ethers by holding L and pressing A, B, X, or Y to assign a button to that item or spell.

Prepare your shortcuts before jumping into the mission, because Roxas has much on his plate today.

For instance, after adding Potion panels to your slots, exit the menu and press X to select Items, then select Potion. Hold L and press A to assign Potions to button A. The next time you're in the heat of battle, you can hold L and press A to quickly use a Potion.

RECONNAISSANCE

Today, Vexen wants to teach Roxas about reconnaissance missions. The objective of reconnaissance missions is to examine certain points of the map to learn more about the world. When Roxas is near a recon point, a "?" icon appears above his head. Continue moving around the area until Roxas's green target reticule appears, then press A to examine the marked area to learn clues about the nature of the world. Each recon point examined is marked on the map on the lower screen. If Heartless appear near a recon point, Roxas must defeat them before he can search for clues.

When enough clues are found to allow Roxas to experience what is called a "breakthrough," or a higher understanding of the world's nature, then the Mission Gauge will fill. New recon points may become available at that point, allowing the mission to proceed.

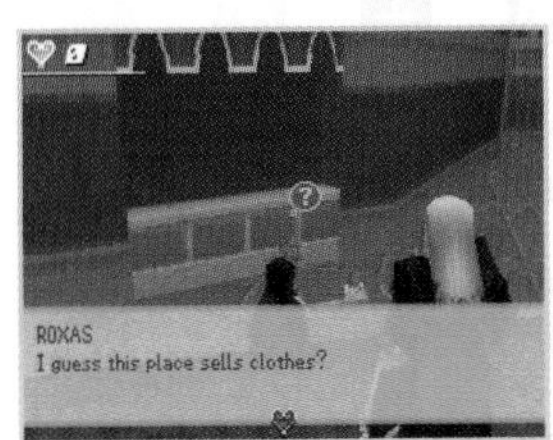

Examine recon points near the starting area until Roxas experiences a "breakthrough."

Start off by searching the southwest portion of the Tram Common. Four recon points are located at several of the shops as well as the dark brick road on the ground. Upon examining all four, Vexen commands Roxas to analyze what he's seeing. Choose "There are a lot of shops," and "This could be the center of town" to reach a breakthrough and proceed.

After examining the first set of recon points, Roxas must figure out what the clues mean.

Escape Possession!

Possessors are Pureblood Heartless that resemble black clouds. They attempt to surround Roxas or his partner. For every second they touch Roxas, they drain HP. Although they can be knocked off, a full combo of strikes may be required to pound them away. Lessen the damage sustained by jumping away from a Possessor's grasp. The Dodge Roll ability gained after this mission is also a good way to escape from Possessors.

EXPLORATION CAUSES BREAKTHROUGHS

Fill the Mission Gauge completely by checking the ground in the enclosed south area.

Next, follow the dark road south and examine the shuttered door with a "4" above it. Then continue to follow the road east and examine the locked door, the staircase, the barricaded hole leading to the woods area, and the shuttered doorway in the northeast corner. This leads to a new breakthrough that fills the Mission Gauge to the goal line. However, there are still a few recon points to find.

Also, investigate the wall behind the shutter where the road stops.

The lone treasure chest is located on the upper level. It contains a **Blazing Shard**.

DAY 13

LEARN ABOUT LIMIT BREAKS

MISSION 06

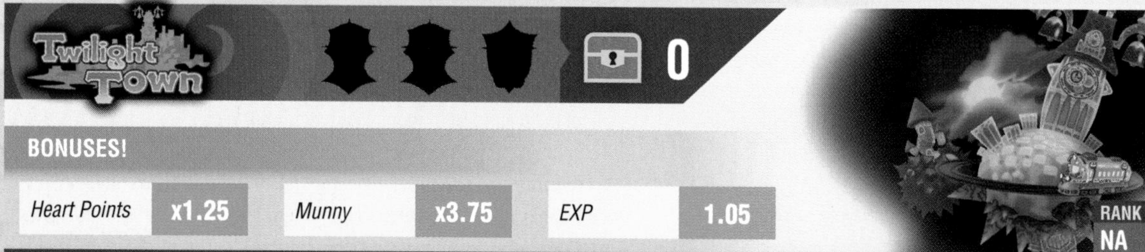

BONUSES!

Heart Points	x1.25	Munny	x3.75	EXP	1.05

RANK NA

ENEMIES

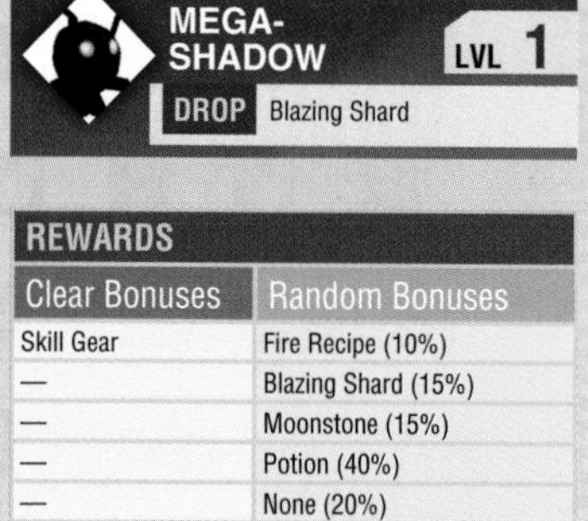

Clear Bonuses	Random Bonuses
Skill Gear	Fire Recipe (10%)
—	Blazing Shard (15%)
—	Moonstone (15%)
—	Potion (40%)
—	None (20%)

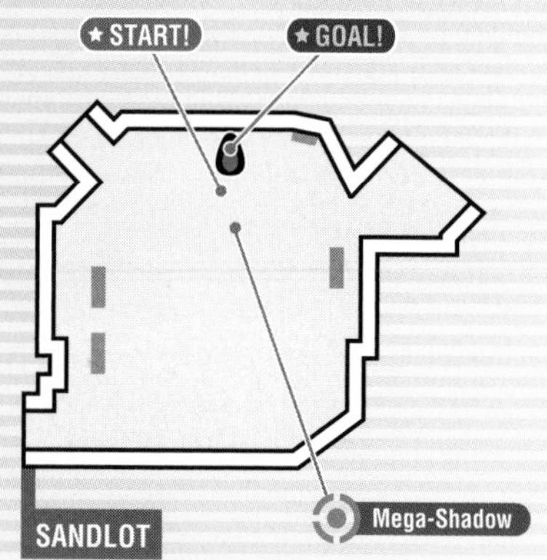

THE SMACK-DOWN

For today's mission, Lexaeus knocks down Roxas's HP to the yellow range of his bar, causing it to flash red and emit a piercing siren. When this occurs, hold A until Roxas's Limit Break activates. While Roxas glows blue, he can attack with wild strikes, inflicting massive damage.

Roxas begins the mission with low health in order to use his Limit Break.

BOSS!

MEGA-SHADOW

Activate Roxas's Limit Break and press A repeatedly to attack the Mega-Shadow. If your Limit Break fails to wipe out this foe, then move away and heal or cast Fire to finish it off from a distance.

DAY 14

HOLO-MISSIONS AVAILABLE

The "Holo-Missions" option becomes available in the menu at this point of the game. This alternate option allows you to revisit previous days to complete missions again.

GEAR UP!

Open the menu and install the Skill Gear panel gained from the last mission to transform Roxas's Keyblade into the Missing Ache, a weapon that improves his strength and critical hit chance. This panel also adds more attacks to your normal ground combo.

Why Complete Missions Again?

Many times during missions, you'll spot treasure chests and badges that are out of reach. When you're unable to reach certain areas, you may not be able to completely fill the Mission Gauge during your first attempt at a mission.

The number of chest items collected is displayed when reviewing mission date in the Holo-Missions screen. Furthermore, missions completed 100% are marked with a yellow "DONE", whereas missions completed less than 100% are marked with a white "DONE."

Missions with a yellow DONE have been completed 100%. Missions with a white DONE were only completed to the point where the Mission Gauge reached the grey goal line.

As you acquire panels that allow Roxas to jump higher and even glide, you'll gain the ability to reach new areas and complete missions more fully than during your first try. And completing all missions 100% unlocks more secrets and bonuses!

THE GIFT OF GAB

Speak to Larxene, seated to the left of the doorway, to obtain a **Potion**. People seated in the Grey Area may offer Roxas additional items or unlock extra missions. But sometimes, the person demands that Roxas complete a certain challenge or meet specific requirements before he or she will be so kind. Speak to the other Organization XIII members every day to find out if they want to help Roxas in some way.

The Organization XIII members sometimes give Roxas panels to help him succeed.

COLLECT HEARTS

MISSION 07

Twilight Town

3

BONUSES!

Heart Points	x1.30	Munny	x3.90	EXP	1.05

RANK
NA

ENEMIES

SHADOW LVL 1
DROP Potion

SCARLET TANGO LVL 13
DROP Blazing Shard

POSSESSOR LVL 16
DROP Blazing Shard

YELLOW OPERA LVL 8
DROP Moonstone

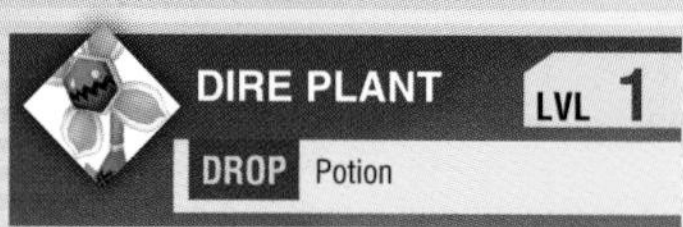

DIRE PLANT LVL 1
DROP Potion

BULKY VENDOR LVL 1
DROP Blazing Shard, Ether, or Iron

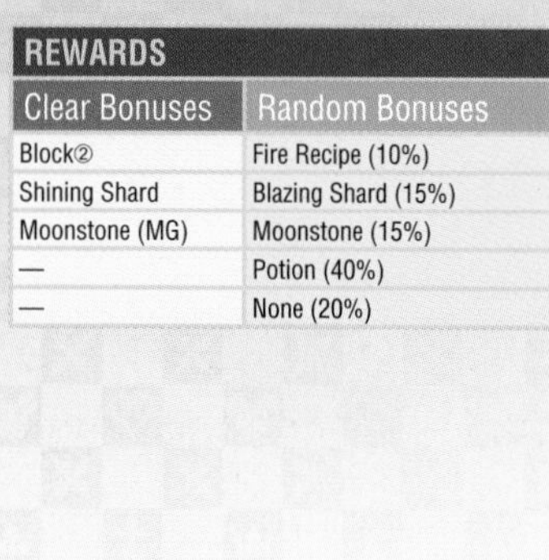

REWARDS

Clear Bonuses	Random Bonuses
Block②	Fire Recipe (10%)
Shining Shard	Blazing Shard (15%)
Moonstone (MG)	Moonstone (15%)
—	Potion (40%)
—	None (20%)

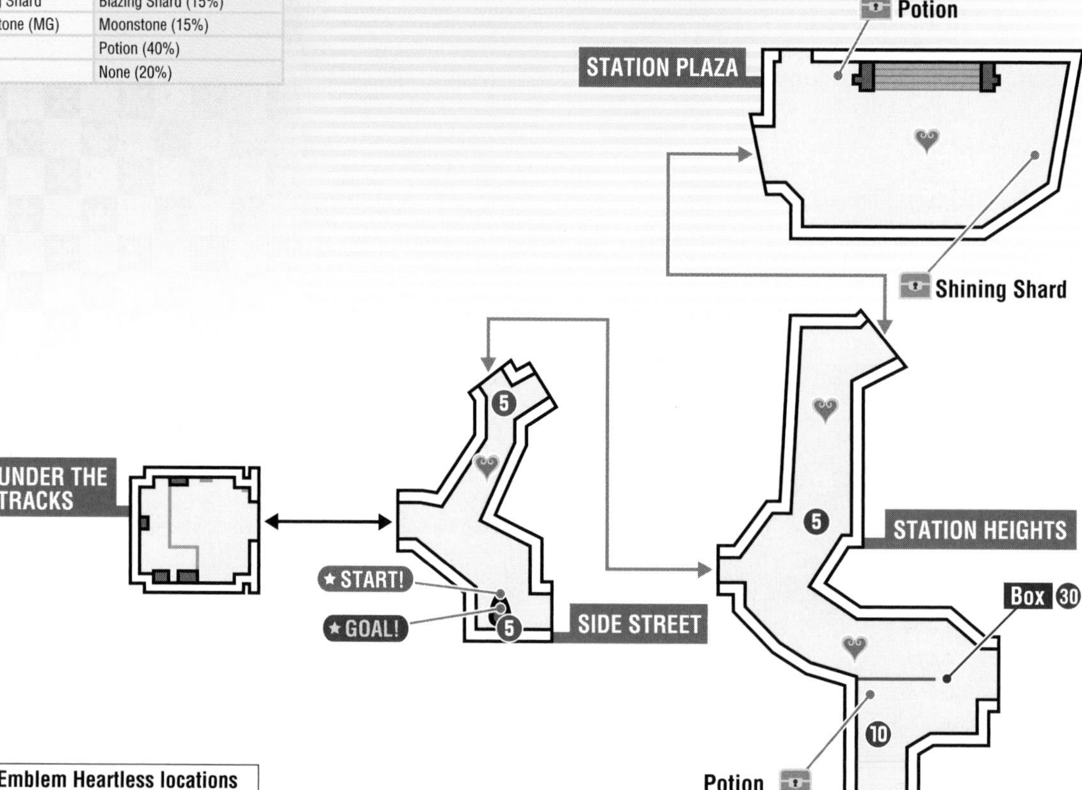

THE MISSIONS SCREEN

Saïx has a mission available, your first real one. After fully preparing your panels in the menu, save your game and speak to Saïx. From this point forward, missions are selected in the Missions menu. Today, only Mission 07 is available. But on some days, there could be as many as four or five missions from which to choose.

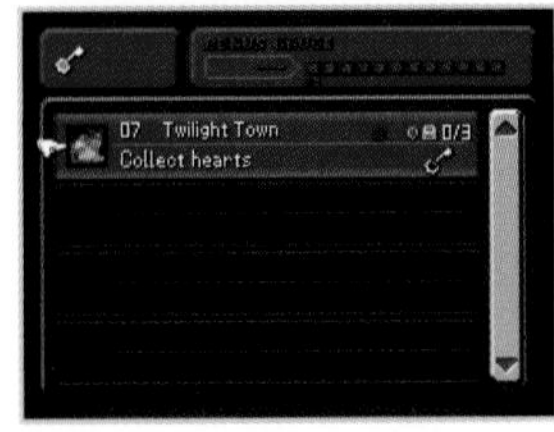

Speak to Saïx every day to view new missions available.

Choose Mission 07 and press A to view a three-page summary about the assignment. Press left or right on the d-pad to view various data. When ready to begin, press A while viewing the summary and confirm starting the mission.

The mission summary pages sometimes contain valuable tips about equipping panels prior to the mission.

COLLECTING HEARTS

The objective of any "collect hearts" mission is to defeat Emblem Heartless until a certain number of heart points accumulate. Enemies such as Shadows and Possessors do not release hearts when destroyed. To complete the mission, you must accumulate at least 121 heart points. To fill the Mission Gauge completely, accumulate at least 199 heart points or defeat every enemy in the stage.

While colorful Heartless bearing emblems release hearts when defeated, black Heartless do not.

Locations of Emblem Heartless are marked on the maps in this section. Defeat the enemies near the starting point and at the bottom and top of Station Heights. Proceed to the Station Plaza and wipe out a group, including the tough Scarlet Tangos that cast bouncing fireballs. By the time you clear out Station Plaza, you should have collected 121 heart points or more even if you fail to defeat enemies in chains.

Scarlet Tangos give extended warnings that they are about to release a fireball. Move away to avoid damage!

CREATE CHAINS TO INCREASE HEART POINTS COLLECTED

Defeating enemies in rapid succession creates a chain, which increases the number of heart points accumulated. Thus, you can reach the required amount much faster by creating chains.

FULL COMPLETION

After filling the Mission Gauge to the goal line, return to the Station Heights and Side Street areas. More Emblem Heartless can be encountered at the same points on the map. Continue defeating enemies until the Mission Gauge is 100% full and the screen flashes. Then RTC to receive the best bonuses, including an extra Moonstone!

New Heartless fill the streets as you return to the exit.

The Elusive Vendors

After filling the Mission Gauge to the goal line, return to Station Heights and proceed to the flat area at the bottom of the hill. Near the south exit, a very strange Heartless materializes. Resembling a gumball machine, the Bulky Vendor is an enemy that doesn't fight back. However, it tries to run away and can vanish if you fail to defeat it quickly. Aside from the large amounts of prizes it drops, the Bulky Vendor also leaves behind a rare item or synthesis material, such as Blazing Shard, Ether, or Iron. Whenever you encounter Bulky Vendors or Rare Vendors, prevent them from escaping!

CHALLENGE MISSION

Objective: Finish in record time!

Restrictions: Enemy level +8

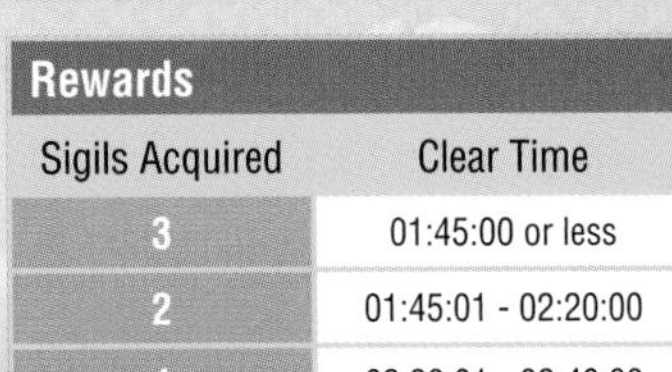

Rewards	
Sigils Acquired	Clear Time
3	01:45:00 or less
2	01:45:01 - 02:20:00
1	02:20:01 - 02:40:00

Replay Mission 07 in Challenge mode and RTC in record time to accumulate up to three Challenge Sigils. As you play, the remaining Sigils are displayed in the upper-right corner of the screen. Try to defeat all the enemies and RTC before they vanish! Use Blizzard spells to quickly defeat the tough Scarlet Tangos at the Station Plaza. Challenge Sigils earned can be redeemed for prizes at the Moogle shop on a later day...

DAY 15-17

MULTIPLE PRIZES AND MISSIONS

The Organization XIII members are impressed with your progress already! Speak to Zexion—the grey-haired man seated to the left of the Grey Area's entrance—to receive a **Panacea** and speak to Marluxia standing behind him to obtain an **Ether**.

Friends in the Grey Area have more presents for Roxas.

During this three-day period, Saïx reveals Missions 08, 09, and 10 simultaneously. These missions can be completed in any order. Only Mission 08 is mandatory, as indicated by the Keyblade mark in its description. Once you have completed Mission 08, you can skip Missions 09 and 10 if you like by choosing the "Advance" option at the top of the screen.

However, skipping too many missions may cause Roxas to become under-powered, making game progression more difficult. ***Therefore, it is strongly recommended to complete all missions without skipping any.***

Missions marked with a Keyblade icon are mandatory, while the rest are optional. Select "Advance" if you want to skip missions without the Keyblade icon.

ELIMINATE THE WATCHERS

MISSION 08

BONUSES!

Heart Points	x1.60	Munny	x4.80	EXP	1.07

ENEMIES

Enemy	LVL	DROP
SHADOW	1	Potion
DIRE PLANT	2	Potion
WATCHER	3	Potion

REWARDS

Clear Bonuses	Random Bonuses
Blazing Shard	Fire Recipe (10%)
Blazing Shard	Blazing Shard (15%)
Potion	Moonstone (15%)
—	Potion (40%)
—	None (20%)

WHO WATCHES THE WATCHERS?

Watchers are Emblem Heartless resembling hovering trashcans. They fire lasers in the direction they face, so watch them closely and run to their sides. Perform aerial combos to defeat them while they are firing in another direction. Their laser attacks can be deflected back at them; simply press Y with the right timing to do so. Be advised, though, that the angered Watcher will retaliate with an even stronger laser blast. However, the Watcher is vulnerable to attack from the sides or rear during this prolonged laser attack.

Larxene helps out immensely by casting Thunder magic against Watchers, so keep this in mind for future encounters.

Heavy Dude!

Watchers' laser attacks can inflict a status called "shoe-glue" that makes Roxas weigh a ton. If this occurs, Roxas can't jump or perform aerial combos. Use a Panacea to cure shoe-glue, or move away to safety until the status subsides.

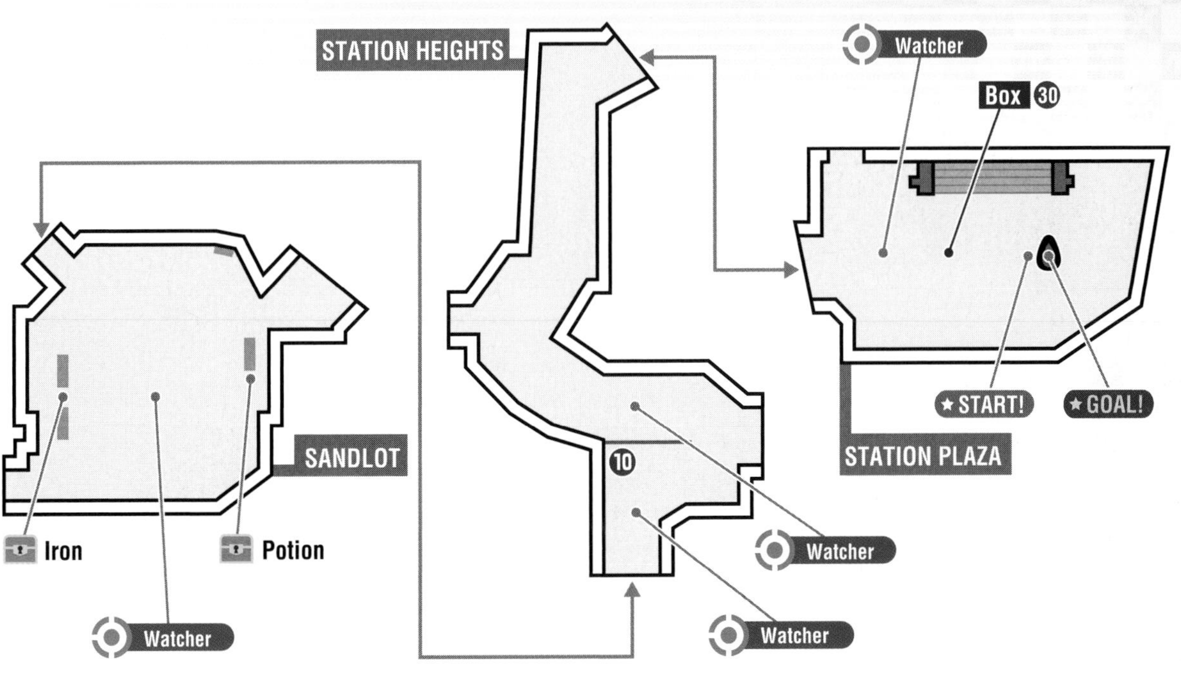

THE WHOLE GANG IS HERE!

Navigate downhill to the Sandlot area, where four Watchers appear at once. Thin their numbers by casting Fire spells from a distance, then move in and destroy those that remain. Open the two chests in the area and fight back to the dark corridor.

Thin the herd by casting Fire spells from a distance.

When only one or two foes remain, move in and use aerial combos to finish off the remaining Watchers.

CHALLENGE MISSION

Objective: Finish in record time!

Restrictions: Enemy level +8

Rewards	
Sigils Acquired	Clear Time
3	01:40:00 or less
2	01:40:01 - 01:55:00
1	01:55:01 - 02:10:00

Ignore all enemies except the Watchers and do the same while racing back to the dark corridor for RTC.

COLLECT HEARTS

MISSION 09

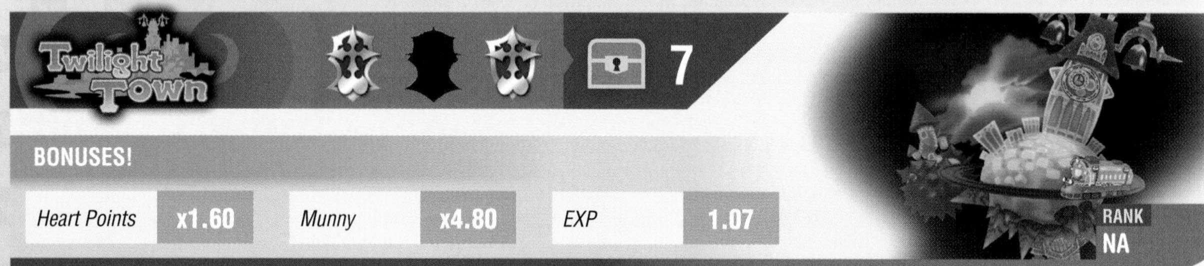

BONUSES!

Heart Points	x1.60	Munny	x4.80	EXP	1.07

ENEMIES

REWARDS	
Clear Bonuses	Random Bonuses
Shining Shard	Fire Recipe (10%)
Ether	Blazing Shard (15%)
Hi-Potion (MG)	Moonstone (15%)
—	Potion (40%)
—	None (20%)

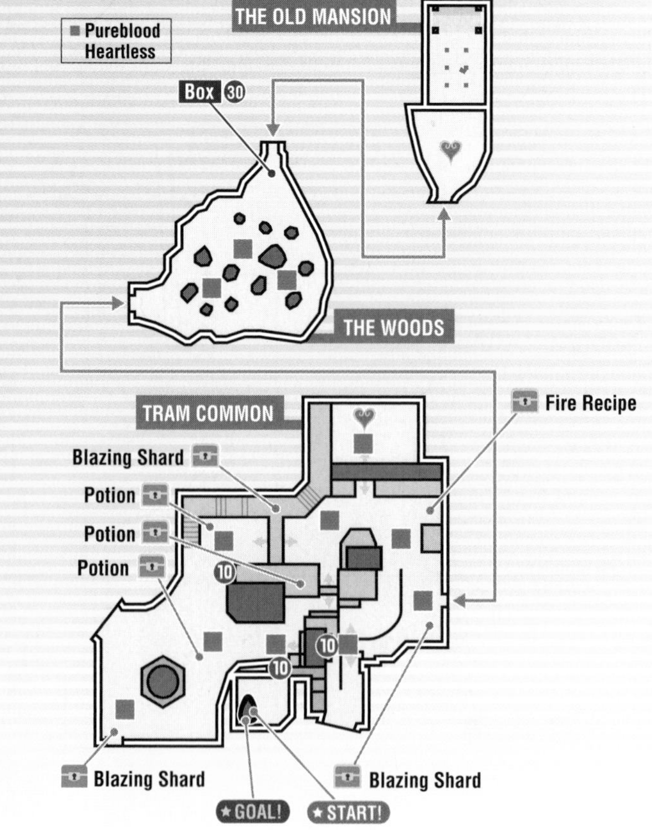

BEYOND THE WOODS

Identical to Mission 07, the objective is to accumulate 104 heart points to fill the Mission Gauge to the goal line, or 148 to fill the gauge 100%. Roxas and Marluxia begin the mission in the Tram Common area, where all seven chests are located. Collect the items and do not discard them in favor of anything dropped by other enemies. While searching, Shadows materialize in various areas. Remember that as Purebloods, though, they do not release hearts when defeated.

Shadows do not release hearts when defeated, which doesn't help you complete this mission.

Blocking by using the right timing can send a Dire Plant's projectile right back at it, inflicting severe damage to the foe.

After collecting items from all the chests, head east and proceed through a hole in the purple wall into the Shadow-infested Woods area. Navigate past the trees to The Old Mansion, where five Dire Plants wait. Defeat them all to accumulate enough heart points to fill the Mission Gauge to the goal line.

THE ZIP SLASHER

To fill the Mission Gauge 100%, you must defeat a dangerous enemy. Return to the Tram Common area after defeating the Dire Plants at The Old Mansion. Head north into an enclosed area to find a Zip Slasher, a very fast and durable armored Heartless. Circle the Zip Slasher until it attacks. After its spin and thrust attack, it remains still for a while so attack when this occurs. Move away when it regains its senses and provoke it into attacking again. Repeat this strategy until it is defeated. Use magic while it is dazed to make the process go faster and only use Limit Breaks while the Zip Slasher is dazed.

Move some distance from the Zip Slasher until it attempts a spinning attack...

Next, assault the armored creature while it recovers from exhaustion.

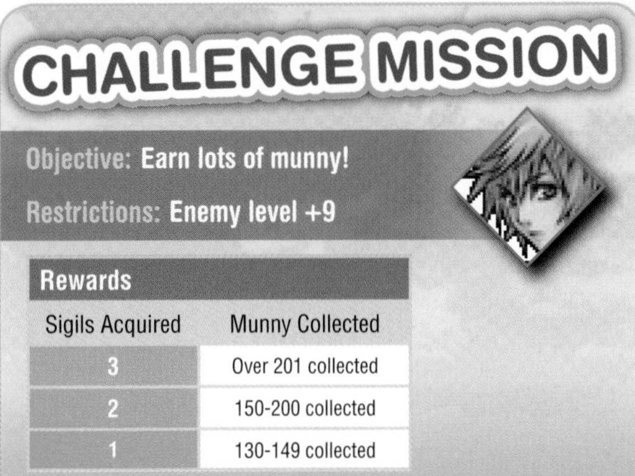

CHALLENGE MISSION

Objective: Earn lots of munny!

Restrictions: Enemy level +9

Rewards	
Sigils Acquired	Munny Collected
3	Over 201 collected
2	150-200 collected
1	130-149 collected

Accumulate large amounts of munny by defeating all of the Shadows in the Tram Common and The Woods areas. Their locations are marked on the maps for convenience. After defeating the Dire Plants at The Old Mansion, return to the Tram Common and defeat the new Shadow that appears nearby to gain the third Challenge Sigil. Defeating the Zip Slasher is not required.

PROVE YOUR ENDURANCE

MISSION 10

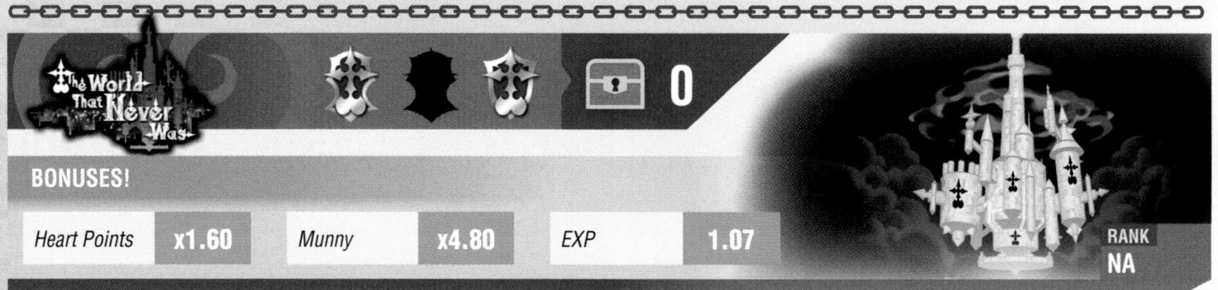

BONUSES!

Heart Points	x1.60	Munny	x4.80	EXP	1.07

RANK
NA

ENEMIES

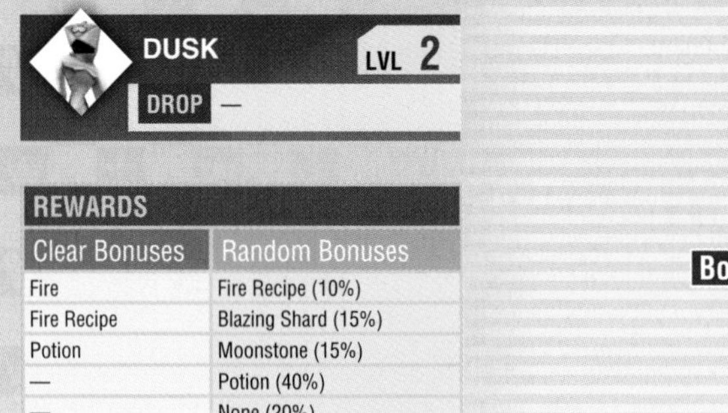

REWARDS	
Clear Bonuses	Random Bonuses
Fire	Fire Recipe (10%)
Fire Recipe	Blazing Shard (15%)
Potion	Moonstone (15%)
—	Potion (40%)
—	None (20%)

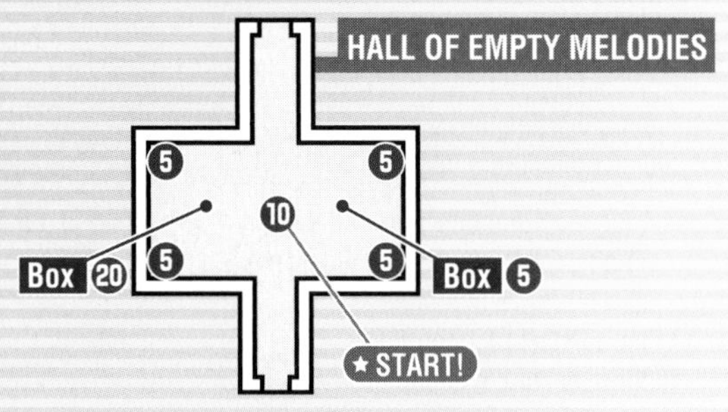

KEEP AWAY!

The objective of this mission is to survive for one minute. A timer appears in the upper-left corner of the upper screen, counting down the remaining seconds. Simply run from corner to corner away from the Dusk enemies; if cornered, use Dodge Rolls to break free.

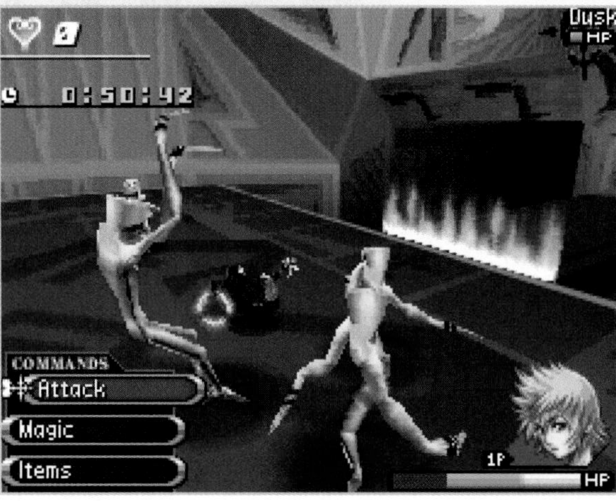

Dodge Roll to break free of Dusks when they draw near.

CHALLENGE MISSION

Objective: Attack as little as possible!

Restrictions: Enemy level +8

Rewards	
Sigils Acquired	Attacks
3	3 attacks or less
2	Attack 4-15 times
1	Attack 16-20 times

Attacking in Challenge mode reduces the number of Sigils earned. Misses also count against your record. As with the Normal Mission, don't bother attacking and use Dodge Rolls to get away.

DAY 22

ELIMINATE THE GUARDIAN

MISSION 11

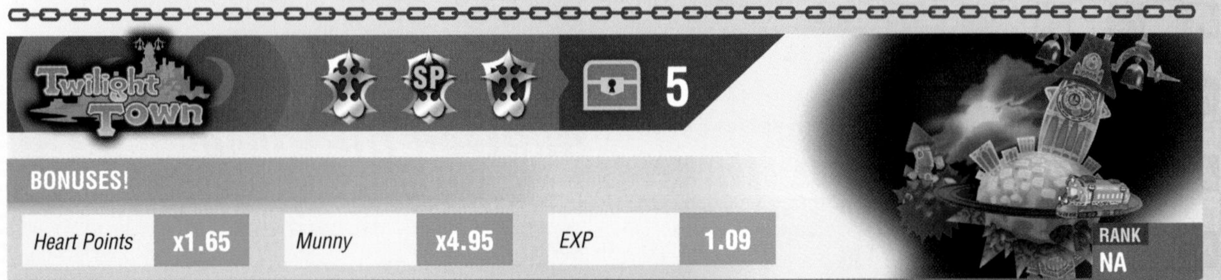

BONUSES!

Heart Points	x1.65	Munny	x4.95	EXP	1.09

ENEMIES

YELLOW OPERA LVL 1 — DROP: Moonstone

WATCHER LVL 3 — DROP: Potion

MINUTE BOMB LVL 2 — DROP: Blazing Shard

GUARDIAN LVL 8 — DROP: Moonstone

REWARDS

Clear Bonuses	Random Bonuses
Doublecast④	Fire Recipe (10%)
Blazing Shard	Blazing Shard (15%)
Blazing Shard	Moonstone (15%)
—	Potion (40%)
—	None (20%)

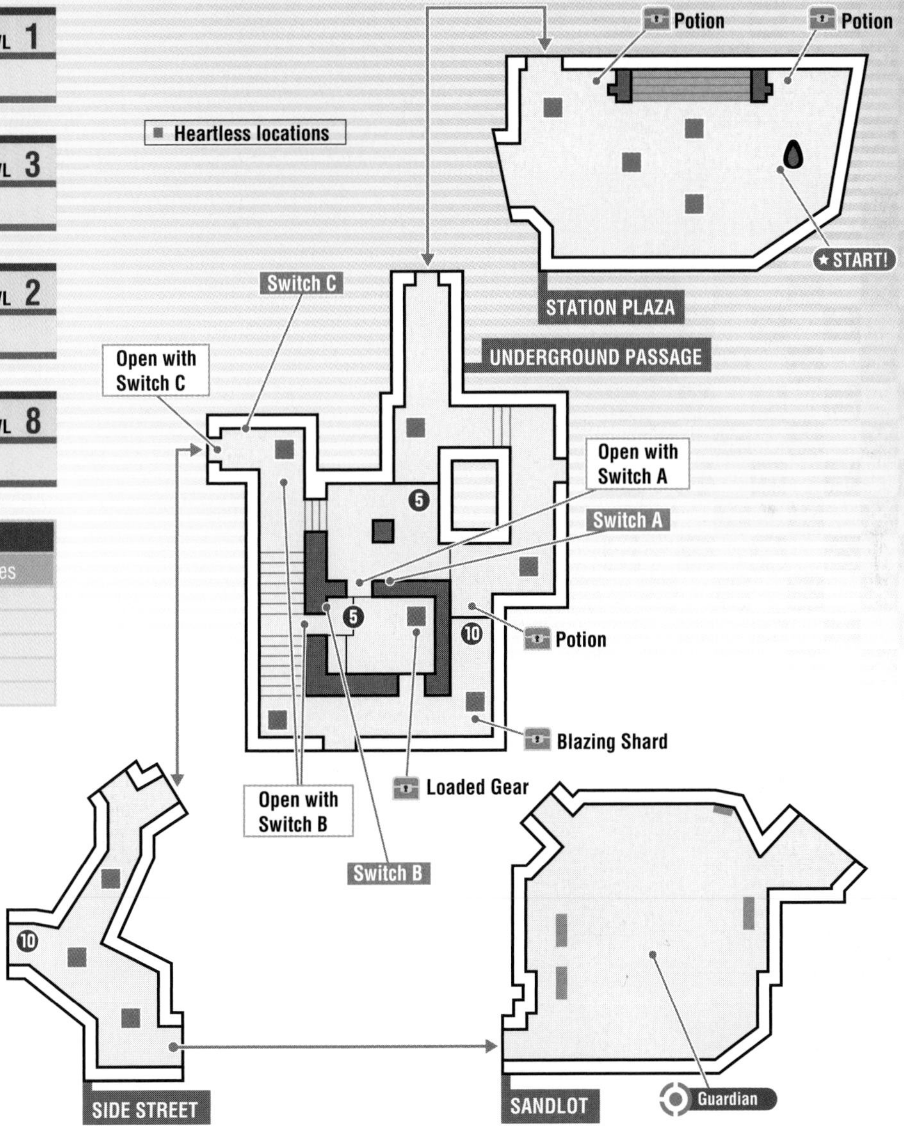

Heartless locations
Potion
Potion
START!
STATION PLAZA
UNDERGROUND PASSAGE
Switch C
Open with Switch C
Open with Switch A
Switch A
Potion
Blazing Shard
Loaded Gear
Open with Switch B
Switch B
SIDE STREET
SANDLOT
Guardian

MINUTE BOMBS!

Moving across the Station Plaza area, Roxas and Axel immediately encounter Minute Bombs. These durable Emblem Heartless can take quite a beating. If they remain around for more than a full minute, a Minute Bomb lights the fuse on top of its head and a countdown appears. Either destroy the Minute Bomb quickly or move away before the countdown expires. Minute Bombs inflict severe damage and may ignite Roxas upon detonation.

When Minute Bombs stop moving and ignite their fuse, a countdown appears over their head...

Finish them off quickly if they're low on HP, or move a safe distance away before they burst.

Roxas and Axel RTC automatically at the end of the mission, so open all chests before proceeding to the Sandlot.

BOSS!

GUARDIAN

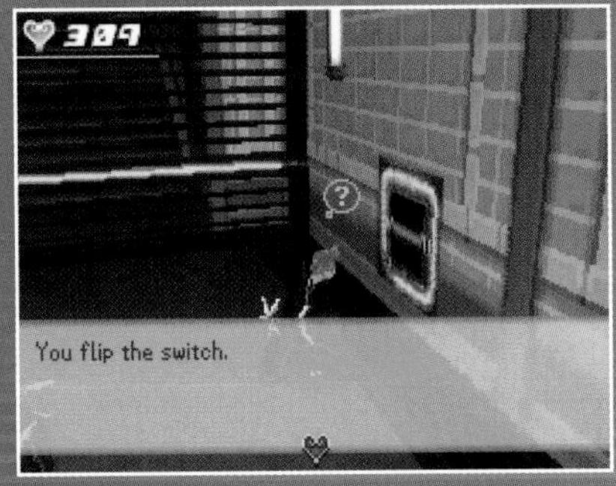

Navigate through the Underground Passage to the northwest exit, and flip the purple switch to open the gate. Continue through the Side Street to the Sandlot, where the Guardian awaits.

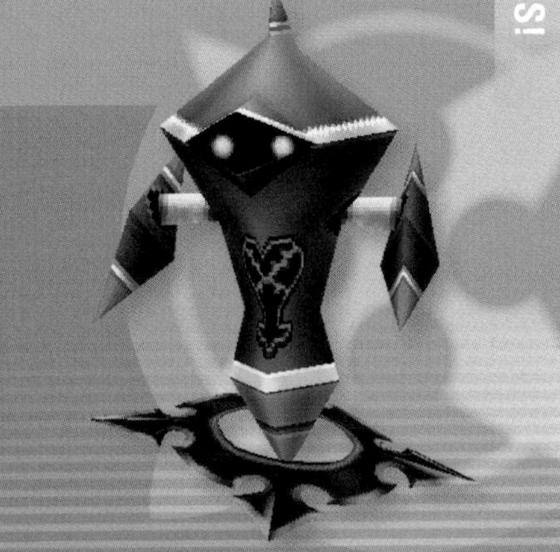

The battle ends when the target is destroyed, so eliminate the three Watcher sidekicks first for extra munny and HP Prizes. Lock on to the Guardian and keep it in your sites at all times. When it puts its "arms" together and faces the ground, prepare to dodge to the left or right before it bisects the ground with its massive beam. Run to its side or behind it and attack it while it prepares for its next attack. Cast Fire spells to inflict additional damage if it floats too far away.

CHALLENGE MISSION

Objective: Earn lots of heart points!

Restrictions: Enemy level +9

Rewards	
Sigils Acquired	Heart Points
3	450 or more
2	430-449
1	400-429

To achieve three Challenge Sigils, equip a stronger gear panel, defeat every Minute Bomb before they explode, and eliminate all other Emblem Heartless in the Underground Passage. During the Guardian boss fight, simply keep defeating Watcher sidekicks until the desired number is nearly reached, then finish off the Guardian while the chain is still active.

SPECIAL CHALLENGE

Objective: Jump as little as possible!

Restrictions: Enemy level +14

Rewards	
Sigils Acquired	Jump
3	Jump 1 time or less
2	Jump 2 times
1	Jump 3 times

To score three Challenge Sigils, you can press B to jump only one time in the entirety of this mission. Roxas automatically leaping up to perform an aerial combo doesn't count as a jump. Your one jump must be used in the Underground Passage to overcome the ledge near the center. After pressing the yellow switch to open the first gate, run diagonally through the doorway so that Roxas lands on the platform where the blue switch is located. Do not drop to the bottom of the central room, or you'll have to jump again to get out. Proceed to the Sandlot and fight the Guardian and three Watchers without jumping, letting Roxas automatically leap up to perform aerial combos.

You must jump to surmount this small ledge in the underground, so avoid leaping at any other time.

DAY 23

Equip the Doublecast④ panel obtained from Mission 11 and link all your Fire panels to it. This enables you to cast Fire six times instead of three. Speak to Demyx to obtain a **Blazing Shard** before beginning this mission.

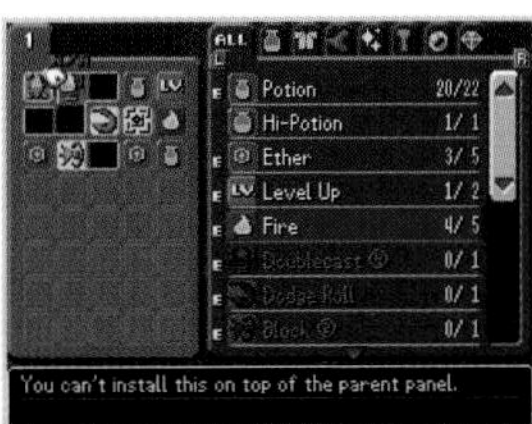

The Doublecast panel immediately increases the number of times spells can be cast during a mission.

Demyx has a present for Roxas today.

ELIMINATE THE POISON PLANT

MISSION 12

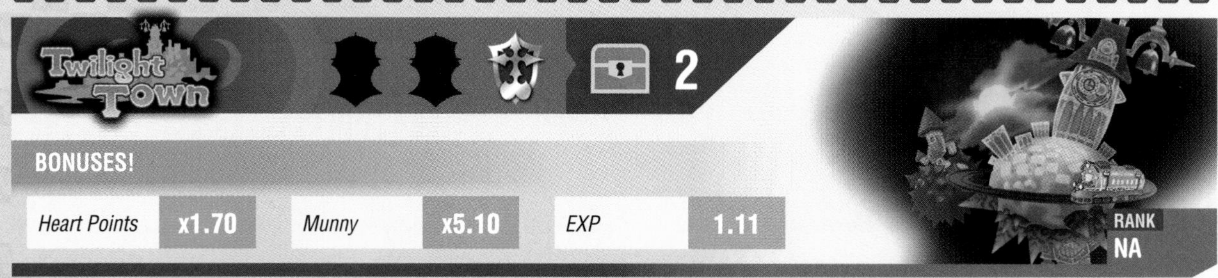

ENEMIES

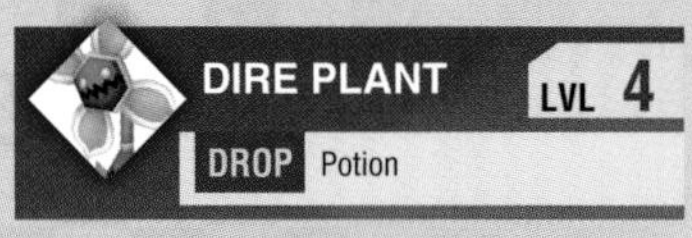

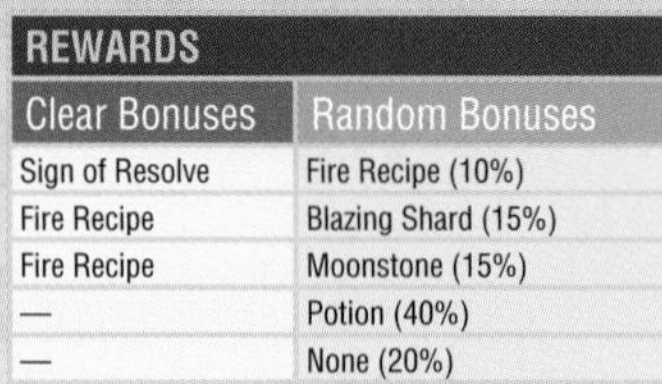

REWARDS	
Clear Bonuses	Random Bonuses
Sign of Resolve	Fire Recipe (10%)
Fire Recipe	Blazing Shard (15%)
Fire Recipe	Moonstone (15%)
—	Potion (40%)
—	None (20%)

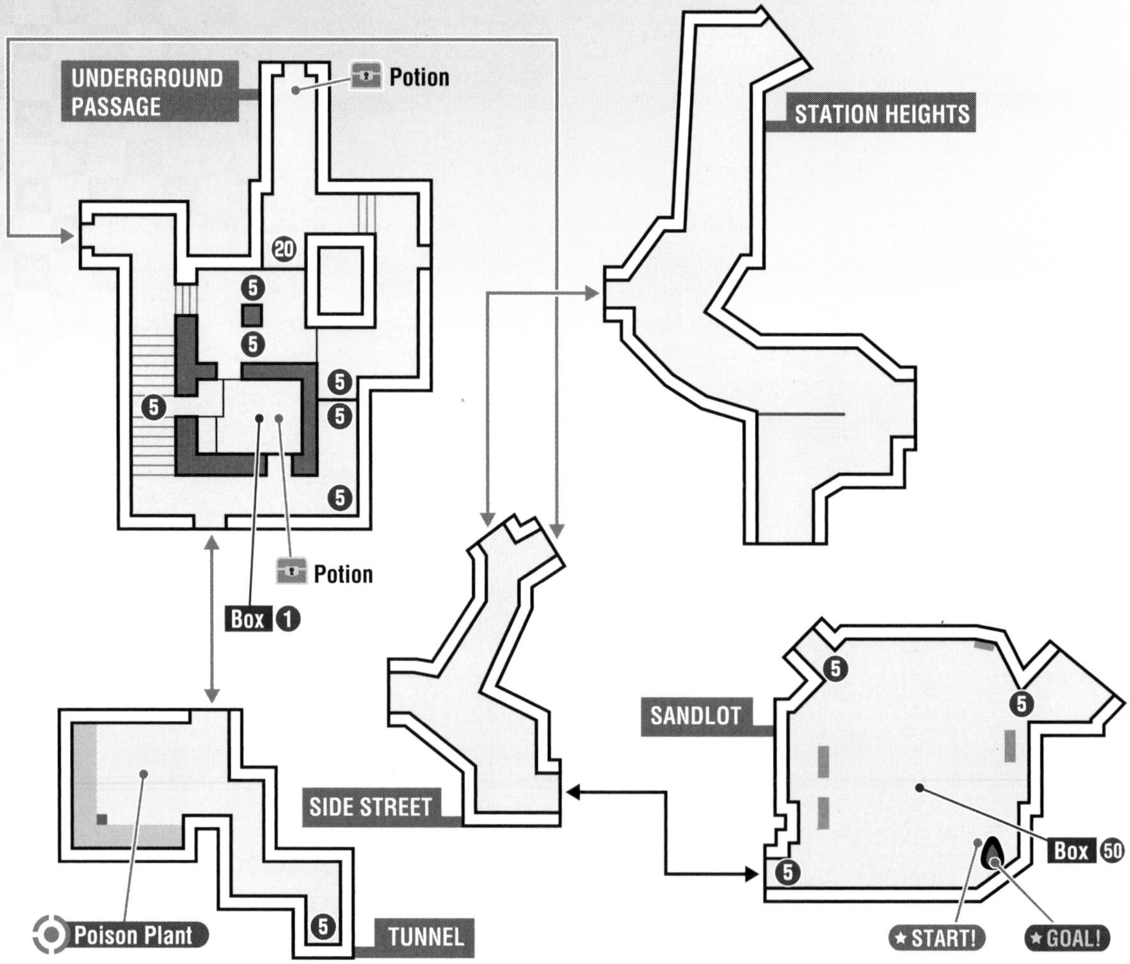

UNDERGROUND PASSAGE
Potion
20
5
5
5
5
5
5
Potion
Box 1
STATION HEIGHTS
SIDE STREET
SANDLOT
5
5
5
Box 50
START!
GOAL!
5
Poison Plant
TUNNEL

MAKING A FRIEND

Lead new recruit Xion to the Side Street area, then into the Underground Passage. The doorway at the south end of the lowest level is now open.

Xion tends to hang back and cast spells. Cover her by engaging enemies with melee attacks.

BOSS!

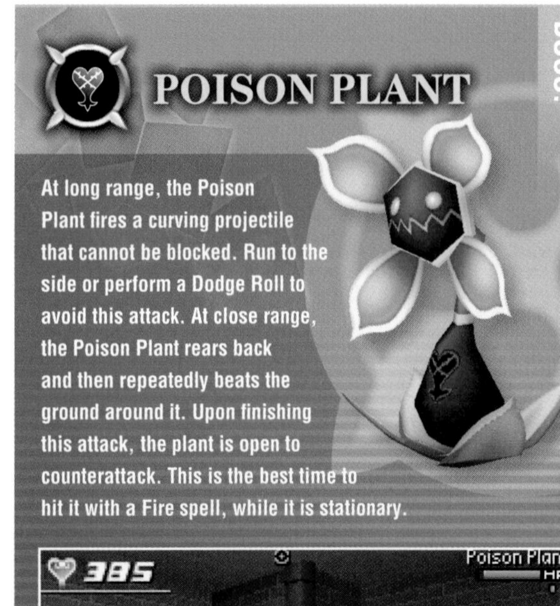

POISON PLANT

At long range, the Poison Plant fires a curving projectile that cannot be blocked. Run to the side or perform a Dodge Roll to avoid this attack. At close range, the Poison Plant rears back and then repeatedly beats the ground around it. Upon finishing this attack, the plant is open to counterattack. This is the best time to hit it with a Fire spell, while it is stationary.

DAY 24

ELIMINATE THE DESERTERS

MISSION 13

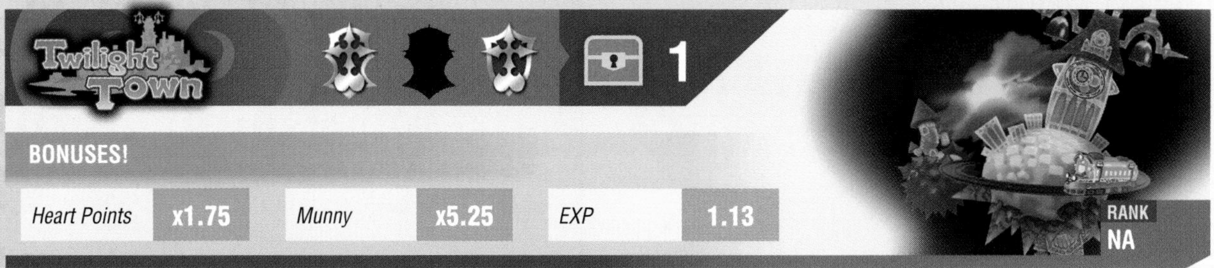

BONUSES!

Heart Points	x1.75	Munny	x5.25	EXP	1.13

RANK NA

ENEMIES

BULKY VENDOR LVL 4
DROP Iron, Shining Shard, or Blazing Shard

DESERTER LVL 3
DROP Potion

REWARDS	
Clear Bonuses	Random Bonuses
Skill Gear+②	Fire Recipe (10%)
Moonstone	Blazing Shard (15%)
Moonstone	Moonstone (15%)
—	Potion (40%)
—	None (20%)

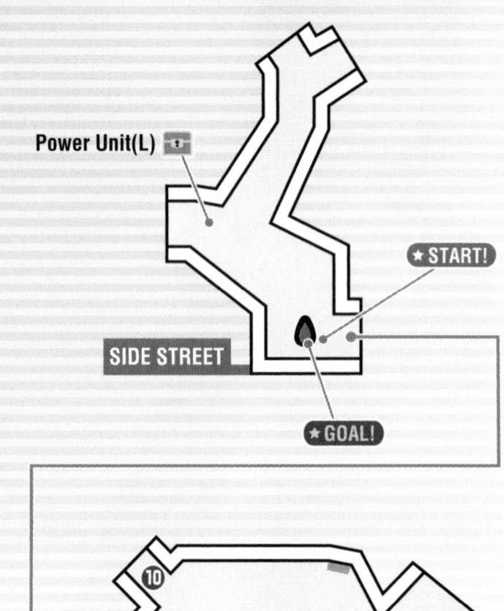

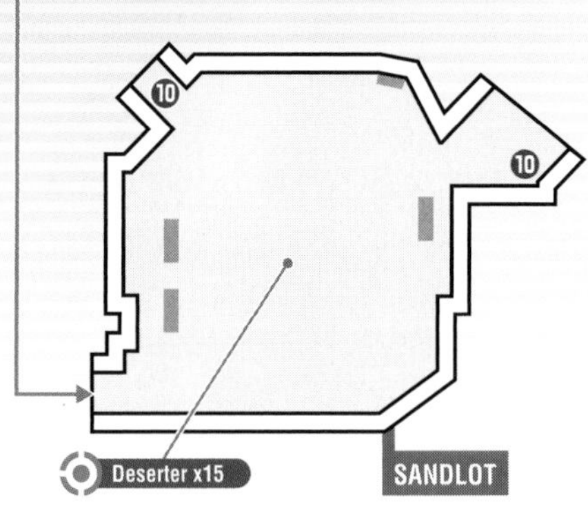

ROUND 'EM UP!

Grab the **Power Unit(L)** from the chest near the starting point before proceeding to the Sandlot. There, 15 lightning-fast Deserters are running amuck.

Head to the top of the Side Street to find a hidden Bulky Vendor.

Deserters run around the area for a few seconds, then stop for a short while. When one Deserter is destroyed, the rest soon approach Roxas and try to attack. Therefore, one way to defeat many Deserters at once is to lock on to one, wait for it to stop, and destroy it with a Fire spell. When the others approach, take out as many of them as possible before they run off again. Repeat until the mission is complete.

Destroying one Deserter brings the wrath of the whole group down on your head. Try to eliminate a few more while they're close.

Cast Fire spells to dispose of Deserters from a distance.

CHALLENGE MISSION

Objective: Finish in record time!

Restrictions: Enemy level +7

Rewards	
Sigils Acquired	Clear Time
3	00:55:00 or less
2	00:55:01 - 01:10:00
1	01:10:01 - 01:30:00

To complete this challenge and win three Sigils, Roxas needs to be at level 30 or higher and have the ability to cast Fire at least 10 or more times. Proceed directly to the Sandlot and start defeating Deserters with Fire spells, without waiting for them to counterattack. Only when they crowd around Roxas should you try to take them out with combos. When they spread out again, resume casting Fire spells.

DAY 25

Speak to Xaldin to receive a **Moonstone** and equip a Block panel before undertaking this day's difficult mission.

The freebies keep coming, so enjoy them while they last.

ELIMINATE THE DARKSIDE

MISSION 14

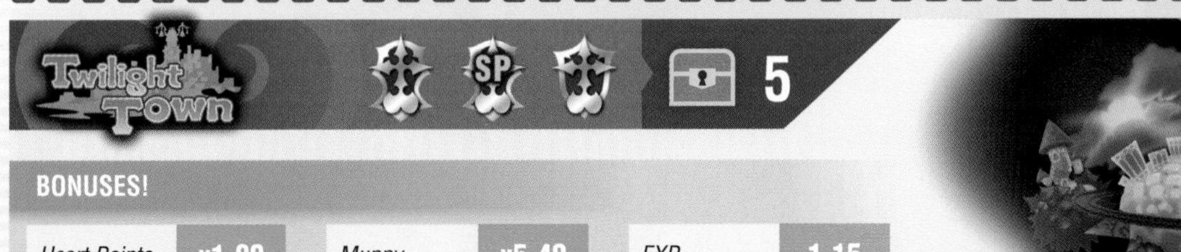

BONUSES!

Heart Points	x1.80	Munny	x5.40	EXP	1.15

RANK NA

ENEMIES

SHADOW* LVL 6
DROP —

*Summoned by Darkside

YELLOW OPERA LVL 3
DROP Moonstone

POSSESSOR LVL 1
DROP Blazing Shard

MINUTE BOMB LVL 2
DROP Blazing Shard

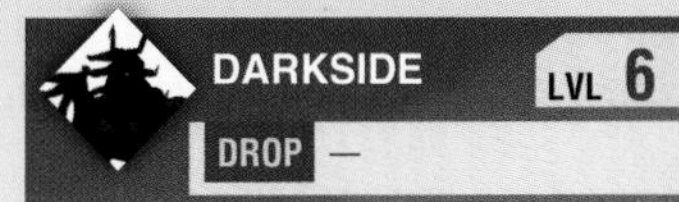
DARKSIDE LVL 6
DROP —

REWARDS	
Clear Bonuses	Random Bonuses
Blizzard	Fire Recipe (10%)
Blizzard	Blazing Shard (15%)
Frost Shard	Moonstone (15%)
—	Potion (40%)
—	None (20%)

HEART OF DARKNESS

Open the chests in the street areas, then hike uphill to the Station Plaza. Proceed across the area until Darkside appears.

*Don't forget to collect the **Moonstone** from the nearby chest during the boss encounter!*

Darkside
Moonstone
STATION PLAZA
★GOAL!
Potion
5
5
STATION HEIGHTS
Potion
5
5
5
★START!
Blazing Shard
SIDE STREET
Potion

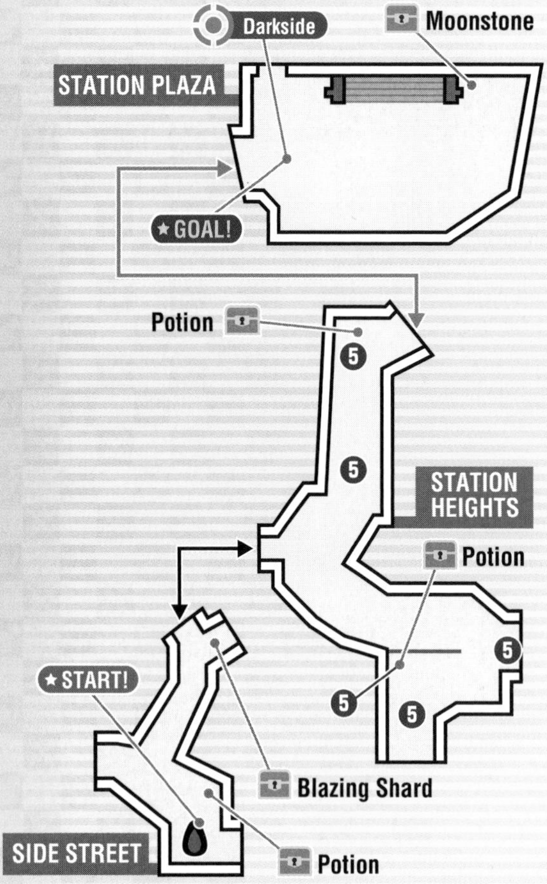

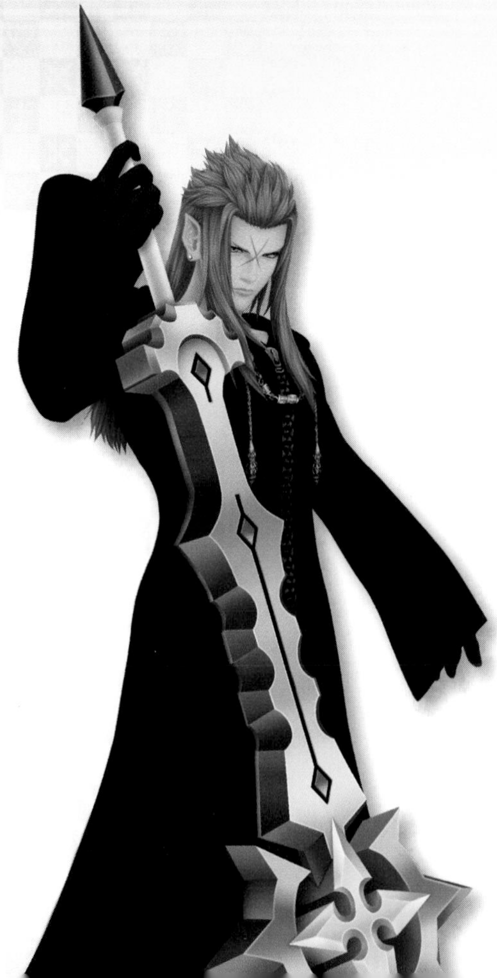

Identifying Darkside's various actions and knowing how to counteract them are critical to minimizing the damage sustained during this battle. If he leans forward and then pulls back with one hand glowing, it indicates he's about to create a pool of darkness and raise Shadows. Destroy these enemies to regain lost HP throughout the battle. If he rears straight back and then slams his hand into the ground, it means he is about to release a shockwave. As the white ring spreads outward, run away or jump over the ring to avoid damage.

In an alternate version of this attack, Darkside leans on one hand and then quickly slams the other into the ground. This shockwave spreads much faster. Darkside pulls a heart out of the ground, then releases it. The heart dissolves and soon black orbs begin raining from the sky. The best defense here is to break off attacking and avoid the orbs.

If Darkside leans back and begins firing purplish orbs from his glowing chest cavity, then move away and align the camera to see the orbs approach. With the right timing, a block can bounce these orbs back and inflict decent damage to Darkside if they connect.

BOSS!

DARKSIDE

While blocking the orbs, lock on to Darkside's head to inflict better damage. Note that failure to block a homing orb inflicts damage equal to half of Roxas's remaining HP. If an orb hits Darkside, he retaliates by releasing double the quantity in his next attack.

Between all of Darkside's attacks, lock on to one hand or the other and repeatedly perform aerial combos. To use magic, wait until just after one of its attacks when its hands lower to its sides and settle.

CHALLENGE MISSION

Objective: Avoid taking damage!

Restrictions: Enemy level +13

Rewards	
Sigils Acquired	Hits Sustained
3	2 or less
2	3 to 5 hits
1	6 to 8 hits

This challenge is tricky and earning three Sigils may take a few tries. The key is to avoid all other enemies on your way to Darkside. When fighting the boss, become familiar with his attacks and how to avoid them, perfecting the methods described in the previous strategy.

SPECIAL CHALLENGE

Objective: Finish in record time!

Restrictions: No attack magic, enemy level +60

Rewards	
Sigils Acquired	Clear Time
3	01:45:00 or less
2	01:45:01 - 03:10:00
1	03:10:01 - 04:10:00

Although at first glance this challenge would appear to be quite forgiving on time, notice that all enemies receive quite a boost in status. Roxas should be extremely high in level (complete the game) and equipped with a weapon panel that boasts a great aerial combo, such as the Lift Gear+ or Nimble Gear+. Proceed directly to the Station Plaza, ignoring all other enemies. Follow the same strategy as normal, only during the rain of black orbs, run from one side of Darkside to the other, attacking the hands. Break this off only when orbs begin to fall in your area.

An alternate strategy is to let the enemies attack on your way to the Station Plaza, especially the Possessors. Let them drain Roxas to the point where he's ready to perform a Limit Break, then break away and proceed to fight Darkside. Attack the boss without regard to your health, triggering three or more Limit Breaks in a row to finish him quickly!

DAY 26

After receiving some bad news, speak to Xaldin twice in the Grey Area with a weapon panel equipped and he'll hand over a **Hi-Potion**.

Speak to Saïx, who promotes Roxas to Novice rank. Higher rank allows you to play more missions in Mission Mode. The Moogle appears near the doorway in the Grey Area. Speak to the Moogle to buy panels with your heart points, to sell panels, or to synthesize new panels by combing two or more and paying a certain amount of munny. Some worthwhile purchases include the Slot Releaser (which opens an extra panel slot in your menu), the Level Up, the Triplecast(3), and the Soldier Ring. Try your hand at synthesis by crafting a Limit Recharge (replenishes the yellow segment of your HP bar) or the Fire Charm.

Higher rank means you can play more missions with other players in Mission Mode.

Introduce yourself to the Moogle and start looking for good deals in its shop.

INVESTIGATE THIS NEW WORLD

MISSION 15

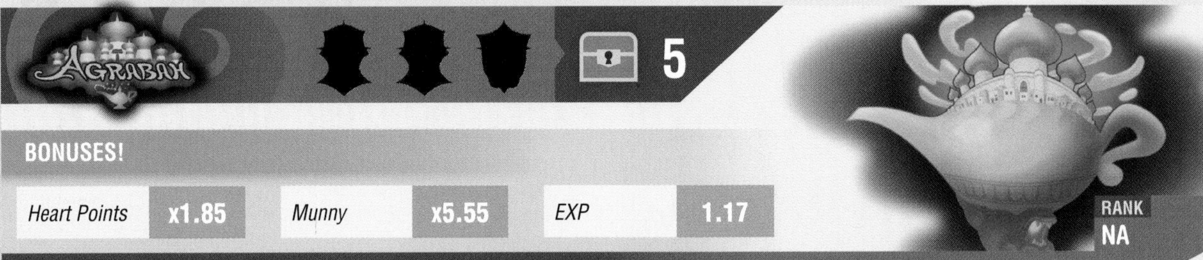

BONUSES!

Heart Points	x1.85	Munny	x5.55	EXP	1.17

RANK NA

ENEMIES

SCARLET TANGO LVL 5
DROP Blazing Shard

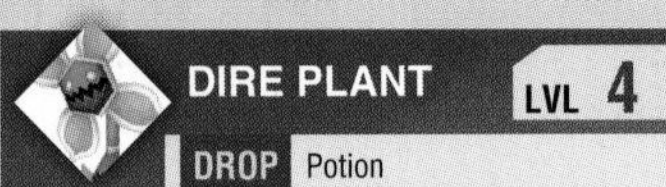
DIRE PLANT LVL 4
DROP Potion

LOUDMOUTH LVL 4
DROP Hi-Potion

REWARDS

Clear Bonuses	Random Bonuses
Ability Unit(L)	Shining Shard (20%)
Shining Shard	Iron (20%)
Blizzard (MG)	Potion (30%)
—	None (30%)

SIFTING THROUGH SAND

Check the map provided in this guide and locate several colors of checkmarks. The hollow red checkmarks denote the locations of optional recon points to search, while the four solid red checkmarks show the locations that must be searched before Roxas has his first breakthrough. These points are marked on the in-game map as they are discovered, so refer often to the lower screen.

Gain knowledge regarding this new world by examining points of interest throughout Agrabah.

To raise the gate blocking the exit, strike the lever on the ground.

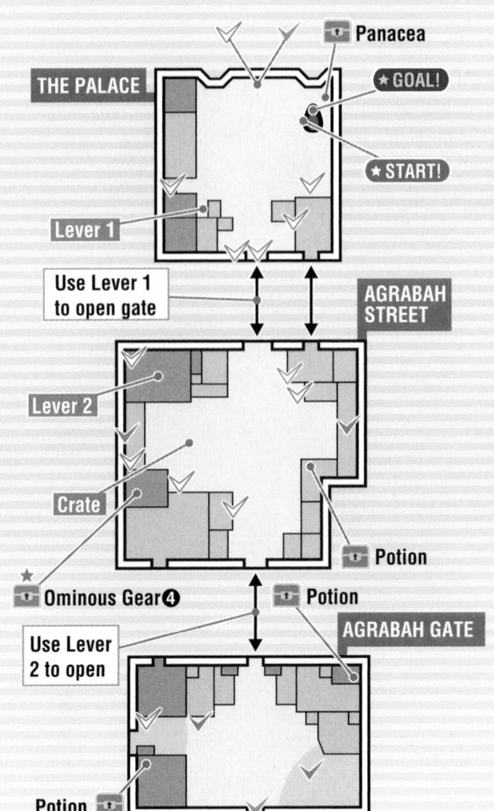

In the Agrabah Street area, use the "steps" in the southeast corner to ascend to the upper level. Search the scaffold floorboards to find a key recon point.

Jump on the "steps" in the southeast corner to explore the east side of the street.

Even a simple scaffold can tell Roxas something about this world.

On the west side of the area, destroy the tower to let the crate fall to the ground. Strike the crate to knock it toward the stack of three crates. Then jump from the mobile crate onto the stack and jump onto the wooden scaffold above. Check the wall to find the other essential clue in this area.

Smash the base beneath the crate to drop it to the ground.

Knock the crate beneath the stack, then jump to the level above.

Hit the switch on the high level to open the second gate.

Before leaping back down, use the crates stacked on the scaffold to reach the northwest platform. Strike the switch there to raise the south gate.

A CHEST OUT OF REACH

*If you look south from this platform, you'll notice a chest that is out of reach. Replay this mission after obtaining the Glide panel later in the game and you can fly from the switch location to the chest with no problem. The chest contains an **Ominous Gear**④.*

SERIES OF BREAKTHROUGHS

Clear the Agrabah Gate area of enemies, then check the boarded door in the northwest corner and the massive sand pile in the southeast corner to trigger a series of questions. The mission proceeds regardless of your answers. Destroy the new Heartless enemies that appear in the area, open the chests on the high platforms, then advance north back toward the dark corridor.

Check the boarded up door in the gate area as well as the nearby sand pile to keep things moving along.

The questions Xigbar asks Roxas can be answered any way you like. Wrong answers have comic responses!

SCENES TRIGGER BREAKTHROUGHS, TOO

Examine the open doorway leading out of the city as well as the palace gate to fill the Mission Gauge 100%.

Upon returning to the Palace area, Xigbar and Roxas overhear Jasmine talking to Aladdin. Following the scene, Roxas has his second breakthrough, filling the Mission Gauge to the goal line. To fill the gauge 100%, examine the palace doors to the north and the city exit at the south end of the Agrabah Gate area, as indicated by green checkmarks on the map in this section.

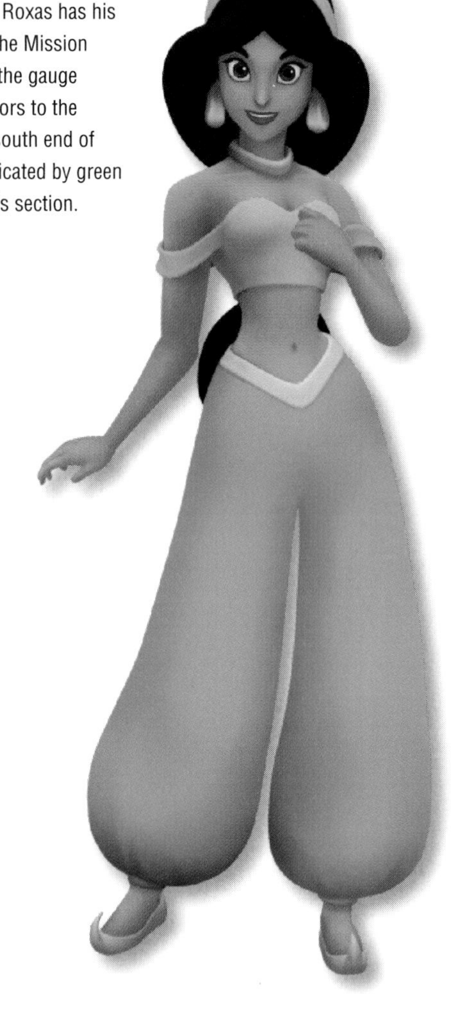

DAY 51-54

Starting with the missions in day 51, you'll start finding red Unity Badges that unlock the same mission in Mission Mode, enabling solo play and multiplayer. Mission Crowns are awarded for completing missions in Mission Mode. The Moogle redeems Mission Crowns for prizes.

Furthermore, completing missions in Story Mode now fills the Bonus Gauge at the top of Saïx's Missions screen. When the gauge rises above the "x2" or "x3" marks, all mission rewards are doubled or tripled accordingly! Mission 18 fills the gauge the most, so completing it first means your rewards already start doubling with the second mission.

Select missions on the Missions screen to see how much each fills the Bonus Gauge when completed. Rewards double and triple as more missions are completed.

Speak to Demyx, who wants Roxas to collect all the chests in Mission 14. If you already have, speak to him again to obtain a **Shining Shard**.

Practice good item gathering in all missions to prepare for demands made by other Organization XIII members.

On Day 52, Saïx gives Roxas a **LV Doubler**⑤. Any Level Up Panels linked to this can raise Roxas's level by two points instead of just one.

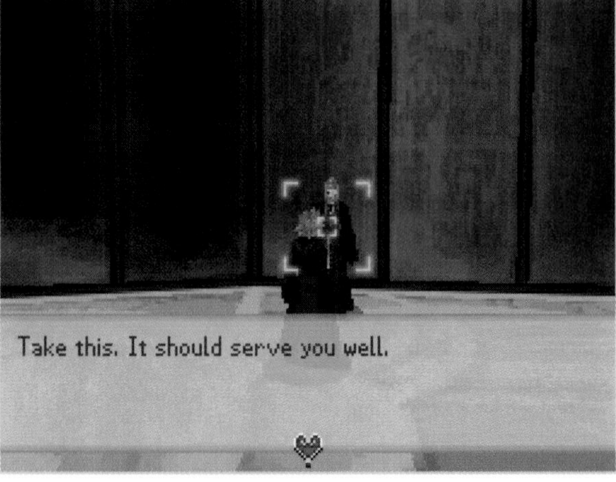

Make room for LV Doubler panels on your slot board. Attach every Level Up panel you accumulate to one of these to maximize Roxas's abilities.

ELIMINATE THE FIRE PLANTS

MISSION 16

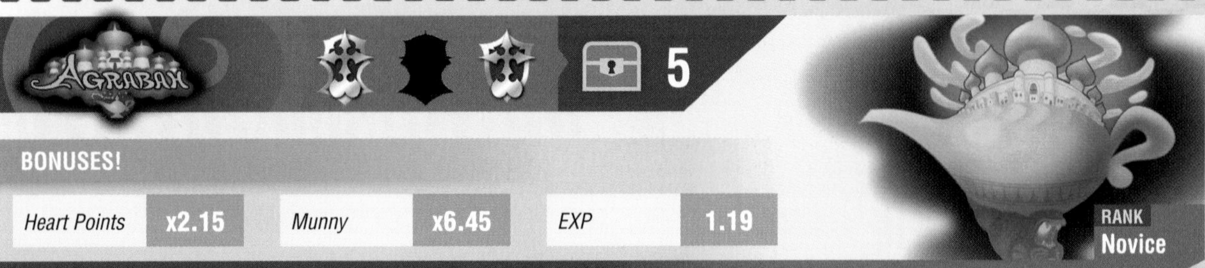

ENEMIES

REWARDS

Clear Bonuses	Random Bonuses
Shining Shard	Shining Shard (20%)
Panacea	Iron (20%)
Elixir Recipe (MG)	Potion (30%)
—	None (30%)

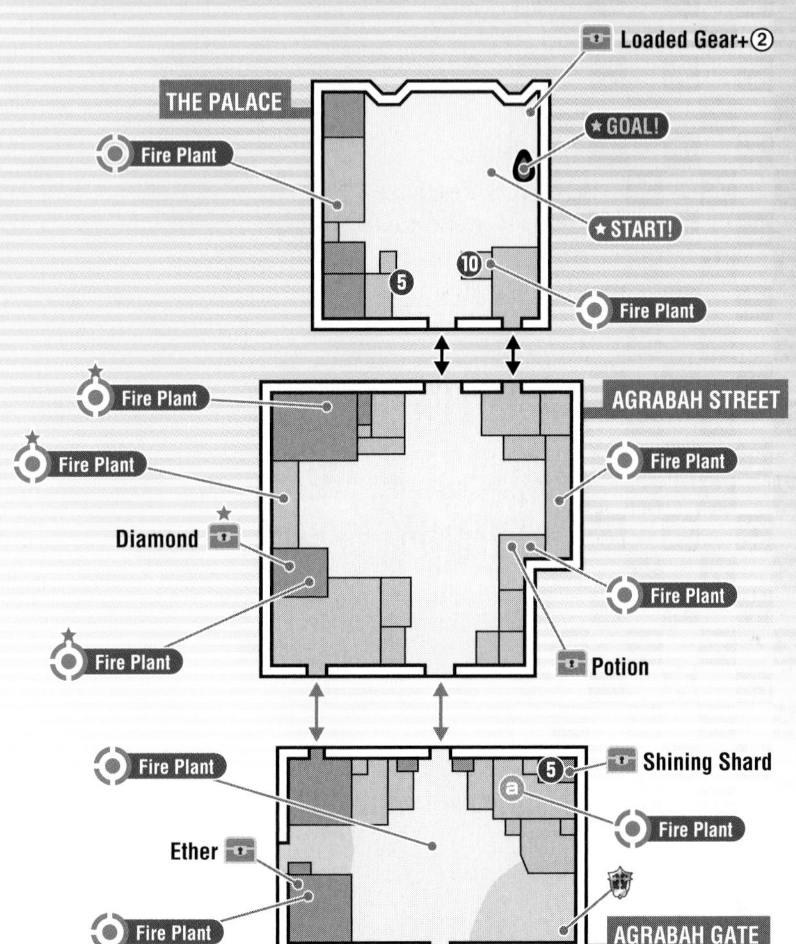

WEED KILLER

Simply move south from location to location in Agrabah, defeating the Fire Plants. A Barrier Master protects the ones in the Agrabah Gate area to the south. Target and wipe out the Barrier Master first to prevent it from protecting the Fire Plants.

Use Blizzard spells to damage Fire Plants severely.

The Barrier Master's spell makes surrounding Heartless invincible. Kill it to remove the protection.

Eliminating the first seven plants raises the Mission Gauge to the goal line. Three more Fire Plants then appear in the hard-to-reach west side of the Agrabah Street area. However, you need the Air Slide or Glide skills to reach them, which means replaying this task later as a Holo-Mission.

Advanced skills acquired later in the game are needed to reach the Fire Plants hidden on the upper levels.

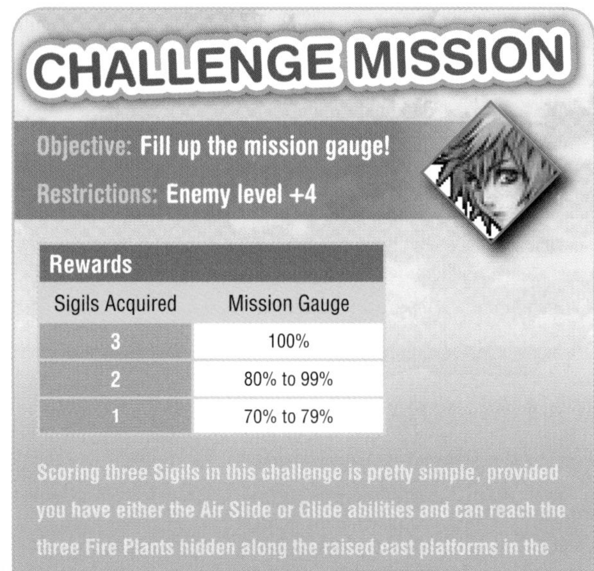

CHALLENGE MISSION

Objective: Fill up the mission gauge!

Restrictions: Enemy level +4

Rewards	
Sigils Acquired	Mission Gauge
3	100%
2	80% to 99%
1	70% to 79%

Scoring three Sigils in this challenge is pretty simple, provided you have either the Air Slide or Glide abilities and can reach the three Fire Plants hidden along the raised east platforms in the Agrabah Street area.

ELIMINATE THE TAILBUNKER

MISSION 17

Twilight Town — 2

BONUSES!

Heart Points	x2.15	Munny	x6.45	EXP	1.19

RANK Novice

ENEMIES

REWARDS	
Clear Bonuses	Random Bonuses
Shining Shard	Fire Recipe (10%)
Blazing Shard	Blazing Shard (15%)
Frost Shard	Moonstone (15%)
—	Potion (40%)
—	Ether (20%)

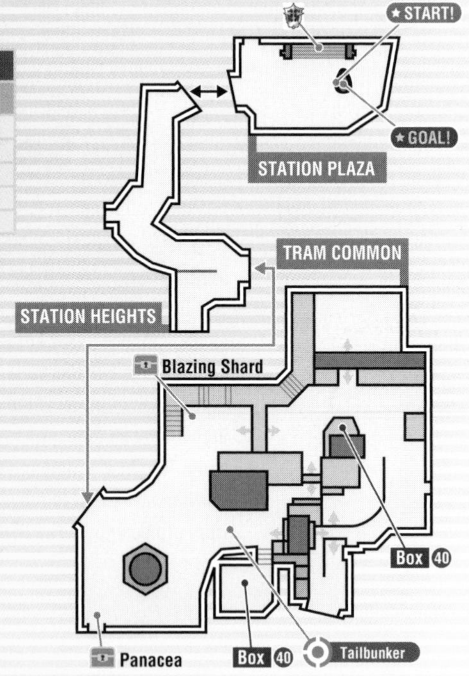

THE SOARING SCOURGE

Eliminate Minute Bombs in the Station Plaza area and pick up the **Unity Badge** hovering near the station doors. Descend the hill to the Tram Common area, where the Tailbunker waits.

TAILBUNKER

BOSS!

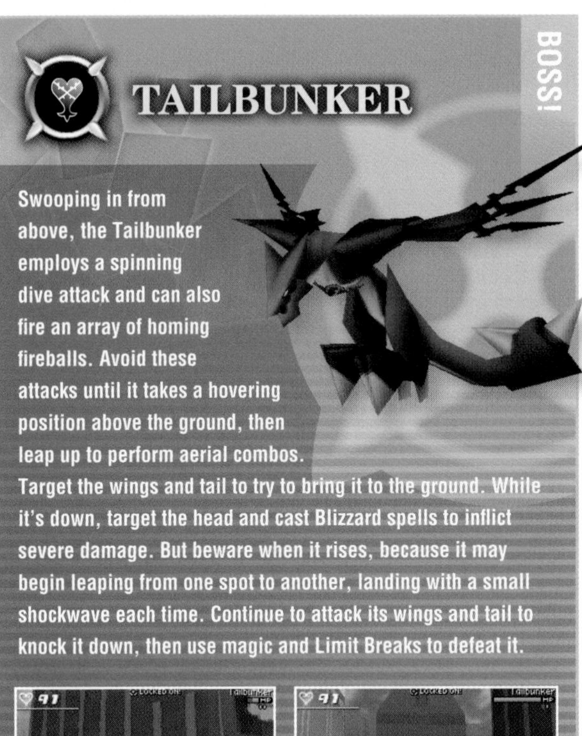

Swooping in from above, the Tailbunker employs a spinning dive attack and can also fire an array of homing fireballs. Avoid these attacks until it takes a hovering position above the ground, then leap up to perform aerial combos. Target the wings and tail to try to bring it to the ground. While it's down, target the head and cast Blizzard spells to inflict severe damage. But beware when it rises, because it may begin leaping from one spot to another, landing with a small shockwave each time. Continue to attack its wings and tail to knock it down, then use magic and Limit Breaks to defeat it.

CHALLENGE MISSION

Objective: Finish in record time!

Restrictions: No recovery items, enemy level +4

Rewards	
Sigils Acquired	Clear Time
3	01:40:00 or less
2	01:40:01 - 02:05:00
1	02:05:01 - 02:30:00

Allow the enemies near the starting point and along the route to the Tram Common to cause damage to Roxas to the point where his Limit Break is ready and then proceed to engage the Tailbunker. Attack the wings and tail to bring it to the ground, then activate Limit Break and attack. Avoid healing Roxas and instead engage his Limit Break again as he takes more damage.

SPECIAL CHALLENGE

Objective: Don't miss with attacks!

Restrictions: No attack magic, take 30% more damage, enemy level +18

Rewards	
Sigils Acquired	Attacks Missed
3	0 misses
2	1 to 3 misses
1	4 to 10 misses

Bring plenty of recovery items, since a single attack from the Tailbunker can immediately reduce Roxas to critical state. The key is to avoid contact with enemies prior to the boss fight. Watch the Tailbunker carefully and time your attacks to ensure they connect. Take your time and avoid stringing together extended attack combos. The Tailbunker could fly away at any time, so don't risk a miss.

DAY
51-54

~MISSING~

COLLECT ORGANIZATION EMBLEMS

MISSION 18

AGRABAH

4

BONUSES!

Heart Points	x2.15	Munny	x6.45	EXP	1.19

RANK
Novice

ENEMIES

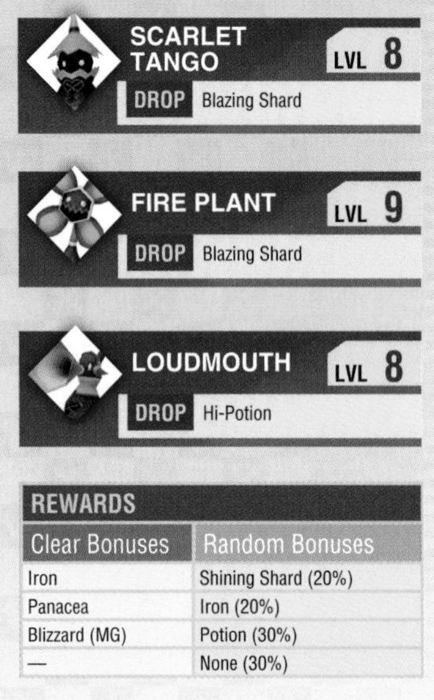

SCARLET TANGO LVL 8
DROP Blazing Shard

FIRE PLANT LVL 9
DROP Blazing Shard

LOUDMOUTH LVL 8
DROP Hi-Potion

REWARDS

Clear Bonuses	Random Bonuses
Iron	Shining Shard (20%)
Panacea	Iron (20%)
Blizzard (MG)	Potion (30%)
—	None (30%)

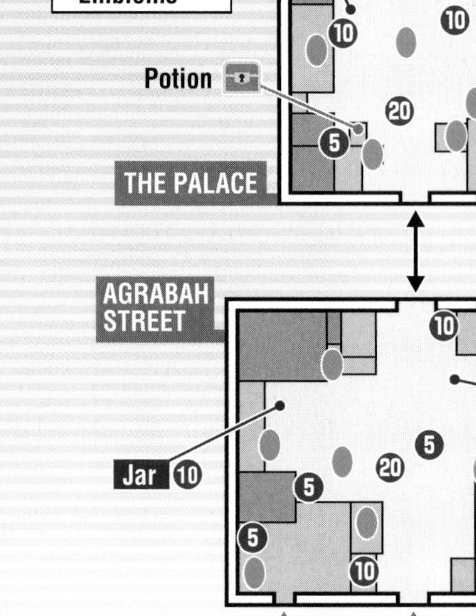

SHRINKING RING SYNDROME

Collecting the silver Organization emblems is easy enough. To guarantee filling the Mission Gauge 100%, however, you must not take any emblems unless a large green ring emanates from them. Over time, the rings shrink and disappear unless you collect another emblem or defeat an enemy. The fewer Organization emblems remaining, the faster the rings shrink.

Collecting emblems while a green ring surrounds them fills the Mission Gauge more than after the ring vanishes.

Climb the platforms in the starting area to reach the two chests and grab the **Unity Badge**. Next, proceed north to the street area. The Organization emblems are all ringed, so try to grab them before the rings vanish. Avoid the enemies on the ground level until the green rings disappear. Then stop collecting emblems, drop to the ground, and defeat an enemy to make the rings reappear. Collect more emblems until the rings vanish again and repeat the process.

Collect any 11 to 13 emblems regardless of their ring appearance to fill the Mission Gauge to the goal line. Collect all 16 emblems while the rings are visible to fill the gauge 100%.

Grab emblems up high first, since the enemies appear low to the ground.

CHALLENGE MISSION

Objective: Finish in record time!

Restrictions: Enemy level +2

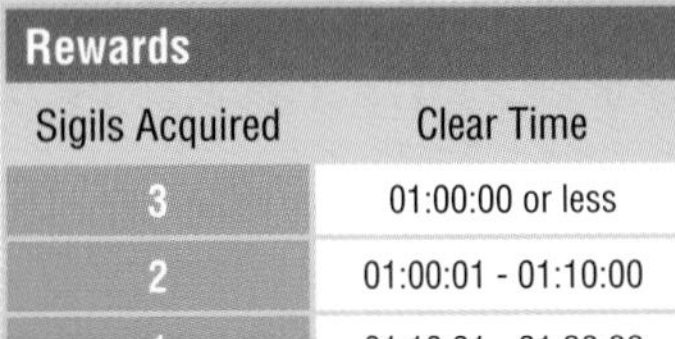

Rewards	
Sigils Acquired	Clear Time
3	01:00:00 or less
2	01:00:01 - 01:10:00
1	01:10:01 - 01:30:00

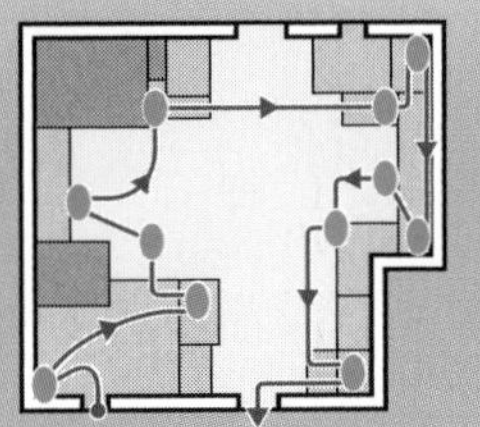

Wait to undertake this challenge until the Glide panel is acquired. The key is to collect as few emblems as possible to fill the Mission Gauge to the goal line, then race back to the dark corridor. Enter the Agrabah street area from the raised northwest doorway and follow the route on the map shown here to collect all 11 emblems in the area while their rings still show. The Glide ability allows you to fly around the area, grab them all, and fly back to RTC in record time.

ELIMINATE THE DESERTERS

MISSION **19**

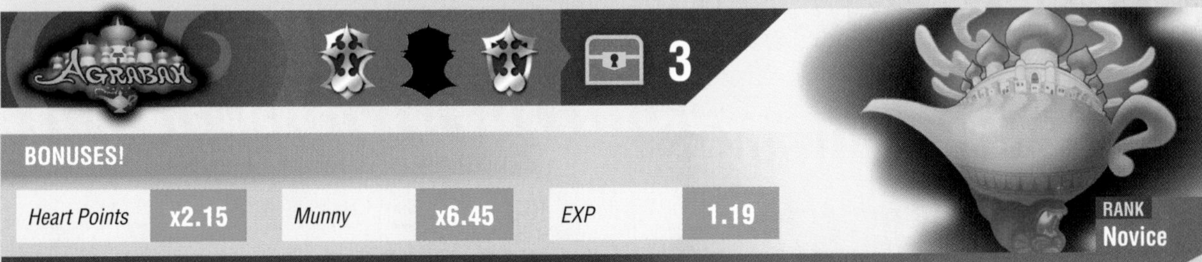

BONUSES!

Heart Points	Munny	EXP	RANK
x2.15	x6.45	1.19	Novice

ENEMIES

DESERTER LVL 8
DROP Shining Shard

REWARDS	
Clear Bonuses	Random Bonuses
Shining Shard	Shining Shard (20%)
Shining Shard	Iron (20%)
Frost Shard	Potion (30%)
—	None (30%)

HEADING TO THE PALACE

A chest on the far side of the street area cannot be reached without advanced abilities.

Open the chest on the raised platform east of the starting point to obtain a **Potion**. The chest containing a **Slot Releaser** cannot be reached without the help of a level 2 Air Slide or the Glide abilities.

Proceed north to the Palace area and begin defeating the 16 Deserters. Without the aid of a partner, Deserter retaliations may be too severe to handle alone. Thus, use Fire and Blizzard spells to eliminate Deserters from the sidelines, then jump away as they attempt to surround Roxas. When only five or fewer foes remain, take out one Deserter and then use a Limit Break to wipe out the last ones.

Until the Deserters are fewer in number, avoid their retaliations after each kill.

*Use the sand piled in front of the yellow awning to reach the upper level on the west side, where the **Unity Badge** is located.*

Deserter x16
Ether
THE PALACE
Slot Releaser
Jar 8
Potion
AGRABAH STREET
GOAL!
START!

CHALLENGE MISSION

Objective: Finish in record time!

Restrictions: Enemy level +2

Rewards	
Sigils Acquired	Clear Time
3	01:00:00 or less
2	01:00:01 - 01:15:00
1	01:15:01 - 01:30:00

The key to gaining three Challenge Sigils in this mission is to load up Roxas with Fire spells as well as the Block panel. Success is easier if Roxas is level 40 and above, with plenty of panel slots available. Start casting Fire spells indiscriminately, and then block the Deserters' counterattacks. Consume a Hi-Ether if necessary, then continue launching fireballs with abandon.

DAY 71

Challenge Missions are added to the Holo-Missions menu, allowing you to replay missions in which you've acquired an Ordeal Badge with new objectives under special restrictions in order to win Challenge Sigils.

Speak to the Moogle, who explains that you can now redeem Challenge Sigils and Mission Crowns earned in Mission Mode for valuable prizes. Simply visit the Moogle after acquiring either and choose the "Redeem" option. The Moogle automatically awards prizes based on how many Challenge Sigils or Mission Crowns you've collected.

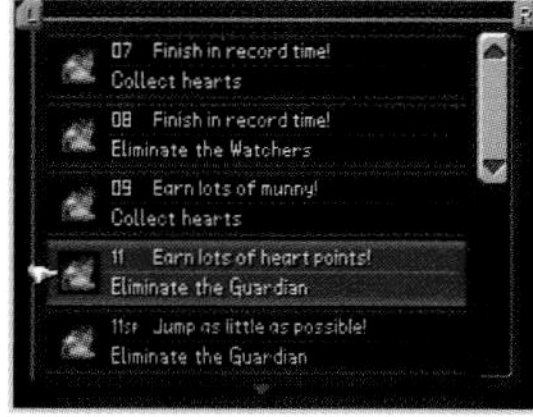

When selecting Holo-Missions to replay, you may now choose Normal Missions or Challenge Missions with extra objectives and restrictions.

The Moogle displays the next three prizes you'll receive for redeeming your Challenge Sigils or Mission Crowns.

*Speak to Xigbar to receive a **Hi-Potion**.*

DESTROY THE SHADOW GLOBS

MISSION 20

BONUSES!

Heart Points	x2.20	Munny	x6.60	EXP	1.22

RANK Novice

ENEMIES

SHADOW	LVL 8
DROP	Potion

POSSESSOR	LVL 8
DROP	Potion

WATCHER	LVL 3
DROP	Ether

GUARDIAN	LVL 8
DROP	Aerial Tech

SHADOW GLOB	LVL 8
DROP	—

REWARDS

Clear Bonuses	Random Bonuses
Iron	Fire Recipe (10%)
Ether	Blazing Shard (15%)
Guard Unit(L) (MG)	Moonstone (15%)
—	Potion (40%)
—	Ether (20%)

FESTERING EVIL

Shadow Globs are easy to destroy, but sometimes they're difficult to reach...

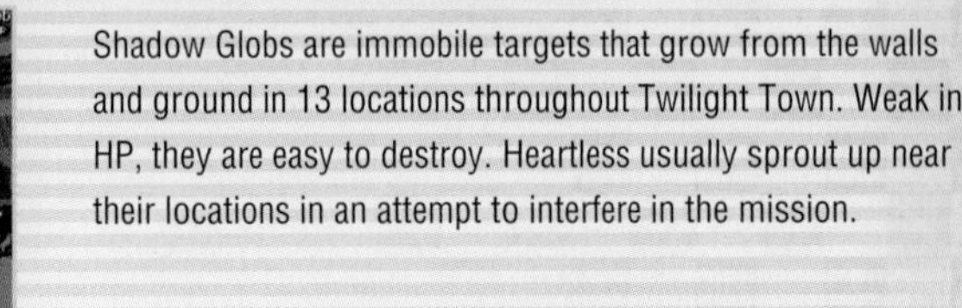

Shadow Globs are immobile targets that grow from the walls and ground in 13 locations throughout Twilight Town. Weak in HP, they are easy to destroy. Heartless usually sprout up near their locations in an attempt to interfere in the mission.

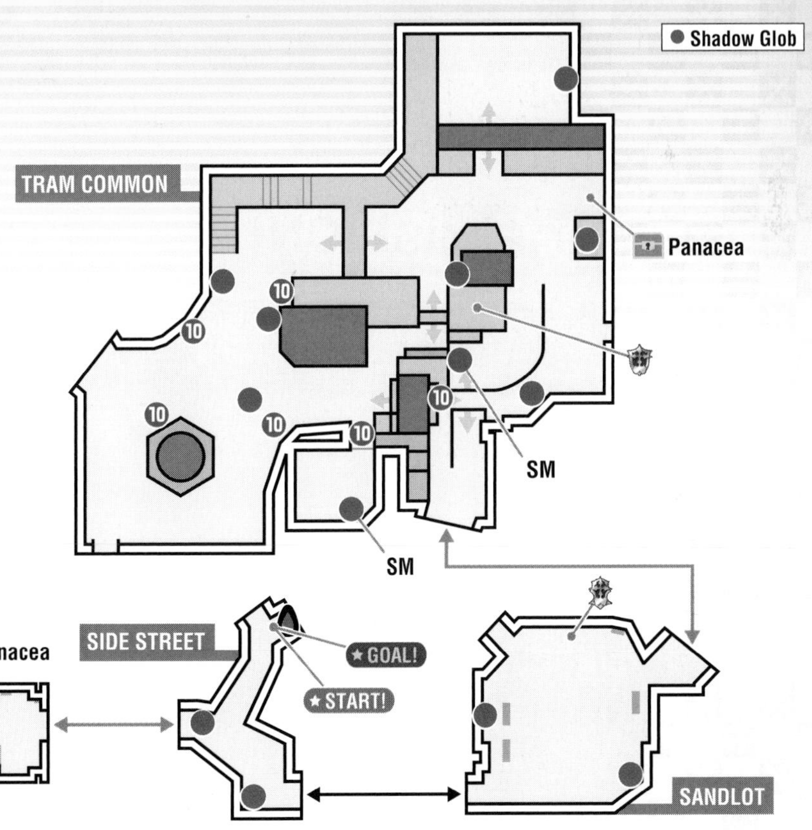

*SM: Appear in Story Mode only, not Mission Mode

While Shadow Globs in the Side Street and Sandlot areas are easily destroyed, many in the Tram Common area are not so easy to reach.

The Shadow Glob high on the wall in the northwest corner can be destroyed with Fire spells cast from the raised ledge on the opposite side.

The Shadow Glob on the slanted blue roof of the easternmost building can be destroyed by casting spells from the green rooftop to the north once you level up your magic.

The one attached to the west side of the tall central building can be destroyed by jumping from the ledge and immediately attacking the glob.

CHALLENGE MISSION

Objective: Finish in record time!

Restrictions: Take 20% more damage, enemy level +4

Rewards

Sigils Acquired	Clear Time
3	01:20:00 or less
2	01:20:01 - 02:10:00
1	02:10:01 - 02:30:00

Equip Roxas with nothing but Fire spells, using Doublecast③, Triplecast③ and Quadcast③ panels to give him dozens of castings. Also, equip Hi-Ethers and the Haste panel, which can be obtained by redeeming 10 Challenge Sigils at the Moogle shop. Instead of attacking Shadow Globs, move to central locations as shown on the map here and cast Fire spells to wipe them out. Ensure that other Heartless don't get in the way by using lock on.

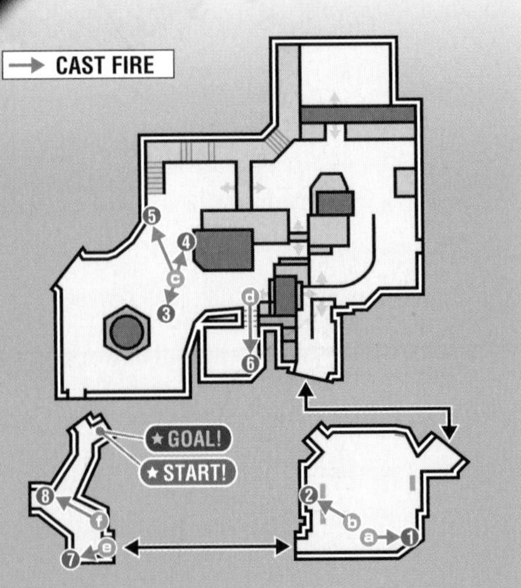

DAY 72

COLLECT HEARTS

MISSION 21

BONUSES!

Heart Points	x2.25	Munny	x6.75	EXP	1.25

RANK Novice

ENEMIES

SHADOW LVL 8
DROP Potion

SCARLET TANGO LVL 8
DROP Blazing Shard

DIRE PLANT LVL 4
DROP Potion

POSSESSOR LVL 8
DROP Potion

LOUDMOUTH LVL 8
DROP Hi-Potion

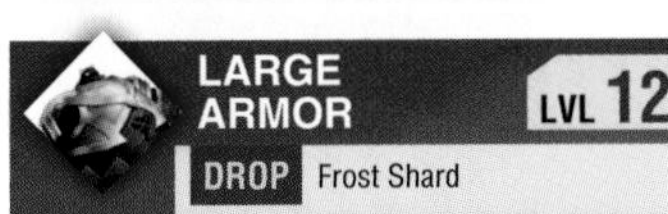
LARGE ARMOR LVL 12
DROP Frost Shard

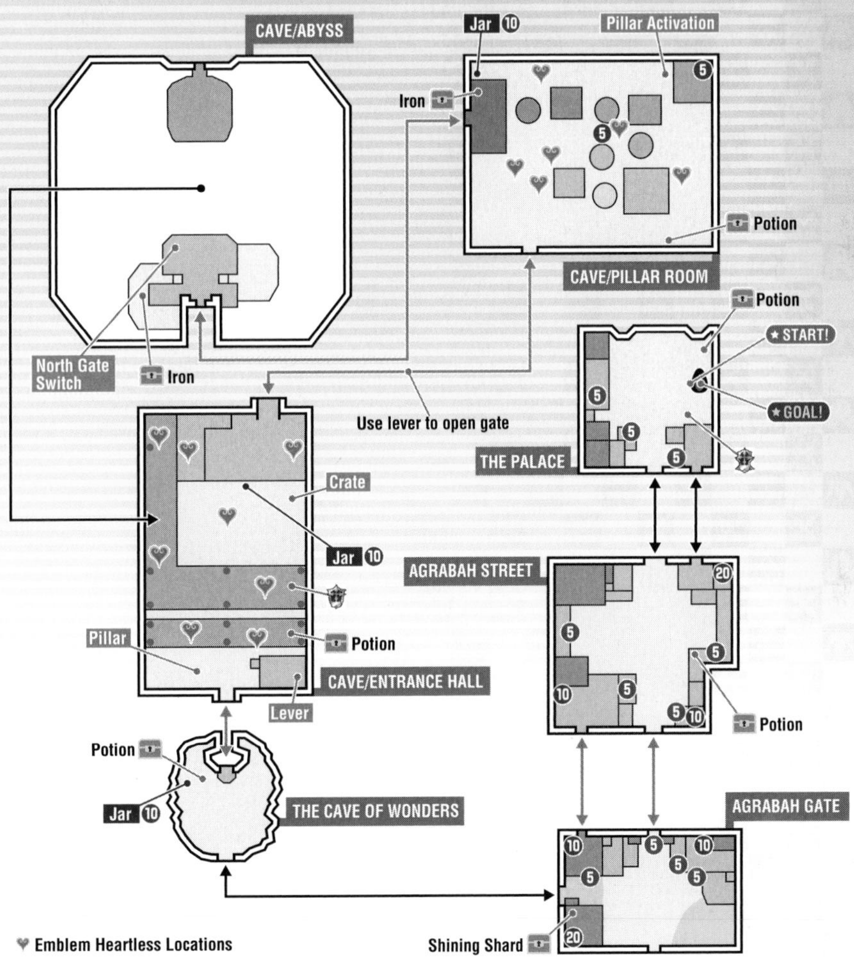

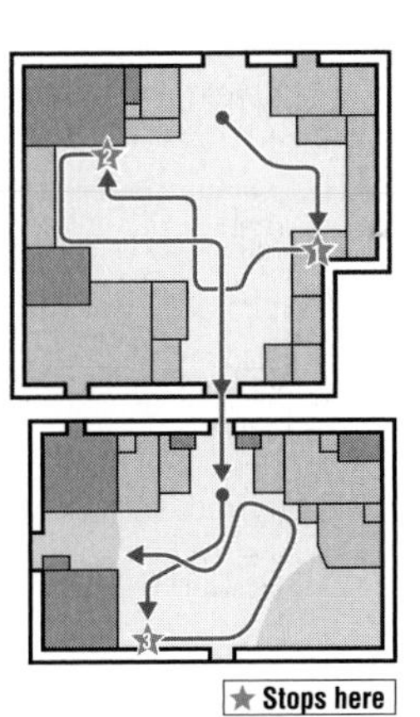

REWARDS	
Clear Bonuses	Random Bonuses
Cure	Shining Shard (20%)
Magic LV2(4)	Iron (20%)
Cure (MG)	Potion (30%)
—	None (30%)

TAIL THE SUSPECT

Open the chest near the dark corridor to obtain a **Potion**. To acquire the nearby **Ordeal Badge**, you must proceed south to the Agrabah Street area, ascend to the upper doorway and return to the Palace area, drop over the side and collect it on the way down.

Make sure Pete stays in your vision zone, while simultaneously staying out of his.

However, Pete is roaming the Agrabah Street area, looking for a hidden doorway. You must keep Pete in view (marked by the blue cone-shaped pattern surrounding Roxas's feet) without falling within his sights (the red area beneath Pete). If he gets out of range for two seconds or you fall within his, you must start over.

As he goes to examine the east wall, stay behind him to his left. When he reaches the northwest wall, stay behind him to his right. Then follow him to the Gate area.

Prepare for Pete's turns by moving to the side opposite where he's going to turn next.

As he examines the south wall, stay behind him to his right. Remain to his side as he makes a short circle and heads toward the west wall, where the secret door is located.

Don't let Pete fall outside of your vision cone for more than two seconds, or you have to start over!

THE CAVE OF WONDERS

Ransack the outdoor area, then jump into the tiger head entrance to the Cave of Wonders. Move around the Entrance Hall to trigger the appearance of Heartless and defeat them to collect hearts.

The Emblem Heartless needed to complete this mission finally appear inside the Cave of Wonders.

Move the crate alongside the tall fixed stone near the entrance.

Once the lower level is cleared out, examine the floor beneath the tall stone to the left of the entrance. As the grooves on the floor indicate, you can move the stone by striking it. However, you must first move the switch on the raised level in the southeast corner. To reach it, move to the north end and strike the crate to move it south. Place it beside the immobile tall stone next to the ledge, then jump to the top. Strike the switch to open the door at the far end.

Jump on the fixed stone to reach the level where the door switch is located. Strike it to open the door on the other ledge.

Bash the lone tall stone to move it north toward the high ledge.

If you cannot move the crate away from the tall stone by the door, leave and reenter the area to reset the crate.

Drop to the ground and bash the tall stone to move it north, to the base of the high platform. Now move the crate beside it and jump from crate to stone to reach the higher level. Defeat more Heartless up here, then examine the large stone by the door before proceeding to the next area.

PILLAR ROOM

Defeat all of the Heartless on the lower level. Once the last is destroyed, a Large Armor appears. While it's upright, the best way to damage this creature is to attack its head from behind. To cast spells on the head, jump high into the air and quickly cast. Occasionally, the Large Armor falls forward and flails about. Rapidly move to the head and launch a combo, but move away when it starts to rise, because the Large Armor immediately begins a brutal retaliation.

Strike the Large Armor's head to knock it over, then unleash the combo attacks.

FULL GAUGE

Although your mission is complete, there are still more hearts to collect from Heartless hidden in the rafters of the Entrance Hall. To reach that area, strike the large square switch in the northeast corner of the Pillar Room. This causes the round pillars in the chamber to start moving up and down.

Knock down the large block to activate a mechanism in the Pillar Room.

Jump onto the central pillar, ride it to the top, and jump to the nearest square pillar. Leap from there to the next closest oscillating round pillar and so forth until you reach the high platform on the west wall.

Vault onto the round pillars as they drop to your level and ride them up to the next.

Drop to the lower ledge on the west side of the platform in the Abyss to reach a chest containing **Iron**. Now jump into the chasm. Roxas and Axel fall into the Entrance Hall, landing on the rafters. Proceed across the upper level, destroying more Heartless without falling over the side. Follow the L-shaped path over to the **Unity Badge**, then bound to the south platform and open the chest containing a **Potion**. Defeat another set of Heartless on this platform, drop to the Entrance Hall below, and return to the Palace area to RTC.

Leap into the Abyss to reach the platforms at the top of the Entrance Room.

Don't fall while battling Heartless in the rafters, or else you'll have to ride the pillars again.

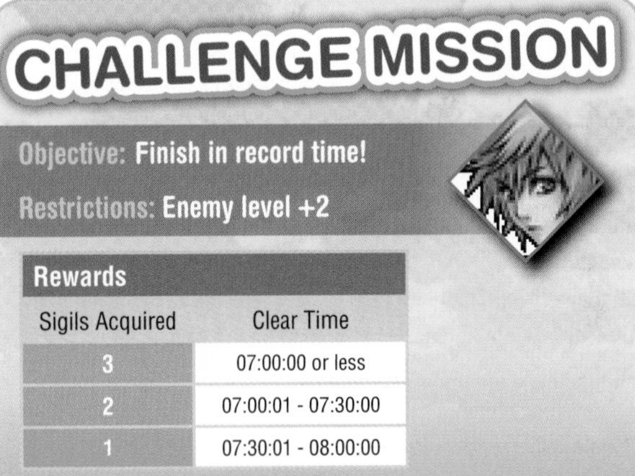

CHALLENGE MISSION

Objective: **Finish in record time!**

Restrictions: **Enemy level +2**

Rewards

Sigils Acquired	Clear Time
3	07:00:00 or less
2	07:00:01 - 07:30:00
1	07:30:01 - 08:00:00

While the time limit to acquire three Challenge Sigils seems to be highly forgiving, the complex mechanics of following Pete, moving the blocks around in the Cave/Entrance Hall area and jumping between oscillation platforms really slow down a player who is ill-equipped. The blocks and moving platforms are easier to deal with when a High Jump③ panel is equipped with two High Jump LV+(L) links attached. That way, you can skip moving the crate next to the tall block and also jump on high platforms before they descend all the way down.

DAY 73

Give Xaldin a Blazing Shard and he'll relinquish a **Frost Shard** in exchange.

ELIMINATE THE SERGEANT

MISSION 22

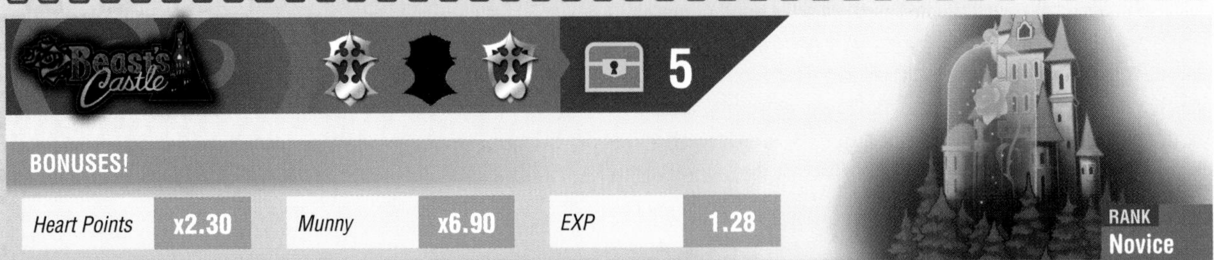

BONUSES!

Heart Points	x2.30	Munny	x6.90	EXP	1.28

ENEMIES

SHADOW LVL 8 — DROP Potion

POSSESSOR LVL 8 — DROP Potion

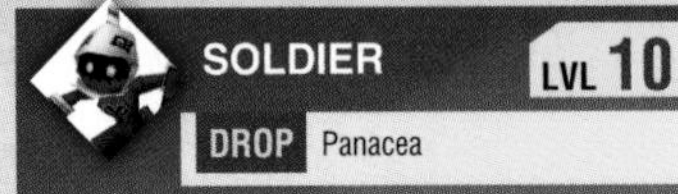

SOLDIER LVL 10 — DROP Panacea

BAD DOG LVL 10 — DROP Iron

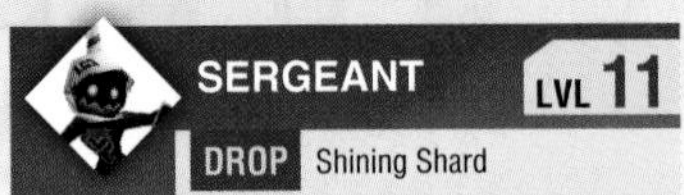

SERGEANT LVL 11 — DROP Shining Shard

REWARDS	
Clear Bonuses	Random Bonuses
Backpack	Frost Shard (25%)
Shining Shard	Ether (40%)
Shining Shard	None (35%)

EXTERIOR DECORATOR

Move forward, defeat the Heartless, and open the chests in the Bridge area. Proceed to the wide-open Courtyard, where three of the statues are out of order. Clear any foes from the area and then strike the three statues to move them each toward the closest pale circle on the ground. When all three statues are stuck in place, a secret door opens to the left of the locked main entrance.

Knock the three loose statues back into place in the Courtyard.

Heartless appear near every statue, hoping to interfere with your task.

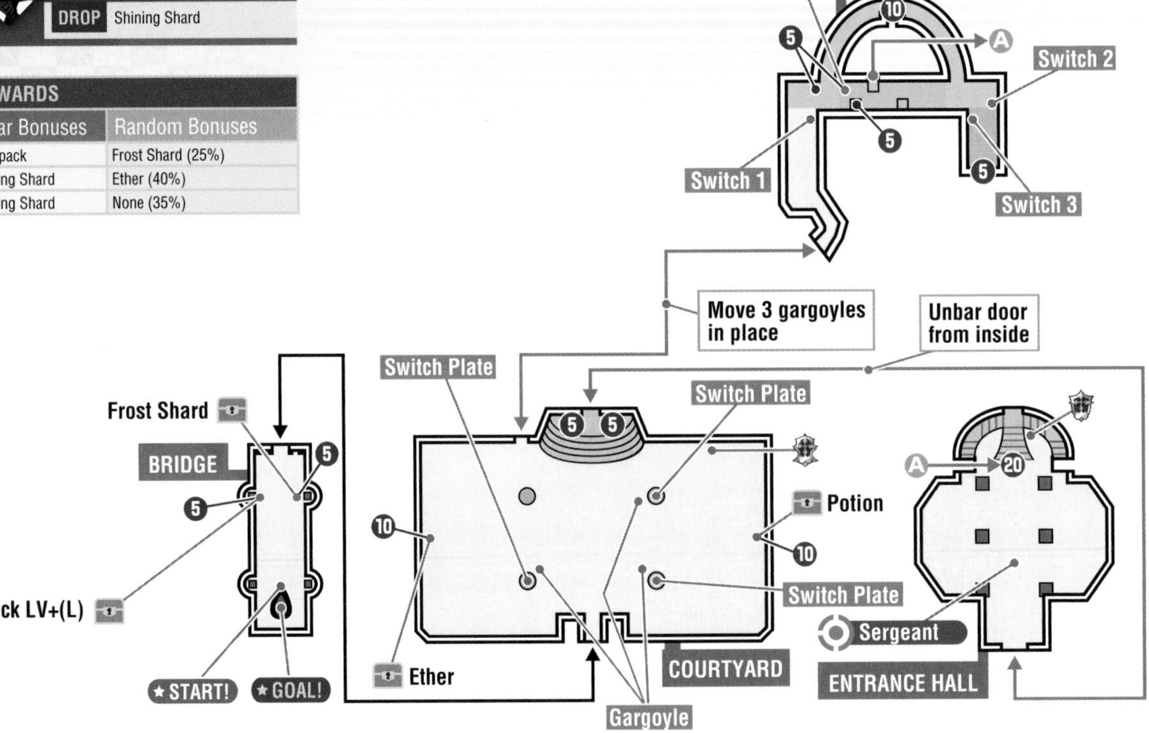

CORRIDOR SEGMENTS

Defeat Soldier Heartless in the passageway, then examine the switch on the wall to raise the divider. Follow the curved segment to the far end, then throw the red switch to open another short segment. Defeat the Soldiers appearing there before using the blue switch to open the central segment.

Examine the wall switches to open new segments of the Upper Level.

Move between the stationary crates and defeat more Heartless. Collect the **Hi-Potion** from the chest at the far end, then jump onto the central crate on the north wall. Step through the fissure here and Roxas then drops into the main Entrance Hall. Move toward the doorway to encounter the Sergeant.

Clear out the zone between the crates.

Jump onto the central crate and move toward the fissure in the wall to drop to the level below.

BOSS!

SERGEANT

Fighting the Sergeant is much like dealing with an oversized Soldier. Simply avoid its spinning kick attacks and bash away at it. When finished, examine the southern door and unbar it, then return to the dark corridor and RTC.

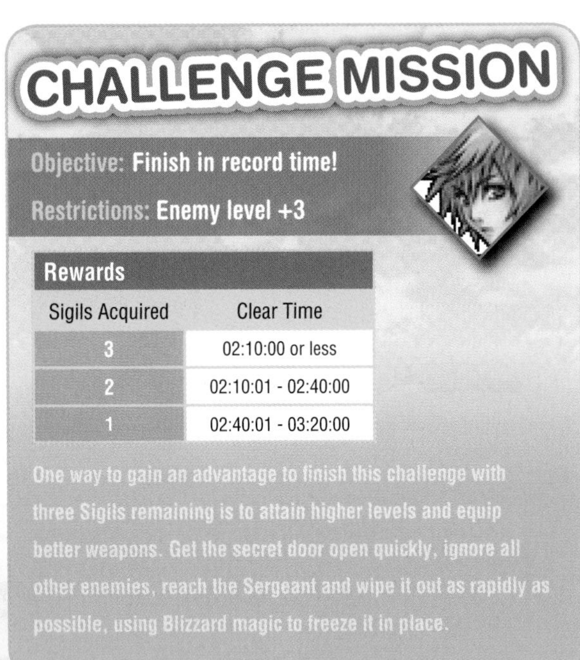

CHALLENGE MISSION

Objective: Finish in record time!

Restrictions: Enemy level +3

Rewards	
Sigils Acquired	Clear Time
3	02:10:00 or less
2	02:10:01 - 02:40:00
1	02:40:01 - 03:20:00

One way to gain an advantage to finish this challenge with three Sigils remaining is to attain higher levels and equip better weapons. Get the secret door open quickly, ignore all other enemies, reach the Sergeant and wipe it out as rapidly as possible, using Blizzard magic to freeze it in place.

DAY 74

Axel now hands over a **Hi-Ether**. Speak to Demyx, who wants Roxas to synthesize something out of two Potions. Visit the Moogle and synthesize a Hi-Potion, then return and speak to Demyx again to receive a **Combo Tech**.

When you acquire too many Potions, use synthesis to combine them into Hi-Potions.

SEARCH FOR XION

MISSION 23

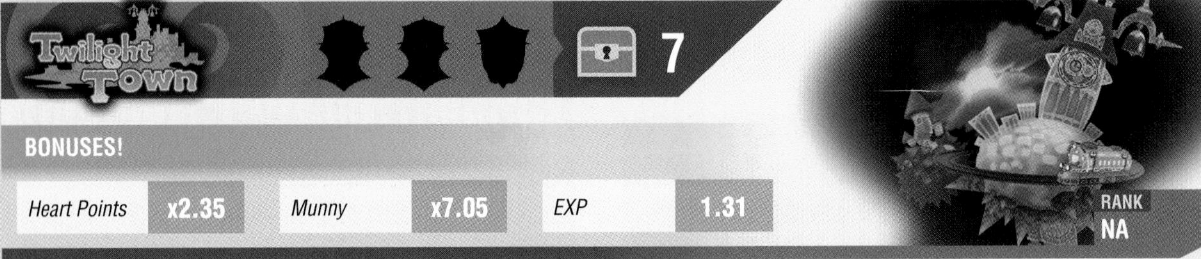

BONUSES!

Heart Points	Munny	EXP
x2.35	x7.05	1.31

ENEMIES

Enemy	LVL	DROP
SHADOW	8	Potion
WATCHER	3	Ether
YELLOW OPERA	10	Moonstone
CYMBAL MONKEY	11	Iron
POISON PLANT	8	Moonstone
ZIP SLASHER	48	Combo Tech
BULKY VENDOR	10	—
VEIL LIZARD	14	Iron

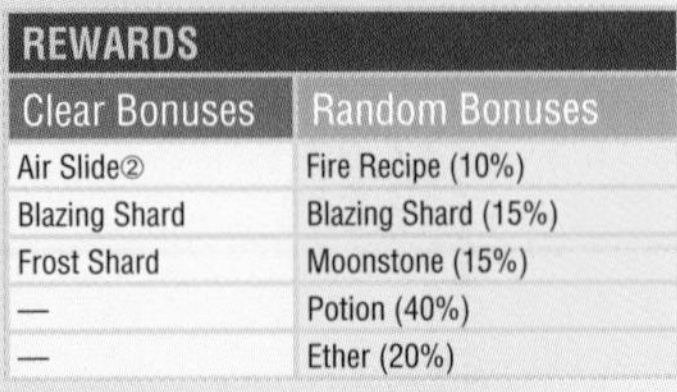

REWARDS	
Clear Bonuses	Random Bonuses
Air Slide②	Fire Recipe (10%)
Blazing Shard	Blazing Shard (15%)
Frost Shard	Moonstone (15%)
—	Potion (40%)
—	Ether (20%)

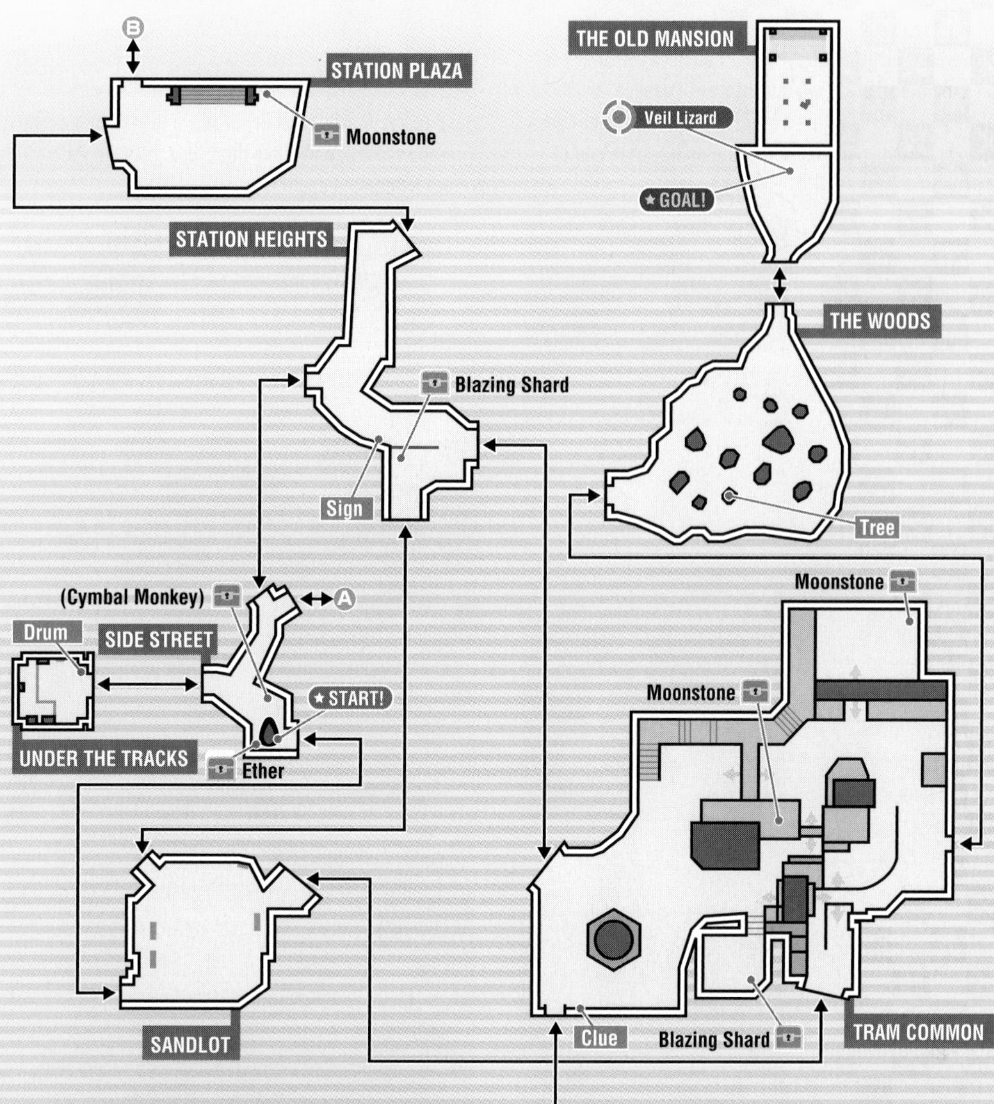

DETECTIVE TIME!

Xion has gone missing. Her last mission was to take out a giant Heartless in Twilight Town. Roxas and Axel must search for clues about the giant Heartless in order to find it, hopefully along with their missing comrade.

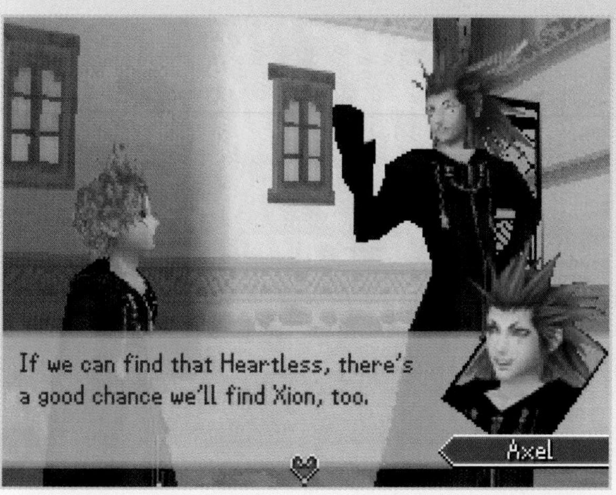

Roxas shares his worries about Xion with Axel.

B
UNDERGROUND PASSAGE
A
Clue
Cure Recipe
Gate down until Sandlot event
TUNNEL

Visit the Sandlot, where Olette and Hayner talk about a noise they heard inside the Tunnel. Before entering the Underground Passage, brush up on your Twilight Town trivia by taking a good look around town. Take special note of what is said on the bulletin board at the south end of Station Heights.

Olette and Hayner drop important clues at the Sandlot.

Check the bulletin at the bottom of Station Heights to learn an important clue.

DISAPPOINTMENT

Roxas and Axel don't find any Heartless inside the Tunnel. Instead, they find Pence. After speaking to him, return to the Sandlot. Olette and Hayner are still talking, but this time they reveal that Pence has a "usual spot" where he likes to hide things.

Pence is the only monster haunting the tunnel below Twilight Town.

The usual spot referred to is "Under the Tracks," the room just off Side Street. Visit that area now and search the room to find lots of clues. Examine the green oil drum in the corner to find a map full of notes.

Check the oil drum in the room near Side Street to find the next important clue.

PENCE'S QUIZ

Correctly answer Pence's trivia questions to learn a valuable clue.

Return to the Tunnel to ask Pence about his notes. He refuses to answer Roxas's and Axel's questions unless they can answer the following questions. In return for the correct answers, Pence talks about a tree in the woods that shakes.

AT THE SOUND OF THE SHAKING TREE

Head to the Woods (east of Tram Commons) and strike the center tree on the south row. Roxas and Axel hear something and quickly run off toward the Old Mansion. Follow the noise to encounter the Veil Lizard.

Strike the tree on the south side of the Woods area to shake something out of it.

BOSS!

VEIL LIZARD

The Veil Lizard is capable of turning invisible. If struck while invisible, it becomes visible again. Thus, your main objective is to attack it frequently enough to prevent it from vanishing. While invisible, it can perform a tongue lash attack that is quite devastating. But successfully blocking this attack stuns the Veil Lizard, rendering it vulnerable to several full combos.

After casting all your spells at it from a distance, move in close and bash it. Watch its movements carefully in the process, though. When it begins to twist, simply roll or jump away before it spins and hits Roxas with its tail.

DAY 75-79

During this four to five day period, Xion becomes your partner for all missions. Speak to her to receive a **Panacea** for good luck. If you completed all missions for days 51 to 54 (Missions 16-19), speak to Axel twice to unlock Mission 28.

Other members of Organization XIII may require Roxas to fulfill certain criteria before they allow him to undertake extra missions.

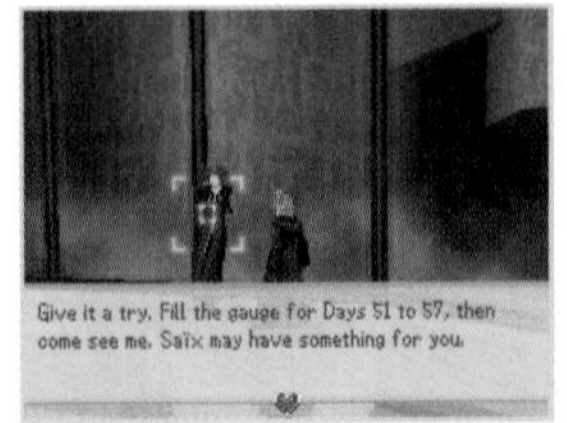

INVESTIGATE THE CAVE

MISSION 24

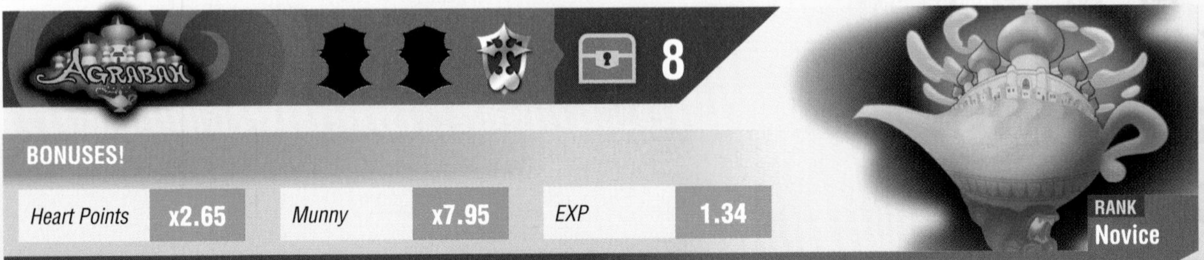

BONUSES!

Heart Points	x2.65	Munny	x7.95	EXP	1.34

RANK Novice

ENEMIES

SCARLET TANGO LVL 8 DROP Blazing Shard

LOUDMOUTH LVL 8 DROP Hi-Potion

FIRE PLANT LVL 9 DROP Blazing Shard

PETE LVL 14 DROP —

REWARDS	
Clear Bonuses	Random Bonuses
Blizzard	Shining Shard (20%)
Frost Shard	Iron (20%)
Frost Shard	Potion (30%)
—	None (30%)

FURTHER INTO THE CAVE

During this reconnaissance mission, there's nothing to investigate outside of the Cave of Wonders so head south to the Agrabah Gate area and enter the secret door. Jump onto the high north ledge in the Entrance Hall and examine the brown stone near the door to the Pillar Room. Xion fits a gem into the stone, raising three objects in the cave and triggering the first breakthrough.

Xion holds the key to unlocking new areas in Agrabah.

THE BURNING BLOCKS

Enter the Pillar Room and strike the switch in the northeast corner to activate the pillars. Jump across the pillars until you reach the northeast corner, then leap over to the corner platform and examine the object Xion raised. Strike the object to ignite it.

Ignite the three blocks in order according to the number of openings on their sides.

Continue crossing the pillar tops to reach the Abyss. The raised object in this area has three openings on each side; it will not ignite when struck. Instead, you must ignite the object with two marks first! Jump into the Abyss so that Roxas and Xion land on the upper levels of the Entrance Hall. Strike the object with two openings on each side to ignite it, collect the items on this level, then drop into the Entrance Hall.

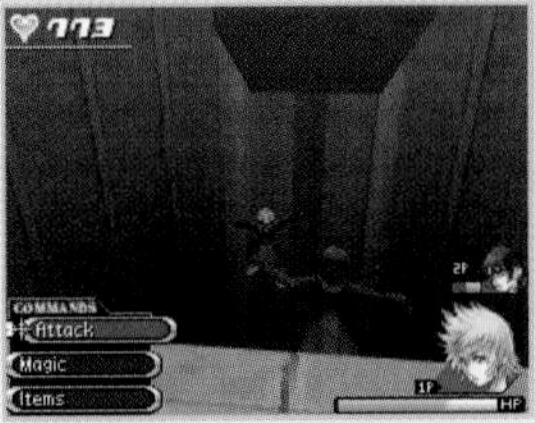

Jump into the Abyss to reach the second block switch located in the upper Entrance Hall.

Roxas notices some construction defects.

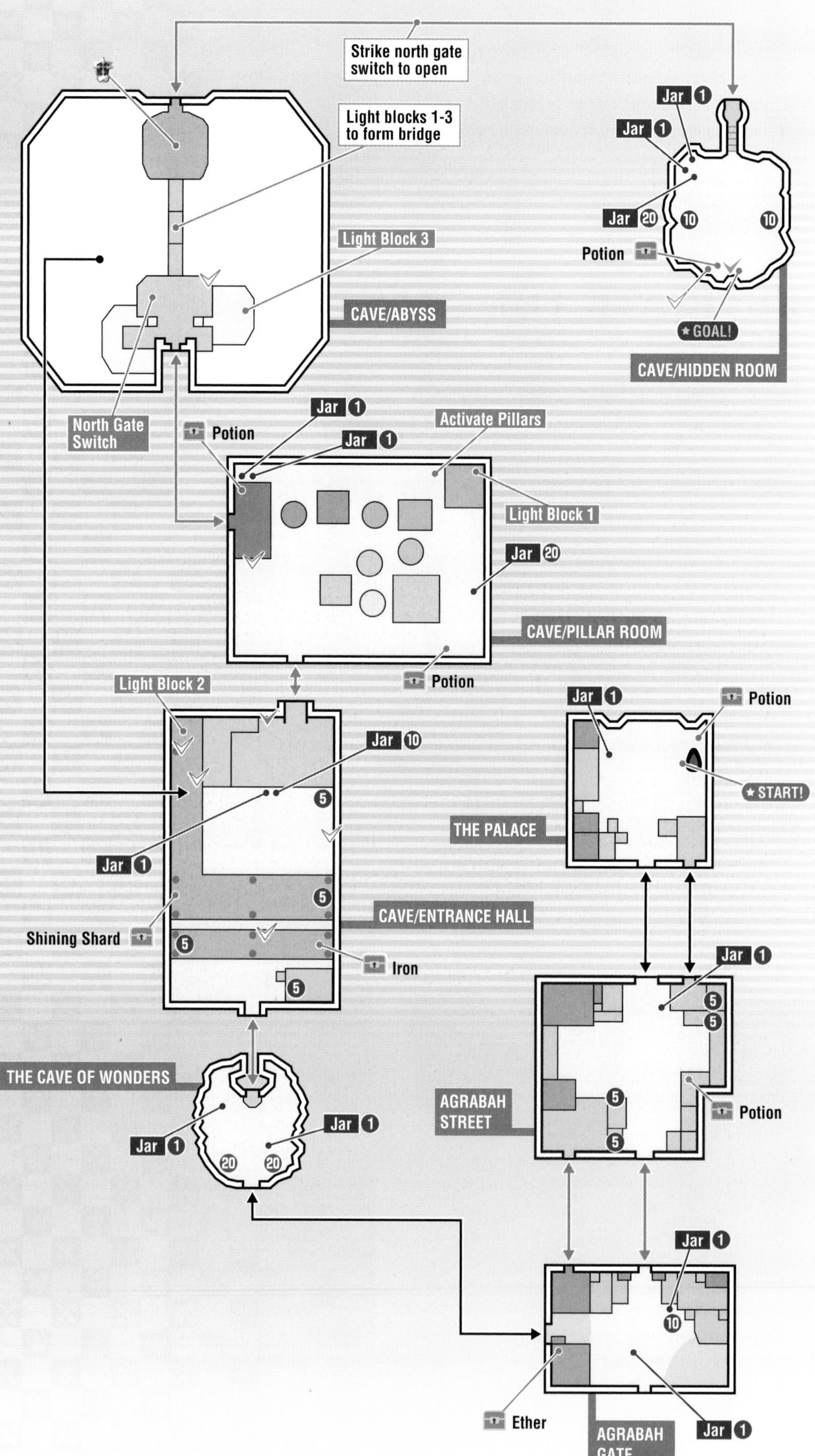
Strike north gate switch to open
Light blocks 1-3 to form bridge
Light Block 3
CAVE/ABYSS
North Gate Switch
Jar 1
Jar 1
Jar 20
10
10
Potion
GOAL!
CAVE/HIDDEN ROOM
Potion
Jar 1
Jar 1
Activate Pillars
Light Block 1
Jar 20
CAVE/PILLAR ROOM
Potion
Light Block 2
Jar 10
5
Jar 1
5
CAVE/ENTRANCE HALL
Shining Shard
5
Iron
5
Jar 1
Potion
START!
THE PALACE
Jar 1
5
5
THE CAVE OF WONDERS
Jar 1
Jar 1
20
20
AGRABAH STREET
5
5
Potion
Jar 1
10
Ether
AGRABAH GATE
Jar 1

Return to the Abyss and strike the object with three openings on each side. A series of platforms rises, connecting to the upper level in the Abyss. Strike the wheel to open the north gate, then jump across the platforms and enter the Hidden Room.

Strike the block with three openings on each side to raise platforms over the Abyss.

Hit the wheel near the entrance to open the gate above. Go into the gate before it closes!

Examine the statue at the back of the room to trigger the final breakthrough, filling the Mission Gauge. However, Pete stumbles upon the two and decides to take matters in his own hands!

Searching the statue at the back of the Hidden Room completes the mission, but there's one last problem to attend to...

PETE

Standing at the sidelines casting spells, Xion can take over this battle if you can keep Pete distracted. Circle around him, remaining close but at arm's length, capable of rolling away if he swings a punch in your direction. Whack him with a single hit, then continue circling before he counterattacks. Attempting to string together a combo just gives him the opportunity to cause serious damage.

COLLECT ORGANIZATION EMBLEMS

MISSION 25

ENEMIES

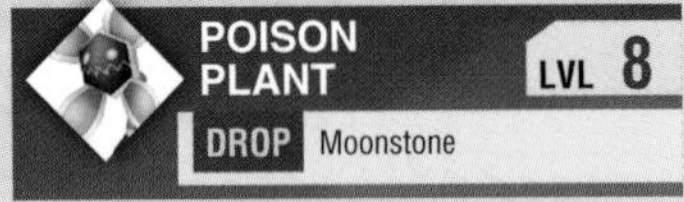

POISON PLANT LVL 8
DROP Moonstone

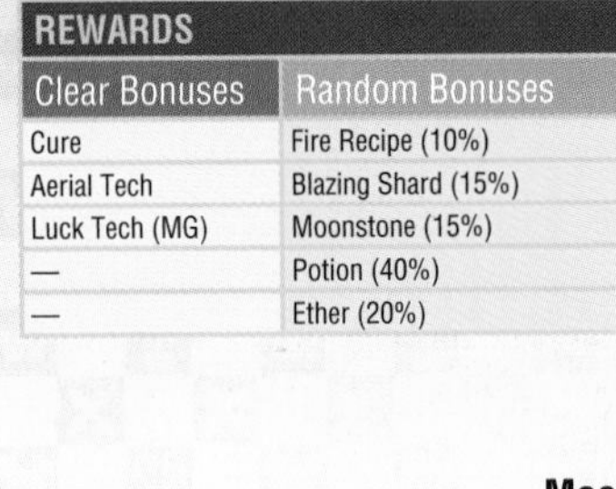

REWARDS	
Clear Bonuses	Random Bonuses
Cure	Fire Recipe (10%)
Aerial Tech	Blazing Shard (15%)
Luck Tech (MG)	Moonstone (15%)
—	Potion (40%)
—	Ether (20%)

SETTLE FOR SECOND BEST

Mission 25 is arguably the toughest emblem-collecting mission in the game. To fill the Mission Gauge 100%, you must collect all 24 emblems while rings encircle them. Due to the heights in the Tram Common area, some of the emblems are unreachable without both High Jump LV3 and Glide LV3 or better. So satisfy yourself that you'll only fill the Mission Gauge to the goal line during your first attempt and try again later.

Grab the emblem near the starting point quickly, before its ring disappears.

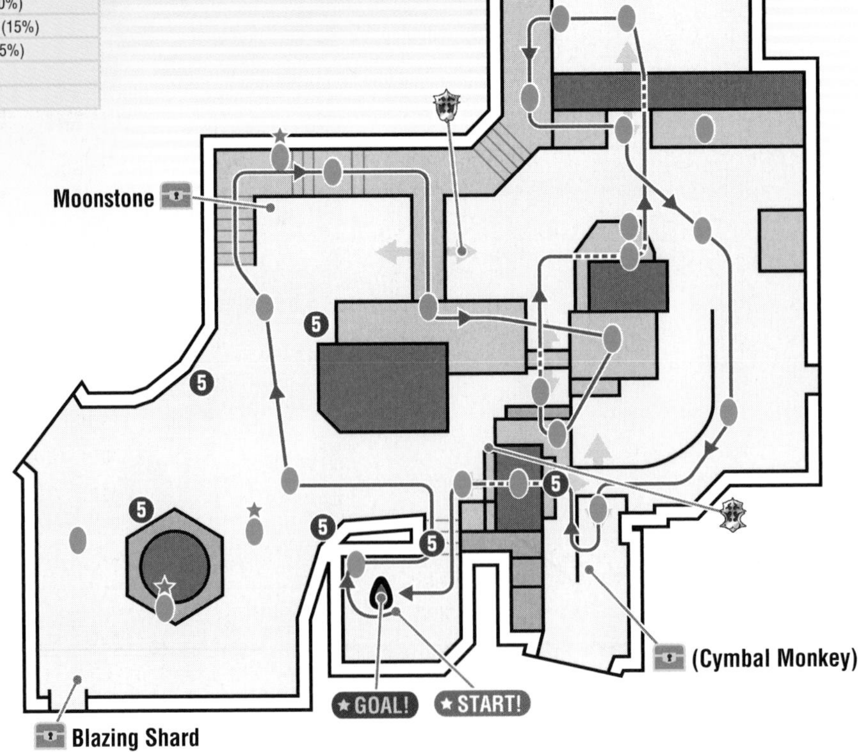

● Organization Emblem
→ Challenge Mission Route

Acquire 16 to 19 emblems regardless of whether their rings are showing to fill the Mission Gauge to the goal line. Pause your game and carefully study the route on the map in this section. The blue lines indicate how to collect 18 of the emblems rather quickly, without the High Jump or Glide abilities. Equipping Air Slide helps Roxas navigate some of the high central rooftops, but it isn't necessary.

Follow the route drawn on the map to quickly collect the necessary number of items.

BACK FOR THE REST

Replay the mission after finishing the game, but this time with the High Jump LV3 and Glide LV3 abilities. After collecting the first emblem near the starting point, exit the south enclosure and defeat the enemies to reinstate the rings around the other emblems. Then head west and collect the next one on the route, before deviating further west. Defeat the enemies that appear, and then collect the emblem on the far side of the hexagonal tower. Return to the route and continue north, vanquishing more enemies to reinstate the rings along the way. Avoid defeating any other enemies, because you'll need them later to bring back the rings.

When trying to fill the Mission Gauge, change the route to collect additional emblems off the usual path. Defeat nearby enemies to make rings reappear.

While climbing out of the northeast enclosure, glide southeast to grab the emblem on the balcony at the back of the green building, then fly northeast to collect the one on the slanted green roof. Quickly backtrack to the gap and drop down to collect the emblem hovering just below. Continue to follow the route by referencing the map in this section.

Glide between rooftops and balconies in the northeast corner to collect more emblems.

After completing the route, return to the rooftops in the center of the area. Defeat some Yellow Operas on the "bridge" spanning the north to center area, then clamber to the ledge on the far right, high jump and glide west and south to the lower side of the hexagonal tower to grab the two emblems before their rings expire.

Jump from the corner of the high ledge and fly toward the hexagonal tower.

Collect two emblems by flying around the south side of the hexagonal southwest tower.

Return to the central rooftops and go east to encounter a Poison Plant. Defeat the Poison Plant, then high jump and glide northwest toward the emblem high above the stairs. With High Jump LV3 and Glide LV3, you should just barely make it.

Defeat the Poison Plant on the east rooftop to make the emblem rings reappear.

Glide over and grab the emblem hovering high above the north stairs before its ring disappears.

CHALLENGE MISSION

Objective: Finish in record time!

Restrictions: Enemy level +2

Rewards

Sigils Acquired	Clear Time
3	01:40:00 or less
2	01:40:01 - 02:00:00
1	02:00:01 - 02:50:00

Simply follow the route on the map in this section. Grab the first emblem near the start point, then collect the other 17 emblems along the route before their rings vanish. As soon as the Mission Gauge fills to the goal line, return to the dark corridor and RTC. Equipping an Air Slide panel accelerates your leaps between a few of the rooftop emblems.

DESTROY THE SHADOW GLOBS

MISSION 26

Agrabah — 6

BONUSES!

Heart Points	x2.65	Munny	x7.95	EXP	1.34

RANK Novice

ENEMIES

SHADOW — LVL 8 — DROP Potion

POSSESSOR — LVL 8 — DROP Potion

LOUDMOUTH — LVL 8 — DROP Hi-Potion

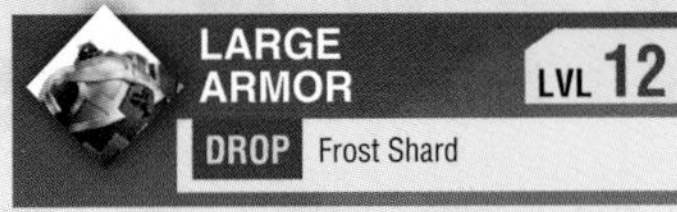

LARGE ARMOR — LVL 12 — DROP Frost Shard

SHADOW GLOB — LVL 11 — DROP —

REWARDS	
Clear Bonuses	Random Bonuses
Fire Recipe	Shining Shard (20%)
Shining Shard	Iron (20%)
Fire (MG)	Potion (30%)
—	None (30%)

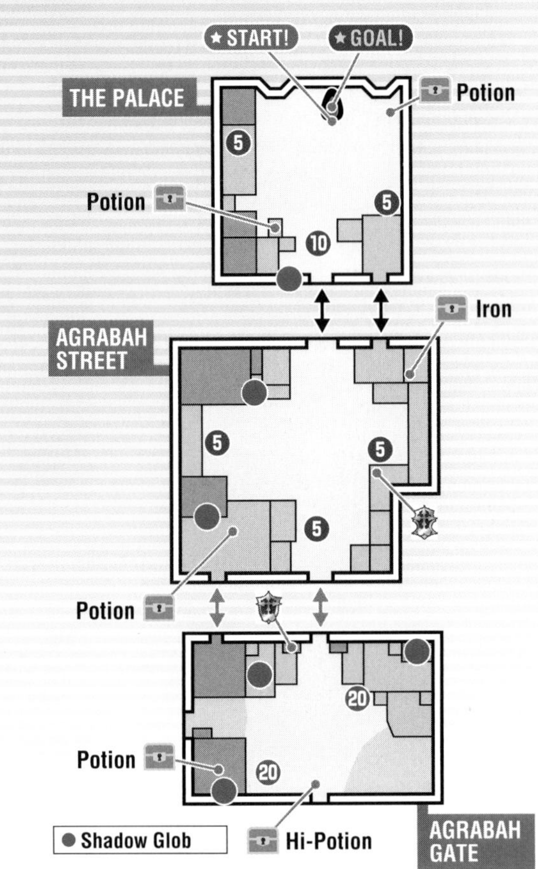

SLIME HUNT

Use Fire spells to dispose of the Shadow Glob positioned high on the south wall in the Palace area. After eliminating all the Shadow Globs within reach, knock down a crate standing on a wooden tower in the Agrabah Street area and push it toward the stack by the west wall. Jump to the upper levels to eliminate the Shadow Globs positioned up high.

Knock down the crate and use it to reach the upper levels of the street area.

Vault across the window shutters in the Agrabah Gate area to reach the ***Unity Badge****.*

CHALLENGE MISSION

Objective: Jump as little as possible!

Restrictions: Level capped at 8

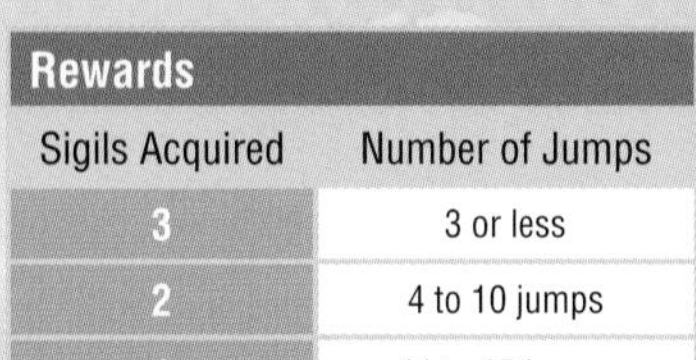

Rewards	
Sigils Acquired	Number of Jumps
3	3 or less
2	4 to 10 jumps
1	11 to 15 jumps

Since your level is capped at 8, prepare for this mission by removing an equivalent number of Level Up panels, freeing those slots to equip extra spell panels. With so many Shadow Globs positioned near the upper level and across chasms, casting Fire spells from a distance helps reduce the number of jumps required in this mission. You won't go wrong if you jump one time in each of the second two areas to reach the high Shadow Globs.

INVESTIGATE BEAST'S CASTLE

MISSION 27

ENEMIES

SHADOW LVL 8 — DROP Potion

SERGEANT LVL 11 — DROP Shining Shard

BAD DOG LVL 10 — DROP Iron

BULKY VENDOR LVL 13 — DROP Frost Shard, Aerial Tech, or Shining Shard

SOLDIER LVL 10 — DROP Panacea

SNAPPER DOG LVL 12 — DROP Ether

REWARDS	
Clear Bonuses	Random Bonuses
Iron	Frost Shard (25%)
Hi-Potion	Ether (40%)
Iron (MG)	None (35%)

ANIMAL HABITAT

Defeat the Heartless surrounding the starting point, then jump onto the crate and slide through the fissure to drop into the Entrance Hall proper. The first important recon point to examine is the claw marks to the right of the south door. The next point is in the Courtyard outside; look for the breadcrumbs on the ground to the southeast.

Examine the claw marks on the wall near the castle entrance.

Breadcrumbs in the Courtyard give Roxas a clue.

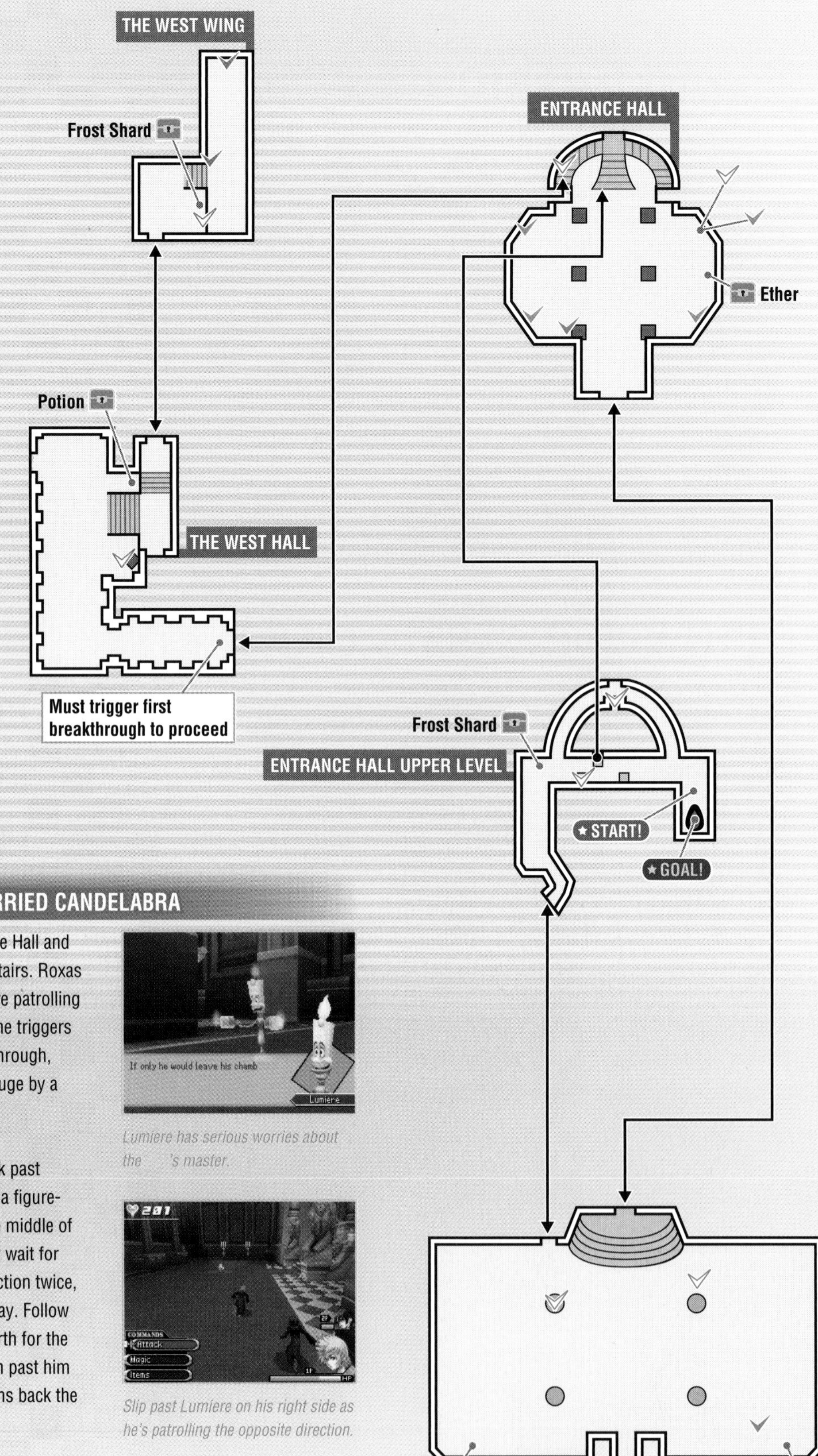

THE WORRIED CANDELABRA

Return to the Entrance Hall and ascend the western stairs. Roxas and Xion spot Lumiere patrolling the corridor. The scene triggers the first recon breakthrough, filling the Mission Gauge by a third.

Lumiere has serious worries about the ’s master.

Now it’s time to sneak past Lumiere. He walks in a figure-eight formation in the middle of the West Hall. Simply wait for him to face your direction twice, then turn the other way. Follow him until he turns north for the second time, then run past him on his right as he turns back the other way.

Slip past Lumiere on his right side as he’s patrolling the opposite direction.

THE BEAST'S LAIR

A Snapper Dog waits in the West Wing. Lock on to it and cast magic spells at it from a distance. These Heartless are extremely weak against magic, so with Xion's help you should eliminate it in no time.

Magic works best against large dogs.

Two key points to examine in the West Wing include the footprints at the top of the stairs and the door at the north end. Roxas then experiences his second breakthrough and must answer some questions for Xion, but the mission's not over yet!

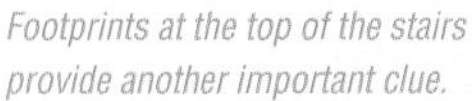

Footprints at the top of the stairs provide another important clue.

Roxas and Xion peek into Beast's room.

EXTRA CREDIT

Fill the Mission Gauge to 100% by returning to the Entrance Hall. Examine the four doors along the east and west walls to trigger another breakthrough. After answering more questions from Xion, it's time to RTC!

Roxas determines that people live in the castle by examining the four doors in the Entrance Hall.

To get back upstairs, you must go through the secret door in the Courtyard.

COLLECT HEARTS

MISSION **28**

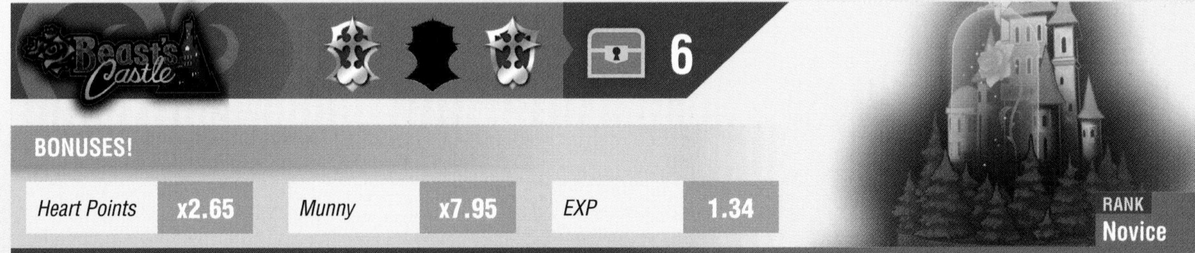

ENEMIES

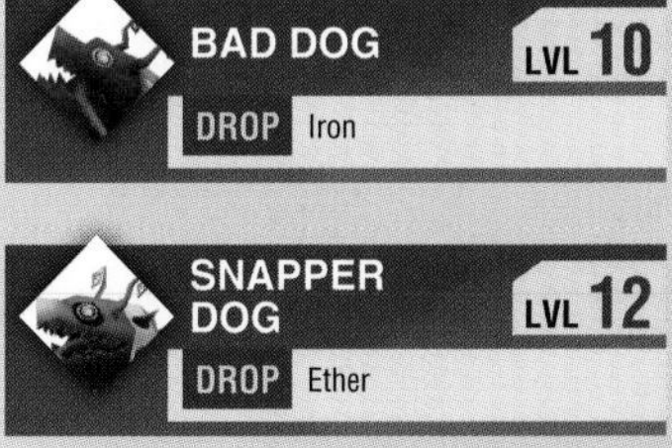

REWARDS	
Clear Bonuses	Random Bonuses
Iron	Frost Shard (25%)
Hi-Potion	Ether (40%)
Combo Tech (MG)	None (35%)

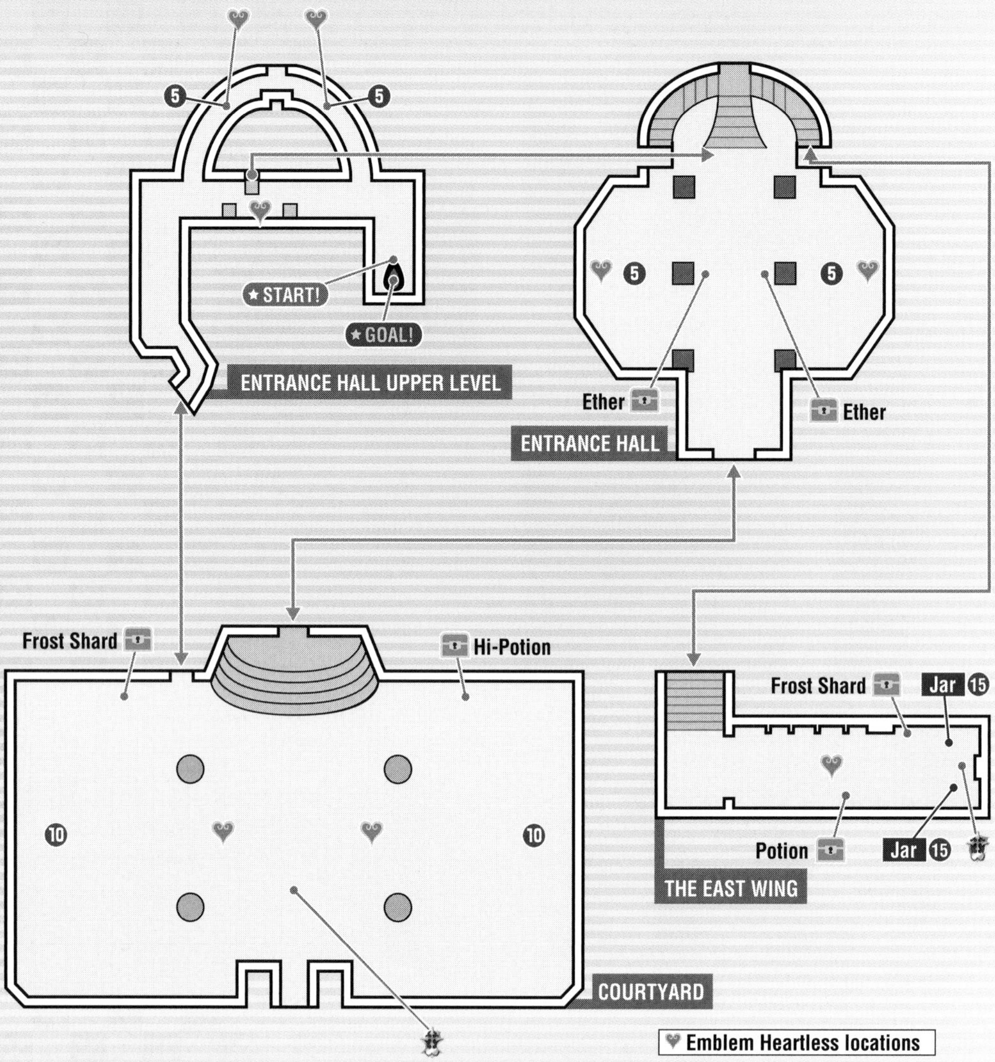

ENTRANCE HALL UPPER LEVEL
START!
GOAL!
5
5

ENTRANCE HALL
5
5
Ether
Ether

COURTYARD
Frost Shard
Hi-Potion
10
10

THE EAST WING
Frost Shard
Jar 15
Potion
Jar 15

Emblem Heartless locations

THE CAREFUL CLOCK

Opening the chests around Cogsworth is easy, as long as you wait for him to face the other direction.

A Snapper Dog appears in the East Wing; use magic to defeat it.

Navigate the castle's outer areas and defeat Heartless. Cogsworth is patrolling the Entrance Hall. If he spots you, it's no big deal; just return to the south door. Watch his simple movement pattern, learn it, and open the chests around him when he isn't looking. Heartless appear at the sides of the room just outside of his vision area.

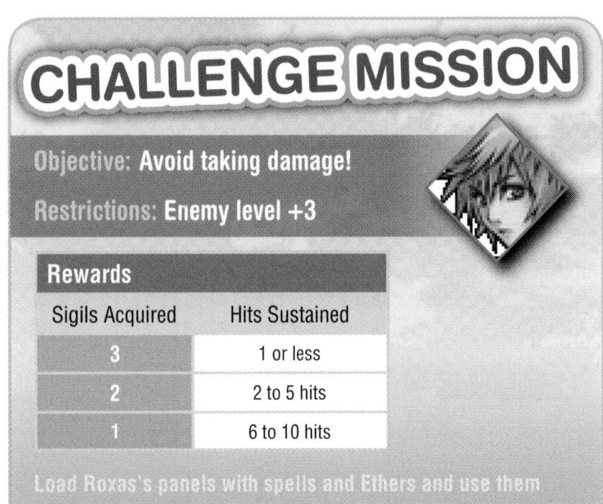

CHALLENGE MISSION

Objective: Avoid taking damage!

Restrictions: Enemy level +3

Rewards	
Sigils Acquired	Hits Sustained
3	1 or less
2	2 to 5 hits
1	6 to 10 hits

Load Roxas's panels with spells and Ethers and use them to weaken enemies from a safe distance. Then move in to deliver only the killing blow, timing your approach to avoid enemy attacks. The leveled up Dodge Roll③ should help you escape a few near misses when dealing with Sergeants and Snapper Dogs.

DAY 94

Talk to Axel twice while in the Grey Area. If you've opened more than 80 chests, he'll surrender a **Lightning Shard**. If not, replay a few missions where you missed some chests and talk to him again.

Axel's keeping count of how many chests you've opened and he rewards diligence.

ELIMINATE THE NEOSHADOWS

MISSION 29

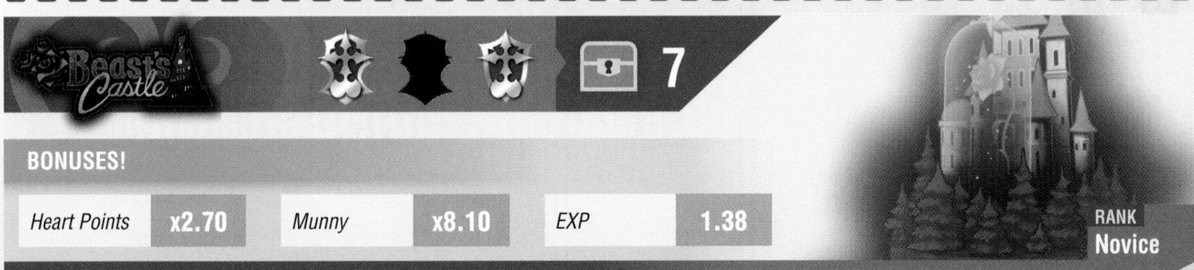

BONUSES!

Heart Points	x2.70	Munny	x8.10	EXP	1.38

RANK **Novice**

ENEMIES

SHADOW LVL 8 — DROP Potion

SNAPPER DOG LVL 12 — DROP Ether

NEOSHADOW LVL 17 — DROP Combo Tech

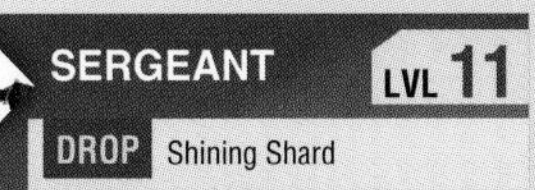

SERGEANT LVL 11 — DROP Shining Shard

CYMBAL MONKEY LVL 13 — DROP Iron

REWARDS	
Clear Bonuses	Random Bonuses
Treasure Magnet	Frost Shard (25%)
Blazing Shard	Ether (40%)
Blazing Shard	None (35%)

SPEED PATROL

When preparing for this mission, equip plenty of Blizzard and Fire panels as well as Ethers. Magic plays a key role in defeating more than just the Neoshadow. Sneaking past Lumiere in the West Hall is optional, but the **Valor Gear**② and **Combo Tech** in the chests at the southeast end make the effort worthwhile. Watch his pattern at least once; when he turns west at the closest point, move in close behind him. Creep up to him slowly as he faces east and then west again, then run around his right side. Repeat the same strategy when returning.

Observation and timing are the keys to sneaking around a patrol.

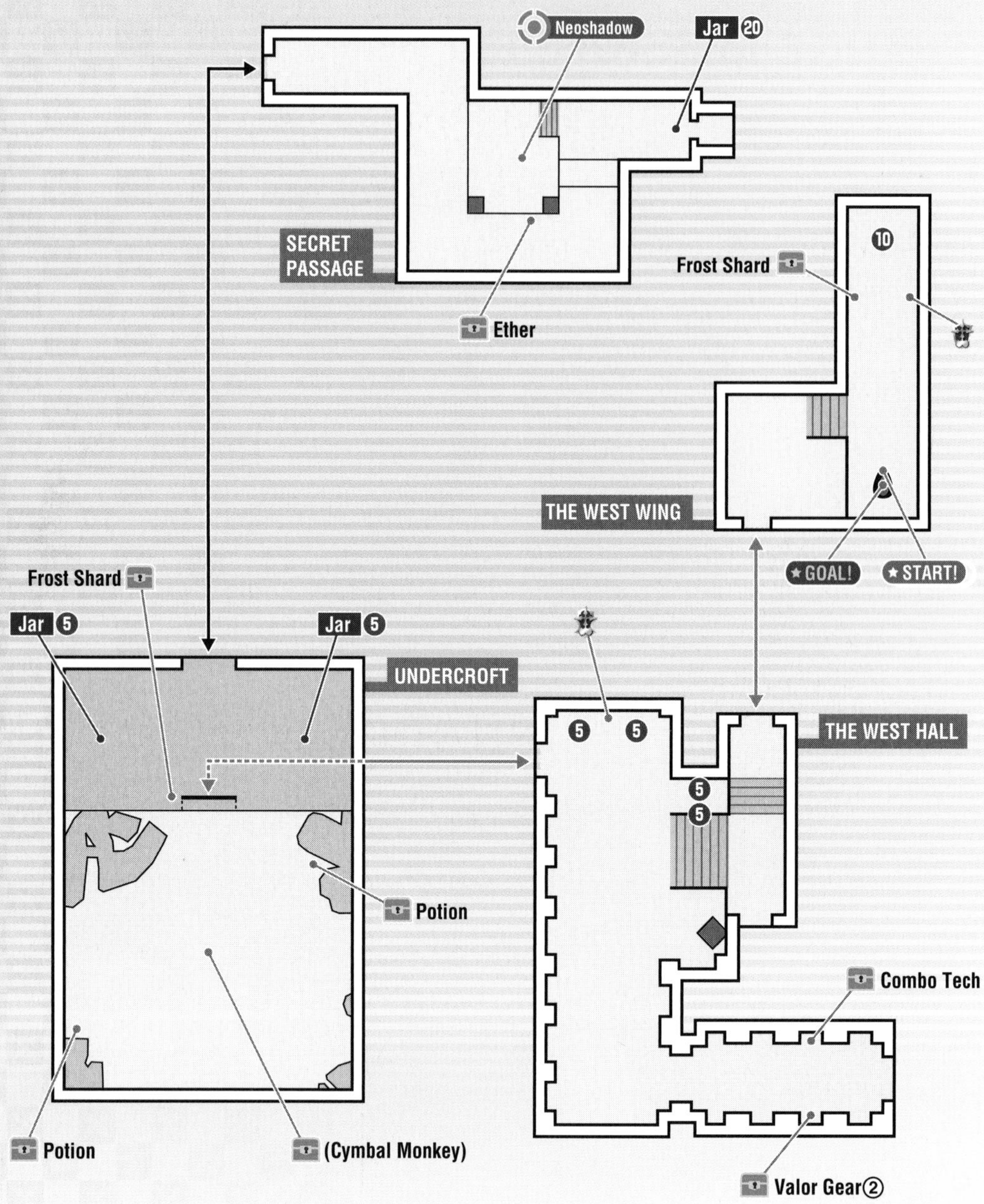

SECRET PASSAGE
Neoshadow
Jar 20
Ether
Frost Shard
10
THE WEST WING
GOAL!
START!
UNDERCROFT
Frost Shard
Jar 5
Jar 5
Potion
Potion
(Cymbal Monkey)
THE WEST HALL
5
5
5
5
Combo Tech
Valor Gear②

CYMBAL MONKEY IN THE BOX!

Cymbal Monkeys inflict the "flip-foot" status with their attacks, which reverses your movement controls!

Proceed through the northwest door in the West Hall to discover a new area. Use magic to defeat the Snapper Dog. Afterward, avoid opening the central chest unless you're dying to see what happens. A Cymbal Monkey pops out of the chest, immediately clashing its cymbals and inflicting the "flip-foot" status, which reverses your movement controls. You can either deal with the reverse controls, wait for the status to subside, or use a Panacea.

NEOSHADOW

BOSS!

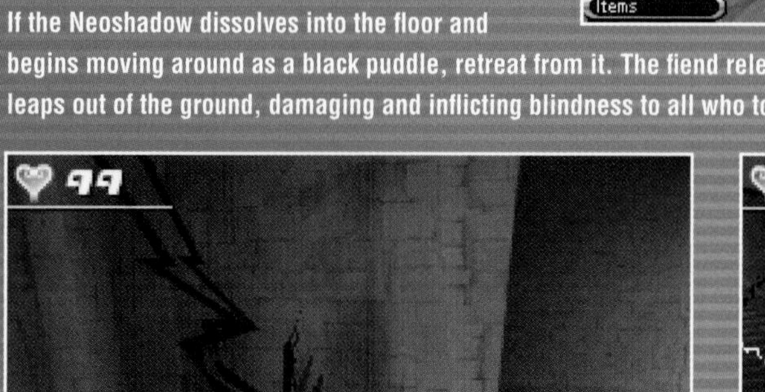

The Neoshadow is an extremely fast and vicious Heartless that is difficult to fight at close range without sustaining great injury. Target it from afar with spells, using Ethers to recharge your castings. Then adopt a "hit and run" strategy: strike it once or twice from behind, but don't combo. After doing so, run away before it claws Roxas.

If the Neoshadow dissolves into the floor and begins moving around as a black puddle, retreat from it. The fiend releases a shockwave as it leaps out of the ground, damaging and inflicting blindness to all who touch the glowing ring.

CHALLENGE MISSION

Objective: Finish in record time!

Restrictions: Level capped at 10, enemy level +2

Rewards	
Sigils Acquired	Clear Time
3	01:55:00 or less
2	01:55:01 - 02:15:00
1	02:15:01 - 02:35:00

Reduce the Level Up panels equipped until Roxas is at level 10. Fill open slots with extra castings of Fire and Blizzard. Proceed immediately to the Neoshadow's location, ignoring all other enemies. Cast Blizzard and Fire from a distance indiscriminately. Leveling up and linking a Magic Unit(L) to your weapon panel should help to completely destroy the Neoshadow and RTC on time.

DAY 95

Xaldin wants Roxas to complete the challenge version of Mission 16. Complete the challenge and score at least one Challenge Sigil to have Xaldin give Roxas an **Iron**.

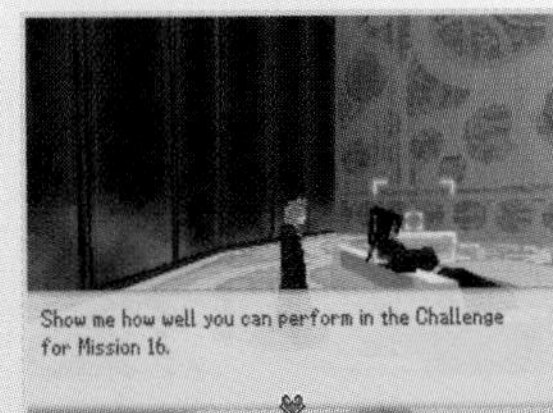

Although you can't yet reach all the Fire Plants, try your hand at Challenge Mission 16 and score at least one Sigil to please Xaldin.

COLLECT HEARTS

MISSION 30

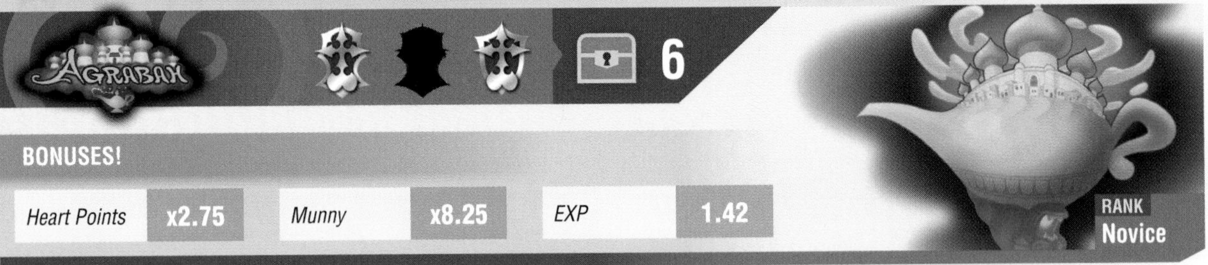

ENEMIES

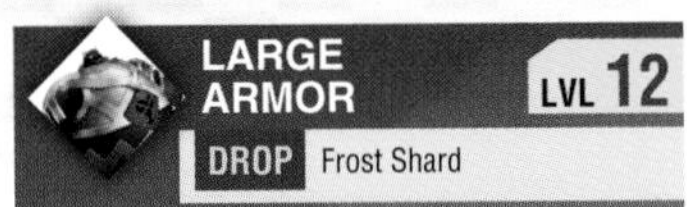

REWARDS	
Clear Bonuses	Random Bonuses
Frost Shard	Shining Shard (20%)
Hi-Potion	Iron (20%)
Ability Unit(L) (MG)	Potion (30%)
—	None (30%)

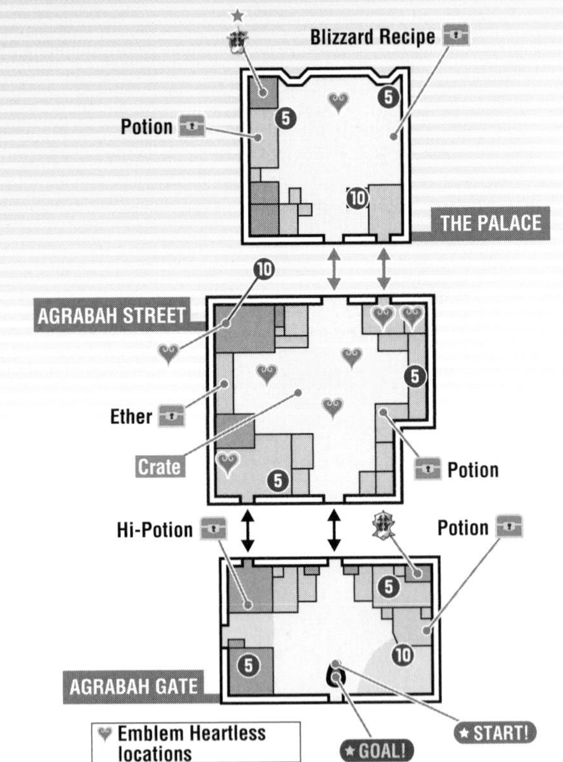

LIKE CANDY FROM A BABY

Heartless hide up high in the Agrabah Street area.

Roam from one area to the next, defeating Heartless to collect heart points. In the Agrabah Street area, knock down the crate and move it adjacent to the stack near the west wall. Use the crates to reach the higher levels and defeat more Heartless hidden up there.

The Heartless in the Palace area is a Large Armor that receives the protection of a Barrier Master. Defeat the Barrier Master to make the Large Armor vulnerable. Use magic against the Barrier Master to prevent the invincible Large Armor from KO'ing Roxas and Xion before the Barrier Master goes down.

The Barrier Master protects the Large Armor, so it must be destroyed first!

Attack the Large Armor's head to bring it down, then attack some more. But watch out for the retaliation!

DAY 96

Xaldin exchanges an **Aerial Tech** for a Moonstone, if you have one handy.

CHALLENGE MISSION

Objective: Fill up the mission gauge!

Restrictions: Take 30% more damage, enemy level +2

Rewards	
Sigils Acquired	Mission Gauge
3	100%
2	90% - 99%
1	81% - 89%

Three Challenge Sigils are easy to achieve in this mission.

ELIMINATE THE BULLY DOG

MISSION 31

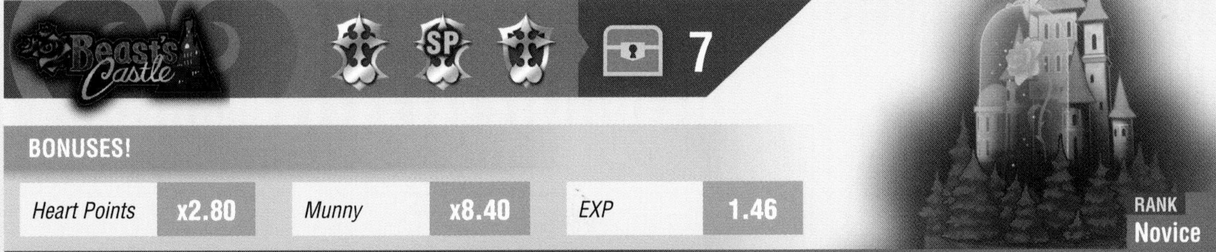

BONUSES!

Heart Points	Munny	EXP
x2.80	x8.40	1.46

RANK Novice

ENEMIES

MEGA-SHADOW LVL 10 — DROP: Combo Tech

SNAPPER DOG LVL 12 — DROP: Ether

BULKY VENDOR LVL 15 — DROP: Frost Shard, Aerial Tech, or Shining Shard

BULLY DOG LVL 14 — DROP: Shining Shard

SERGEANT LVL 11 — DROP: Shining Shard

REWARDS

Clear Bonuses	Random Bonuses
Pack Extender(4)	Frost Shard (25%)
Shining Shard	Ether (40%)
Frost Shard	None (35%)

BALLROOM
Ether
Ether
Ether
START!
20
SECRET PASSAGE
Ether
GOAL!
THE WEST HALL
20
Bully Dog
Frost Shard
Ether
20
Ether
ENTRANCE HALL

TWIG BOY TO THE RESCUE!

With Roxas wielding only a tree branch, it's time to rely on magic.

Roxas hands his Keyblade over to Xion throughout this mission, opting to fight with a mere twig. Reliance on magic is essential for completing this mission, so equip plenty of spell panels and Ethers. Even in the first area, you'll encounter vicious Snapper Dogs. Go ahead and use magic to defeat them, then recharge your castings using the **Ether** in the nearby chest.

Cogsworth patrols the south segment of the West Hall. He follows a block figure-eight pattern. Wait for him to approach and then turn away and start heading the other direction. Wait for him to face right and then left, then run past him on his right side.

Slip past Cogsworth when he reaches the far end of his route.

BULLY DOG

BOSS!

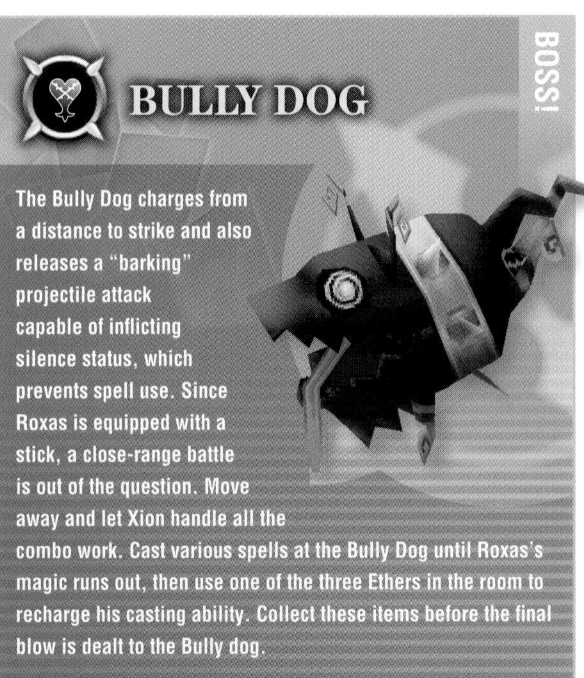

The Bully Dog charges from a distance to strike and also releases a "barking" projectile attack capable of inflicting silence status, which prevents spell use. Since Roxas is equipped with a stick, a close-range battle is out of the question. Move away and let Xion handle all the combo work. Cast various spells at the Bully Dog until Roxas's magic runs out, then use one of the three Ethers in the room to recharge his casting ability. Collect these items before the final blow is dealt to the Bully dog.

CHALLENGE MISSION

Objective: Finish in record time!

Restrictions: Level capped at 5, no recovery items

Rewards

Sigils Acquired	Clear Time
3	00:45:00 or less
2	0:45:01 - 01:00:00
1	01:00:01 - 01:20:00

With Roxas's level capped at 5, remove all extra Level Up panels and replace them with extra castings of Blizzard, Fire, and Aero. With not a second to spare, you must roll right past Cogsworth and reach the ballroom. If spotted, it's best to simply start over. Higher levels and equipping a Magic Unit(L) on your weapon panel should help defeat the Bully Dog in quick fashion. Completing the game and equipping the Zero Gear⑤ with three or more Magic Unit(L) links makes this challenge a bit easier.

DAY 97-100

Axel wants Roxas to open all the chests in Mission 29 (Eliminate the Neoshadows). Do so and he'll unlock Mission 35.

Give Demyx a Shining Shard, and he'll relinquish a ***Rune Tech****.*

VANQUISH THE HEARTLESS THREAT

MISSION 32

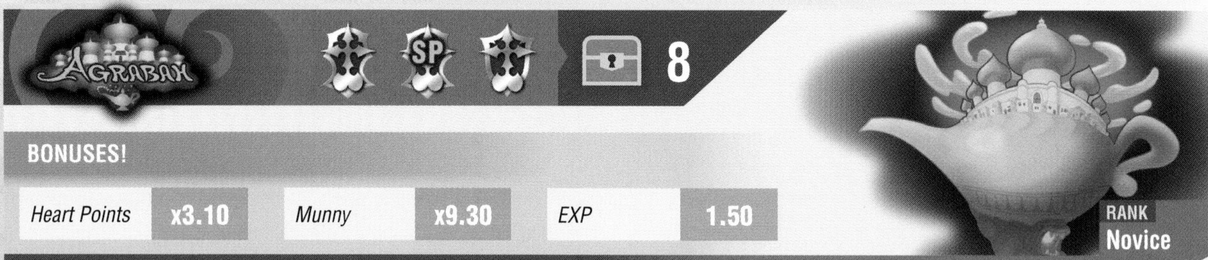

BONUSES!

Heart Points	x3.10	Munny	x9.30	EXP	1.50

ENEMIES

Enemy	LVL	DROP
SCARLET TANGO	8	Blazing Shard
LOUDMOUTH	8	Hi-Potion
BULKY VENDOR	15	Frost Shard, Aerial Tech, or Shining Shard
ANTLION	12	None

REWARDS

Clear Bonuses	Random Bonuses
Aero	Shining Shard (20%)
Gear Component A	Iron (20%)
Moonstone	Potion (30%)
—	None (30%)

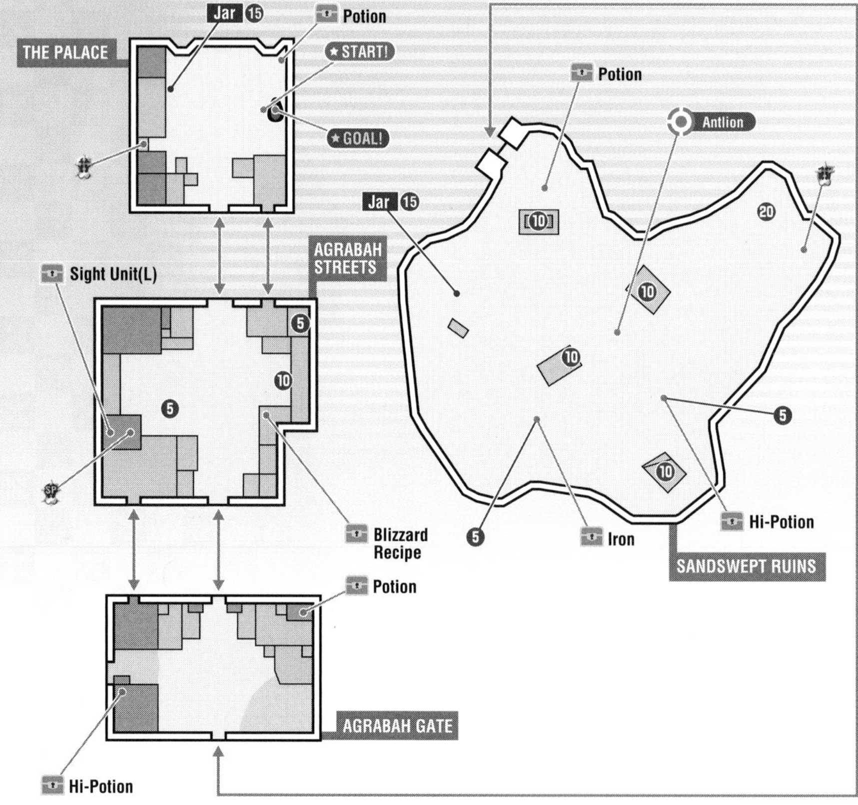

A TRULY CHALLENGING BOSS

Avoid using too many recovery items or spells while fighting insignificant Heartless in the street areas.

Head south, collect the items in the first three areas, and exit through the open gate to the Sandswept Ruins. This is where you'll encounter the massive Heartless, an Antlion.

Out of Reach Items

*The **Ordeal Blazon** and **Sight Unit(L)** are located on the raised platform on the west side of the Agrabah Street area. Unfortunately, these items remain out of reach until you have the panels necessary to equip the High Jump LV2 and Air Slide LV2 abilities, or the Glide ability for greater simplicity. Replay Mission 32 at a later time to collect these items.*

BOSS!

ANTLION

The Antlion seems to ignore Roxas at first, but that soon changes. Lock on to the Antlion and chase it across the sands, battering the "cogs" that emerge from its back. To inflict greater damage, move slightly in front of it and cast Blizzard.

Occasionally, the villain stops with its head emerging from the sands. Move left or right to avoid the blocks rising in a line, and then move in to attack the head before it submerges again.

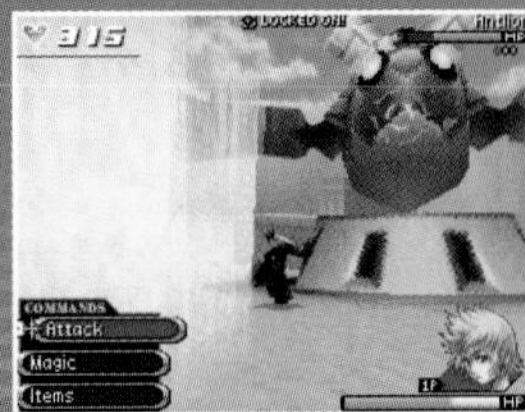

After sustaining enough damage, the Antlion stops moving and its head emerges from the sand, swirling with purple clouds to indicate it's stunned. Quickly approach and attack it, using repeated Air Slides to reach the head faster. Move away when it awakens and avoid the exploding blocks it fires from its head.

When the Antlion's HP is reduced to two bars or less, it completely changes tactics. Hovering upright over the sand, the Antlion surrounds itself with a custom Aero spell, making it impossible to approach or melee attack. If it begins to move toward Roxas, use Dodge Rolls and Air Slides to escape from it. Stay locked on and watch for a purple orb to surround its head, followed by a glow emanating from its mouth. When this occurs, Dodge Roll or Air Slide quickly to the left or right to avoid the massive beam it spews.

When gold blocks begin swirling in the Antlion's tornado, prepare for it to start hurling the blocks your way. The blocks cause damage if they strike, and they can knock into one another just like balls on a pool table. Afterward, position Roxas behind the blocks and strike them to launch them back at the Antlion, causing damage. Each block causes only a small amount of damage. However, after a minute the block begins to flash red before exploding; strike the blocks while they're flashing red to inflict greater damage. When it takes enough damage, the Antlion drops to the ground, dazed. Approach and strike the head or launch Blizzard spells to damage it until it wakes up. Continue to knock the blocks at it and strike its exposed head until you're victorious.

CHALLENGE MISSION

Objective: Attack as little as possible!

Restrictions: No recovery items, enemy level +14

Rewards	
Sigils Acquired	Attacks
3	10 or less
2	11 to 20 attacks
1	21 to 35 attacks

Avoid all other enemies and head straight for the Antlion battle. Use spells to damage it until the first part of the battle, when it begins hovering in the air and spewing blocks. Use your 10 hits to knock blocks back at it. After knocking it from the sky, use your Limit Break to attack its stunned head, since this won't count against your attacks.

SPECIAL CHALLENGE

Objective: Finish in record time!

Restrictions: Enemy level +55, HP drains while on the ground

Rewards	
Sigils Acquired	Clear Time
3	01:20:00 or less
2	01:20:01 - 01:35:00
1	01:35:01 - 03:00:00

Roxas takes damage every half-second he stands on the ground, so equip the Glide panel and fly as often as possible. Glide directly to the Antlion battle. For the first half of the battle, use Glide to catch up to the Antlion and attack and heal with Hi-Potions as necessary. For the second part of the battle, cast Cura repeatedly to fight the effects of losing life while standing, since you must stand in order to knock the blocks back at the Antlion.

BREAK THE JARS

MISSION 33

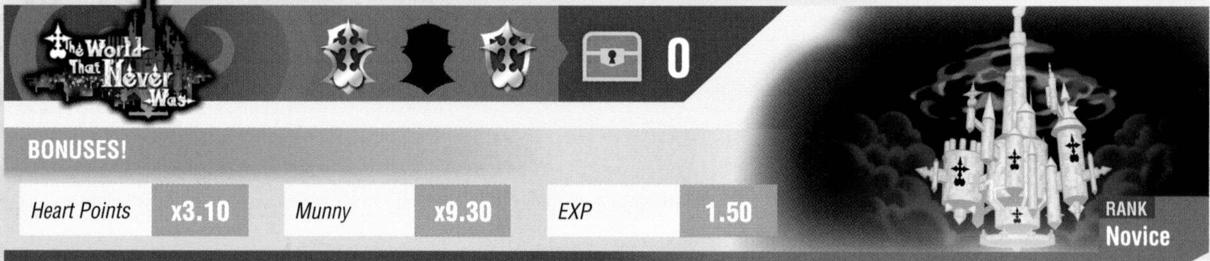

ENEMIES

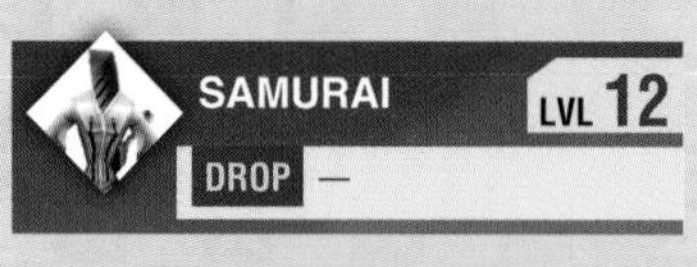

REWARDS	
Clear Bonuses	Random Bonuses
Fire Recipe	Potion (40%)
Blazing Shard	Ether (40%)
Frost Shard	None (20%)

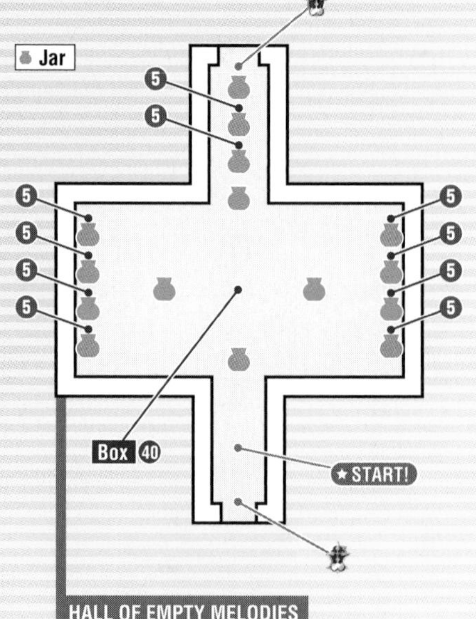

SMASH LOUNGE

The objective of this mission is to destroy all of the giant jars in the room. The jars are quite durable, with each requiring several bashes to break. Therefore, equip a weapon panel that enhances Strength above all else, so that Roxas can break the jars faster.

Equip a weapon panel with improved Strength to smash the jars more quickly.

Samurais are tough Nobodies best avoided at this relatively early stage in the game.

Jar Contents (15 Jars Total)	
Number	Contents
3	HP Prizes & munny
2	Potion
1	Hi-Potion
3	Samurai x2
6	Nothing

Random jars release a pair of Samurais when destroyed. These monsters may be a bit tougher than you can handle during Days 97-100, so use Air Slides and Dodge Rolls to escape from them. Move to the other side of the room and destroy jars until the Samurais catch up, then escape again and smash some jars in another clear area. Repeat this until done. Other jars release prizes and items when destroyed.

CHALLENGE MISSION

Objective: Finish in record time!

Restrictions: Enemy level +2

Rewards	
Sigils Acquired	Clear Time
3	01:05:00 or less
2	01:05:01 - 01:25:00
1	01:25:01 - 01:45:00

Equip Roxas with a weapon panel that boosts Strength, such as the Ominous Gear, Valor Gear, Prestige Gear, or the Crisis Gear, or their better versions. This makes it easier to destroy the jars using fewer attacks. Avoid equipping the Auto-Lock ability so that Roxas does not target the Samurai enemies. Then, blow through the jars as you normally would.

ELIMINATE THE AERIAL MASTERS

MISSION 34

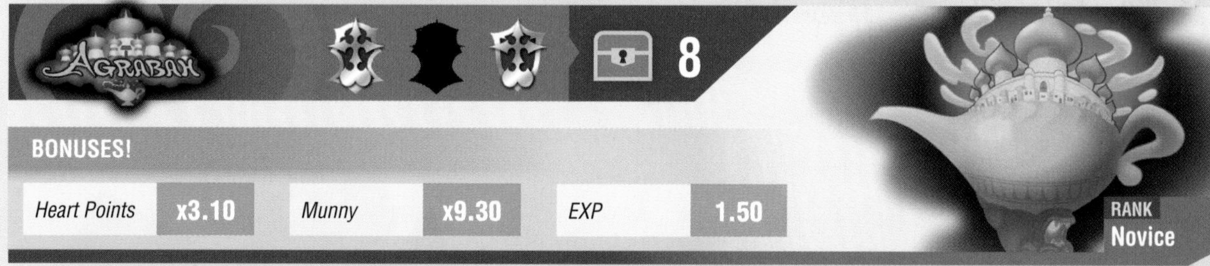

BONUSES!

Heart Points	x3.10	Munny	x9.30	EXP	1.50

RANK Novice

ENEMIES

SCARLET TANGO LVL 8 — DROP Blazing Shard

LOUDMOUTH LVL 8 — DROP Hi-Potion

LARGE ARMOR LVL 12 — DROP Frost Shard

ZIP SLASHER LVL 40 — DROP Combo Tech

AERIAL MASTER LVL 20 — DROP Aerial Tech

REWARDS	
Clear Bonuses	Random Bonuses
Cure	Shining Shard (20%)
Shining Shard	Iron (20%)
Blazing Shard	Potion (30%)
—	None (30%)

★START!
★GOAL!
Backpack
5
5
AGRABAH STREETS
Potion
Aerial Master
Jar 30
Potion
Iron
AGRABAH GATE
Jar 30
Aerial Master
Potion
Aerial Master
Potion
10
10
10
SANDSWEPT RUINS
Ether
Aerial Master
Shining Shard

WING HUNT

A chest near the starting point contains a **Backpack**, but it's difficult to reach without the Air Slide LV2 plus High Jump LV2 or higher abilities, or Glide. If you have the Lift Gear +, Air Slide Lvl.1 and a bit of luck, you can make it onto the ledge. If that seems too hard at this level, just keep this chest in mind as you continue in the game that you'll need to replay this mission later to claim this item.

Return for the Backpack in the chest on the upper level after finding more suitable ability panels.

The Agrabah Gate area is where you'll encounter the first Aerial Master foe. Use aerial combos coupled with Fire and Blizzard spells to destroy it. Loudmouths appearing in the area often try to heal it, so decide whether you want to destroy them first before finishing off the target.

Destroy Loudmouths to prevent them from healing other Heartless with their songs.

Continue to the Sandswept Ruins and locate three more Aerial Masters. Once each is encountered, try to avoid moving too far away from that area so that only one Aerial Master appears at a time.

The three Aerial Masters in the Sandswept Ruins area appear at the locations marked on the map in this guide.

While returning to the RTC point, you will encounter a Large Armor in the Agrabah Gate area.

CHALLENGE MISSION

Objective: Finish in record time!

Restrictions: Level capped at 10, enemy level +1

Rewards

Sigils Acquired	Clear Time
3	02:40:00 or less
2	02:40:01 - 03:40:00
1	03:40:01 - 05:00:00

Use the map to head straight to the locations of each Aerial Master, eliminating them quickly by casting Fire spells and hitting them with your best weapon. A level 2 or 3 High Jump helps immensely in reaching them when they drift too high up.

COLLECT HEARTS

MISSION 35

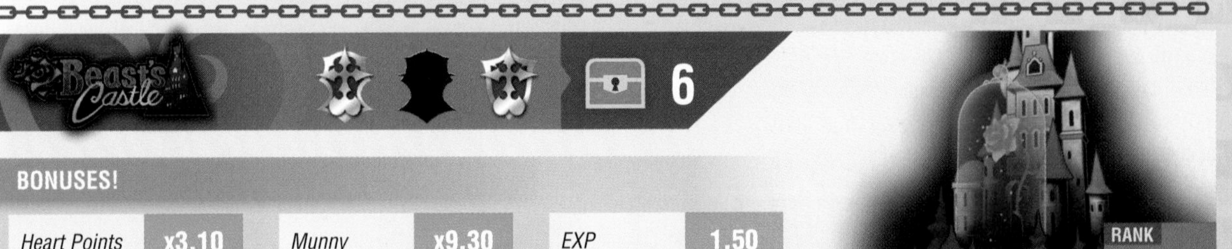

BONUSES!

Heart Points	x3.10	Munny	x9.30	EXP	1.50

RANK
Novice

ENEMIES

SHADOW LVL 12
DROP Potion

ICY CUBE LVL 1
DROP Iron

MASSIVE POSSESSOR LVL 12
DROP Panacea

SNOWY CRYSTAL LVL 12
DROP Ether

SNAPPER DOG LVL 12
DROP Ether

REWARDS	
Clear Bonuses	Random Bonuses
Blizzard Recipe	Frost Shard (25%)
Frost Shard	Ether (40%)
Bronze	None (35%)

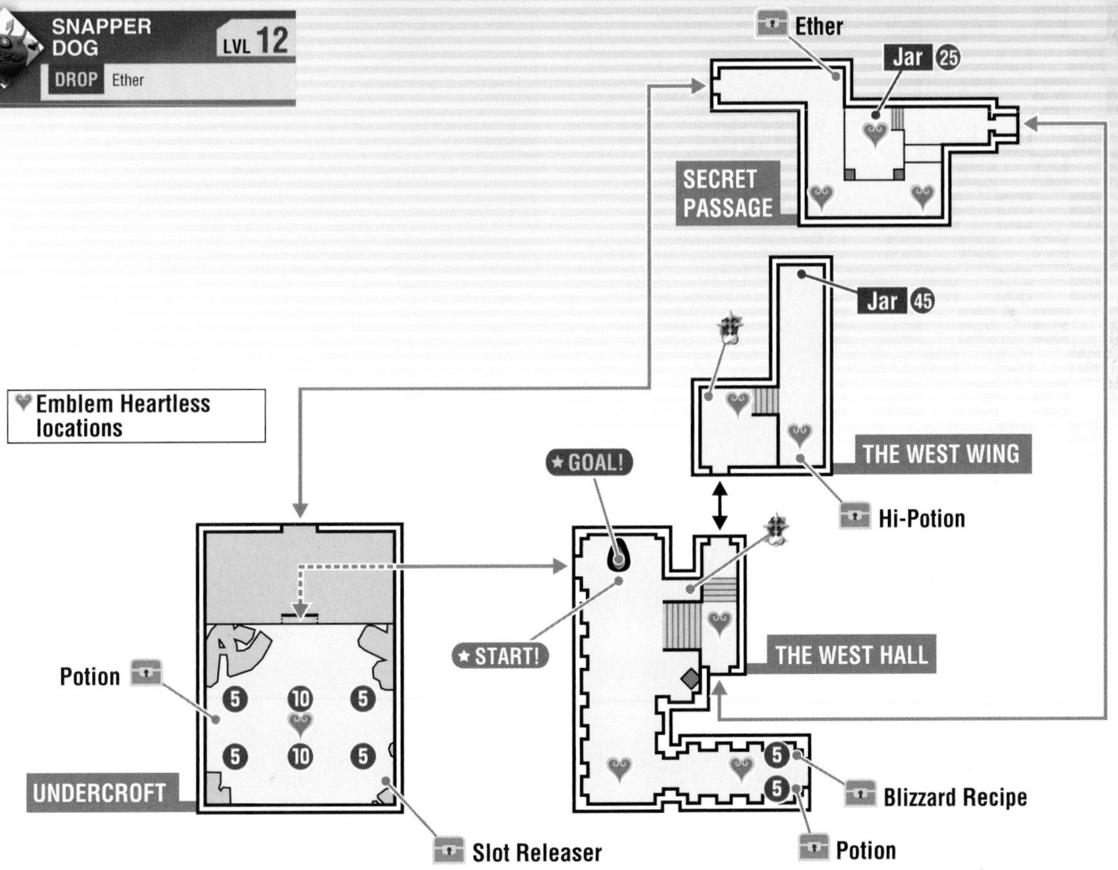

Ether
Jar 25
SECRET PASSAGE
Jar 45
Emblem Heartless locations
THE WEST WING
GOAL!
Hi-Potion
START!
THE WEST HALL
Potion
UNDERCROFT
Blizzard Recipe
Slot Releaser
Potion

SWEEP AND CLEAR

Roam from one hall to the next defeating Heartless. Save your Fire and Fira spells to use against Icy Cubes and Snowy Crystals, and use Blizzard or Aero magic to defeat Snapper Dogs. All other Heartless are inconsequential, although they make good target practice and release additional prizes and munny when defeated.

Hit Icy Cubes and Snowy Crystals with Fire magic for a quick kill.

CHALLENGE MISSION

Objective: **Finish in record time!**

Restrictions: **Enemy level +2**

Rewards	
Sigils Acquired	Clear Time
3	02:45:00 or less
2	02:45:01 - 03:20:00
1	03:20:01 - 04:20:00

The best advice is to head straight into the Undercroft, then go through the Secret Passage back to the West Hall. Proceed straight up to the West Wing, then return to the West Hall and use the Glide ability to reach the enemies to the south. Equip plenty of Fire and Fira panels to deal with Icy Cubes and Snowy Crystals and use other spells to defeat Snapper Dogs. Ignore Shadows and Massive Possessors during the hunt and you should make it in time to acquire three Sigils.

DAY 117

After Roxas speaks to Saïx, Saïx bestows the Rookie rank upon Roxas. Visit the Moogle to see that new items are available to purchase and synthesize. Furthermore, Xion becomes a playable character in Mission Mode, both in Solo and Multiplayer.

Give Demyx an Iron and he'll hand over a **Power Tech** in exchange!

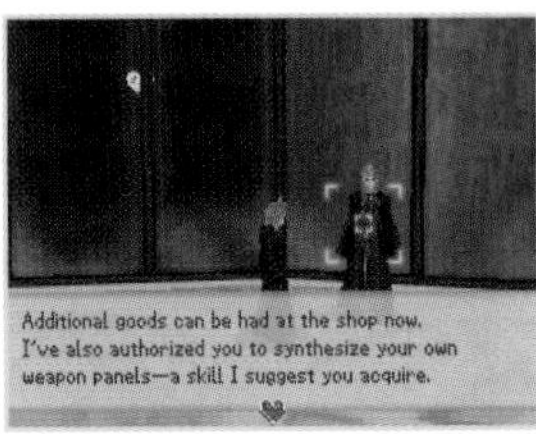

Saïx has decided Roxas is ready for tougher missions.

Rookies get access to more items in the Moogle shop!

INVESTIGATE THIS NEW WORLD

MISSION 36

BONUSES!

Heart Points	x3.15	Munny	x9.45	EXP	1.54

RANK NA

ENEMIES

FLARE NOTE LVL 13
DROP Blazing Shard

LI'L CANNON LVL 13
DROP Gear Component A

REWARDS	
Clear Bonuses	Random Bonuses
Thunder	Lightning Shard (30%)
Lightning Shard	Panacea (35%)
Thunder (MG)	None (35%)

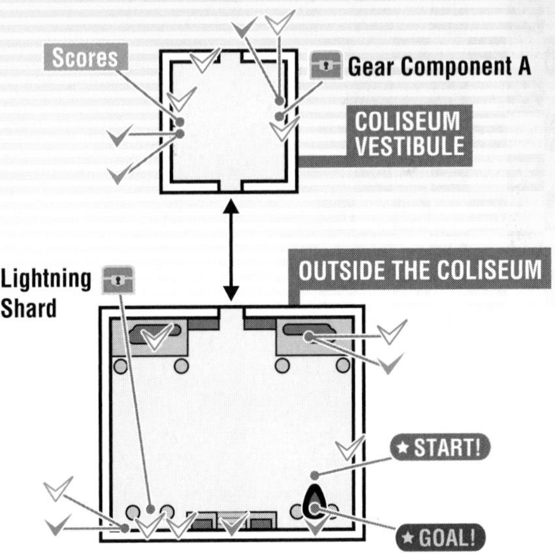

HOME OF CHAMPIONS

Clear the entrance area of Heartless and Phil soon comes out to talk. He and Xigbar leave afterward. Search the area for clues until Roxas has his first breakthrough. While many clues are available at first, only the five marked with solid red checkmarks on the map in this section are crucial to the breakthrough.

Check the rosters and leaderboards on either side of the south wall to uncover major clues.

The south door also provides Roxas with food for thought.

Enter the Coliseum Vestibule and open the nearby chest to obtain a **Gear Component A**. Then check the horned trophy on the east wall and the gold trophy on the west wall to trigger the first breakthrough. Answer the questions correctly to proceed.

Examine the trophies in the vestibule until Roxas has his first breakthrough.

TRAINING TIME!

Speak to Phil to begin training for the Coliseum. The training involves smashing barrels for points, scoring as high as possible within one minute. The more barrels you destroy at one time, the more points you score. Therefore, you must try to knock one barrel into another. Position Roxas behind a barrel, facing other barrels, then strike it until it flies over and smashes the other barrel. Standard barrels are capable of destroying one other barrel if properly aimed, while dark brown exploding barrels can take out large clusters of barrels. Equip a weapon panel that knocks enemies upward within the first 1-2 hits of a combo, such as the Lift Gear or Nimble Gear, to lift the barrels off the ground faster.

Strike one barrel to knock it into another one.

Destroy additional barrels before their chain rings expire to score higher.

The key to scoring high is to use the exploding barrels wisely. If no exploding barrels are available, then knock one barrel into another barrel repeatedly, as quickly as possible before the chain ring around the target collapses. However, aim carefully. Strike a barrel that is far away from the others and knock it into another lone barrel or one that is at the edge of a group. As more barrels appear, allow them to gather in clusters and continue smashing the loners. Then when an exploding barrel appears, knock it into the center of the group to score up to eight points per barrel!

Avoid destroying clusters of barrels until an exploding barrel appears. When this occurs, knock the exploding barrel into the group to score big.

Points Per Barrel Destroyed, Per Chain

Chain	Points
1	2
2	3
3	4
4	5
5	6
6	7
7 or more	8

SCORE 100!

Score 100 points or higher in this training exercise and you'll be rewarded by another Organization XIII member on Day 149!

FINISH RECONNAISSANCE

Tell Phil you've had enough when you're ready to give up on training. Roxas experiences his second breakthrough, filling the Mission Gauge to the goal line. To max out the Mission Gauge, examine the gold trophy on the west wall again, then go outside. After a brief encounter with Hercules, jump onto the northeast platform and examine the giant gold statue. Roxas has his final breakthrough, filling the Mission Gauge.

Avoid getting too close to the gold statue, or Roxas may miss this vital recon point.

DAY 118

Roxas enters the Grey Area as usual, only to find a note that Organization XIII is closed for vacation. Not knowing what to do, he heads to Twilight Town to kill some time.

Rarely (if ever) does a video game give you a vacation. Enjoy!

VACATION

MISSION **37**

Twilight Town

0

BONUSES!

Heart Points	x3.20	Munny	—	EXP	—

RANK
Rookie

REWARDS	
Clear Bonuses	Random Bonuses
None	None

EYES ON THE BALL

On vacation, Roxas finds Olette, Hayner, and Pence playing a fun game called "Grandstander." The objective is to knock a giant ball into the air with a large foam bat and keep it from touching the ground. See how many times you can hit it before it reaches the ground; each hit is worth a point. The ball can touch the ground five times before your game ends.

Whack the ball into the air with the foam bat, then see how many more times you can hit it before it touches the ground.

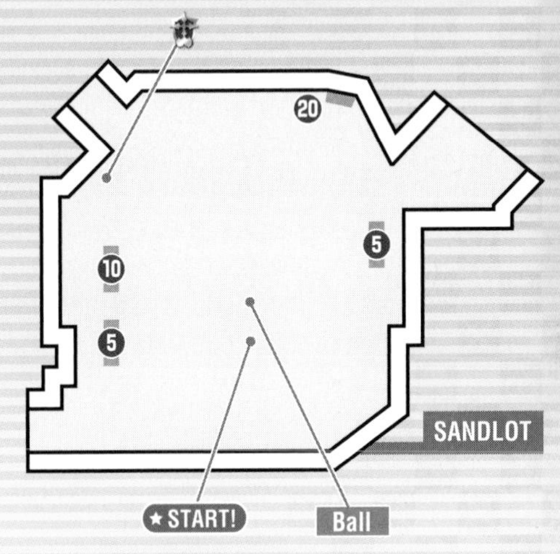

The key to scoring high is to knock the ball way into the air. The foam bat allows you to execute a three-hit combo where the last blow knocks the ball out of sight. Then hit the ball again while it's airborne, knocking it into the sky again before you fall back to the ground. Continue launching aerial combos on the ball for as long as possible.

The key to scoring high is using aerial combos launched with the right timing.

Follow the ball's shadow on the ground if it rises out of view.

Unfortunately, the ball usually soars out of view. However, by keeping the camera behind Roxas, you should be able to track the ball's shadow on the ground. After knocking it high, follow the shadow to the point where it stops, and then immediately launch another aerial combo.

TRY TO SCORE 50

Go for a score of 50 or higher in Grandstander to unlock an extra mission on day 153.

DAY 119-122

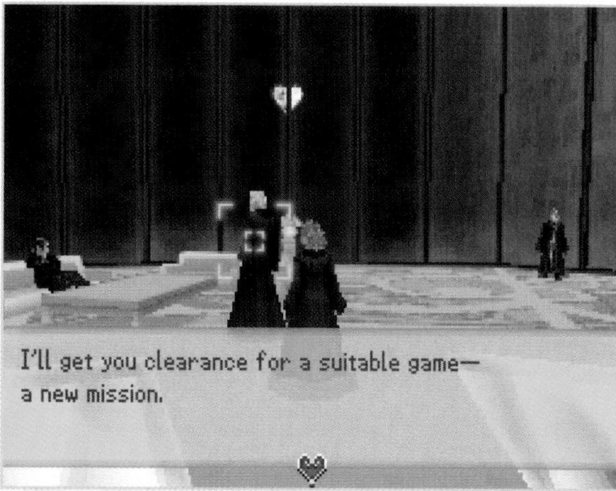

Equip a weapon panel with three or more slots and link two or more units to it, such as Power Units, Magic Units, Guard Units, and so on. Then speak to Luxord and he'll add Mission 41 to the day's roster. Complete all missions between Days 97 to 116 (Missions 32-35) and speak to Xigbar to receive a **Gust Shard**.

Equip a weapon panel and link two units of any kind to it to impress Luxord enough to add another mission.

INVESTIGATE THE CASTLE'S MASTER — MISSION 38

BONUSES!

Heart Points	x3.50	Munny	x10.50	EXP	1.63

RANK
NA

ENEMIES

MEGA-SHADOW — LVL 10 — DROP: Combo Tech

SERGEANT — LVL 11 — DROP: Shining Shard

NEOSHADOW — LVL 17 — DROP: Lightning Shard

MASSIVE POSSESSOR — LVL 12 — DROP: Gust Shard

SNAPPER DOG — LVL 12 — DROP: Power Tech

BULKY VENDOR — LVL 18 — DROP: Elixir Recipe

BULLY DOG — LVL 14 — DROP: Lightning Shard

REWARDS

Clear Bonuses	Random Bonuses
Thunder Recipe	Elixir Recipe (10%)
Aerora Recipe	Gear Component A (10%)
Thunder (MG)	Bronze (10%)
—	Hi-Potion (20%)
—	Potion (15%)
—	Ether (15%)
—	None (20%)

FIND BELLE'S CHAMBERS

It's time to get to the bottom of what's transpiring at Beast's Castle. Refer to the map in this section and find the locations marked by four solid red checkmarks. Search in the Entrance Hall, the Courtyard, and the Ballroom. Then return to the Entrance Hall and head up to the East Wing.

The door behind the starting point provides a major recon clue.

The recon point in the Ballroom is in the center of the dance floor.

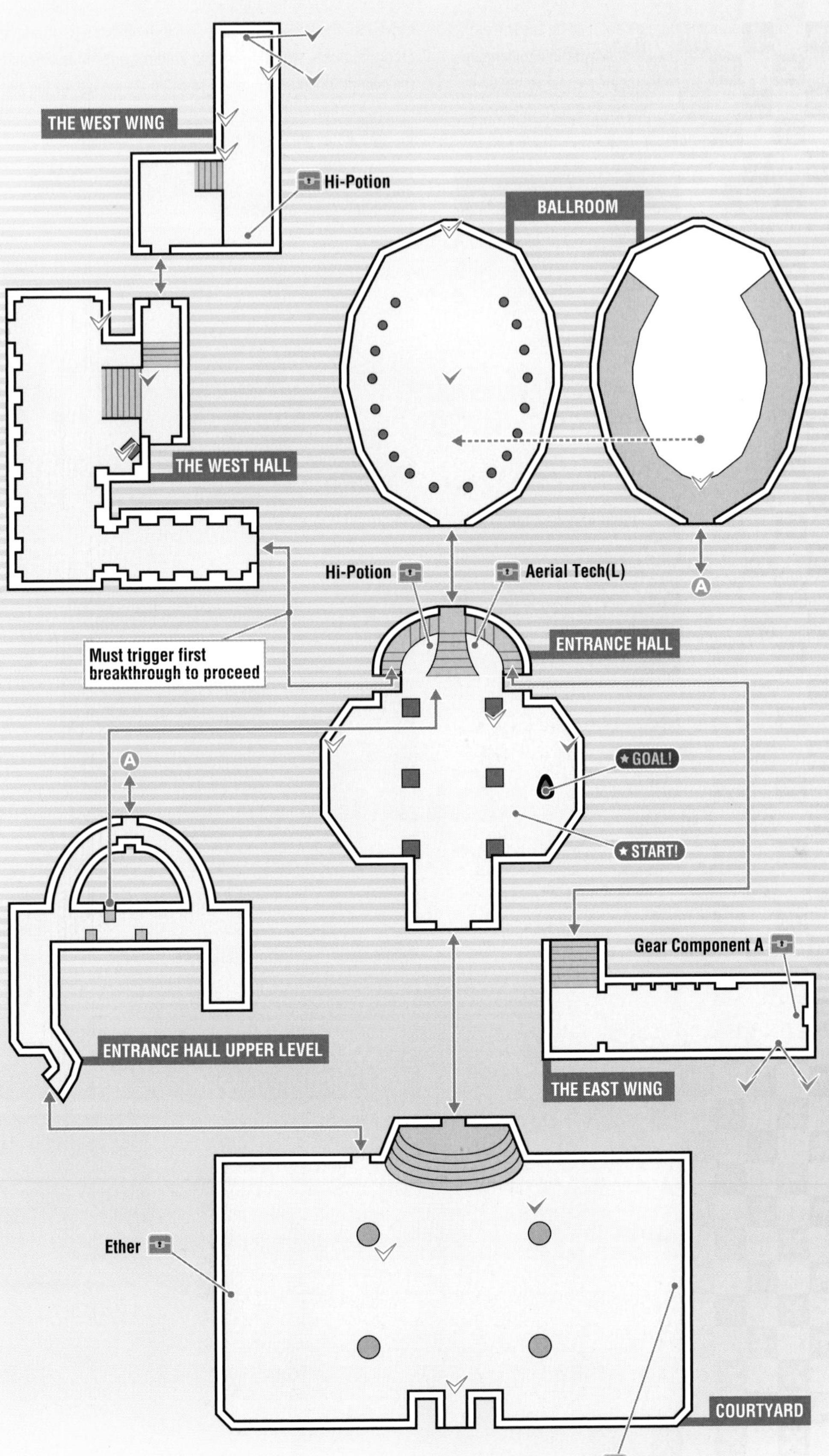

THE WEST WING
Hi-Potion
BALLROOM
THE WEST HALL
Hi-Potion
Aerial Tech(L)
A
Must trigger first breakthrough to proceed
ENTRANCE HALL
A
GOAL!
START!
Gear Component A
ENTRANCE HALL UPPER LEVEL
THE EAST WING
Ether
COURTYARD
Elixir Recipe

Cogsworth is patrolling the East Wing, making a slow circle around the center. Simply run past him on his right as soon as he turns from your direction. Defeat the Sergeants at the far end without accidentally falling back into Cogsworth's sight. Open the nearby chest to obtain a **Gear Component A** and examine the door. Answer Xaldin's questions correctly to trigger the first breakthrough.

Sneak past Cogsworth on his right as he circles around.

Examine Belle's door and answer Xaldin's questions correctly to have a breakthrough.

THE BEAST'S ROOM

Sneak past Lumiere in the West Hall. On his route, he faces south (your direction) for a long time, then turns west before curving south to east. The best time to pass him is when he turns west again, but you must stick very close to the east wall and get up the stairs quickly.

Start heading toward Lumiere once he reaches this point, then dash past him as he heads west, then north.

Check the floor at the top of the stairs to find an important clue, then move into the West Wing and check the Beast's door, along with any other locations. After answering Xaldin's questions correctly to trigger the second breakthrough, the Mission Gauge fills to the goal line.

The carpet at the top of the stairs tells Roxas something. In recon, no clue is too small.

Examine the Beast's door twice before heading back, once to trigger a breakthrough and again to get a start on the next one.

DIGGING DEEPER

Fill the Mission Gauge 100% by checking the Beast's door again. Next, sneak past Lumiere and Cogsworth again and go to Belle's door in the East Wing again. Answer Xaldin's final set of questions, then return to the Entrance Hall to RTC.

Sneak back to Belle's room in the East Wing and examine her door to fill the Mission Gauge.

COLLECT HEARTS

MISSION 39

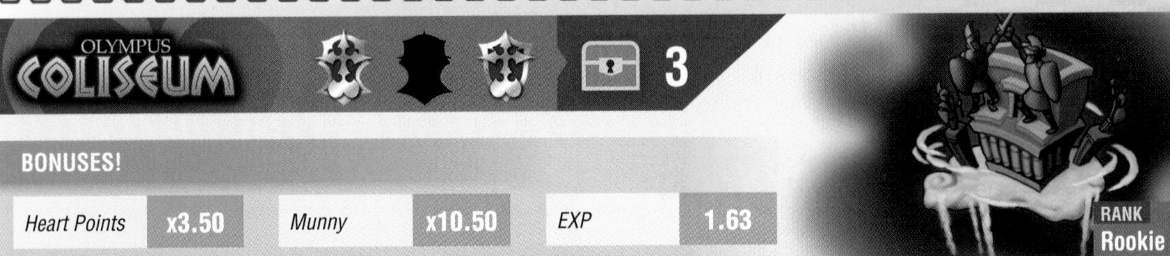

BONUSES!

Heart Points	x3.50	Munny	x10.50	EXP	1.63

RANK
Rookie

ENEMIES

SHADOW LVL 10
DROP —

FLARE NOTE LVL 13
DROP Blazing Shard

CLAY ARMOR LVL 15
DROP —

JUMBO CANNON LVL 15
DROP Lightning Shard

REWARDS	
Clear Bonuses	Random Bonuses
Gear Component A	Lightning Shard (30%)
Shield Tech	Panacea (35%)
Rune Tech (MG)	None (35%)

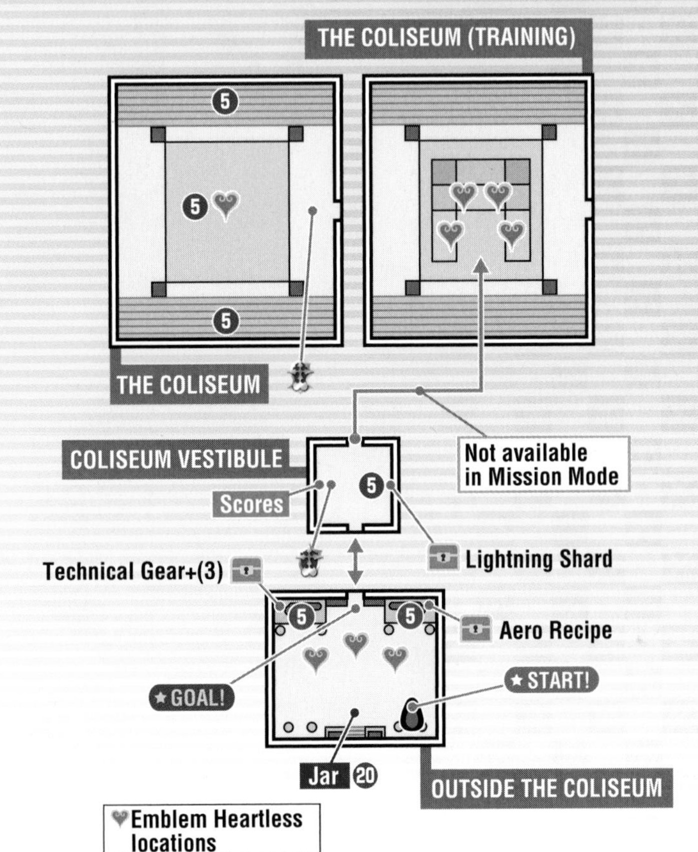

CLEAR THE COLISEUM

Wipe out the enemies appearing outside the Coliseum. Phil soon comes calling for Roxas, demanding he take out the Heartless inside. The Clay Armor is virtually identical to a Large Armor, except it's larger and has a more vicious retaliation after being knocked down. Cast a Thunder spell to knock down the Clay Armor for longer than usual.

Attack the back of the Clay Armor's head to ensure your attacks won't bounce off.

TRAINING WITH SOLDIERS

In this training session, you can gain points the same way as before, but this time you can smash barrels into other barrels or into Soldiers to score points. Work quickly to build your chain to score more points per enemy defeated.

Keep knocking barrels into Soldier Heartless to score points and accumulate hearts simultaneously.

Maximize your scoring potential with exploding barrels by using them immediately.

Accumulate 250 heart points during training to complete the mission and 500 to fill the Mission Gauge 100%. Phil provides you with as many chances as it takes to fill the Mission Gauge. But once that's done, he leaves for the day.

SCORE 130 POINTS!

Try to score at least 130 points before Phil leaves to receive an extra gift on Day 171. If you fail to do it during your first try, then you must complete the entire mission again—including defeating the Clay Armor—just to have another shot at the prize!

CHALLENGE MISSION

Objective: Jump as little as possible!

Restrictions: Level capped at 13, enemy level +1

Rewards	
Sigils Acquired	Jumps
3	1 or less
2	2 to 3 jumps
1	4 to 6 jumps

Thanks to the flat of the land in and around the Coliseum, this challenge should prove easy. In training, simply don't use the barrels at all; just defeat the Soldiers as they step off the platforms. Although your score won't raise any eyebrows, you still get to RTC with three Challenge Sigils!

ELIMINATE THE DESERTERS

MISSION 40

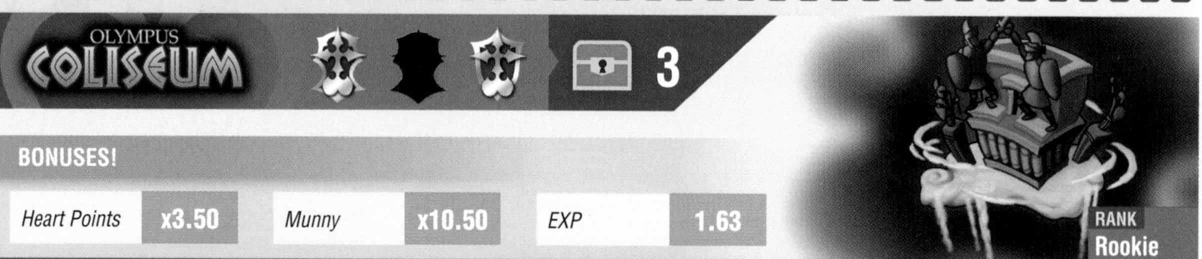

BONUSES!

Heart Points	x3.50	Munny	x10.50	EXP	1.63

RANK Rookie

ENEMIES

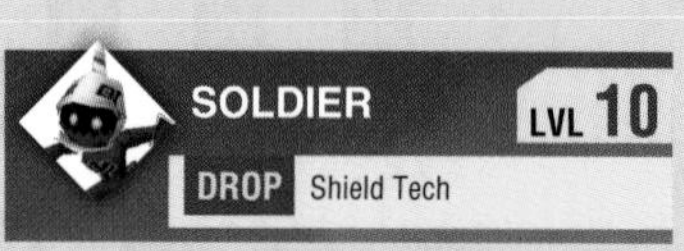

SOLDIER LVL 10 — DROP Shield Tech

CYMBAL MONKEY LVL 16 — DROP Range Tech

DESERTER LVL 15 — DROP Gust Shard

REWARDS	
Clear Bonuses	Random Bonuses
Cure Recipe	Lightning Shard (30%)
Lightning Shard	Panacea (35%)
Lightning Shard	None (35%)

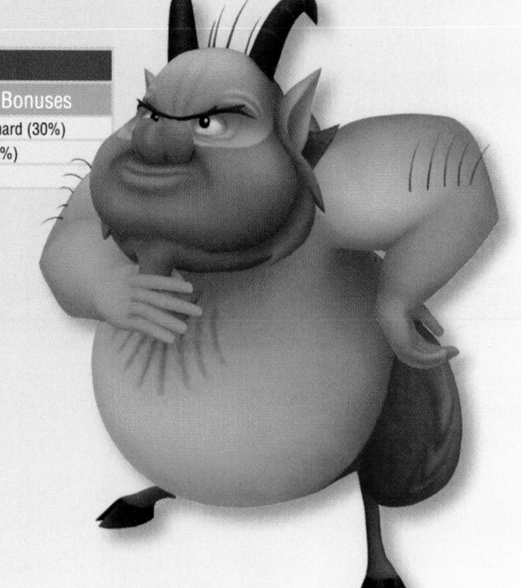

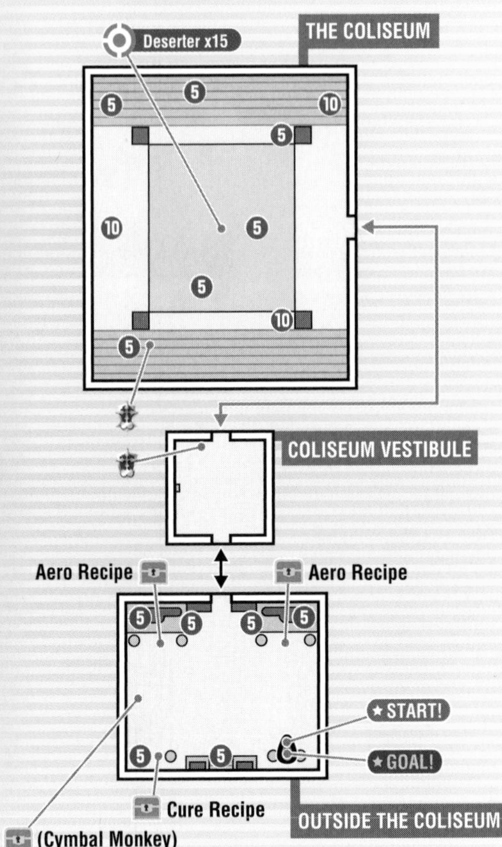

KILLING FLOOR

Open all the chests near the dark corridor. The one near the west wall contains a Cymbal Monkey, but this enemy typically drops a useful **Range Tech** when defeated. Phil's still not back from chasing nymphs, so venture into the Coliseum. Destroy all the Deserters and the Soldiers, who drop **Shield Techs** on a regular basis here. Shield Techs are highly useful in synthesis.

Knock barrels into the Soldiers and Deserters for easy kills!

ORDEAL BADGE UP HIGH!

*To reach the **Ordeal Badge** floating high above the ground in the Coliseum, perform a High Jump from the top of the audience and Air Slide toward the badge.*

CHALLENGE MISSION

Objective: Finish in record time!

Restrictions: Take 20% more damage, enemy level +2

Rewards	
Sigils Acquired	Clear Time
3	02:25:00 or less
2	02:25:01 - 02:40:00
1	02:40:01 - 03:10:00

At slightly higher levels, this challenge isn't very difficult. Enter the Coliseum and launch Fire spells at Deserters and use lock on to avoid wasting spells on Soldiers. When the Deserters gather, continue swinging away using a ground combo.

ELIMINATE THE MORNING STAR

MISSION 41

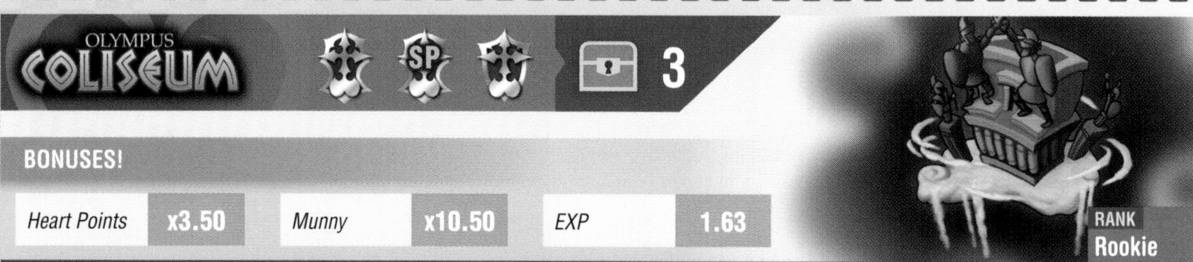

BONUSES!

Heart Points	x3.50	Munny	x10.50	EXP	1.63

ENEMIES

REWARDS

Clear Bonuses	Random Bonuses
Aero	Lightning Shard (30%)
Shield Tech	Panacea (35%)
Gust Shard	None (35%)

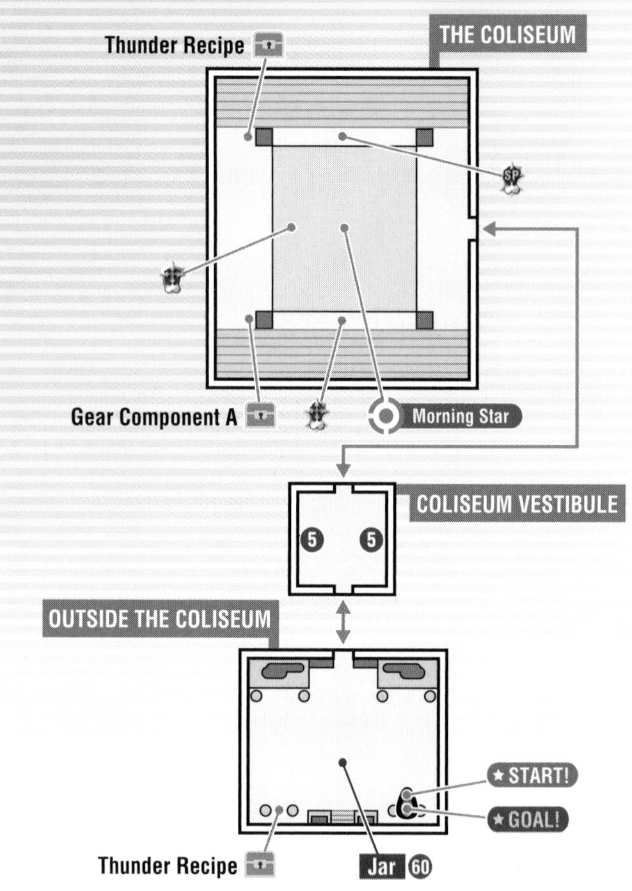

WELCOME PARTY

Defeat the enemies near the entrance and head through the vestibule into the arena. Take out the Morning Star and all of its Li'l Cannon sidekicks. Once you return outside, a Zip Slasher appears. Whittle down its HP, then collect the **Elixir Recipe** it drops.

After the challenging encounter with the Morning Star, seek out the Zip Slasher waiting in the courtyard. Fight it using Blizzard spells to freeze it in place.

MORNING STAR

BOSS!

Avoid focusing on the Li'l Cannons, since replacements immediately appear for each one that you destroy. If a target appears below Roxas, use Air Slides or Dodge Rolls to get out of the way before the projectile lands.

Lock on to the Morning Star and track its spinning movements around the ring. Block with the right timing when it spins in to attack, and you might just knock it off balance and stop its spin. When it's stopped, hit it with barrels to inflict severe damage; otherwise, attack its head until it is destroyed.

When the Morning Star launches and flies out of view, look for its shadow on the ground and move away before it lands to avoid taking damage.

Once the Morning Star is destroyed, the Mission Gauge fills 100%. However, you can destroy the Li'l Cannons for extra munny and Gear Component A items. It's best that you eliminate them and all their replacements using the barrels to help.

CHALLENGE MISSION

Objective: Finish in record time!

Restrictions: No attack magic, enemy level +2

Rewards	
Sigils Acquired	Clear Time
3	01:40:00 or less
2	01:40:01 - 02:00:00
1	02:00:01 - 02:20:00

Use Block LV2 or higher to stop the Morning Star in its tracks, then unleash a Limit Break attack as often as possible. If this proves too challenging, come back and try again at a much higher level.

SPECIAL CHALLENGE

Objective: Don't miss with attacks!

Restrictions: No attack magic, enemy level +19

Rewards	
Sigils Acquired	Misses
3	1 or less
2	2 to 5 misses
1	6 to 10 misses

Avoid attacking any enemy other than the Morning Star. Don't risk trying to attack when it retracts its arms inside its shell; simply break away until it jumps and lands again. With extreme diligence, you can avoid missing a big target like the Morning Star with no problem.

DAY 149

Xigbar rewards you with a piece of **Bronze** if you manage to score 100 points or more during training in Mission 36. Replay it from the Holo-Missions menu if needed.

Xigbar is very interested in Roxas's progress at Olympus Coliseum.

COLLECT HEARTS

MISSION 42

HALLOWEEN TOWN — 3

BONUSES!

Heart Points	x3.55	Munny	x10.65	EXP	1.69

RANK Rookie

ENEMIES

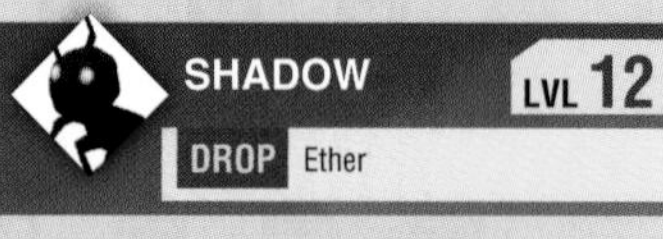

SHADOW LVL 12
DROP Ether

BULKY VENDOR LVL 19
DROP Elixir Recipe, Gear Component A, or Iron

SKATER BOMB LVL 16
DROP Gust Shard

CREEPWORM LVL 16
DROP —

HOVER GHOST LVL 16
DROP Lightning Shard

REWARDS

Clear Bonuses	Random Bonuses
LV Doubler®	Gust Shard (40%)
Gust Shard	Potion (40%)
Sliding Dash (MG)	None (20%)

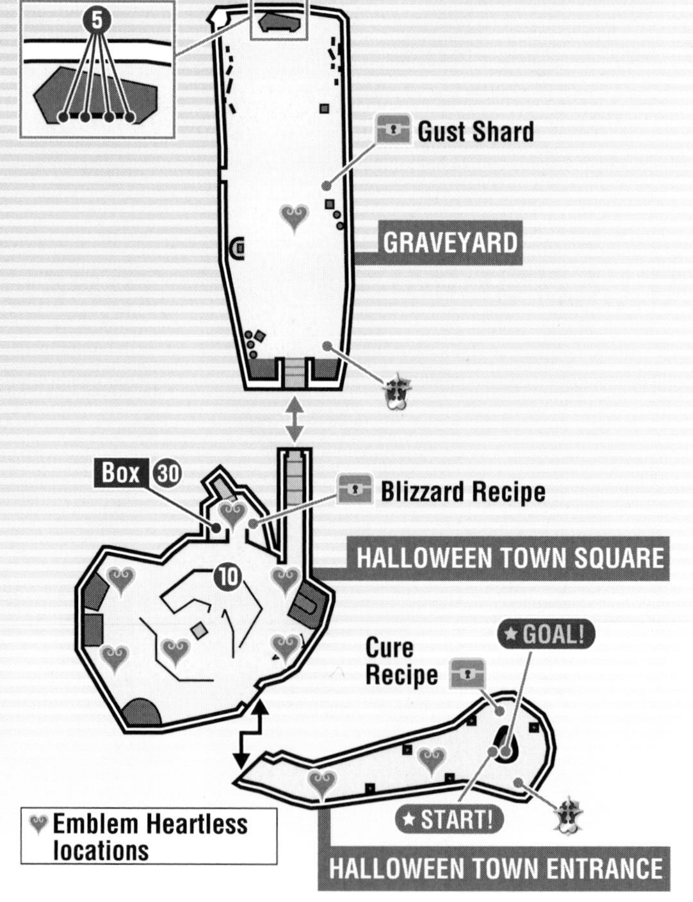

WORLD OF NIGHTMARES

Use the Air Slide to keep up with Hover Ghosts as they try hit-and-run tactics against Roxas.

Simply move to each location marked on the map in this section and defeat Emblem Heartless. Collect 200 hearts to complete the mission and 255 or more to fill the Mission Gauge 100%.

CHALLENGE MISSION

Objective: Finish in record time!

Restrictions: Deal 20% less damage

Rewards	
Sigils Acquired	Clear Time
3	01:45:00 or less
2	01:45:01 - 02:15:00
1	02:15:01 - 03:00:00

The restriction to Roxas's damage doesn't apply to pumpkin bombs, so use them to destroy your foes quickly and efficiently. A good quantity of attack magic panels equipped doesn't hurt either.

USE THE PUMPKIN BOMBS!

Striking red or blue pumpkins lying on the ground around Halloween Town ignites their fuses, triggering five-second countdowns until they explode. Red pumpkins burst into flames, damaging nearby enemies and possibly igniting them. Blue pumpkins (encountered in later missions) burst into ice, inflicting cold damage and possibly freezing nearby targets. Move away before pumpkin bombs explode, or Roxas will take damage as well!

DAY 150

ELIMINATE THE GIANT HEARTLESS

MISSION 43

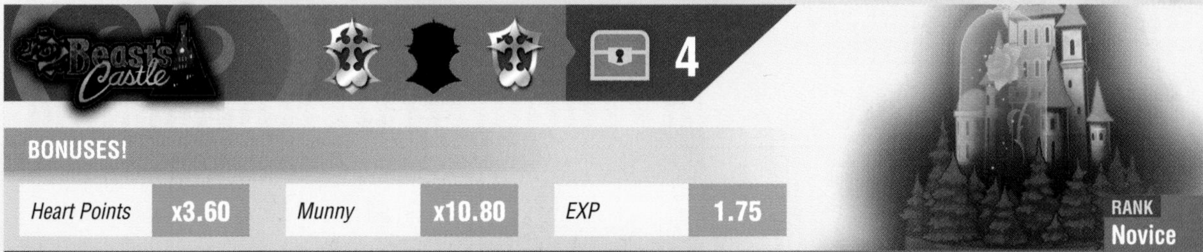

BONUSES!

Heart Points	x3.60	Munny	x10.80	EXP	1.75

RANK Novice

ENEMIES

SHADOW LVL 12 — DROP Ether

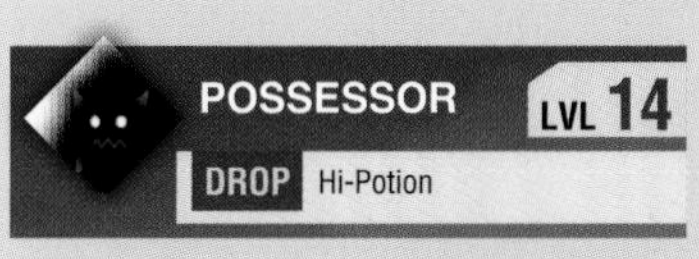

POSSESSOR LVL 14 — DROP Hi-Potion

MEGA-SHADOW LVL 10 — DROP Combo Tech

MASSIVE POSSESSOR LVL 12 — DROP Gust Shard

GIGAS SHADOW LVL 21 — DROP Elixir Recipe

DARK FOLLOWER LVL 21 — DROP —

REWARDS	
Clear Bonuses	Random Bonuses
Fira	Elixir Recipe (10%)
Lightning Shard	Gear Component A (10%)
Lightning Shard	Bronze (10%)
—	Hi-Potion (20%)
—	Potion (15%)
—	Ether (15%)
—	None (20%)

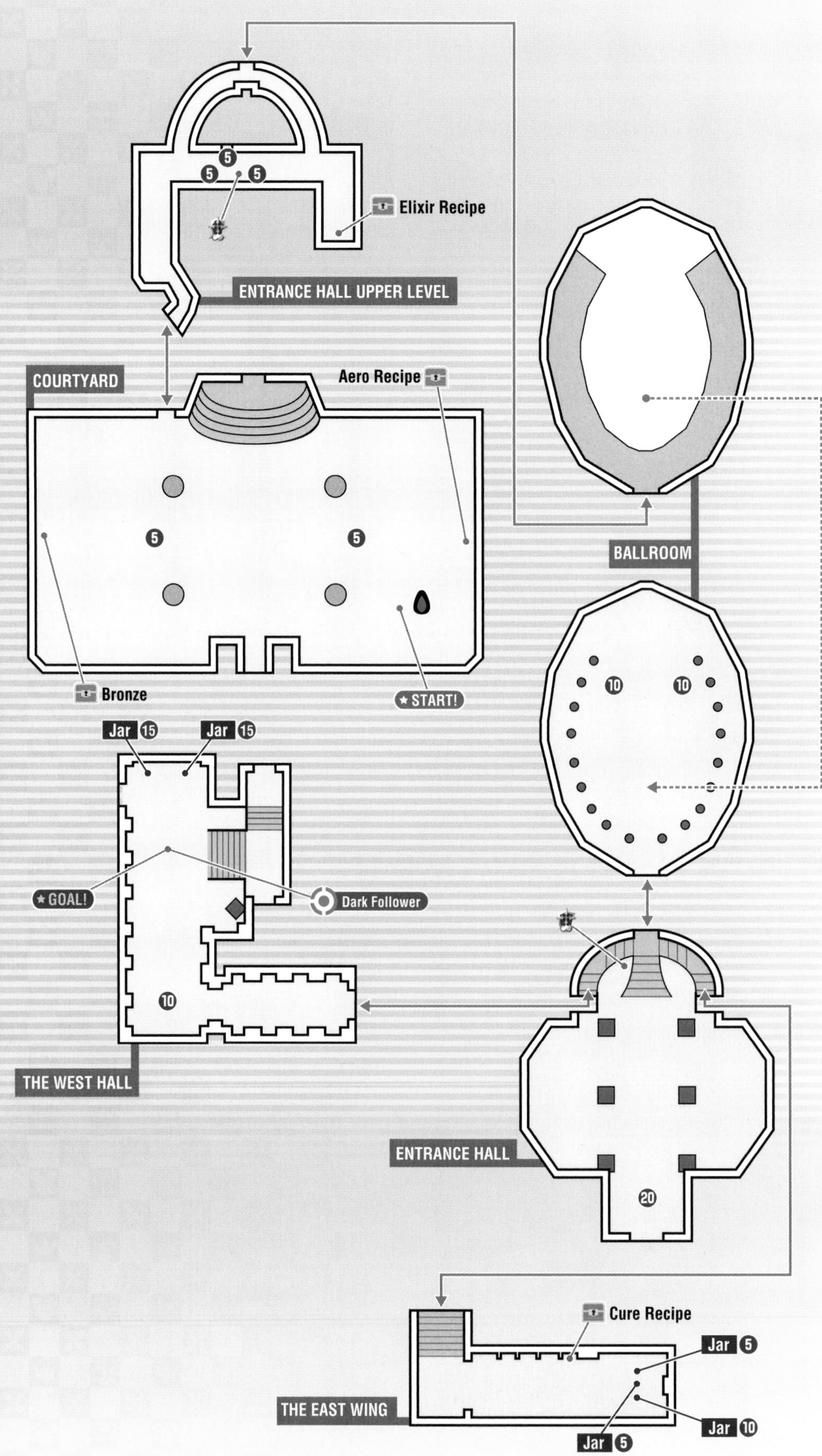
5
5
5
Elixir Recipe
ENTRANCE HALL UPPER LEVEL
COURTYARD
Aero Recipe
5
5
Bronze
START!
BALLROOM
10
10
Jar 15
Jar 15
GOAL!
Dark Follower
10
THE WEST HALL
ENTRANCE HALL
20
Cure Recipe
Jar 5
THE EAST WING
Jar 10
Jar 5

BARRICADE

Unable to open the castle doors, you must navigate through the secret door to the Upper Level. Next, enter the Ballroom and drop to the lower level to reach the Entrance Hall. Don't forget to eliminate the Heartless in the East Wing and open the chest there, which contains a **Cure Recipe**. Finally, visit the West Hall to find the Dark Follower.

Massive Possessors break into six regular Possessors.

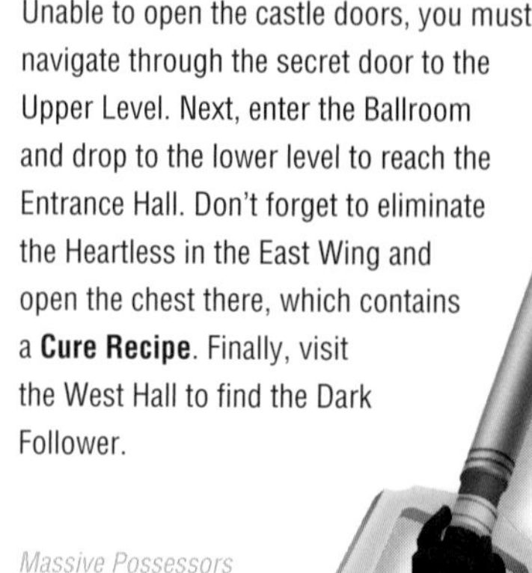

DARK FOLLOWER

BOSS!

The Dark Follower is identical to the Darkside in terms of its attacks and weaknesses. It is simply tougher to eliminate and its homing orb attacks inflict status impairments when they hit. The purplish orbs emanating from its chest inflict blindness, while the black orbs that rain from the sky inflict shoe-glue, preventing Roxas from jumping or performing aerial combos.

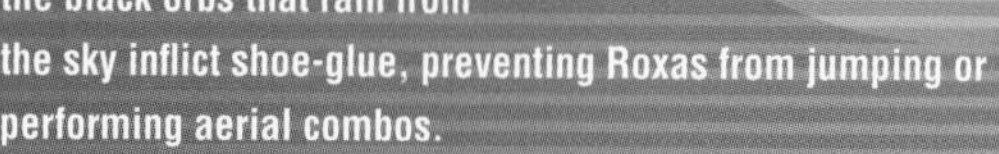

Pay attention to this boss's attacks, avoiding them as you learned previously when fighting the Darkside. Block with the right timing to knock back the purplish orbs emanating from its chest, but beware the retaliation of landing a hit. When black orbs rain from the sky, break off from attacking and move away. Otherwise, target either one of its hands or the head and launch repeated aerial attacks.

CHALLENGE MISSION

Objective: Finish in record time!

Restrictions: Take 10% more damage

Rewards	
Sigils Acquired	Clear Time
3	03:10:00 or less
2	03:10:01 - 03:25:00
1	03:25:01 - 04:00:00

Only large amounts of equipped magic panels can help you defeat both the enemies in the Ballroom as well as the Dark Follower in time. Clear the Ballroom quickly using Fire spells, then cast Thunder and Thundaga repeatedly to help weaken the Dark Follower to the point where the usual tactics allow you to defeat it in time.

DAY 151

Speak to Axel, who believes Roxas should have 130 chests open by now. If this is the case, he hands over a **Shield Tech**.

Continue meeting Axel's high standards to keep the prizes and extra missions coming.

ELIMINATE THE AVALANCHE

MISSION 44

BONUSES!

Heart Points	x3.65	Munny	x10.95	EXP	1.81

RANK Rookie

ENEMIES

MEGA-SHADOW LVL 21 — DROP: Combo Tech

CYMBAL MONKEY LVL 22 — DROP: Range Tech

GIGAS SHADOW LVL 10 — DROP: Elixir Recipe

NEOSHADOW LVL 17 — DROP: Lightning Shard

POISON PLANT LVL 20 — DROP: Lightning Shard

AVALANCHE LVL 25 — DROP: Frost Shard

BULKY VENDOR LVL 24 — DROP: Elixir Recipe, Shield Tech, or Iron

REWARDS

Clear Bonuses	Random Bonuses
High Jump	Fire Recipe (10%)
Fira Recipe	Moonstone (10%)
Sight Unit(L)	Hi-Potion (10%)
—	Potion (15%)
—	Hi-Ether (10%)
—	Ether (15%)
—	Panacea (15%)
—	None (15%)

DOUBLE MISSION!

The best way to change a friend's bad day is to work together.

Xion teams up with Roxas to combine objectives. Her mission is to collect Organization emblems around Twilight Town, while Roxas's mission is to defeat the Avalanche.

Luckily, there are enemies near every emblem location, so collecting them while their rings are visible is no problem. If the emblem rings disappear, move away and defeat some Heartless to make them reappear. Otherwise, ignore the enemies unless you need to make the rings come back. Grab all the emblems with their rings showing so that the Mission Gauge fills 100% when you defeat the Avalanche.

Defeat enemies near emblem locations as needed to make the rings visible again.

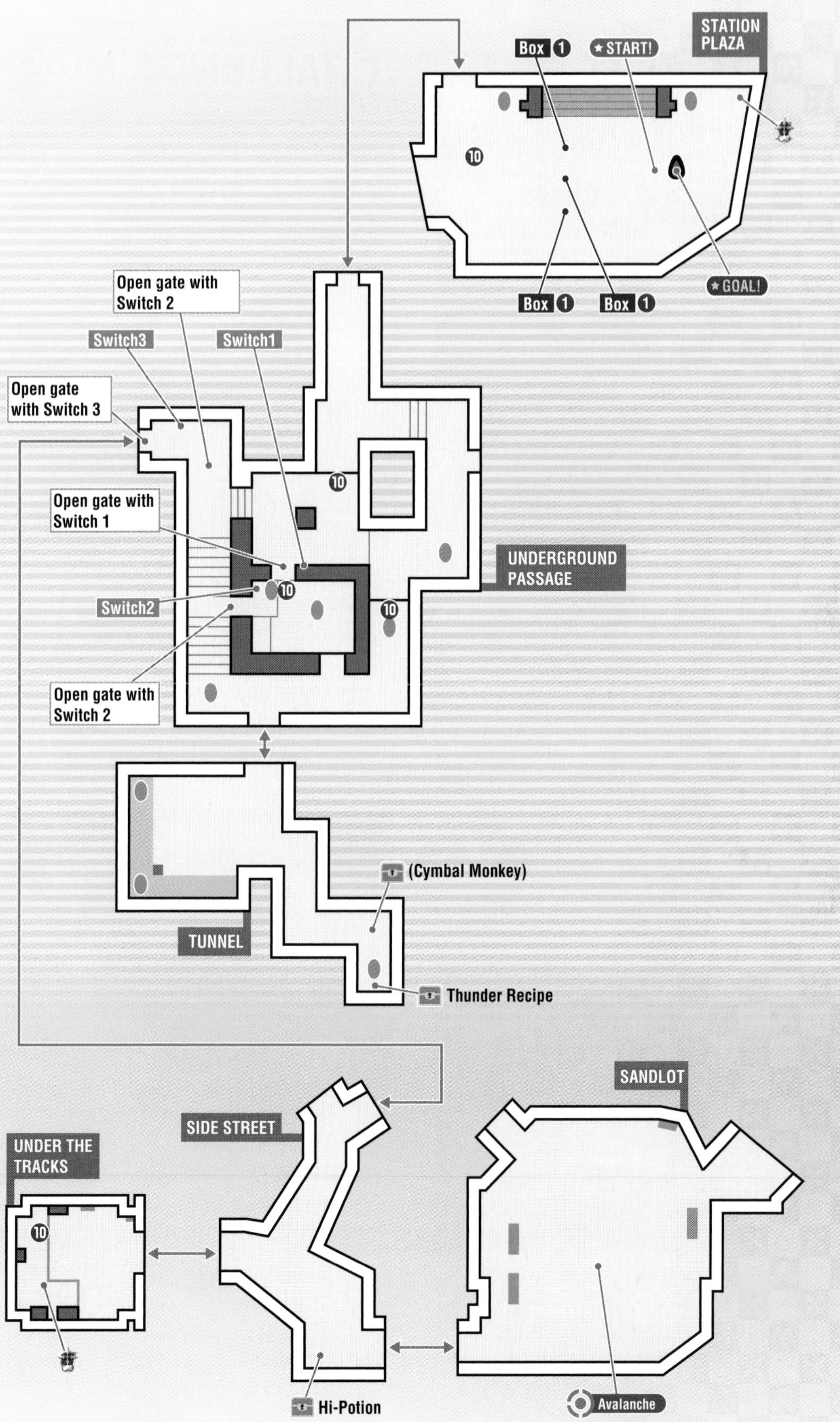

STATION PLAZA
Box 1
START!
Box 1
Box 1
GOAL!
10
Open gate with Switch 2
Switch3
Switch1
Open gate with Switch 3
10
Open gate with Switch 1
UNDERGROUND PASSAGE
10
Switch2
10
Open gate with Switch 2
(Cymbal Monkey)
TUNNEL
Thunder Recipe
SANDLOT
SIDE STREET
UNDER THE TRACKS
10
Hi-Potion
Avalanche
Organization Emblems

Navigate through the Underground Passage to the Tunnel. The two emblems near the doorway should be easy to grab while their rings still show; however, the one at the end of the snaking corridor is a bit trickier. Open the nearby chest to reveal a Cymbal Monkey and defeat it to make the emblem's ring reappear.

Defeat the Cymbal Monkey in the Tunnel in order to reactivate the emblem at the south end.

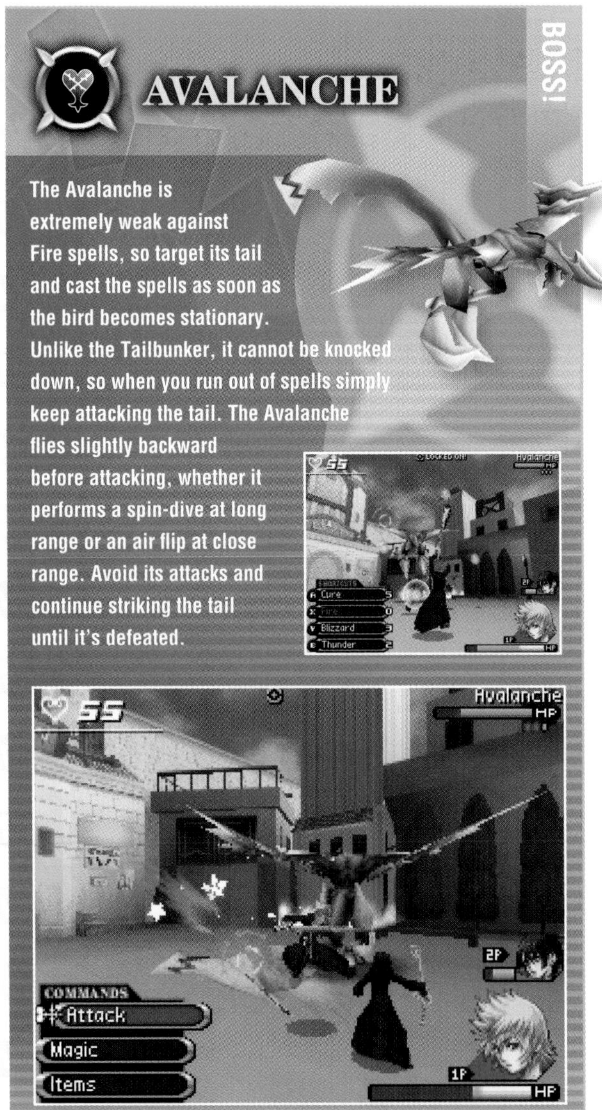

BOSS!

AVALANCHE

The Avalanche is extremely weak against Fire spells, so target its tail and cast the spells as soon as the bird becomes stationary. Unlike the Tailbunker, it cannot be knocked down, so when you run out of spells simply keep attacking the tail. The Avalanche flies slightly backward before attacking, whether it performs a spin-dive at long range or an air flip at close range. Avoid its attacks and continue striking the tail until it's defeated.

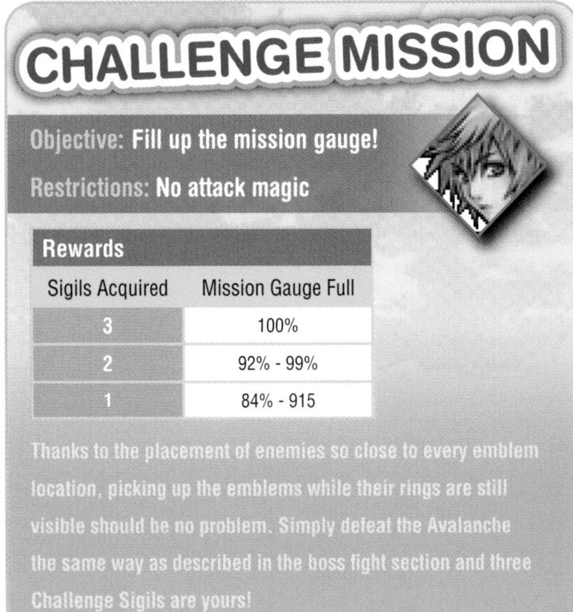

CHALLENGE MISSION

Objective: Fill up the mission gauge!

Restrictions: No attack magic

Rewards	
Sigils Acquired	Mission Gauge Full
3	100%
2	92% - 99%
1	84% - 915

Thanks to the placement of enemies so close to every emblem location, picking up the emblems while their rings are still visible should be no problem. Simply defeat the Avalanche the same way as described in the boss fight section and three Challenge Sigils are yours!

DAY 152-156

Speak to Xaldin to receive a **Combo Tech**, this time with no requirements or challenges involved! On Day 153 (after completing any one of the available missions), Luxord appears in the Grey Area. If you scored 50 points or more playing Grandstander during your vacation, then Luxord adds Mission 49 to Saïx's Mission screen. If not, replay Mission 37 from the Holo-Missions screen.

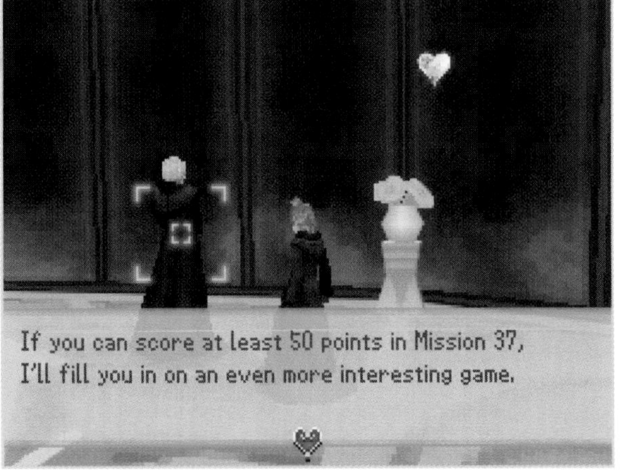

Luxord wants Roxas to excel even while on vacation before he'll authorize an additional mission.

COLLECT HEARTS

MISSION **45**

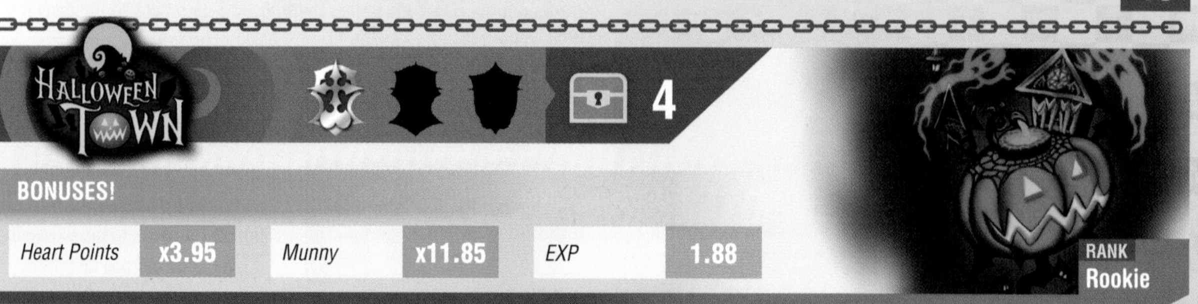

BONUSES!

Heart Points	x3.95	Munny	x11.85	EXP	1.88

RANK **Rookie**

ENEMIES

MEGA-SHADOW LVL 10
DROP Combo Tech

SNOWY CRYSTAL LVL 22
DROP Frost Shard

CREEPWORM LVL 16
DROP —

HOVER GHOST LVL 12
DROP Lightning Shard

REWARDS	
Clear Bonuses	Random Bonuses
Thunder Recipe	Gust Shard (40%)
Gust Gem	Potion (40%)
Gear Component A (MG)	None (20%)

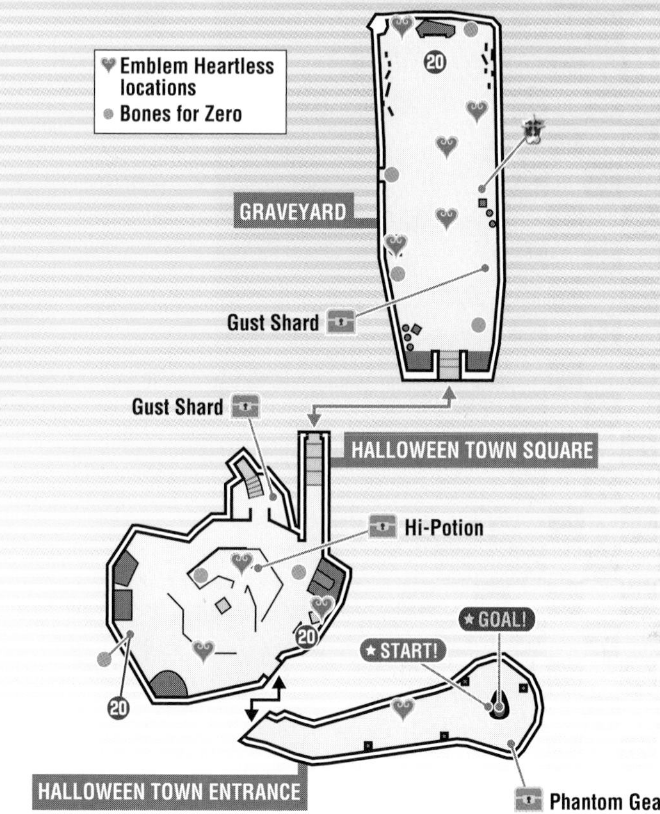

HEARTLESS SNIFFER ZERO

Jump up to examine Jack's scary balloons, some of which contain Heartless.

Follow the entrance to the gate, where Roxas notices a strange balloon. Continue into the Town Square where Jack explains the balloons to Dr. Finklestein. Follow Jack to the northeast exit and enter the Graveyard.

Pick up the **Bones** in the Graveyard and feed them to Zero. When Roxas has a bone, an icon appears above his head. Approach Zero until a green interaction reticule appears around him, then press A to feed him a bone. For each bone he's fed, Zero will fly to a location where a Heartless hides. Find a search point in that area, which is usually located at jumping height. With the reticule visible, press A to find a Heartless. Additionally, jump and search the balloons to reveal more Heartless.

*Pick up a **Bone** to give to Zero.*

While a Bone icon floats over Roxas's head, approach Zero and press A while the reticule shows to give him the bone.

Happily fed, Zero floats to where a Heartless is hiding and circles around the location.

If you approach the south exit, Lock, Shock, and Barrel make an appearance.

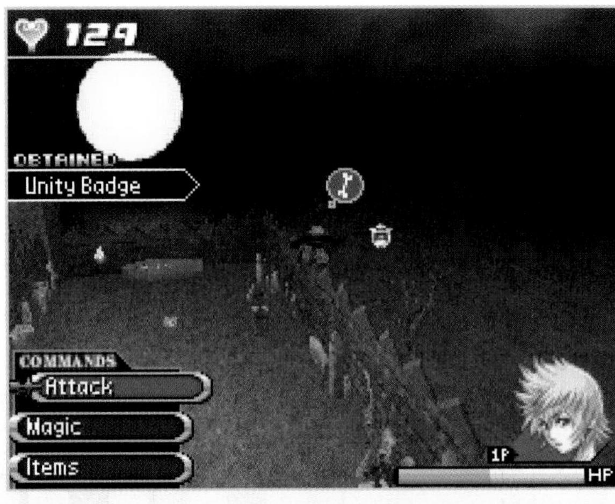

To reach the **Unity Badge** hovering over the Graveyard, you'll need the High Jump and Glide abilities.

If you give Zero a Bone and he leaves the Graveyard, it means there are no more Heartless to find there. Follow Zero back to Halloween Town Square and continue feeding him Bones to make him show you the locations of hidden Snowy Crystals. Use Fire spells to eradicate the foes.

Zero finds one last Heartless hiding near the dark corridor.

When you give Zero a Bone and he leaves Town Square, follow him back to the Entrance. Zero points out one last Snowy Crystal hiding in a lamppost. Defeat it and your Mission Gauge should fill to 100%. Time to say goodbye to Zero and RTC!

COLLECT HEARTS

MISSION 46

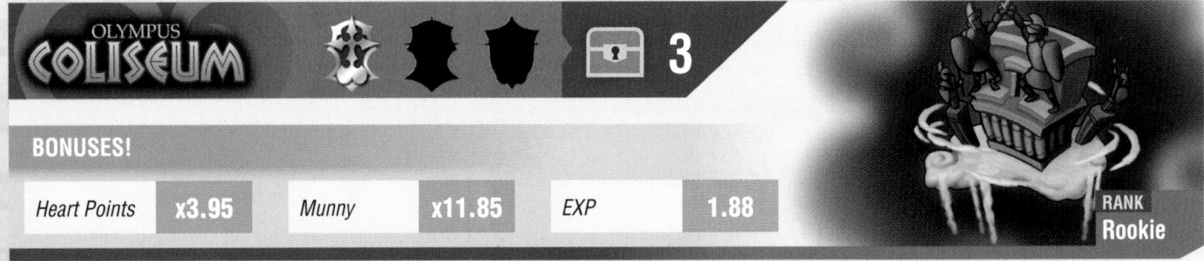

ENEMIES

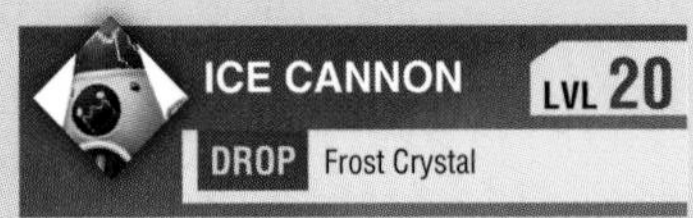

REWARDS	
Clear Bonuses	Random Bonuses
Elixir Recipe	Lightning Shard (30%)
Hi-Potion	Panacea (35%)
Thunder (MG)	None (35%)

CHAMP'S CHALLENGE

Work with Demyx to clear the cannons away from the entrance.

Demyx is your partner until you enter the Coliseum. Defeat the Heartless near the entrance, then enter the vestibule. After Phil emerges from his training session with Herc, open the nearby chest to collect a **Lightning Shard**, then speak to the satyr to begin the day's training.

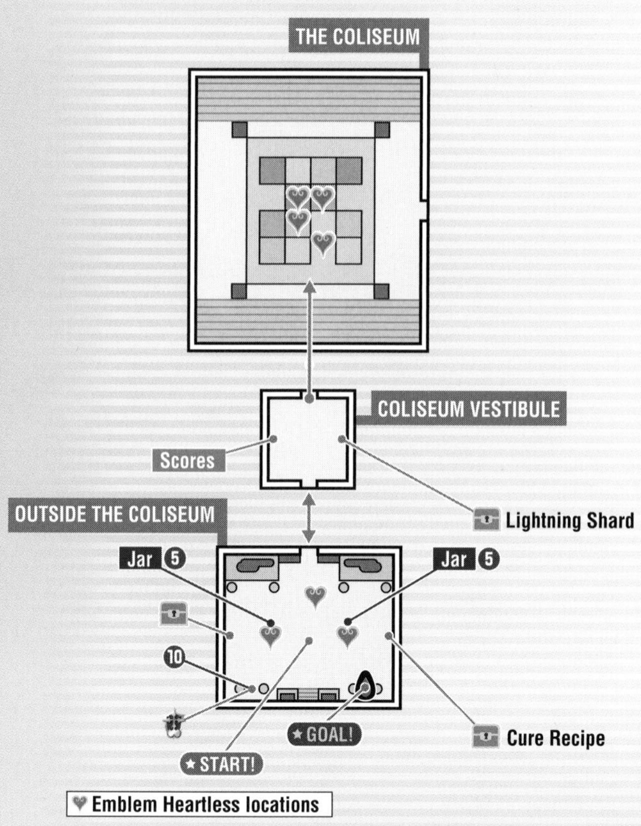

Known as the Champ's Challenge, this training session is much the same as previous ones. Smack the barrels toward groups of Heartless to destroy them. Kill additional Heartless before the chain rings surrounding them disappear to score higher. Collecting 230 heart points while training is enough to complete the mission, but Phil offers additional opportunities to train until you've collected 460 or more heart points and filled the Mission Gauge 100%. Once the Mission Gauge is full, Phil leaves. It should be noted that you get three attempts to fill the gauge; if you don't achieve 100% at that time, then the mission ends.

Use barrels on higher levels to destroy Heartless on lower levels.

COLLECT HEARTS

MISSION 47

WONDERLAND

3

BONUSES!

Heart Points	x3.95	Munny	x11.85	EXP	1.88

RANK Rookie

ENEMIES

GREY CAPRICE LVL 20 — DROP Aerial Tech

SAPPHIRE ELEGY LVL 7 — DROP Rune Tech

STRIPED ARIA LVL 20 — DROP Gust Shard

LURK LIZARD LVL 22 — DROP Lightning Shard

REWARDS	
Clear Bonuses	Random Bonuses
Blizzara	Iron (40%)
Gust Gem	Ether (40%)
Lightning Shard	None (20%)

BIZARRO WORLD

Roxas's mission is to defeat Heartless and collect heart points in Wonderland, a strange world where nothing makes sense. Collect the **Iron** from the chest behind the dark corridor, then enter the next room.

The White Rabbit is in too big a hurry to greet new visitors.

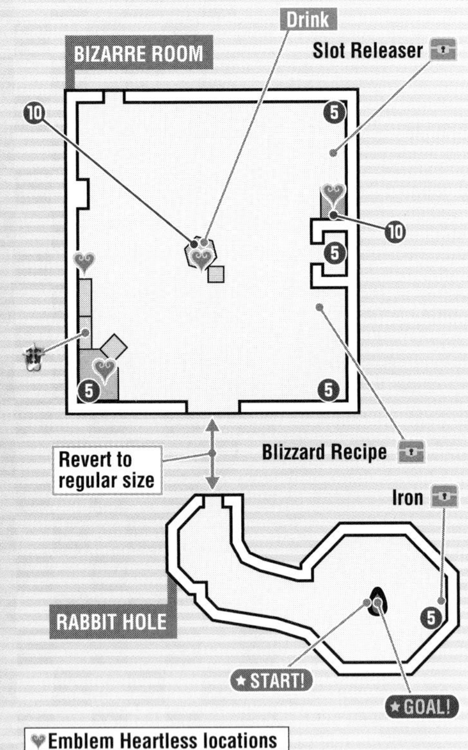

Drinking from the bottles on the central table shrinks or enlarges Roxas as needed.

The mysterious White Rabbit has shrunk and flees through a tiny door. Lucky for Roxas, the Doorknob tells him to drink from the bottle on the central table to decrease in size.

Now that Roxas is small, move around the Bizarre Room and take out the Heartless that appear. Remember to jump atop the central table as well as the stove on the east wall. When the room is clear, approach the brown chairs along the west wall. Strike the chair on the right and it reveals itself to be a Lurk Lizard in disguise!

Sapphire Elegies can warp away the instant you attack, while Grey Caprices can trade places with you if their missiles strike!

Examine the brown chair to reveal the Lurk Lizard.

BOSS!

LURK LIZARD

The Lurk Lizard is essentially a bigger, tougher version of the Veil Lizard fought at Twilight Town. Occasionally, the beast vanishes, attacking with its tongue and glowing eyes. If caught by the tongue, press the attack button repeatedly to escape. Try to use the footstep sounds to locate it, then bash it to make it reappear. Also, it's glowing eye attack gives away its location, if you can trace the attack to its source.

At close range, it attacks by spinning. This attack can inflict shoe-glue status on Roxas, making him unable to jump or perform aerial combos. Avoid this by casting spells at close distance, just outside the range of its tail. Blizzard and Fire spells are particularly effective.

After defeating the Lurk Lizard, drink from the bottle on the table to return to normal size and then RTC.

ELIMINATE THE SOLID ARMOR

MISSION 48

ENEMIES

LOUDMOUTH LVL 17
DROP Shining Shard

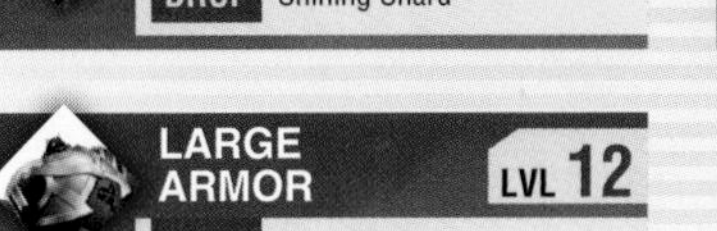

REWARDS

Clear Bonuses	Random Bonuses
Rune Tech	Blizzard Recipe (20%)
Blizzard Recipe	Hi-Potion (20%)
Lightning Shard	Potion (30%)
—	None (30%)

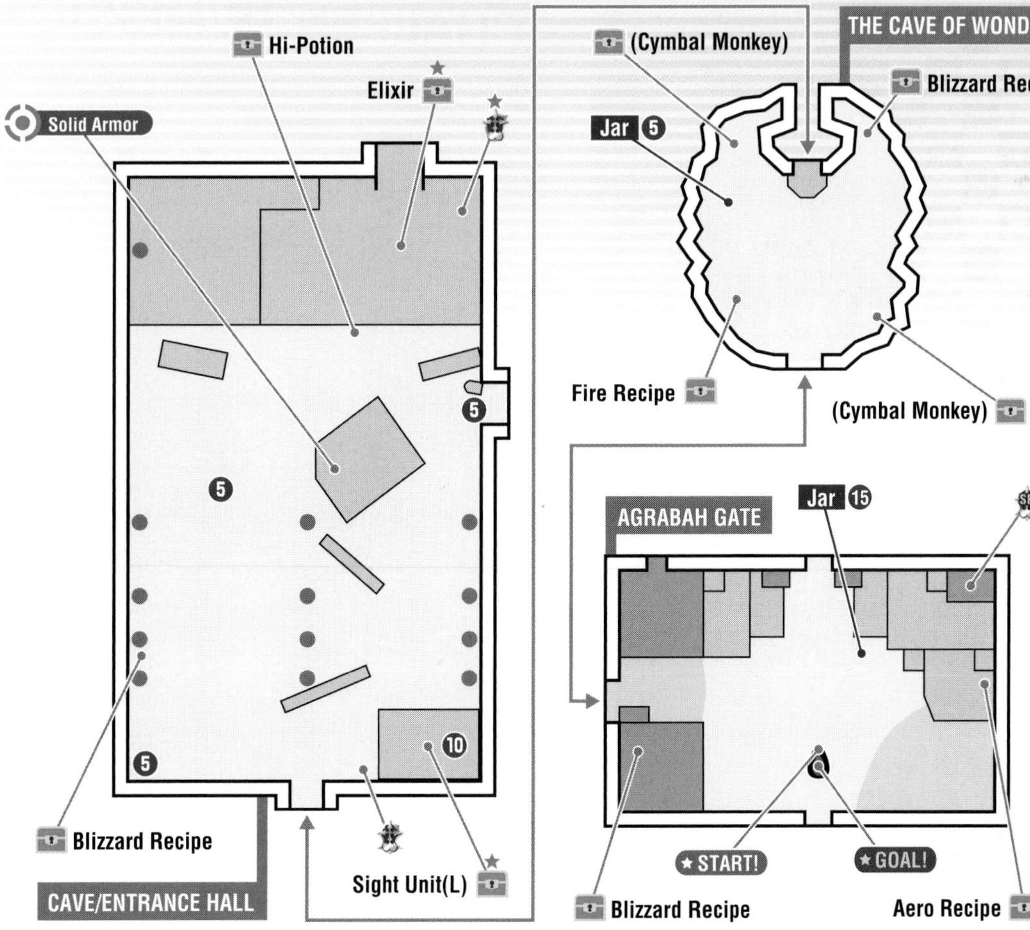

TARGET ACQUIRED

Enemies attack outside the Cave of Wonders.

Collect the **Aero Recipe**, **Blizzard Recipe,** and **Ordeal Blazon** in the Agrabah Gate area. Then enter the secret door to the Cave of Wonders; the Solid Armor is waiting just inside the Entrance Hall.

SOLID ARMOR

BOSS!

Although larger, tougher and more durable, the Solid Armor is really no different than a Large Armor. Jump to cast Blizzard spells on its head to knock it over for a longer duration. While it's down, target the head with additional spells or combo attacks. When the Solid Armor rises, it swings its arms and performs a cannonball jump in retaliation, so move away. The head is difficult to hit with aerial combos unless you attack from behind.

Try to contain your movement in the Entrance Hall while fighting. Stepping into various zones triggers the appearance of additional Large Armors, who work with the Solid Armor to defeat Roxas and Xaldin. The Large Armor locations are marked on the map in this section. Also, avoid fighting near the debris on the floor so that your movements and attacks are more accurate.

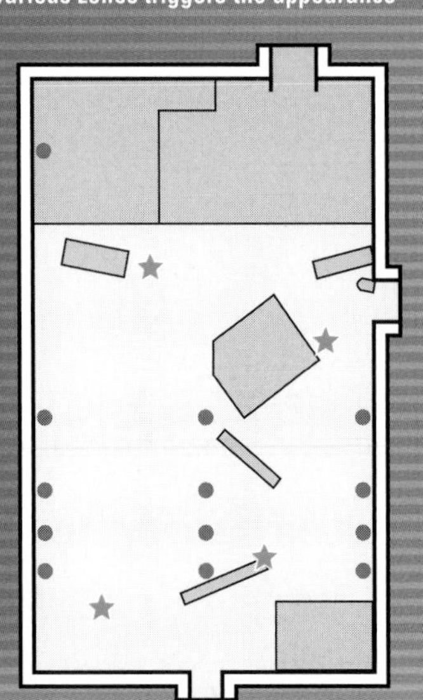

Chests Out of Reach

To reach the north ledge with a High Jump, stand on the very edge of the pink and gold column, as shown.

*After grabbing the Elixir and Unity Badge, jump and glide over to the platform beside the exit to get the **Sight Unit(L)**.*

*During your first attempt at this mission, you'll be unable to reach the **Sight Unit(L)** on the high ledge near the doorway or the **Elixir** and **Unity Badge** on the high north area. Try this mission again as a Holo-Mission after attaining the High Jump LV3 and Glide abilities. After defeating the Solid Armor and Large Armors, jump onto the tip of the overturned pink and gold column below the north rise. High Jump and grab hold of the ledge, then climb up.*

CHALLENGE MISSION

Objective: **Finish in record time!**

Restrictions: **Level capped at 20, enemy level +2**

Rewards	
Sigils Acquired	Clear Time
3	02:20:00 or less
2	02:20:01 - 03:20:00
1	03:20:01 - 04:20:00

Proceed directly to the Cave and fight the Solid Armor, ignoring all other foes to the best of your abilities. Strike it until it falls, then target it's head with Blizzard spells to empty its life bars.

SPECIAL CHALLENGE

Objective: Don't miss with attacks!

Restrictions: No attack magic, enemy level +12

Rewards	
Sigils Acquired	Misses
3	10 or less
2	11 to 15 misses
1	16 to 20 misses

Unfortunately, a deflected attack counts as a miss in this challenge. Trying to strike the Solid Armor from the front means your attacks are more likely to bounce off its chest. Therefore, always attack its head from behind while it is standing, even though this means you must run around to attack its head when it falls over.

COLLECT HEARTS

MISSION 49

BONUSES!

Heart Points	x3.95	Munny	x11.85	EXP	1.88

RANK Rookie

ENEMIES

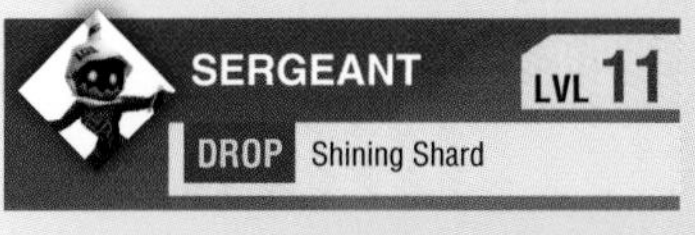

Enemy	LVL	DROP
SERGEANT	11	Shining Shard
BULLY DOG	14	Lightning Shard
SOLDIER	10	Shield Tech
CYMBAL MONKEY	23	Range Tech
BAD DOG	10	Bronze
ICY CUBE	20	Frost Shard
SNAPPER DOG	12	Power Tech
SNOWY CRYSTAL	22	Frost Shard

REWARDS	
Clear Bonuses	Random Bonuses
Cure	Elixir Recipe (10%)
Bronze	Gear Component A (10%)
Gear Component A (MG)	Bronze (10%)
—	Hi-Potion (20%)
—	Potion (15%)
—	Ether (15%)
—	None (20%)

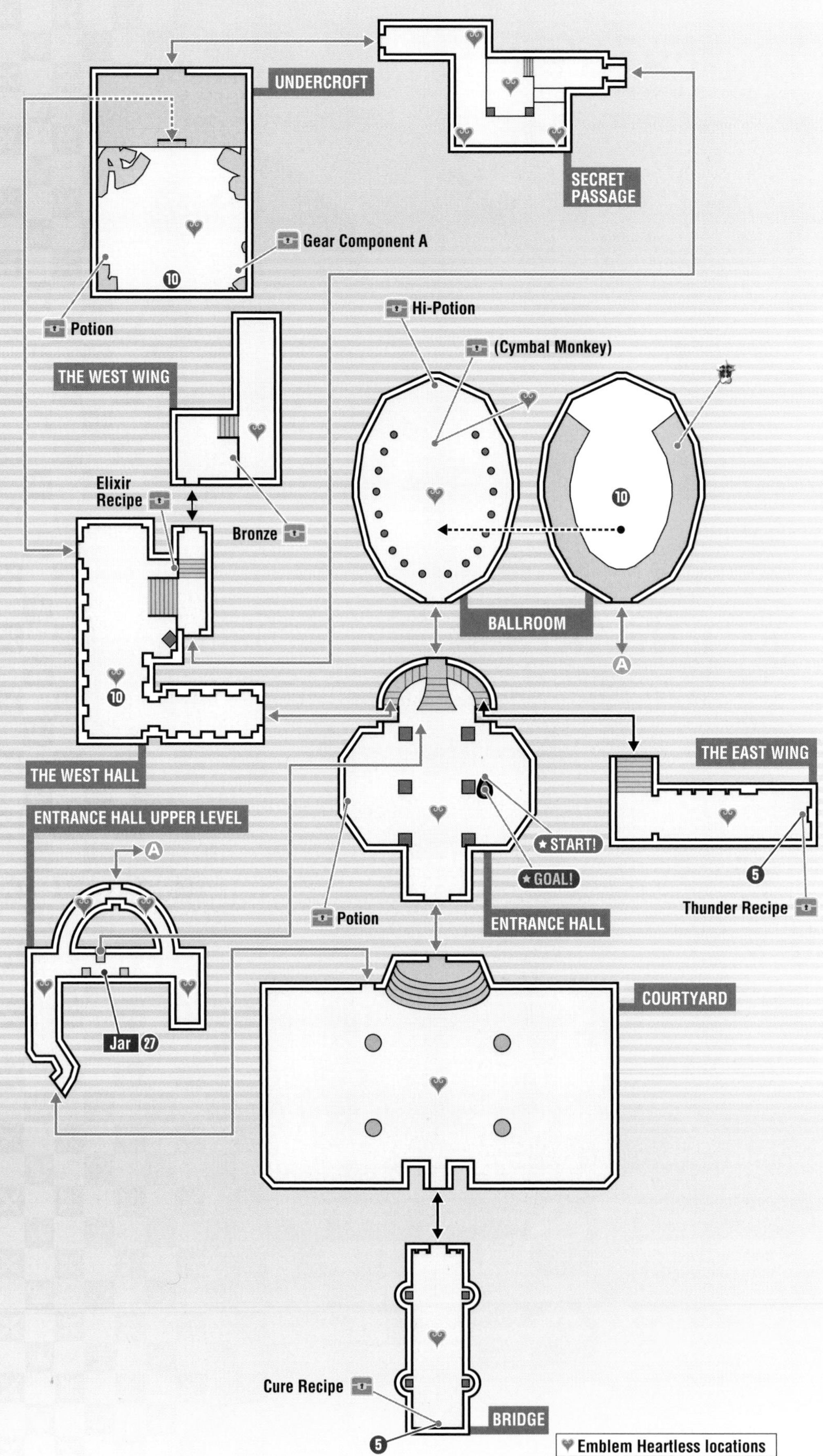
UNDERCROFT
SECRET PASSAGE
Gear Component A
Potion
Hi-Potion
(Cymbal Monkey)
THE WEST WING
Elixir Recipe
Bronze
BALLROOM
THE WEST HALL
THE EAST WING
ENTRANCE HALL UPPER LEVEL
START!
GOAL!
Thunder Recipe
Potion
ENTRANCE HALL
Jar
COURTYARD
Cure Recipe
BRIDGE
Emblem Heartless locations

COME PREPARED

In spite of Xigbar's accompaniment on this mission, prepare by equipping as much magic as possible. You'll need to cast Fire multiple times to deal with Icy Cubes and Snowy Crystals and use plenty of Aero and Blizzard spells for dealing with Snapper Dogs and Bully Dogs, especially when they come in pairs. In spite of the plentiful items in the area, Ethers and Hi-Ethers are sorely lacking. Equip both types of panels to ensure you can cast magic as much as needed. Use the map in this section to locate Emblem Heartless and items, then clean out the entire stage.

Fighting a pair of Bully Dogs can be quite daunting.

DAY 171

Xigbar wants Roxas to score at least 130 points during training in Mission 39. Do so in the Holo-Missions screen if needed, then speak to him again to receive a **Blazing Gem**. Scoring that high can be a bit tough, especially in Standard Mode or Proud Mode.

Before he'll hand over another prize, Xigbar has another Coliseum-related challenge for Roxas to achieve.

VANQUISH THE HEARTLESS THREAT

MISSION 50

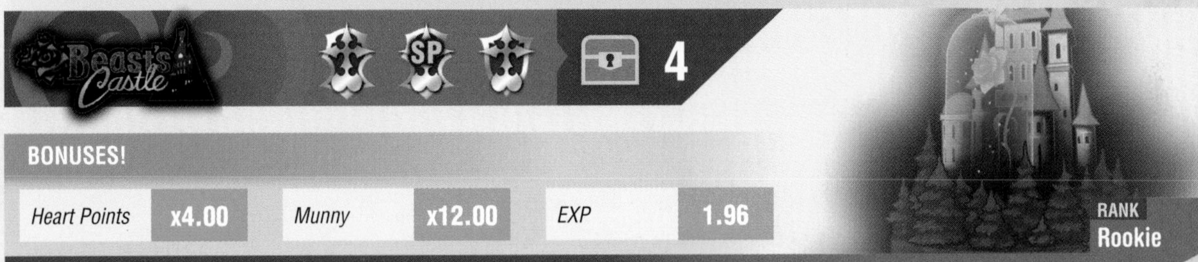

BONUSES!

Heart Points	x4.00	Munny	x12.00	EXP	1.96

RANK Rookie

ENEMIES

Enemy	LVL	DROP
SOLDIER	22	—
BAD DOG	10	Bronze
SNAPPER DOG	12	Power Tech
BULLY DOG	14	Lightning Shard
INFERNAL ENGINE	22	—

REWARDS

Clear Bonuses	Random Bonuses
Cura	Elixir Recipe (10%)
Rune Tech+	Gear Component A (10%)
Bronze	Bronze (10%)
—	Hi-Potion (20%)
—	Potion (15%)
—	Ether (15%)
—	None (20%)

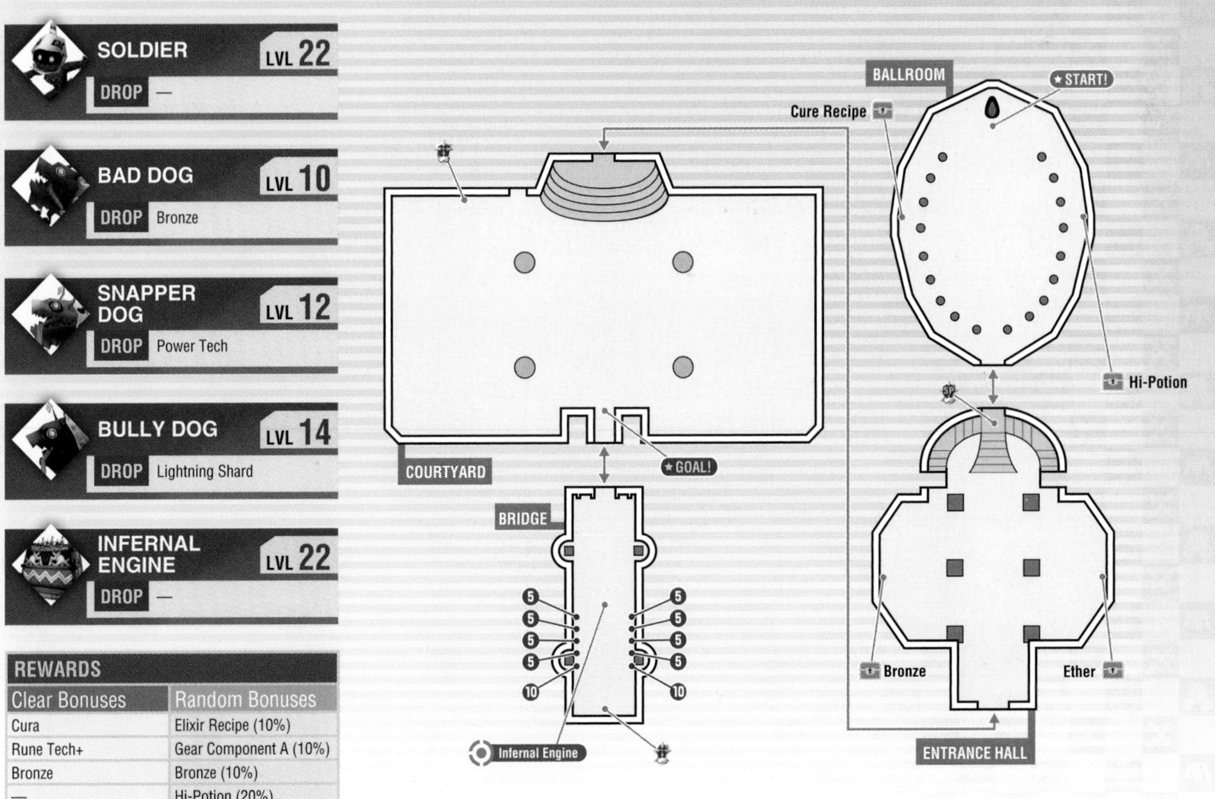

AVOID UNNECESSARY FIGHTS

If the Beast can't handle what's on the other side of the front gate, can Roxas?

Collect items and make your way south. Avoid tangling with enemies as much as possible and conserve your use of magic and recovery items for the upcoming boss battle. While in the courtyard, Roxas hears a terrible noise coming from the Bridge.

BOSS!

INFERNAL ENGINE

The ultimate Heartless war machine is on the Bridge, attempting to storm the castle! Each of its attacks requires a virtually separate strategy, so pay close attention.

Although running up and attacking the mouth is somewhat successful, this leaves Roxas extremely vulnerable to counterattack. Instead, stay away from the Infernal Engine and use Air Slides and Dodge Rolls to avoid missile attacks lobbed by the three Heartless dancing on its top. By remaining at medium range, you'll incite the Infernal Engine into opening its mouth and firing its cannon. Block these shots with the right timing to send them flying up to the top, taking out one of the Heartless with each shot.

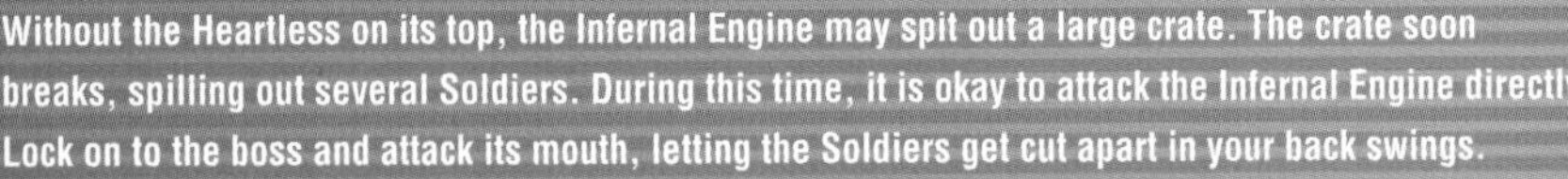

Without the Heartless on its top, the Infernal Engine may spit out a large crate. The crate soon breaks, spilling out several Soldiers. During this time, it is okay to attack the Infernal Engine directly. Lock on to the boss and attack its mouth, letting the Soldiers get cut apart in your back swings.

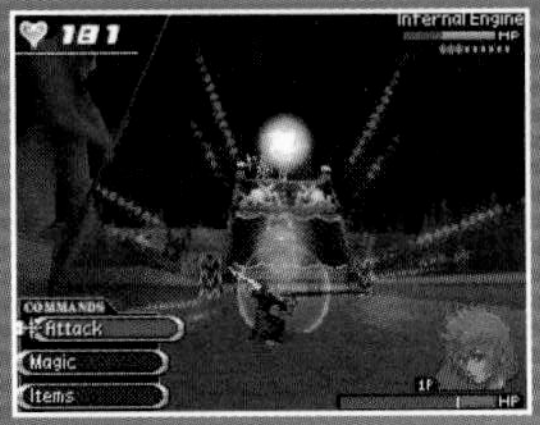

Another good time for a direct assault occurs when the boss opens its mouth and charges its battering ram attack. Move in and attack the ram itself, which is extremely weak, until fully charged. Once the glowing blue energy fades, move to the side and use Air Slides to dash away. The entire engine launches forward with the ram, but the damage is less severe if only the tires hit Roxas.

Probably the most difficult attack to avoid is its hammer, which the boss may extend from its open mouth if Roxas remains at close range for too long. The only defense against this attack is to stay at medium range and prod it into performing its previously mentioned attacks.

Other times, the mouth opens and causes exploding drums to roll out. Back away from the Infernal Engine and Dodge Roll left and right to avoid these drums. Kill the Heartless atop the engine at your first chance and take each opportunity to attack the battering ram. After the Infernal Engine is defeated, collect the **Ordeal Emblem** behind it and return to the Courtyard to complete the mission.

CHALLENGE MISSION

Objective: Finish in record time!

Restrictions: Take 50% more damage, enemy level +12

Rewards	
Sigils Acquired	Clear Time
3	02:30:00 or less
2	02:30:01 - 02:50:00
1	02:50:01 - 03:30:00

Race to the boss fight by using the Glide and Haste abilities. Equip plentiful Thunder and Thundara spells as well as Ethers or Hi-Ethers. Call down lightning into the mouth whenever it opens; otherwise, follow the tactics outlined previously and hope to be fast enough. Finishing the game before taking on this challenge is sure to make winning three Sigils easier.

SPECIAL CHALLENGE

Objective: Avoid taking damage!

Restrictions: Take 50% more damage, enemy level +30

Rewards	
Sigils Acquired	Hits Sustained
3	3 or less
2	4 to 10 hits
1	11 to 15 hits

As with the other special challenges, finishing the game before attempting this challenge helps greatly. Maintain your distance from the Infernal Engine and cast Thunder and Thundara spells to damage it without risking a hit. Otherwise, follow the strategies listed previously and bounce back those projectiles like a champ to reduce your hits sustained.

DAY 172

Saïx promotes Roxas to Agent, so speak to him before visiting the Moogle shop. That way, several new items are added to the purchase and synthesis inventories.

Riku becomes a playable character in Mission Mode. Now that you're more than halfway through the Story Mode missions, it's a good time to replay some missions in both Mission Mode and as Challenges. Panels available only by redeeming Challenge Sigils and Mission Crowns certainly provide an edge, making mission completion easier and less frustrating. Demyx wants Roxas to do his assignment by defeating every hidden Heartless in Mission 45. If you've found them all, speak to him again to receive a **Frost Gem**.

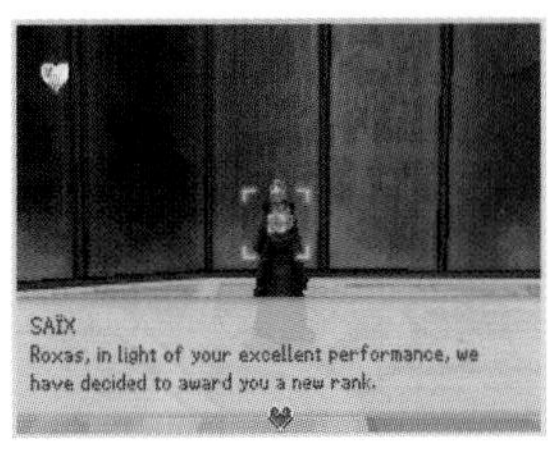

Roxas is doing well in Organization XIII by lasting 172 days.

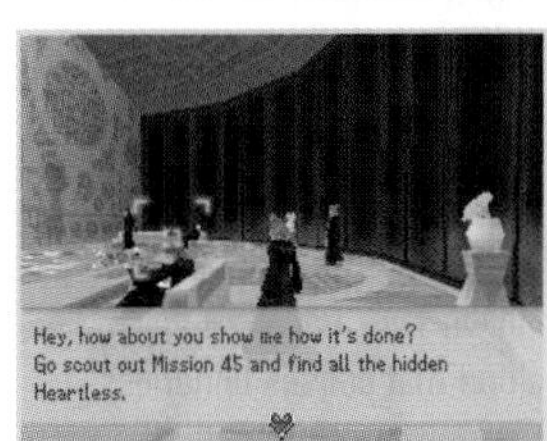

*Find all the Heartless hidden around Halloween Town in Mission 45 to receive a **Frost Gem** from Demyx.*

LIGHT THE LANTERNS

If you used all the pumpkin bombs to defeat Heartless in the Graveyard, leave the area and return to make them reappear. Hit the bombs and knock them toward the four lanterns in the area. The lanterns light up when a bomb explodes near them. When all four lanterns are lit, the grave opens at the north end. Jump atop the grave to proceed to the Boneyard 1 area.

Knock the bombs toward the lanterns to light them. Stay far enough away when the bombs explode to avoid taking damage.

Lighting all four lanterns opens the coffin at the north end, which is how you get to the next area.

As before, knock the pumpkin bombs toward the four lanterns in the area to light them. Light all four of them to open the exit in the northwest corner. At Moonlight Hill, Lock, Shock, and Barrel attack Roxas.

Light more lanterns using pumpkin bombs in the Boneyard.

LOCK, SHOCK, & BARREL

BOSS!

Lock on to one kid at a time and attack until their HP is depleted. All three throw pumpkin bombs at Roxas. Strike these bombs before they explode to knock them away, or block them when thrown to knock them right back at the assailant.

BACK TO YOUR ASSIGNMENT

After chasing off the kids, return to the task of revealing hidden Heartless and defeating them for hearts. Zero is now hanging around, if you'd like his help in finding their locations. Otherwise, just search at the locations marked on the maps in this guide. Fill the Mission Gauge 100% before you RTC.

Wipe out the Heartless hidden around Moonlight Hill with Zero's help.

ELIMINATE THE WAVECREST

MISSION 53

BONUSES!

Heart Points	x4.35	Munny	x13.05	EXP	2.15

RANK Agent

ENEMIES

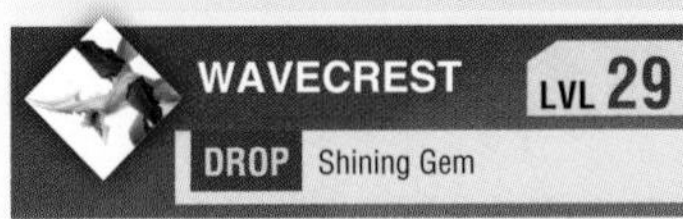

REWARDS	
Clear Bonuses	Random Bonuses
Luck Tech	Elixir Recipe (10%)
Cura Recipe	Combo Tech(30%)
Bronze	Potion (40%)
—	None (20%)

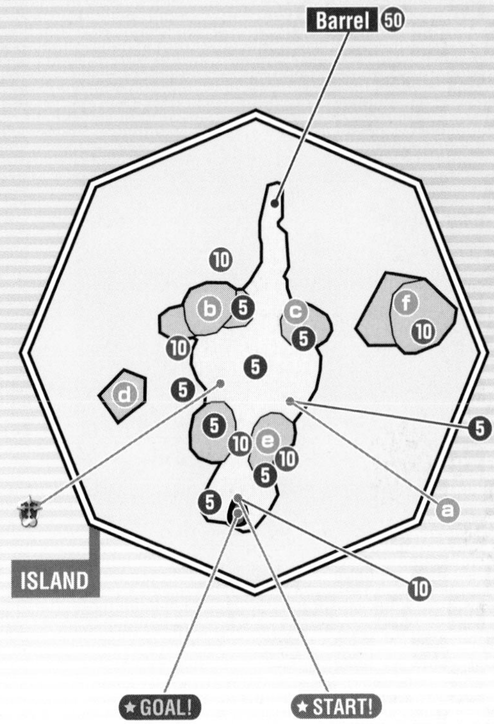

THE TREASURE HUNTERS

Travel north from the dark corridor until Roxas runs across Hook and Smee digging for treasure, but unfortunately they unearth Heartless instead. Defeat the Turquoise Marches and Air Battler to trigger another scene, then go north toward the pirate ship.

LEARNING TO FLY

Roxas meets Tinker Bell, who gives him the temporary ability to Auto-Glide. Jump off the ground and press Y to float. Use the d-pad while floating to fly in any direction. While floating or flying, hold Y to rise or B to descend.

Tinker Bell gives Roxas the ability to fly in the hopes that he will help. But he has a mission to attend to...

Fly to each location marked on the map provided here, examining the dug-up treasure boxes to reveal hidden Heartless. Additional enemies other than what are listed in this section may automatically appear in the nearby area. After defeating the enemies, Roxas automatically returns to the location. Check the dug-up box again to find an item. The target Wavecrest appears when you search location "f," atop the tall rock to the northeast. Defeat it, collect the remaining items, and RTC.

Land at each dig site and examine the treasure box to find Heartless.

Defeat the Heartless at each dig site, then return to claim the item.

Enemies Appearing at Each Map Location & Items Found		
Letter Callout	Enemies	Item Found
a	Air Battler, Turquoise March x2	Gust Shard
b	Air Battler	Potion
c	Air Battler	Panacea
d	Turquoise March x2	Frost Gem
e	Air Battler	Panacea
f	Wavecrest	Lightning Shard

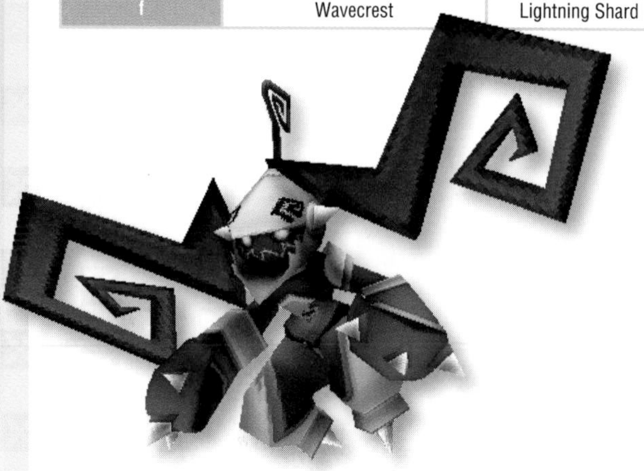

WAVECREST

BOSS!

The Wavecrest cannot be brought to the ground, so this is a battle that must be fought in midair. Fly after the Wavecrest and lock on to its tail. Execute melee combos until the Wavecrest pulls back, then fly away before it flips or dives to avoid taking damage. The Wavecrest is extremely strong against magic, so don't cast spells. Simply fly after it and strike the tail repeatedly until you're victorious.

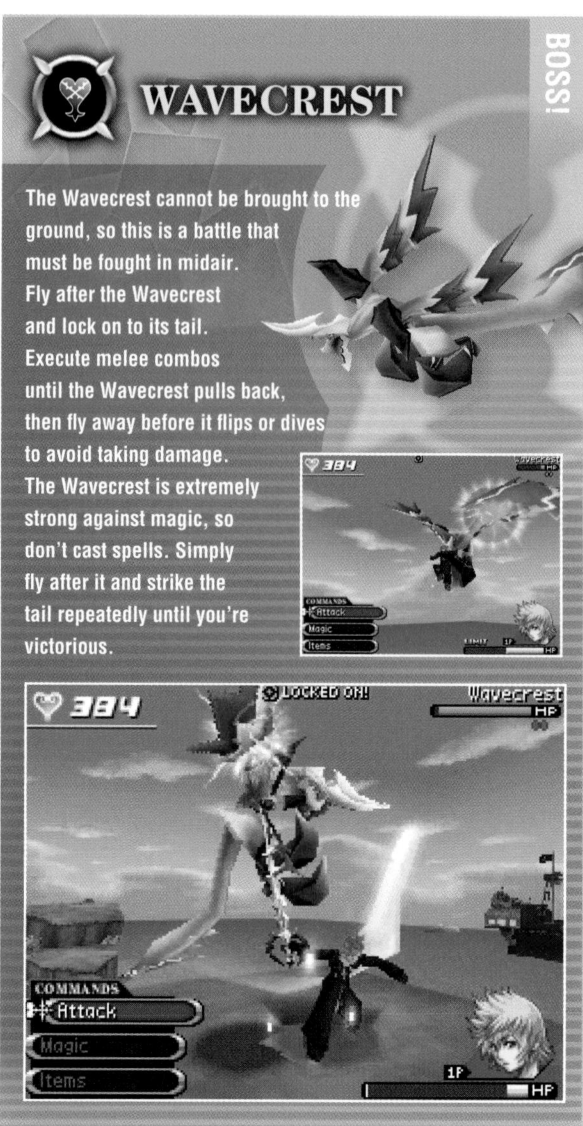

GLIDE TIME!

*The **Glide**③ panel is obtained by completing this mission. Look for it in your "Items Collected" column, a little secret present added to your stash by Tink. Equip it to fly as long as the Y button is held after a jump. While it doesn't function the same as in Never Land, you can now replay previous missions to open chests and collect badges that were previously out of reach.*

ELIMINATE THE DUAL BLADE

MISSION 54

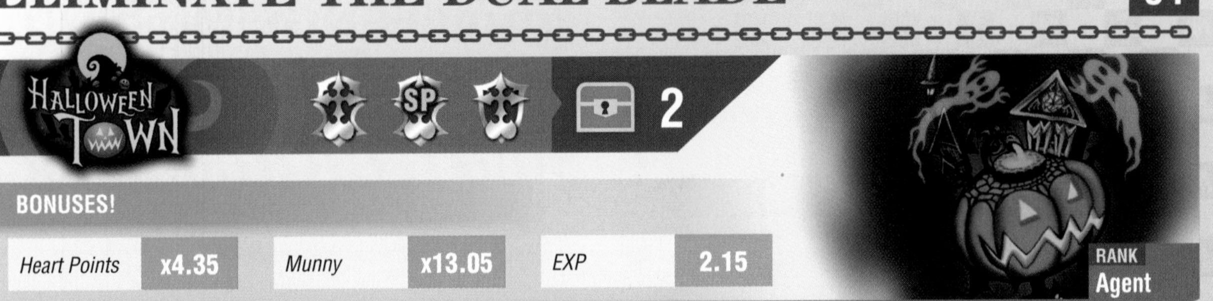

BONUSES!

Heart Points	x4.35	Munny	x13.05	EXP	2.15

ENEMIES

RARE VENDOR LVL 24
DROP Elixir Recipe, Shield Tech, or Iron

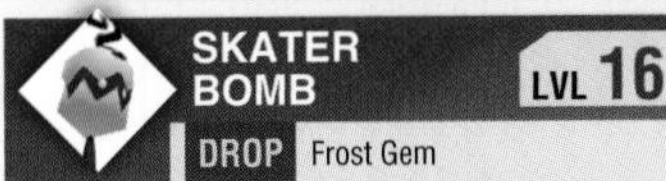

SKATER BOMB LVL 16
DROP Frost Gem

DUAL BLADE LVL 24
DROP Lightning Gem

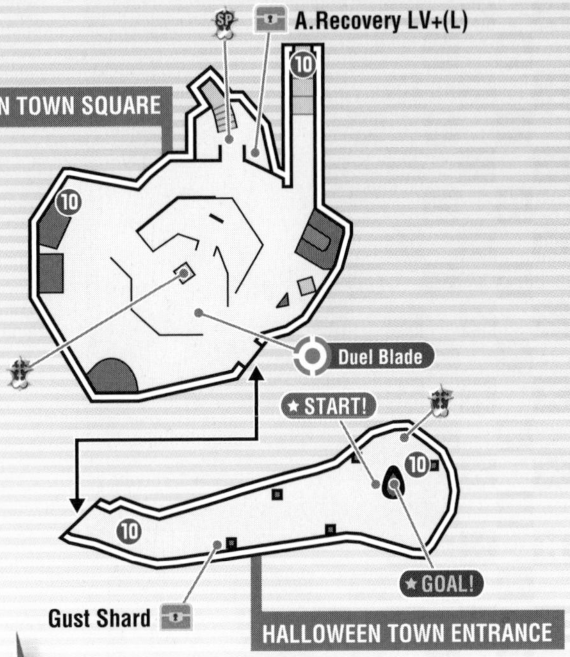

REWARDS

Clear Bonuses	Random Bonuses
Frost Gem	Blizzara Recipe (15%)
Gust Shard	Thunder Recipe (20%)
Gust Shard	Gust Shard (15%)
—	Frost Gem (10%)
—	Blazing Gem (10%)
—	Gust Gem (10%)
—	Ether (10%)
—	None (20%)

A.Recovery LV+(L)
HALLOWEEN TOWN SQUARE
Duel Blade
START!
GOAL!
Gust Shard
HALLOWEEN TOWN ENTRANCE

QUITE A CHALLENGE!

Axel's little extra mission proves to be quite a showstopper. Equip a lot of Thunder magic to deal with the boss in a more effective manner. If you want to come back and try later, Thundara and Thundaga will speed up the process even more.

DAY 173-176

~LIES~

DUAL BLADE

BOSS!

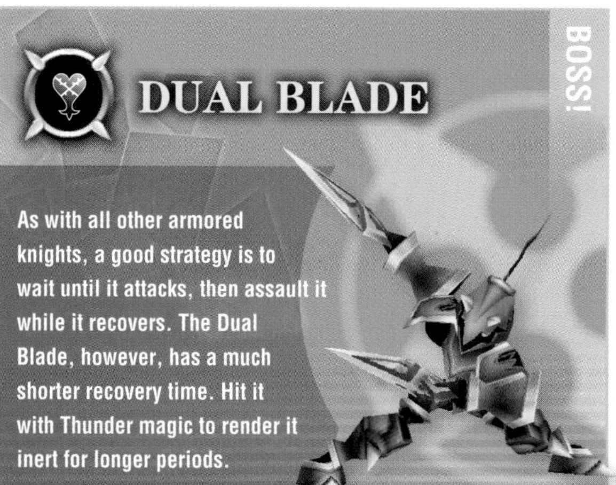

As with all other armored knights, a good strategy is to wait until it attacks, then assault it while it recovers. The Dual Blade, however, has a much shorter recovery time. Hit it with Thunder magic to render it inert for longer periods.

Avoid defeating the Skater Bomb sidekicks, since replacements immediately appear. Focus on taking out the Dual Blade first, and then you can eliminate the Skater Bombs one by one until they stop appearing.

CHALLENGE MISSION

Objective: Finish in record time!

Restrictions: No attack magic, enemy level +5

Rewards	
Sigils Acquired	Clear Time
3	01:00:00 or less
2	01:00:01 - 01:15:00
1	01:15:01 - 01:30:00

Being timely with your blocks against the Dual Blade's focused blade attack creates additional opportunities to strike. Generate as many extra openings as possible, because you can't wait to attack between its attacks!

SPECIAL CHALLENGE

Objective: Avoid taking damage!

Restrictions: Level capped at 10, deal 30% less damage

Rewards	
Sigils Acquired	Hits Sustained
3	1 or less
2	2 to 5 hits
1	6 to 10 hits

More a test of your patience than anything else, this challenge wants to determine if you're willing to wait to attack between its attacks, only to inflict minimal damage. Hit it with Thunder and Thundara spells to provide extra chances to attack. Otherwise, jump or Dodge Roll out of the path of its thrust and attack conservatively, with only two or three hits per combo.

COLLECT ORGANIZATION EMBLEMS

MISSION 55

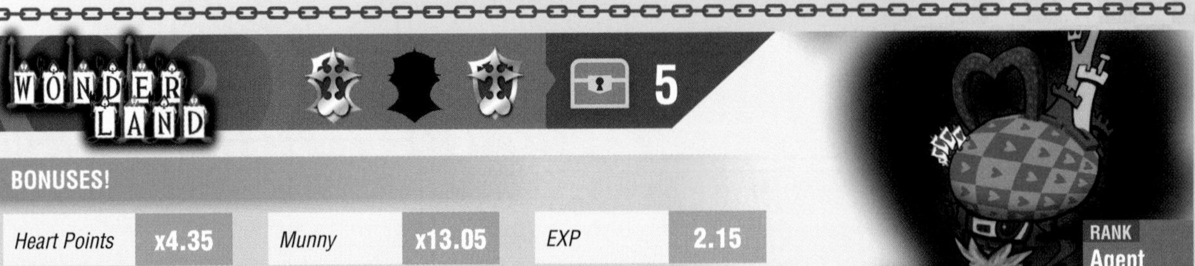

ENEMIES

Enemy	LVL	DROP
GIGAS SHADOW	21	Elixir Recipe
SAPPHIRE ELEGY	20	Rune Tech
GREY CAPRICE	20	Gear Component B
PINK CONCERTO	26	Range Tech
STRIPED ARIA	20	Bronze
TRICKY MONKEY	24	Gear Component B

REWARDS

Clear Bonuses	Random Bonuses
Shining Gem	Aero Recipe (15%)
Dark Ingot	Cure Recipe (15%)
Gear Component B (MG)	Cura Recipe (10%)
—	Elixir Recipe (10%)
—	Shining Gem (10%)
—	Dark Ingot (5%)
—	Hi-Potion (20%)
—	None (20%)

PLEASANT DAY FOR A GLIDE PARTY

Enter the Bizarre Room and drink from the central bottle to shrink in size. The Organization emblems appear afterward, with their rings visible. Use the Glide ability to fly around the room and grab the emblems before their rings vanish. Ignore enemies that appear unless you fail to reach an emblem in time. Defeat an enemy to make the emblem rings reappear, then grab the remaining emblems.

Collect the Organization emblems while their rings still show to better fill the Mission Gauge.

Grab the emblems in the Hedge Maze Entrance and the Queen's Castle areas in a similar manner, and then enter the Lotus Forest. Grab as many emblems as possible while their rings are still visible, then defeat a Heartless to make the rings reappear. After grabbing all the emblems on the ground floor, defeat a Heartless and use the mushrooms in the southwest corner to reach the upper level. Glide across the upper level and collect all the emblems in one flight for greater efficiency.

The Glide ability makes emblem gathering a cinch, both in this mission and previous ones.

Enter the Tea Party Garden via the northeast door in the Lotus Forest. Glide around the room to gather the hovering emblems, then drop to the central table and collect the last ones. If you gathered the emblems only when their rings were showing, your Mission Gauge should be 100% full at this point. If not, try again in a Holo-Mission!

Fly to the emblems hovering high above the ground first.

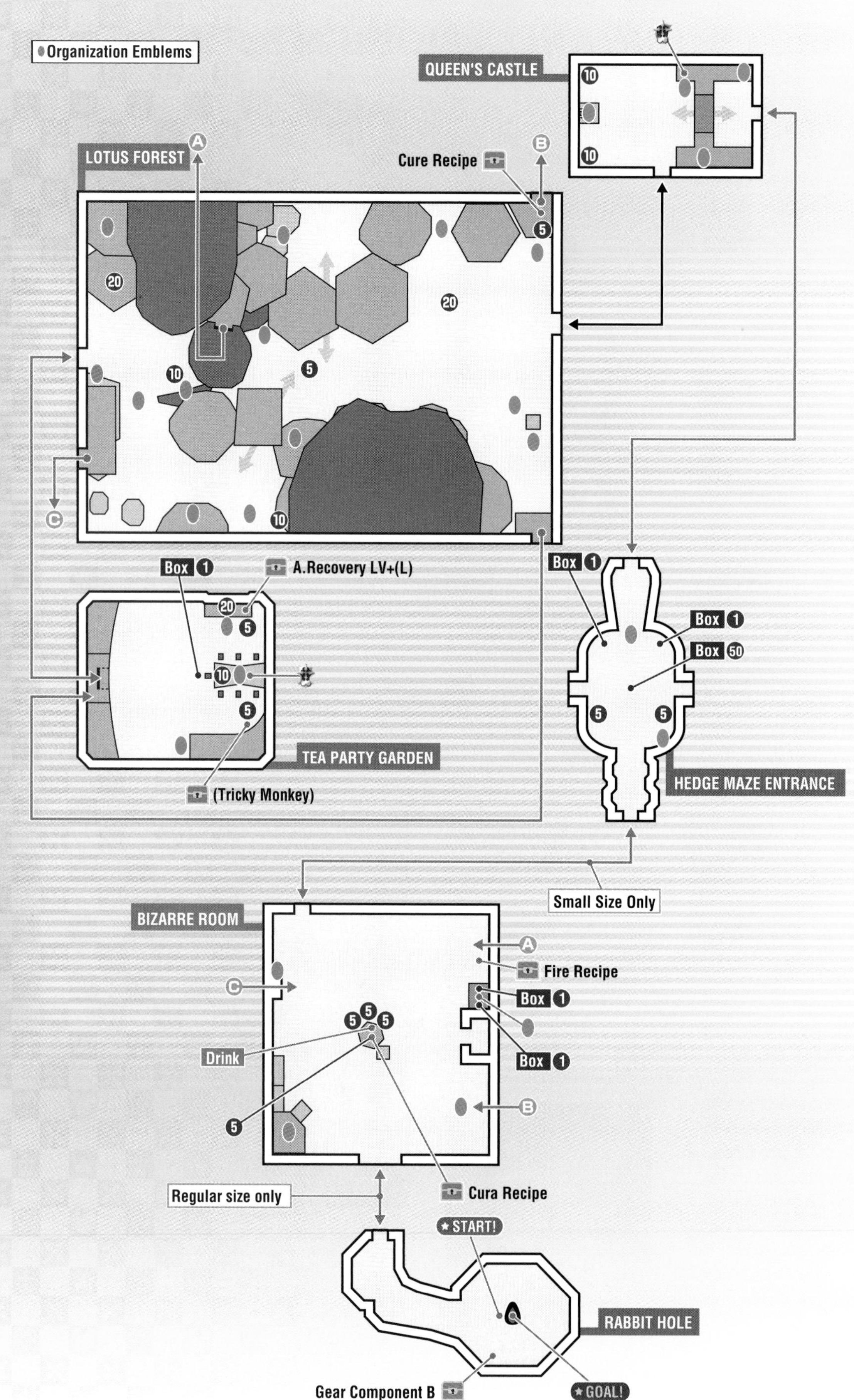
Organization Emblems
QUEEN'S CASTLE
LOTUS FOREST
Cure Recipe
Box 1
A.Recovery LV+(L)
Box 1
Box 50
TEA PARTY GARDEN
(Tricky Monkey)
HEDGE MAZE ENTRANCE
Small Size Only
BIZARRE ROOM
Fire Recipe
Box 1
Drink
Box 1
Regular size only
Cura Recipe
START!
RABBIT HOLE
Gear Component B
GOAL!

CHALLENGE MISSION

Objective: Finish in record time!

Restrictions: Take 20% more damage, enemy level +1

Rewards	
Sigils Acquired	Clear Time
3	02:25:00 or less
2	02:25:01 - 03:00:00
1	03:00:01 - 03:40:00

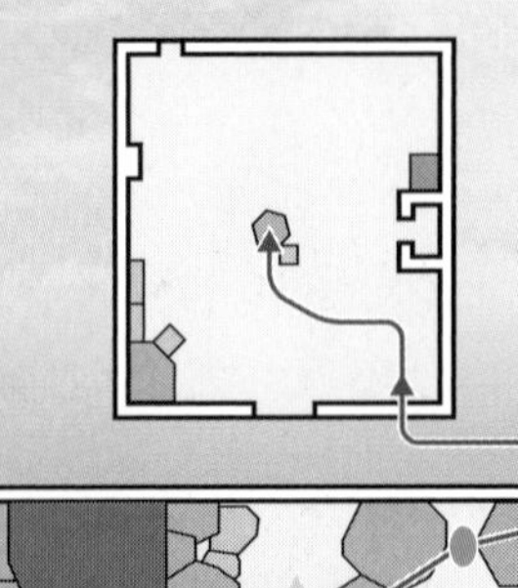

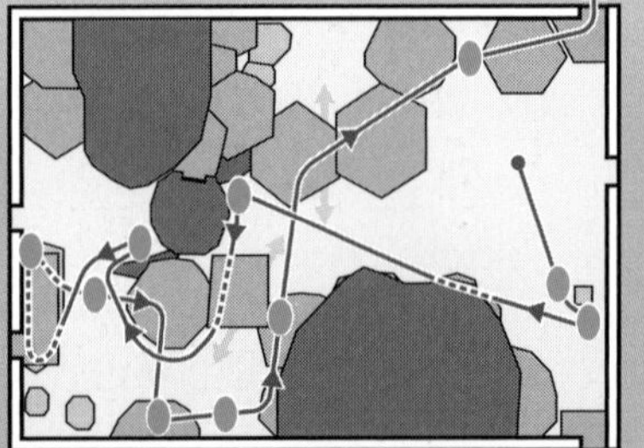

Visit the Bizarre Room, take the pill to shrink, and begin collecting emblems as rapidly as possible without regard to the enemies. Collect all 10 on your way to the Lotus Forest. Inside the Lotus Forest, use the route drawn on the map in this section to collect 10 more emblems in the area. Next, exit via the northeast door on the upper level to warp back to the Bizarre Room. Quickly take the pill without triggering any Heartless appearances and RTC before losing a Sigil.

DAY 193

Xaldin wants Roxas to combine a Moonstone and Shield Tech via synthesis to create a Perfect Block(L) panel. He'll provide a **Range Tech** for a successful combination.

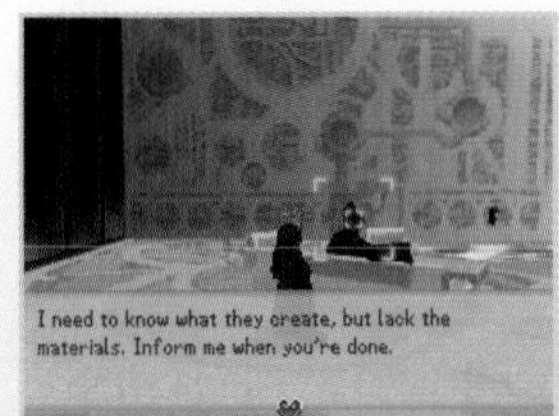

ELIMINATE BOTH GIANT HEARTLESS

MISSION 56

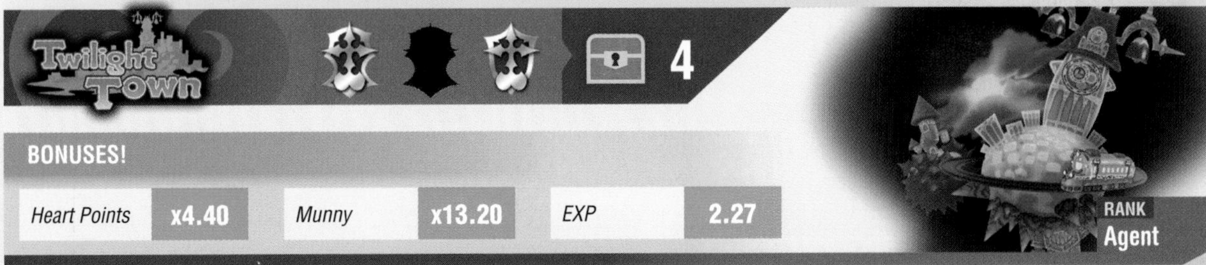

BONUSES!

Heart Points	x4.40	Munny	x13.20	EXP	2.27

ENEMIES

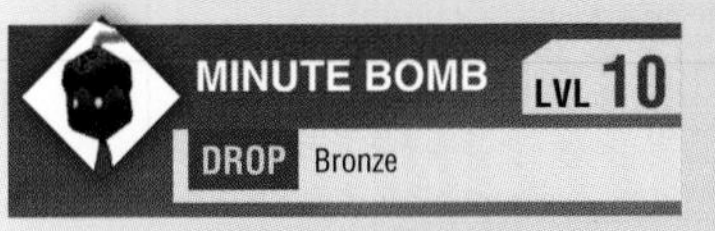

MINUTE BOMB LVL 10 — DROP Bronze

DETONATOR LVL 26 — DROP Gear Component B

BARRIER MASTER LVL 26 — DROP Shield Tech

TRICKY MONKEY LVL 26 — DROP Gear Component B

HEAT SABER LVL 30 — DROP Power Tech

DESTROYER LVL 26 — DROP Shining Gem

REWARDS

Clear Bonuses	Random Bonuses
Thundara	Elixir Recipe (15%)
LV Doubler⑥	Bronze (10%)
Blizzara	Moonstone (15%)
—	Hi-Potion (20%)
—	Potion (20%)
—	None (20%)

TRIO TANGO

Axel's and Xion's help comes in handy during this difficult mission.

Axel and Xion accompany Roxas on this mission. Gather the items in the Side Street area before entering the Sandlot. After defeating the Heat Saber, ascend Station Heights to battle the Destroyer at Station Plaza.

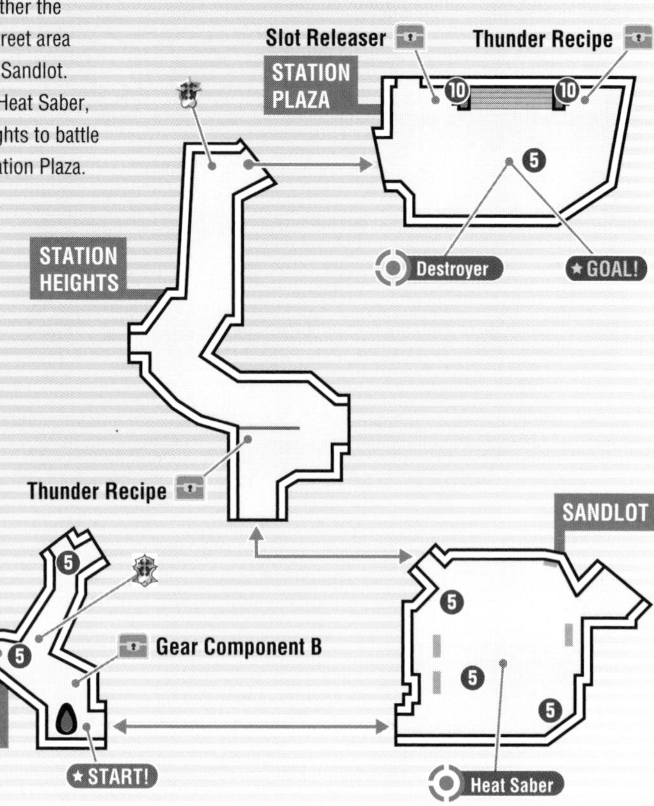

HEAT SABER

BOSS!

The Heat Saber is rendered virtually invulnerable by the protection of a Barrier Master. Lock on to the Barrier Master and attack it until it drops its book. When the Heat Saber closes in, lead it away from the Barrier Master to the other side of the Sandlot. After doing so, return to the Barrier Master and continue attacking it. Repeat this until the Barrier Master is destroyed.

Unlike other armored Heartless, the Heat Saber doesn't really become exhausted between its attacks; instead, it continues to block and dodge while standing still. The only way to stun it is to hit it with Blizzard or Blizzara spells. If you run out of spells, use Ethers to recharge your magic and cast again. Limit Breaks are effective but can be deadly if Roxas fails to eliminate the Heat Saber. Refrain from using Limit Breaks until the boss's HP is down to one bar. Use Limit Break only one time, since another boss roams elsewhere in Twilight Town.

BOSS!

DESTROYER

Avoid fighting the Minute Bombs on the ground, except to jump away from them if they begin to countdown to detonation. The Destroyer fights exactly like a stronger, tougher version of the Guardian. When it puts its "arms" together and bends to the ground, move left or right to get out of the path of its cutting beam. Move beneath it or to its rear, attacking it while it fires.

The Destroyer also fires twin beams from both arms simultaneously for extended periods, tracking Roxas on the ground. Again, move underneath it and attack from below. Casting Thunder magic on the boss can disrupt any of its laser attacks, inflicting great damage in the process.

CHALLENGE MISSION

Objective: Finish in record time!

Restrictions: No recovery items, take 30% more damage

Rewards

Sigils Acquired	Clear Time
3	03:30:00 or less
2	03:30:01 - 04:00:00
1	04:00:01 - 05:00:00

Start the battle against the Heat Saber by repeatedly casting Blizzard magic against it, especially Blizzaga. These spells cause it to stagger, allowing for more opportunities to strike within a short time. If Roxas's HP drops to the Limit Break range, save it for the battle against the Destroyer. Avoid healing and hit it with one Limit Break after another. Gaining three Sigils depends on it!

DAY 194-197

Mission 59 remains unavailable until you use a Limit Break to defeat 30 enemies and speak to Xigbar. The enemy must succumb during the Limit Break. The simplest way to achieve this feat is to repeat Mission 06 until Xigbar's happy. Xion's sorry for worrying you and consequently hands over a **Bronze**.

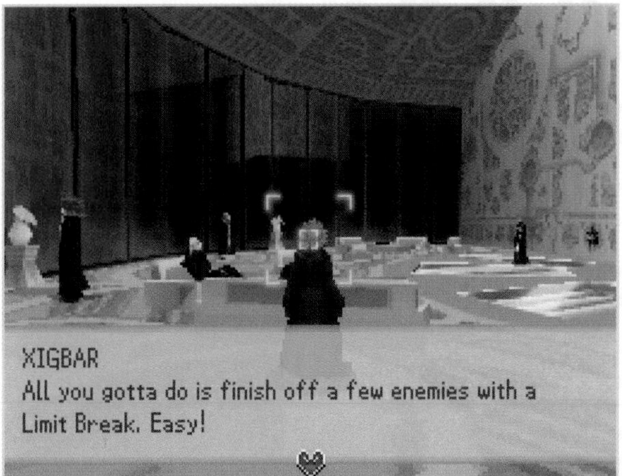

Roxas starts with low HP in Mission 06, so complete this mission repeatedly to meet Xigbar's demands.

ELIMINATE THE COMMANDERS

MISSION 57

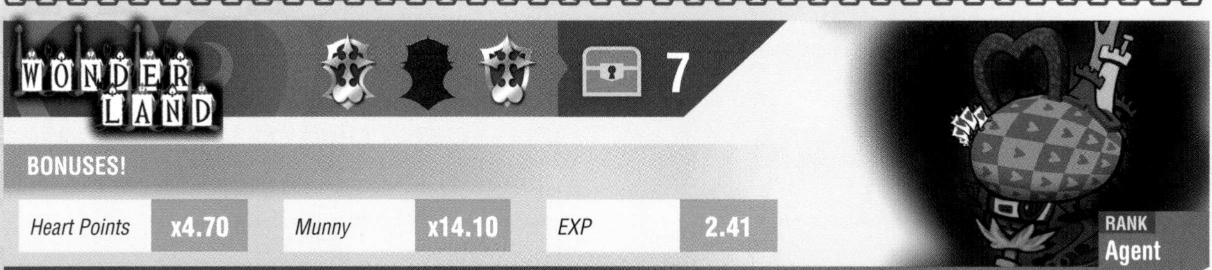

ENEMIES

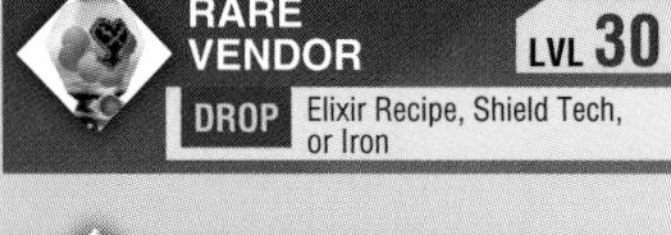

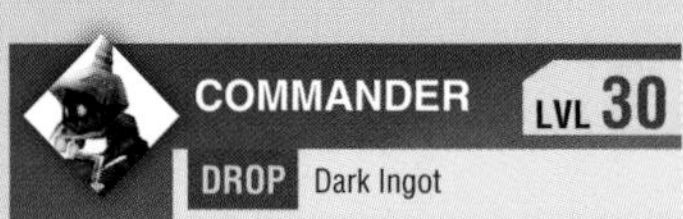

REWARDS	
Clear Bonuses	Random Bonuses
Blizzara	Aero Recipe (15%)
Gear Component B	Cure Recipe (15%)
Dark Ingot	Cura Recipe (10%)
—	Elixir Recipe (10%)
—	Shining Gem (10%)
—	Dark Ingot (5%)
—	Hi-Potion (20%)
—	None (20%)

PARANOID LAND

The Queen of Hearts is highly upset over recent intrusions in her domain.

Follow the White Rabbit north to the Queen's Castle area. It seems a trio of suspects has Wonderland in a tizzy. Following the scene, clear the area of Heartless and return to the Hedge Maze Entrance. The east door is now open.

PAST WATCHFUL EYES

Proceed through the White Rose Hedge Maze until Roxas and Luxord discover a card soldier on patrol. Every few seconds, the soldier closes his eyes to yawn. When its field of sight diminishes, run quickly past the guard's domain.

The guard's field of sight is displayed on the ground. Stay out of it to avoid detection.

Just past the first card guard, you'll encounter the first Commander. These enemies are just larger, sturdier versions of Soldiers and Sergeants. Block their spinning kick attacks to stun them and just keep melee attacking them until they succumb.

Commanders are simple to eliminate. Reaching them is the hard part...

Sneak past another card guard when its eyes are closed. Grab the **Ordeal Badge** right in front of it, then dash to the right to encounter yet another Commander.

*The **Ordeal Badge** sits right in front of a guard. Get the item and continue to the right once the guard's eyes close.*

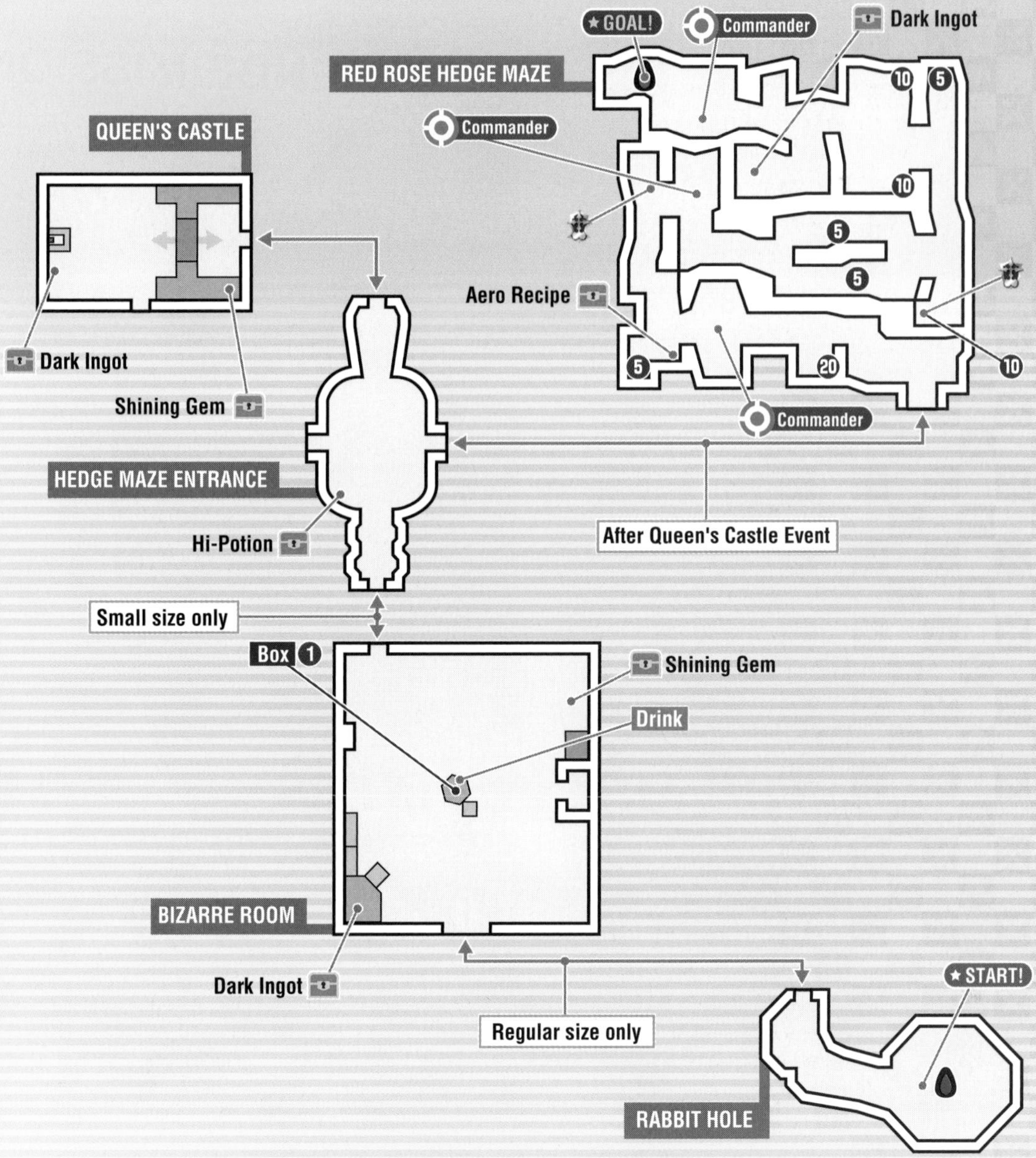

RED ROSE HEDGE MAZE

★ GOAL!

Commander

Dark Ingot

Commander

Aero Recipe

Commander

QUEEN'S CASTLE

Dark Ingot

Shining Gem

HEDGE MAZE ENTRANCE

Hi-Potion

After Queen's Castle Event

Small size only

Box 1

Shining Gem

Drink

BIZARRE ROOM

Dark Ingot

Regular size only

★ START!

RABBIT HOLE

CARD SANDWICH

Continue east and stop at the corner. Look east to spot two card guards patrolling. The easier guard to sneak past is the one patrolling to the southwest. Wait until it heads your direction before turning north. Stop before falling within sight of the guard patrolling to the northeast, wait for him to turn away, and continue.

Watch the two guards patrol before moving past the one on the right.

Avoid running into the second guard when leaving the area.

CONTINUE NORTH, THEN NORTHWEST

Patience is a virtue for those who can keep their eyes open.

Luxord decides to open a closer dark corridor after Roxas defeats the final Commander.

Head north until you spot the sight lines of two more card guards in the northeast corner of the map. They both close their eyes at the same time, so glide between them when that happens.

Grab a **Dark Ingot** from the chest in a nook off to the left, then continue toward the northwest corner of the map. After defeating the final Commander, Luxord creates a dark corridor for convenience. Use it to RTC.

CHALLENGE MISSION

Objective: Finish in record time!

Restrictions: No recovery items, take 30% more damage

Rewards

Sigils Acquired	Clear Time
3	01:25:00 or less
2	01:25:01 - 02:00:00
1	02:00:01 - 02:30:00

The best advice here is to complete the game before attempting this challenge. Use the Glide ability (or preferably the Rocket Glide ability) to fly through every area, speeding travel. A high-powered weapon and a high level Block ability help speed along the Commanders' individual demise. Try to block their spin kicks so that you don't have to wait to attack, and use spells to quickly reduce their HP.

ELIMINATE THE ARTFUL FLYERS

MISSION 58

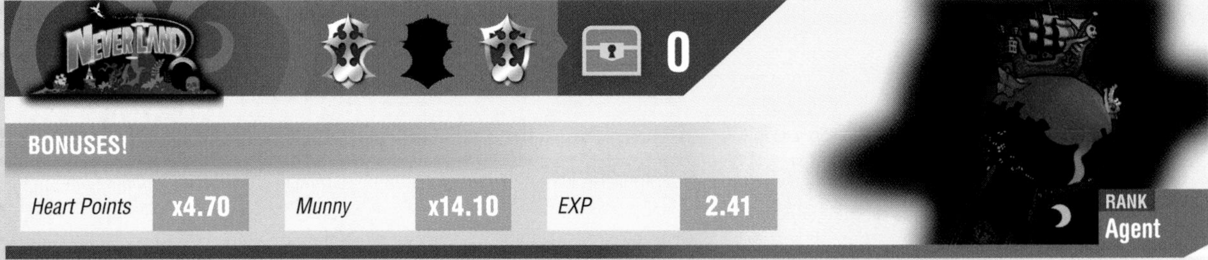

BONUSES!

Heart Points	x4.70	Munny	x14.10	EXP	2.41

RANK Agent

ENEMIES

TURQUOISE MARCH LVL 20 — DROP Shining Gem

AIR BATTLER LVL 20 — DROP Gust Shard

BUBBLE BEAT LVL 30 — DROP Frost Shard

ARTFUL FLYER LVL 30 — DROP Power Tech+

REWARDS

Clear Bonuses	Random Bonuses
Cure	Elixir Recipe (10%)
Cura Recipe	Combo Tech(30%)
Dark Ingot	Potion (40%)
—	None (20%)

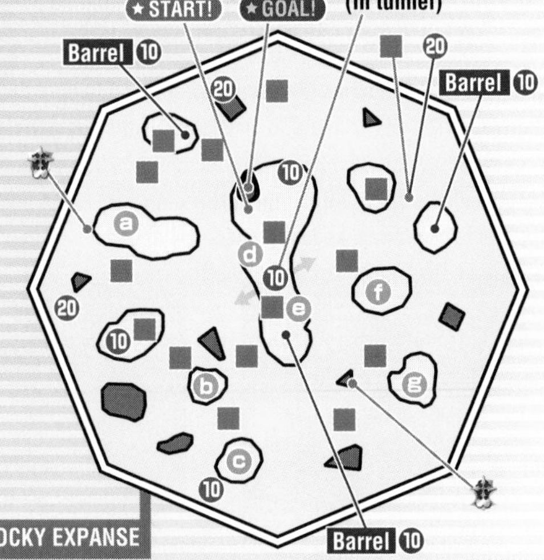

■ Emblem Heartless locations in Challenge Mission

CONSTANT BARRAGE

Proceed south across the central isle until Tinker Bell arrives and sprinkles Axel and Roxas with fairy dust. But even though problem number one is handled, the duo must now operate under constant threat of cannon fire from Hook's pirate ship. A cannonball fires every 10 to 15 seconds. Avoid damage by either moving or blocking the cannonballs with the right timing. If enemies are nearby, bounce cannonballs at them to knock them out!

Hook's cannon fires on Roxas intermittently throughout this mission.

RESUME CHECKING BOXES

As with your previous visit to Never Land, fly to the locations marked on the map and check the dug-up boxes to find Heartless. After defeating the Heartless, Roxas and Axel automatically return to the location. Check the box again to find the item located there. The Artful Flyers are located at positions "a", "e", and "g" marked on the map in this section. These creatures are essentially bigger, more resilient versions of the Air Battlers, slightly weak against Blizzard and Fire magic. When all three are defeated, it's time to RTC.

Search Hook's dig sites to find Heartless and other items.

Enemies Appearing at Each Map Location & Items Found

Mark	Enemies	Item Found
a	Artful Flyer	Potion
b	Bubble Beat x2	Frost Gem
c	Bubble Beat x2	Shining Gem
d	Bubble Beat x2	Bronze
e	Artful Flyer	Potion
f	Bubble Beat x2	Iron
g	Artful Flyer	Panacea

CHALLENGE MISSION

Objective: Earn lots of heart points!

Restrictions: Take 30% more damage, deal 30% less damage

Rewards

Sigils Acquired	Heart Pts. Accumulated
3	570 or more
2	500 - 569
1	450 - 499

Three Challenge Sigils are already yours, so simply take your time and clear the area. Switch lock on between multiple enemies to weaken them all to the breaking point, then finish them off quickly in a chain to collect bonus hearts.

COLLECT SHINING SHARDS

MISSION 59

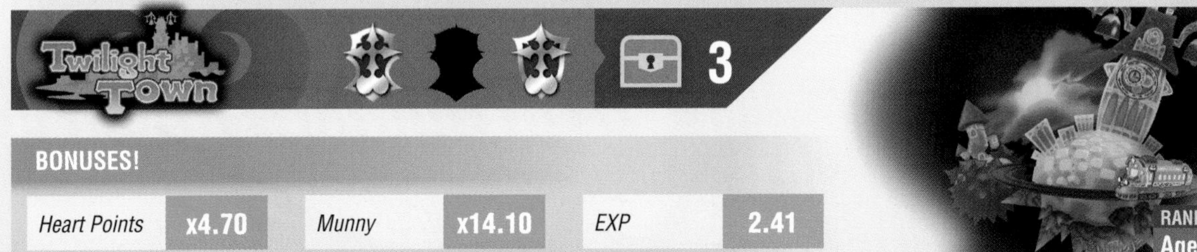

BONUSES!

Heart Points	x4.70	Munny	x14.10	EXP	2.41

RANK Agent

ENEMIES

SHADOW LVL 25 — DROP: Moonstone

MEGA-SHADOW LVL 15 — DROP: Dark Ingot

POISON PLANT LVL 20 — DROP: Lightning Shard

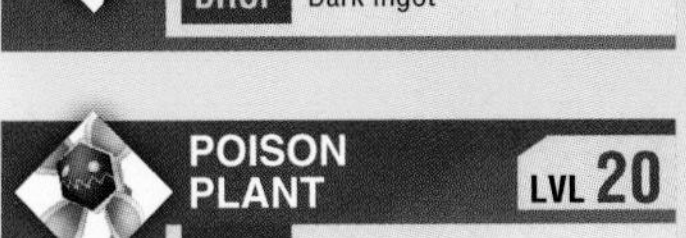

RARE VENDOR LVL 30 — DROP: Elixir Recipe, Power Tech, or Iron

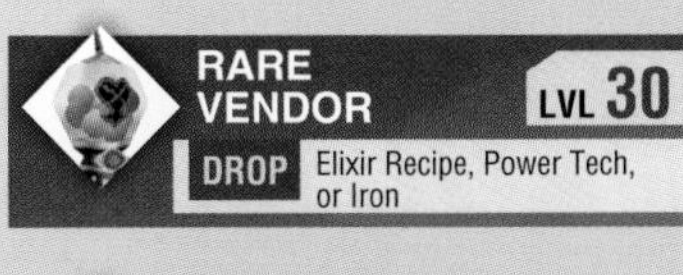

GUARDIAN LVL 8 — DROP: Shining Shard

TAILBUNKER LVL 30 — DROP: Gear Component B

REWARDS

Clear Bonuses	Random Bonuses
Lightning Gem	Elixir Recipe (15%)
Moonstone	Bronze (10%)
Power Tech (MG)	Moonstone (15%)
—	Hi-Potion (20%)
—	Potion (20%)
—	None (20%)

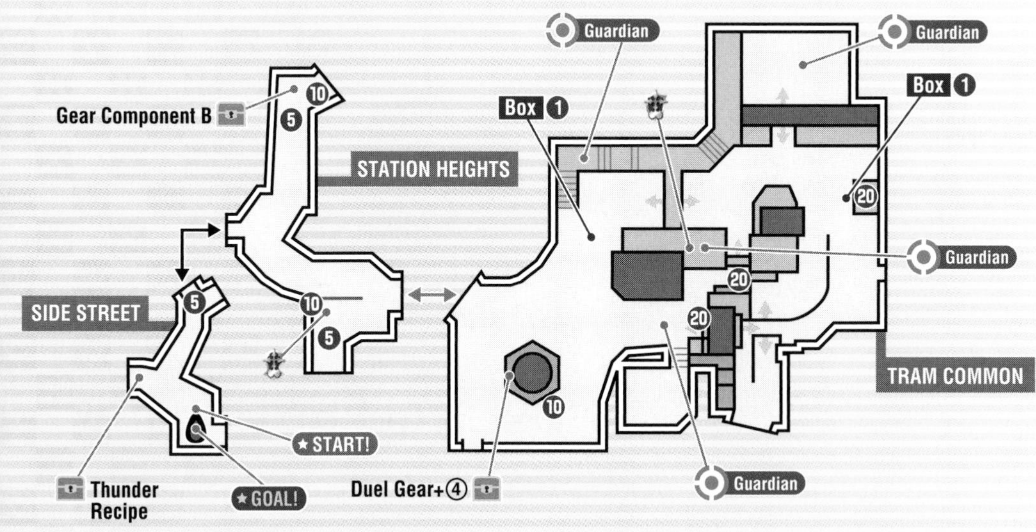

GRUDGE MATCH

The Shining Shards in this mission can only be gained by defeating four Guardians that appear in specific locations in the Tram Common. Unfortunately, there's also a Tailbunker to worry about . Dispose of the Tailbunker by striking its tail and wings to drive it to the ground, then attack its head and cast Blizzard magic to defeat it.

Shoot down the Tailbunker before moving to other parts of the Tram Common.

Afterward, find and defeat three Guardians and pick up the Shining Shards they drop to complete the mission. Being such low-level enemies at this late point in the game, the Guardians aren't too difficult to defeat. Defeat a fourth Guardian and obtain the shard it drops, filling the Mission Gauge 100% before you RTC.

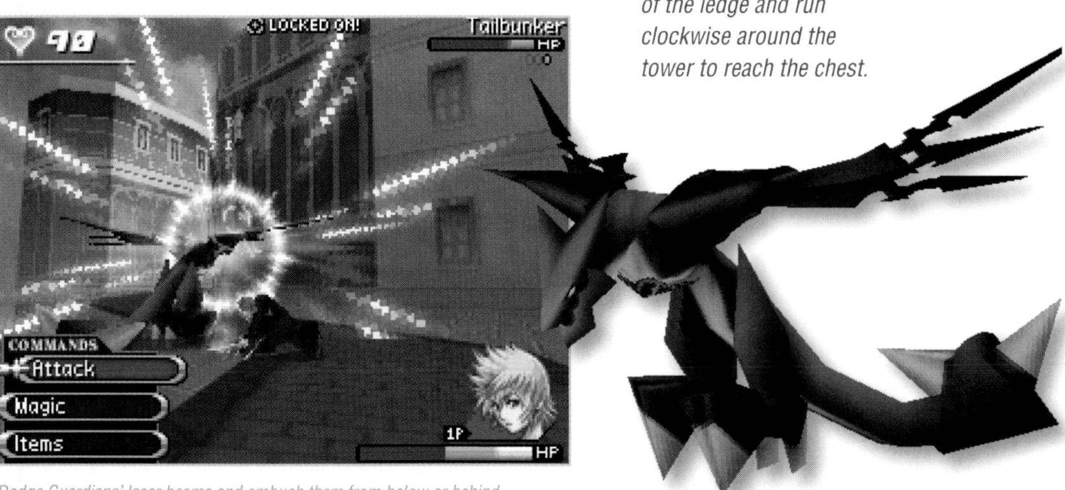

Dodge Guardians' laser beams and ambush them from below or behind.

GLIDE TO THE DUEL GEAR+④

*To collect the **Duel Gear+④** from a chest atop the hexagonal tower in the southwest corner of the Tram Common, ascend the north stairs and cross the "bridge." Head to the right, jump from the ledge, and glide southwest all the way over to the hexagonal tower. Land on the south portion of the ledge and run clockwise around the tower to reach the chest.*

CHALLENGE MISSION

Objective: Finish in record time!

Restrictions: No recovery items, enemy level +1

Rewards	
Sigils Acquired	Clear Time
3	02:10:00 or less
2	02:10:01 - 02:40:00
1	02:40:01 - 03:10:00

Eliminate three Guardians in the Tram Common area to procure Shining Shards, then return to the dark corridor. Use Thunder attacks against each to quicken the battles, consuming Ethers as needed to keep your magic going. Upon entering the Tram Common, follow the curve to the left and up the stairs to take out the first. Then cross the "bridge" to fight the next one on the rooftop before dropping over the south side and taking out the third.

ELIMINATE THE AVALANCHE

MISSION 60

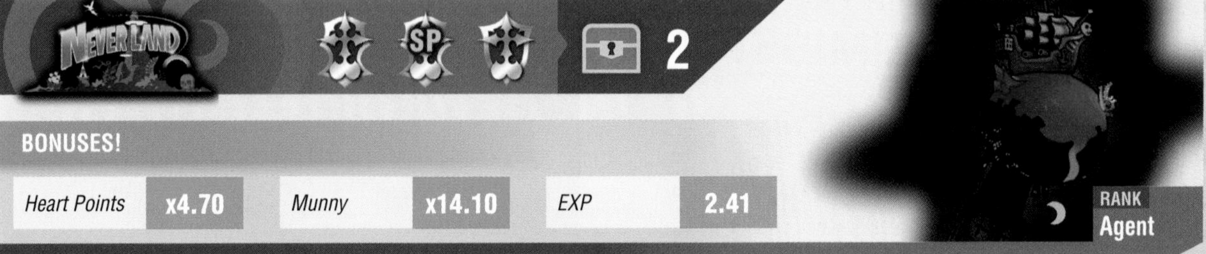

BONUSES!

Heart Points	x4.70	Munny	x14.10	EXP	2.41

ENEMIES

TURQUOISE MARCH — LVL 20 — DROP: Shining Gem

AVALANCHE — LVL 26 — DROP: Frost Gem

REWARDS	
Clear Bonuses	Random Bonuses
Range Tech	Elixir Recipe (10%)
Combo Tech	Combo Tech(30%)
Gust Shard	Potion (40%)
—	None (20%)

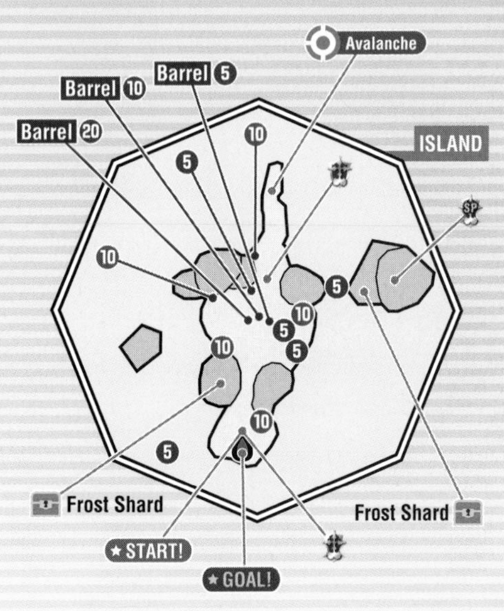

BLIZZARD WING

During this trip to Never Land, you can fly without Tink's help, so get cracking. The Avalanche hovers over the northern tip of the central isle, attacking as Roxas flies into range. Chase the Avalanche through the air and assault its wings and tail as before. Whenever the Avalanche pulls back, swoop out of the way to avoid its impending attack. Cast Fire LV3 or LV4 spells while it's stationary to inflict severe damage. Once it's defeated, collect the items in the area, eliminate any remaining Turquoise Marches if you like, then RTC.

Turquoise March enemies frequently attempt to interfere in your battle, but don't worry about them until the Avalanche is knocked out.

CHALLENGE MISSION

Objective: Finish in record time!

Restrictions: Level capped at 27, no attack magic

Rewards	
Sigils Acquired	Clear Time
3	01:25:00 or less
2	01:25:01 - 01:55:00
1	01:55:01 - 02:30:00

A really strong weapon is the best way to bring down this perpetually flying monster in time to meet the objective. Without the ability to target it's head, you must anticipate its swoops and dives and resume your assault as quickly as possible.

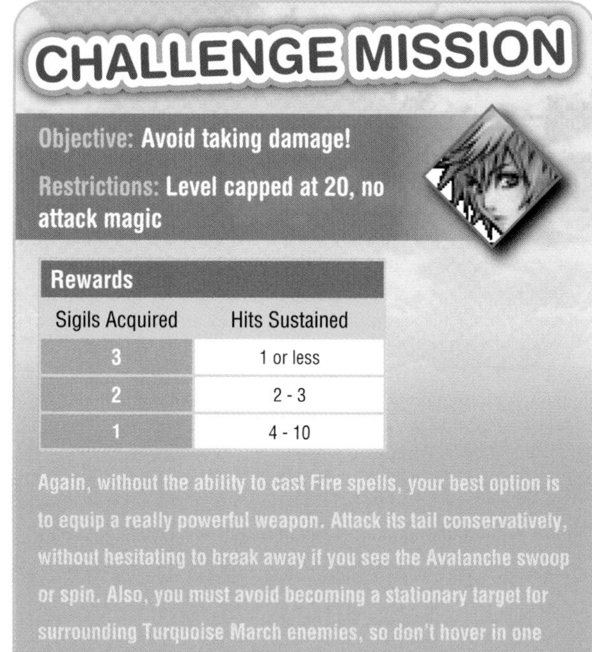

CHALLENGE MISSION

Objective: Avoid taking damage!

Restrictions: Level capped at 20, no attack magic

Rewards	
Sigils Acquired	Hits Sustained
3	1 or less
2	2 - 3
1	4 - 10

Again, without the ability to cast Fire spells, your best option is to equip a really powerful weapon. Attack its tail conservatively, without hesitating to break away if you see the Avalanche swoop or spin. Also, you must avoid becoming a stationary target for surrounding Turquoise March enemies, so don't hover in one position for too long.

DAY 224

Demyx needs help finishing his assignment again. Find all the Heartless hiding in Mission 52 (collecting hearts in Halloween Town) and speak to him again to receive a **Dark Ingot**.

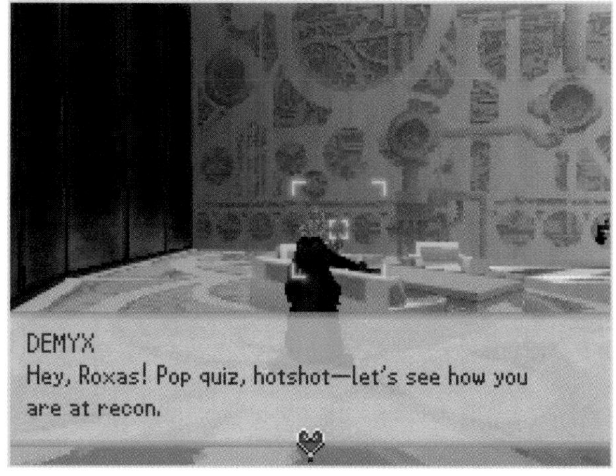

Lazy, lazy, lazy!

VANQUISH THE HEARTLESS THREAT

MISSION 61

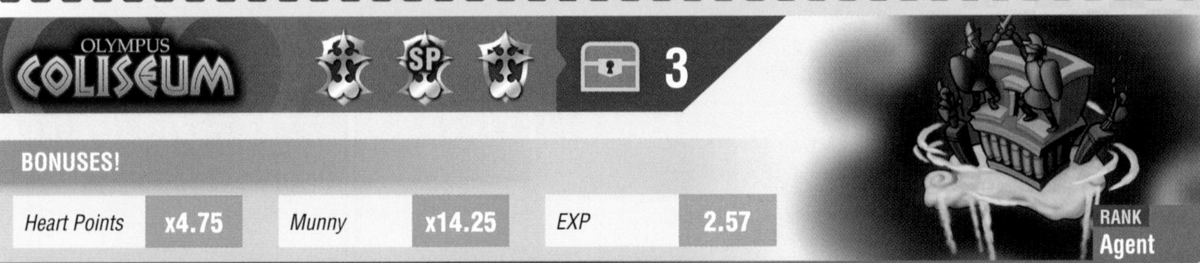

BONUSES!

Heart Points	x4.75	Munny	x14.25	EXP	2.57

ENEMIES

SHADOW LVL 25
DROP —

FLARE NOTE LVL 20
DROP Blazing Gem

XIGBAR LVL 31
DROP —

YELLOW OPERA LVL 20
DROP Moonstone

ICE CANNON LVL 20
DROP Frost Gem

GUARD ARMOR LVL 31
DROP —

STRIPED ARIA LVL 20
DROP Bronze

JUMBO CANNON LVL 15
DROP Lightning Shard

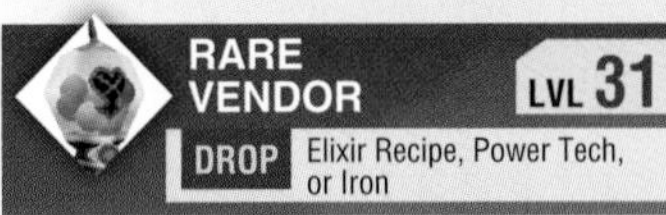
RARE VENDOR LVL 31
DROP Elixir Recipe, Power Tech, or Iron

HOVER GHOST LVL 20
DROP Lightning Gem

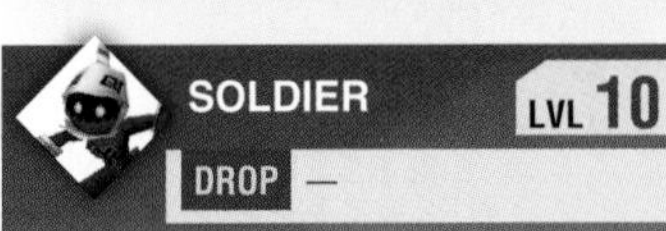
SOLDIER LVL 10
DROP —

TAILBUNKER LVL 30
DROP Gear Component B

REWARDS

Clear Bonuses	Random Bonuses
Firaga	Fira Recipe (10%)
Cura Recipe	Lightning Shard (16%)
Gust Gem	Lightning Gem (10%)
—	Gear Component B (16%)
—	Hi-Potion (10%)
—	Ether (16%)
—	None (22%)

RELUCTANT ENTRANT

Roxas must participate in the tournament to complete his mission.

Defeat the Heartless appearing outside the Coliseum, then enter the vestibule. Phil informs Roxas that the games are already underway. The only way to enter the Coliseum and search for Heartless is to walk right in. Speak to Phil again when you're ready.

The objective is to defeat five rounds of enemies. Whether you use barrels or not to achieve this is left to your discretion. However, keep in mind that hitting an enemy with a barrel is usually an instant kill.

The barrels make enemy disposal easier, so use them!

Round four features a Tailbunker that seems harder to bring to the ground than usual. Jump on the top platform and knock barrels at it to inflict severe damage and ground it. Follow up with a quick combo before it rises, then return to the top platform and launch another barrel. Repeat until you're victorious.

Knock barrels toward the hovering Tailbunker from atop the central platform.

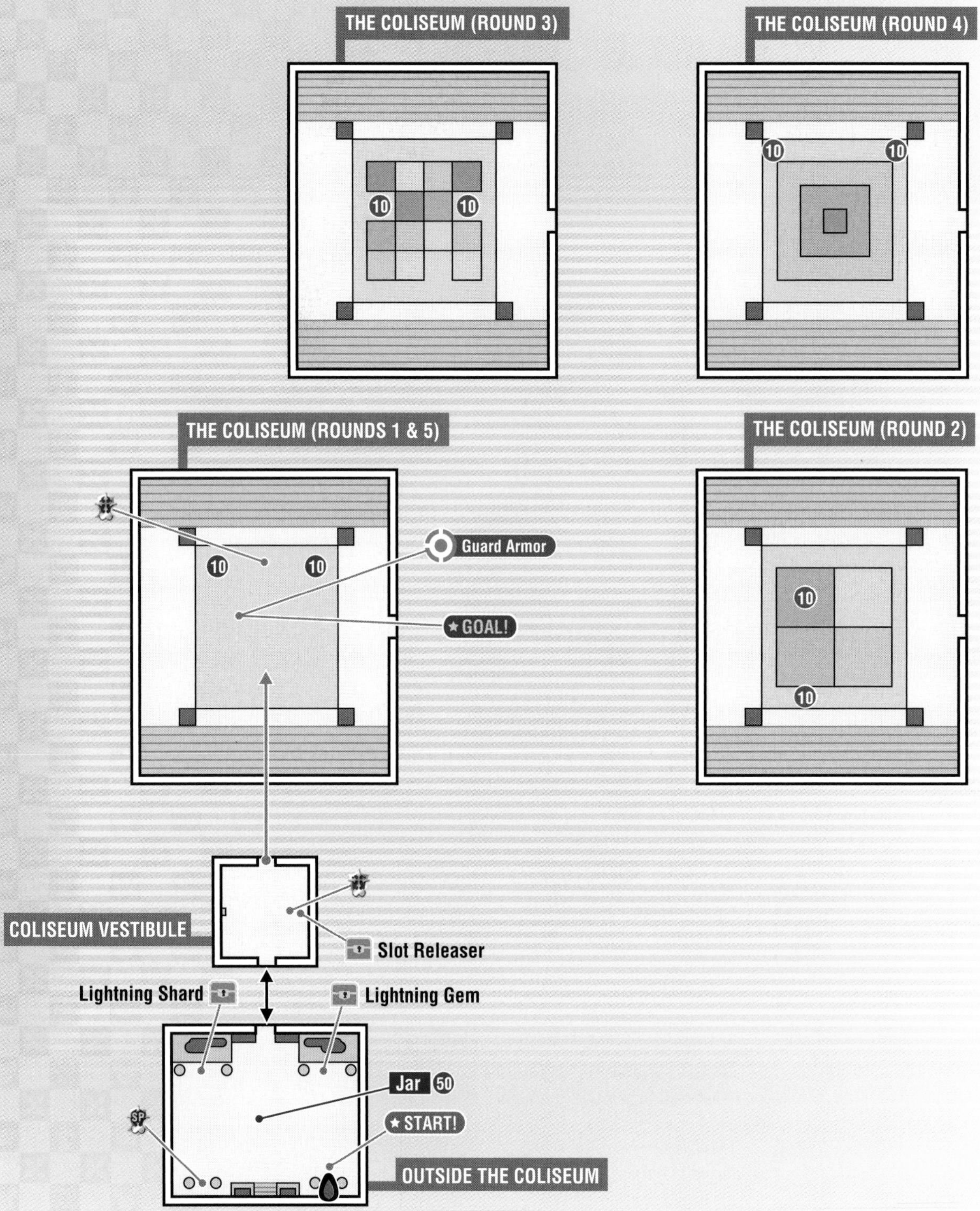

THE COLISEUM (ROUND 3)

THE COLISEUM (ROUND 4)

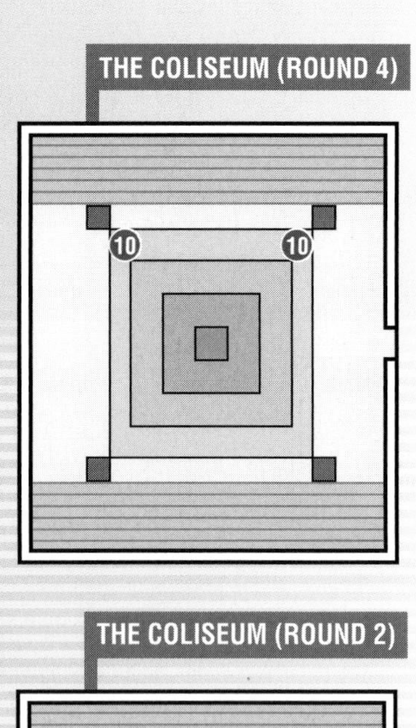

THE COLISEUM (ROUNDS 1 & 5)

Guard Armor

GOAL!

THE COLISEUM (ROUND 2)

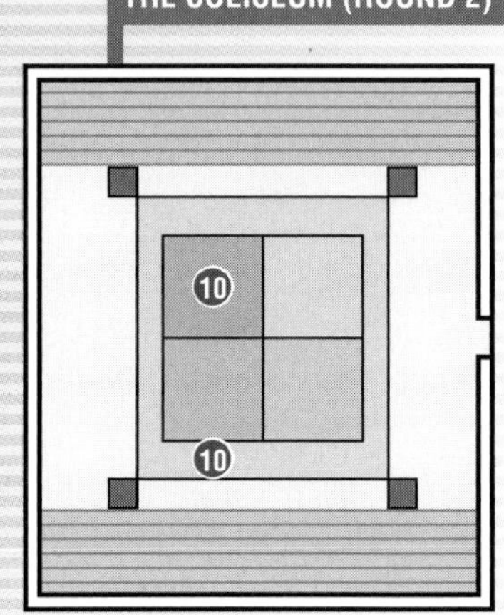

COLISEUM VESTIBULE

Slot Releaser

Lightning Shard

Lightning Gem

Jar 50

START!

OUTSIDE THE COLISEUM

XIGBAR

BOSS!

No, Xigbar is not the final contestant in the games. However, he does want to determine Roxas's progress. Dodge Roll to avoid shots he fires, then Air Slide over to him. He seems extremely weak against aerial combos, so use Aero magic to inflict severe damage to him. Xigbar surrenders when his HP drops to about half.

GUARD ARMOR

BOSS!

The Guard Armor is extremely resilient against all forms of magic, so use melee attacks to overcome it. Jump and attack its head. Move away when it begins to march and swat at the ground, then circle behind it to continue attacking its head.

Sometimes the Guard Armor leaps into the air and crashes to the ground, releasing a mild shockwave that causes minor damage. When this happens, it's head falls off! While it scrambles to recover its head, run up and melee attack the helmet on the ground.

Afterwards, the Guard Armor reattaches its head, but the damage inflicted causes its arms and legs to separate from the torso and act independently. Lock on to the arms and attack them fiercely, using Limit Breaks if possible. The idea is to destroy both limbs before the Guard Armor reassembles itself. Otherwise, if you destroy one limb and not the other, then the missing limb regenerates after the boss reassembles. The Guard Armor also regains some HP during this regeneration process.

Eliminate both arms, then do the same thing with the legs. When the legs and arms are gone, the floating torso becomes helpless. Continue smacking the helmet until the Guard Armor collapses.

CHALLENGE MISSION

Objective: Avoid taking damage!

Restrictions: Level capped at 20, no attack magic

Rewards	
Sigils Acquired	Hits Sustained
3	6 or less
2	7 - 35 hits
1	36 - 50 hits

The key here is to position the barrels between Roxas and the enemies and knock them into the enemies to defeat them. Avoid fighting the enemies directly as much as possible until the Guard Armor battle. Try to remember how many hits you've taken and withdraw if you take more than six. If you just want to complete the challenge, note that the criteria are much more forgiving for winning two Sigils.

SPECIAL CHALLENGE

Objective: Finish in record time!

Restrictions: No attack magic, enemy level +30

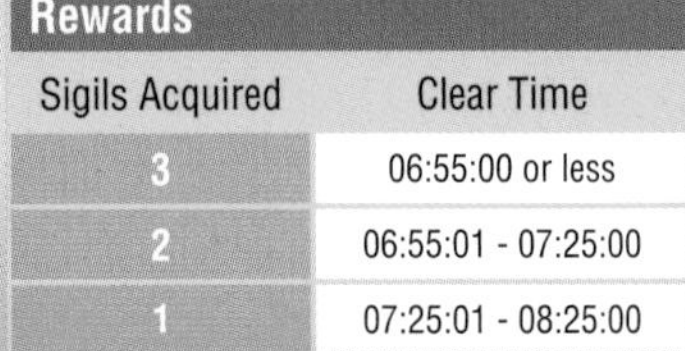

Rewards	
Sigils Acquired	Clear Time
3	06:55:00 or less
2	06:55:01 - 07:25:00
1	07:25:01 - 08:25:00

Forget using the barrels; just take out enemies directly. However, save your Limit Breaks for the Guard Armor battle. Launch them against the hands and feet when the Guard Armor falls apart.

DAY 225-227

Saïx promotes Roxas to Expert and also presents him with the **Final Limit** panel. When equipped, Roxas finishes his Final Limit with three blinding blasts of light and his Limit Breaks last longer. Visit the Moogle to find all sorts of new items to buy in the shop, including another Slot Releaser and Level Up, Thundara, Magic LV3④ and Quadcast③, Glide LV+(L), Treasure Magnet③, the Rainforce Ring, Critical Ring, and Silver. Furthermore, Donald becomes a playable character in Mission Mode!

Becoming an Expert, Roxas gets an upgrade for his Limit Breaks.

Note that two missions are absent from the roster. Speak to Axel and Demyx to add Missions 63 and 64 to the Missions screen. Axel wants Roxas to score at least one Challenge Sigil in the Mission 58 Challenge (eliminate the Artful Flyers in Never Land, earning lots of Heart Points). Achieve that and speak to him again to get Mission 63 added to your choices.

Axel and Demyx require Roxas to prove himself if he wants more assignments.

Passing off yet more assignments, Demyx wants Roxas to open all the chests in Mission 51 (eliminating the Pink Concertos in Wonderland). He adds Mission 64 to the roster upon successful completion.

ELIMINATE THE CARRIER GHOST

MISSION 62

HALLOWEEN TOWN

8

BONUSES!

Heart Points	x5.05	Munny	x15.15	EXP	2.77

RANK Expert

ENEMIES

MEGA-SHADOW LVL 15
DROP Gust Gem

SNOWY CRYSTAL LVL 22
DROP Frost Gem

CREEPWORM LVL 16
DROP —

HOVER GHOST LVL 12
DROP Lightning Gem

TENTACLAW LVL 32
DROP Gear Component C

CARRIER GHOST LVL 32
DROP Aerial Tech+

REWARDS	
Clear Bonuses	Random Bonuses
Combo Tech+	Blizzara Recipe (15%)
Shield Tech+	Thunder Recipe (10%)
Diamond	Blazing Gem (10%)
—	Gust Gem (10%)
—	Shining Crystal (10%)
—	Shield Tech+ (20%)
—	Silver (20%)
—	None (5%)

GHOST TRAP

Navigate through Halloween Town as usual, jumping on the coffin in the Graveyard to continue. Roxas becomes sealed in the Boneyard 1 area, Meaning you must defeat 20 Hover Ghosts before you can continue. Use Jack's newly perfected blizzard pumpkin bombs to help.

Defeat Hover Ghosts one after another to set Roxas free from the Boneyard. Staying airborne is the best strategy.

THE DOOR TO BONEYARD 2

At Moonlight Hill, knock pumpkin bombs toward the four lanterns in the area. Once all four lanterns are lit, the east door opens. Proceed to Boneyard 2. Open the chests and examine the black balloon at the back to reveal the Carrier Ghost.

Use pumpkin bombs to light the four lanterns around Moonlight Hill once again.

Examine the floating balloon in Boneyard 2 to make the Carrier Ghost appear.

DAY

225-227

~QUIETUDE~

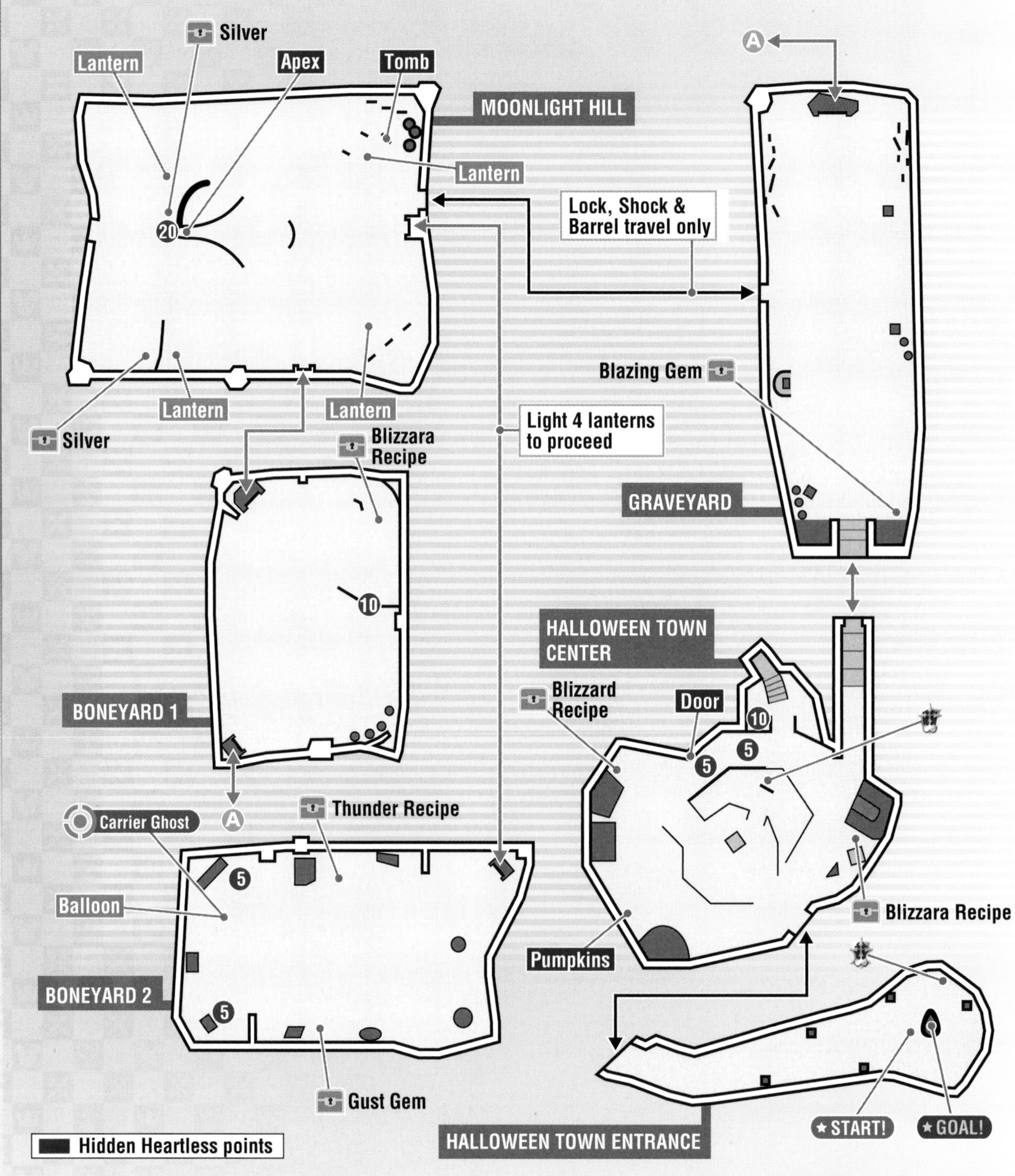

CARRIER GHOST

BOSS!

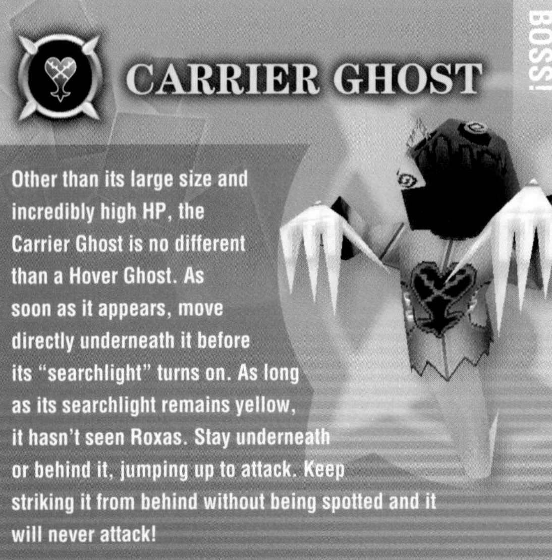

Other than its large size and incredibly high HP, the Carrier Ghost is no different than a Hover Ghost. As soon as it appears, move directly underneath it before its "searchlight" turns on. As long as its searchlight remains yellow, it hasn't seen Roxas. Stay underneath or behind it, jumping up to attack. Keep striking it from behind without being spotted and it will never attack!

If the searchlight turns red, it means Roxas has been spotted. Dodge Roll underneath or behind it and strike from below or behind to knock it to the ground. Occasionally, the Carrier Ghost may drift too high out of range. If so, move away and allow it to vanish and materialize elsewhere, closer to the ground. Cast Blizzara and Blizzaga spells to inflict a decent amount of damage.

STRANGE NEW ENEMY

Return to the Halloween Town Entrance. Just as Roxas is about to RTC, a Tentaclaw appears. Destroy this creature by smashing its red center. Spells are extremely effective, but only when fired from a distance and after the Tentaclaw has settled into a more stationary position. RTC when finished.

The Tentaclaw's appearance is an omen of things to come in Halloween Town.

CHALLENGE MISSION

Objective: Finish in record time!

Restrictions: Enemy level +2, HP drains while on the ground

Rewards	
Sigils Acquired	Clear Time
3	03:00:00 or less
2	03:00:01 - 03:30:00
1	03:30:01 - 04:00:00

Glide as often as possible to reduce damage sustained and cast Cura to fight the damaging effects during instances when you must stay on the ground often, such as when fighting the 20 Hover Ghosts in Boneyard 1. Use the blizzard bombs on the ground as well as Blizzard spells to freeze Hover Ghosts in place, making them easier to dispatch. Don't hesitate to use your Limit Breaks to get through the 20 Hover Ghosts. When you encounter the Carrier Ghost, attack it from behind and try to avoid detection until you've destroyed it.

DAY 225-227

~QUIETUDE~

DESTROY THE SHADOW GLOBS

MISSION 63

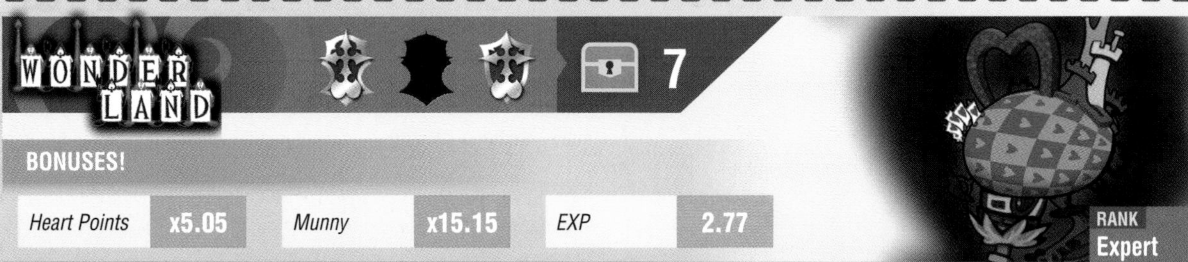

ENEMIES

REWARDS	
Clear Bonuses	Random Bonuses
Diamond	Aero Recipe (15%)
Moonstone	Cure Recipe (10%)
Rune Tech+ (MG)	Cura Recipe (15%)
—	Gust Crystal (10%)
—	Shining Gem (10%)
—	Diamond (10%)
—	Premium Orb (10%)
—	None (20%)

SPOT REMOVER

Dispose of all the Shadow Globs in the Rabbit Hole, then proceed into the Bizarre Room and drink from the bottle on the table to shrink in size. The Shadow Globs then appear on the enlarged version of the room. Destroy them all and continue through Wonderland, dispatching all you find. Thanks to the Glide ability, there really are none out of reach.

Destroy Shadow Globs around Wonderland.

Enter the northeast door on the upper level of the Lotus Forest so that Roxas and Xion enter the Tea Party Garden atop the hedges. Glide over to the Shadow Glob on the hedge in the southeast corner, then destroy the rest of the foes. When the last Shadow Glob is destroyed, a Lurk Lizard appears. Thanks to Xion's help, it should be much easier to defeat it this time.

Glide between hedges above the Tea Party Garden to reach all the Shadow Globs.

The Lurk Lizard appearing when the Tea Party Garden is clear is an optional foe.

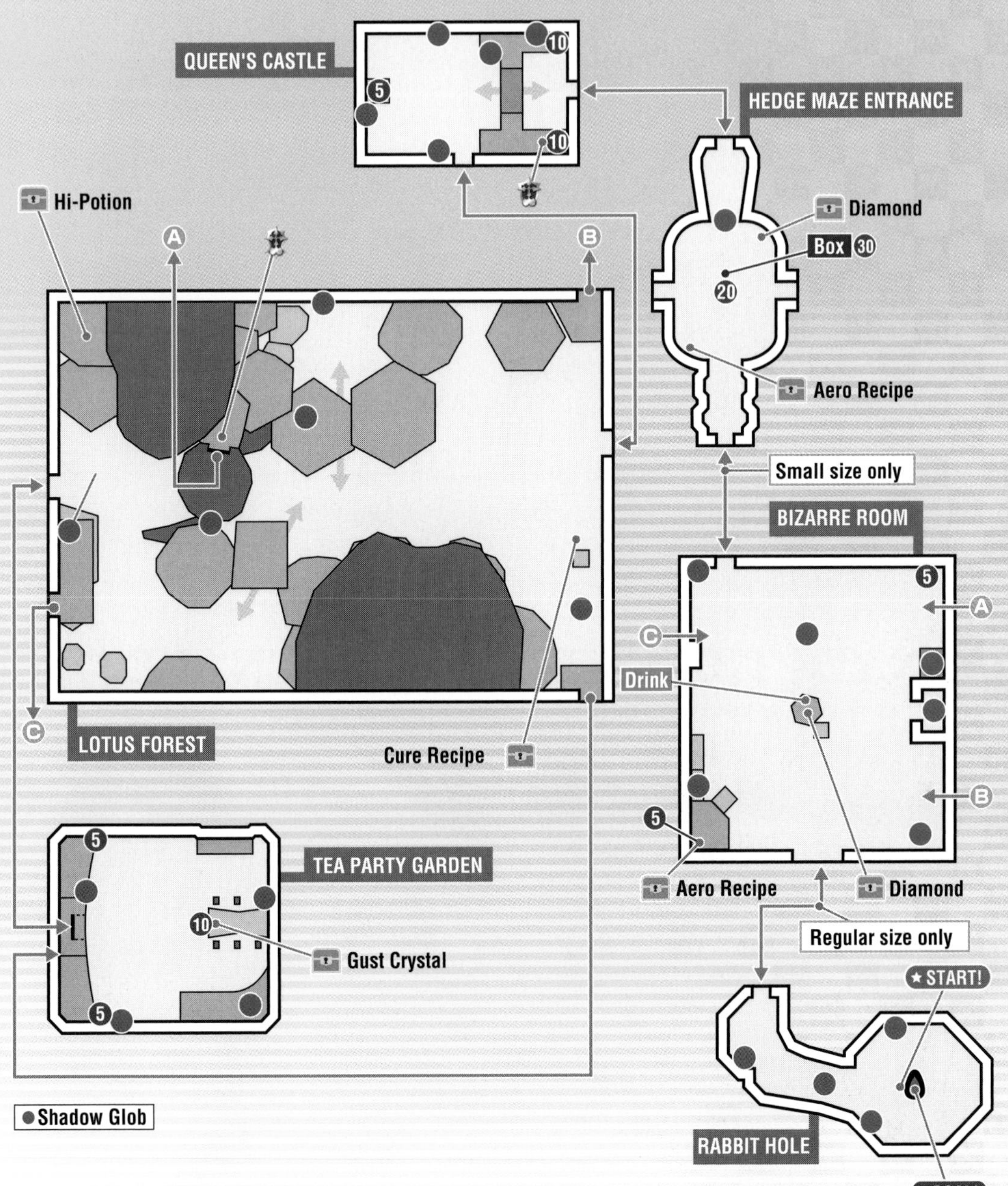
QUEEN'S CASTLE
HEDGE MAZE ENTRANCE
Hi-Potion
Diamond
Box 30
Aero Recipe
Small size only
BIZARRE ROOM
Drink
LOTUS FOREST
Cure Recipe
TEA PARTY GARDEN
Gust Crystal
Aero Recipe
Diamond
Regular size only
START!
RABBIT HOLE
GOAL!
Shadow Glob

CHALLENGE MISSION

Objective: Finish in record time!

Restrictions: No recovery magic, HP drains while on the ground level +1

Rewards	
Sigils Acquired	Clear Time
3	02:30:00 or less
2	02:30:01 - 03:00:00
1	03:00:01 - 03:30:00

It's important to equip a very powerful weapon, lots of Hi-Potions, and the Glide ability. The route illustrated on the map in this section highlights a very successful way to eliminate the Shadow Globs and use the central exit in the Lotus Forest (in the tree trunk on the upper level) to warp back to the Bizarre Room, return to normal size, and exit. However, after shrinking you must destroy the Mega-Shadow that appears whenever you stand on the center table; otherwise, you can never return to normal size in time. Use strong Fire or Fira spells to quickly knock it out.

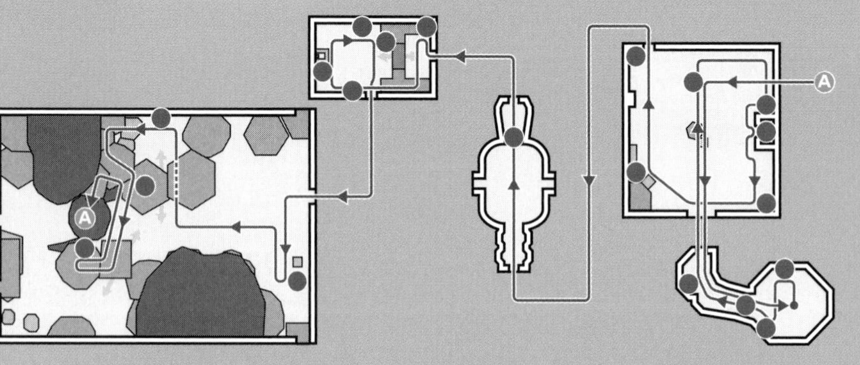

ELIMINATE THE EMERALD SERENADE

MISSION 64

BONUSES!

Heart Points	x5.05	Munny	x15.15	EXP	2.77

RANK Expert

ENEMIES

TURQUOISE MARCH LVL 20
DROP Shining Gem

AIR BATTLER LVL 20
DROP Combo Tech+

EMERALD SERENADE LVL 32
DROP Silver

REWARDS	
Clear Bonuses	Random Bonuses
Megalixir Recipe	Aeroga Recipe (15%)
Combo Tech++	Gear Component C (15%)
Silver	Hi-Potion (15%)
—	Ether (15%)
—	Elixir (20%)
—	None (20%)

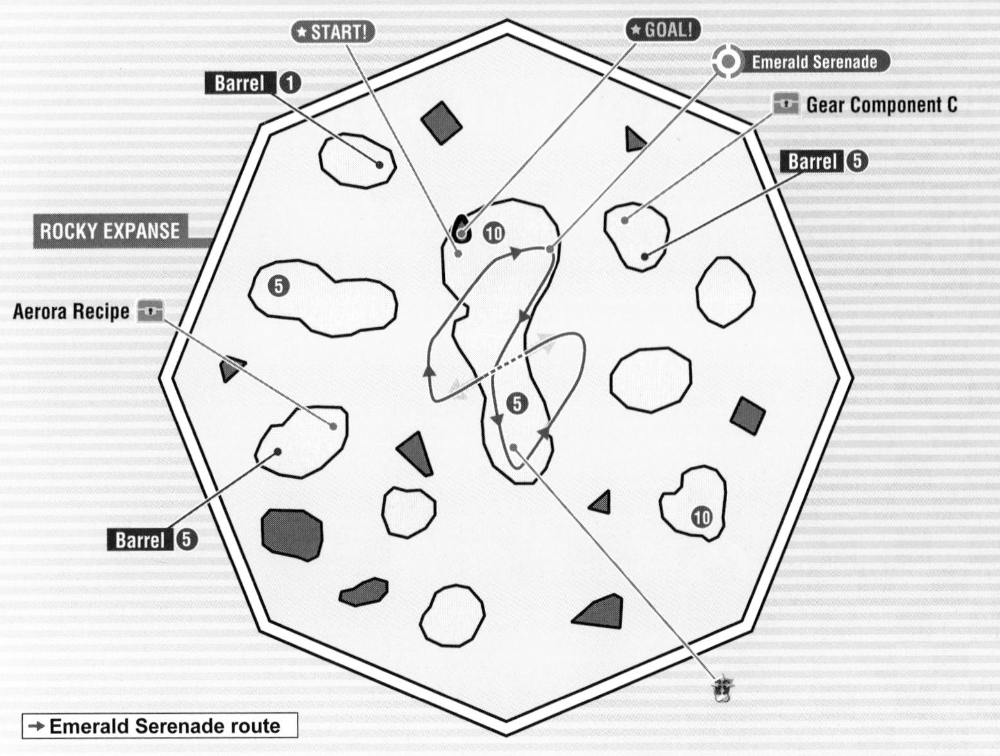

THE OBLIVIOUS TRAVELER

When Roxas and Axel arrive in Never Land, the Emerald Serenade is already traveling along the route drawn on the map shown above. It does not attack, nor does it stop traveling its route. Due to its speed, pursuing the Emerald Serenade is a fruitless endeavor. One way to destroy it is to set up an ambush. The best ambush location in Never Land is inside the tunnel below the central Island. Position Roxas at the west tunnel entrance. When the Emerald Serenade comes into view, fire a Blizzard spell at it to momentarily freeze it in place. Strike it while it's frozen to inflict extra damage. Stay inside the tunnel until it comes around again. Repeat freezing it and attacking it until it is destroyed, then collect the items available and RTC.

Wait in ambush in the tunnel under the center isle...

When the Emerald Serenade comes into view, freeze it in place with a Blizzard spell.

Attack the Emerald Serenade, then wait for its next pass.

DAY 255

ELIMINATE THE NOVASHADOW

MISSION 65

WONDERLAND 8

BONUSES!

Heart Points	Munny	EXP
x5.10	x15.30	2.99

RANK Expert

ENEMIES

NOVASHADOW LVL 40
DROP Shield Tech+

REWARDS	
Clear Bonuses	Random Bonuses
LV Tripler④	Aero Recipe (15%)
Gear Component B	Cure Recipe (15%)
Rune Tech+	Cura Recipe (10%)
—	Gust Crystal (10%)
—	Shining Gem (10%)
—	Diamond (10%)
—	Premium Orb (10%)
—	None (20%)

ENTER THE MAZE

The Queen has her hands full in Wonderland.

Drink from the bottle in the Bizarre Room to shrink, then head north to the Queen's Castle area. Seems the Queen's cards still haven't located the intruders they are looking for. Afterward, clear the room of Heartless if you want, or return back to the Hedge Maze Entrance. The west exit is now unblocked.

FIRST LAMP SWITCH

Because the guard in the passageway north of the entrance never closes his eyes, you cannot go that way. Instead, head west and examine the crystal switch on the ground. This switch activates the first of four lamps in the Bizarre Room. When all four are lit, the Novashadow (your target) becomes revealed.

The four switches throughout the maze activate lights in the Bizarre Room, eventually revealing the boss.

A card patrols the southwest corner of the Red Rose Hedge Maze. Wait out of range until he stops, facing your direction. When he turns and heads the other way, follow him. As he turns into the cubby to the south, go north and turn back to watch. Wait for him to leave the area, then go into the south niche to find a chest containing a **Cura Recipe**. Go through the southwest exit.

Follow the card west until he makes a turn south.

*Hide in the nook to the far north, then go south to find a **Cura Recipe**.*

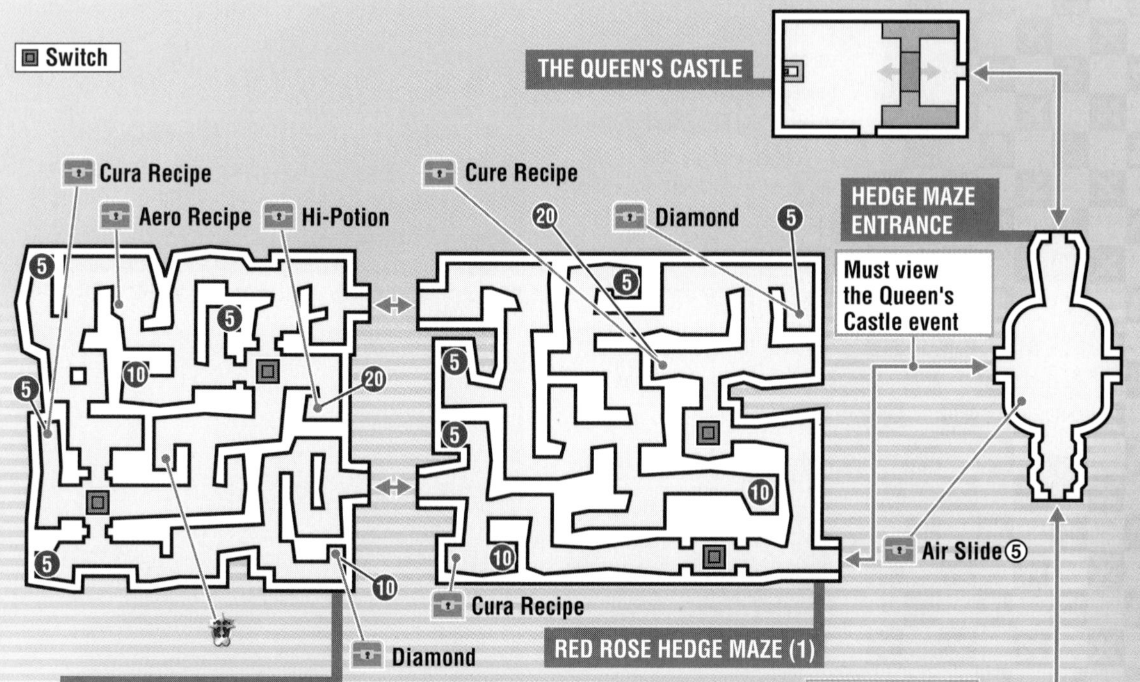

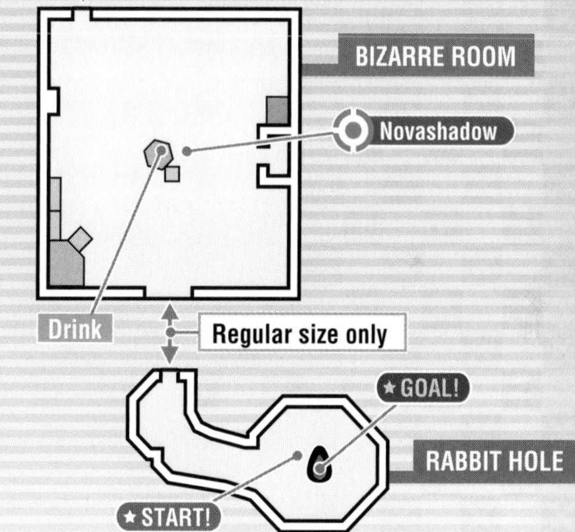

ROUNDABOUT

Wait just southwest of the dividing hedge wall. When the card comes into view...

Run around the east side of the dividing wall and follow the passage to a **Diamond**.

Upon entering the west segment of the Red Rose Hedge Maze, you are in danger of being spotted by a card that patrols the area near the exit. On the in-game map, he's represented by the white and green dot. If spotted, you'll be sent back to the starting point of the *previous* area! Avoid this by waiting in the southwest corner of the area divided by a freestanding hedge wall. When the card comes into view, run around the east side of the hedge and proceed down the corridor before he turns and spots Roxas. Quickly open the southeast chest to obtain a **Diamond** and dash west before he returns.

SNEAKY SNEAKY

Wait for stationary cards to close their eyes. Run past when their vision cone is not extended.

Wait for the card at the corner to close his eyes, then run past. Follow the route west and then north to find the second switch.

Find the third switch in the northeast part of the second area.

Continue north, then stop and wait for the patrolling card to move around one side of the freestanding hedge so that you can run around the other. Collect the items to the north, then head east after waiting for a card to close its eyes. Navigate east to the third switch and press it.

Pressing the third switch causes all of the cards to leave the area. Defeat the Heartless appearing near the northeast door, then enter it to reach the north part of the first area.

The cards have a meeting to attend, allowing free passage to the fourth switch.

However, the Heartless have other plans. Use magic to prevent Sapphire Elegies from wasting your time.

THE FINAL LAMP SWITCH

Follow the hedge maze south, then north, then east, defeating Heartless along the route. Next, go south and press the final switch. Continue south to the exit and return to the Bizarre Room.

Pressing the fourth switch in the hedge maze activates the final lamp in the Bizarre Room.

BOSS!

NOVASHADOW

The Novashadow's claw swipes are capable of inflicting flip-foot status on Roxas, reversing the game's controls. Frequently it submerges into the ground, then bursts out, releasing a powerful shockwave. Hit it with various Thunder spells from a distance to minimize your risk.

Afterward, clear the Bizarre Room of Heartless so that you can drink from the bottle on the table. After doing so, return to the entrance and RTC.

DAY 256-258

Speak to Luxord to receive a **Combo Tech++**. Next, acquire a **Diamond** and visit the Moogle to synthesize those items into an Auto-Dodge(L). You're only allowed one of this panel, so if you already synthesized one, show it to Luxord and keep the extra Combo Tech++. In return for succeeding at his challenge, he'll hand over a piece of **Silver**. However, is this reward really better than having an extra Combo Tech++? If you don't want the Auto-Dodge(L), you're probably better off not synthesizing it, and keeping Combo Tech++ for yourself.

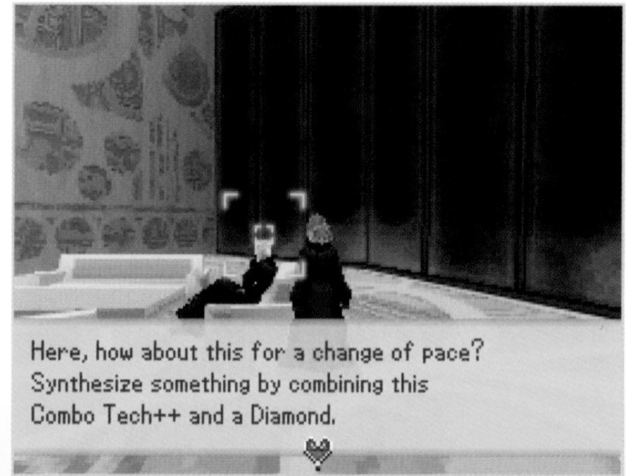

Consider the reward before using valuable resources in Synthesis.

RESTORE THE TOWN'S HEARTLESS

MISSION 66

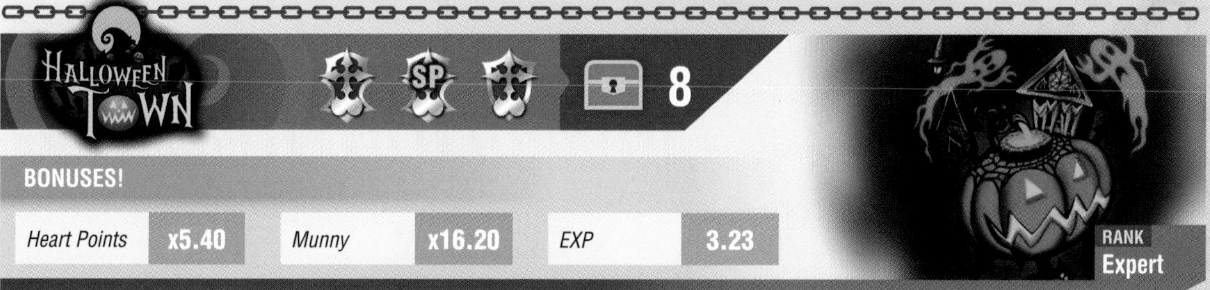

BONUSES!

Heart Points	x5.40	Munny	x16.20	EXP	3.23

RANK Expert

ENEMIES

TRICKY MONKEY LVL 40
DROP Shining Gem

TENTACLAW LVL 40
DROP Gear Component C

LEECHGRAVE LVL 40
DROP —

REWARDS	
Clear Bonuses	Random Bonuses
Curaga	Blizzara Recipe (15%)
Power Tech+	Thunder Recipe (10%)
Silver	Blazing Gem (10%)
—	Gust Gem (10%)
—	Shining Crystal(10%)
—	Shield Tech+ (20%)
—	Silver (20%)
—	None (5%)

HEARTLESS EATERS

Set plenty of Fire panels prior to this mission, along with many Hi-Ethers. Entering the Halloween Town Square, Roxas sees where all the Heartless have gone. The town is now "infested" with Tentaclaws and you must defeat all of them in the square before you can proceed. Quite soon you'll figure out that wiping them out by using aerial combos takes a very long time. Casting Fire spells from a distance takes them down much more quickly, but you should conserve your magic for the upcoming boss fight.

Tentaclaws become agitated when they sense Roxas at close range.

Continue through Halloween Town to Moonlight Hill, where you must wipe out another group of Tentaclaws.

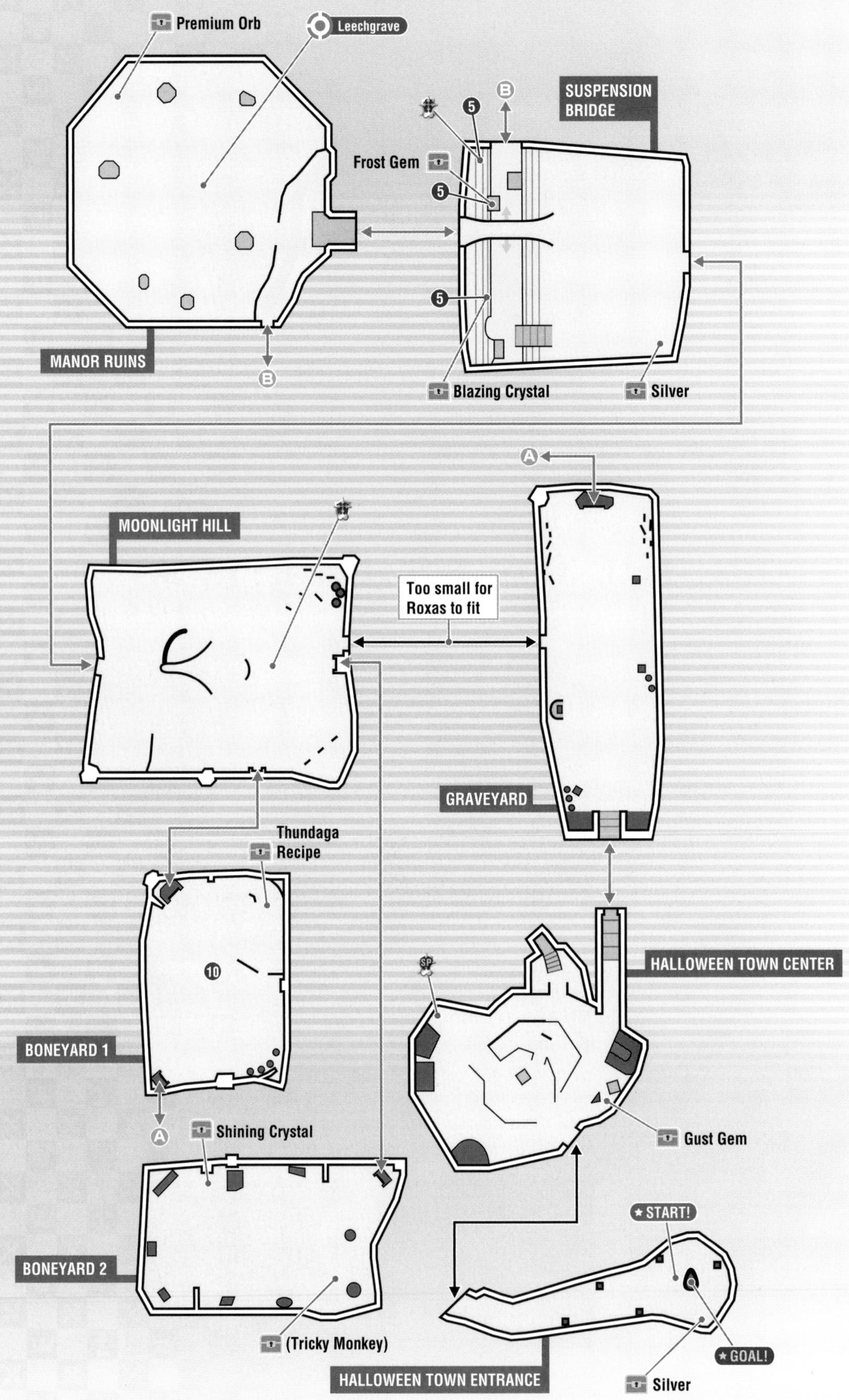
Premium Orb
Leechgrave
MANOR RUINS
B
5
B
SUSPENSION BRIDGE
Frost Gem
5
5
Blazing Crystal
Silver
A
MOONLIGHT HILL
Too small for Roxas to fit
GRAVEYARD
Thundaga Recipe
10
BONEYARD 1
A
Shining Crystal
HALLOWEEN TOWN CENTER
Gust Gem
BONEYARD 2
(Tricky Monkey)
START!
GOAL!
HALLOWEEN TOWN ENTRANCE
Silver

REACHING THE ORDEAL BLAZON

*To reach the **Ordeal Blazon** hovering high above the northwest corner of the square, jump from the top step in front of Jack's house to the north and glide south and then east to the blazon. Follow a similar strategy to collect the **Unity Badge** at Moonlight Hill, gliding from the top of the hill to reach it.*

BOSS!

LEECHGRAVE

Four Tentaclaws surround the stationary Leechgrave. During this battle, the Tentaclaws have an extra attack wherein they attempt to "swallow" Roxas and feed him to the Leechgrave. The Tentaclaws rear way back before attempting this attack, allowing time to roll away or jump clear.

The Leechgrave's weak point is the coffin swinging beneath its body. However, attacking the coffin directly is unwise due to its unavoidable counterattacks. Instead, destroy all the Tentaclaws in the area. When the last Tentaclaw is defeated, the Leechgrave becomes stunned for a short period of time. This is your chance to attack. Activate a Limit Break to maximize the damage you can inflict before it revives.

When the Leechgrave comes to, it raises four new Tentaclaws from the ground. Speed up the battle by casting Fire spells at Tentaclaws from a short distance away to eliminate them more rapidly. By staying out of Tentaclaws' reach, they grow still and become easier targets for spells. However, the Tentaclaws occasionally relocate themselves to other parts of the area. There is little warning of this, so a few spells may miss.

If you're not ready to activate Limit Break before destroying the last Tentaclaw, simply let it swallow Roxas. Defeat the last Tentaclaw to knock out the Leechgrave, then unleash holy retribution on its coffin. Repeat this process until you're victorious. Exit the Manor Ruins area via the south cave, return to the entrance, and RTC.

CHALLENGE MISSION

Objective: Finish in record time!

Restrictions: Level capped at 35, no recovery magic

Rewards	
Sigils Acquired	Clear Time
3	05:10:00 or less
2	05:10:01 - 06:40:00
1	06:40:01 - 09:30:00

Completing the game and equipping the Zero Gear⑤ plus three Ability Unit(L) panels gives Roxas the mobility needed to take out the Tentaclaws quickly and defeat the Leechgrave fast enough to win three Challenge Sigils. The Princess's Crown ring should provide a needed boost in status.

SPECIAL CHALLENGE

Objective: Avoid taking damage!

Restrictions: Take 20% more damage, enemy level +50

Rewards	
Sigils Acquired	Hits Sustained
3	5 or less
2	6 to 20 hits
1	21 to 35 hits

Hit the Tentaclaws with repeated Thundaga spells to eliminate them, rather than exposing everyone to the danger of their vicious digestive counterattacks. Combo the Leechgrave with really powerful weapons as described in the previous challenge. Move away the instant it recovers from losing all its Tentaclaws, minimizing any damage the beast deals to Roxas.

ELIMINATE THE EMERALD SERENADE

MISSION 67

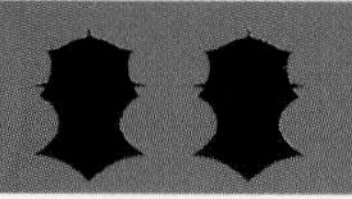

7

RANK Expert

BONUSES!

Heart Points	x5.40	Munny	x16.20	EXP	3.23

ENEMIES

Enemy	LVL	DROP
SAPPHIRE ELEGY	30	Rune Tech+
BLIZZARD PLANT	23	Combo Tech+
POSSESSOR	20	Blazing Crystal
EMERALD SERENADE	40	Silver

REWARDS	
Clear Bonuses	Random Bonuses
Rune Tech+	Aero Recipe (15%)
Lightning Gem	Cure Recipe (15%)
Silver	Cura Recipe (10%)
—	Gust Crystal (10%)
—	Shining Gem (10%)
—	Diamond (10%)
—	Premium Orb (10%)
—	None (20%)

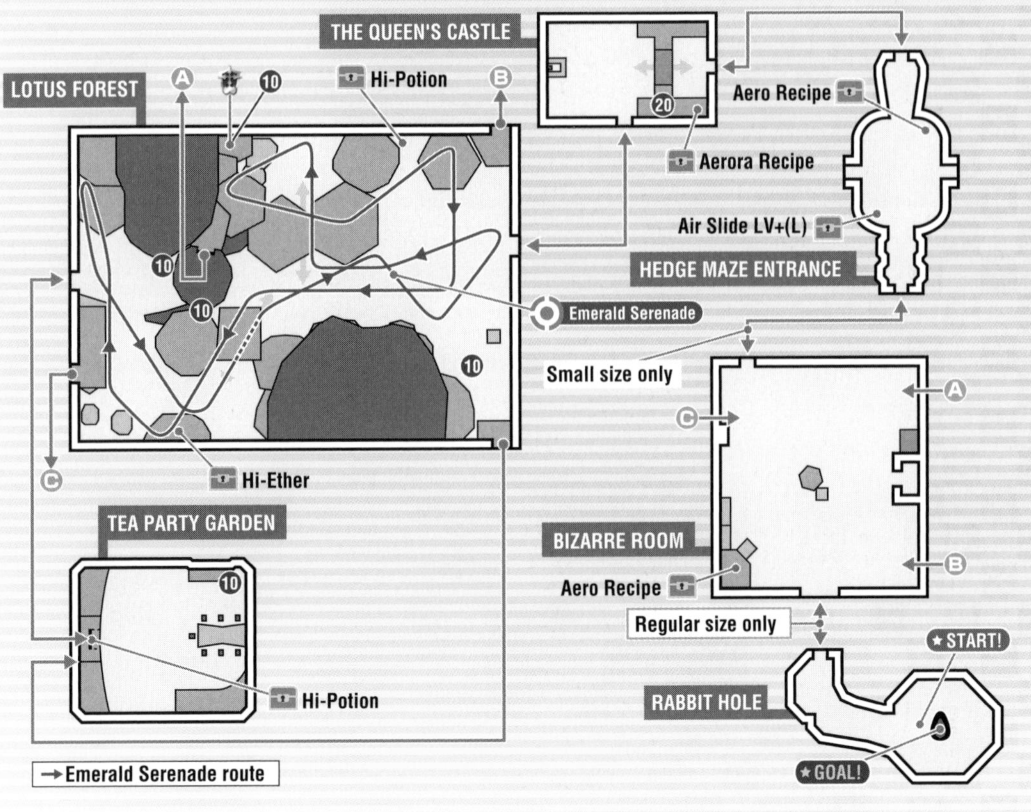

COMING ROUND THE MOUNTAIN

Simply fight to the Lotus Forest, then set up an "ambush" for the Emerald Serenade, much as you did during a previous mission in Never Land. The best place is on the ground level, at the east end of the narrow passage between the trees. Cast Blizzard to freeze it as it approaches, then hit it with a Fire spell to maximize damage. With good timing, it's possible to turn around and freeze it again before it ascends to the upper level. Otherwise, wait for it to come around again and repeat the ambush until it's defeated.

Freeze the Emerald Serenade each time it passes through the Lotus Garden, then attack it again.

COLLECT HEARTS

MISSION 68

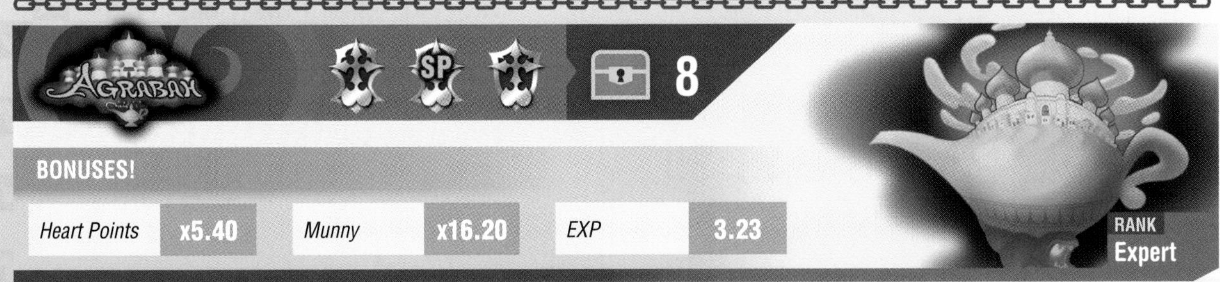

ENEMIES

REWARDS	
Clear Bonuses	Random Bonuses
Fire Recipe	Blizzard Recipe (30%)
Blizzard Recipe	Elixir Recipe (5%)
Curaga Recipe (MG)	Hi-Potion (35%)
—	None (30%)

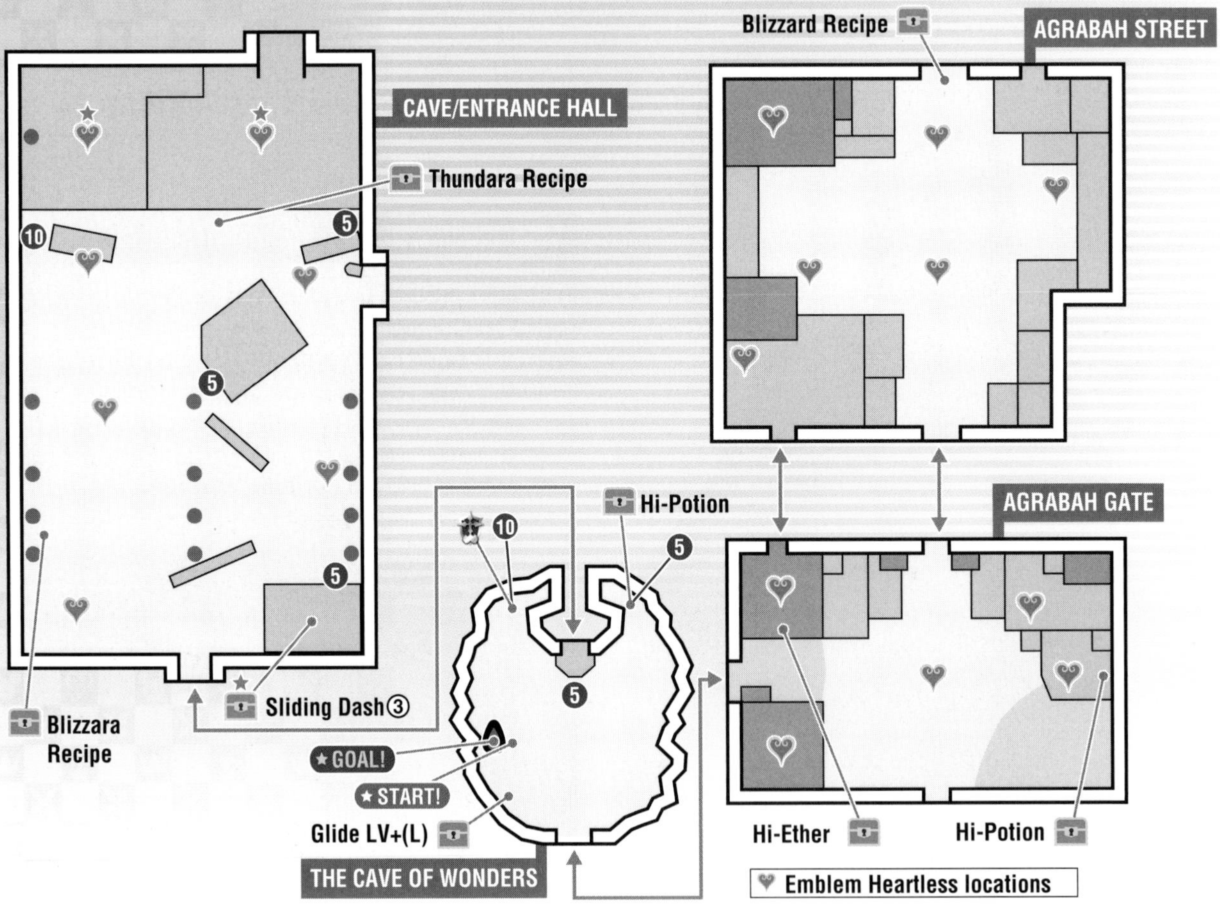

CAVE/ENTRANCE HALL
Thundara Recipe
Blizzara Recipe
Sliding Dash③
Blizzard Recipe
AGRABAH STREET
Hi-Potion
AGRABAH GATE
GOAL!
START!
Glide LV+(L)
THE CAVE OF WONDERS
Hi-Ether
Hi-Potion
Emblem Heartless locations

THE GOAL IS GOOD ENOUGH

Patrol Agrabah and defeat Heartless to collect heart points. Locations of Emblem Heartless are marked on the map in this section. However, you can't complete this mission 100% until you possess the High Jump LV3 ability, which is achieved by equipping the High Jump③ panel and two High Jump LV+(L) links, acquired later. This ability is required to reach the Heartless hidden on the raised north ledges of the Cave/Entrance Hall.

Take out all the Heartless in Agrabah to fill your Mission Gauge.

Once you attain the High Jump LV3 ability, replay this mission from the Holo-Missions screen. Climb onto the overturned pink and gold column at the base of the north ledge. Position Roxas at the uppermost tip of the column, then jump over to grab the ledge. After defeating the Heartless up there, glide southeast to the raised platform, where a chest contains a **Slide Dash**③ panel. Now you should be able to achieve 100%!

Jump from the very tip of the overturned column, as shown.

Glide from the north ledge to the platform beside the south door.

DAY 277-280

Demyx needs Roxas's help filling in for Xion. Find and defeat all the Heartless hidden in Mission 62 (eliminate the Carrier Ghost in Halloween Town). Do so, then speak to Demyx again and he'll add Mission 71 to the roster.

Will Demyx ever get his act together?

VANQUISH THE HEARTLESS THREAT

MISSION 69

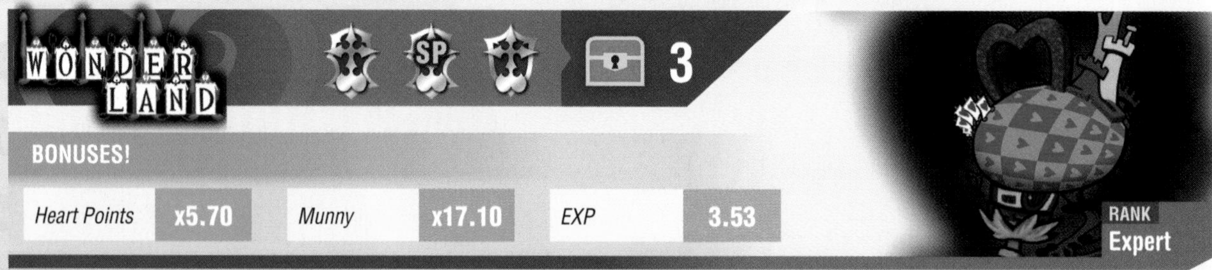

BONUSES!

Heart Points	x5.70	Munny	x17.10	EXP	3.53

ENEMIES

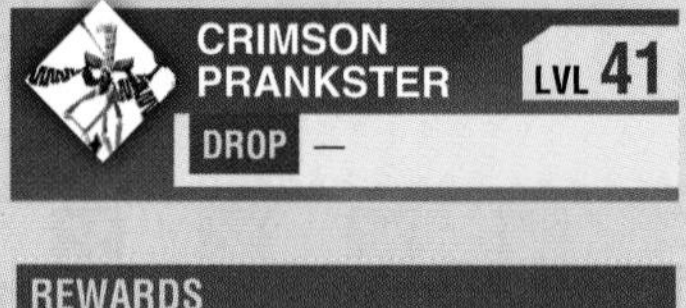

REWARDS

Clear Bonuses	Random Bonuses
Thundaga	Aero Recipe (15%)
Thundara Recipe	Cure Recipe (15%)
Silver	Cura Recipe (10%)
—	Gust Crystal (10%)
—	Shining Gem (10%)
—	Diamond (10%)
—	Premium Orb (10%)
—	None (20%)

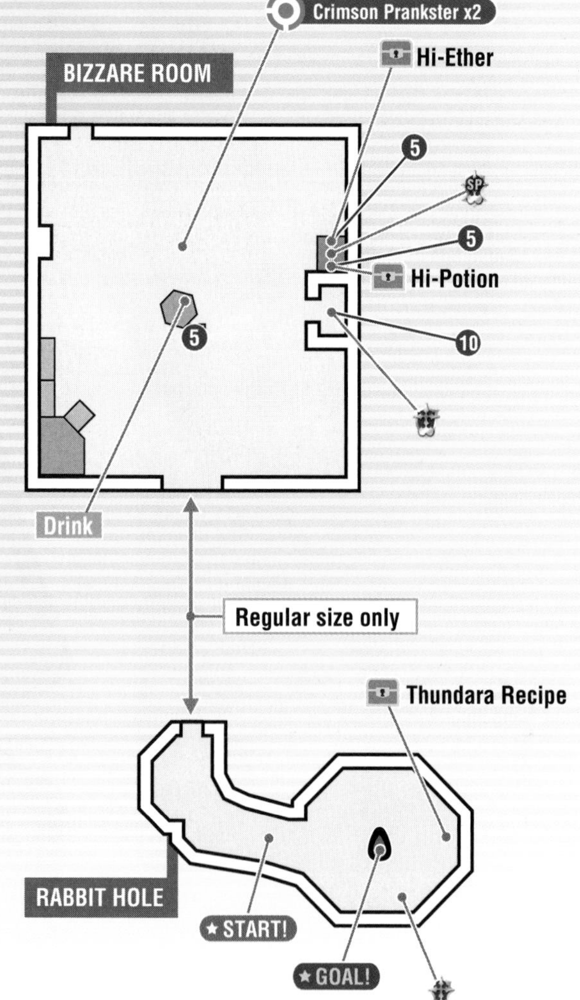

BOSS!

CRIMSON PRANKSTER X2

The main prank these twin bosses play is that they appear to be two separate bosses. However, you cannot eliminate them one at a time. If you eliminate one without immediately defeating the other, then the survivor brings the fallen twin back to life, replacing some of its lost HP as well.

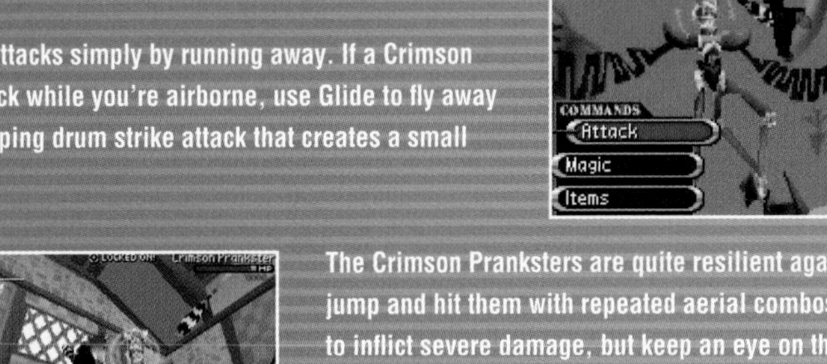

With the Scan ability equipped, lock on to one Crimson Prankster and attack it until its HP is nearly depleted, to where you can eliminate it with only a few more hits. Then tap the R button to switch lock on and attack the other Crimson Prankster until it is defeated. Quickly attack the remaining twin before it can resurrect its sibling, and the battle is won!

Meanwhile, avoid their fire-breathing attacks simply by running away. If a Crimson Prankster initiates a fire-breathing attack while you're airborne, use Glide to fly away from danger. Also watch out for the leaping drum strike attack that creates a small damage area.

The Crimson Pranksters are quite resilient against most magic, so jump and hit them with repeated aerial combos. Use Limit Breaks to inflict severe damage, but keep an eye on the health of the one you're attacking. If a Crimson Prankster's HP drops close to the line during a Limit Break, switch the lock on target and chase after the other one.

CHALLENGE MISSION

Objective: Avoid taking damage!

Restrictions: Enemy level +22, HP drains while on the ground

Rewards

Sigils Acquired	Hits Sustained
3	10 or less
2	11 to 15 hits
1	16 to 20 hits

Avoid direct contact with either Crimson Prankster and instead cast Blizzard, Thunder, and Aero magic at them. Jump before each casting and use jumps to dodge all their attacks. When you run out of castings, use Elixirs to recover health and magic.

SPECIAL CHALLENGE

Objective: Finish in record time!

Restrictions: Enemy level +30, HP drains while on the ground

Rewards

Sigils Acquired	Clear Time
3	02:15:00 or less
2	02:15:01 - 03:20:00
1	03:20:01 - 05:00:00

Use Blizzard, Aero, and Thunder magic to stop or stun the Crimson Pranksters. Remember to damage one to near-death, then switch your lock on and defeat the other, then switch back and finish the battle.

ELIMINATE THE DESERTERS

MISSION 70

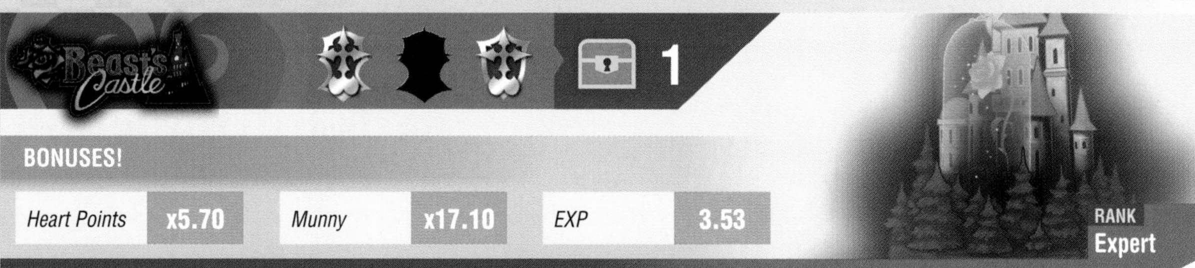

BONUSES!

Heart Points	x5.70	Munny	x17.10	EXP	3.53

RANK
Expert

ENEMIES

REWARDS

Clear Bonuses	Random Bonuses
Shining Crystal	Elixir Recipe (10%)
Shining Gem	Blazing Crystal (15%)
Blazing Gem	Frost Gem (15%)
—	Hi-Potion (15%)
—	Ether (15%)
—	Panacea (20%)
—	None (10%)

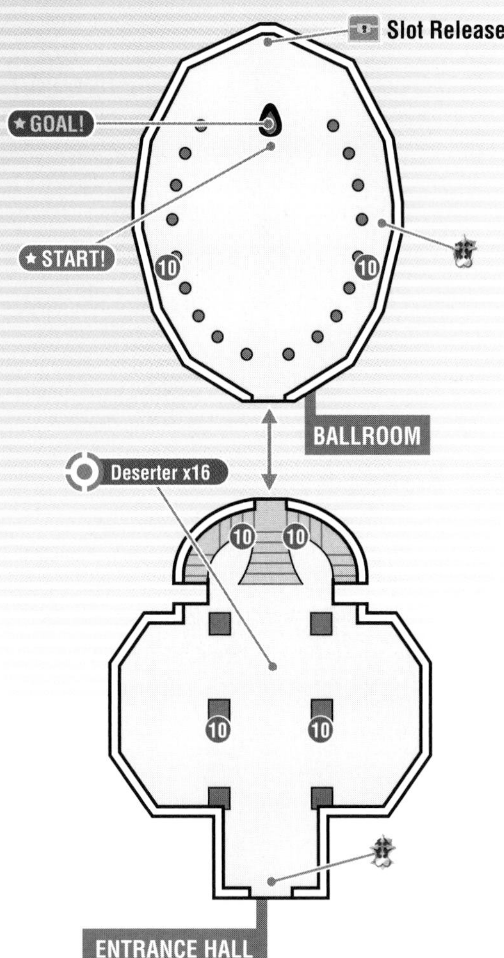

SHIELDED REFUGEES

Grab the all-important **Slot Releaser** from the chest behind the entrance point in the Ballroom and enter the Entrance Hall. The Deserters benefit from the protection of a Barrier Master. Lock on to the Barrier Master and eliminate it first, using Blizzard and Aero magic to dispatch it more quickly. Then begin eliminating Deserters by hitting them with Fire spells.

Defeat the Barrier Master so that it can't protect the Deserters.

The Deserters attack when one falls. During the first few counterattacks, when there are more Deserters, run away from them until they resume "deserting." Continue killing them and running away until there are only five or so left. By then, their retribution won't be so bad. Continue killing them as they gather around Roxas to finish them off.

The Deserters notice Roxas only when one of their numbers is killed.

THE INVISIBLE

On your way back to the dark corridor, an Invisible appears in the Ballroom. Thank goodness there's only one, because these creatures are tougher to eliminate than most bosses! Note that you can still RTC if the Invisible is still hanging around, if you want. Staying aerial for a good portion of the time helps to avoid most of its attacks, such as its rain of purple orbs and its shockwave attack. Performing the shockwave leaves it stunned for several moments thereafter, which is a great time to hit it with a Limit Break or Fire spells. When it vanishes and its sword begins crisscrossing the room, use Dodge Rolls to avoid it.

The Invisible is a powerful enemy on the level of a sub-boss.

Use Dodge Rolls to evade the sword when it streaks across the area.

CHALLENGE MISSION

Objective: Finish in record time!

Restrictions: No recovery magic, Take 30% more damage

Rewards	
Sigils Acquired	Clear Time
3	01:25:00 or less
2	01:25:01 - 01:50:00
1	01:50:01 - 02:30:00

Load up Roxas with Fire spells, Blizzard, and Aero spells, then head directly to the Entrance Hall. Eliminate the Barrier Master quickly by hitting it with Blizzard and Aero spells. Once the Barrier Master is no longer protecting the Deserters, begin shooting Fire spells indiscriminately. Use Ethers to regain magic casts. With the first few kills, you should dodge the remaining Deserters' retribution. However, once the pack has thinned to about four or five, keep shooting Fire spells at them to beat the clock.

PROVE YOUR ENDURANCE

MISSION 71

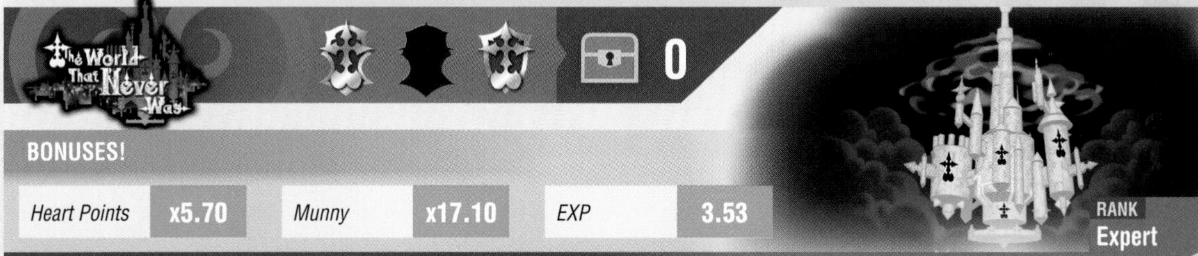

BONUSES!

Heart Points	x5.70	Munny	x17.10	EXP	3.53

RANK Expert

ENEMIES

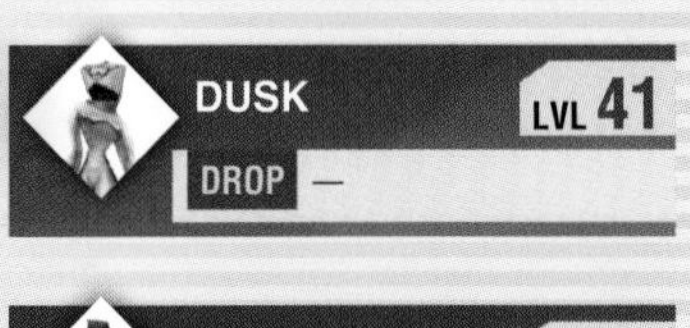

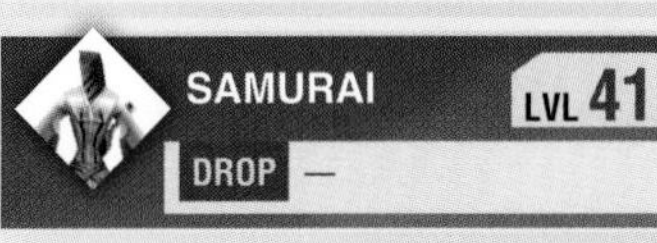

REWARDS	
Clear Bonuses	Random Bonuses
Gear Component B	Thundara Recipe (20%)
Aerora Recipe	Aerora Recipe (20%)
Gust Gem	Elixir Recipe (10%)
—	Ether (30%)
—	None (20%)

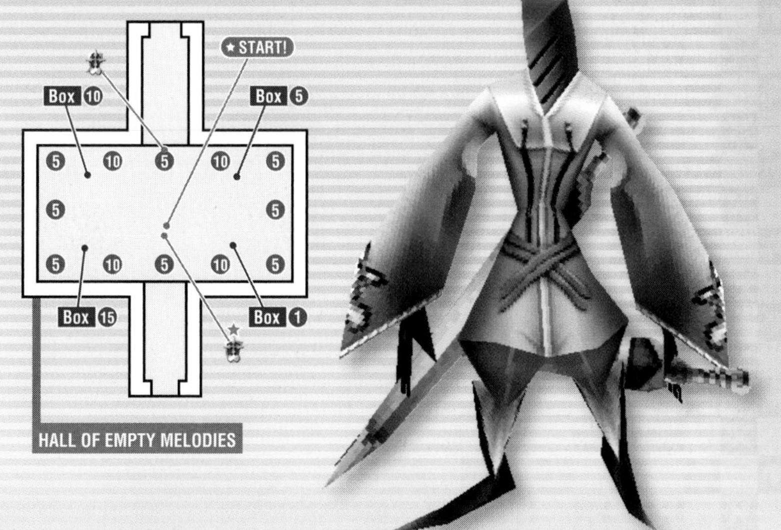

ROLL ON THROUGH

Roll through the enemies for two minutes with the Dodge Rush ability.

By linking the Dodge Rush(L) panel to a Dodge Roll③, you can roll between the advancing Dusks and Samurai with ease, without fear of being attacked mid-roll. Simply repeat this until the mission is complete.

Attacking or using Limit Breaks only leaves Roxas open to counterattacks from Samurais.

CHALLENGE MISSION

Objective: Earn lots of munny!

Restrictions: No recovery magic

Sigils Acquired	Munny Earned
3	200 or more
2	180 - 199
1	150 - 179

Use Limit Breaks and Fire spells to defeat the Dusks and accumulate a lot of munny. The creatures don't drop very much in prizes, so you must eliminate them very efficiently; Fire spells can do the trick. Use an Elixir to regain health and your magic castings.

COLLECT HEARTS

MISSION 72

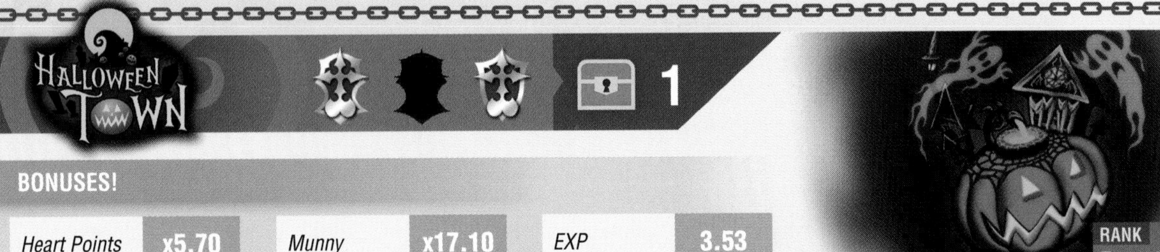

BONUSES!

Heart Points	x5.70	Munny	x17.10	EXP	3.53

ENEMIES

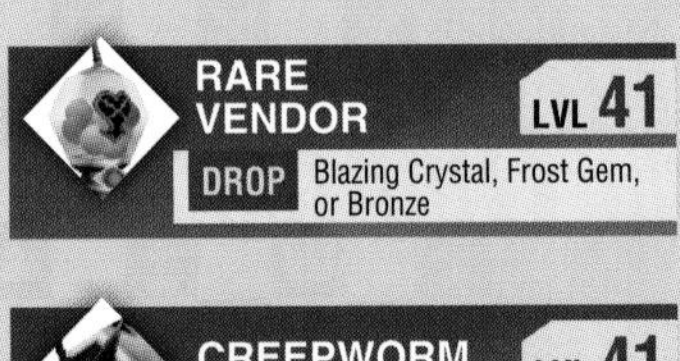

CREEPWORM LVL 41
DROP —

DUAL BLADE LVL 41
DROP Gear Component C

REWARDS

Clear Bonuses	Random Bonuses
Combo Tech+	Blizzara Recipe (15%)
Lightning Gem	Thunder Recipe (10%)
Power Tech+	Blazing Gem (10%)
—	Gust Gem (10%)
—	Shining Crystal(10%)
—	Shield Tech+ (20%)
—	Silver (20%)
—	None (5%)

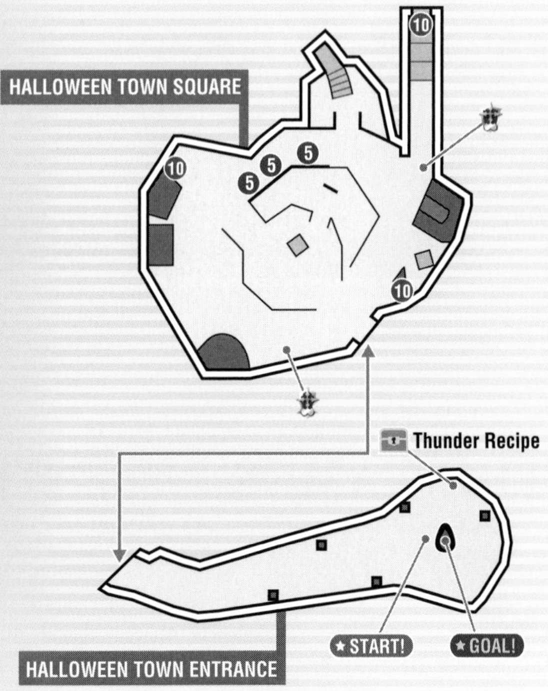

CHALLENGE MISSION

Objective: Finish in record time!

Restrictions: No attack magic, enemy level +25

Rewards	
Sigils Acquired	Clear Time
3	03:05:00 or less
2	03:05:01 - 03:35:00
1	03:35:01 - 04:05:00

The HP of each Dual Blade is too high to consider taking them out in time to win three Challenge Sigils. Instead, focus on defeating the Creepworms that appear in the area. Use Glide to reach them quickly and eliminate them while the chain ring still shows to score higher heart points. Once you've scored roughly 110 hearts, the Mission Gauge fills to the goal line and you can RTC.

FOUR BLADES ARE TOUGHER THAN ONE

The Dual Blades waiting in the Halloween Town Square fight the same as those previously encountered, only now there are two of them. Remember tactics such as blocking their thrusts with the right timing or casting Thundaga to stun them for longer periods, during which Roxas can tear them up with his Limit Breaks. Also keep in mind that this is a quest to collect hearts, not to eliminate a target. That means breaking away to wipe out the Creepworms that periodically run through the area. Score roughly 110 points to complete the mission, and eliminate all the Creepworms and Dual Blades to fill the Mission Gauge 100%.

Attack from the "outside" of the duo, meaning positioning your target between Roxas and the other Dual Blade. This prevents ambushes.

Avoid the Dual Blades' thrusts and counter attack with magic and aerial combos.

There is a Rare Vendor near Jack's house. Eliminate it to acquire rare synthesis items.

DAY 296

Speak with Saïx to be promoted to Master rank. New items are available in the Moogle's shop, such as Mega-Potions, Mega-Ethers, a Slot Releaser, Magic LV2④ in a new configuration, Block④ and Block LV+(L), level up links for Air Slide, High Jump, and Treasure Magnet, the Champion Gear+⑤, the Lucky Star ring, and Gold. Three new rings can be synthesized, along with some other items. Lastly, Goofy is now playable in Mission Mode!

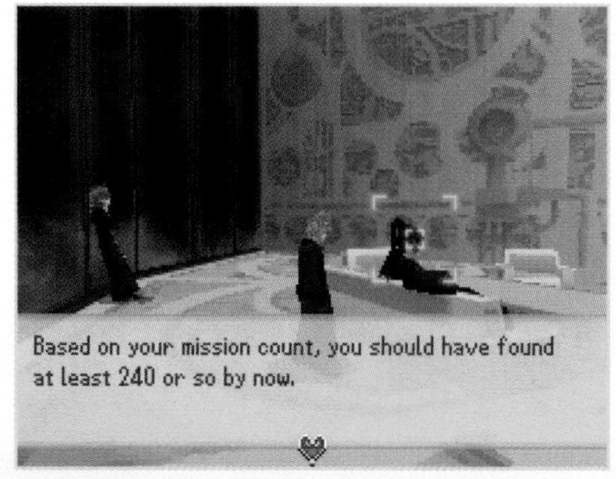

*If you've opened 240 chests or more, Xaldin rewards your thoroughness with a **Blazing Crystal**.*

DEFEAT HEARTLESS IN THE GAMES

MISSION 73

BONUSES!

Heart Points	Munny	EXP
x5.75	x17.25	3.93

ENEMIES

WATCHER LVL 20 — DROP Gust Gem

LI'L CANNON LVL 14 — DROP Ankharite

STALWART BLADE LVL 50 — DROP Adamantite

AIR BATTLER LVL 20 — DROP Gust Crystal

ICE CANNON LVL 20 — DROP Gold

SKY GRAPPLER LVL 42 — DROP Premium Orb

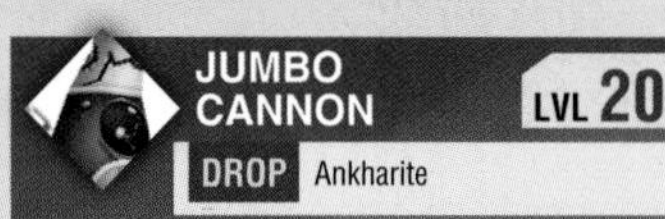

SWITCH LAUNCHER LVL 40 — DROP Shining Crystal

SNOWY CRYSTAL LVL 30 — DROP Frost Crystal

JUMBO CANNON LVL 20 — DROP Ankharite

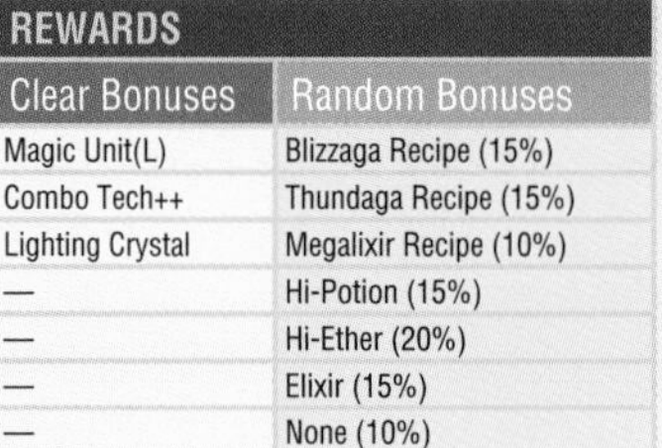

REWARDS

Clear Bonuses	Random Bonuses
Magic Unit(L)	Blizzaga Recipe (15%)
Combo Tech++	Thundaga Recipe (15%)
Lighting Crystal	Megalixir Recipe (10%)
—	Hi-Potion (15%)
—	Hi-Ether (20%)
—	Elixir (15%)
—	None (10%)

CHANGE OF LINEUP

Notice how nice Phil gets when he's in a bind?

Enter the Coliseum and speak to Phil. He's desperately in need of a challenger for today's games and Roxas fits the bill. You must survive five rounds in the arena, culminating in a battle against a powerful boss.

AERIAL FOES

The first round pits Roxas against a couple of Air Battlers (which should be cannon fodder by now) and a Sky Grappler. Inflict severe damage to the Sky Grappler by knocking the barrels into it from the top platforms on either side.

Knock barrels from the tops of the platforms on either side of the arena to take out the flying enemies.

WALL OF CANNONS

Knock the barrels into the cannons mounted on the high wall to eliminate them. Notice that the **Ordeal Badge** for this mission is located behind the wall, so take a lap around the ring before destroying the final cannon.

"Fire" the barrels as counter salvos against the cannons on the high wall.

*Seek out the **Ordeal Badge** behind the cannon wall.*

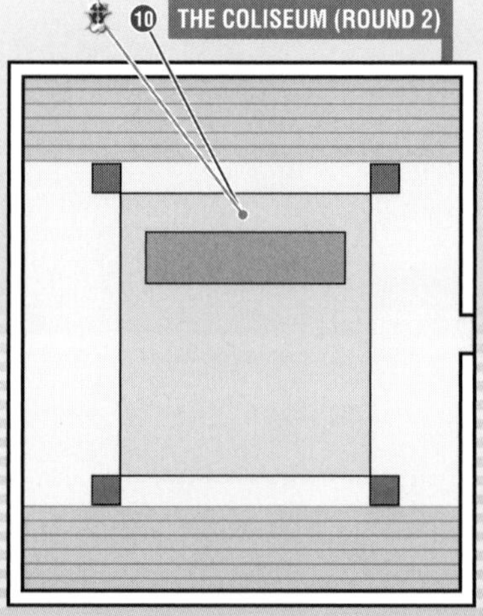

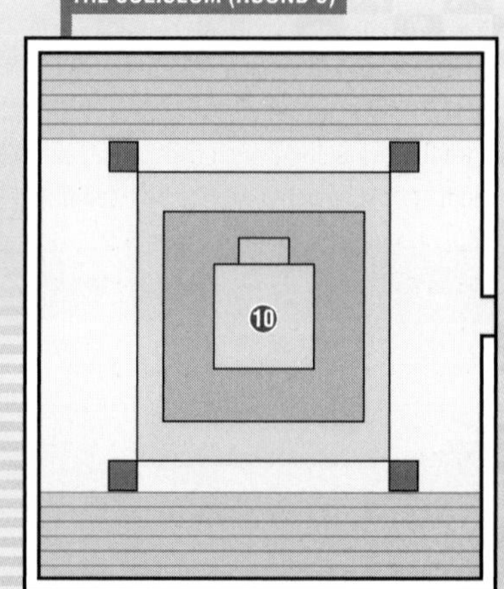

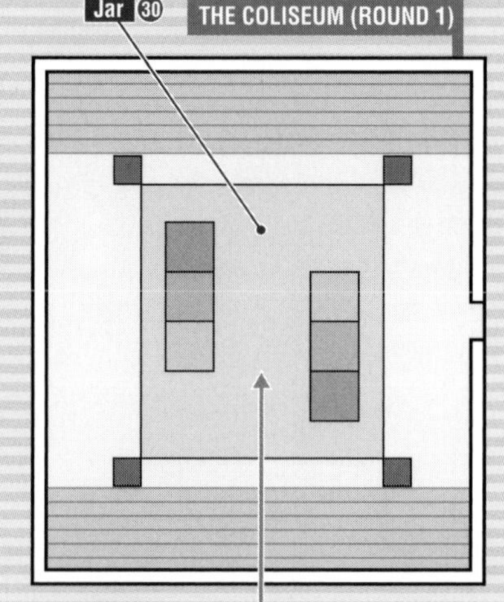

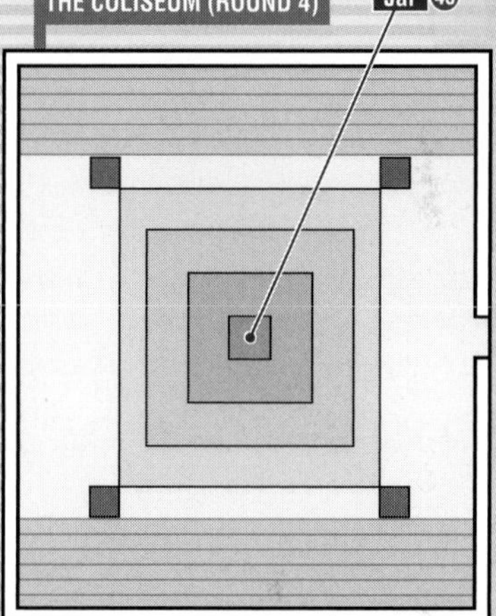

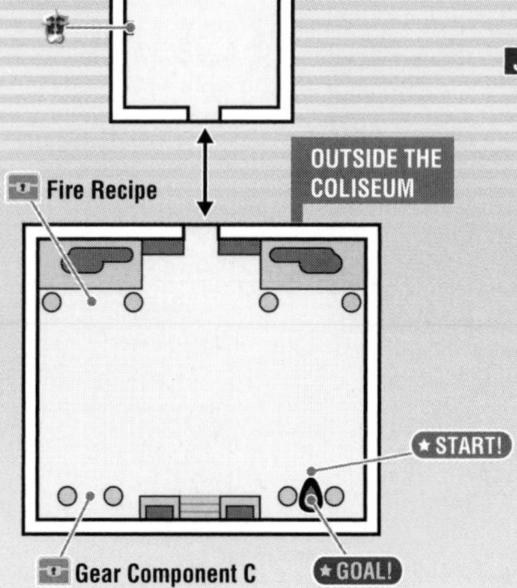

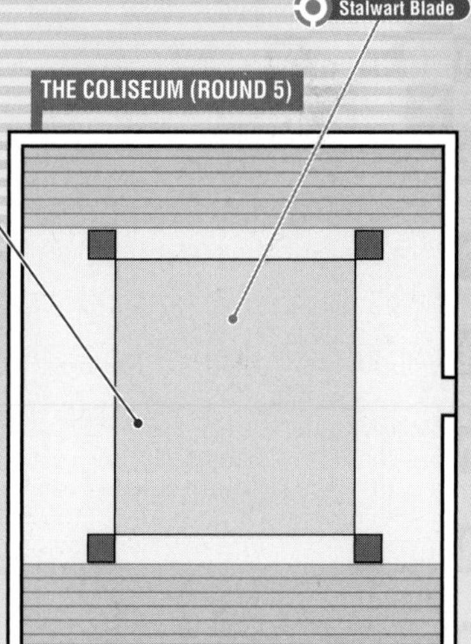

PIT OF DESPAIR

Use Fire spells to dispose of the Snowy Crystals and use the barrels against the Switch Launcher. The latter's projectiles teleport Roxas to the ground below the Switch Launcher, just before it squashes him. Avoid its shots by using Air Slide or well-timed Dodge Rolls.

Knock barrels from the sides into the pit.

Eliminate the Snowy Crystals quickly by casting Fire.

THE HOVER CROWD

Goad the Watchers into pursuing Roxas to the lower levels, where it is more difficult for the Ice Cannon to target.

Use Thunder spells to eliminate the Watchers as quickly as possible. If Roxas gets inflicted with shoe-glue, use Panaceas to recover. You can't afford to be a sitting duck for the Ice Cannon. When only the cannon remains, ascend to the high platform and use Fire spells to weaken it for the kill.

Eliminate all Watchers before jumping to the Ice Cannon's platform to fight it.

BOSS! STALWART BLADE

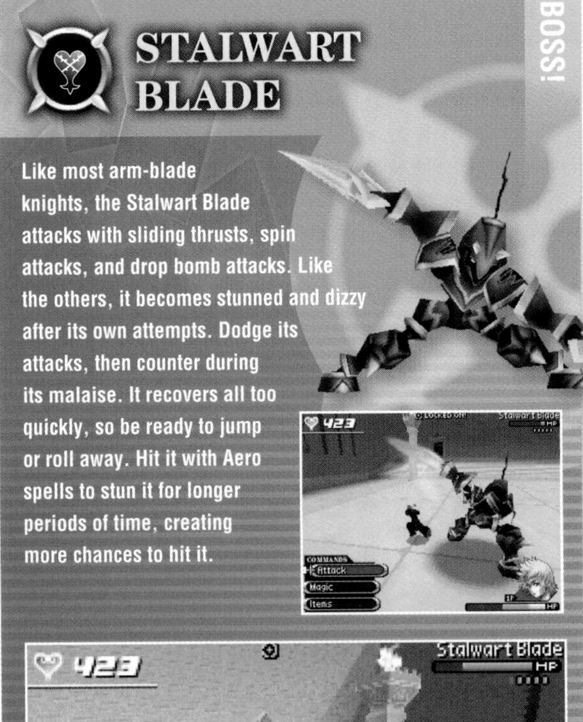

Like most arm-blade knights, the Stalwart Blade attacks with sliding thrusts, spin attacks, and drop bomb attacks. Like the others, it becomes stunned and dizzy after its own attempts. Dodge its attacks, then counter during its malaise. It recovers all too quickly, so be ready to jump or roll away. Hit it with Aero spells to stun it for longer periods of time, creating more chances to hit it.

CHALLENGE MISSION

Objective: Finish in record time!

Restrictions: No recovery magic, enemy level +3

Rewards	
Sigils Acquired	Clear Time
3	03:30:00 or less
2	03:30:01 - 05:00:00
1	05:00:01 - 06:00:00

Wipe out the Air Battlers and take out the Sky Grappler using the barrels. Use the barrels to destroy the cannons on the raised platform, then use Fire spells to wipe out the Snowy Crystals and circle the Switch Launcher while attacking. Use Fire and Thunder spells against the Ice Cannon and Watchers respectively, then take down the Stalwart Blade by casting Aeroga multiple times while fighting.

DAY 297

SEARCH FOR THE IMPOSTOR

MISSION 74

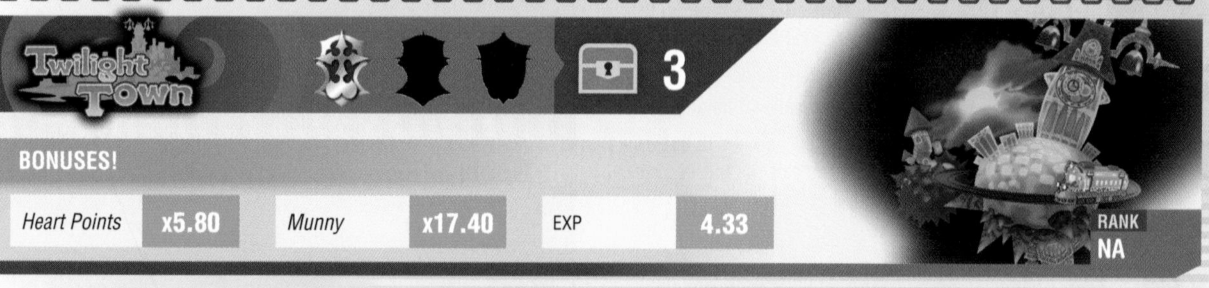

BONUSES!

Heart Points	x5.80	Munny	x17.40	EXP	4.33

RANK NA

ENEMIES

SHADOW LVL 30
DROP Blazing Gem

SCARLET TANGO LVL 20
DROP Blazing Crystal

DIRE PLANT LVL 20
DROP Frost Crystal

RARE VENDOR LVL 42
DROP Luck Tech, Adamantite, or Dark Ingot

INVISIBLE LVL 45
DROP Shield Tech++

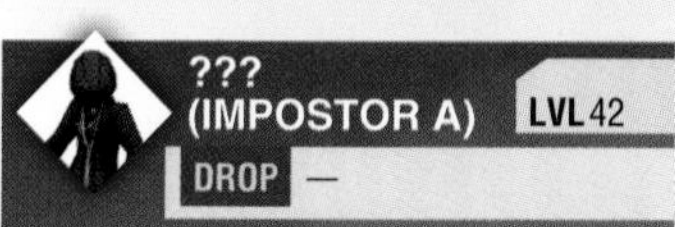

??? (IMPOSTOR A) LVL 42
DROP —

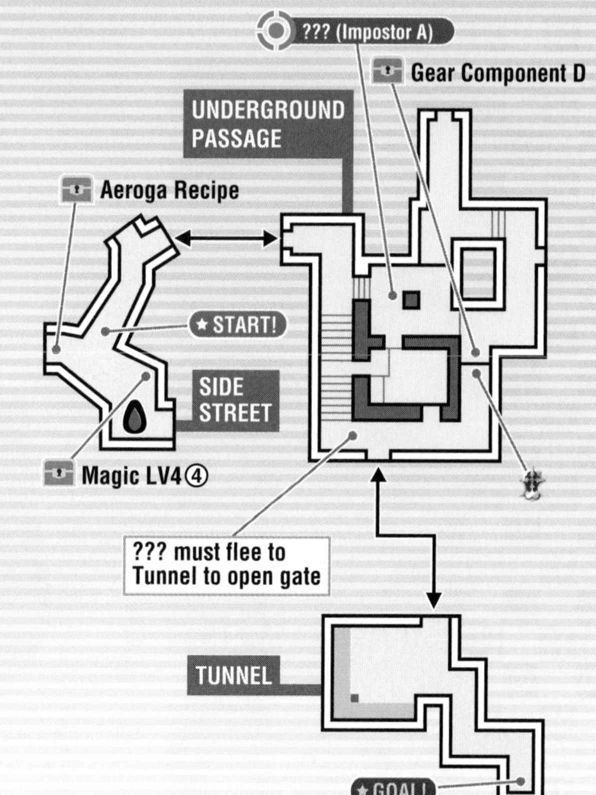

REWARDS

Clear Bonuses	Random Bonuses
High Jump③	Aeroga Recipe (10%)
Lightning Crystal	Gear Component D (5%)
Adamantite	Orichalcum (10%)
—	Hi-Potion (20%)
—	Hi-Ether (20%)
—	Panacea (15%)
—	None (20%)

FUTILE PURSUIT

Search the starting area for items and a Rare Vendor before moving on!

Speak to Saïx when you're ready to begin this mission. When Roxas is unable to enter Castle Oblivion, Axel spirits him away to Twilight Town, only they manage to bump into the impostor they seek!

Chase and attack the impostor throughout the Underground Passage. Cast spells to break his block.

Follow the impostor into the underground. Striking the impostor causes him to vanish from one location and reappear elsewhere. Look for the orange-red colored dot to appear on the in-game map to determine his next location. He doesn't attack back, so there's nothing to fear. When he finally appears by the south blue gate, he moves to the Tunnel.

Enter the Tunnel and chase the impostor from the southeast corner into the main room and back again. When the impostor slips through the south gate and out of Twilight Town, it's time to call it a day.

Pursue the impostor into the tunnel.

CHALLENGE MISSION

Objective: Finish in record time!

Restrictions: No recovery magic, no recovery items, HP drains while on the ground

Rewards	
Sigils Acquired	Clear Time
3	01:30:00 or less
2	01:30:01 - 02:00:00
1	02:00:01 - 02:30:00

Although the impostor is easy to track on the map once you enter the Underground Passage, the person may still cause you to lose Challenge Sigils by blocking attacks. Cast Aeroga frequently to damage the impostor and prevent it from blocking so much at each location. Use Glide to quickly fly to the impostor and attack.

DAY 298

Speak to Saïx to trigger a conversation with him and Axel. Then, speak to Saïx once again to embark on the mission to slay the impostor.

Saïx's and Axel's history sometimes gets in the way of Organization business.

ELIMINATE THE IMPOSTOR

MISSION 75

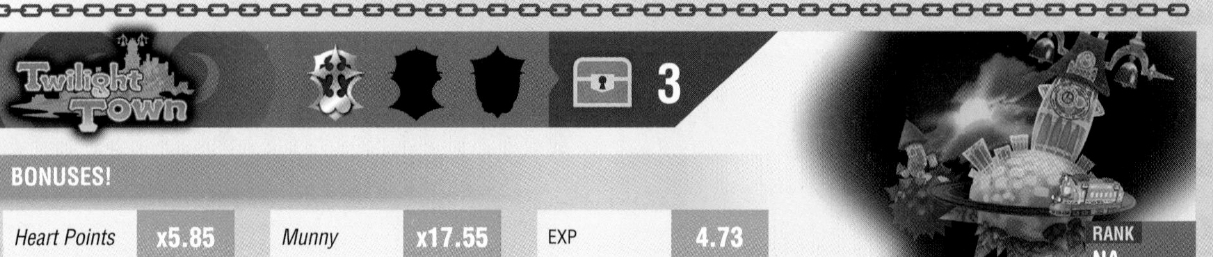

BONUSES!

Heart Points	x5.85	Munny	x17.55	EXP	4.73

ENEMIES

MEGA-SHADOW LVL 20
DROP: Range Tech+

SCARLET TANGO LVL 20
DROP: Blazing Crystal

STORM BOMB LVL 20
DROP: Combo Tech++

TRICKY MONKEY LVL 42
DROP: Shining Crystal

??? (IMPOSTOR B) LVL 42
DROP: —

REWARDS

Clear Bonuses	Random Bonuses
Gear Component C	Aeroga Recipe (10%)
Gear Component C	Gear Component D (5%)
Frost Crystal	Orichalcum (10%)
—	Hi-Potion (20%)
—	Hi-Ether (20%)
—	Panacea (15%)
—	None (20%)

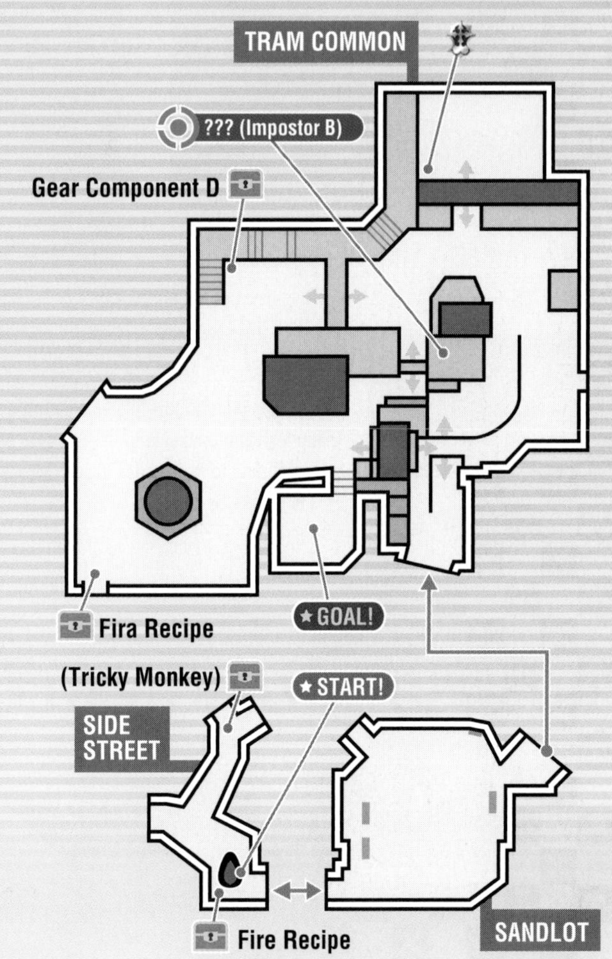

SHADOW RING

Attacking the Mega-Shadows from above helps Roxas avoid damage.

Collect items near the starting point in the Side Street, then enter the Sandlot. Roxas becomes sealed inside the area with a gaggle of Mega-Shadows. Staying airborne and attacking with aerial combos proves conducive to Roxas's continuing health. Defeat all Mega-Shadows to unseal the area.

TRAM COMMON CHASE

Track the movements of the elusive impostor on the lower screen's map.

As in the previous mission, the impostor's location appears on the map on the lower screen. Strike the person whenever it stops, and pursue it to its next stop. Scores of Heartless appear near the impostor's stopping points. Take out those who stand in the way and look for nearby chests.

After chasing the impostor and striking it enough times, it vanishes and reappears in the enclosed south area. Follow it there for a closing scene.

The impostor circles the Tram Common before reaching the final stop.

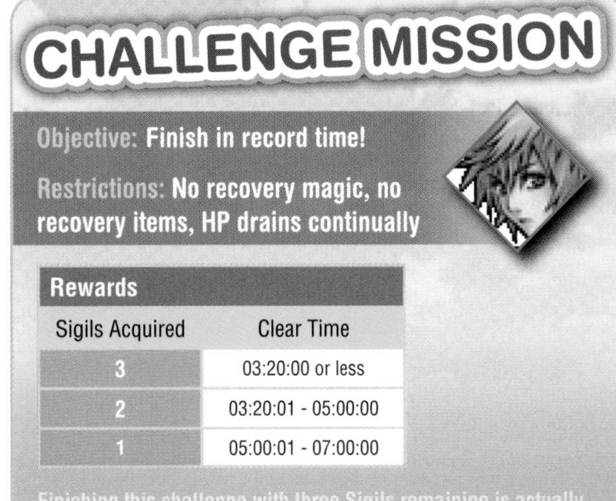

CHALLENGE MISSION

Objective: Finish in record time!

Restrictions: No recovery magic, no recovery items, HP drains continually

Rewards	
Sigils Acquired	Clear Time
3	03:20:00 or less
2	03:20:01 - 05:00:00
1	05:00:01 - 07:00:00

Finishing this challenge with three Sigils remaining is actually quite a bit easier than Mission 74. Simply ignore the enemies and stay after the impostor. If enemy damage activates Roxas's Limit Break, use it to strike the impostor and speed along the mission.

DAY 299

Try to keep your edge while heavy stuff goes down today. Equip a weapon panel with five or more slots and link four or more units to it. Impress Xigbar with it and he'll give Roxas a piece of **Gold**!

Xigbar wants to see some real weaponry in action before he'll be impressed.

DESTROY THE SHADOW GLOBS

MISSION 76

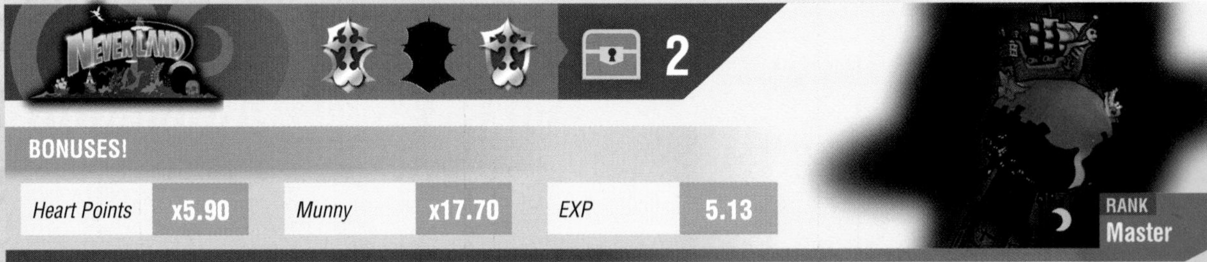

ENEMIES

TURQUOISE MARCH LVL 14 — DROP: Shining Crystal

WAVECREST LVL 24 — DROP: Gust Crystal

RARE VENDOR LVL 43 — DROP: Luck Tech, Adamantite, or Dark Ingot

SHADOW GLOB LVL 43 — DROP: —

BUBBLE BEAT LVL 24 — DROP: Frost Crystal

REWARDS	
Clear Bonuses	Random Bonuses
Rune Tech+	Curaga Recipe (20%)
Power Tech+	Megalixir Recipe (10%)
Glide LV+(L)	Frost Crystal (20%)
—	Mithril (25%)
—	Hi-Potion (15%)
—	None (10%)

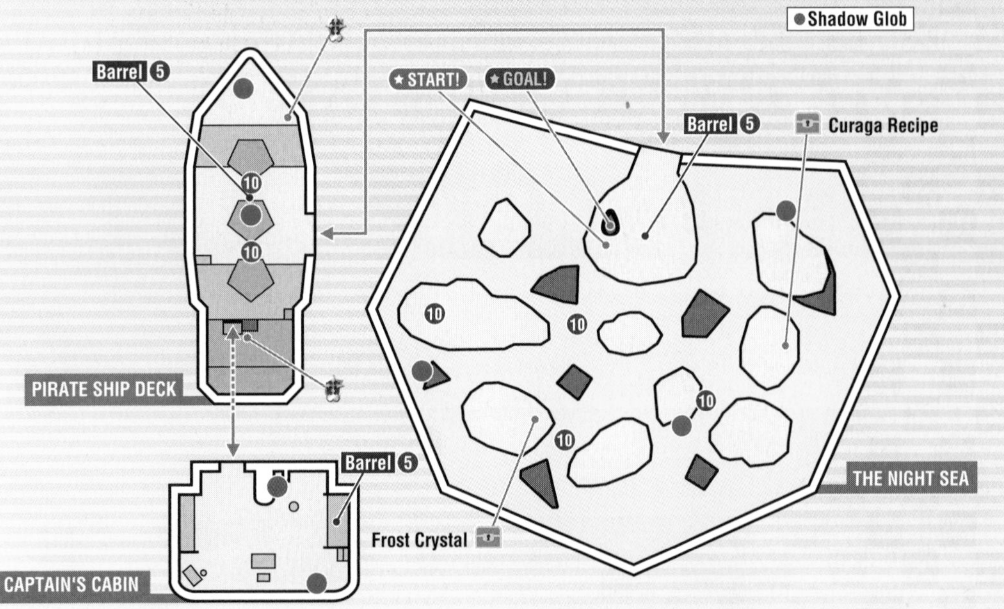

GLOB HUNT

The Shadow Globs are well hidden in the Night Sea area. Many are on the far sides of rocks jutting from the water's surface. There's also the danger of triggering Wavecrest appearances while flying around. Use the map in this section to locate the Shadow Globs in the Night Sea area. Go to those locations and look at the sides of the rocks positioned there.

Use the map here to find the locations of the Shadow Globs, hidden on the backsides of many rocks and islands.

Clear out the sea area, then proceed to the pirate ship and do the same thing. By the time you eliminate the ones on the deck and the mast, you'll have completed the mission. But don't let that stop you! Enter the Captain's Cabin and destroy the two in there to achieve 100%.

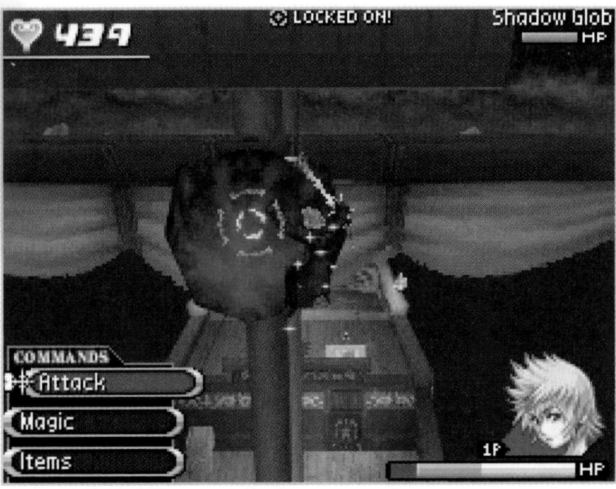

Look for a Shadow Glob high up on the center mast.

A Rare Vendor appears near the Shadow Glob at the bow of the ship!

Eliminate the Shadow Globs in Hook's quarters to fill your Mission Gauge.

CHALLENGE MISSION

Objective: Finish in record time!

Restrictions: Level capped at 30, HP drains continually

Rewards	
Sigils Acquired	Clear Time
3	01:00:00 or less
2	01:00:01 - 02:00:00
1	02:00:01 - 03:00:00

Although Roxas constantly loses HP, he will not perish from it. Just avoid any enemy attacks and go after the Shadow Globs. Use Thundaga spells to wipe out the Shadow Globs instantly. Head to the pirate ship first and eliminate the Shadow Globs on the bow, the mast, and in the cabin. Then simply head back to the open area. Fly to the far east rock and destroy the Shadow Glob there, then fly directly back to the dark corridor and RTC before you lose a Challenge Sigil.

DAY 300

ELIMINATE THE PHANTOMTAIL

MISSION 77

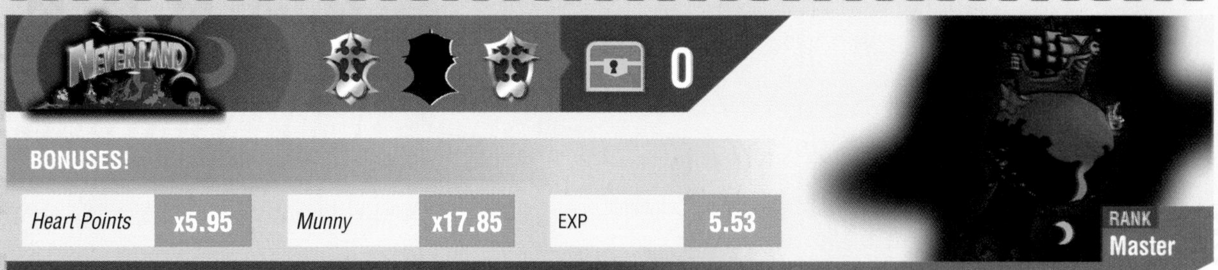

BONUSES!

Heart Points	x5.95	Munny	x17.85	EXP	5.53

ENEMIES

REWARDS	
Clear Bonuses	Random Bonuses
LV Tripler④	Curaga Recipe (20%)
Thundaga Recipe	Megalixir Recipe (10%)
Gold	Frost Crystal (20%)
—	Mithril (25%)
—	Hi-Potion (15%)
—	None (10%)

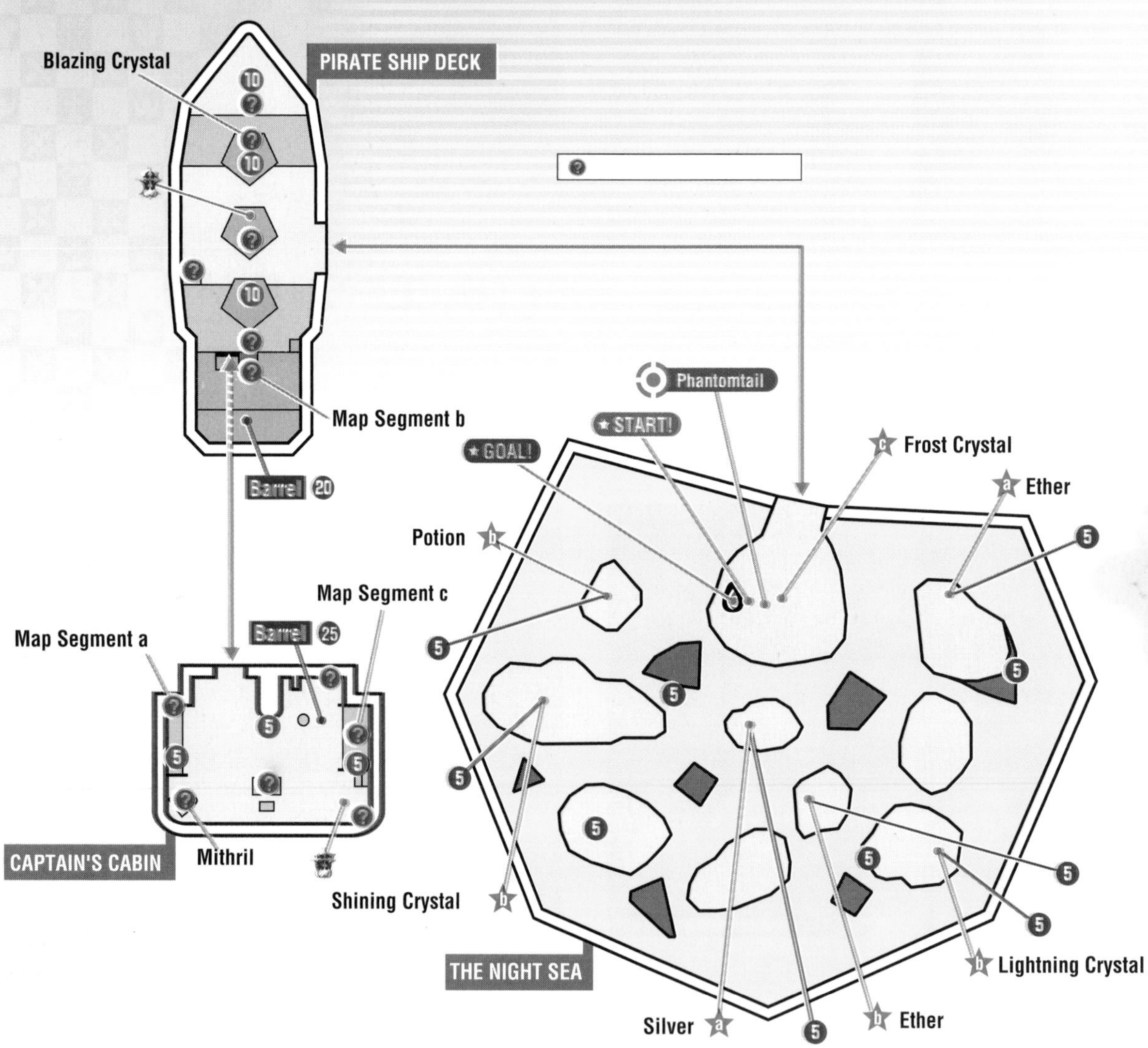

PIRATE SHIP DECK
Blazing Crystal
Map Segment b
Barrel 20

CAPTAIN'S CABIN
Map Segment a
Map Segment c
Barrel 25
Mithril
Shining Crystal

THE NIGHT SEA
Phantomtail
START!
GOAL!
Frost Crystal
Ether
Potion
Lightning Crystal
Silver
Ether

TINKER BELL IN PERIL

Hook and Smee have finally captured Tinker Bell! Follow them back to the pirate ship and enter the Captain's Cabin. Roxas frees Tink, who finds a map marked with a digging spot. Check the corner of the sofa on the west side of Hook's quarters to find another piece of the map. While there are other points of interest to examine, some of them release Heartless so it's not recommended to go exploring off the map.

Check the northwest corner of the couch to find a map piece.

Examine the roll-top desk in the corner to obtain a piece of **Mithril**.

MORE OF THE MAP

Exit the Captain's Cabin and fly up to the helm. Examine the steering wheel to find another map segment. Now you're ready to return to the Night Sea area knowing just where to dig!

Check the wheel to find a map piece.

Search the forward crow's nest to find a **Blazing Crystal**.

Fly to the locations marked in red on your lower screen and strike the ground there to dig up a treasure box. During Roxas's first attempt, he's disappointed to find that no Heartless pop out. At that point, Hook and Smee appear on the north central island near the dark corridor. Land on that island when you want to begin the battle against the Phantomtail, before or after collecting items.

Strike the ground at map-marked locations with the Keyblade to dig up treasures.

Approach Hook and Smee near the dark corridor to trigger the Phantomtail's entrance.

BOSS!

PHANTOMTAIL

Avoid attacking the Phantomtail's head, which makes it vanish momentarily. As with other flyers, lock on to the tail, fly after it, and attack. Cast Aero and Fire spells at the tail when the beast is relatively stationary to inflict greater than normal damage. Fly away from the floating blue orbs it releases, then resume pursuing the tail.

When the Phantomtail is defeated, the final map piece appears on the bed in the Captain's Cabin. This marks the location of the Frost Crystal on the map.

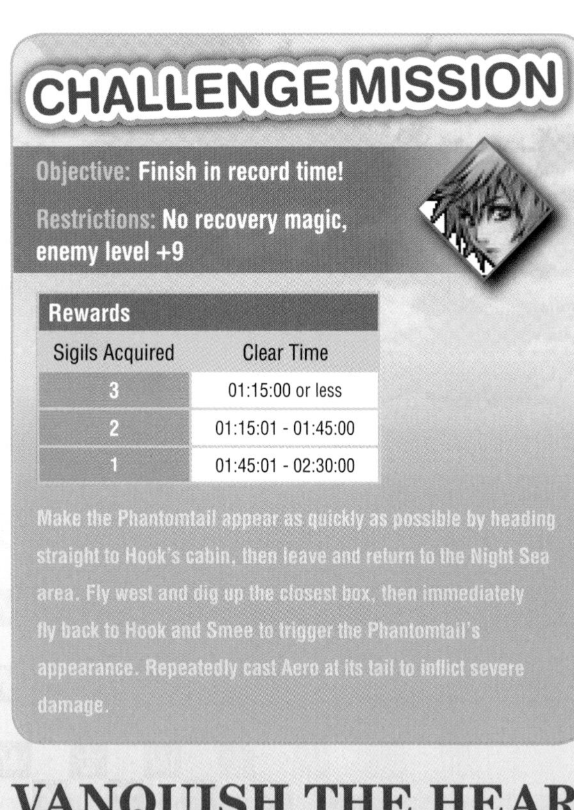

CHALLENGE MISSION

Objective: Finish in record time!

Restrictions: No recovery magic, enemy level +9

Rewards	
Sigils Acquired	Clear Time
3	01:15:00 or less
2	01:15:01 - 01:45:00
1	01:45:01 - 02:30:00

Make the Phantomtail appear as quickly as possible by heading straight to Hook's cabin, then leave and return to the Night Sea area. Fly west and dig up the closest box, then immediately fly back to Hook and Smee to trigger the Phantomtail's appearance. Repeatedly cast Aero at its tail to inflict severe damage.

DAY 301-304

Xaldin wants Roxas to fill the Bonus Gauge (complete all missions) for days 256 to 275. Speak to him after accomplishing this task and he'll add Mission 80 to the day's roster.

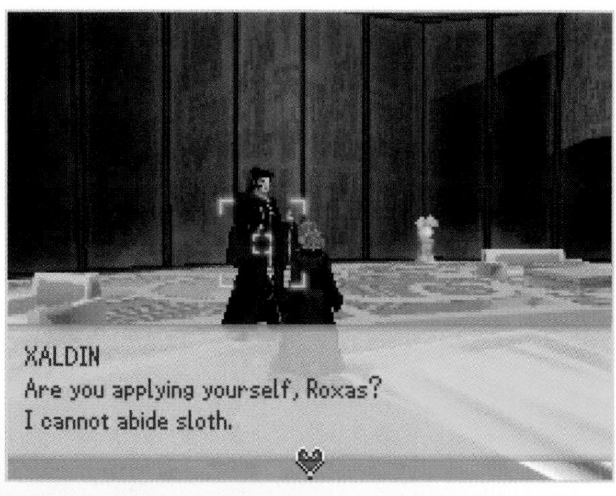

Remember to speak to Xaldin after completing all missions to receive a new mission.

VANQUISH THE HEARTLESS THREAT

MISSION **78**

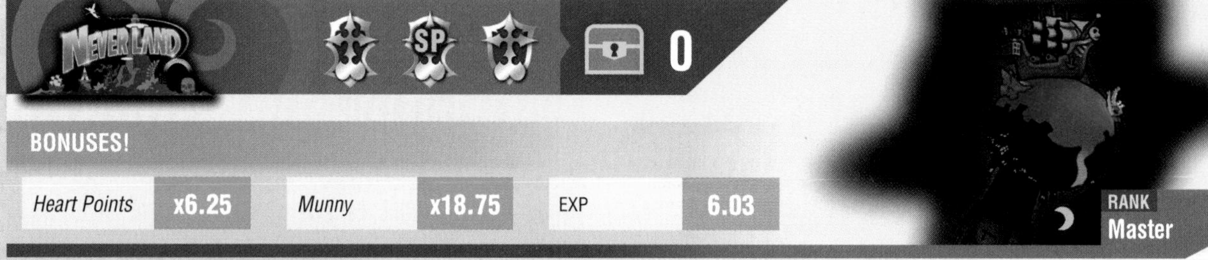

BONUSES!

Heart Points	x6.25	Munny	x18.75	EXP	6.03

RANK Master

ENEMIES

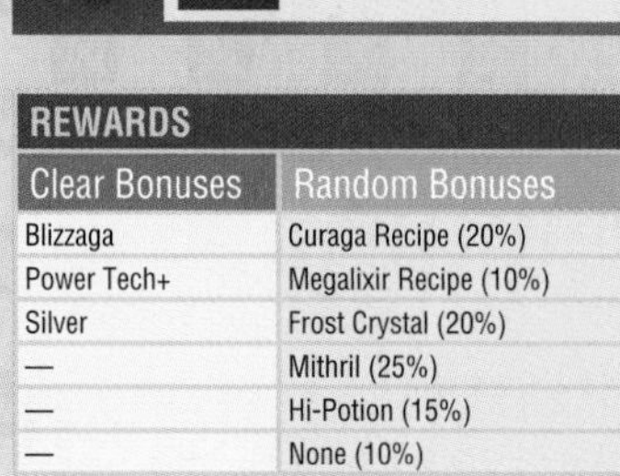

REWARDS	
Clear Bonuses	Random Bonuses
Blizzaga	Curaga Recipe (20%)
Power Tech+	Megalixir Recipe (10%)
Silver	Frost Crystal (20%)
—	Mithril (25%)
—	Hi-Potion (15%)
—	None (10%)

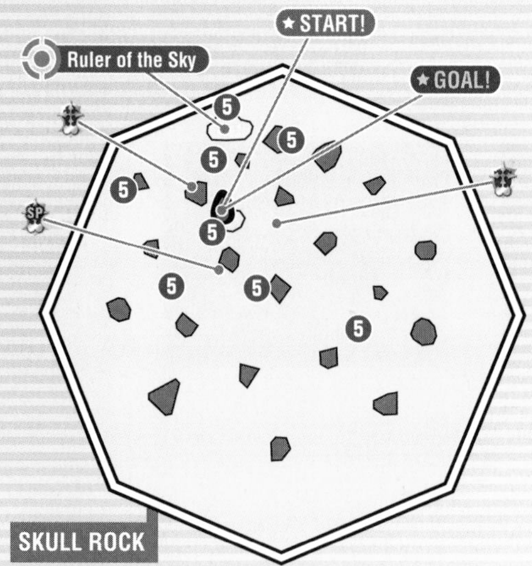

AIR DOMINION

After Tink restores Roxas's ability to fly, collect the badges and blazon hovering over the water's surface in various places. Then fly toward the island where Hook and Smee are busy working to initiate the boss fight.

Tink gives Roxas what he needs to reach Hook and Smee.

Seek the badges and blazons scattered around the islands before approaching the pirates.

BOSS!

RULER OF THE SKY

The Ruler flies continuously at first, causing iceberg columns to shoot up from the water's surface in its wake. It also releases slow flying orbs that are easy to avoid by flying off to the left or right.

Catch up to the Ruler and attack the last segment of its tail. The best time to do this occurs when the creature is turning; strike the tail segment repeatedly to destroy it.

When a tail segment is destroyed, the Ruler becomes enraged. Pulling back, the Ruler begins to swoop back and forth, trying to hit Roxas. If you fall too low to the water's surface before its swoop, it releases an array of frost orbs as it flies past. These are hard to avoid, so stay airborne. As it swoops in, fly to the left or right out of its path. Press Y or B to fly higher or swoop lower, above or below its wing line.

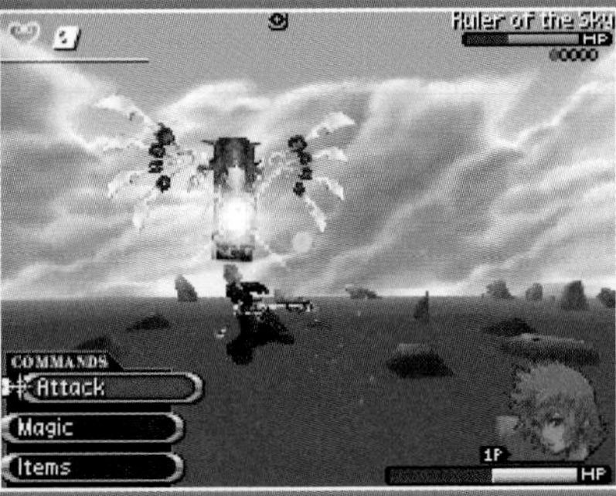

After diving at Roxas a half dozen times, the Ruler plunges into the ocean. During this time, descend to the ocean's surface and double-tap the R button occasionally to lock on to the Ruler when it surfaces, usually outside of your view. The Ruler then takes a position in the sky and begins firing coins at Roxas, machine gun style. The good news is that if any of these coins hit Roxas, he collects munny. The bad news is they hurt!

While the Ruler is firing coins, fly low just above the water's surface and beneath the Ruler. Rise underneath its belly and resume attacking the next tail segment until it flies away again. Then pursue it as before, attempting to cut off the next tail segment and start the whole cycle over again.

When the final tail segment is destroyed, the Ruler becomes super-enraged and begins flying around the area, creating circles of icebergs around Roxas and firing one blue orb after another. The best tactic is to circle in the direction opposite the Ruler. So as it's flying to the right, you should fly left and vice versa.

Once the Ruler stops circling and starts firing coins, fly underneath its belly and attack the core. Fire spells inflict extra damage, so hit it with as many as possible while it's stationary. If the Ruler moves back and down so that Roxas ends up above it, you can still attack its core from above and cast Fire spells to damage it.

After firing coins, it begins clawing at the air. The best defense here is to fly directly away from it; otherwise, the attacks are unavoidable. After the claw swipes, it remains stationary for a moment before flying off again. Try to finish it off by hitting it with one or two more Fire spells before it gets away. Otherwise, fly counter to its circle and attack again when it stops to fire.

CHALLENGE MISSION

Objective: **Attack as little as possible!**

Restrictions: **Level capped at 40, no recovery magic**

Rewards

Sigils Acquired	Attacks
3	0 attacks
2	1 - 20 attacks
1	21 - 60 attacks

Use Limit Breaks and magic spells to defeat the Ruler of the Sky. Fly near its tail and cast Fire spells to break off the pieces. After doing so, hit it with more powerful Fire magic when it becomes stationary. Take your time and use Hi-Potions to recover when needed. The instant you press the Attack button, you lose a Sigil, so be careful when pressing A to cast magic.

SPECIAL CHALLENGE

Objective: **Finish in record time!**

Restrictions: **Level capped at 20, take 30% more damage**

Rewards

Sigils Acquired	Clear Time
3	07:45:00 or less
2	07:45:01 - 09:15:00
1	09:15:01 - 10:15:00

Get it to stop flying as usual, then cast Fire spells to inflict extra damage to its core. Only higher levels and better weaponry can help you bring down the Ruler of the Sky in time to acquire three Challenge Sigils.

ELIMINATE THE GIANT HEARTLESS

MISSION 79

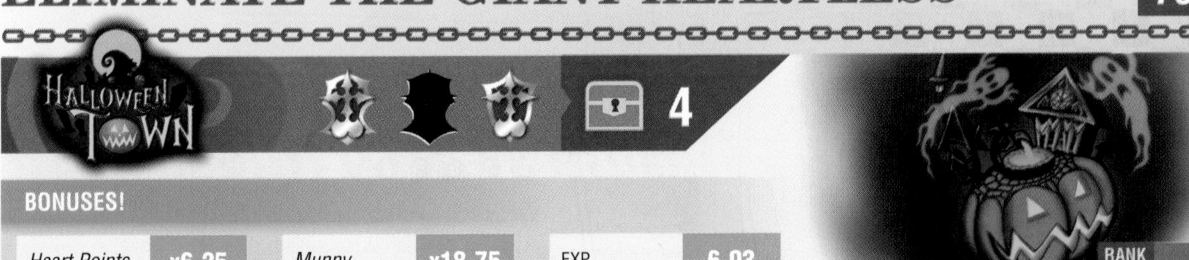

BONUSES!

Heart Points	x6.25	Munny	x18.75	EXP	6.03

RANK Master

ENEMIES

Enemy	LVL	DROP
DETONATOR	26	Megalixir Recipe
HOVER GHOST	15	Lightning Crystal
TRICKY MONKEY	49	Shining Crystal
CARRIER GHOST	32	Aerial Tech++
ICY CUBE	49	Frost Crystal
CHILL RIPPER	55	Range Tech++
SNOWY CRYSTAL	22	Frost Crystal

REWARDS

Clear Bonuses	Random Bonuses
Frost Crystal	Firaga Recipe (15%)
Mithril	Megalixir Recipe (20%)
Adamantite	Lightning Crystal (20%)
—	Shining Crystal(20%)
—	Hi-Ether (15%)
—	None (10%)

DEFEAT THE RANDOM ENEMIES

Hover Ghosts and Icy Cubes trap Roxas in the town square area. Defeat them with the help of Thunder and Fire spells respectively, then meet Xigbar in the Graveyard. He partners up at this point to make the rest of this mission easier.

Eliminate all enemies to unseal the town square.

Xigbar and Roxas team up in the Graveyard.

Fight through the Boneyards and Moonlight Hill to the Suspension Bridge area. Use Fire to clear away the Icy Cubes and Snowy Crystals to make room for the boss.

Xigbar is extremely helpful in getting through the Moonlight Hill area.

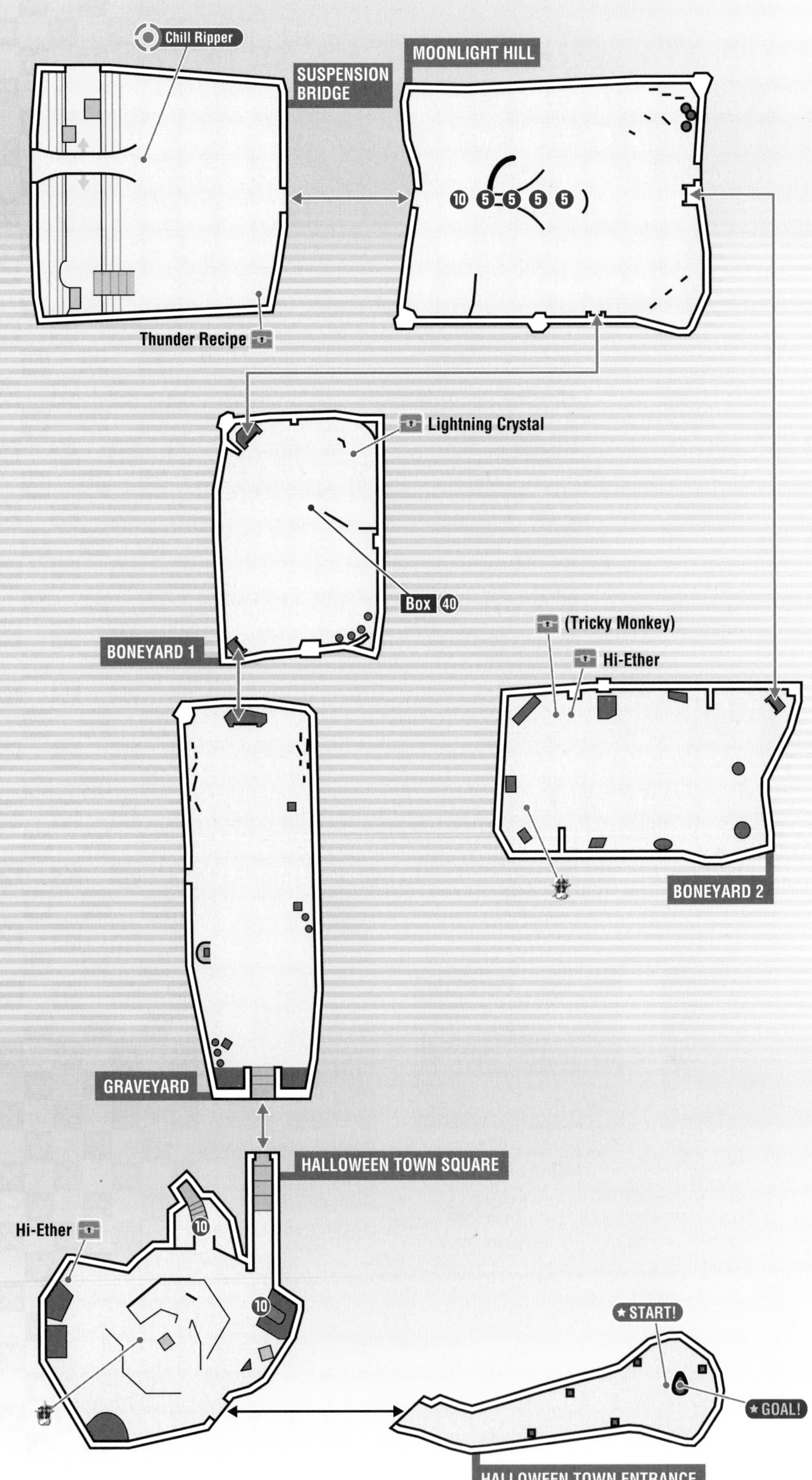
Chill Ripper
SUSPENSION BRIDGE
MOONLIGHT HILL
Thunder Recipe
Lightning Crystal
Box 40
BONEYARD 1
(Tricky Monkey)
Hi-Ether
BONEYARD 2
GRAVEYARD
HALLOWEEN TOWN SQUARE
Hi-Ether
START!
GOAL!
HALLOWEEN TOWN ENTRANCE

CHILL RIPPER

BOSS!

Use Fire, Fira, and Firaga spells liberally, especially when the Chill Ripper is stationary, to help bring down its massive amount of HP. As with all blade-arm knights, avoid or block its thrust attacks, attack while it's exhausted, and use Air Slides to avoid the shockwave of its drop bomb attack. The Chill Ripper is also capable of erecting icicles in a straight line, which can be easily avoided by Dodge Rolling left or right out of the line. But the best strategy is to keep lighting it on fire until defeated.

CHALLENGE MISSION

Objective: Finish in record time!

Restrictions: Level capped at 60, enemy level +13

Rewards

Sigils Acquired	Clear Time
3	04:20:00 or less
2	04:20:01 - 05:00:00
1	05:00:01 - 06:00:00

Link every Fire, Fira, and Firaga panel you own, along with Elixirs and Hi-Ethers. Reach the boss location quickly by casting Fire spells to eliminate Hover Ghosts and Icy Cubes that try to postpone your journey. Then take an Elixir and wipe out the Chill Ripper by casting Fire magic until it dies. With enough magic and Elixirs, you can acquire three Challenge Sigils.

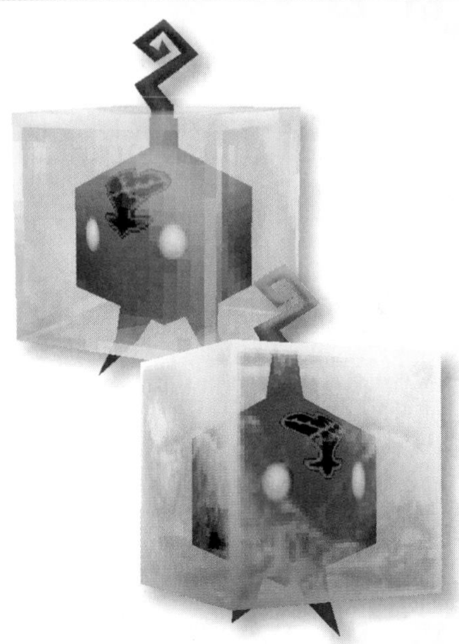

BREAK THE JARS

MISSION 80

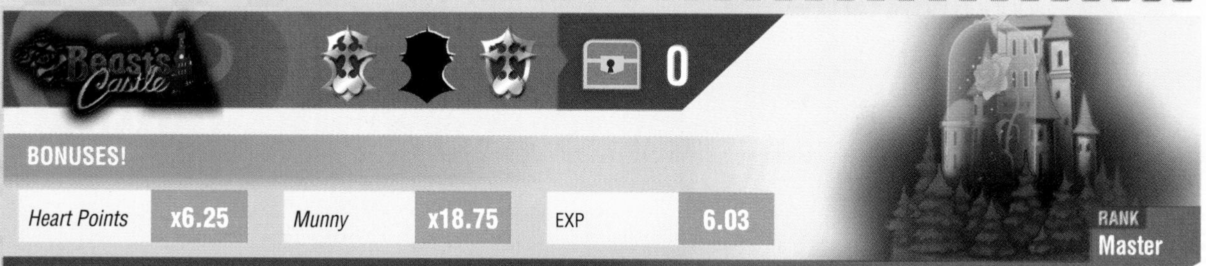

ENEMIES

REWARDS	
Clear Bonuses	Random Bonuses
Shining Crystal	Curaga Recipe (10%)
Shining Gem	Blazing Crystal (10%)
Luck Tech (MG)	Hi-Potion (20%)
—	Hi-Ether (20%)
—	Elixir (20%)
—	None (20%)

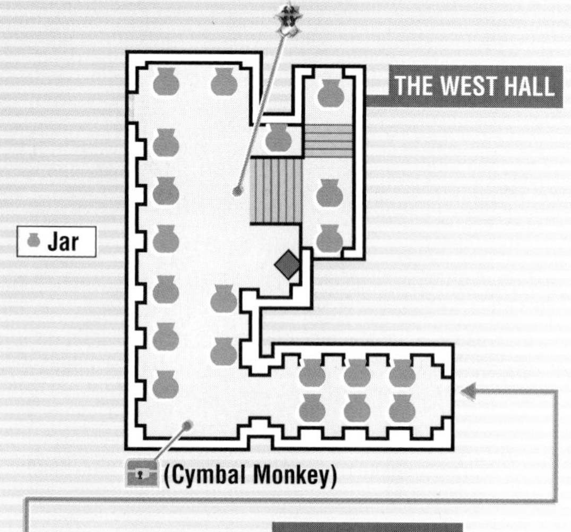

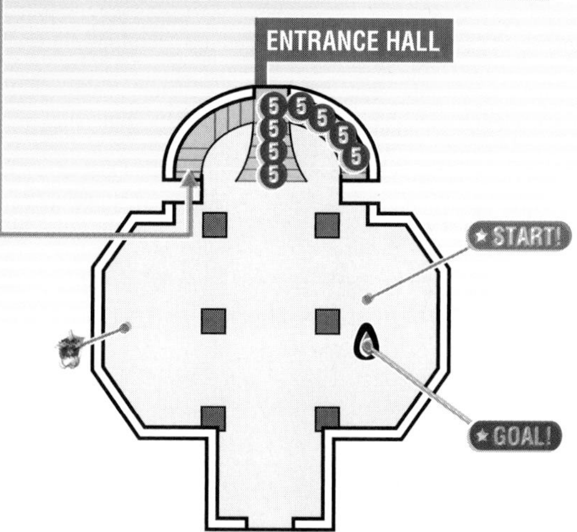

THE POD JARS

Simply head up to the West Hall and begin smashing jars. Several of the jars release Living Pods when broken. These are the toughest of the ghost-type Emblem Heartless, capable of warping above Roxas and draining his health in a single lift. Use Aero spells to knock them away and try to eliminate one before smashing more jars and releasing another one. Otherwise, the mission becomes too difficult to complete.

Living Pods are truly evasive and formidable opponents, slowing down the jar-breaking process.

THE JAR ABOVE THE DOOR

Mission Gauge still not full? One jar is located in a tricky place above the south doorway above the stairs. Jump from the top of the north stairs and glide over to it to have a shot at breaking it. Repeat this as needed until it smashes to bits. Remember to get out of the way before the Living Pods have their way with Roxas any further.

CHALLENGE MISSION

Objective: Fill up the mission gauge!

Restrictions: Level capped at 30

Rewards	
Sigils Acquired	Mission Gauge Full
3	100%
2	89% - 99%
1	75% - 88%

Simply destroy all jars to fill the Mission Gauge 100%, easily gaining three Sigils. As for the Living Pods, use Air Slides to escape from them and go up or down the stairs as needed to avoid detection.

ELIMINATE THE EMERALD SERENADE

MISSION **81**

WONDERLAND

6

BONUSES!

Heart Points	x6.25	Munny	x18.75	EXP	6.03

RANK **Master**

ENEMIES

GREY CAPRICE LVL 20
DROP Aerial Tech++

RARE VENDOR LVL 49
DROP Luck Tech, Diamond, Dark Ingot

EMERALD SERENADE LVL 49
DROP Gold

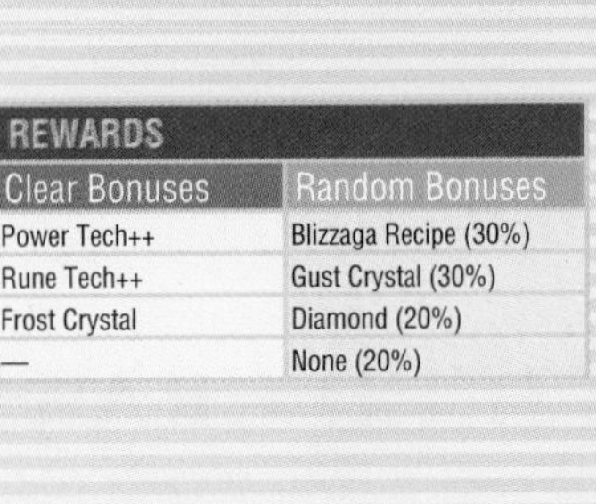

REWARDS	
Clear Bonuses	Random Bonuses
Power Tech++	Blizzaga Recipe (30%)
Rune Tech++	Gust Crystal (30%)
Frost Crystal	Diamond (20%)
—	None (20%)

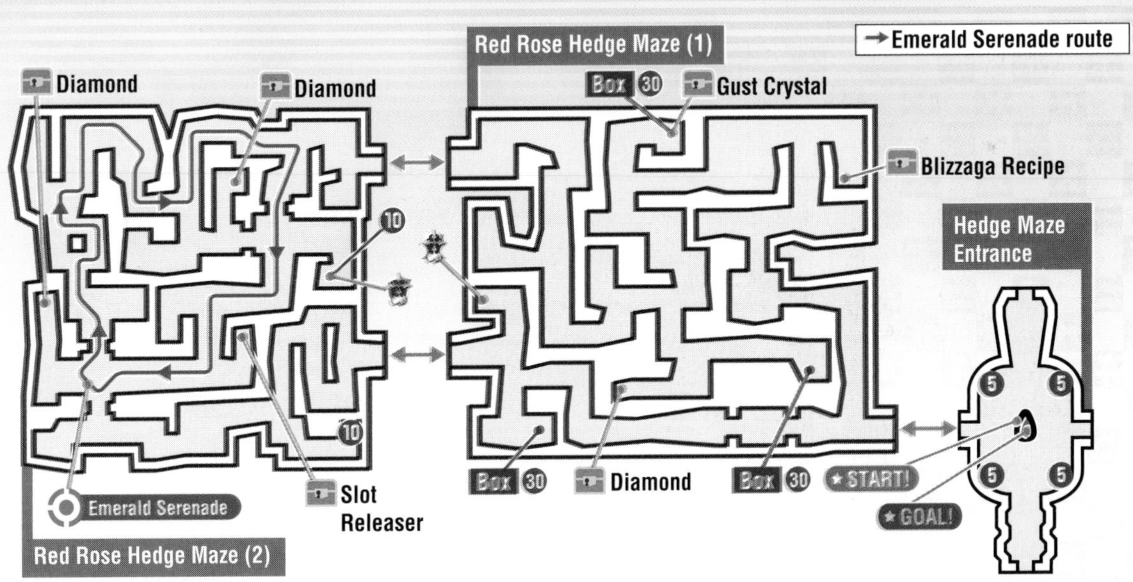

FOLLOWING A SINGLE PATH

Another Emerald Serenade has popped up, this time in the Red Rose Hedge Maze. Navigate through the first area, collecting items from chests and eliminating any additional Heartless that appear. Do the same in the second area, then plant Roxas in the path of the Emerald Serenade.

Ambush the Emerald Serenade as it navigates the west segment of the hedge maze.

Cast Blizzard to freeze the Emerald Serenade in place, then hit it with another LV5 spell to inflict damage. Repeat this each time it passes until the mission is complete.

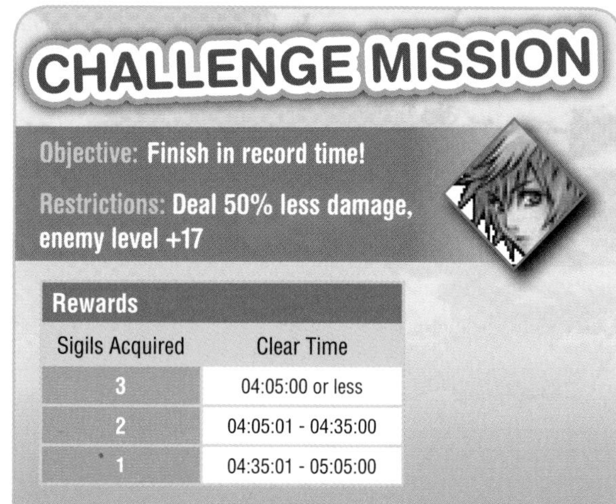

CHALLENGE MISSION

Objective: **Finish in record time!**

Restrictions: **Deal 50% less damage, enemy level +17**

Rewards	
Sigils Acquired	Clear Time
3	04:05:00 or less
2	04:05:01 - 04:35:00
1	04:35:01 - 05:05:00

When playing for time, freeze the Emerald Serenade in place with a Blizzard spell and then hit it with Fire for extreme damage. Run counterclockwise along its route to quickly meet up with it again.

DAY 321

Xigbar awards Roxas a **Frost Crystal** for scoring 150 points or more during Phil's training in Mission 46. That's quite a bit of exertion just for a crystal!

Xigbar's challenges are all a bit exacting, to match his personality.

ELIMINATE THE SPIKED CRAWLER — MISSION 82

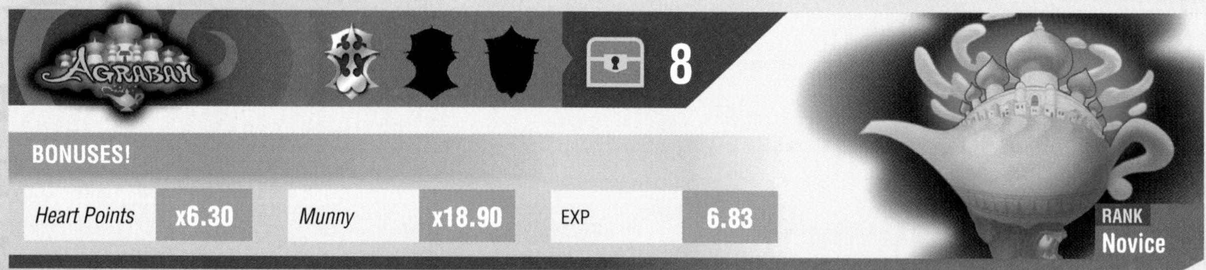

BONUSES!

Heart Points	x6.30	Munny	x18.90	EXP	6.83

RANK Novice

ENEMIES

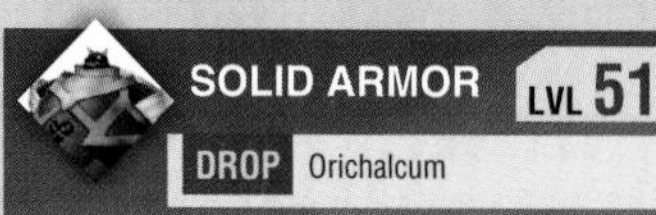

SPIKED CRAWLER LVL 51
DROP —

REWARDS	
Clear Bonuses	Random Bonuses
Sliding Dash LV+(L)	Firaga Recipe (10%)
Lightning Gem	Gold (10%)
Lightning Shard	Hi-Potion (30%)
—	Hi-Ether (20%)
—	None (30%)

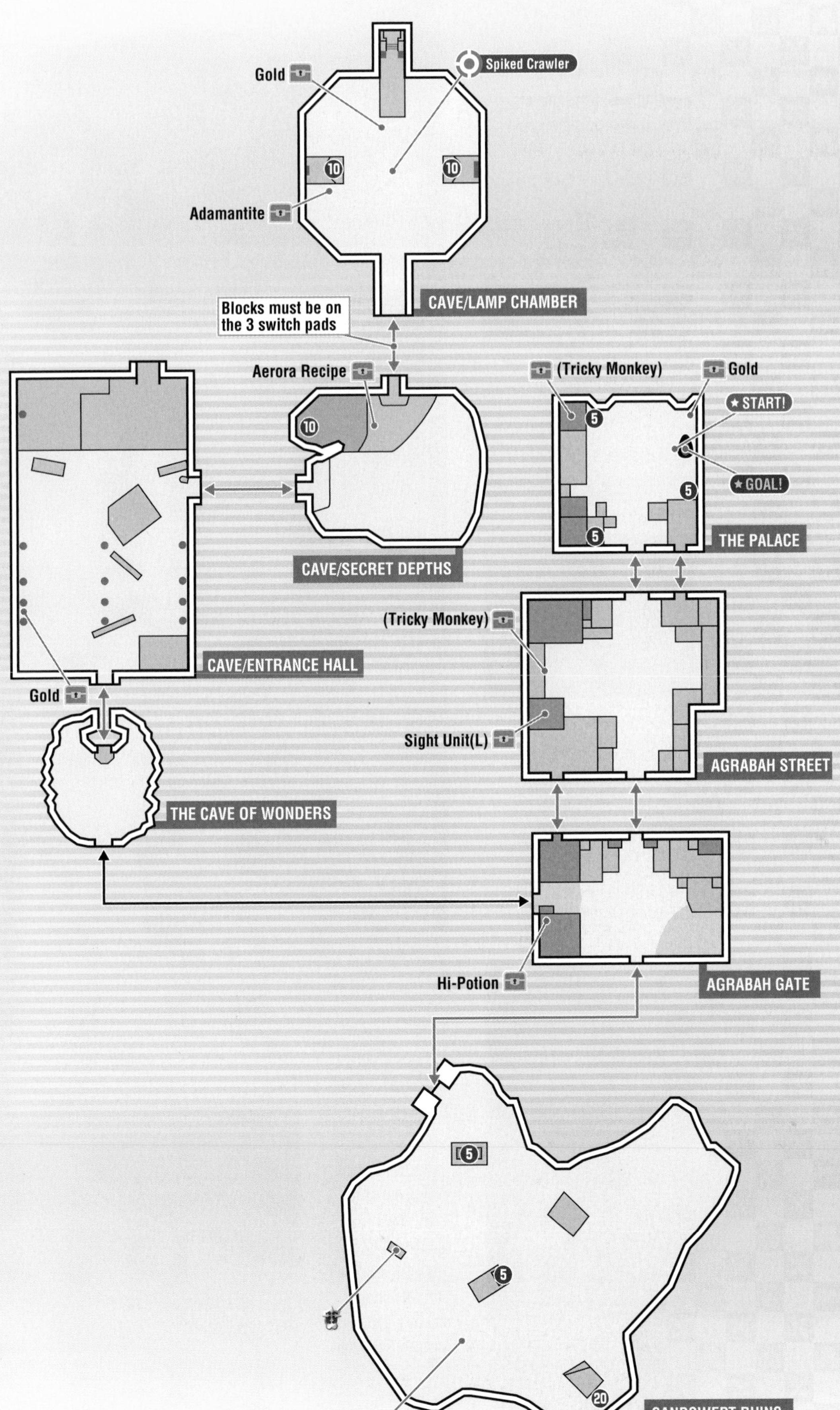
Gold
Spiked Crawler
Adamantite
CAVE/LAMP CHAMBER
Blocks must be on the 3 switch pads
Aerora Recipe
(Tricky Monkey)
Gold
START!
GOAL!
THE PALACE
CAVE/SECRET DEPTHS
(Tricky Monkey)
CAVE/ENTRANCE HALL
Gold
Sight Unit(L)
AGRABAH STREET
THE CAVE OF WONDERS
Hi-Potion
AGRABAH GATE
Hi-Ether
SANDSWEPT RUINS

AN OFF DAY

Roxas's level is halved because he's not feeling well, which means defeating enemies requires more attacks and higher-powered spells. Be sure to link most of your spells to LV2, LV3, and LV4 Magic panels.

Roxas is half his usual level today, significantly reducing his Strength and other combat factors.

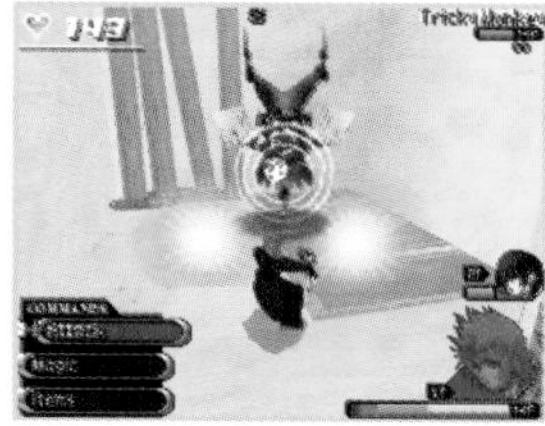

Avoid the Tricky Monkey that pops out of the chest above the shops.

Loot and pillage the street and Sandswept Ruins areas, then head toward the Cave of Wonders. The hole in the east wall of the Entrance Hall is now open.

As if one Tricky Monkey per mission wasn't enough, there's another lurking in the chest on the east side of the Agrabah Street.

Heartless attack on your way in and out of the Cave.

Inside you'll find many breakable jars and a golden elephant statue. Strike the statue and four crates drop from the ceiling. Knock three of the crates south onto the square pressure pads in the floor. When finished, the gate on the mid-level opens. Enter the Lamp Chamber to find your target.

Hit three boxes to knock them onto the three pressure pads on the ground level.

SPIKED CRAWLER

BOSS!

Open the chests in the chamber, then approach the north keyhole door to trigger the appearance of the Spiked Crawler.

This is a timed battle. The Spiked Crawler simply spins around back and forth, so block with the right timing to try to avoid damage. If HP runs low, smash any of the pots near the walls to recover. After time elapses, Xion automatically eliminates the boss. Exit Agrabah via the dark corridor at the Palace.

DAY 322-326

Luxord doesn't care whether Roxas feels good or not, he wants every chest in Mission 82 opened. Speak to him when done and he'll add Mission 84 to the list.

Worried about Roxas, Xion gives him an ***Elixir Recipe***.

SEARCH FOR XALDIN

MISSION 83

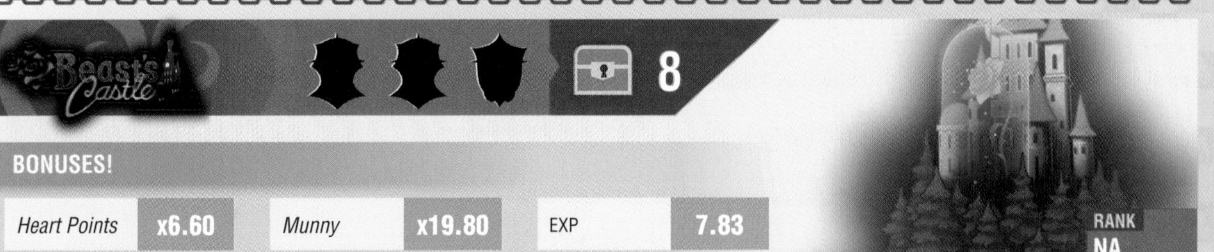

BONUSES!

Heart Points	x6.60	Munny	x19.80	EXP	7.83

RANK NA

ENEMIES

SHADOW LVL 30
DROP Blazing Gem

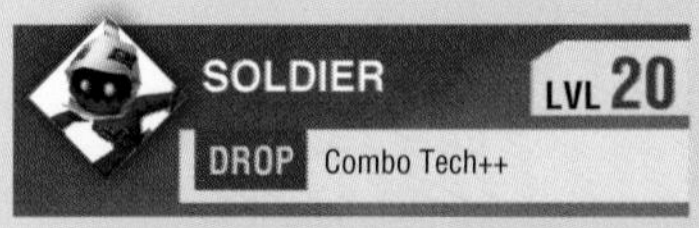
SOLDIER LVL 20
DROP Combo Tech++

SNOWY CRYSTAL LVL 30
DROP Frost Crystal

GIGAS SHADOW LVL 40
DROP Megalixir Recipe

BAD DOG LVL 10
DROP Power Tech++

BLITZ SPEAR LVL 58
DROP Lightning Crystal

POSSESSOR LVL 30
DROP Lightning Crystal

BULLY DOG LVL 30
DROP Diamond

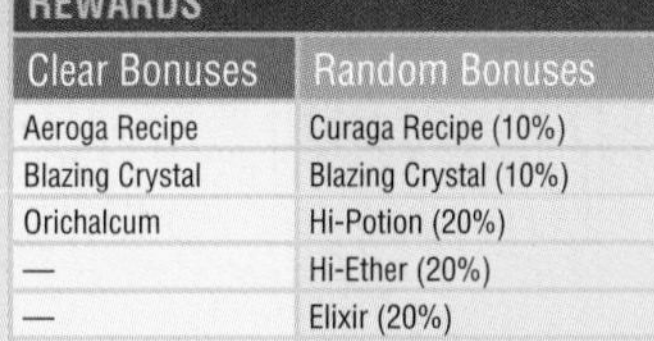
REWARDS

Clear Bonuses	Random Bonuses
Aeroga Recipe	Curaga Recipe (10%)
Blazing Crystal	Blazing Crystal (10%)
Orichalcum	Hi-Potion (20%)
—	Hi-Ether (20%)
—	Elixir (20%)
—	None (20%)

SERGEANT LVL 30
DROP Shield Tech+

ICY CUBE LVL 20
DROP Frost Crystal

WHERE'S XALDIN?

Clear the Courtyard and Bridge areas, then head inside and up to the East Wing. Cogsworth and Lumiere discuss recent events at the castle. Afterward, you can tangle with a squad of Sergeants and collect an **Elixir** from the far end.

*Collecting the **Hi-Ether** in the Bridge area comes at a steep price.*

Sergeants protect an Elixir.

Fight over to the West Wing, using Blizzard spells to help defeat a pair of Bully Dogs encountered together outside the Beast's door. Next, peek in on the Beast to uncover another clue to Xaldin's whereabouts. After the scene, use Firaga spells to defeat a trio of Snowy Crystals. Return to the Courtyard to find Xaldin near the dark corridor. With him found, Roxas's mission here is done. RTC when ready.

Use Blizzard to help freeze one of the Bully Dogs temporarily so that Roxas can deal double damage.

*Enter the secret passage in the Courtyard to reach the upper balcony of the Ballroom, where a chest contains a **Blazing Crystal**.*

*What was Xaldin doing at Beast's Castle? Play **Kingdom Hearts II** to find out!*

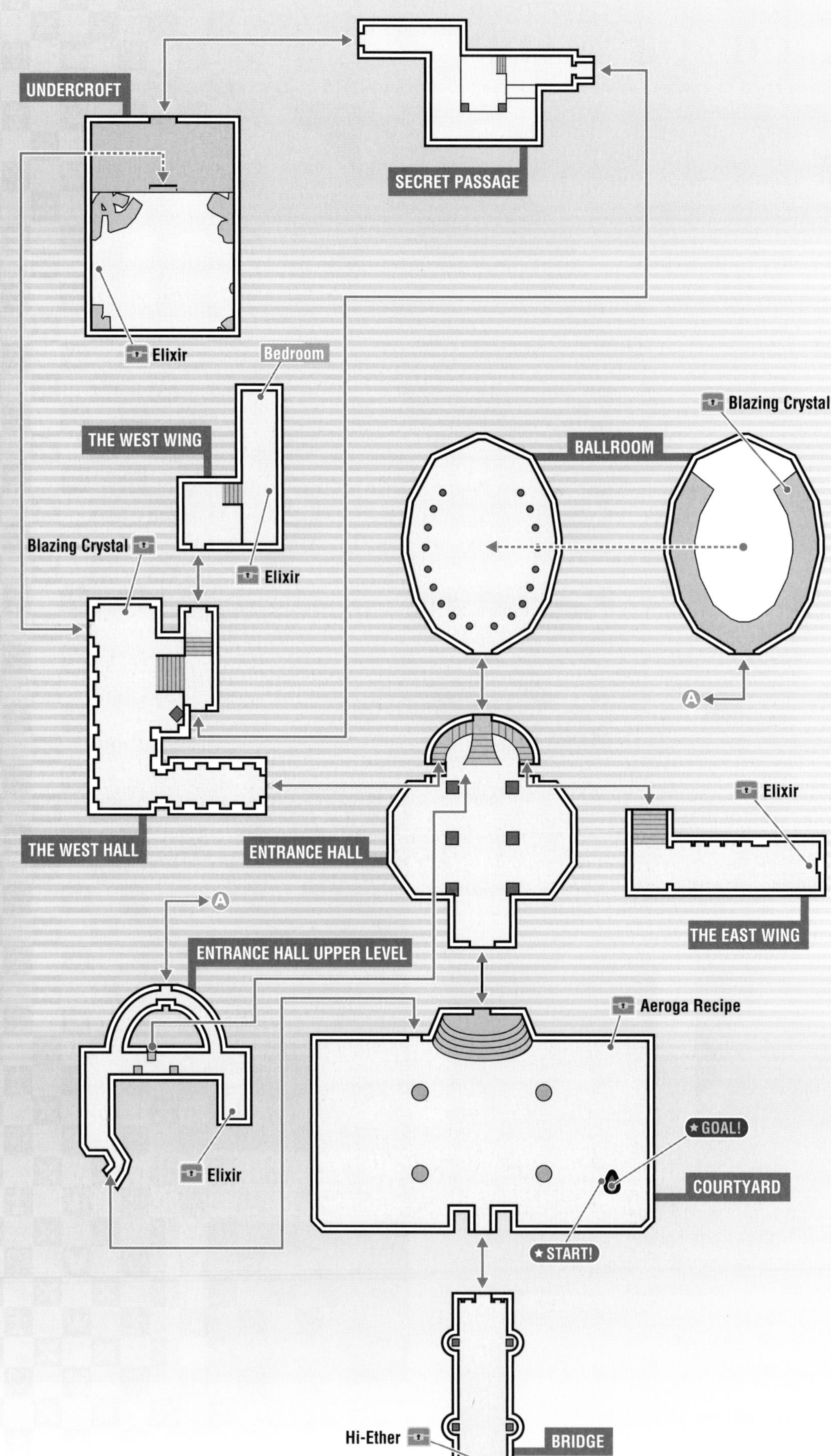
UNDERCROFT
SECRET PASSAGE
Elixir
Bedroom
THE WEST WING
Blazing Crystal
BALLROOM
Blazing Crystal
Elixir
A
THE WEST HALL
ENTRANCE HALL
Elixir
THE EAST WING
A
ENTRANCE HALL UPPER LEVEL
Aeroga Recipe
GOAL!
COURTYARD
Elixir
START!
Hi-Ether
BRIDGE

ELIMINATE THE SCORCHING SPHERE

MISSION 84

BONUSES!

Heart Points	x6.60	Munny	x19.80	EXP	7.83

ENEMIES

TRICKY MONKEY LVL 52
DROP Shining Crystal

SCORCHING SPHERE LVL 52
DROP Gear Component D

REWARDS	
Clear Bonuses	Random Bonuses
Firaga Recipe	Blizzaga Recipe (15%)
Mithril	Thundaga Recipe (15%)
Mithril	Megalixir Recipe (10%)
—	Hi-Potion (15%)
—	Hi-Ether (20%)
—	Elixir (15%)
—	None (10%)

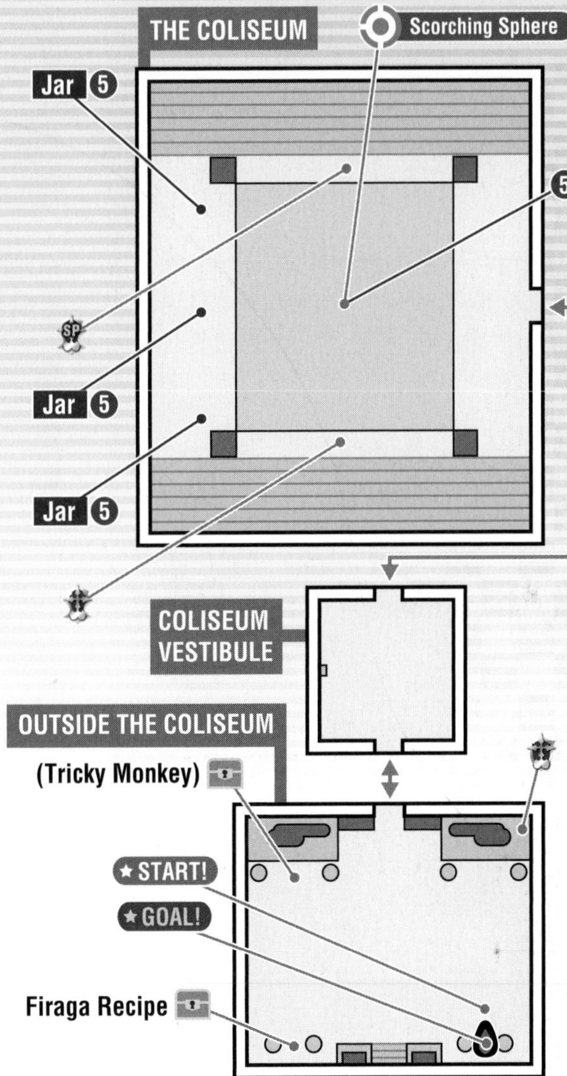

BIG RED BALL

Xigbar is Roxas's partner in taking down the Scorching Sphere. Enter the Coliseum and proceed directly into the arena. After the Scorching Sphere appears, move to the tops of the stands and use Glide to reach the hovering **Ordeal Badge** and **Ordeal Blazon**.

Glide from the tops of the stands to snatch the emblems in the air.

SCORCHING SPHERE

BOSS!

Like all sphere enemies, you must block with the correct timing to deflect its spinning attack and use Air Slides to get away from its drop bomb attacks. Cast Blizzara and stand behind the icy cloud to draw it into a trap, breaking its spin attacks. Knock the barrels at it while it's relatively stationary to inflict massive damage.

CHALLENGE MISSION

Objective: Avoid taking damage!

Restrictions: Level capped at 45, take 50% more damage

Rewards	
Sigils Acquired	Hits Sustained
3	0 hits
2	1 hit
1	2 hits

Hit the Scorching Sphere with high-level Blizzard spells to freeze it in place, reducing your chances of being hit by a jumping attack. Otherwise, Air Slide should help Roxas escape harm during its jump attacks.

SPECIAL CHALLENGE

Objective: Finish in record time!

Restrictions: Level capped at 40, HP drains continually

Rewards	
Sigils Acquired	Clear Time
3	00:45:00 or less
2	00:45:01 - 01:00:00
1	01:00:01 - 01:30:00

Blizzard magic is the only kind of magic that damages the Scorching Sphere, but it does so in a weak manner at best. Link Blizzard spells to LV2 and LV4 panels to cast Blizzard LV5, and inflict some real damage. Then add other Blizzard panels to Quadcast③, Triplecast③, and Doublecast④ panels to maximize your Blizzard LV5 castings. Every time it drops, hit it with Blizzard to quickly knock it out.

COLLECT HEARTS

MISSION 85

BONUSES!

Heart Points	x6.60	Munny	x19.80	EXP	7.83

RANK
Master

ENEMIES

GREY CAPRICE LVL 20
DROP Aerial Tech++

NOVASHADOW LVL 50
DROP Shield Tech++

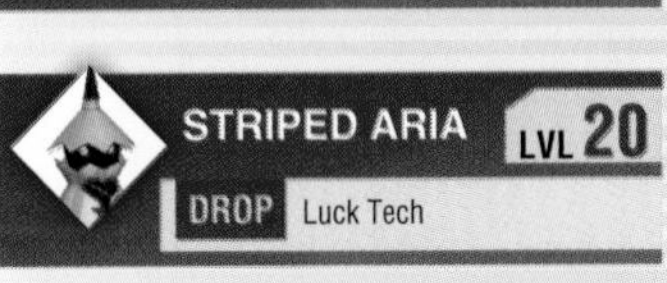

STRIPED ARIA LVL 20
DROP Luck Tech

LURK LIZARD LVL 52
DROP Mithril

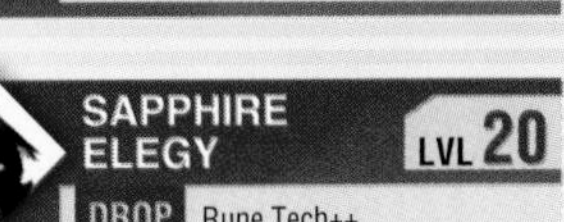

SAPPHIRE ELEGY LVL 20
DROP Rune Tech++

REWARDS	
Clear Bonuses	Random Bonuses
Blizzaga Recipe	Blizzaga Recipe (30%)
Blizzara Recipe	Gust Crystal (30%)
Combo Tech++	Diamond (20%)
—	None (20%)

AN IMPRACTICAL LITTLE STROLL

Another Novashadow lurks in the Hedge Maze Entrance. Use Aero magic to defeat it quickly.

Lurk Lizards provide the wrong kind of surprise.

Tour Wonderland and clear every area of Heartless in the process. Use Fire spells to snuff out Sapphire Elegies, preventing them from unnecessarily overextending combat.

The Mission Gauge fills to the goal line after you collect 596 hearts. But why stop there? Continue through the Lotus Forest clearing out all enemies. A Lurk Lizard appears when the Tea Party Garden is clear. Defeating it is sure to raise your heart total above 1241, filling the Mission Gauge to max.

CHALLENGE MISSION

Objective: Finish in record time!

Restrictions: No recovery magic, HP drains while on the ground

Rewards	
Sigils Acquired	Clear Time
3	05:00:00 or less
2	05:00:01 - 06:00:00
1	06:00:01 - 06:30:00

Ignore the Novashadow and Veil Lizard for the time being. Sapphire Elegies prolong battles with their warp skill, so disregard them too. Eliminate Grey Caprice and Striped Aria enemies throughout Wonderland until you fill the Mission Gauge. RTC quickly by using the door in the tree in the Lotus Forest to return to the Bizarre Room, change size and head home.

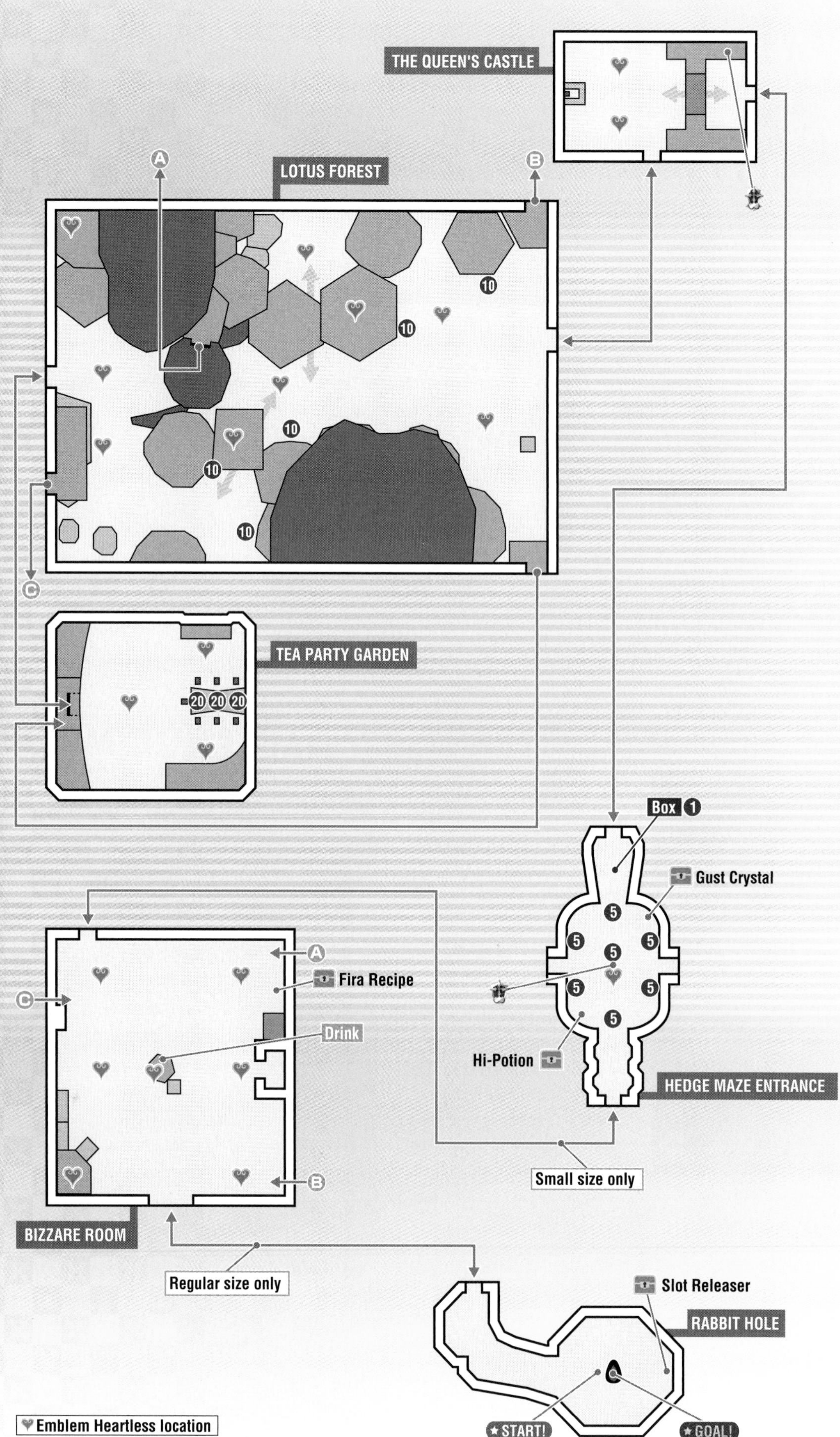
THE QUEEN'S CASTLE
LOTUS FOREST
A
B
C
10
TEA PARTY GARDEN
20
Box 1
Gust Crystal
5
Hi-Potion
HEDGE MAZE ENTRANCE
Small size only
Fira Recipe
Drink
BIZZARE ROOM
Regular size only
Slot Releaser
RABBIT HOLE
START!
GOAL!
Emblem Heartless location

COLLECT ORGANIZATION EMBLEMS

MISSION 86

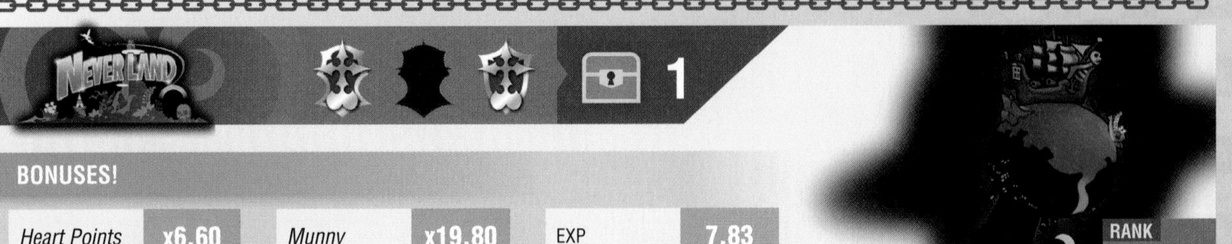

BONUSES!

Heart Points	x6.60	Munny	x19.80	EXP	7.83

RANK Master

ENEMIES

TURQUOISE MARCH LVL 20
DROP Shining Crystal

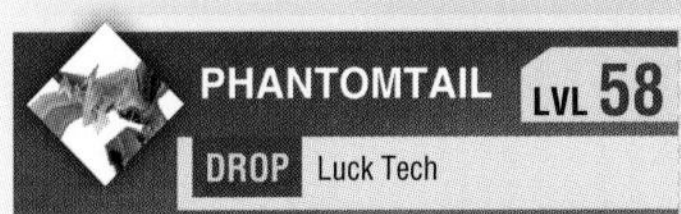

PHANTOMTAIL LVL 58
DROP Luck Tech

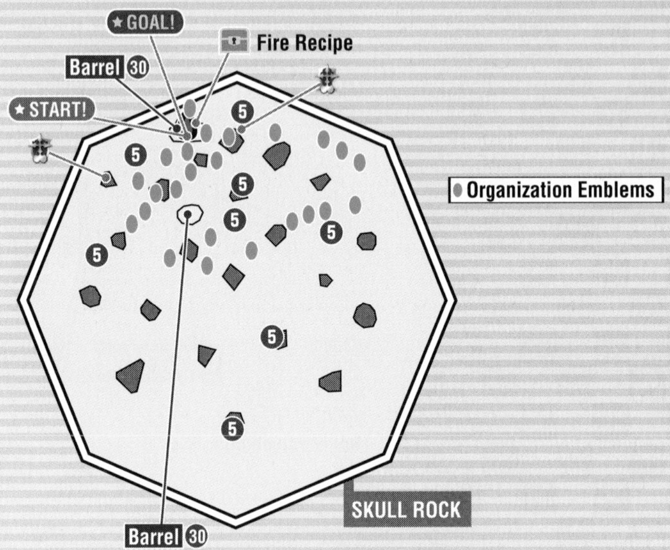

REWARDS

Clear Bonuses	Random Bonuses
Curaga Recipe	Curaga Recipe (20%)
Curaga Recipe	Megalixir Recipe (10%)
Ankharite (MG)	Frost Crystal (20%)
—	Mithril (25%)
—	Hi-Potion (15%)
—	None (10%)

CAREFUL FLIGHT PATH

Luxord tags along to help Roxas collect emblems in the Skull Rock area of Never Land. Lucky thing too, since Roxas will be haunted by at least one Phantomtail the entire time. If the rings do collapse before you can collect them all, it's best to skim close to an island. Turquoise Marches appear near land formations and can be defeated quicker than a Phantomtail. After defeating the Turquoise March, resume collecting emblems.

Fly through emblems while their ring shows to fill the Mission Gauge.

Defeat Turquoise March enemies before collecting emblems without rings.

CHALLENGE MISSION

Objective: Finish in record time!

Restrictions: Level capped at 45, HP drains continually

Rewards

Sigils Acquired	Clear Time
3	01:10:00 or less
2	01:10:01 - 01:30:00
1	01:30:01 - 02:00:00

Simply fly the route shown in this section, grabbing every emblem along the way. There are enough emblems to fill the Mission Gauge, if all are grabbed while their rings show. Flying the route accurately definitely requires memorizing the route and keeping an eye on the map on the lower screen, along with a bit of practice.

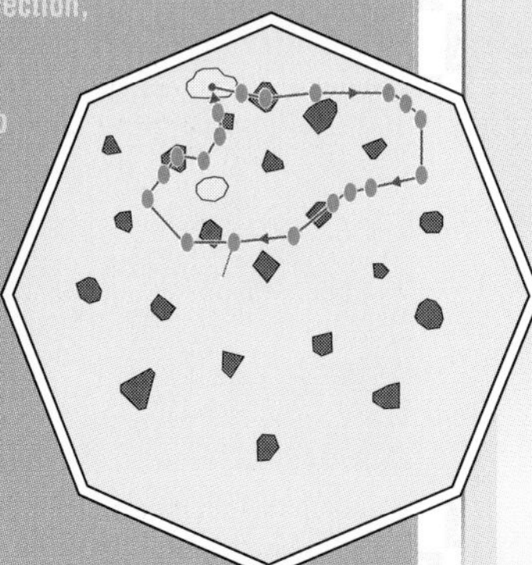

ELIMINATE THE WINDSTORMS

MISSION 87

BONUSES!

Heart Points	x6.60	Munny	x19.80	EXP	7.83

RANK
Master

ENEMIES

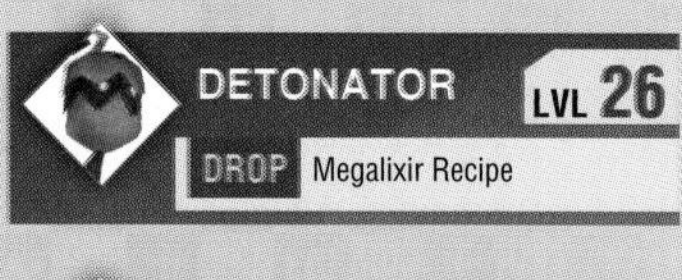

Enemy	Level	Drop
DETONATOR	LVL 26	Megalixir Recipe
INVISIBLE	LVL 52	Shield Tech++
WINDSTORM	LVL 52	Gust Crystal

REWARDS

Clear Bonuses	Random Bonuses
Lightning Crystal	Firaga Recipe (15%)
Mithril	Megalixir Recipe (20%)
Diamond	Lightning Crystal (20%)
—	Shining Crystal(20%)
—	Hi-Ether (15%)
—	None (10%)

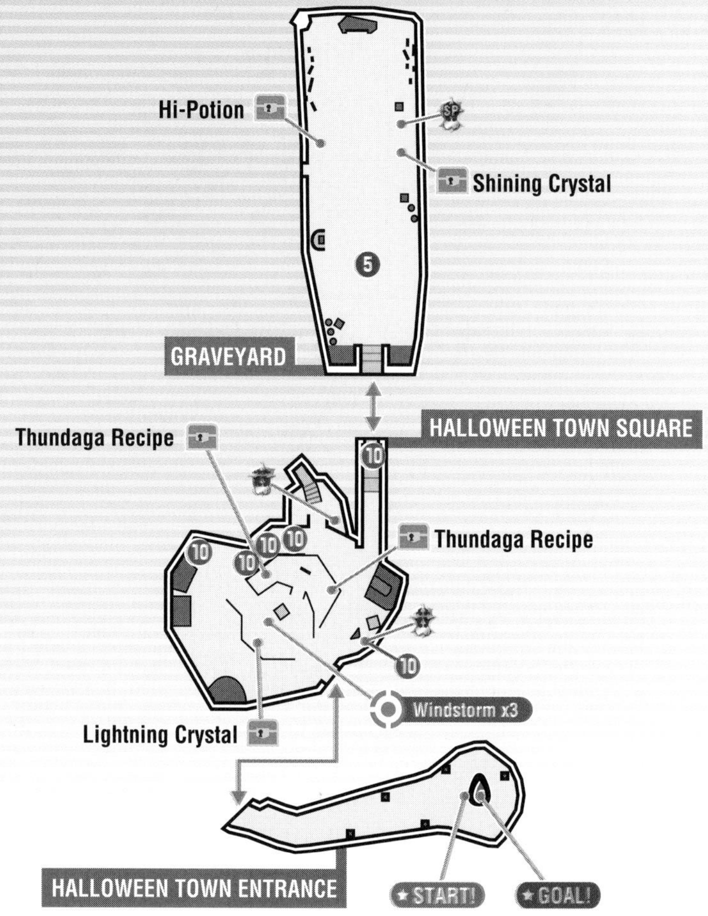

ILL BREEZE

Why does each Invisible encountered have to be scarier and more powerful than the last?

Head to Halloween Town Square to take on three Windstorms at once and a host of Detonators. When finished there, continue to the Graveyard to encounter an Invisible. It watches guard over a **Hi-Potion** and a **Shining Crystal** in nearby chests.

WINDSTORM X3

BOSS!

Having defeated every flying dragon type thus far, you should be good to go. Strike the Windstorms in the wings or tail to knock them to the ground, then target the head. Cast Thunder spells to stun them, rendering them prone to extra damage.

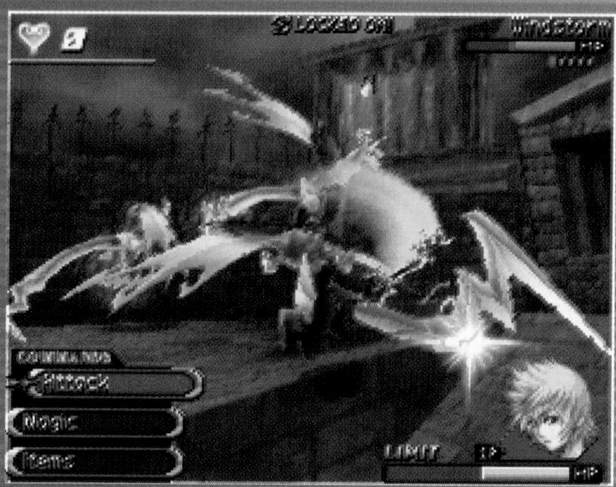

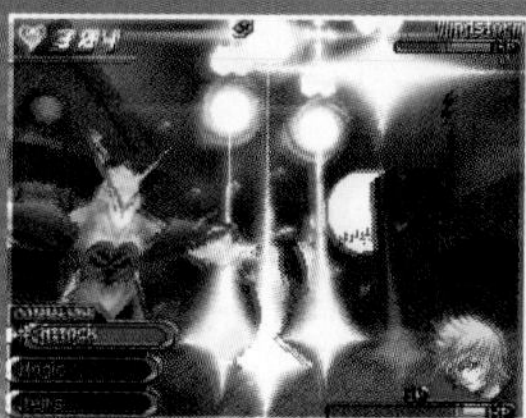

Avoid letting your Limit Breaks "rip" until you're dealing with just one Windstorm. Otherwise, you can find yourself quickly pecked apart from all sides.

CHALLENGE MISSION

Objective: Finish in record time!

Restrictions: Take 50% more damage, enemy level +3

Rewards	
Sigils Acquired	Clear Time
3	01:00:00 or less
2	01:00:01 - 01:30:00
1	01:30:01 - 02:00:00

Equip Roxas with nothing more than Thundaga spells linked to every multi-cast panel, as well as LV2 and LV4 panels for added strength. Wield a gear panel that boosts magic and as many Magic Units as you can link to it. Lock on to the Windstorms and cast LV5 Thundaga spells like a madman. Achieving three Challenge Sigils is extremely difficult unless Roxas is near level 100.

SPECIAL CHALLENGE

Objective: Avoid taking damage!

Restrictions: Enemy level +20

Rewards	
Sigils Acquired	Hits Sustained
3	5 or less
2	6 - 10 hits
1	11 - 15 hits

Keep an eye on the map to keep track of Windstorms flying off-screen, and cast Thundaga spells instead of using melee attacks to decrease the risk of suffering a counter blow.

DAY 352

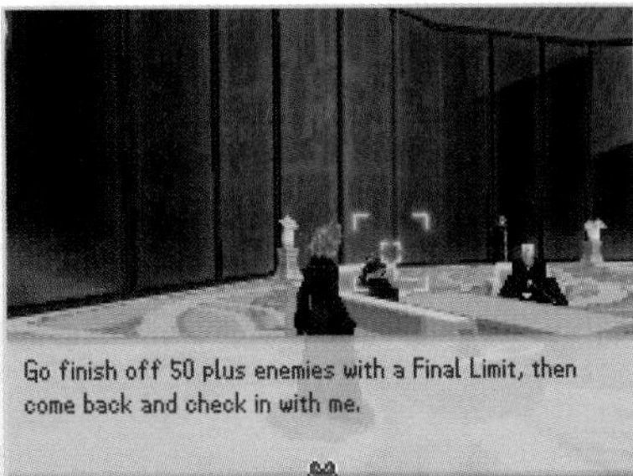

Xigbar wants Roxas to finish off 50 enemies with his Final Limit and will give Roxas a **Lightning Crystal** if he does. Again, your best bet is to replay Mission 06 50 times, finishing off the Mega-Shadow with your Final Limit attack each time.

Will Xigbar ever stop coming up with hurdles for Roxas?

ELIMINATE THE GIANT HEARTLESS

MISSION 88

HALLOWEEN TOWN

1

BONUSES!

Heart Points	x6.61	Munny	x19.83	EXP	9.03

RANK Master

ENEMIES

ORCUS LVL 54
DROP Gold

REWARDS	
Clear Bonuses	Random Bonuses
LV Quadrupler③	Firaga Recipe (15%)
Blizzaga Recipe	Megalixir Recipe (20%)
Blizzaga Recipe	Lightning Crystal (20%)
—	Shining Crystal(20%)
—	Hi-Ether (15%)
—	None (10%)

QUIET...TOO QUIET

Collect the **Slot Releaser** and **Unity Badge** near the entrance. Proceed to the Graveyard.

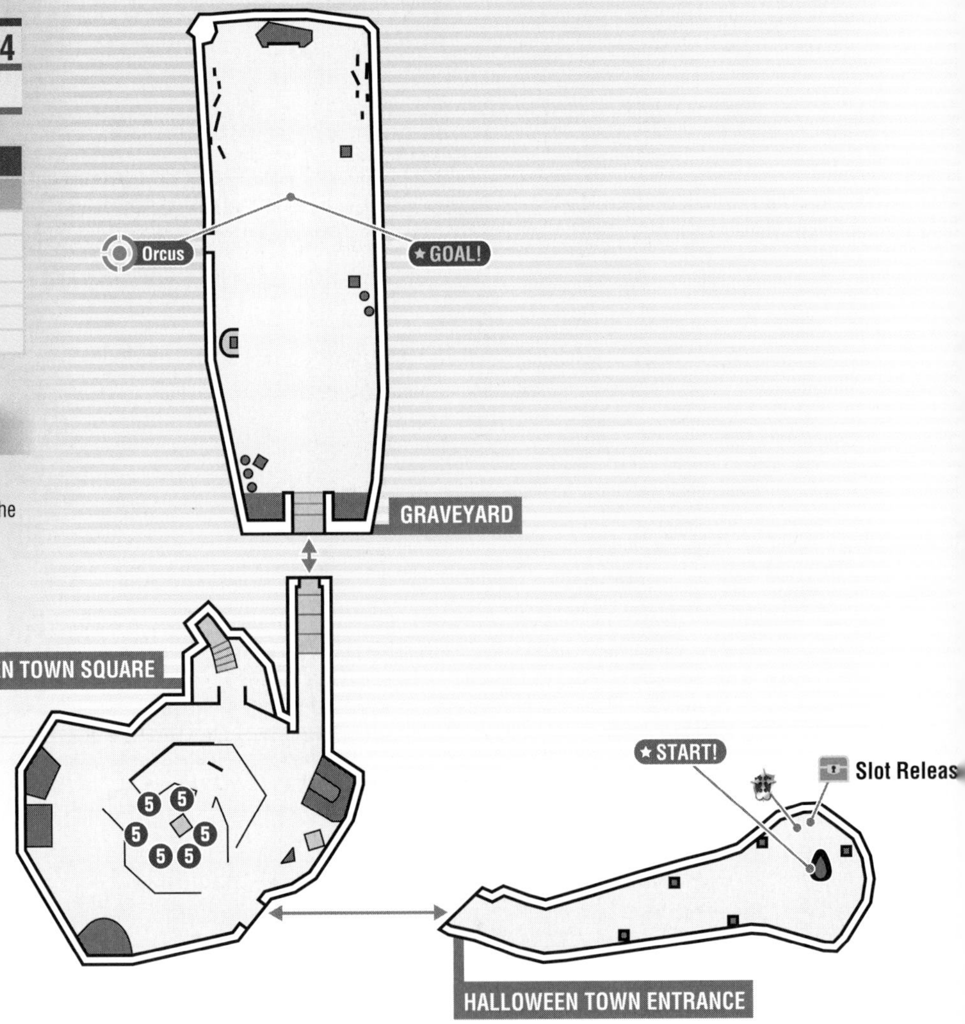

Orcus
★GOAL!
GRAVEYARD
HALLOWEEN TOWN SQUARE
★START!
Slot Releas
HALLOWEEN TOWN ENTRANCE

ORCUS

BOSS!

The Orcus is a weaker version of an Invisible. When it throws its sword and vanishes, use Dodge Rolls to avoid the sword thrusts. It releases a shockwave when reappearing, so jump off the ground and attack the minute it appears. The Orcus usually goes limp after that, which is a good time to unleash a Limit Break. Move away when it awakens, however, since it casts a kind of lightning field around itself. This is not a real battle; after knocking two life bars off the Orcus, then the battle is over.

DAY 353

ELIMINATE SIX GIANT HEARTLESS

MISSION 89

8

BONUSES!

Heart Points	x6.62	Munny	x19.86	EXP	10.63

RANK Master

ENEMIES

Enemy	LVL	DROP
SHADOW	30	Blazing Gem
GIGAS SHADOW	40	Megalixir Recipe
ORCUS	50	Gold
SCARLET TANGO	20	Blazing Crystal
POISON PLANT	20	Adamantite
DUSTFLIER	45	Premium Orb
POSSESSOR	30	Lightning Crystal
STALWART BLADE	50	Adamantite
STORM BOMB	20	Combo Tech++
VEIL LIZARD	50	Rune Tech++

TRICKY MONKEY LVL 59 DROP Shining Crystal

POWERED ARMOR LVL 50 DROP —

REWARDS

Clear Bonuses	Random Bonuses
Orichalcum	Aeroga Recipe (10%)
Diamond	Gear Component D (5%)
Premium Orb (MG)	Orichalcum (10%)
—	Hi-Potion (20%)
—	Hi-Ether (20%)
—	Panacea (15%)
—	None (20%)

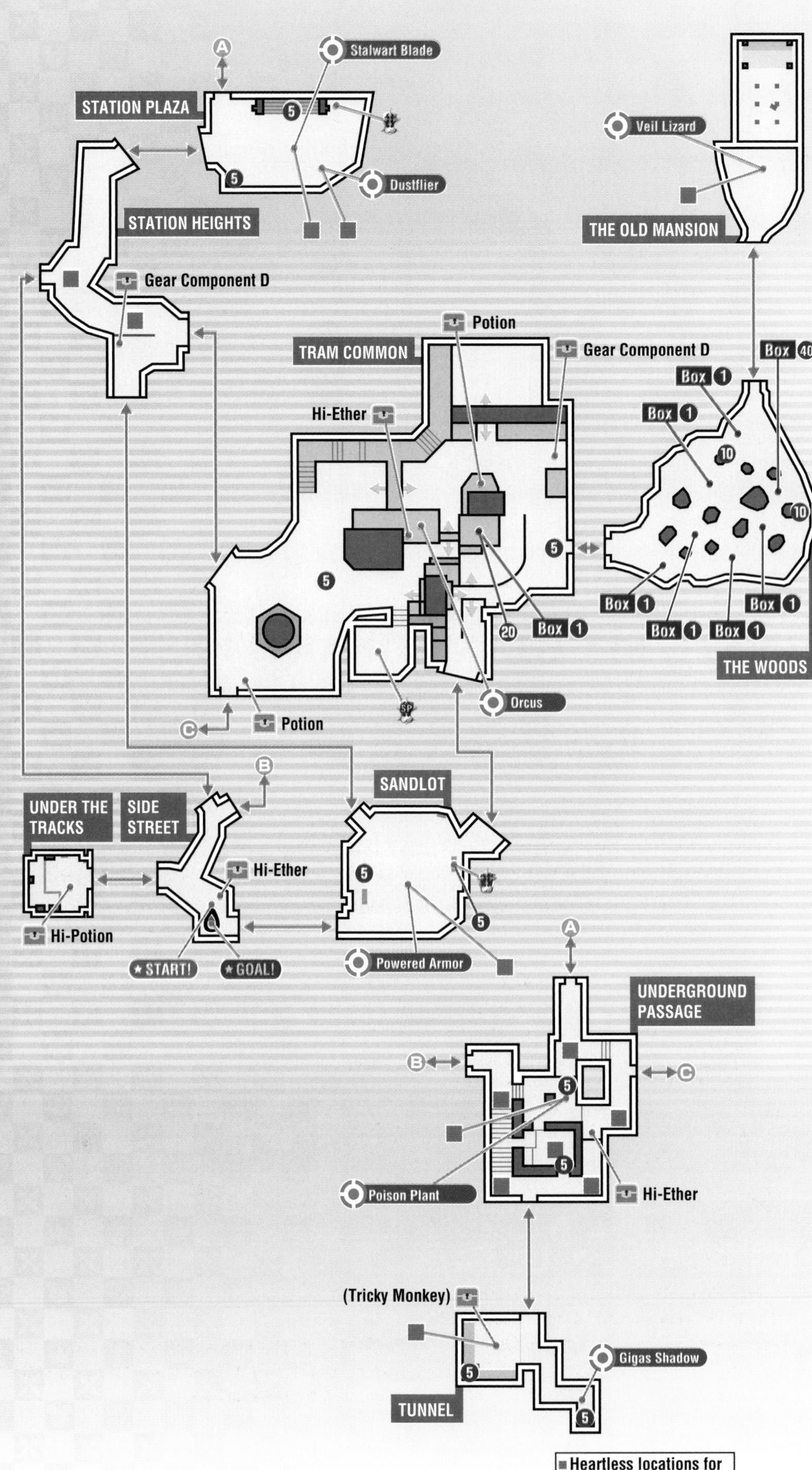
STATION PLAZA
Stalwart Blade
Dustflier
STATION HEIGHTS
Gear Component D
THE OLD MANSION
Veil Lizard
TRAM COMMON
Potion
Gear Component D
Hi-Ether
Box 40
Box 1
Box 1
Box 1
Box 1
Box 1
Box 1
Box 1
THE WOODS
Orcus
Potion
SANDLOT
UNDER THE TRACKS
SIDE STREET
Hi-Ether
Hi-Potion
START!
GOAL!
Powered Armor
UNDERGROUND PASSAGE
Poison Plant
Hi-Ether
(Tricky Monkey)
Gigas Shadow
TUNNEL
Heartless locations for Challenge Mission

A BOY ALONE

This mission requires Roxas to fight five previously encountered bosses and one new one, alone! Equip plenty of Hi-Ethers and Mega-Ethers to retain spell-casting abilities throughout. Head up to Station Plaza to battle a Stalwart Blade. Simply avoid its attacks, then counterstrike while it's dazed. Cast Aero spells on it to increase stun time.

Familiar territory can still prove challenging.

SUBTERRANEAN TARGETS

Enter the Underground Passage and defeat a Poison Plant near the center. Avoid its head-beating attack, then counter with Fire spells while it recovers.

Let the Poison Plant beat its head on the ground all it likes, then counterstrike.

Aerial combos work best against the Gigas Shadow.

Descend further into the Tunnel and take out a Gigas Shadow. Use any form of magic, especially Aero, to weaken it before finishing the job. Return to the Underground Passage and take the east exit to the Tram Common.

THE SWORDSLINGER

Another Orcus awaits in the Tram Common. Stay airborne to avoid damage from most of its attacks. Watch for when it throws its sword; when this occurs, dodge the sword slashes, then jump and attack as soon as the Orcus reappears. If its HP is low, that's the best time to unleash a Limit Break to finish it off.

Avoid the Orcus's rain of homing orbs or lightning strike attacks by chaining aerial combos.

BEHIND YOU!

Take the east exit from the Tram Common and through the Woods to reach the Old Mansion. There you'll fight a Veil Lizard, much as you have several times before. Hit it with Blizzard and Aero magic to bring it down faster or to make it visible again. Attack and then roll away before its spin attack connects to win the battle.

Attack, roll away, and attack again.

THE POWERED ARMOR

Return to the Tram Common and enter the southeast exit to reach the Sandlot. Although the Powered Armor is a new enemy, it fights exactly like the Guard Armor. Watch for it to jump and drop its helmet, which you should strike several times before it replaces. Then attack its dismembered limbs and destroy them before it can put them back on, or it can regenerate HP. Finally, whack away at the head until the hollow armor gives up.

Strike the Powered Armor's helm to knock it off, then continue attacking it on the ground.

Destroy the limbs before they can reattach themselves.

By this point the mission should be complete, so feel free to RTC if you want. However, if you're up for a little more and really want to fill that gauge, return to the Station Plaza.

DUSTFLIER

BOSS!

The honest truth is that the Dustflier is extremely difficult to defeat, so you're probably better off trying again after clearing the game, with the Zero Gear and multiple Sight Unit(L) panels linked to improve your chances of critical hits. Magic is virtually pointless, so there's no standing back and fighting. Equip plenty of Cura spells so that you can receive healing without recasting so often.

The main danger is the Dustflier's insane area-wide shockwave attacks, which it creates every time it lands. Therefore, you must jump and glide to the Dustflier's tail and attack from above. This move goads it into staying airborne, where it's much less harmful. However, it drops to the ground when you do this, so move away and jump and glide toward it again. Try to stay airborne as long as possible by gliding between each aerial combo. This is the only viable strategy for defeating it, so repeat it until you're victorious.

A constant swarm of Shadows cover the ground. Ignore them until you want to heal, then switch your lock on to a Shadow and break it open to release some HP. Otherwise, cast Cura on yourself and get airborne again as quickly as possible to heal.

Limit Breaks aren't quite as effective against the Dustflier as they are against most enemies. And never in this battle do you want to leave Roxas exposed to instant defeat. Refrain from using a Limit Break until you have the boss on the ropes with less than an HP bar and about to fall, then go to town on it.

CHALLENGE MISSION

Objective: **Avoid taking damage!**

Restrictions: **Take 50% more damage, enemy level +10**

Rewards	
Sigils Acquired	Hits Sustained
3	5 or less
2	6 - 15 hits
1	16 - 20 hits

With so many target enemies to go up against, there's not much more advice to give other than what is already provided for the normal mission. Avoid the Dustflier and RTC right after defeating the last of the target six.

SPECIAL CHALLENGE

Objective: **Earn lots of heart points!**

Restrictions: **Level capped at 60, no recovery magic**

Rewards	
Sigils Acquired	Heart Points Earned
3	800 or more
2	600 - 799 hearts
1	210 - 599 hearts

Collecting 800 heart points without having to fight the Dustflier is easy if you follow a certain route and defeat enemies in chains. Also, don't allow Storm Bombs to detonate themselves. Start in Station Heights, defeat those enemies, return to the Side Street, enter the Underground Passage, clear it while heading north, then take out the Stalwart Blade normally in the Station Plaza. Backtrack on this route to the dark corridor and RTC without lifting much of a finger! Don't forget to get all six Giant Heartless, or you won't be allowed to RTC.

DAY 354

Speak to Luxord to receive a **Rune Tech++**. Xaldin's not so easy. He gives Roxas a piece of **Adamantite**, but wants him to supply a Combo Tech+ and combine the two in synthesis. But he'll give Roxas a rare **Luck Tech** for doing so. Either show him a Dodge Combo(L), or visit the Moogle and synthesize one for 8800 munny.

Synthesize an additional Dodge Combo(L) for Xaldin today.

PLACE THE DEVICE

MISSION **90**

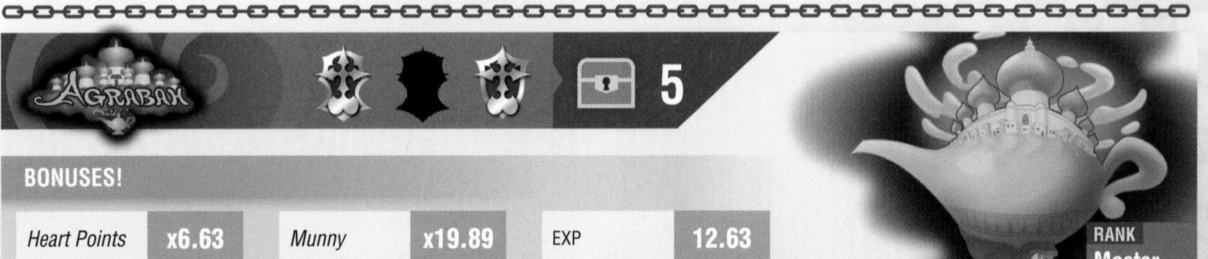

BONUSES!

Heart Points	x6.63	Munny	x19.89	EXP	12.63

RANK **Master**

ENEMIES

Enemy	LVL	Drop
GIGAS SHADOW	40	Megalixir Recipe
INVISIBLE	60	Shield Tech++
SCARLET TANGO	20	Blazing Crystal
LAND ARMOR	65	Mithril
LOUDMOUTH	20	Gear Component D
AERIAL MASTER	30	Diamond

REWARDS

Clear Bonuses	Random Bonuses
Sight Unit(L)	Firaga Recipe (10%)
Power Tech++	Gold (10%)
Blazing Crystal	Hi-Potion (30%)
—	Hi-Ether (20%)
—	None (30%)

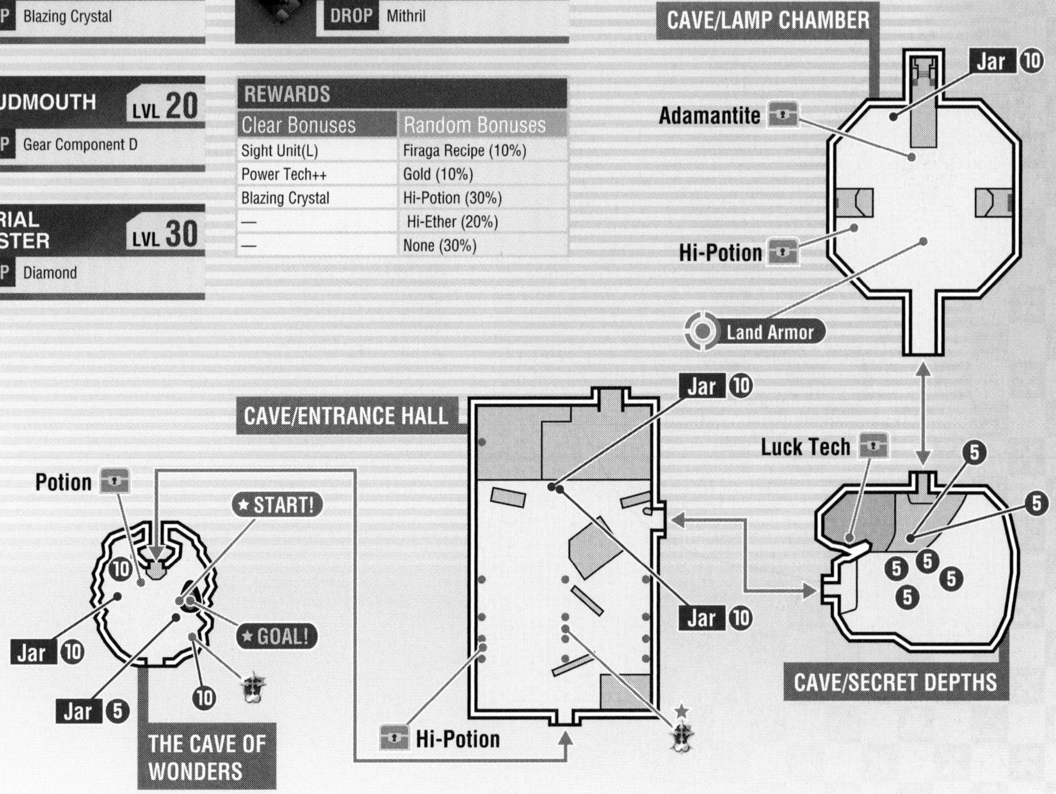

CAVE/LAMP CHAMBER
Jar 10
Adamantite
Hi-Potion
Land Armor

CAVE/ENTRANCE HALL
Jar 10
Jar 10
Hi-Potion

CAVE/SECRET DEPTHS
Luck Tech
5 5 5 5 5 5

THE CAVE OF WONDERS
Potion
START!
GOAL!
10
Jar 10
Jar 5
10

XIII BEACON

No need to high jump in the Entrance Hall today; there are plenty of enemies on the ground floor.

Defeat Heartless in every room while traveling to the Lamp Chamber. Roxas sets up a device in the chamber on behalf of the Organization. However, Heartless arrive intent on stealing or destroying the device. Roxas must protect it from them.

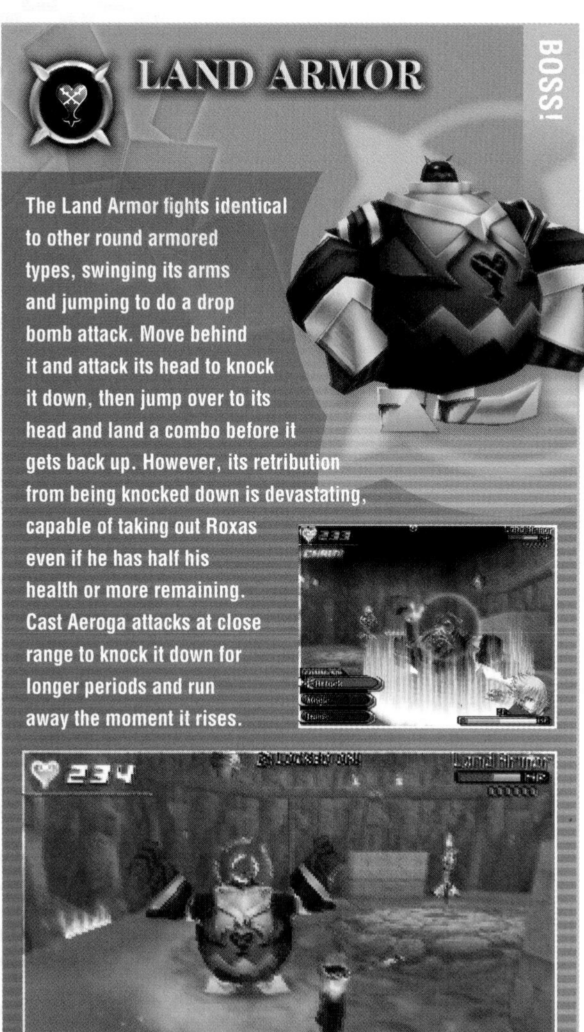

LAND ARMOR

BOSS!

The Land Armor fights identical to other round armored types, swinging its arms and jumping to do a drop bomb attack. Move behind it and attack its head to knock it down, then jump over to its head and land a combo before it gets back up. However, its retribution from being knocked down is devastating, capable of taking out Roxas even if he has half his health or more remaining. Cast Aeroga attacks at close range to knock it down for longer periods and run away the moment it rises.

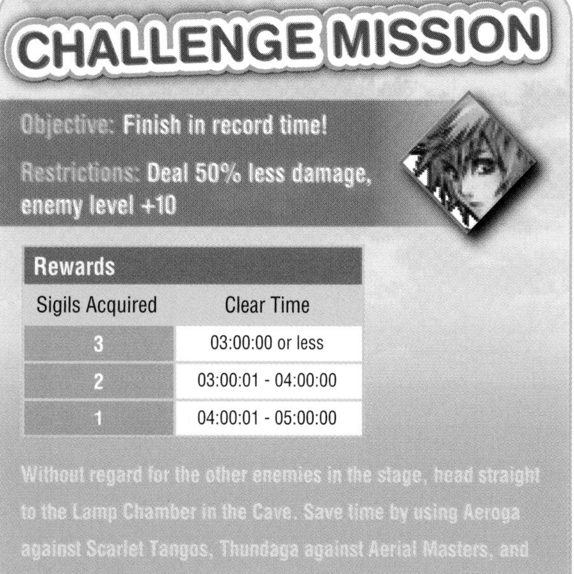

CHALLENGE MISSION

Objective: Finish in record time!

Restrictions: Deal 50% less damage, enemy level +10

Rewards

Sigils Acquired	Clear Time
3	03:00:00 or less
2	03:00:01 - 04:00:00
1	04:00:01 - 05:00:00

Without regard for the other enemies in the stage, head straight to the Lamp Chamber in the Cave. Save time by using Aeroga against Scarlet Tangos, Thundaga against Aerial Masters, and Aeroga on the Land Armor.

DAY 355

Synthesize the Ultimate Gear+⑥ if possible and equip it on Roxas. Save your game, set your panel slots as you like, and then speak to Axel.

Prepare for the final missions by synthesizing the best gear available.

ESCAPE THE CASTLE

MISSION 91

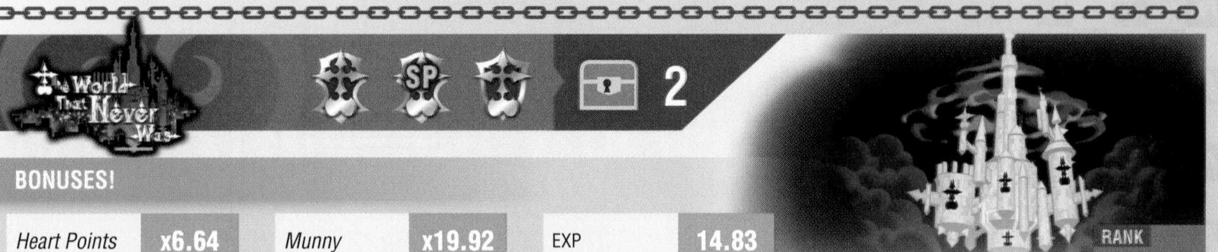

BONUSES!

Heart Points	x6.64	Munny	x19.92	EXP	14.83

RANK Master

ENEMIES

DUSK LVL 23 DROP Range Tech++

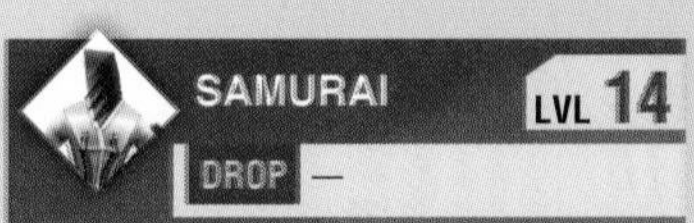

SAMURAI LVL 14 DROP —

SAÏX LVL 61 DROP —

REWARDS	
Clear Bonuses	Random Bonuses
None	Thundara Recipe (20%)
—	Aerora Recipe (20%)
—	Megalixir Recipe (10%)
—	Hi-Potion (5%)
—	Hi-Ether (20%)
—	None (25%)

LEAVING XIII

The path out of The Castle That Never Was is very linear and easy to follow. The Dusks encountered along the way are easily dispatched by no special means.

What does it say about being a Nobody when they very nearly break apart with one hit?

To reach the **Ordeal Blazon** in Naught's Skyway, jump from the top of the dual ramp and glide over to it.

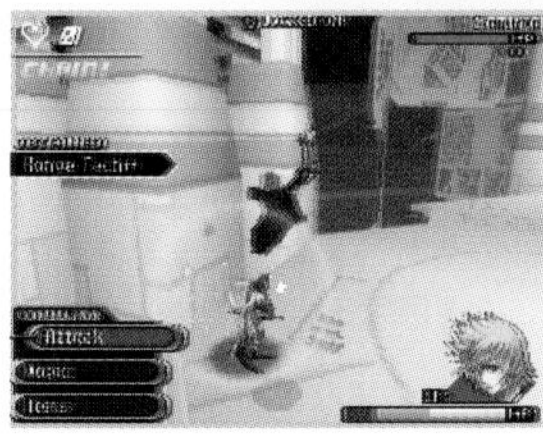

Samurais encountered randomly are much easier to dispatch than the ones previously encountered.

After taking the elevator at Crooked Ascension, head south through Nothing's Call. Samurais dot your path, but they are easily eliminated with a weapon that boasts strength, such as the Ultimate Gear+⑥. Continue south to meet Saïx.

BOSS!

SAÏX

Saïx attacks swiftly with his claymore and also casts Blizzara spells. He can warp to various points and leap right behind Roxas and attack. What he doesn't seem to be very good at is getting away during a Limit Break. Thanks to the many hits he inflicts, you'll have plenty of opportunities to trigger a Limit Break. After each one, move away and cast Cure or use a Hi-Potion to recover before attacking again.

When Saïx stands still and begins gathering energy, it means he's about to launch a berserker attack. The best thing to do is move far away so that when he launches this multi-combo assault, Roxas is nowhere near him. Use Air Slides and Dodge Rolls to avoid all his strikes. He becomes dazed afterward, so launch a Limit Break or attack him when this occurs.

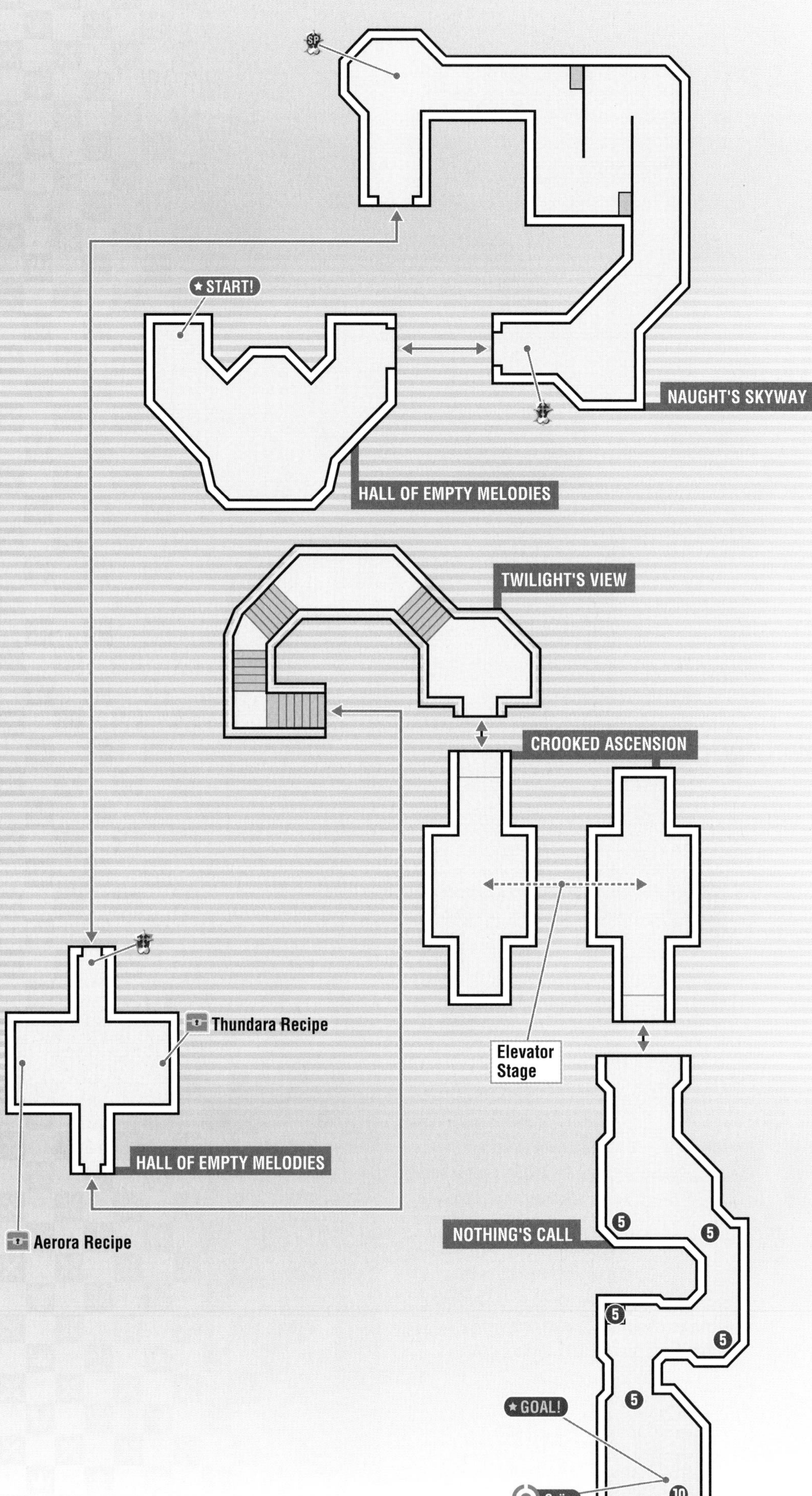
START!
NAUGHT'S SKYWAY
HALL OF EMPTY MELODIES
TWILIGHT'S VIEW
CROOKED ASCENSION
Thundara Recipe
Elevator Stage
HALL OF EMPTY MELODIES
NOTHING'S CALL
Aerora Recipe
GOAL!
Saïx

CHALLENGE MISSION

Objective: Avoid taking damage!

Restrictions: No recovery magic, no recovery items, enemy level +20

Rewards	
Sigils Acquired	Hits Sustained
3	10 or less
2	11 - 20 hits
1	21 - 30 hits

Proceed directly to the battle with Saïx and use LV5 Aero and Aerora spells to attack him from a distance. Although it's not the most powerful, Thundaga spells also help inflict damage from a distance, improving the chances that Roxas will take less damage.

SPECIAL CHALLENGE

Objective: Finish in record time!

Restrictions: Enemy level +25, HP drains continually

Rewards	
Sigils Acquired	Clear Time
3	01:55:00 or less
2	01:55:01 - 02:30:00
1	02:30:01 - 04:00:00

Finish the game, equip the Zero Gear and three Ability Unit(L) panels, and the Auto-Life Panel with two Auto-Life LV+(L) links. With your HP dropping to zero, you won't have time to heal against Saïx and still claim three Challenge Sigils. Though your life drains, it stops a few points shy of zero. However, one hit can kill Roxas. The Auto-Life takes care of the hits you're sure to take, but only once.

DAY 357

On this day, Roxas is alone in Twilight Town. The place is devoid of Heartless, so head straight up to Station Plaza. There you'll find the Moogle, along with the ability to access the menu and save your game. When you're ready to proceed, examine the doors of the clock tower and choose to go up.

Having Twilight Town all to yourself is kinda nice...or kinda creepy, depending on your perspective.

XION

MISSION 92

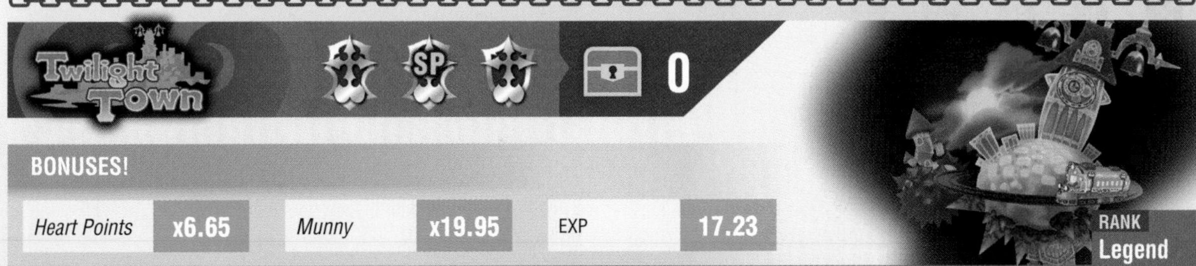

BONUSES!

Heart Points	x6.65	Munny	x19.95	EXP	17.23

ENEMIES

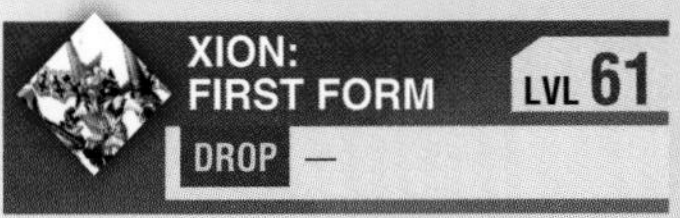

XION: FIRST FORM — LVL 61 — DROP —

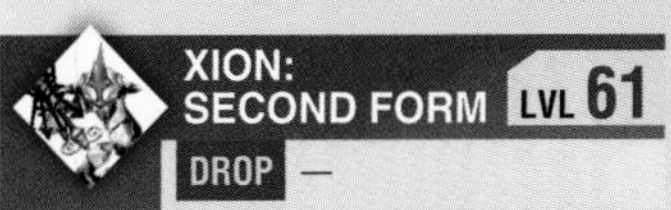

XION: SECOND FORM — LVL 61 — DROP —

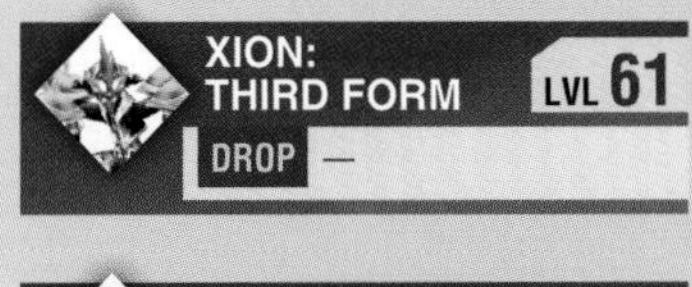

XION: THIRD FORM — LVL 61 — DROP —

XION: FINAL FORM — LVL 61 — DROP —

REWARDS	
Clear Bonuses	Random Bonuses
None	Aeroga Recipe (10%)
—	Gear Component D (5%)
—	Orichalcum (10%)
—	Hi-Potion (20%)
—	Hi-Ether (20%)
—	Panacea (15%)
—	None (20%)

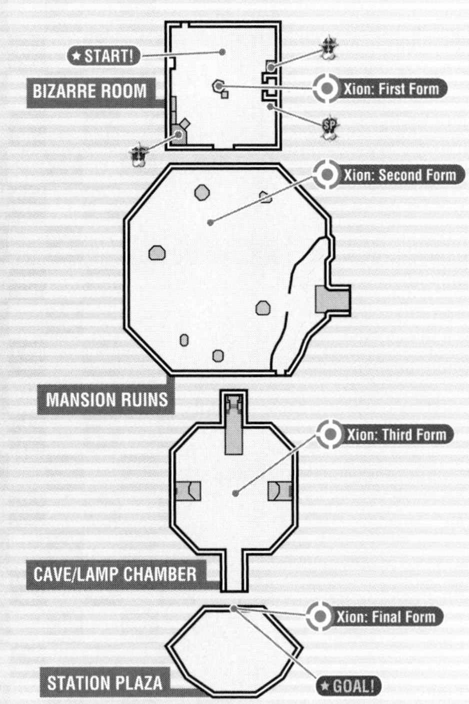

XION: FIRST FORM

BOSS!

Glide around the Bizarre Room and collect the two badges and blazon. Xion's first form is somewhat easy to defeat since she starts drawing sparkly energy before all her attacks. Move away when she attacks, then jump toward her and attack her from above. You can avoid most of her swift hits and retributions by staying airborne through a majority of the battle.

XION: SECOND FORM

BOSS!

Things get trickier at the Manor Ruins in Halloween Town, as Xion starts employing vortex attacks to hold Roxas in place. As soon as these begin to form, jump and glide or Air Slide away. Try to make your way back to Xion and perform aerial combos against her. When she pulls back her scythe, it means she's about to launch a combo. Dodge and jump away from her attacks, then immediately retaliate. The best strategy is to run in a small circle around her as she swings, then counterattack as soon as she's through.

Another new attack occurs when she rises in the air and gathers energy in her new scythe. Whenever she's preparing this attack, move far away to get a head start on the homing missiles. Dodge the missiles by Air Sliding away from them until they dissolve. Getting hit by a cloud of these can take Roxas's health from full to almost empty. While Air Sliding away from the missiles, curve back toward Xion so that you can hit her before she tries to launch another round, or she'll keep you running circles around the ring.

Using a Limit Break during this battle provides an advantage, but be sure to use only one. Two more battles are coming up!

XION: THIRD FORM

BOSS!

Now wielding four blades, Xion takes on many characteristics of the blade-arm type enemies. If she leaps off the ground, start performing Air Slides to get away before she drops right on top of Roxas, inflicting massive damage.

When her blades begin to glow, she launches into a complete combo. Avoid all her slashes, then get in a quick combo before running away. She'll launch her next attack soon.

She still uses the vortex traps from the previous battle, so jump and glide or Air Slide to break free of these. Since she leaves so little time for counterattack, go ahead and use Limit Breaks as often as you like to reach the final battle. Knock back Xion when she starts to form an energy bubble around herself; if you don't, then she'll regain full health. Be careful though, if she's attacked after the bubble is already formed, then Roxas will take the damage instead.

XION: FINAL FORM

BOSS!

Now massive in size, Xion attacks with two giant swords. But between all her attacks, she remains still for a time. Glide over and attack the torso, then flee when she pulls back and gets ready to swing. Keep your eyes on her arms and Dodge Roll left or right as needed, or jump and Air Slide away. She aims her slashes at Roxas's last position, so the best evasive maneuver is to run from her one side to the other in a wide curve along the outskirts of the invisible barrier.

When a quarter of her health is gone, Xion adds an attack where she crosses her blades and her shoulder points twinkle.

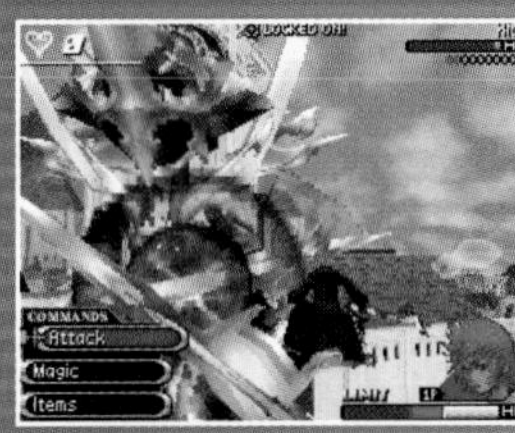

This comes just before an invisible force that knocks Roxas away, inflicting minor damage. However, this is damage you can avoid by breaking off your attack and moving back a few steps.

After losing more than half her health, Xion sometimes places her blades together and summons lightning bolts. Perform Dodge Rolls to evade these strikes as best you can, but even then it's going to be hairy.

Continue to glide up to the torso and attack until her health is at three bars or less. At this point, she adds an attack where she knocks Roxas away from her and into a vortex trap. Jump and glide away from it quickly, because she soon summons a ring of intense energy to explode up from the surface. Air Slide to get outside the ring before it goes off.

As her health dips below two bars, she begins attacking faster, providing less time to strike the torso. This is the best time to use a Limit Break since the finish is so near!

CHALLENGE MISSION

Objective: Avoid taking damage!

Restrictions: Level capped at 60, enemy level +15

Rewards	
Sigils Acquired	Hits Sustained
3	48 or less
2	49 - 72 hits
1	73 - 88 hits

Getting hit 48 times or less is quite possible, as long as you can jump to avoid some of Xion's special attacks.

SPECIAL CHALLENGE

Objective: Finish in record time!

Restrictions: No recovery magic, enemy level +30

Rewards	
Sigils Acquired	Clear Time
3	10:00:00 or less
2	10:00:01 - 12:10:00
1	12:10:01 - 14:10:00

Finish the game, purchase the Zero Gear, equip it and link three Ability Unit(L). Use Limit Breaks liberally to get through the first three forms, then use a Limit Recharge against the fourth. Know the signs of Xion's attacks well and avoid taking damage as much as possible.

DAY 358

BELIEVE

MISSION 93

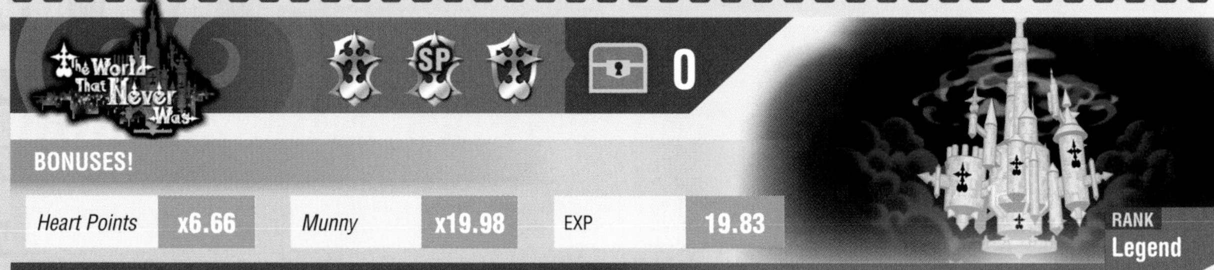

Heart Points	Munny	EXP
x6.66	x19.98	19.83

ENEMIES

Enemy	LVL	DROP
NEOSHADOW	17	—
RIKU	61	—

REWARDS	
Clear Bonuses	Random Bonuses
None	Thundara Recipe (20%)
—	Aerora Recipe (20%)
—	Megalixir Recipe (10%)
—	Hi-Potion (5%)
—	Hi-Ether (20%)
—	None (25%)

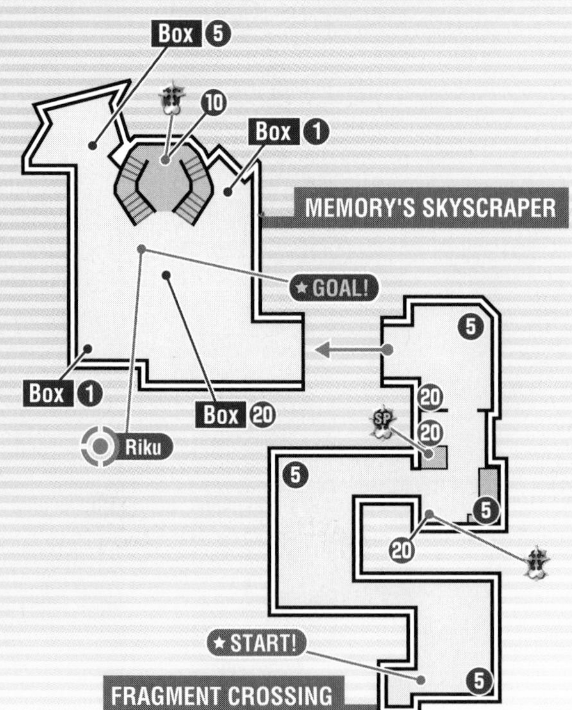

DUAL WIELD!

Equipped with two Keyblades and a bad attitude, Roxas can now cut through Neoshadows like butter! Have fun making your way north through Fragment Crossing. Chop down the Neoshadows outside Memory's Skyscraper and prepare for the final battle!

Roxas's newfound double-weapon power won't last long, so enjoy it.

*Collect the **Ordeal Badge** and **Ordeal Blazon** hovering over the machinery.*

RIKU

BOSS!

Quickly run up to the building front to acquire the Unity Badge, then glide back to Riku. Good luck trying to dodge any of his first strikes, but use Dodge Rolls and jumps to get away quickly afterward. His glowing blade attacks can be blocked if you employ the right timing. Otherwise, trigger your Limit Break each time he knocks down Roxas's health and deplete his health as fast as possible.

CHALLENGE MISSION

Objective: Don't miss with attacks!

Restrictions: Level capped at 60, enemy level +25

Rewards	
Sigils Acquired	Missed Attacks
3	0 misses
2	1 - 5 misses
1	6 - 10 misses

As it says, don't let your dual Keyblades swing at empty air even once! It doesn't matter if your Limit Break attack misses, since that doesn't count as a standard attack. Just be sure to stop pressing A when your Limit Break is done; otherwise, cast Thundaga to hit with accuracy.

SPECIAL CHALLENGE

Objective: Finish in record time!

Restrictions: No recovery magic, no recovery items, enemy level +35

Rewards	
Sigils Acquired	Clear Time
3	04:42:00 or less
2	04:42:01 - 06:00:00
1	06:00:01 - 07:00:00

Equip the Zero Gear with three Ability Unit(L) links and use your Limit Breaks and Limit Recharge items to cut Riku down as fast as possible.

COMPLETION BONUSES

After the final mission, allow the credits to roll and then save your game. Load this save and you'll find Roxas back at Station Plaza, on day 357 just before the final battles. However, many changes occur.

LEGEND RANK

Completing the game earns you the Legend rank. Missions 92 and 93 are now playable in the Holo-Missions screen, and more items are added to the Moogle Shop.

MOOGLE SHOP EXTRAS

Clear the game and check the Moogle shop for great new items!

Extra items are now available in the Moogle shop, such as the Zero Gear⑤, more Slot Releasers, another LV Quadrupler③, and three new rings. Depending on the criteria achieved, Sora's Awakening and The King's Return may also be available to purchase.

The synthesis menu now includes the thirteen best rings in the game. Additionally, more items are added to the Redeem list as prizes for redeeming Challenge Sigils and Mission Crowns.

By collecting a crown mark for completing every mission available in Mission Mode, the **Limit Pass** item is added to the shop. Purchasing this item adds a feature to the Config screen, making it possible to turn Limit Breaks on/off.

SORA'S AWAKENING AND THE KING'S RETURN

Also available to buy, depending on the criteria completed, are two status items that unlock additional characters in Mission Mode. Complete all missions, including those that are only unlocked when completing certain characters' requests and The King's Return item is added to the shop. Purchase this to make The King (Mickey) playable in Mission Mode.

Purchase The King's Return in the shop to make Mickey playable in Mission Mode.

Complete all missions with the Mission Gauge at 100% and the Sora's Awakening item is added to the shop. Purchase this to make Sora playable in Mission Mode.

SECRET REPORTS UNLOCKED

Days in Roxas's Diary with Secret Reports available are marked with an A icon.

The Secret Reports are extra files that become attached to certain days in Roxas's Diary. Days with a Secret Report attached are marked with an A button icon. Press A to view the Secret Report attached to that day. Reading them one by one, you'll get a behind-the-scenes look into events from the villain's point of view.

One Secret Report is available per day. To acquire the Secret Report for each day, fill the Mission Gauge 100%. If a Challenge Mission exists, obtain one or more Challenge Sigils.

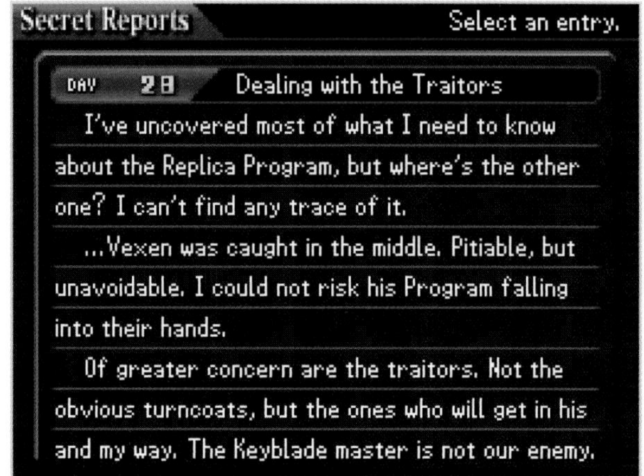

The Secret Reports reveal additional storyline aspects, as told by the members of Organization XIII.

THEATER MODE UNLOCKED

Completing the game adds Theater Mode to the title screen, allowing you to view all the scenes shown between missions during the game.

Theater Mode allows you to review of all the scenes shown between missions in Mission Mode.

MISSION MODE

Mission Mode is identical to Story Mode, except that players can either play solo or in multiplayer sessions. New missions become available to play as the player obtains Unity Badges and higher ranks in Story Mode.

The main difference between the two modes is that players can earn Mission Crowns in Mission Mode, redeemable for prizes in the Moogle shop. The number of Mission Crowns a player receives is based on how many Mission Points the player collects. Mission Points appear when enemies are defeated, and can also be found in various quantities on the map (as marked throughout this chapter).

Collect white or blue crystals called Mission Points to increase the number of Mission Crowns received for each mission completed!

Furthermore, Mission Mode contains an extra tutorial mission, Mission 00, covered in the following section. Once the mission criteria are accomplished, a countdown begins. You must return to the dark corridor before the countdown ends, or you will fail to earn the bonus points for the mission.

Play as Dual-Wielding Roxas

In Story Mode, Roxas can only dual-wield during Mission 93. However, with certain equipment, he can dual-wield during any mission in Mission Mode. Purchase the Zero Gear⑤ weapon panel from the shop, equip it and link three Ability Unit(L) panels. Then start Mission Mode and choose Roxas as your character; he now dual-wields just like in Mission 93!

MISSION MODE TUTORIAL

MISSION **00**

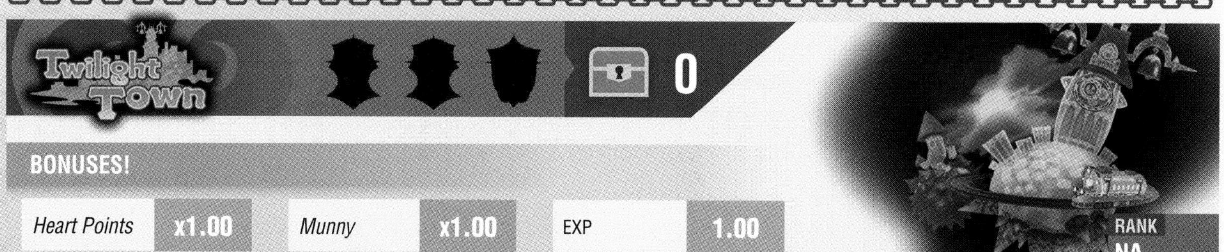

ENEMIES

Enemy	LVL	DROP
SHADOW	1	Potion
YELLOW OPERA	1	Moonstone
SCARLET TANGO	1	Blazing Shard

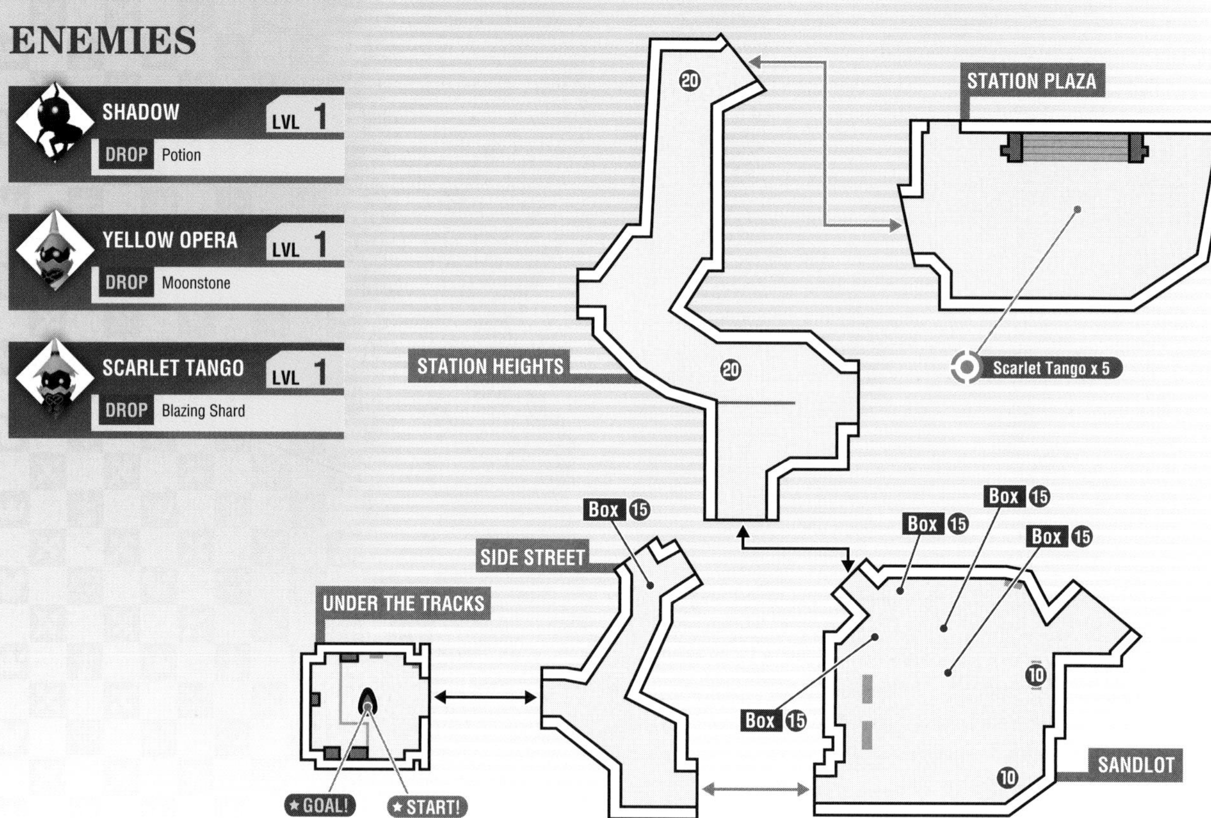

COLLECTING MISSION POINTS

The objective of Mission 00 is to navigate through Twilight Town to Station Plaza and defeat five Scarlet Tangos. Exit the storage room Under the Tracks and head north on Side Street to find a crate. Smash the crate to obtain 15 Mission Points. In Multiplayer, several characters can "compete" to pick up the points. The more Mission Points you pick up, the more Mission Crowns you're awarded at the end. However, no Mission Crowns are awarded for completing Mission 00.

Extra crates appear in many missions. Smash them to collect Mission Points.

GATHERING GATES

Move to the south end of Side Street, where a Gathering Gate blocks the exit. In Multiplayer mode, all characters must stand at the gate in order for the group to proceed to the next area. Standing at the gate also provides protection from other characters' attacks. In Solo mode, you'll proceed immediately as usual.

Gathering Gates prevent players from moving ahead of the group. All players must convene at the Gathering Gate in order for the group to move on.

TO THE STATION!

After each enemy you defeat, collect the Mission Points before resuming the battle.

Defeat Shadows, smash crates, and pick up the floating blue crystals to obtain Mission Points. Take the northwest exit out of the Sandlot to Station Heights. Proceed uphill, taking out enemies and collecting points.

TARGET TANGO

If ignited or inflicted with another status, you begin to drop Mission Points; remember that other players can steal them!

The targets appear two at a time. Perform aerial combos and cast Blizzard magic to defeat the Scarlet Tangos. Avoid their fire attacks at all costs.

LOSING POINTS TO STATUS

Note that if a player is ignited, he or she starts dropping collected Mission Points until the status subsides. Use a Panacea to cure most statuses immediately. If you're another player in a multiplayer game, follow characters inflicted with status ailments and steal their points!

COUNTDOWN TO FAILURE

When the last Scarlet Tango is destroyed, a countdown appears on-screen. You have 120 seconds to return to the dark corridor. Normally failure to return in the allotted time results in the loss of bonus Mission Points and gives another player the chance to steal the Mission Crowns. However, no Mission Crowns are awarded for Mission 00. But to get a Crown for Mission 00, you must return to the store room Under the Tracks in time to receive the bonus Mission Points. In Mission Mode, the search reticule does not appear on the dark corridor. Simply step onto the dark corridor to complete your mission.

In other missions, the countdown appears as soon as the Mission Gauge is filled to the goal line. You must complete extra tasks to fill the gauge 100% and revisit the dark corridor before the countdown expires to receive the Bonus Points.

GIVE IT YOUR BEST SHOT!

Now you're ready to replay missions in Mission Mode, keeping these differences in mind!

CHAPTER 4 PANELS & ABILITIES

PANELS MENU

All of the abilities that your character can use during missions are determined by the panels that you equip in the Panels Menu. To access the Panels Menu, select "Panels" from the Main Menu before accepting a mission.

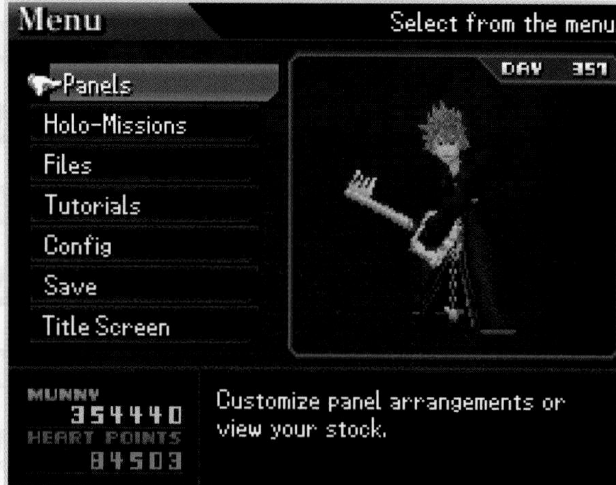

While in the Panels Menu, your character's stats appear on the top screen and his/her panel grid appears on the bottom screen. Use the following commands to navigate the various parts of the Panels Menu.

Panels Menu Commands

Command	Effect
D-pad	*Highlight various panels and menu options*
A	*Select highlighted item*
B	*Undo selection/Return selected panel to panel list/Return to Main Menu*
X	*Toggle between abilities window and stats on the top screen*
X + d-pad	*Navigate abilities window*
Y	*Change panel page*
L and R	*Change panel list*
START	*Open submenu*

PANEL TYPES

There are eight tabs situated along the top of the lower screen in the Panels Menu, representing eight different panel lists. You can cycle between them by pressing L or R. The leftmost panel ("All") displays every panel in your possession. The other seven contain the following panels:

Item Menu: Equipping these panels provides access to healing and restorative abilities during missions.

Support Menu: Allows you to level up your character and increase the number of items you can collect from the battlefield and carry with you.

Magic Menu: All of your character's magic abilities stem from equipping these panels. You can also increase the level and number of uses of your magic with these panels.

Ability Menu: Equipping these panels offers additional abilities in combat, including dodging, blocking and gliding.

Weapon Menu: The panels in this list transform your character's weapon, granting additional combat techniques and increasing your character's stats. You can only equip one weapon panel at a time.

Ring Menu: Ring panels give your character additional abilities and increase certain stats. You can only equip one ring at a time.

Material Menu: By collecting recipe and material panels, you can synthesize new items at the Moogle Shop. You cannot equip these panels in the Panel Menu (for more information on panel synthesis, see the next chapter).

EQUIPPING PANELS

Aside from material panels, which you cannot equip, there are essentially two main types of panels: base panels and link panels. The type of panel determines how you equip it.

BASE PANELS

Base panels include magic spells, weapons, healing items and abilities. You can equip these by highlighting them in a panel list (use the d-pad), selecting them (press A), choosing any empty slot on a panel page (use the d-pad) and pressing A again to equip the selected panel in that slot.

To view the abilities that you gain from equipping base panels (or lose by unequipping them), press X to view the Abilities window on the top screen. As you add and remove base panels, you can see which abilities you gain and lose from doing so. Panels can also be equipped using the stylus by draging a panel from the Panel Menu to an open slot.

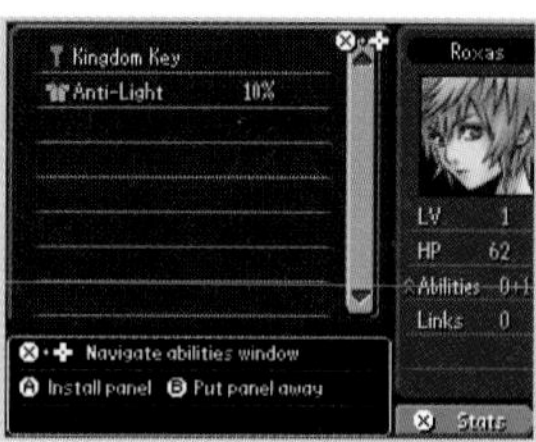

If a base panel's name has a circled number at the end of it (i.e.: Dodge Roll③), that number indicates the size of the base panel's link area. You must have that number of free slots in a panel page to equip the panel. The link grid icon that appears in the bottom-right corner when you highlight the panel shows the shape of the link area.

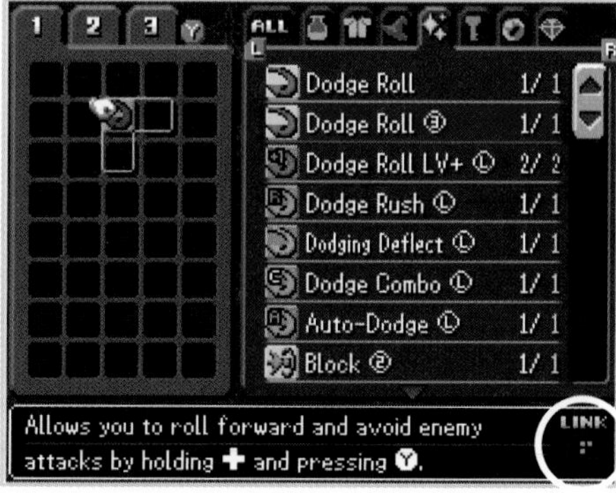

MAKING THE PIECES FIT

Link areas from two different panels cannot overlap. Some panels, such as LV Doubler⑥ come in several different varieties, where the only difference is the configuration of the link areas. Use the ones that fit best in your panel pages.

LINK PANELS

Link panels have an (L) at the end of their name and can only be equipped in the link area of a specific type of base panel. For example, Dodging Deflect(L) can only be equipped in an empty panel slot within the link area of a Dodge Roll panel.

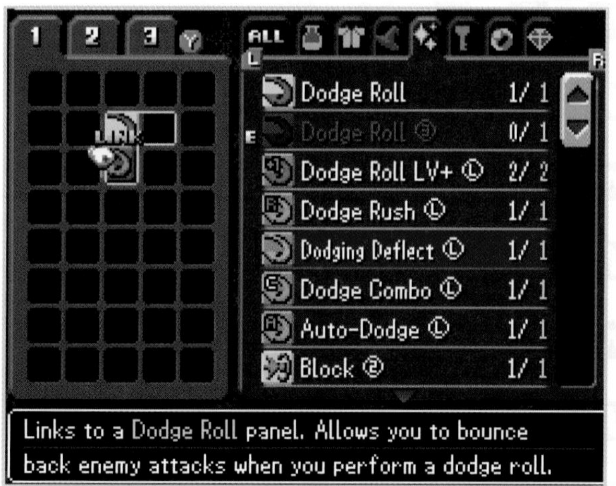

Equipping link panels improves the ability bestowed upon your character by the base panel. Sometimes it simply levels up the ability and sometimes it grants your character an entirely new ability. It's a good idea to keep the abilities window open while you equip link panels to see the effects they have (see the "Abilities" section in this chapter for more information on gaining new abilities by equipping link panels).

Panels that provide the ability to cast magic spells (like Firaga and Cura) behave like base and link panels, depending on how you equip them. Equipping a magic panel in an empty panel slot gives your character the ability to cast that spell at LV1 once during the next mission. But placing the panel inside the link area of another magic panel (like Doublecast④ or Magic LV4④) powers up the spell by increasing its level or the number of times it can be cast during the next mission (for more information, see the "Magic" section in this chapter).

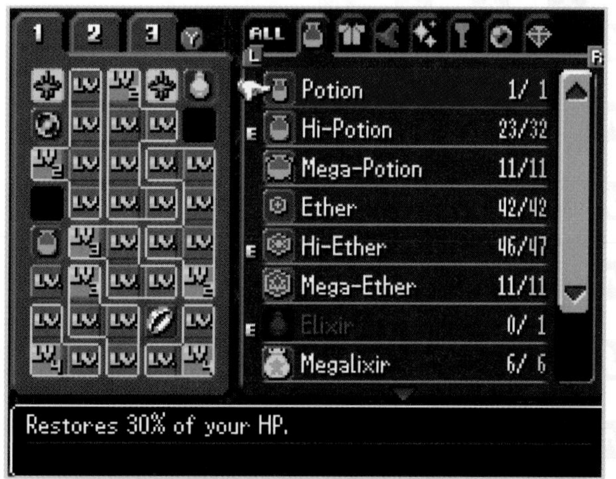

PANEL LISTS

The next several pages detail the 277 different panels that you can collect over the course of your adventure. Panels are divided into the seven categories that they're sorted into on the Panels Menu, with specific strategies and information about each.

ITEM MENU PANELS

Item panels are the most basic and straightforward panels in the Panels Menu. They are all base panels with a link area of one slot, so no other panels can be linked to them.

For each item panel you place on a panel page, you can use that item's ability once during your next mission. For example, if you place three Ethers and a Mega-Potion on a panel page, you will be able to use Ether three times and Mega-Potion once during the next mission.

Starting another mission resets the number of uses for each panel item. However, Item panels can only be used once, so if you use two of the three Ethers in one mission and start another mission without changing your panel layout, you will only have access to the one remaining Ether for that next mission.

- ★ ***Icon:*** *The panel's icon, as it appears in the Panels Menu.*
- ★ ***Name:*** *The name of the panel.*
- ★ ***Sell Price:*** *The amount of munny earned by selling the panel in the Moogle Shop. A "—" means the item cannot be sold.*
- ★ ***Shop Price:*** *Price of the panel (in hearts) at the Moogle Shop, as well as the rank required to buy it and the number of times you can purchase it.*
- ★ ***How to Get It:*** *Other methods for obtaining the panel, with mission numbers for each method. Refer to the Mission Walkthrough, Panel Synthesis and Bestiary chapters of this guide for more information.*
- ★ ***Effect:*** *The item panel's effect on your character when equipped.*

MENU PANELS

Icon	Name	Sell Price	Shop Price	How to Get It	Effect
	Potion	10	*90 (Novice; unlimited)*	*Completion reward (04, 08, 10, 28); random reward (multiple); treasure chest (multiple); enemy (multiple); Moogle Shop freebie*	*Restores 30% of your HP*
	Hi-Potion	20	*360 (Agent; unlimited)*	*Completion reward (09, 27, 30, 46); random reward (multiple); treasure chest (multiple); enemy (43); Synthesis; Moogle Shop freebie*	*Restores 50% of your HP*
	Mega-Potion	200	*400 (Master; unlimited)*	*Synthesis; Moogle Shop freebie*	*Restores 40% HP to all comrades on the same map*
	Ether	40	*180 (Rookie; unlimited)*	*Completion reward (04, 09, 20); random reward (multiple); treasure chest (multiple); enemy (multiple); Moogle Shop freebie*	*Restores one cast of each of your magic*
	Hi-Ether	100	*480 (Agent; unlimited)*	*Random reward (multiple); treasure chest (67, 68, 69, 79, 82, 83, 89); Synthesis; Moogle Shop freebie*	*Restores two casts of each of your magic*
	Mega-Ether	400	*640 (Master; unlimited)*	*Synthesis; Moogle Shop freebie*	*Restores one cast of each magic to all comrades on the same map*
	Elixir	1000	—	*Random reward (64, 73, 80, 83, 84); treasure chest (48, 83); Synthesis; Moogle Shop freebie*	*Fully restores your HP and magic*
	Megalixir	2000	—	*Synthesis; Moogle Shop freebie*	*Fully restores HP and magic to all comrades on the same map*
	Panacea	1400	*120 (Rookie; unlimited)*	*Completion reward (16, 18); random reward (multiple); treasure chest (15, 17, 20); enemy (22, 27, 28, 35); Moogle Shop freebie*	*Cures all negative status effects*
	Limit Recharge	1000	—	*Synthesis; Moogle Shop freebie*	*Replenishes the threshold at which you can use a Limit Break up one notch*

SUPPORT MENU PANELS

The panels in the Support Menu do one of two things: they increase your character's level (Level Up, LV Doubler⑤, etc.), or they increase the number of items you can pick up in a mission and carry in your backpack (Backpack and Pack Extender④).

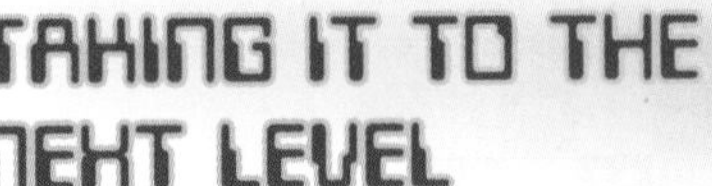

TAKING IT TO THE NEXT LEVEL

You can place a Level Up panel in any empty slot on a panel page to boost your character's level by 1, but you'll get much more out of them if you use them as link panels in the link area of a LV Doubler, LV Tripler or LV Quadrupler panel.

MENU PANELS

Icon	Name	Link	Sell Price	Shop Price	How to Get It	Effect
	Level Up	—	—	*180 (Novice; x1); 1200 (Rookie, x1); 2500 (Expert, x1)*	*Moogle Shop freebie*	*Increases your level by 1*
	LV Doubler⑤	LINK	—	—	*After talking to Saïx in Day 52*	*Increases your level by 2 for each linked Level Up panel*
	LV Doubler⑥	LINK	—	—	*Completion reward (42)*	*Increases your level by 2 for each linked Level Up panel*
	LV Doubler⑥	LINK	—	—	*Completion reward (56)*	*Increases your level by 2 for each linked Level Up panel*
	LV Doubler⑥	LINK	—	—	*Moogle Shop freebie*	*Increases your level by 2 for each linked Level Up panel*
	LV Doubler⑥	LINK	—	—	*Moogle Shop freebie*	*Increases your level by 2 for each linked Level Up panel*
	LV Tripler④	LINK	—	—	*Completion reward (77)*	*Increases your level by 3 for each linked Level Up panel*
	LV Tripler④	LINK	—	—	*Completion reward (65)*	*Increases your level by 3 for each linked Level Up panel*
	LV Tripler④	LINK	—	—	*Moogle Shop freebie*	*Increases your level by 3 for each linked Level Up panel*
	LV Quadrupler③	LINK	—	—	*Completion reward (88)*	*Increases your level by 4 for each linked Level Up panel*
	LV Quadrupler③	LINK	—	*6000 (Legend; x1)*	—	*Increases your level by 4 for each linked Level Up panel*
	LV Quadrupler③	LINK	—		*Moogle Shop freebie*	*Increases your level by 4 for each linked Level Up panel*
	Backpack	—	—	*480 (Rookie; x1)*	*Completion reward (22); treasure chest (34)*	*Lets you carry two additional items in your backpack*
	Pack Extender④	LINK	—	—	*Completion reward (31)*	*Lets you carry four additional items for each Backpack panel you link to it*

MAGIC MENU PANELS

All magic panels without a link area represent the various types of magic that you can cast in combat (Fire, Blizzard, Cure, and so on). For every one of these panels that you place on a panel page, you can cast that magic once in combat at LV1.

KNOW YOUR ENEMY

Always customize your magic for the enemies that you will be fighting in a mission. Refer to the "Bestiary" section of this guide to view enemy profiles and their elemental weaknesses before determining what type of magic to equip.

To increase the number of times that you can cast a particular type of magic, either place multiple panels of that magic on a panel page, or place the magic panels within the link area of a Doublecast④, Triplecast③ or Quadcast③ panel.

To increase the potency of a particular type of magic, place its magic panel within the link area of a Magic LV2④, Magic LV3④ or Magic LV④ panel. The effects are cumulative and LV5 is the maximum level for any type of magic. So if you place a Magic LV2④ panel and a Magic LV3④ panel on the panel grid and you place the same magic panels in each, you will wind up with three types of LV5 magic.

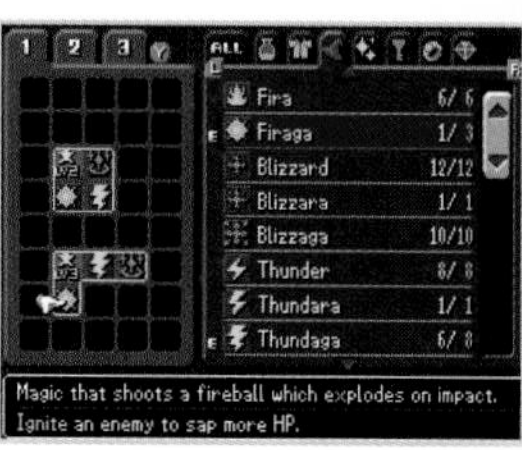

The best way to create multiple uses of the same magic is to link magic panels to Doublecast④, Triplecast③ and Quadcast③ to increase the number of times you can cast that particular type of magic by two, three or four.

Whenever possible, link the types of magic that you leveled up to these panels because the effects are cumulative. For example, placing one Thunder panel in a Doublecast④ link area and another Thunder panel in a Magic LV3④ link area generates three casts of Thunder at LV3.

WASTE NOT, WANT NOT

If you have one empty slot that you're not using on the panel grid, it's best to drop a magic panel into it to create one additional magical attack.

Here's a quick example of placing magic panels:

★ *Placing a Fire panel anywhere on a panel page creates one use of Fire at LV1.*

★ *Placing a Fire panel within the link area of a Magic LV2④ panel generates one use of Fire at LV2.*

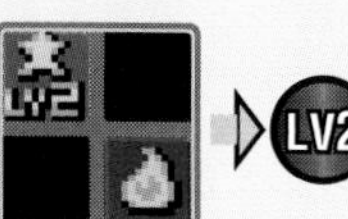

★ *Placing two Fire panels within the link area of a Magic LV2④ panel makes two uses of Fire at LV4 (because you placed two Fire panels in the panel page).*

★ *Placing three Fire panels within the link area of a Magic LV2④ panel creates three uses of Fire at LV5 (because LV5 is the highest level).*

★ *Placing a Fire panel within the link area of a Magic LV3④ panel generates one use of Fire at LV3.*

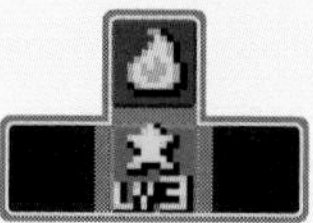

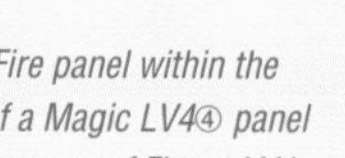

★ *Placing a Fire panel within the link area of a Magic LV4④ panel provides one use of Fire at LV4.*

★ *Placing two Fire panels within the link area of a Magic LV3④ panel creates two uses of Fire at LV5 (again, because LV5 is the highest magic level possible).*

★ *Placing a Fire panel within the link area of a Magic LV2④ panel and another Fire panel within the link area of a Magic LV3④ panel produces two uses of Fire (because you placed two Fire panels) at LV5 (one in the LV2 area and one in the LV3 area).*

MENU PANELS

Icon	Name	Link	Sell Price	Shop Price	How to Get It	Effect
	Fire	—	200	*90 (Rookie, x1); 180 (Rookie, x1)*	*Completion reward (03, 05, 10, 26, 52); Synthesis; Moogle Shop freebie*	*Magic that shoots a homing ball of flame; ignite an enemy to sap more HP*
	Fira	—	300	*480 (Agent, x1); 960 (Agent, x1)*	*Completion reward (43, 52); Synthesis; Moogle Shop freebie*	*Magic that shoots a ball of flame straight ahead; ignite an enemy to sap more HP*
	Firaga	—	400	—	*Completion reward (61); Synthesis*	*Magic that shoots a fireball which explodes on impact; ignite an enemy to sap more HP*
	Blizzard	—	200	*90 (Rookie, x1); 180 (Rookie, x1)*	*Completion reward (14, 15, 18, 24); Synthesis; Moogle Shop freebie*	*Magic that shoots an ice crystal which pursues foes; frozen enemies take triple damage*
	Blizzara	—	300	*480 (Agent, x1); 960 (Agent, x1)*	*Completion reward (47, 56, 57); Synthesis; Moogle Shop freebie*	*Magic that shoots an ice crystal which stays in place; frozen enemies take triple damage*
	Blizzaga	—	400	—	*Completion reward (78); Synthesis*	*Magic that shoots an ice mine which explodes on contact; frozen enemies take triple damage*
	Thunder	—	200	*360 (Rookie, x1); 720 (Rookie, x1)*	*Completion reward (36, 38, 46); Synthesis; Moogle Shop freebie*	*Magic that rains down a row of lightning bolts; jolt enemies to set them up for additional damage*
	Thundara	—	300	*600 (Expert, x1); 1200 (Expert, x1)*	*Completion reward (56); Synthesis; Moogle Shop freebie*	*Magic that hits a broad area with many lightning bolts; jolt enemies to set them up for additional damage*
	Thundaga	—	400	—	*Completion reward (69); Synthesis*	*Magic that strikes a foe directly with lightning; jolt enemies to set them up for additional damage*
	Aero	—	200	*360 (Rookie, x1); 720 (Rookie, x1)*	*Completion reward (32, 41); Synthesis; Moogle Shop freebie*	*Magic that shoots a swift gust of wind at a foe; air-tossed enemies take triple damage*
	Aerora	—	300	—	*Synthesis; Moogle Shop freebie*	*Magic that sends a gust of wind to stalk your foes; air-tossed enemies take triple damage*
	Aeroga	—	400	—	*Synthesis; Moogle Shop freebie*	*Magic that generates a huge whirlwind; air-tossed enemies take triple damage*
	Cure	—	200	*480 Rookie, x1); 960 (Rookie, x1)*	*Completion reward (21, 25, 34, 49, 58); Synthesis; Moogle Shop freebie*	*Magic that restores some of your HP*
	Cura	—	300	*720 (Agent, x1); 1440 (Agent, x1)*	*Completion reward (50); Synthesis; Moogle Shop freebie*	*Magic that continues to restore your HP over time*
	Curaga	—	400	—	*Completion reward (66); Synthesis*	*Magic that creates an HP recovery field for you and your comrades*
	Magic LV2④	LINK	—	—	*Completion reward (21)*	*Doubles the level of magic panels linked to it; link more of the same magic to stack the effect*
	Magic LV2④	LINK	—	*2400 (Master, x1)*	—	*Doubles the level of magic panels linked to it; link more of the same magic to stack the effect*
	Magic LV2④	LINK	—	*840 (Rookie, x1)*	—	*Doubles the level of magic panels linked to it; link more of the same magic to stack the effect*
	Magic LV3④	LINK	—	*840 (Agent, x1)*	—	*Triples the level of magic panels linked to it; link more of the same magic to stack the effect*
	Magic LV3④	LINK	—	*1400 (Expert, x1)*	—	*Triples the level of magic panels linked to it; link more of the same magic to stack the effect*
	Magic LV4④	LINK	—	—	*Treasure chest (74)*	*Quadruples the level of magic panels linked to it; link more of the same magic to stack the effect*
	Doublecast④	LINK	—	—	*Completion reward (11)*	*Arms you with two casts of each magic panel you link to it*
	Triplecast③	LINK	—	*450 (Novice, x1)*	—	*Arms you with three casts of each magic panel you link to it*
	Quadcast③	LINK	—	*2000 (Expert, x1)*	—	*Arms you with four casts of each magic panel you link to it*

ABILITY MENU PANELS

As the category name implies, ability panels endow your character with additional abilities or enhance the character's current ones. Base ability panels give your character an extra ability. Some—but not all—base panels have a link area. Placing link ability panels in that link area produces a wide variety of effects.

Each ability link panel only corresponds to one specific type of ability base panel. For example, Haste LV+(L) can only be used to level up Haste③.

WATCH THOSE ABILITIES!

Because the effects of adding different combinations of link panels to abilities produces different effects, it's a good idea to have the abilities window open when you add and remove ability link panels.

MENU PANELS

Icon	Name	Link	Sell Price	Shop Price	How to Get It	Effect
	Dodge Roll	LINK	—	—	*Completion reward (05)*	*Allows you to roll forward and avoid enemy attacks*
	Dodge Roll③	LINK	—	—	*Completion reward (51)*	*Allows you to roll forward and avoid enemy attacks*
	Dodge Roll LV+(L)	—	—	*600 (Agent, x1)*	—	*Links to a Dodge Roll panel and raises its level*
	Dodge Rush(L)	—	100	—	*Synthesis*	*Links to a Dodge Roll panel; allows you to knock enemies aside when you perform a dodge roll*
	Dodging Deflect(L)	—	100	—	*Synthesis*	*Links to a Dodge Roll panel; allows you to bounce back enemy attacks when you perform a Dodge Roll*
	Dodge Combo(L)	—	100	—	*Synthesis*	*Links to a Dodge Roll panel; allows you to transition swiftly from a Dodge Roll back to the offensive*
	Auto-Dodge(L)	—	100	—	*Synthesis*	*Links to a Dodge Roll panel; allows you to automatically avoid enemy attacks sometimes*
	Block②	LINK	—	—	*Completion reward (07)*	*Allows you to block and bounce back enemy attacks*
	Block④	LINK	—	*2400 (Master, x1)*	—	*Allows you to block and bounce back enemy attacks*
	Block LV+(L)	—	—	*2400 (Master, x1); 6000 (Legend, x1)*	—	*Links to a Block panel and raises its level*
	Perfect Block(L)	—	100	—	*Synthesis*	*Links to a Block panel; allows you to block just as an attack hits to eliminate recoil*
	Block-Counter(L)	—	100	—	*Synthesis*	*Links to a Block panel; allows you to respond with a powerful counterattack immediately after blocking*

MENU PANELS

Icon	Name	Link	Sell Price	Shop Price	How to Get It	Effect
	Block-Retreat(L)	—	100	—	Synthesis	Links to a Block panel; allows you to recoil farther after you block an attack
	Sliding Block(L)	—	100	—	Synthesis	Links to a Block panel; allows you to quickly slide forward as you block
	Block-Jump(L)	—	100	—	Synthesis	Links to a Block panel; allows you to jump right after you block without any delay
	Fire Block(L)	—	100	—	Synthesis	Links to a Block panel; allows you to ignite enemies sometimes when blocking
	Blizzard Block(L)	—	100	—	Synthesis	Links to a Block panel; allows you to freeze enemies sometimes when blocking
	Thunder Block(L)	—	100	—	Synthesis	Links to a Block panel; allows you to jolt enemies sometimes when blocking
	Aero Block(L)	—	100	—	Synthesis	Links to a Block panel; allows you to air-toss enemies sometimes when blocking
	Block Bonus(L)	—	100	—	Synthesis	Links to a Block panel; allows you to generate HP Prizes sometimes when blocking
	Round Block(L)	—	100	—	Synthesis	Links to a Block panel; allows you to block any attack, even if it comes from behind
	Auto-Block(L)	—	100	—	Synthesis	Links to a Block panel; allows you to automatically block frontal attacks
	Aerial Recovery	LINK	—	270 (Novice, x1)	—	Allows you to regain your balance after you are sent flying
	Aerial Recovery③	LINK	—	2400 (Agent, x1)	—	Allows you to regain your balance after you are sent flying
	A. Recovery LV+(L)	—	—	—	Treasure chest (54, 55)	Links to an Aerial Recovery panel and raises its level
	Quick Recovery(L)	—	100	—	Synthesis	Links to an Aerial Recovery panel; allows you to AR more quickly
	Aerial Payback(L)	—	100	—	Synthesis	Links to an Aerial Recovery panel; allows you to respond with a powerful counterattack after an AR
	Smash Recovery(L)	—	100	—	Synthesis	Links to an Aerial Recovery panel; allows you to knock away nearby enemies when you perform an AR
	Air Slide②	LINK	—	—	Completion reward (23)	Allows you to perform an Aerial Dash in midair
	Air Slide⑤	LINK	—	—	Treasure chest (65)	Allows you to perform an Aerial Dash in midair
	Air Slide LV+(L)	—	—	1200 (Master, x1); 6000 (Legend, x1)	Treasure chest (38, 67)	Links to an Air Slide panel and raises its level
	Air Rush(L)	—	100	—	Synthesis	Links to an Air Slide panel; allows you to knock enemies aside when you perform an Air Slide
	Sliding Dash	LINK	—	—	Completion reward (42)	Allows you to quickly close in on a target and attack
	Sliding Dash③	LINK	—	—	Treasure chest (68)	Allows you to quickly close in on a target and attack
	Sliding Dash LV+(L)	—	—	—	Completion reward (82); Moogle Shop freebie	Links to a Sliding Dash panel and raises its level

MENU PANELS

Icon	Name	Link	Sell Price	Shop Price	How to Get It	Effect
	Glide③	LINK	—	—	Completion reward (53)	Allows you to ride the wind in midair; you will stay airborne while the button is pressed
	Glide⑤	LINK	—	—	Moogle Shop freebie	Allows you to ride the wind in midair; you will stay airborne while the button is pressed
	Glide LV+(L)	—	—	1000 (Expert, x1)	Completion reward (76); treasure chest (68); Moogle Shop freebie	Links to a Glide panel and raises its level
	Homing Glide(L)	—	100	—	Synthesis	Links to a Glide panel; allows you to lock on to a target while gliding to automatically move toward it
	Rocket Glide(L)	—	100	—	Synthesis	Links to a Glide panel; allows you to slam past foes by gliding right after you begin an Air Slide
	Haste	LINK	—	—	Moogle Shop freebie	Allows you to run more quickly
	Haste③	LINK	—	—	Moogle Shop freebie	Allows you to run more quickly
	Haste LV+(L)	—	—	—	Moogle Shop freebie	Links to a Haste panel and raises its level
	High Jump	LINK	—	—	Completion reward (44)	Allows you to jump higher
	High Jump③	LINK	—	—	Completion reward (74)	Allows you to jump higher
	High Jump LV+(L)	—	—	2400 (Master, x1); 6000 (Legend, x1)	—	Links to a High Jump panel and raises its level
	Float(L)	—	100	—	Synthesis	Links to a High Jump panel; allows you to slow your descent in midair
	Treasure Magnet	LINK	—	—	Completion reward (29)	Allows you to easily scoop up prizes lying around you
	Treasure Magnet③	LINK	—	1500 (Expert, x1)	—	Allows you to easily scoop up prizes lying around you
	T. Magnet LV+(L)	—	—	800 (Master, x1); 1600 (Master, x1)	—	Links to a Treasure Magnet panel and raises its level
	Auto-Life③	LINK	—	4800 (Rookie, x1)	—	Allows you to recover if all your HP runs out; only works once
	Auto-Life LV+(L)	—	—	1200 (Agent, x1); 2400 (Master, x1)	—	Links to an Auto-Life panel and raises its level
	Limit Boost	LINK	—	1440 (Agent, x1)	—	Increases the upper limit of your yellow gauge so you can use Limit Breaks sooner
	Final Limit	LINK	—	—	Speak to Saïx on Day 225	Allows you to use your Final Limit, a powered-up version of the Limit Break
	Scan	LINK	—	—	Completion reward (04)	Displays the HP of targets
	Range Extender	LINK	—	1200 (Rookie, x1)	—	Allows you to lock on to enemies even if they are far away
	Auto-Lock	LINK	—	960 (Agent, x1)	—	Allows you to automatically lock on to available targets while attacking
	Ultima Weapon	LINK	—	—	Moogle Shop freebie	Allows you to use the Ultima Weapon ability

WEAPON MENU PANELS

Most weapon panels are base "gear" panels that modify your character's weapon. Note that these panels are not weapons in and of themselves; you can only equip one gear weapon panel at a time. There are also a handful of link weapon panels that can be used to modify any gear that has a link area.

Each gear weapon panel affects each character's stats and abilities differently. The following table only represents the effects of each weapon panel when equipped on Roxas during Story Mode. Refer to the "Characters" chapter in this guide for details on how each panel affects each character during Mission Mode.

★ ***Strength:*** *The first number represents the bonus to your character's Strength when the panel is equipped. The second number represents the additional Strength bonus for every Power Unit(L) linked to the gear.*

★ ***Magic:*** *The first number represents the bonus to your character's Magic when the panel is equipped. The second number represents the additional Magic bonus for every Magic Unit(L) linked to the gear.*

★ ***Defense:*** *The first number represents the bonus to your character's Defense when the panel is equipped. The second number represents the additional Defense bonus for every Guard Unit(L) linked to the gear.*

★ ***Crit %:*** *The first number represents the bonus to your character's Critical% when the weapon is equipped. The second number represents the additional Critical% bonus for every Sight Unit(L) linked to the gear.*

★ ***Crit Bonus:*** *The first number represents the bonus to your character's Crit Bonus when the weapon is equipped. The second number represents the additional Critical Bonus for every Sight Unit(L) linked to the gear.*

★ ***Abilities:*** *Linking Ability Units(L) to a gear panel unlocks additional abilities, listed in this column alongside the number of Ability Units(L) required to unlock them.*

MENU PANELS

Icon	Name	Link	Str.	Mag.	Def.	Crit %	Crit Bonus	Abilities	Sell Price	Shop Price	How to Get It
	Skill Gear	LINK	*+5/—*	*—/—*	*—/—*	*+3/—*	*—/—*	—	—	—	*Completion reward (06)*
	Skill Gear+②	LINK	*+7/+1*	*—/+1*	*—/+1*	*+4/+1*	*—/+1*	*1(L): Combo Boost*	—	—	*Completion reward (13)*
	Technical Gear③	LINK	*+30/+1*	*—/+1*	*—/+1*	*+6/+1*	*+1/+1*	*1(L): Combo Boost; 2(L): Combo-Jump*	—	*720 (Novice; x1)*	—
	Technical Gear+③	LINK	*+35/+1*	*—/+1*	*—/+1*	*+8/+2*	*+2/+1*	*1(L): Chain Power; 2(L): Chain Time*	—	—	*Treasure chest (39)*
	Duel Gear④	LINK	*+56/+1*	*—/+1*	*—/+1*	*+12/+2*	*+6/+1*	*1(L): Chain Power; 2(L): Chain Time; 3(L): Heart Bonus*	1800	—	*Synthesis*
	Duel Gear+④	LINK	*+61/+1*	*—/+1*	*—/+1*	*+9/+2*	*+4/+1*	*1(L): Combo Boost; 2(L): Combo-Jump; 3(L): Critical Boost*	—	—	*Treasure chest (59)*
	Duel Gear++⑤	LINK	*+47/+1*	*—/+1*	*—/+1*	*+12/+5*	*+5/+0*	*1(L): Combo Boost; 2(L): Combo-Jump; 3(L): Critical Boost*	3200	—	*Synthesis*
	Loaded Gear	LINK	*+9/—*	*+12/—*	*—/—*	*+2/—*	*+1/—*	—	—	—	*Treasure chest (11)*
	Loaded Gear+②	LINK	*+40/+1*	*+15/+1*	*—/+1*	*+2/+1*	*+3/+1*	*1(L): Fire Finish*	—	—	*Treasure chest (16)*

MENU PANELS

Icon	Name	Link	Str.	Mag.	Def.	Crit %	Crit Bonus	Abilities	Sell Price	Shop Price	How to Get It
	Chrono Gear③	LINK	+45/+1	+18/+2	—/+1	+4/+1	+2/+1	1(L): Thunder Finish; 2(L): Magic Bracer	—	720 (Novice; x1)	—
	Chrono Gear+③	LINK	+47/+1	+25/+2	—/+1	+4/+1	+4/+1	1(L): Blizzard Finish; 2(L): Magic Bracer	360	—	Synthesis
	Phantom Gear④	LINK	+52/+1	+29/+1	—/+2	+6/+1	+4/+1	1(L): Fire Finish; 2(L): Magic Bracer; 3(L): Magic Finale	—	—	Treasure chest (45)
	Phantom Gear+④	LINK	+58/+1	+36/+1	—/+2	+6/+1	+7/+1	1(L): Thunder Finish; 2(L): Magic Bracer; 3(L): Magic Finale	—	—	Moogle Shop freebie
	Phantom Gear++⑤	LINK	+61/+1	+39/+5	—/+1	+8/+1	+9/+1	1(L): Magic Bracer; 2(L): Magic Finale; 3(L): Magical Strike	3200	—	Synthesis
	Lift Gear③	LINK	+40/+1	—/+1	—/+1	+4/+1	+2/+2	1(L): Combo Boost; 2(L): Combo-Jump	—	1080 (Novice; x1)	—
	Lift Gear+③	LINK	+45/+1	—/+1	—/+1	+4/+1	+1/+2	1(L): Chain Power; 2(L): Combo-Jump	—	—	Moogle Shop freebie
	Nimble Gear④	LINK	+39/+1	—/+1	—/+1	+6/+1	+2/+2	1(L): Chain Power; 2(L): Combo-Jump; 3(L): Combo-Air Slide	—	3600 (Rookie; x1)	—
	Nimble Gear+④	LINK	+55/+1	—/+1	—/+1	+6/+1	+2/+2	1(L): Combo Boost; 2(L): Combo-Jump; 3(L): Combo-Air Slide	1800	—	Synthesis
	Wild Gear③	LINK	+40/+1	—/+1	+4/+2	+2/+1	+1/+1	1(L): Offensive Block; 2(L): Defender	—	1080 (Novice; x1)	—
	Wild Gear+③	LINK	+50/+1	—/+1	+4/+2	+2/+1	+2/+1	1(L): Offensive Block; 2(L): Defender	—	—	Moogle Shop freebie
	Ominous Gear④	LINK	+37/+1	—/+1	+6/+2	+3/+1	+4/+1	1(L): Offensive Block; 2(L): Defender; 3(L): Second Chance	—	—	Treasure chest (15)
	Ominous Gear+④	LINK	+55/+1	—/+1	+6/+2	+3/+1	+3/+1	1(L): Offensive Block; 2(L): Defender; 3(L): Damage Control	1800	—	Synthesis
	Valor Gear②	LINK	+55/+1	—/+1	+1/+1	+2/+1	+3/+1	1(L): Defender	—	—	Treasure chest (29)
	Valor Gear+②	LINK	+60/+1	—/+1	+1/+1	—/+1	+4/+1	1(L): Striker	—	—	Moogle Shop freebie
	Fearless Gear③	LINK	+55/+2	—/+1	+2/+1	+4/+1	+4/+1	1(L): Defender; 2(L): Striker	—	2400 (Rookie; x1)	—
	Fearless Gear+③	LINK	+63/+2	—/+1	+2/+1	—/+1	+4/+1	1(L): Defender; 2(L): Striker	1200	—	Synthesis
	Prestige Gear④	LINK	+50/+2	—/+1	+3/+1	—/+1	+8/+1	1(L): Defender; 2(L): Striker; 3(L): Combo Block	—	3600 (Agent; x1)	—
	Prestige Gear+④	LINK	+55/+2	—/+1	+3/+1	+6/+1	+9/+1	1(L): Defender; 2(L): Striker; 3(L): Brick Wall	1800	—	Synthesis
	Crisis Gear⑤	LINK	+49/+3	+23/+3	+4/+1	+8/+1	+7/+1	1(L): Defender; 2(L): Combo-Block; 3(L): Brick Wall	3200	—	Synthesis
	Crisis Gear+⑤	LINK	+55/+3	+28/+3	+4/+1	—/+1	+8/+1	1(L): Defender; 2(L): Combo-Block; 3(L): Brick Wall	3200	—	Synthesis
	Omega Gear⑥	LINK	+85/+3	+31/+3	+5/+1	—/+1	+12/+1	1(L): Striker; 2(L): Grand Slam; 3(L): Damage Control	—	—	Moogle Shop freebie

MENU PANELS

Icon	Name	Link	Str.	Mag.	Def.	Crit %	Crit Bonus	Abilities	Sell Price	Shop Price	How to Get It
	Omega Gear+⑥	LINK	+95/+3	+34/+3	+5/+1	+10/+1	+13/+1	1(L): Magic Bracer; 2(L): Brick Wall; 3(L): Vitality Barrier	6200	—	Synthesis
	Hazard Gear⑤	LINK	+60/+1	+37/+3	+8/+3	+4/+1	+8/+1	1(L): Magic Bracer; 2(L): Vitality Barrier; 3(L): Damage Control	3200	—	Synthesis
	Hazard Gear+⑤	LINK	+85/+1	+45/+3	+8/+3	+4/+1	+10/+1	1(L): Fire Finish; 2(L): Thunder Finish; 3(L): Blizzard Finish	3200	—	Synthesis
	Rage Gear⑤	LINK	+73/+1	—/+1	—/+1	+10/+3	+6/+3	1(L): Chain Power; 2(L): Combo-Jump; 3(L): Combo-Air Slide	—	—	Moogle Shop freebie
	Rage Gear+⑤	LINK	+78/+1	—/+1	—/+1	+10/+3	+7/+3	1(L): Combo Boost; 2(L): Combo-Jump; 3(L): Combo-Air Slide	3200	—	Synthesis
	Champion Gear⑤	LINK	+65/+3	—/+1	+2/+1	+12/+3	+9/+1	1(L): Combo Boost; 2(L): Combo-Jump; 3(L): Critical Boost	3200	—	Synthesis
	Champion Gear+⑤	LINK	+85/+3	—/+1	+2/+1	+16/+3	+9/+1	1(L): Chain Power; 2(L): Chain Time; 3(L): Heart Bonus	—	6400 (Master; x1)	—
	Ultimate Gear⑥	LINK	+105/+3	—/+1	+3/+1	+20/+3	+12/+1	1(L): Combo-Jump; 2(L): Combo-Block; 3(L): Critical Boost	—	—	Moogle Shop freebie
	Ultimate Gear+⑥	LINK	+110/+3	—/+1	+3/+1	+15/+3	+14/+1	1(L): Combo Boost; 2(L): Chain Power; 3(L): Chain Time	6200	—	Synthesis
	Pandora's Gear⑤	LINK	+75/+5	+30/+5	—/+5	+10/+5	+9/+5	0(L): Risky Play; 1(L): Vitality Surge; 2(L): Vitality Barrier; 3(L): Alive 'n' Kicking	—	—	Moogle Shop freebie
	Pandora's Gear+⑤	LINK	+80/+1	+34/+1	—/+1	+10/+1	+10/+1	1(L): Vitality Surge; 2(L): Vitality Barrier; 3(L): Alive 'n' Kicking	3200	—	Synthesis
	Zero Gear⑤	LINK	+109/+4	+30/+4	—/+4	+10/+4	+17/+4	1(L): Defender; 2(L): Damage Control; 3(L): Second Chance	—	30,000 (Legend; x1)	—
	Casual Gear②	LINK	+25/+1	—/+1	—/+1	—/+1	+2/+1	1(L): Offensive Block	—	—	Moogle Shop freebie
	Mystery Gear③	LINK	+65/+1	—/+1	—/+1	+4/+5	+7/+5	1(L): Striker; 2(L): Grand Slam	—	—	Moogle Shop freebie

WEAPON PANELS (LINK PANELS)

Icon	Name	Sell Price	Shop Price	How to Get It	Effect
	Ability Unit(L)	—	360 (Rookie, 1x)	Completion reward (15, 30)	Links to your weapon panel and unlocks one of its hidden abilities
	Power Unit(L)	—	180 (Novice, 1x); 480 (Agent, 1x); 2500 (Legend; 1x)	Treasure chest (13); Moogle Shop freebie	Links to your weapon panel and increases Strength; the amount varies between weapons
	Magic Unit(L)	—	480 (Rookie, 1x); 800 (Expert, 1x); 2500 (Legend, 1x)	Completion reward (73); Moogle Shop freebie	Links to your weapon panel and increases Magic; the amount varies between weapons
	Guard Unit(L)	—	480 (Agent, 1x); 800 (Expert, 1x); 2500 (Legend, 1x)	Completion reward (20), Moogle Shop freebie	Links to your weapon panel and increases Defense; the amount varies between weapons
	Sight Unit(L)	—	—	Completion reward (44, 90); treasure chest (32, 48, 82)	Links to your weapon panel and increases Critical% and Crit Bonus; the amount varies between weapons

TIPS FOR PLACING WEAPON PANELS

Each weapon has different abilities for every character who uses it. This isn't immediately obvious at the start of the game, but as you proceed through your adventure, you will notice that the weapon panels can be customized significantly by linking other panels to them. The "Characters" section of the guide has detailed information about the weapon abilities for each playable character.

RING MENU PANELS

There are 54 different ring panels, but you can only equip one at a time. A ring panel is an accessory panel that bestows a stat boost and/or additional abilities on your character. These are the panels that you are most apt to change between missions, since a simple substitution can radically enhance your character's ability to fight certain enemies and resist their attacks.

MENU PANELS

Icon	Name	Sell Price	Shop Price	How to Get It	Effect
	Sign of Resolve	—	—	*Completion reward (12)*	*HP +10, Strength +1, Magic +1, Defense +4*
	Brawl Ring	—	*270 (Novice, x1)*	—	*Defense +8, Combo-Jump*
	Magic Ring	225	—	*Synthesis*	*Magic +3, Defense +6, Ether Boost*
	Soldier Ring	—	*450 (Novice, x1)*	—	*Strength +3, Defense +8, Combo Boost*
	Fencer's Ring	600	—	*Synthesis*	*HP +20, Defense +8, Potion Boost LV1*
	Fire Charm	600	—	*Synthesis*	*Defense +8, 30% Fire resistance, Magic Bracer*
	Flower Charm	—	*1200 (Rookie, x1)*	—	*HP +15, Strength +2, Defense +10, 30% flower resistance, Magic Bracer*
	Strike Ring	1200	—	*Synthesis*	*Defense +10, Critical% +5, Crit Bonus +5*
	Lucky Ring	1200	—	*Synthesis*	*Defense +16, Prize Power LV1, Heart Bonus*
	Blizzard Charm	—	*2400 (Rookie, x1)*	—	*Strength +4, Defense +12, 30% ice resistance, Magic Bracer*
	White Ring	1200	—	*Synthesis*	*Magic +4, Defense +12, Prize Power LV2*
	Knight's Defense	—	*2400 (Agent, x1)*	—	*Defense +12, Combo-Block, EXP Boost LV1*
	Raider's Ring	1400	—	*Synthesis*	*Defense +18, Combo-Jump, Combo-Block*
	Thunder Charm	1400	—	*Synthesis*	*Defense +14, 30% lightning resistance, Magic Bracer*
	Recovery Ring	1400	—	*Synthesis*	*HP +40, Defense +16, Vitality Barrier, Potion Boost LV1*
	Vitality Ring	1400	—	*Synthesis*	*Magic +6, Defense +16, Vitality Surge, Ether Boost*
	Rainforce Ring	—	*3000 (Expert, x1)*	—	*Strength +6, Defense +16, Thunder Finish*
	Double Up	1500	—	*Synthesis*	*Defense +18, EXP Boost LV2*
	Storm's Eye	1500	—	*Synthesis*	*Defense +18, 30% Wind resistance, 30% Water resistance, Magic Bracer*
	Critical Ring	—	*4000 (Expert, x1)*	—	*Defense +20, Critical% +8, Crit Bonus +8, Striker*

MENU PANELS

Icon	Name	Sell Price	Shop Price	How to Get It	Effect
	Fairy Circle	2000	—	Synthesis	Defense +20, 30% Space resistance, 30% flip-foot resistance, 30% Time resistance
	Full Circle	2000	—	Synthesis	Defense +24, 20% resistance to all elements
	Lucky Star	—	4400 (Master, x1)	—	Defense +24, Prize Power LV2, Lucky Strike
	Charge Ring	2200	—	Synthesis	Defense +26, Potion Boost LV1, Ether Boost
	Eternal Ring	2200	—	Synthesis	HP +30, Strength +4, Defense +28, Chain Time
	Carmine Blight	2200	—	Synthesis	Strength +8, Defense +30, Fire Finish
	Frozen Blight	2200	—	Synthesis	Magic +8, Defense +30, Blizzard Finish
	Safety Ring	2200	—	Synthesis	Defense +30, Potion Boost LV2
	Princess's Crown	—	10,000 (Legend, x1)	—	HP +60, Defense +30, Potion Boost LV1, EXP Boost LV2
	Lunar Strike	3000	—	Synthesis	Defense +30, Critical% +10, Crit Bonus +10, 30% Moon resistance
	Crimson Blood	—	—	Moogle Shop reward	Strength +8, Defense +30, Grand Slam
	Deep Sky	—	12,000 (Legend, x1)	—	Magic +8, Defense +30, Combo-Air Slide, Aero Finish
	Protect Ring	3000	—	Synthesis	Defense +30, Defender
	Might Crown	3000	—	Synthesis	HP +80, Defense +30, 10% resistance to all elements, EXP Boost LV1
	Critical Sun	—	13,000 (Legend, x1)	—	Defense +10, Critical% +15, Crit Bonus +20, Critical Boost
	Three Stars	3000	—	Synthesis	Defense +30, Potion Boost LV1, Lucky Strike, EXP Boost LV1
	Imperial Crown	3000	—	Synthesis	HP +100, Defense +10, Brick Wall, Magic Finale
	Witch's Chaos	3000	—	Synthesis	Strength +20, Defense +10, Damage Control, Elemental Curse
	Rune Ring	—	—	Moogle Shop reward	Magic +20, Defense +10, Second Chance, Elemental Curse
	Extreme	3000	—	Synthesis	One HP, Hi-EXP Boost
	Master's Circle	—	—	Moogle Shop reward	Defense +30, 100% resistance to all elements, Risky Play, Perma-Plight
	Nothing to Fear	3000	—	Synthesis	Defense +30, 100% Nil resistance
	Space in Its Place	3000	—	Synthesis	Defense +30, 100% Space resistance
	Flagging Winds	3000	—	Synthesis	Defense +30, 100% Wind resistance
	Ice Breaker	3000	—	Synthesis	Defense +30, 100% Ice resistance
	Down to Earth	3000	—	Synthesis	Defense +30, 100% Earth resistance

MENU PANELS

Icon	Name	Sell Price	Shop Price	How to Get It	Effect
	Lose Your Illusion	3000	—	*Synthesis*	*Defense +30, 100% flip-foot resistance*
	Sighing of the Moon	3000	—	*Synthesis*	*Defense +30, 100% Moon resistance*
	Tears of Flame	3000	—	*Synthesis*	*Defense +30, 100% Fire resistance*
	Parting of Waters	3000	—	*Synthesis*	*Defense +30, 100% Water resistance*
	Test of Time	3000	—	*Synthesis*	*Defense +30, 100% Time resistance*
	Flowers Athirst	3000	—	*Synthesis*	*Defense +30, 100% Flower resistance*
	Stolen Thunder	3000	—	*Synthesis*	*Defense +30, 100% Lightning resistance*
	Dying of the Light	3000	—	*Synthesis*	*Defense +30, 100% Light resistance*

MATERIAL MENU PANELS

Material panels are the only panels that you don't equip on the Panels Menu. Instead, they are used in the Moogle Shop where you can synthesize new panels from them. For more information on panel synthesis, see the "Synthesis" chapter that follows this one.

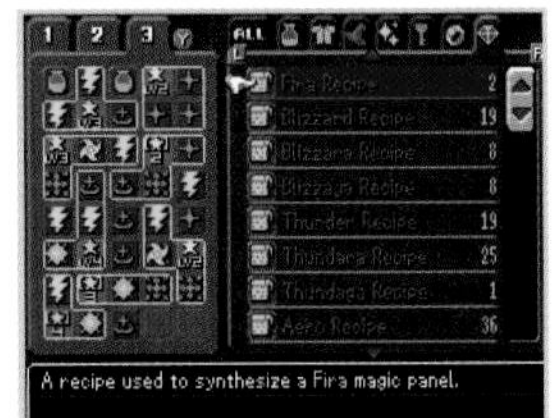

MENU PANELS

Icon	Name	Sell Price	Shop Price	How to Get It
	Fire Recipe	100	—	*Completion reward (10, 12, 26, 33, 68); random reward (01-14, 17, 20, 23, 25, 44); treasure chest (09, 48, 55, 73, 75, 86)*
	Fira Recipe	150	—	*Completion reward (44); random reward (61), treasure chest (75, 85)*
	Firaga Recipe	200	—	*Completion reward (84); random reward (79, 82, 87, 88, 90); treasure chest (84)*
	Blizzard Recipe	100	—	*Completion reward (35, 48, 68); random reward (48, 68); treasure chest (30, 32, 35, 42, 47, 48, 62, 68)*
	Blizzara Recipe	150	—	*Completion reward (85); random reward (52, 54, 62, 66, 72); treasure chest (52, 62, 68)*
	Blizzaga Recipe	200	—	*Completion reward (85, 88); random reward (73, 81, 84, 85); treasure chest (81)*
	Thunder Recipe	100	—	*Completion reward (38, 45); random reward (52, 54, 62, 66, 72); treasure chest (41, 44, 49, 52, 56, 59, 62, 72, 79)*
	Thundara Recipe	150	—	*Completion reward (69); random reward (71, 91, 93); treasure chest (68, 69, 91)*
	Thundaga Recipe	200	—	*Completion reward (77); random reward (73, 84); treasure chest (66, 87)*
	Aero Recipe	100	—	*Random reward (51, 55, 57, 63, 65, 67, 69); treasure chest (39, 40, 43, 48, 51, 57, 63, 65, 67)*

MENU PANELS

Icon	Name	Sell Price	Shop Price	How to Get It
	Aerora Recipe	150	—	Completion reward (38, 71); random reward (71, 91, 93); treasure chest (64, 67, 82, 91)
	Aeroga Recipe	200	—	Completion reward (83); random reward (64, 74, 75, 89, 92); treasure chest (74, 83)
	Cure Recipe	100	—	Completion reward (40); random reward (51, 55, 57, 63, 65, 67, 69); treasure chest (23, 40, 42, 43, 46, 49, 50, 55, 63, 65)
	Cura Recipe	150	—	Completion reward (53, 58, 61); random reward (51, 55, 57, 63, 65, 67, 69); treasure chest (51, 55, 65)
	Curaga Recipe	200	—	Completion reward (68, 86); random reward (76, 77, 78, 80, 83, 86); treasure chest (76)
	Elixir Recipe	100	—	Completion reward (16, 46); random reward (38, 43, 49, 50, 51, 53, 55-60, 68, 70, 71); treasure chest (38, 43, 49); enemy (38, 41-44, 54, 55, 57, 59, 61)
	Megalixir Recipe	200	—	Completion reward (64); random reward (73, 76, 77, 78, 79, 84, 86, 87, 88, 91, 93); enemy (79, 83, 87, 89, 90)
	Blazing Shard	100	—	Completion reward (08, 11, 17, 23, 29, 33, 34); random reward (01-14, 17, 20, 23, 25); treasure chest (05, 09, 11, 14, 17, 23, 25); enemy (05, 06, 07, 11, 12, 14, 15, 16, 18, 21, 24, 30, 32, 34, 36, 39, 48)
	Blazing Gem	400	—	Completion reward (52, 70); random reward (52, 54, 62, 66, 72); treasure chest (52, 62); enemy (51, 61, 68, 74, 77, 83, 89)
	Blazing Crystal	800	—	Completion reward (83, 90); random reward (70, 80, 83); treasure chest (66, 83); enemy (63, 67, 72, 74, 75, 82, 89, 90)
	Frost Shard	100	—	Completion reward (14, 17, 19, 23, 24, 28, 30, 31, 33, 35); random reward (22, 27, 28, 29, 31, 35); treasure chest (22, 27, 28, 29, 31, 60); enemy (17, 21, 23, 26, 27, 30, 31, 32, 34, 42, 44, 45, 46, 48, 52, 58)
	Frost Gem	400	—	Completion reward (54); random reward (52, 54, 70); treasure chest (52, 66); enemy (51, 52, 53, 54, 57, 58, 60, 61, 62, 72)
	Frost Crystal	800	—	Completion reward (75, 79, 81); random reward (76, 77, 78, 86); treasure chest (76); enemy (73, 74, 76, 77, 79, 83)
	Lightning Shard	100	—	Completion reward (36, 40, 43, 47, 48, 82); random reward (36, 39, 40, 41, 46, 61); treasure chest (36, 39, 46, 61); enemy (38, 42, 44, 45, 46, 47, 50, 59, 61)
	Lightning Gem	400	—	Completion reward (59, 67, 72, 82); random reward (61); treasure chest (61); enemy (52, 54, 61, 62, 68)
	Lightning Crystal	800	—	Completion reward (73, 74, 87); random reward (79, 87, 88); treasure chest (79, 87); enemy (77, 79, 83, 89)
	Gust Shard	100	—	Completion reward (41, 42, 54, 60); random reward (42, 45, 52, 54); treasure chest (42, 45, 52, 54); enemy (38, 40, 43, 47, 53, 58)
	Gust Gem	400	—	Completion reward (45, 47, 61, 71); random reward (52, 54, 62, 66, 72); treasure chest (52, 62, 66); enemy (62, 63, 70, 73)
	Gust Crystal	800	—	Random reward (63, 65, 67, 69, 81, 85); treasure chest (63, 81, 85); enemy (73, 76, 87)
	Shining Shard	100	—	Completion reward (07, 09, 15, 16, 17, 19, 22, 26, 31, 34); random reward (15, 16, 18, 19, 21, 24, 26, 30, 32, 34); treasure chest (7, 16, 21, 24, 34); enemy (13, 17, 19, 22, 23, 27, 28, 29, 31, 32, 38, 48, 49, 59)
	Shining Gem	400	—	Completion reward (55, 70, 80); random reward (51, 55, 57, 63, 65, 67, 69); treasure chest (51, 57); enemy (53, 56, 58, 60, 64, 66)
	Shining Crystal	800	—	Completion reward (70, 80); random reward (62, 66, 72, 79, 87, 88); treasure chest (66, 87); enemy (73, 75, 76, 77, 79, 82, 84, 86, 89)
	Gear Component A	100	—	Completion reward (32, 39, 45, 49, 51); random reward (38, 43, 49, 50); treasure chest (36, 38, 41, 49); enemy (36, 38, 41, 42)
	Gear Component B	300	—	Completion reward (55, 57, 65, 71); random reward (61); treasure chest (55, 56, 59); enemy (51, 55, 56, 57, 59, 61)
	Gear Component C	600	—	Completion reward (75); random reward (64); treasure chest (64, 73); enemy (62, 63, 65, 66, 72)
	Gear Component D	1000	—	Random reward (74, 75, 89, 92); treasure chest (74, 75, 89); enemy (82, 84, 90)

MENU PANELS

Icon	Name	Sell Price	Shop Price	How to Get It
	Combo Tech	500	—	Completion reward (28, 60); random reward (53, 58, 60); treasure chest (29); enemy (23, 29, 31, 34, 38, 43, 44, 45)
	Combo Tech+	800	—	Completion reward (62, 72); enemy (64, 67)
	Combo Tech++	1200	—	Completion reward (64, 73, 85); enemy (63, 75, 83, 89)
	Shield Tech	500	—	Completion reward (39, 41); enemy (40, 44, 48, 49, 54, 56, 57)
	Shield Tech+	800	—	Completion reward (62); random reward (62, 66, 72); enemy (65, 70, 83)
	Shield Tech++	1200	—	Enemy (74, 85, 87, 90)
	Rune Tech	500	—	Completion reward (39, 48); enemy (47, 55)
	Rune Tech+	800	—	Completion reward (50, 63, 65, 67, 76); enemy (65, 67)
	Rune Tech++	1200	—	Completion reward (81); enemy (85, 89)
	Power Tech	500	—	Completion reward (59); enemy (38, 48, 49, 50, 56, 59, 61)
	Power Tech+	800	—	Completion reward (66, 72, 76, 78); enemy (58)
	Power Tech++	1200	—	Completion reward (81, 90); enemy (83)
	Aerial Tech	500	—	Completion reward (25); enemy (17, 20, 23, 27, 31, 32, 34, 47)
	Aerial Tech+	800	—	Enemy (62, 65)
	Aerial Tech++	1200	—	Enemy (79, 81, 85)
	Range Tech	500	—	Completion reward (60); enemy (40, 44, 48, 49, 51, 55, 57)
	Range Tech+	800	—	Enemy (63, 68, 75)
	Range Tech++	1200	—	Enemy (79, 91)
	Ankharite	3000	—	Completion reward (86); enemy (73)
	Luck Tech	3000	—	Completion reward (25, 53, 80); treasure chest (90); enemy (74, 76, 77, 81, 85, 86)
	Iron	100	200 (Novice, x1)	Completion reward (18, 20, 27); random reward (15, 16, 18, 19, 21, 24, 26, 30, 32, 34, 37); treasure chest (08, 21, 24, 26, 32, 34, 47); enemy (07, 13, 16, 22, 23, 25, 27, 28, 29, 30, 35, 38, 42, 44, 54, 57, 59, 61)
	Bronze	300	600 (Rookie, x1)	Completion reward (35, 49, 50, 51, 53); random reward (38, 43, 49, 50, 56, 59); treasure chest (43, 46, 49, 50); enemy (49, 50, 55, 56, 58, 61, 72)
	Dark Ingot	600	1200 (Agent, x1)	Completion reward (55, 57, 58); random reward (51, 55, 57); treasure chest (51, 57); enemy (52, 57, 59, 74, 76, 81)
	Silver	1200	2400 (Expert, x1)	Completion reward (64, 66, 67, 69, 78); random reward (62, 66, 72); treasure chest (62, 66); enemy (64, 67, 80)
	Gold	2400	4800 (Master, x1)	Completion reward (77); random reward (82, 90); treasure chest (82); enemy (73, 81, 88, 89)
	Mithril	3800	—	Completion reward (79, 84, 87); random reward (76, 77, 78, 86); enemy (85, 90)

MENU PANELS

Icon	Name	Sell Price	Shop Price	How to Get It
	Orichalcum	5300	—	Completion reward (83, 89); random reward (74, 75, 89, 92); enemy (82)
	Moonstone	50	100 (Novice, unlimited)	Completion reward (07, 13, 32, 59, 63); random reward (01-14, 17, 20, 23, 25, 44, 56, 59); treasure chest (14, 23, 25); enemy (02, 03, 04, 07, 09, 11, 12, 14, 17, 23, 25, 59, 61)
	Diamond	1000	2000 (Expert, unlimited)	Completion reward (62, 63, 87, 89); random reward (63, 65, 67, 69, 81, 85); treasure chest (16, 63, 65, 81); enemy (81, 82, 83, 90)
	Adamantite	2500	5000 (Master, unlimited)	Completion reward (74, 79); treasure chest (82, 90); enemy (73, 74, 76, 89)
	Premium Orb	5800	—	Completion reward (89); random reward (63, 65, 67, 69); treasure chest (66); enemy (73, 89)

CREATING & STORING PANEL DECKS

Once you get into the more advanced missions, it's a real time-saver to customize decks of panels for use against certain enemies and save them for future reference. For example, if you know from the mission description that you'll be facing a lot of enemies that are vulnerable to fire, you can customize panel decks specifically for that purpose. Saving a deck is also a good idea if you have a good deck that you want to improve upon, without running the risk of losing it.

To save a panel deck, press START at the Panels Menu to open the submenu, and then choose "Store This Deck." You can have up to three saved decks at a time. To load a deck, choose "Retrieve a Deck" from the submenu. If you want to create a deck from scratch, choose "Clear All Slots."

GENERAL TIPS FOR PLACING PANELS

Deck customization and experimentation are strongly encouraged, but there are a few panels that you'll almost always want to be sure to equip:

- ★ ***Level Up.*** *Link Level Up panels to LV Doubler, LV Tripler and LV Quadrupler panels as often as possible. This boosts your character's level, and the higher it is, the higher your character's stats will be across the board.*
- ★ ***Backpack.*** *This increases the number of rewards you can bring back from missions. Linking it to a Pack Extender④ expands it even further.*
- ★ ***Block②*** *or* ***Block④****. This allows you to block enemy attacks (if the attack can be blocked) during combat. Removing Dodge Roll makes it easier to execute Blocks. Blocking some attacks deflects them back at the enemy or interrupts the enemy's attack. See the enemy profiles for more information about whether or not an enemy's attacks can be blocked.*
- ★ ***Air Slide②*** *or* ***Air Slide⑤****. Enables your character to perform an aerial dash while in mid-air. Link Air Slide LV+(L) to level it up. You can use it in conjunction with Glide to boost airspeed.*
- ★ ***Glide③*** *or* ***Glide⑤****. With this ability active, your character can glide through the air while in midair, which is a great technique for avoiding enemy attacks that you cannot block. Link Glide LV+(L) to level it up.*
- ★ ***High Jump*** *or* ***High Jump③****. There are certain areas that you cannot reach without this ability. Plus, it also makes it easier to navigate areas that have many different levels, like Agrabah and Wonderland. You can boost High Jump③ by placing High Jump LV+(L) in its link area.*
- ★ ***Limit Boost.*** *This valuable ability increases the upper limit of your character's yellow HP gauge, making it possible to use powerful Limit Breaks sooner than usual.*
- ★ ***Final Limit.*** *This ability enables your character to add a much more powerful Final Limit attack to his/her normal Limit Break.*
- ★ ***Scan.*** *As long as you have this in your panel grid, an enemy's HP is displayed and information about it will appear in the Enemy Profiles after you defeat that type of foe for the first time.*

ABILITIES

What follows is a comprehensive list of all the abilities available during the Story Mode adventure. All of the non-weapon panel abilities apply universally to every character in Mission Mode. Refer to the "Characters" chapter at the start of this guide to see how the various weapon panels modify their weapons and abilities in Mission Mode.

Abilities

Ability	Panels	Description
Dodge Roll LV1-3	Dodge Roll or Dodge Roll③	Hold d-pad and press Y to roll forward and avoid enemy attacks; level up by linking Dodge Roll LV+(L)
Dodge Rush	Dodge Roll③ & Dodge Rush(L)	Knock enemies aside when you perform a Dodge Roll
Dodging Deflect	Dodge Roll③ & Dodging Deflect(L)	Bounce back enemy attacks when you do a Dodge Roll
Dodge Combo	Dodge Roll③ & Dodge Combo(L)	Transition swiftly from a Dodge Roll back to the offensive
Auto-Dodge	Dodge Roll③ & Auto-Dodge(L)	Automatically avoid enemy attacks sometimes
Block LV1-4	Block② or Block ④	Press Y to block and bounce back enemy attacks; level up by linking Block LV+(L)
Perfect Block	Block②/④ & Perfect Block(L)	Block just as an attack hits to eliminate recoil and transition into your next move
Block-Counter	Block②/④ & Block-Counter(L)	Respond with a powerful counterattack immediately after blocking
Block-Retreat	Block②/④ & Block-Retreat(L)	Recoil farther after you block an attack
Sliding Block	Block②/④ & Sliding Block(L)	Quickly slide forward as you block
Block-Jump	Block②/④ & Block-Jump(L)	Jump right after you block with no delay
Fire Block	Block②/④ & Fire Block(L)	Ignite enemies sometimes when blocking (15% base chance)
Blizzard Block	Block②/④ & Blizzard Block(L)	Freeze enemies sometimes when blocking (15% base chance)
Thunder Block	Block②/④ & Thunder Block(L)	Jolt enemies sometimes when blocking (15% base chance)
Aero Block	Block②/④ & Aero Block(L)	Air-toss enemies sometimes when blocking (15% base chance)
Block Bonus	Block②/④ & Block Bonus(L)	Generate HP Prizes sometimes when blocking
Round Block	Block②/④ & Round Block(L)	Block any attack, even if it comes from behind
Auto-Block	Block②/④ & Auto-Block(L)	Automatically block frontal attacks
Aerial Recovery LV1-3	Aerial Recovery or Aerial Recovery③	Press B if you are sent flying to regain your balance; level up by linking A. Recovery LV+(L)
Quick Recovery	Aerial Recovery③ & Quick Recovery(L)	Recover more quickly by pressing B as soon as you are sent flying
Aerial Payback	Aerial Recovery③ & Aerial Payback(L)	Respond with a powerful counterattack immediately after you perform an Air Recovery
Smash Recovery	Aerial Recovery③ & Smash Recovery(L)	Knock away nearby enemies when you perform an Air Recovery
Air Slide LV1-5	Air Slide② or Air Slide⑤	Press B while in midair to perform an aerial dash; level up with Air Slide LV+(L)
Air Rush	Air Slide②/⑤ & Air Rush(L)	Knock enemies aside when you perform an Air Slide

Abilities

Ability	Panels	Description
Sliding Dash LV1-3	Sliding Dash or Sliding Dash③	Press A to quickly close in on a target and attack; level up with Sliding Dash LV+(L)
Glide LV1-5	Glide③ or Glide⑤	Hold Y while in midair to ride the wind; you will stay airborne until you release the button; level up with Glide LV+(L)
Homing Glide	Glide③/⑤ & Homing Glide(L)	Lock on to a target while gliding to automatically move toward it
Rocket Glide	Glide③/⑤ & Rocket Glide(L)	Slam past enemies by gliding right after you perform an Air Slide (Air Slide ability must be equipped)
Haste LV1-3	Haste or Haste③	Run faster; level up with Haste LV+(L)
High Jump LV1-3	High Jump or High Jump③	Jump higher; level up with High Jump LV+(L)
Float	Float(L)	Hold B while in midair to slow your descent
Treasure Magnet LV1-3	Treasure Magnet or Treasure Magnet③	Scoop up prizes lying around you; level up with T. Magnet LV+(L)
Auto-Life LV1-3	Auto-Life③	Recover if all your character's HP runs out; only works once per mission; level up with Auto-Life LV+(L)
Limit Boost	Limit Boost	Use Limit Breaks sooner by increasing the upper limit of your yellow gauge
Final Limit	Final Limit	Use your Final Limit, a more powerful version of the Limit Break
Scan	Scan	View the HP of targets
Range Extender	Range Extender	Lock on to enemies even if they are far away
Auto-Lock	Auto-Lock	Automatically lock on to available targets while attacking
Ultima Weapon	Ultima Weapon	Increases weapon's attack power by 15
Brick Wall	Prestige Gear+④ & 3x Ability Unit(L); OR Crisis Gear⑤/+⑤ & 3x Ability Unit(L); OR Omega Gear+⑥ & 2x Ability Unit(L); OR Imperial Crown	Continue a combo without interruption even if you take minor damage
Offensive Block	Wild Gear③/+③ & Ability Unit(L); OR Ominous Gear④/+④ & Ability Unit(L); OR Casual Gear② & Ability Unit(L)	Bounce back incoming attacks with your combos
Combo-Jump	Technical Gear③ & Ability Unit(L) x2; OR Duel Gear+④/++⑤ & Ability Unit(L) x2; OR Lift Gear③/+③ & Ability Unit(L) x2; OR Nimble Gear④/+④ & Ability Unit(L) x2; OR Rage Gear⑤/+⑤ & Ability Unit(L) x2; OR Champion Gear⑤ & Ability Unit(L) x2; OR Ultimate Gear⑥ & Ability Unit(L); OR Brawl Ring; OR Raider's Ring	Jump in the middle of a combo
Combo-Block	Prestige Gear④ & Ability Unit(L) x3; OR Crisis Gear⑤/+⑤ & Ability Unit(L) x2; OR Ultimate Gear⑥ & Ability Unit(L) x2; OR Knight's Defense; OR Raider's Ring	Block mid-combo by releasing d-pad and pressing Y (Block ability must be equipped)
Combo Air-Slide	Nimble Gear④/+④ & Ability Unit(L) x3; OR Rage Gear⑤/+⑤ & Ability Unit(L) x3; OR Deep Sky	Air Slide in the middle of an aerial combo by pressing B (Air Slide ability must be equipped)
Risky Play	Pandora's Gear⑤ or Master's Circle	Lose HP when your attacks miss; allows you to intentionally drain your own HP to trigger Limit Break
Magical Strike	Phantom Gear++⑤ & Ability Unit(L) x3	Gain a slight boost in Strength if your Magic is higher
Critical Boost	Duel Gear+④/++⑤ & Ability Unit(L) x3; OR Champion Gear⑤ & Ability Unit(L) x3; OR Ultimate Gear⑥ & Ability Unit(L) x3; OR Critical Sun	Potentially deal critical hits with any kind of attack
Combo Boost	Skill Gear+② & Ability Unit(L); OR Technical Gear③ & Ability Unit(L); OR Duel Gear+④/++④ & Ability Unit(L); OR Lift Gear③ & Ability Unit(L); OR Nimble Gear+④ & Ability Unit(L); OR Rage Gear+⑤ & Ability Unit(L); Champion Gear⑤ & Ability Unit(L); OR Soldier Ring	Dish out increasingly higher damage as your combo continues
Vitality Surge	Pandora's Gear⑤/+⑤ & Ability Unit(L); OR Vitality Ring	Gain a boost in Strength when your HP is full
Vitality Barrier	Omega Gear+⑥ & Ability Unit(L) x3; OR Hazard Gear⑤ & Ability Unit(L) x2; OR Pandora's Gear⑤/+⑤ & Ability Unit(L) x2; OR Recovery Ring	Take one-third the usual damage when your HP is full
Alive 'n' Kicking	Pandora's Gear⑤/+⑤ & Ability Unit(L) x3	Attack enemies when your HP is full, and they will always stagger

Abilities

Ability	Panels	Description
Striker	Valor Gear+② & Ability Unit(L); OR Fearless Gear③/+③ & Ability Unit(L) x2; Prestige Gear④/+④ & Ability Unit(L) x2; OR Crisis Gear+⑤ & Ability Unit(L); OR Omega Gear⑥ & Ability Unit(L); Mystery Gear③ & Ability Unit(L); OR Critical Ring	Gain a boost in Strength when your HP is low
Defender	Wild Gear③/+③ & Ability Unit(L) x2; OR Ominous Gear④/+④ & Ability Unit(L) x2; Valor Gear② & Ability Unit(L); OR Fearless Gear③/+③ & Ability Unit(L); OR Prestige Gear④/+④ & Ability Unit(L); Crisis Gear⑤ & Ability Unit(L); Zero Gear⑤ & Ability Unit(L); OR Protect Ring	Gain a boost in Defense when your HP is low
Grand Slam	Omega Gear⑥ & Ability Unit(L) x2; OR Mystery Gear③ & Ability Unit(L) x2; OR Crimson Blood	Deals critical hits more often when your HP is low
Damage Control	Ominous Gear+④ & Ability Unit(L) x3; OR Omega Gear⑥ & Ability Unit(L) x3; OR Hazard Gear⑤ & Ability Unit(L) x3; Zero Gear⑤ & Ability Unit(L) x2; OR Witch's Chaos	Take half the usual damage when your HP is low
Second Chance	Ominous Gear④ & Ability Unit(L) x3; OR Zero Gear⑤ & Ability Unit(L) x3; OR Rune Ring	Retain 1 HP after being hit with an otherwise fatal attack
Perma-Plight	Master's Circle	Lose the ability to recover HP when it is low, and remain in constant peril
One HP	Extreme	Fight with only 1 HP; you cannot recover more than this
Fire Finish	Loaded Gear+② & Ability Unit(L); OR Phantom Gear④ & Ability Unit(L); OR Hazard Gear+⑤ & Ability Unit(L); OR Carmine Blight	Ignite enemies sometimes with the finishing blow of your combos
Blizzard Finish	Chrono Gear+③ & Ability Unit(L); OR Hazard Gear+⑤ & Ability Unit(L) x2; OR Frozen Blight	Freeze enemies sometimes with the finishing blow of your combos
Thunder Finish	Chrono Gear③ & Ability Unit(L); OR Phantom Gear+④ & Ability Unit(L); OR Hazard Gear+⑤ & Ability Unit(L) x2; OR Rainforce Ring	Jolt enemies sometimes with the finishing blow of your combos
Aero Finish	Deep Sky	Air-toss enemies sometimes with the finishing blow of your combos
Elemental Curse	Witch's Chaos or Rune Ring	Randomly incur negative status independently of enemy attacks
Magic Finale	Phantom Gear④/+④ & Ability Unit(L) x3; OR Phantom Gear++⑤ & Ability Unit(L) x2; OR Imperial Crown	Increase the power of the last cast you have left of any given magic
Magic Bracer	Chrono Gear③/+③ & Ability Unit(L) x2; OR Phantom Gear④/+④ & Ability Unit(L) x2; OR Phantom Gear++⑤ & Ability Unit(L); OR Omega Gear+⑥ & Ability Unit(L); Hazard Gear⑤ & Ability Unit(L); OR Fire Charm; OR Flower Charm; OR Blizzard Charm; OR Thunder Charm; OR Storm's Eye	Always finish casting magic, even if you are hit in the process
Potion Boost LV1	Fencer's Ring; OR Recovery Ring; OR Charge Ring; OR Princess's Crown; OR Three Stars	Recover more HP than usual from items
Potion Boost LV2	Safety Ring	Recover even more HP than usual from items
Ether Boost	Magic Ring; OR Vitality Ring; OR Charge Ring	Recover more magic casts than usual from items
Prize Power LV1	Lucky Ring	Recover more HP when you pick up HP prizes
Prize Power LV2	White Ring or Lucky Star	Recover even more HP when you pick up HP prizes
Lucky Strike	Lucky Star or Three Stars	Force enemies to drop items more quickly
Chain Time	Technical Gear+③ & Ability Unit(L) x2; OR Duel Gear④ & Ability Unit(L) x2; OR Champion Gear+⑤ & Ability Unit(L); Ultimate Gear+⑥ & Ability Unit(L) x3; OR Eternal Ring	Give yourself a longer time window for continuing chains
Chain Power	Technical Gear+③ & Ability Unit(L); OR Duel Gear④ & Ability Unit(L); OR Lift Gear③ & Ability Unit(L); OR Nimble Gear④ & Ability Unit(L); OR Rage Gear⑤ & Ability Unit(L); OR Champion Gear+⑤ & Ability Unit(L); OR Ultimate Gear+⑥ & Ability Unit(L) x2	Deal extra damage with attacks once you've maxed out a chain
Heart Bonus	Duel Gear④ & Ability Unit(L) x3; OR Champion Gear+⑤ & Ability Unit(L) x3; OR Lucky Ring	Fully recover HP every time you collect 300 hearts
EXP Boost LV1	Knight's Defense; OR Might Crown; OR Three Stars	Receive more EXP than usual (10% bonus)
EXP Boost LV2	Double Up or Princess Crown	Receive even more EXP than usual (20% bonus)
Hi-EXP Boost	Extreme	Receive twice as much EXP as usual
Backpack	Backpack	Collect more items while in the field

THE MOOGLE SHOP

The Moogle Shop is an extremely important destination for your panel needs. Many panels can be purchased at the Moogle Shop, but you must have enough hearts to pay for them. Some panels are not available for purchase until you have attained a certain ranking. (See the previous panel tables for information on which panels can be purchased, their cost, and what rank your character needs to be in order to buy them.)

If you have a surplus of panels that you want to cash in, you can sell them at the Moogle Shop as well. Note that you buy panels with hearts, but you sell them for munny.

Instead of selling panels, you can transform them into other panels using the Synthesize option. See the "Synthesis" chapter that follows this one for more information on panel synthesis.

Finally, as you earn Challenge Sigils and Mission Crowns, you can claim "freebie" panels from the Moogle Shop. Choose the "Redeem" option from the Moogle Shop menu to see if any new freebies are available. You can only claim a freebie item once. (Refer to the "Mission Walkthrough" chapter for more information on how to earn Challenge Sigils and Mission Crowns.)

SLOT RELEASERS

A Slot Releaser is a special item that opens up another slot on your panel pages, allowing you to equip an additional panel on your character.

Challenge Sigil Freebies

Freebie	Sigils Required
Slot Releaser	5
Haste	10
Casual Gear②	15
Fire x3	20
Cure x3	25
Slot Releaser	30
Thunder x3	35
Wild Gear+③	40
Fira x2	45
Slot Releaser	50
Thundara x2	60
Phantom Gear④	70
Slot Releaser	80
Level Up	90
Haste③	100
Haste LV+(L)	110
Rage Gear⑤	120
Slot Releaser	130
Level Up	140
Glide⑤	150
Omega Gear⑥	160
Glide LV+(L)	170
LV Doubler⑥	180
Slot Releaser	190
Haste LV+(L)	200
Level Up	210
LV Tripler④	220
Level Up	230
Slot Releaser	250
Ultima Weapon	255

Mission Crown Freebies

Freebie	Crowns Required
Slot Releaser	1
Valor Gear+②	2
Potion x10	5
Ether x10	8
Lift Gear+③	10
Blizzard x3	15
Slot Releaser	20
Aero x3	25
Panacea x10	30
Cura x2	35
Blizzara x2	40
Slot Releaser	45
Hi-Potion x10	50
Hi-Ether x10	55
Mystery Gear③	60
Slot Releaser	65
Elixir x10	70
Limit Recharge x5	75
Aerora x3	80
Slot Releaser	85
Mega-Potion x10	90
Mega-Ether x10	100
Ultimate Gear⑥	110
Megalixir x5	120
Aeroga	130
Premium Orb	140
Sliding Dash LV+(L)	150
Crimson Blood	160
Power Unit(L)	170
Adamantite x2	180
Magic Unit(L)	190
Rune Ring	200
LV Quadrupler③	220
Guard Unit(L)	240
LV Doubler⑥	260
Slot Releaser	280
Master's Circle	358

CHAPTER 5

PANEL SYNTHESIS

Throughout the game, you may find yourself collecting panels that you have no use for, either because you've already moved on to more powerful versions of those panels, or because they don't fit in with your overall strategy. Although some panels can be sold at the Moogle Shop, you should explore the possibility of turning them into other panels through the Synthesis option in the Moogle Shop. In order to synthesize a panel, you need to meet three conditions:

1. You must have the required panels listed in the "Ingredients" list on the top screen.

2. You must have the amount of munny listed to the right of the panel that you want to synthesize.

3. In some cases, you must have attained a certain rank, or the panel to be synthesized will not appear as an option on the bottom screen.

If all three conditions are met, simply highlight the panel that you want to synthesize and press A to trade in the required munny and ingredients, and the newly synthesized panel appears in your inventory in the Panels Menu. It's just that easy!

- ★ ***Icon:*** *The image of the panel to be synthesized, as it appears in the Panels Menu.*
- ★ ***Panel:*** *The name of the panel to be synthesized.*
- ★ ***Rank:*** *The rank required in order to synthesize the panel; a "—" means that there is no rank requirement.*
- ★ ***Ingredients:*** *The other panels that you must have in your inventory; these panels will be consumed if you use them to synthesize the panel.*
- ★ ***Munny:*** *The munny required to synthesize the panel.*

ITEM PANEL SYNTHESIS

Icon	Panel	Rank	Ingredients	Munny
	Hi-Potion	—	Potion x2	800
	Mega-Potion	—	Hi-Potion x2	1500
	Hi-Ether	—	Ether x2	1200
	Mega-Ether	—	Hi-Ether x2	1800
	Elixir	—	Elixir Recipe, Hi-Potion, Hi-Ether, Shining Shard	1600
	Megalixir	—	Megalixir Recipe, Mega-Potion, Mega-Ether, Shining Crystal	2500
	Limit Recharge	—	Moonstone, Shining Shard, Blazing Shard	2000

MAGIC PANEL SYNTHESIS

Icon	Panel	Rank	Ingredients	Munny
	Fire	—	Fire Recipe, Blazing Shard x2	700
	Fira	—	Fira Recipe, Fire, Blazing Gem x2	1000
	Firaga	—	Firaga Recipe, Fira, Blazing Crystal x2	1400
	Blizzard	—	Blizzard Recipe, Frost Shard x2	1200
	Blizzara	—	Blizzara Recipe, Blizzard, Frost Gem x2	1300
	Blizzaga	—	Blizzaga Recipe, Blizzara, Frost Crystal x2	2000
	Thunder	—	Thunder Recipe, Lighting Shard x2	1400
	Thundara	—	Thundara Recipe, Thunder, Lighting Gem x2	1400
	Thundaga	—	Thundaga Recipe, Thundara, Lightning Crystal x2	2000
	Aero	—	Aero Recipe, Gust Shard x2	1400
	Aerora	—	Aerora Recipe, Aero, Gust Gem x2	1600
	Aeroga	—	Aeroga Recipe, Aerora, Gust Crystal x2	2000
	Cure	—	Cure Recipe, Shining Shard x2	1600
	Cura	—	Cura Recipe, Cure, Shining Gem x2	2000
	Curaga	—	Curaga Recipe, Cura, Shining Crystal x2	2600

ABILITY PANEL SYNTHESIS

Icon	Panel	Rank	Ingredients	Munny
	Dodge Rush(L)	—	Moonstone x2, Combo Tech x3, Power Tech+ x2, Premium Orb	4500
	Dodging Deflect(L)	—	Diamond, Range Tech+ x3	6800
	Dodge Combo(L)	—	Adamantite, Combo Tech+	8800
	Auto-Dodge(L)	—	Diamond, Combo Tech++	6800
	Perfect Block(L)	—	Moonstone x2, Shield Tech x2	3300
	Block-Counter(L)	—	Moonstone x2, Shield Tech x3, Shield Tech+ x2	4500
	Block-Retreat(L)	—	Moonstone x2, Shield Tech x3, Perfect Block(L)	4500
	Sliding Block(L)	—	Diamond, Shield Tech+, Range Tech+ x2	6800
	Block-Jump(L)	—	Diamond, Shield Tech+, Aerial Tech+ x2	6800
	Fire Block(L)	—	Moonstone x2, Shield Tech x3, Blazing Shard x3, Rune Tech x3	4500
	Blizzard Block(L)	—	Moonstone x2, Shield Tech x3, Frost Shard x3, Rune Tech x3	4500
	Thunder Block(L)	—	Diamond, Shield Tech+, Lightning Gem x3, Rune Tech+ x2	6800
	Aero Block(L)	—	Diamond, Shield Tech+, Gust Gem x3, Rune Tech+ x2	6800
	Block Bonus(L)	—	Adamantite, Shield Tech+, Luck Tech	8800
	Round Block(L)	—	Moonstone x2, Shield Tech+ x2	4500
	Auto-Block(L)	—	Adamantite, Shield Tech+, Round Block(L)	8800
	Quick Recovery(L)	—	Moonstone x2, Rune Tech+ x2	4500
	Aerial Payback(L)	—	Diamond, Combo Tech+ x3	6800
	Smash Recovery(L)	—	Adamantite, Power Tech++ x2	8800
	Air Rush(L)	—	Moonstone x2, Aerial Tech+ x2	4500
	Homing Glide(L)	—	Adamantite, Aerial Tech++ x2, Range Tech++ x2	8800
	Rocket Glide(L)	—	Adamantite, Aerial Tech++ x2, Combo Tech++ x2, Range Tech x5	8800
	Float(L)	—	Adamantite, Aerial Tech++ x2	8800

WEAPON PANEL SYNTHESIS

Icon	Panel	Rank	Ingredients	Munny
	Duel Gear④	Rookie	Gear Component A x3, Combo Tech x3, Bronze x2	4600
	Duel Gear++⑤	Rookie	Gear Component B x4, Combo Tech x5, Dark Ingot	7800
	Chrono Gear+③	Rookie	Gear Component A x3, Rune Tech x2, Bronze	2000
	Phantom Gear++⑤	Rookie	Gear Component B x4, Rune Tech+ x2, Dark Ingot	7800
	Nimble Gear+④	Rookie	Gear Component A x3, Aerial Tech x2, Bronze x2	3700
	Ominous Gear+④	Rookie	Gear Component A x3, Range Tech x2, Bronze x2	3700
	Fearless Gear+③	Rookie	Gear Component A x3, Power Tech x2, Bronze x2	2000
	Prestige Gear+④	Rookie	Gear Component B x4, Power Tech x3, Dark Ingot	4600
	Crisis Gear⑤	Rookie	Gear Component B x4, Rune Tech+ x2, Power Tech+ x2, Dark Ingot x2	7800
	Crisis Gear+⑤	Rookie	Gear Component C x4, Rune Tech+ x2, Power Tech+ x2, Silver x2	11700
	Omega Gear+⑥	Rookie	Gear Component D x4, Rune Tech++ x3, Power Tech++ x3, Mithril x2	30000
	Hazard Gear⑤	Rookie	Gear Component C x4, Rune Tech+ x2, Range Tech+ x2, Silver x2	7800
	Hazard Gear+⑤	Rookie	Gear Component D x4, Rune Tech++ x2, Range Tech++ x2, Gold	11700
	Rage Gear+⑤	Rookie	Gear Component C x4, Combo Tech+ x2, Aerial Tech+ x2, Silver x2	7800
	Champion Gear⑤	Rookie	Gear Component C x4, Combo Tech+ x2, Power Tech+ x2, Silver x2	7800
	Ultimate Gear+⑥	Rookie	Gear Component D x4, Combo Tech++ x3, Power Tech++ x3, Orichalcum x2	30000
	Pandora's Gear+⑤	Rookie	Gear Component D x4, Luck Tech x2, Premium Orb, Mithril x2	19500

RING PANEL SYNTHESIS

Icon	Panel	Rank	Ingredients	Munny
	Magic Ring	—	Iron x3, Moonstone	3600
	Fencer's Ring	—	Iron x3, Moonstone, Shining Shard x2	3600
	Fire Charm	—	Iron x3, Moonstone, Blazing Shard x2, Aerial Tech x2	3600
	Strike Ring	—	Iron x4, Bronze x3, Moonstone, Combo Tech x3	4500
	Lucky Ring	—	Iron x4, Bronze x3, Moonstone, Shield Tech x2	4500
	White Ring	—	Iron x4, Bronze x3, Moonstone, Power Tech x4	4500
	Raider's Ring	—	Dark Ingot x2, Moonstone, Lucky Ring	5900
	Thunder Charm	—	Dark Ingot x2, Moonstone x2, Lightning Gem x2, Aerial Tech x4	5900
	Recovery Ring	—	Dark Ingot x2, Moonstone x2, Combo Tech+	5900
	Vitality Ring	—	Dark Ingot x2, Moonstone x2, Combo Tech++	5900
	Double Up	—	Silver, Diamond, Luck Tech	6800
	Storm's Eye	—	Silver, Diamond, Gust Gem x2	6800
	Fairy Circle	—	Silver, Diamond, Range Tech+ x2, Aerial Tech+ x2	6800
	Full Circle	—	Silver, Diamond, Shield Tech x2, Shield Tech+	6800
	Charge Ring	—	Gold, Diamond x2, Full Circle	8800
	Eternal Ring	—	Gold, Diamond x2, Recovery Ring	8800
	Carmine Blight	—	Gold, Adamantite, Power Tech++ x2, Ankharite x2	8800
	Frozen Blight	—	Gold, Diamond x2, Rune Tech++ x2	8800
	Safety Ring	—	Gold, Diamond x2, Shield Tech+	8800
	Lunar Strike	Legend	Mithril x2, Adamantite x4, Premium Orb	10100
	Protect Ring	Legend	Mithril x2, Adamantite x4, Shield Tech++ x2	10100
	Might Crown	Legend	Mithril x2, Adamantite x4, Combo Tech++ x2	10100
	Three Stars	Legend	Mithril x2, Adamantite x4, Luck Tech x4	10100
	Imperial Crown	Legend	Mithril x2, Adamantite x4, Ankharite x2, Premium Orb	14800
	Witch's Chaos	Legend	Mithril x2, Adamantite x4, Shield Tech++ x2, Premium Orb	14800
	Extreme	Legend	Orichalcum, Moonstone x8, Dark Ingot x20, Luck Tech x4	12500
	Nothing to Fear	Legend	Orichalcum, Adamantite x4, Frozen Blight	12500
	Space in Its Place	Legend	Orichalcum, Moonstone x8, Combo Tech++ x3, Aerial Tech++ x3	12500
	Flagging Winds	Legend	Orichalcum, Moonstone x8, Gust Crystal x2, Gust Shard x5	12500
	Ice Breaker	Legend	Orichalcum, Moonstone x8, Frost Crystal x2, Frost Gem x3	12500
	Down to Earth	Legend	Orichalcum, Moonstone x8, Eternal Ring	12500
	Lose Your Illusion	Legend	Orichalcum, Adamantite x4, Charge Ring	12500
	Sighing of the Moon	Legend	Orichalcum, Diamond x6, Strike Ring	12500
	Tears of Flame	Legend	Orichalcum, Diamond x6, Blazing Crystal x2, Blazing Gem x3	12500
	Parting of Waters	Legend	Orichalcum, Diamond x6, Storm's Eye	12500
	Test of Time	Legend	Orichalcum, Adamantite x4, Fairy Circle	12500
	Flowers Athirst	Legend	Orichalcum, Moonstone x8, Double Up	12500
	Stolen Thunder	Legend	Orichalcum, Moonstone x8, Lightning Crystal x2, Lightning Shard x5	12500
	Dying of the Light	Legend	Orichalcum, Moonstone x8, Imperial Crown, Shining Gem x3	12500

CHAPTER 6

BESTIARY

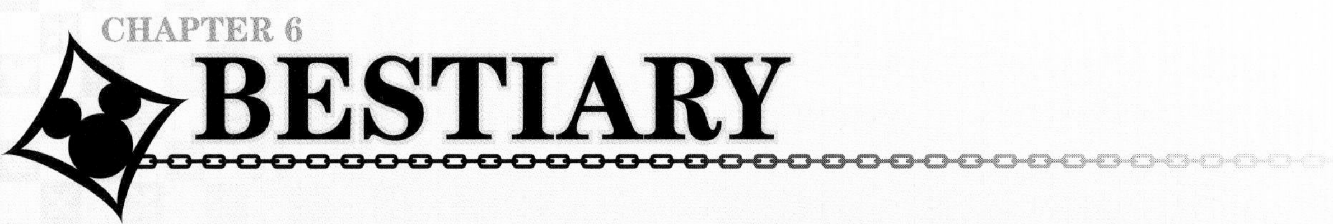

The bulk of this chapter contains profiles for each enemy you will encounter over the course of this game. But before you dig into this section, you should become familiar with the following information.

ENEMY ATTACK COUNTERS

Certain enemies have special attacks that automatically allow them to guard against melee attacks, as performed with the Attack command. Three of these four attacks prevent your character and the enemy from attacking for a brief moment. The fourth attack, Tailspin Charge, allows the enemy to keep attacking after blocking your character's attack.

Countering Attack	Enemies Who Use It
Headbutt	Sapphire Elegy, Pink Concerto, Minute Bomb
Rolling Shockwaves	Snowy Crystal
Tailspin Charge	Tailbunker, Avalanche, Wavecrest, Phantomtail, Windstorm
Lunge	Dusk

ENEMY STATS BY LEVEL

Although you face the same enemies in multiple missions over the course of the game, those enemies level up just as your character does. So when you face a Shadow in Mission 02, it's a lowly level 1 enemy, but when you see it again in Mission 59, it's a much tougher level 25 creature.

You can determine an enemy's level for a mission by viewing its detailed profile on the pages that follow. Once you figure out its level, you can use that information to refer to the following table to calculate its Base HP and Base Strength/Defense.

★ ***Calculating HP:*** *To figure out an enemy's actual HP for a mission, take the Base HP value and multiply it by its HP Factor.*

★ ***Calculating Attack Damage:*** *To determine the damage that an enemy's attacks will inflict, multiply the Base Strength/Defense for its level by the Power Factors of its attacks.*

★ ***Calculating Defense:*** *Multiply the Base Strength/Defense value for an enemy's level by its Defense Factor to calculate its defense rating. Some enemies have multiple areas that you can target, each with its own defense rating.*

Base Enemy Stats By Level

Level	Base HP	Base Str./Def.
1	62	8
2	65	9
3	68	11
4	71	12
5	74	14
6	77	15
7	80	17
8	83	18
9	86	20
10	89	21
11	92	23
12	95	24
13	98	26
14	101	27
15	104	29
16	107	30
17	110	32
18	113	33
19	116	35
20	119	36
21	122	38
22	125	39
23	128	41
24	131	42
25	134	44
26	137	45
27	140	47
28	143	48
29	146	50
30	149	51
31	152	53
32	155	54
33	158	56
34	161	57
35	164	59
37	170	62
39	176	65

Base Enemy Stats By Level

Level	Base HP	Base Str./Def.
40	179	66
41	182	68
42	185	69
43	188	71
44	191	72
45	194	74
46	197	75
48	203	78
49	206	80
50	209	81
51	212	83
52	215	84
53	218	86
54	221	87
55	224	89
58	233	93
59	236	95
60	239	96
61	242	98
62	245	99
63	248	101
64	251	102
65	254	104
66	257	105
67	260	107
68	263	108
69	266	110
70	269	111
71	272	113
72	275	114
75	284	119
76	287	120
81	302	128
86	317	135
90	329	141
91	332	143
96	347	150

MISSION POINTS AND MISSION PRIZES

During Mission Mode, most defeated enemies drop mission prizes and award mission points to the player who defeats them. However, certain types of enemies drop mission prizes each time they lose 20 percent of their maximum HP, which gives every player a chance to earn rewards in combat against them.

Enemies That Drop Mission Prizes Only When Defeated

Name	Points Earned From Prizes	Total Points Earned
Shadow	1[1]	1
Mega-Shadow	3	2
Gigas Shadow	5	3
Yellow Opera	1	1
Scarlet Tango	2	1
Grey Caprice	3	2
Striped Aria	3	2
Sapphire Elegy	3	2
Pink Concerto	3	2
Turquoise March	2	1
Emerald Serenade	1	1
Dire Plant	1	1
Fire Plant	2	1
Blizzard Plant	2	1
Poison Plant	4	2
Possessor	1	1
Massive Possessor	4[2]	2
Bulky Vendor	20	5
Rare Vendor	40	5
Watcher	3	2
Guardian	20	10
Destroyer	20	10
Minute Bomb	2	1
Skater Bomb	2	1
Detonator	4	2
Deserter	2	1
Sergeant	4	2
Soldier	2	1
Commander	5	3
Loudmouth	1	1
Flare Note	2	1
Bubble Beat	2	1
Barrier Master	30	3
Shadow Glob	30	10
Large Armor	5	3
Clay Armor	5	3
Solid Armor	4	2
Land Armor	10	5
Bad Dog	2	1
Snapper Dog	4	2
Bully Dog	20	10
Cymbal Monkey	3	2

Enemies That Drop Mission Prizes Only When Defeated

Name	Points Earned From Prizes	Total Points Earned
Tricky Monkey	4	2
Neoshadow	3	2
Novashadow	4	2
Air Battler	3	2
Aerial Master	13	4
Artful Flyer	13	4
Sky Grappler	13	4
Icy Cube	1	1
Snowy Crystal	4	2
Li'l Cannon	2	1
Ice Cannon	2	1
Jumbo Cannon	10	5
Morning Star	10	5
Spiked Crawler	10	5
Scorching Sphere	10	5
Creepworm	1	1
Hover Ghost	2	1
Carrier Ghost	5	3
Living Pod	5	3
Zip Slasher	13	4
Dual Blade	5	3
Heat Saber	10	5
Chill Ripper	10	5
Stalwart Blade	10	5
Tailbunker	5	3
Avalanche	10	5
Wavecrest	5	3
Phantomtail	10	5
Windstorm	5	3
Veil Lizard	20	10
Lurk Lizard	13	4
Powered Armor	20	10
Invisible	10	5
Orcus	20[3]	10
Dusk	3	2
Samurai	5	3
Darkside	—	100
Pete	20	20
Lock	10	0
Shock	10	0
Barrel	10	0
???	3	2[4]

Enemies That Drop Mission Prizes For Each 20 Percent of HP Lost

Name	20% Lost	40% Lost	60% Lost	80% Lost	Defeated	Mission Points
Dustflier	10	10	10	20	50	15
Guard Armor	10	10	10	20	50	10
Dark Follower	10	10	30	50	—	30
Antlion	10	10	10	20	50	10
Infernal Engine	10	10	10	20	50	10
Leechgrave	10	10	10	20	50	10
Crimson Prankster	10	10	10	20	50	10

Enemies That Drop Mission Prizes For Each 20 Percent of HP Lost

Name	20% Lost	40% Lost	60% Lost	80% Lost	Defeated	Mission Points
Ruler of the Sky	10	10	10	20	50	10
Anti-Saïx[5]	6	6	6	12	30	20
Xion: First Form	10	10	30	50	—	30
Xion: Second Form	10	10	30	50	—	30
Xion: Third Form	10	10	30	50	—	30
Xion: Final Form	10	10	30	50	—	30
Anti-Riku[6]	6	6	18	30	—	30

[1] Shadows summoned by the Dark Follower are worth two points, not one.

[2] Drops points when dividing into Possessors.

[3] During Mission 88, Orcus drops two mission prizes for the first 20 percent of its HP lost, two mission prizes for the second 20 percent, two for the third, four for the fourth and 10 mission prizes for the final 20 percent.

[4] This number is 0 when the enemy appears with Leechgrave.

[5] Appears instead of Saïx in Mission Mode.

[6] Appears instead of Riku in Mission Mode.

ENEMY PROFILES

The following pages contain detailed information about the 104 enemies in *Kingdom Hearts 358/2 Days*. These enemy profiles provide the strengths and weaknesses of every foe in the game, along with tips for how to defeat them.

❶ **Enemy Type**: *This symbol indicates whether the enemy is a Heartless, a Nobody or Other.*

❷ **Enemy Description**: *Straight from the enemy's in-game Enemy Profile, this brief summary describes the most important details about the foe.*

❸ **Worlds**: *You'll find the enemy in these worlds during the course of your adventure.*

❹ **Hearts**: *Defeating the enemy results in this number of hearts.*

❺ **HP Factor**: *Multiply this number by the enemy's Base HP for its level to determine its HP in Story Mode (see "Enemy Stats By Level" section). In Mission Mode, multiply the Story Mode HP total again by 3 to determine the enemy's Mission Mode HP.*

❻ **EXP Factor**: *Multiply this number by the base EXP value for the mission that you're playing to determine how much EXP you can earn from defeating the enemy in that mission.*

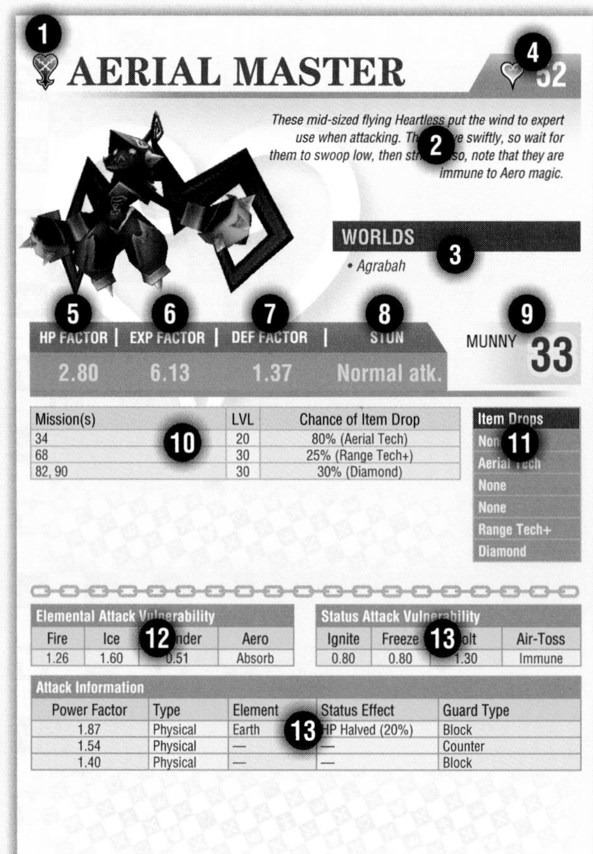

❼ **Defense Factor**: *Multiply this number by the enemy's Base Strength/Defense to determine its defense rating (see "Enemy Stats By Level" section). Some enemies have several body parts that you can target, each with their own Defense Factors.*

❽ **Stun**: *Some enemies can be stunned with any regular attacks ("Normal attack"). Others can only be stunned with special Stun attacks ("Stun attack"). Large and powerful enemies cannot be stunned at all ("None").*

❾ **Munny**: *This indicates the amount of munny earned for defeating the enemy. This number stays constant, no matter what level the enemy is or what mission you're playing.*

❿ **Enemy Level & Item Drop Chances**: *Consult this table to determine the enemy's level in each mission that it appears, as well as the chance of getting a dropped item from the enemy once it's defeated.*

⓫ **Item Drops**: *These are the items that the enemy may drop once it's defeated. Low-level enemies drop items near the top of the list, while high-level enemies drop items toward the bottom of it.*

⓬ **Elemental Attack Vulnerability**: *This table lists the damage multipliers for when you hit the enemy with an elemental attack. For example, Shadows have a fire attack vulnerability of 2.20, so hitting them with a fire-based attack does more than twice the damage than the attack's base damage. However, Shadows also have an electricity attack vulnerability of 0.60, so electrical attacks only hit them for slightly more than half of the attack's base damage. If the field says "Absorb," then hitting the enemy with that type of elemental attack will heal them for 10 percent of the attack's base damage!*

⓭ **Status Attack Vulnerability**: *This table shows the likelihood that you'll cause a status effect on the enemy by hitting it with an attack that can cause a status effect. A number below 1.00 means that it's less likely that the enemy will suffer the status attack. A number above 1.00 means it's more likely, while 1.00 means that the attack is no more or less likely to cause a status effect than usual.*

⓮ **Attack Information**: *All of the enemy's attacks are listed in this table, along with the following information for each:*

Power Factor: *Multiply by the Base Strength/Defense value for the enemy's level to determine how much damage the attack inflicts on your character's HP (see "Enemy Stats By Level" section).*

Type: *Determines whether the attack is physical or magical.*

Element: *If the attack has an elemental alignment, it is shown here.*

Status Effect: *Lists the status effect (if any) that the attack can cause.*

Guard Type: *Shows what kind of defense you can use against the attack. "Counter" means that ranged attacks can be deflected and melee attacks can be interrupted if you guard against them. "Block" means that the attack can be blocked, but ranged attacks are not deflected and melee attacks are not interrupted. "None" means that you cannot guard against the attack and must avoid it.*

The enemy profiles appear in alphabetical order for easy reference. The following table lists them in the order that they appear in the Enemy Profiles section of the Main Menu, if you'd like to figure out which enemies you haven't yet scanned.

Enemy Profiles Checklist

	Name	Page
	Shadow	p. 312
	Mega-Shadow	p. 307
	Gigas Shadow	p. 301
	Yellow Opera	p. 319
	Scarlet Tango	p. 311
	Grey Caprice	p. 302
	Striped Aria	p. 315
	Sapphire Elegy	p. 311
	Pink Concerto	p. 309
	Turquoise March	p. 316
	Emerald Serenade	p. 301
	Dire Plant	p. 300
	Fire Plant	p. 301
	Blizzard Plant	p. 296
	Poison Plant	p. 309
	Possessor	p. 309
	Massive Possessor	p. 307
	Bulky Vendor	p. 296
	Rare Vendor	p. 310
	Watcher	p. 317
	Guardian	p. 302
	Destroyer	p. 299
	Minute Bomb	p. 307
	Skater Bomb	p. 313
	Storm Bomb	p. 315
	Detonator	p. 299

Enemy Profiles Checklist

	Name	Page
	Deserter	p. 299
	Sergeant	p. 312
	Soldier	p. 314
	Commander	p. 297
	Loudmouth	p. 306
	Flare Note	p. 301
	Bubble Beat	p. 296
	Barrier Master	p. 295
	Shadow Glob	p. 312
	Large Armor	p. 305
	Clay Armor	p. 297
	Solid Armor	p. 314
	Land Armor	p. 304
	Bad Dog	p. 295
	Snapper Dog	p. 313
	Bully Dog	p. 296
	Cymbal Monkey	p. 298
	Tricky Monkey	p. 316
	Neoshadow	p. 308
	Novashadow	p. 308
	Air Battler	p. 294
	Aerial Master	p. 294
	Artful Flyer	p. 294
	Sky Grappler	p. 313
	Icy Cube	p. 303
	Snowy Crystal	p. 313

Enemy Profiles Checklist

	Name	Page
	Li'l Cannon	p. 305
	Ice Cannon	p. 303
	Switch Launcher	p. 315
	Jumbo Cannon	p. 304
	Morning Star	p. 307
	Spiked Crawler	p. 314
	Scorching Sphere	p. 312
	Creepworm	p. 298
	Hover Ghost	p. 303
	Carrier Ghost	p. 297
	Living Pod	p. 305
	Zip Slasher	p. 319
	Dual Blade	p. 300
	Heat Saber	p. 303
	Chill Ripper	p. 297
	Blitz Spear	p. 295
	Stalwart Blade	p. 314
	Tailbunker	p. 315
	Avalanche	p. 295
	Wavecrest	p. 317
	Phantomtail	p. 309
	Windstorm	p. 317
	Dustflier	p. 300
	Veil Lizard	p. 316
	Lurk Lizard	p. 306
	Guard Armor	p. 302

Enemy Profiles Checklist

	Name	Page
	Powered Armor	p. 310
	Invisible	p. 304
	Orcus	p. 308
	Dusk	p. 300
	Samurai	p. 311
	Darkside	p. 299
	Dark Follower	p. 298
	Pete	p. 308
	Lock	p. 306
	Shock	p. 306
	Barrel	p. 306
	Xigbar	p. 317
	Unknown	p. 319
	Unknown	p. 319
	Antlion	p. 294
	Infernal Engine	p. 304
	Tentaclaw	p. 316
	Leechgrave	p. 305
	Crimson Prankster	p. 298
	Ruler of the Sky	p. 310
	Saïx	p. 311
	Xion: First Form	p. 318
	Xion: Second Form	p. 318
	Xion: Third Form	p. 318
	Xion: Final Form	p. 318
	Riku	p. 310

AERIAL MASTER

♡ 52

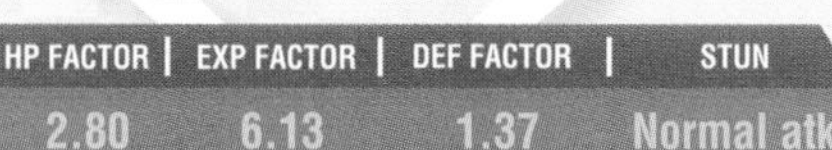

These mid-sized flying Heartless put the wind to expert use when attacking. They move swiftly, so wait for them to swoop low, then strike. Also, note that they are immune to Aero magic.

WORLDS

- *Agrabah*

HP FACTOR	EXP FACTOR	DEF FACTOR	STUN	MUNNY
2.80	6.13	1.37	Normal atk.	33

Mission(s)	LVL	Chance of Item Drop
34	20	80% (Aerial Tech)
68	30	25% (Range Tech+)
82, 90	30	30% (Diamond)

Item Drops
None
Aerial Tech
None
None
Range Tech+
Diamond

Elemental Attack Vulnerability			
Fire	Ice	Thunder	Aero
1.26	1.60	0.51	Absorb

Status Attack Vulnerability			
Ignite	Freeze	Jolt	Air-Toss
0.80	0.80	1.30	Immune

Attack Information				
Power Factor	Type	Element	Status Effect	Guard Type
1.87	Physical	Earth	HP Halved (20%)	Block
1.54	Physical	—	—	Counter
1.40	Physical	—	—	Block

AIR BATTLER

♡ 23

These mid-sized flying Heartless put the wind to expert use when attacking. They move swiftly, so wait for them to swoop low, then strike. Also, note that they are immune to Aero magic.

WORLDS

- *Olympus Coliseum*
- *Never Land*

HP FACTOR	EXP FACTOR	DEF FACTOR	STUN	MUNNY
1.60	3.53	1.28	Normal atk.	22

Mission(s)	LVL	Chance of Item Drop
53, 58	20	40% (Gust Shard)
64	20	45% (Combo Tech+)
73	20	20% (Gust Crystal)

Item Drops
None
None
None
Gust Shard
Combo Tech+
Gust Crystal

Elemental Attack Vulnerability			
Fire	Ice	Thunder	Aero
4.40	4.80	1.80	Immune

Status Attack Vulnerability			
Ignite	Freeze	Jolt	Air-Toss
0.80	0.80	1.30	Immune

Attack Information				
Power Factor	Type	Element	Status Effect	Guard Type
1.40	Physical	—	—	Block
0.96	Physical	—	—	Block
1.30	Physical	Aero	Air-Toss (100%)	Block

ANTLION

♡ 93

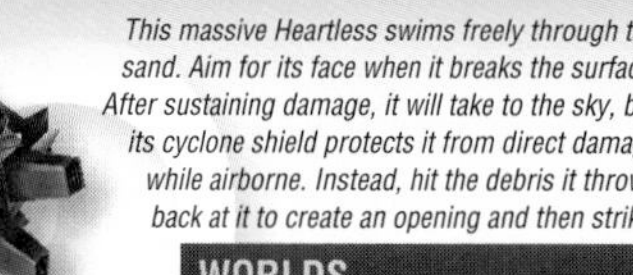

This massive Heartless swims freely through the sand. Aim for its face when it breaks the surface. After sustaining damage, it will take to the sky, but its cyclone shield protects it from direct damage while airborne. Instead, hit the debris it throws back at it to create an opening and then strike.

WORLDS

- *Agrabah*

HP FACTOR	EXP FACTOR	DEF FACTOR	STUN	MUNNY
8.80	54.14	3.00~3.20	None	—

Mission(s)	LVL	Chance of Item Drop
32	12	—

Item Drops
None
None
None
None
None
None

Elemental Attack Vulnerability			
Fire	Ice	Thunder	Aero
0.56	1.00	0.23	0.69

Status Attack Vulnerability			
Ignite	Freeze	Jolt	Air-Toss
Immune	Immune	Immune	Immune

Attack Information				
Power Factor	Type	Element	Status Effect	Guard Type
0.98	Physical	—	—	Block
1.70	Physical	Aero	Air-Toss (90%)	None
0.30	Physical	Aero	Air-Toss (90%)	Block
0.98	Physical	—	—	Block
0.98	Physical	—	—	Block
2.10	Physical	—	—	None

ARTFUL FLYER

♡ 50

These large flying Heartless put the wind to expert use when attacking. They move swiftly, but are vulnerable just after kicking, so be ready to mount a counteroffensive. They also retain their kind's immunity to Aero magic.

WORLDS

- *Never Land*

HP FACTOR	EXP FACTOR	DEF FACTOR	STUN	MUNNY
2.80	5.90	1.37	Normal atk.	27

Mission(s)	LVL	Chance of Item Drop
58	30	100% (Power Tech+)

Item Drops
None
None
None
Power Tech+
None
None

Elemental Attack Vulnerability			
Fire	Ice	Thunder	Aero
1.08	1.14	0.60	Absorb

Status Attack Vulnerability			
Ignite	Freeze	Jolt	Air-Toss
0.80	0.80	1.30	Immune

Attack Information				
Power Factor	Type	Element	Status Effect	Guard Type
1.60	Physical	—	—	Block
1.40	Physical	—	—	Counter
1.17	Physical	—	—	Block
1.25	Physical	Aero	Air-Toss (100%)	Block

AVALANCHE ♡ 70

These large aerial Heartless use their potent ice breath to attack their prey. Strike their wings and tail to force them to land, then focus attacks on their head, which is weak against Fire magic.

WORLDS

- Twilight Town
- Never Land

HP FACTOR	EXP FACTOR	DEF FACTOR	STUN	MUNNY
6.80	9.18	1.70~2.20	None	33

Mission(s)	LVL	Chance of Item Drop
44	25	30% (Frost Shard)
60	25	50% (Frost Gem)

Item Drops
None
None
Frost Shard
Frost Gem
None
None

Elemental Attack Vulnerability			
Fire	Ice	Thunder	Aero
1.65	Immune	Immune	Immune

Status Attack Vulnerability			
Ignite	Freeze	Jolt	Air-Toss
0.10	Immune	Immune	Immune

Attack Information				
Power Factor	Type	Element	Status Effect	Guard Type
1.70	Physical	—	—	None
1.54	Physical	—	—	Block
2.02	Physical	—	—	Block
1.87	Physical	—	—	Counter
1.63	Physical	—	—	Block
1.43	Physical	Ice	Freeze (35%)*	Block

* Chance of Freeze drops to 30% when the Avalanche has landed.

BAD DOG ♡ 15

Small and canine in appearance, these Heartless wander aimlessly until a target draws near. Their bark is bad, but not worse than their bite; they'll snap at you if you hit them. Deflect this attack with a block to stagger them.

WORLDS

- Beast's Castle

HP FACTOR	EXP FACTOR	DEF FACTOR	STUN	MUNNY
2.39	1.73	1.25	Normal atk.	11

Mission(s)	LVL	Chance of Item Drop
22, 27, 28	10	20% (Iron)
49, 50	10	21% (Bronze)
83	10	45% (Power Tech++)

Item Drops
None
Iron
Bronze
None
None
Power Tech++

Elemental Attack Vulnerability			
Fire	Ice	Thunder	Aero
3.30	4.00	1.50	4.25

Status Attack Vulnerability			
Ignite	Freeze	Jolt	Air-Toss
1.00	1.00	1.00	1.00

Attack Information				
Power Factor	Type	Element	Status Effect	Guard Type
1.63	Physical	—	—	Counter
0.93	Physical	—	—	Block

BARRIER MASTER ♡ 16

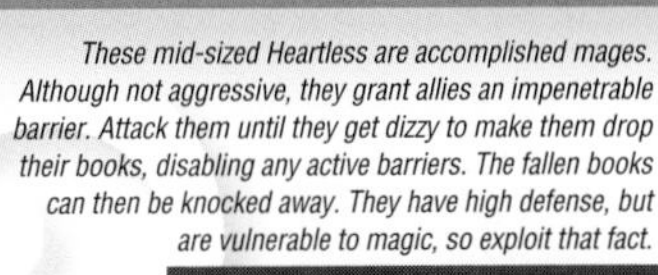

These mid-sized Heartless are accomplished mages. Although not aggressive, they grant allies an impenetrable barrier. Attack them until they get dizzy to make them drop their books, disabling any active barriers. The fallen books can then be knocked away. They have high defense, but are vulnerable to magic, so exploit that fact.

WORLDS

- Twilight Town
- Agrabah
- Beast's Castle

HP FACTOR	EXP FACTOR	DEF FACTOR	STUN	MUNNY
10.40	2.20	1.95	Stun atk.	35

Mission(s)	LVL	Chance of Item Drop
16	8	20% (Iron)
30	12	20% (Iron)
56	26	45% (Shield Tech)
70	41	—

Item Drops
None
Iron
None
Shield Tech
None
None

Elemental Attack Vulnerability			
Fire	Ice	Thunder	Aero
5.28	6.08	2.28	6.80

Status Attack Vulnerability			
Ignite	Freeze	Jolt	Air-Toss
1.20	1.20	1.20	1.20

Attack Information				
Power Factor	Type	Element	Status Effect	Guard Type
—	—	—	—	—

BLITZ SPEAR ♡ 65

This lightning knight Heartless's skillful defense makes it tough to finish off. Although its focused slash can be stopped with a block, blasting the knight with Aeroga while it is storing up energy will stagger it, opening it up to extra damage, especially from magic.

WORLDS

- Beast's Castle

HP FACTOR	EXP FACTOR	DEF FACTOR	STUN	MUNNY
9.20	8.05	1.55	None	28

Mission(s)	LVL	Chance of Item Drop
83	58	100% (Lightning Crystal)

Item Drops
None
None
None
None
None
Lightning Crystal

Elemental Attack Vulnerability			
Fire	Ice	Thunder	Aero
0.97	1.11	Absorb	1.22

Status Attack Vulnerability			
Ignite	Freeze	Jolt	Air-Toss
Immune	Immune	Immune	Immune

Attack Information				
Power Factor	Type	Element	Status Effect	Guard Type
1.41	Physical	—	—	Block
0.61	Physical	—	—	Block
0.73	Physical	Thunder	Jolt (100%)	None
2.02	Physical	Thunder	Jolt (100%)	Counter
1.43	Physical	Thunder	Jolt (50%)	None
1.70	Physical	Thunder	Jolt (100%)	None

BLIZZARD PLANT

These large plant Heartless are rooted to the ground. They strike from afar with homing ice shots that ricochet off walls, but they can be returned with a block. At close range, they'll attempt a head-butt, after which they'll be wide open for a counter attack.

WORLDS

- *Wonderland*

HP FACTOR	EXP FACTOR	DEF FACTOR	STUN
2.80	4.45	1.35	Normal atk.

MUNNY **22**

Mission(s)	LVL	Chance of Item Drop
51, 57	23	40% (Frost Gem)
67	23	45% (Combo Tech+)

Item Drops
None
None
None
Frost Gem
Combo Tech+
None

Elemental Attack Vulnerability			
Fire	Ice	Thunder	Aero
4.40	Absorb	Immune	Immune

Status Attack Vulnerability			
Ignite	Freeze	Jolt	Air-Toss
1.50	Immune	Immune	Immune

Attack Information				
Power Factor	Type	Element	Status Effect	Guard Type
0.56	Physical	Ice	Freeze (5%)	Block
1.17	Physical	Ice	Freeze (20%)	Counter

BUBBLE BEAT

These mid-sized Heartless cause the most trouble when they toot their horns to heal themselves and their cohorts. Block and you can deflect the homing water missiles they spew.

WORLDS

- *Never Land*

HP FACTOR	EXP FACTOR	DEF FACTOR	STUN
2.00	3.05	1.32	Stun atk.

MUNNY **21**

Mission(s)	LVL	Chance of Item Drop
58	30	30% (Frost Shard)
76	24	30% (Frost Crystal)

Item Drops
None
None
None
Frost Shard
None
Frost Crystal

Elemental Attack Vulnerability			
Fire	Ice	Thunder	Aero
2.20	2.13	2.40	2.27

Status Attack Vulnerability			
Ignite	Freeze	Jolt	Air-Toss
1.50	0.30	1.00	1.00

Attack Information				
Power Factor	Type	Element	Status Effect	Guard Type
0.32	Physcial	Ice	Freeze (50%)	Block

BULKY VENDOR

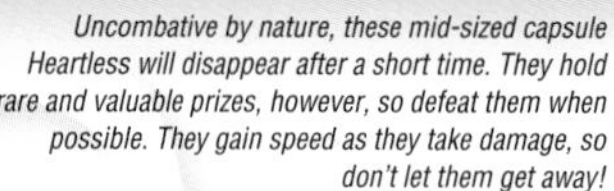

Uncombative by nature, these mid-sized capsule Heartless will disappear after a short time. They hold rare and valuable prizes, however, so defeat them when possible. They gain speed as they take damage, so don't let them get away!

WORLDS

- *N/A*

HP FACTOR	EXP FACTOR	DEF FACTOR	STUN
1.19	1.00	1.30	Stun atk.

MUNNY **40**

Mission(s)	LVL	Chance of Item Drop
07	1	100% (60%: Ether, 30%: Blazing Shard, 10%: Iron)
13	4	100% (60%: Blazing Shard, 30%: Shining Shard, 10%: Iron)
17	8	100% (60%: Blazing Shard, 30%: Shining Shard, 10%: Iron)
23	10	100% (60%: Blazing Shard, 30%: Shining Shard, 10%: Iron)
27	13	100% (60%: Blazing Shard, 30%: Shining Shard, 10%: Iron)
31, 32	15	100% (60%: Shining Shard, 30%: Aerial Tech, 10%: Frost Shard)
38	18	100% (60%: Iron, 30%: Gear Component A, 10%: Elixir Recipe)
42	19	100% (60%: Iron, 30%: Gear Component A, 10%: Elixir Recipe)
44	24	100% (60%: Iron, 30%: Shield Tech, 10%: Elixir Recipe)

Item Drops
Iron
Frost Shard
Elixir Recipe
None
None
None

Elemental Attack Vulnerability			
Fire	Ice	Thunder	Aero
1.47	1.60	0.60	1.70

Status Attack Vulnerability			
Ignite	Freeze	Jolt	Air-Toss
1.00	1.00	1.00	1.00

Attack Information				
Power Factor	Type	Element	Status Effect	Guard Type
—	—	—	—	—

BULLY DOG

Larger and faster than the Bad Dog, but these canine Heartless bark just the same. Physical attacks won't knock them off balance; exploit their weakness to magic instead.

WORLDS

- *Beast's Castle*

HP FACTOR	EXP FACTOR	DEF FACTOR	STUN
4.80	5.23	1.45	None

MUNNY **32**

Mission(s)	LVL	Chance of Item Drop
31	14	100% (Shining Shard)
38, 49, 50	14	50% (Lightning Shard)
83	30	Diamond

Item Drops
None
Shining Shard
Lightning Shard
None
None
Diamond

Elemental Attack Vulnerability			
Fire	Ice	Thunder	Aero
1.65	1.80	0.68	2.13

Status Attack Vulnerability			
Ignite	Freeze	Jolt	Air-Toss
0.80	0.80	0.80	0.50

Attack Information				
Power Factor	Type	Element	Status Effect	Guard Type
1.87	Physical	—	—	Counter
1.43	Physical	Moon	Silence (3%)	Block
0.73	Physical	Moon	Silence (25%)	Block

CARRIER GHOST

30

These large flying Heartless can spontaneously appear behind their targets and possess them. Although they behave similarly to Hover Ghosts, physical attacks won't stagger them.

WORLDS

- *Halloween Town*

HP FACTOR	EXP FACTOR	DEF FACTOR	STUN
12.80	4.35	2.40	None

MUNNY 26

Mission(s)	LVL	Chance of Item Drop
62	32	30% (Aerial Tech+)
79	32	25% (Aerial Tech++)

Item Drops
None
None
None
None
Aerial Tech+
Aerial Tech++

Elemental Attack Vulnerability			
Fire	Ice	Thunder	Aero
0.90	1.10	0.25	0.24

Status Attack Vulnerability			
Ignite	Freeze	Jolt	Air-Toss
0.40	0.40	0.40	0.40

Attack Information				
Power Factor	Type	Element	Status Effect	Guard Type
1.25	Physical	Illusion	Flip-Foot (10%)	Block
0.20	Magical	Light	Radar Zap (15%)	None

CHILL RIPPER

66

This icy knight Heartless's skillful defense makes it tough to finish off. Although its focused slash can be stopped with a block, blasting the knight with Firaga while it is storing up energy will stagger it, opening it up to extra damage, especially from magic.

WORLDS

- *Halloween Town*

HP FACTOR	EXP FACTOR	DEF FACTOR	STUN
10.00	8.33	1.55	None

MUNNY 28

Mission(s)	LVL	Chance of Item Drop
79	55	100% (Range Tech++)

Item Drops
None
None
None
None
None
Range Tech++

Elemental Attack Vulnerability			
Fire	Ice	Thunder	Aero
0.97	Absorb	Immune	Immune

Status Attack Vulnerability			
Ignite	Freeze	Jolt	Air-Toss
0.10	Immune	Immune	Immune

Attack Information				
Power Factor	Type	Element	Status Effect	Guard Type
1.53	Physical	—	—	Block
0.23	Physical	—	—	Block
2.02	Physical	Ice	Freeze (100%)	Counter
1.63	Physical	Ice	Freeze (100%)	None
1.63	Physical	Ice	Freeze (100%)	Block

CLAY ARMOR

43

Armor covers every inch of these large Heartless, allowing them to deflect blows from every direction. To inflict damage, aim for the head and knock them down to render them vulnerable to further attack. Use Thunder magic to keep them down longer.

WORLDS

- *Olympus Coliseum*

HP FACTOR	EXP FACTOR	DEF FACTOR	STUN
15.19	4.85	2.20	None

MUNNY 32

Mission(s)	LVL	Chance of Item Drop
39	15	—

Item Drops
None
None
None
None
None
None

Elemental Attack Vulnerability			
Fire	Ice	Thunder	Aero
1.65	1.79	0.90	1.99

Status Attack Vulnerability			
Ignite	Freeze	Jolt	Air-Toss
Immune	Immune	0.12	0.12

Attack Information				
Power Factor	Type	Element	Status Effect	Guard Type
1.10	Physical	—	—	Block
1.96	Physical	Earth	HP halved (100%)	None
1.50	Physical	—	—	None
1.43	Physical	Flower	Darkness (30%)	Block

COMMANDER

32

As aggressive as they are large, these foes still rely on kick attacks that can be deflected with a well-timed block. Note, however, that their size prevents normal attacks from knocking them off balance.

WORLDS

- *Wonderland*

HP FACTOR	EXP FACTOR	DEF FACTOR	STUN
2.80	4.68	1.60	None

MUNNY 26

Mission(s)	LVL	Chance of Item Drop
57	30	50% (Dark Ingot)

Item Drops
None
None
None
Dark Ingot
None
None

Elemental Attack Vulnerability			
Fire	Ice	Thunder	Aero
0.61	0.67	0.25	0.78

Status Attack Vulnerability			
Ignite	Freeze	Jolt	Air-Toss
0.30	0.30	0.30	0.30

Attack Information				
Power Factor	Type	Element	Status Effect	Guard Type
1.43	Physical	—	—	Block
1.87	Physical	—	—	Counter
1.43	Physical	—	—	Counter

CREEPWORM

10

Although fast, these Heartless are unfit for combat and low in HP. A single blow should be enough to take them out.

WORLDS

- Halloween Town

HP FACTOR	EXP FACTOR	DEF FACTOR	STUN
0.07	1.00	1.00	Normal atk.

MUNNY 10

Mission(s)	LVL	Chance of Item Drop
42, 45, 52, 62	16	—
72	41	—

Item Drops
None
None
None
None
None
None

Elemental Attack Vulnerability			
Fire	Ice	Thunder	Aero
1.00	1.00	1.00	1.00

Status Attack Vulnerability			
Ignite	Freeze	Jolt	Air-Toss
1.00	1.00	1.00	1.00

Attack Information				
Power Factor	Type	Element	Status Effect	Guard Type
—	—	—	—	—

CRIMSON PRANKSTER

98

This newcomer to Wonderland splits in two, attacking as a pair. Unless both halves are defeated at the same time, they will continue the cycle of merging and splitting. Counter its flamethrower with ice magic—Blizzaga if possible. Aeroga will halt its fiery spin attack.

WORLDS

- Wonderland

HP FACTOR	EXP FACTOR	DEF FACTOR	STUN
5.76	69.53	1.90	None

MUNNY —

Mission(s)	LVL	Chance of Item Drop
69	41	—

Item Drops
None
None
None
None
None
None

Elemental Attack Vulnerability			
Fire	Ice	Thunder	Aero
Immune	0.71	0.20	0.57

Status Attack Vulnerability			
Ignite	Freeze	Jolt	Air-Toss
Immune	Immune	Immune	Immune

Attack Information				
Power Factor	Type	Element	Status Effect	Guard Type
0.90	Physical	—	—	Block
1.43	Physical	Fire	Ignite	Block
1.17	Physical	Fire	Ignite	Block
0.98	Physical	Fire	Ignite	Block

CYMBAL MONKEY

11

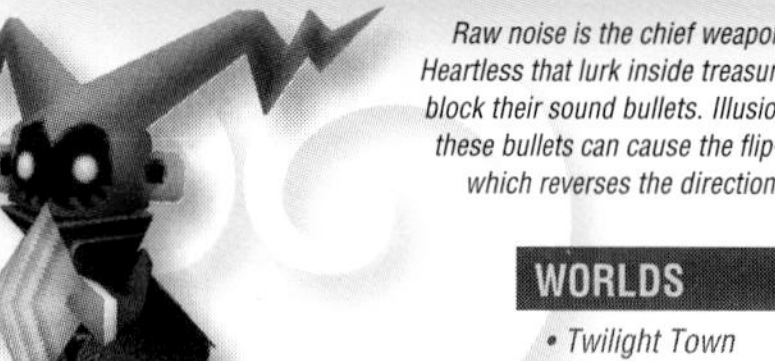

Raw noise is the chief weapon of these mid-sized Heartless that lurk inside treasure chests. Be sure to block their sound bullets. Illusion-based attacks like these bullets can cause the flip-foot status ailment, which reverses the directional controls for basic movement.

WORLDS

- Twilight Town
- Agrabah
- Beast's Castle

HP FACTOR	EXP FACTOR	DEF FACTOR	STUN
1.27	1.00	1.04	Stun atk.

MUNNY 25

Mission(s)	LVL	Chance of Item Drop
23	11	20% (Iron)
25	12	20% (Iron)
29	13	20% (Iron)
40	16	40% (Range Tech)
44	22	40% (Range Tech)
48, 49	23	40% (Range Tech)
80	50	35% (Silver)

Item Drops
None
Iron
Range Tech
None
None
Silver

Elemental Attack Vulnerability			
Fire	Ice	Thunder	Aero
1.80	3.80	0.72	2.20

Status Attack Vulnerability			
Ignite	Freeze	Jolt	Air-Toss
1.00	1.00	1.00	1.00

Attack Information				
Power Factor	Type	Element	Status Effect	Guard Type
1.64	Physical	Illusion	Flip-Foot (30%)	Counter

DARK FOLLOWER

—

A stronger form of the Darkside. Although more powerful, it follows the same basic patterns as its predecessor. Send back the dark homing blasts fired from its chest with a block, then attack either its hands or, if possible, its head for maximum damage.

WORLDS

- Beast's Castle

HP FACTOR	EXP FACTOR	DEF FACTOR	STUN
16.00	41.25	2.00~4.50	None

MUNNY —

Mission(s)	LVL	Chance of Item Drop
43	21	—

Item Drops
None
None
None
None
None
None

Elemental Attack Vulnerability			
Fire	Ice	Thunder	Aero
0.68	0.76	0.28	0.28

Status Attack Vulnerability			
Ignite	Freeze	Jolt	Air-Toss
Immune	Immune	Immune	Immune

Attack Information				
Power Factor	Type	Element	Status Effect	Guard Type
1.90	Physical	—	—	Block
0.98	Physical	Flower	Darkness (15%)	Counter
1.02	Magical	Nil	Null Defense (100%)	None
1.02	Magical	Nil	Null Defense (100%)	None
1.17	Physical	Space	Shoe-Glue (25%)	None

DARKSIDE

—

This giant Heartless will devour all around it if left unchecked. The dark homing blasts fired from its chest can be turned back on it with a block. Target its hands or, if possible, its head. Earth-based attacks like its homing blast can halve your character's current HP.

WORLDS

- *Twilight Town*

HP FACTOR	EXP FACTOR	DEF FACTOR	STUN	MUNNY
6.00	12.65	1.74~3.55	None	—

Mission(s)	LVL	Chance of Item Drop
14	6	—

Item Drops
None
None
None
None
None
None

Elemental Attack Vulnerability			
Fire	Ice	Thunder	Aero
0.59	0.67	0.25	0.77

Status Attack Vulnerability			
Ignite	Freeze	Jolt	Air-Toss
Immune	Immune	Immune	Immune

Attack Information				
Power Factor	Type	Element	Status Effect	Guard Type
1.70	Physical	—	—	Block
0.75	Physical	Flower	Darkness (10%)	Counter
0.74	Magical	Nil	Null Defense (100%)	None
0.74	Magical	Nil	Null Defense (100%)	None
0.82	Physical	Earth	HP Halved (20%)	None

DESERTER

12

Quick to flee from threats, these small Heartless will attack anyone who takes down another of their number with a flurry of kicks. Block to send them sprawling.

WORLDS

- *Twilight Town*
- *Agrabah*
- *Beast's Castle*

HP FACTOR	EXP FACTOR	DEF FACTOR	STUN	MUNNY
0.37	1.10	1.20	Normal atk.	30

Mission(s)	LVL	Chance of Item Drop
13	3	10% (Potion)
19	8	10% (Shining Shard)
40	15	30% (Gust Shard)
70	41	40% (Shield Tech+)

Item Drops
Potion
Shining Shard
Gust Shard
None
Shield Tech+
None

Elemental Attack Vulnerability			
Fire	Ice	Thunder	Aero
1.40	1.60	0.60	1.70

Status Attack Vulnerability			
Ignite	Freeze	Jolt	Air-Toss
1.00	1.00	1.00	1.00

Attack Information				
Power Factor	Type	Element	Status Effect	Guard Type
2.61	Physical	—	—	Counter

DESTROYER

46

These large, flying drone Heartless fire a super laser that tears apart anything in its path, friend or foe. While regular attacks will not stagger the Destroyer, jolting it with Thunder magic will disable its super and double laser.

WORLDS

- *Twilight Town*

HP FACTOR	EXP FACTOR	DEF FACTOR	STUN	MUNNY
4.80	5.55	1.65	None	36

Mission(s)	LVL	Chance of Item Drop
56	26	18% (Shining Gem)

Item Drops
None
None
None
Shining Gem
None
None

Elemental Attack Vulnerability			
Fire	Ice	Thunder	Aero
0.69	0.80	0.68	0.89

Status Attack Vulnerability			
Ignite	Freeze	Jolt	Air-Toss
0.10	0.10	0.80	Immune

Attack Information				
Power Factor	Type	Element	Status Effect	Guard Type
1.09	Physical	Light	Radar Zap (20%)	None
2.13	Magical	Nil	Null Defense (100%)	None

DETONATOR

30

These large versions of the Minute Bomb act similarly, but produce a much broader blast radius when they self-detonate. They also won't stagger from regular attacks, making them a dangerous foe. Take ample care when facing them.

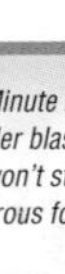

WORLDS

- *Twilight Town*
- *Halloween Town*

HP FACTOR	EXP FACTOR	DEF FACTOR	STUN	MUNNY
2.39	4.30	1.45	None	26

Mission(s)	LVL	Chance of Item Drop
56	26	80% (Gear Component B)
79, 87	26	10% (Megalixir Recipe)

Item Drops
None
None
None
Gear Component B
None
Megalixir Recipe

Elemental Attack Vulnerability			
Fire	Ice	Thunder	Aero
Immune	2.66	0.70	2.13

Status Attack Vulnerability			
Ignite	Freeze	Jolt	Air-Toss
Immune	1.50	0.40	0.40

Attack Information				
Power Factor	Type	Element	Status Effect	Guard Type
1.70	Physical	—	—	Counter
2.17	Physical	Fire	Ignite (100%)	Block
2.17	Physical	Fire	Ignite (100%)	Block

DIRE PLANT

These small plant Heartless are rooted to the ground. They strike from afar using a seed cannon that can be turned on other foes with a well-timed block, or even used to destroy the Dire Plant itself. Flower-based attacks like their seeds can cause blindness, which causes your character's attacks to miss.

WORLDS

- Twilight Town
- Agrabah

HP FACTOR	EXP FACTOR	DEF FACTOR	STUN	MUNNY
0.71	1.33	1.08	Normal atk.	11

Mission(s)	LVL	Chance of Item Drop
03, 04, 07	1	10% (Potion)
08, 09	2	10% (Potion)
12	4	10% (Potion)
15, 16, 21	4	15% (Potion)
74	20	9% (Frost Crystal)

Item Drops
Potion
Potion
None
None
None
Frost Crystal

Elemental Attack Vulnerability			
Fire	Ice	Thunder	Aero
2.20	3.20	1.20	3.40

Status Attack Vulnerability			
Ignite	Freeze	Jolt	Air-Toss
2.00	0.70	0.70	Immune

Attack Information

Power Factor	Type	Element	Status Effect	Guard Type
0.98	Physical	Flower	Darkness (5%)	Counter

DUAL BLADE

This large and aggressive knight Heartless's skillful defense makes it tough to finish off. Although its focused slash can be stopped with a block, blasting the knight with Thundaga while it is storing up energy will stagger it, opening it up to extra damage, especially from magic.

WORLDS

- Halloween Town

HP FACTOR	EXP FACTOR	DEF FACTOR	STUN	MUNNY
9.60	6.23	1.50	None	22

Mission(s)	LVL	Chance of Item Drop
54	24	100% (Lightning Gem)
72	41	100% (Gear Component C)

Item Drops
None
None
None
Lightning Gem
Gear Component C
None

Elemental Attack Vulnerability			
Fire	Ice	Thunder	Aero
0.81	0.91	0.52	Absorb

Status Attack Vulnerability			
Ignite	Freeze	Jolt	Air-Toss
Immune	Immune	0.15	Immune

Attack Information

Power Factor	Type	Element	Status Effect	Guard Type
1.41	Physical	—	—	Block
0.61	Physical	—	—	Block
2.02	Physical	Aero	Air-Toss (100%)	Counter
1.63	Physical	—	—	None
1.43	Physical	Aero	Air-Toss (100%)	Block

DUSK

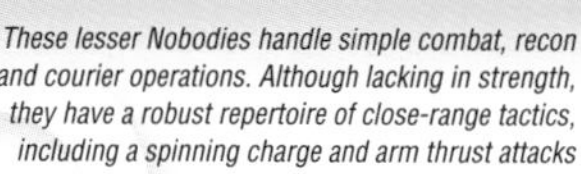

These lesser Nobodies handle simple combat, recon and courier operations. Although lacking in strength, they have a robust repertoire of close-range tactics, including a spinning charge and arm thrust attacks

WORLDS

- The Castle That Never Was

HP FACTOR	EXP FACTOR	DEF FACTOR	STUN	MUNNY
0.48	2.53	1.18	Normal atk.	6

Mission(s)	LVL	Chance of Item Drop
10	2	—
71	41	—
91	23	20% (Range Tech++)

Item Drops
None
None
None
None
None
Range Tech++

Elemental Attack Vulnerability			
Fire	Ice	Thunder	Aero
1.30	2.00	0.60	1.70

Status Attack Vulnerability			
Ignite	Freeze	Jolt	Air-Toss
1.00	1.00	1.00	Immune

Attack Information

Power Factor	Type	Element	Status Effect	Guard Type
2.10	Physical	—	—	Block
1.30	Physical	—	—	Block

DUSTFLIER

Large and deadly, these flying Heartless pack extreme power and high HP levels. Their arsenal includes Meteor breath and an invincible charge, and all of their attacks can inflict negative status effects on contact. This specimen is easily in the strongest class of Heartless. Prepare accordingly.

WORLDS

- Twilight Town

HP FACTOR	EXP FACTOR	DEF FACTOR	STUN	MUNNY
12.00	51.85	7.20~12.00	None	33

Mission(s)	LVL	Chance of Item Drop
89	45	100% (Premium Orb)

Item Drops
None
None
None
None
None
Premium Orb

Elemental Attack Vulnerability			
Fire	Ice	Thunder	Aero
0.08	0.11	0.03	Absorb

Status Attack Vulnerability			
Ignite	Freeze	Jolt	Air-Toss
Immune	Immune	0.01	Immune

Attack Information

Power Factor	Type	Element	Status Effect	Guard Type
3.10	Physical	Earth	HP halved (100%)	Block
2.50	Physical	Aero	Air-Toss (100%)	Block
2.60	Physical	—	Random (100%)	None
3.00	Physical	Fire	Ignite (80%)	Block

EMERALD SERENADE

14

These large flying Heartless travel along a set path, making ambush a useful tactic. Their speed grows faster as their HP drops, rendering them increasingly tricky to finish off.

WORLDS

- Wonderland
- Never Land

HP FACTOR	EXP FACTOR	DEF FACTOR	STUN	MUNNY
7.06	1.55	1.70	Normal atk.	40

Mission(s)	LVL	Chance of Item Drop
64	32	20% (Silver)
67	40	20% (Silver)
81	49	80% (Gold)

Item Drops
None
None
None
None
Silver
Gold

Elemental Attack Vulnerability			
Fire	Ice	Thunder	Aero
0.28	0.28	0.28	0.28

Status Attack Vulnerability			
Ignite	Freeze	Jolt	Air-Toss
1.50	1.50	1.50	1.50

Attack Information				
Power Factor	Type	Element	Status Effect	Guard Type
—	—	—	—	—

FIRE PLANT

15

These mid-sized plant Heartless are rooted to the ground. They strike from afar with bouncing fireballs, but are slow to react. A nimble fighter can easily get behind them and eliminate them from the rear.

WORLDS

- Agrabah

HP FACTOR	EXP FACTOR	DEF FACTOR	STUN	MUNNY
1.59	1.83	1.32	Normal atk.	16

Mission(s)	LVL	Chance of Item Drop
16, 18, 24, 30	9	10% (Blazing Shard)
48	9	30% (Blazing Shard)
68	20	60% (Blazing Gem)

Item Drops
None
Blazing Shard
Blazing Shard
None
Blazing Gem
None

Elemental Attack Vulnerability			
Fire	Ice	Thunder	Aero
Absorb	8.00	1.00	3.00

Status Attack Vulnerability			
Ignite	Freeze	Jolt	Air-Toss
Immune	1.50	0.50	Immune

Attack Information				
Power Factor	Type	Element	Status Effect	Guard Type
0.98	Physical	Fire	Ignite (30%)	Block

FLARE NOTE

17

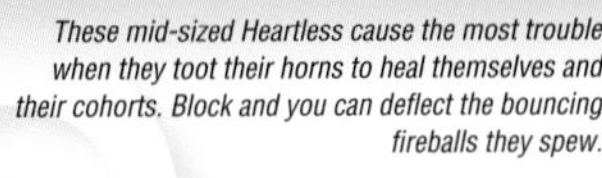

These mid-sized Heartless cause the most trouble when they toot their horns to heal themselves and their cohorts. Block and you can deflect the bouncing fireballs they spew.

WORLDS

- Olympus Coliseum

HP FACTOR	EXP FACTOR	DEF FACTOR	STUN	MUNNY
4.00	2.85	1.25	Stun atk.	17

Mission(s)	LVL	Chance of Item Drop
36, 39	13	24% (Blazing Shard)
61	20	18% (Blazing Gem)

Item Drops
None
None
Blazing Shard
Blazing Gem
None
None

Elemental Attack Vulnerability			
Fire	Ice	Thunder	Aero
Absorb	11.20	1.40	6.80

Status Attack Vulnerability			
Ignite	Freeze	Jolt	Air-Toss
Immune	1.50	1.00	1.00

Attack Information				
Power Factor	Type	Element	Status Effect	Guard Type
1.30	Physical	Fire	Ignite (40%)	Block

GIGAS SHADOW

—

These large Pureblood Heartless take the Mega-Shadow attack pattern and add even more muscle. The only way to knock them off guard is to deflect their tackles with a block.

WORLDS

- Twilight Town
- Beast's Castle
- Wonderland

HP FACTOR	EXP FACTOR	DEF FACTOR	STUN	MUNNY
7.19	4.55	1.15	None	26

Mission(s)	LVL	Chance of Item Drop
43, 55	21	30% (Elixir Recipe)
44	10	30% (Elixir Recipe)
63	13	45% (Combo Tech++)
83, 89, 90	40	10% (Megalixir Recipe)

Item Drops
None
None
Elixir Recipe
Elixir Recipe
Combo Tech++
Megalixir Recipe

Elemental Attack Vulnerability			
Fire	Ice	Thunder	Aero
2.93	3.20	1.20	3.40

Status Attack Vulnerability			
Ignite	Freeze	Jolt	Air-Toss
0.40	0.40	0.40	0.40

Attack Information				
Power Factor	Type	Element	Status Effect	Guard Type
0.98	Physical	—	—	Block
1.82	Physical	—	—	Block
2.11	Physical	Space	Shoe-Glue (100%)	Counter

GREY CAPRICE

These small flying Heartless strike with special warp missiles that make your character trade positions with them. Their magic can't be interrupted by attacking, so try to take them out early on!

WORLDS

- *Wonderland*

HP FACTOR	EXP FACTOR	DEF FACTOR	STUN
2.80	5.45	1.09	Stun atk.

MUNNY **27**

Mission(s)	LVL	Chance of Item Drop
47	20	60% (Aerial Tech)
51, 55, 57	20	30% (Gear Component B)
65	20	30% (Aerial Tech+)
81, 85	20	25% (Aerial Tech++)

Item Drops
None
None
Aerial Tech
Gear Component B
Aerial Tech+
Aerial Tech++

Elemental Attack Vulnerability			
Fire	Ice	Thunder	Aero
2.55	2.66	1.00	2.83

Status Attack Vulnerability			
Ignite	Freeze	Jolt	Air-Toss
1.20	1.20	1.20	1.20

Attack Information				
Power Factor	Type	Element	Status Effect	Guard Type
1.30	Physical	—	—	Block

GUARDIAN

These large flying drone Heartless fire a super laser that damages anything in its path, friend or foe. Regular attacks will not stagger the Guardian. To disable its super laser, jolt it with Thunder. Nil-based attacks like the super laser can null your character's defense, increasing the damage incurred.

WORLDS

- *Twilight Town*

HP FACTOR	EXP FACTOR	DEF FACTOR	STUN
2.23	3.38	1.55	None

MUNNY **30**

Mission(s)	LVL	Chance of Item Drop
11	8	24% (Moonstone)
20	8	100% (Aerial Tech)
59	8	100% (Shining Shard)

Item Drops
Moonstone
Aerial Tech
None
Shining Shard
None
None

Elemental Attack Vulnerability			
Fire	Ice	Thunder	Aero
0.70	0.80	0.60	0.92

Status Attack Vulnerability			
Ignite	Freeze	Jolt	Air-Toss
0.40	0.40	1.80	Immune

Attack Information				
Power Factor	Type	Element	Status Effect	Guard Type
0.93	Magical	Nil	Null Defense	None

GUARD ARMOR

Large and heavily armored, these Heartless will jump and then crash into the ground, creating a powerful shockwave. They drop their heads after landing, however; strike then and the body will eventually fall to pieces, with each piece acting autonomously. Start with the limbs and take them all out.

WORLDS

- *Olympus Coliseum*

HP FACTOR	EXP FACTOR	DEF FACTOR	STUN
4.16	39.60	1.00~2.04	None

MUNNY —

Mission(s)	LVL	Chance of Item Drop
61	31	—

Item Drops
None
None
None
None
None
None

Elemental Attack Vulnerability			
Fire	Ice	Thunder	Aero
0.39	0.43	0.33	0.47

Status Attack Vulnerability			
Ignite	Freeze	Jolt	Air-Toss
Immune	Immune	0.10	Immune

Attack Information				
Power Factor	Type	Element	Status Effect	Guard Type
0.80	Physical	—	—	Block
0.98	Physical	—	—	Block
1.17	Physical	—	—	Block
1.62	Physical	—	—	None
1.49	Physical	Moon	Silence (10%)	Block

GUARD ARMOR ACTION PATTERN FLOW

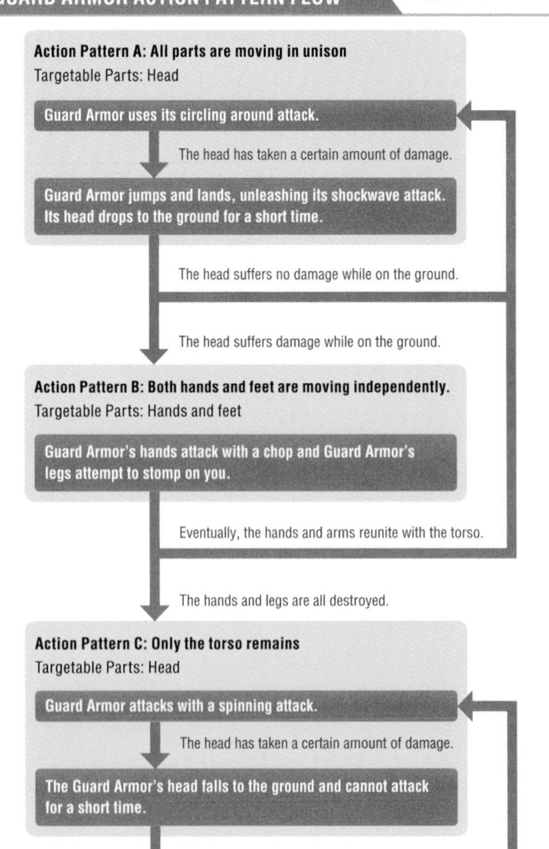

HEAT SABER ♡ 68

This fiery knight Heartless's skillful defense makes it tough to finish off. Although its focused slash can be stopped with a block, blasting the knight with Blizzaga while it is storing up energy will stagger it, opening it up to extra damage.

WORLDS

- *Twilight Town*

HP FACTOR	EXP FACTOR	DEF FACTOR	STUN	MUNNY
8.80	8.60	1.55	None	28

Mission(s)	LVL	Chance of Item Drop
56	30	100% (Power Tech)

Item Drops
None
None
None
Power Tech
None
None

Elemental Attack Vulnerability			
Fire	Ice	Thunder	Aero
Absorb	1.11	Immune	Immune

Status Attack Vulnerability			
Ignite	Freeze	Jolt	Air-Toss
Immune	0.10	Immune	Immune

Attack Information				
Power Factor	Type	Element	Status Effect	Guard Type
1.57	Physical	—	—	Block
0.67	Physical	—	—	Block
2.05	Physical	Fire	Ignite (100%)	Circle
1.70	Physical	Fire	Ignite (100%)	None
1.54	Physical	Fire	Ignite (100%)	Block

HOVER GHOST ♡ 16

These small flying Heartless can spontaneously appear behind their targets and possess them. If you are ensnared, rapidly press buttons to shake loose. Hover Ghosts are quick to blink out of harm's way, but negative status effects will prevent them from vanishing.

WORLDS

- *Olympus Coliseum*
- *Halloween Town*

HP FACTOR	EXP FACTOR	DEF FACTOR	STUN	MUNNY
3.20	2.38	1.06	Normal atk.	16

Mission(s)	LVL	Chance of Item Drop
42, 45	12	40% (Lightning Shard)
52	12	30% (Lightning Gem)
61	20	30% (Lightning Gem)
62	12	5% (Lightning Gem)
79	15	30% (Lightning Crystal)

Item Drops
None
None
Lightning Shard
Lightning Gem
Lightning Gem
Lightning Crystal

Elemental Attack Vulnerability			
Fire	Ice	Thunder	Aero
4.40	4.80	1.80	5.67

Status Attack Vulnerability			
Ignite	Freeze	Jolt	Air-Toss
1.00	1.00	1.00	1.00

Attack Information				
Power Factor	Type	Element	Status Effect	Guard Type
0.90	Physical	—	—	Block
0.18	Magical	Flower	Darkness (5%)	None

ICE CANNON ♡ 29

These mid-sized cannon Heartless fire shots that rain down from above. Use dodge rolls or air slides to evacuate the target area. Their head-on shots can freeze victims, but can also be batted back with a block. Regular attacks won't throw them off balance.

WORLDS

- *Olympus Coliseum*

HP FACTOR	EXP FACTOR	DEF FACTOR	STUN	MUNNY
3.60	4.15	1.70	None	17

Mission(s)	LVL	Chance of Item Drop
46	20	40% (Frost Shard)
61	20	30% (Frost Gem)
73	20	30% (Gold)

Item Drops
None
None
Frost Shard
Frost Gem
None
Gold

Elemental Attack Vulnerability			
Fire	Ice	Thunder	Aero
4.40	Absorb	1.05	2.98

Status Attack Vulnerability			
Ignite	Freeze	Jolt	Air-Toss
1.50	Immune	1.00	Immune

Attack Information				
Power Factor	Type	Element	Status Effect	Guard Type
1.63	Physical	Ice	Freeze (25%)	None
1.63	Physical	Ice	Freeze (25%)	Counter

ICY CUBE ♡ 15

These small Heartless are encased in ice and strike with a tackle that can be blocked and deflected, knocking them off balance. Hit them while they're down to send them careening into other enemies, freezing them on the spot.

WORLDS

- *Beast's Castle*
- *Halloween Town*

HP FACTOR	EXP FACTOR	DEF FACTOR	STUN	MUNNY
1.02	1.93	1.28	Normal atk.	11

Mission(s)	LVL	Chance of Item Drop
35	1	20% (Iron)
49	20	50% (Frost Shard)
79	49	15% (Frost Crystal)
83	20	15% (Frost Crystal)

Item Drops
None
Iron
Frost Shard
None
None
Frost Crystal

Elemental Attack Vulnerability			
Fire	Ice	Thunder	Aero
6.00	Absorb	0.65	2.00

Status Attack Vulnerability			
Ignite	Freeze	Jolt	Air-Toss
2.00	Immune	Immune	Immune

Attack Information				
Power Factor	Type	Element	Status Effect	Guard Type
1.17	Physical	Ice	Freeze (10%)	Counter
0.98	Physical	Ice	Freeze (30%)	Block
0.73	Physical	Ice	Freeze (100%)	None

INFERNAL ENGINE 96

The cannonballs that this heavy tank Heartless fires can be returned with a block to take out the archers perched atop it. The battering ram that emerges from its mouth before it charges is especially weak. Capitalize on that vulnerability, but get out of there before it begins its advance.

WORLDS

- Beast's Castle

HP FACTOR	EXP FACTOR	DEF FACTOR	STUN	MUNNY
19.20	61.80	0.60~4.50	None	—

Mission(s)	LVL	Chance of Item Drop
50	22	—

Item Drops
None
None
None
None
None
None

Elemental Attack Vulnerability			
Fire	Ice	Thunder	Aero
0.59	0.45	0.16	0.49

Status Attack Vulnerability			
Ignite	Freeze	Jolt	Air-Toss
Immune	Immune	Immune	Immune

Attack Information				
Power Factor	Type	Element	Status Effect	Guard Type
0.20	Physical	Thunder	Jolt (20%)	None
1.36	Physical	Fire	Ignite (2%)	Block
0.90	Physical	Fire	Ignite (10%)	Counter
1.30	Physical	—	—	Counter
1.98	Physical	—	—	None
3.42	Physical	—	—	None

INVISIBLE —

Both fast and strong, these Heartless pose a serious threat. They attack with a fearsome shockwave. Time your combo finisher so it connects right after they catch their sword. This will cancel the shockwave and leave them open.

WORLDS

- Twilight Town
- Beast's Castle
- Halloween Town

HP FACTOR	EXP FACTOR	DEF FACTOR	STUN	MUNNY
12.00	16.05	3.24	None	—

Mission(s)	LVL	Chance of Item Drop
70	41	100% (Gust Gem)
74	45	100% (Shield Tech++)
87	52	100% (Shield Tech++)
90	60	100% (Shield Tech++)

Item Drops
None
None
None
None
Gust Gem
Shield Tech++

Elemental Attack Vulnerability			
Fire	Ice	Thunder	Aero
0.72	0.80	Absorb	0.90

Status Attack Vulnerability			
Ignite	Freeze	Jolt	Air-Toss
Immune	0.05	Immune	Immune

Attack Information				
Power Factor	Type	Element	Status Effect	Guard Type
1.45	Physical	—	—	Block
1.46	Physical	—	—	Block
1.03	Physical	—	—	Block
1.64	Magical	Nil	Null Defense (100%)	None
1.64	Physical	Thunder	Jolt (100%)	None
0.67	Physical	Time	Defense Lv. 1 (50%)	Block

JUMBO CANNON 29

Mid-sized versions of the Li'l Cannon, these foes fire shots that rain down from above. Use dodge rolls or air slides to evacuate the target area. Although strong across the board and immune to being stunned by attacks, their head-on shots can be batted back with a block.

WORLDS

- Olympus Coliseum

HP FACTOR	EXP FACTOR	DEF FACTOR	STUN	MUNNY
5.60	4.23	1.70	None	26

Mission(s)	LVL	Chance of Item Drop
39, 46	15	30% (Lightning Shard)
61	15	50% (Lightning Shard)
73	20	20% (Ankharite)

Item Drops
None
None
Lightning Shard
Lightning Shard
None
Ankharite

Elemental Attack Vulnerability			
Fire	Ice	Thunder	Aero
Immune	2.29	0.86	2.67

Status Attack Vulnerability			
Ignite	Freeze	Jolt	Air-Toss
Immune	0.30	1.00	Immune

Attack Information				
Power Factor	Type	Element	Status Effect	Guard Type
1.82	Physical	Fire	Ignite (100%)	None
1.82	Physical	Fire	Ignite (100%)	Counter

LAND ARMOR 47

Armor covers every inch of these large Heartless, allowing them to deflect blows from every direction. Instead, aim for the head and knock them down, rendering them vulnerable to further attack. Use Aero magic to keep them down longer.

WORLDS

- Agrabah

HP FACTOR	EXP FACTOR	DEF FACTOR	STUN	MUNNY
6.56	5.83	2.40	None	36

Mission(s)	LVL	Chance of Item Drop
90	65	80% (Mithril)

Item Drops
None
None
None
None
None
Mithril

Elemental Attack Vulnerability			
Fire	Ice	Thunder	Aero
0.50	0.56	0.20	0.85

Status Attack Vulnerability			
Ignite	Freeze	Jolt	Air-Toss
Immune	Immune	Immune	0.12

Attack Information				
Power Factor	Type	Element	Status Effect	Guard Type
1.25	Physical	—	—	Block
1.90	Physical	Earth	HP Halved (100%)	None
1.60	Physical	Space	Shoe-Glue (100%)	None
1.40	Physical	Flower	Darkness (40%)	Block

LARGE ARMOR

22

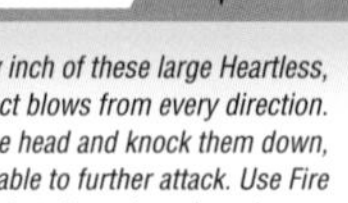

Armor covers every inch of these large Heartless, allowing them to deflect blows from every direction. Instead, aim for the head and knock them down, rendering them vulnerable to further attack. Use Fire magic to keep them down longer.

WORLDS

- *Agrabah*

HP FACTOR	EXP FACTOR	DEF FACTOR	STUN	MUNNY
6.80	3.28	2.10	None	22

Mission(s)	LVL	Chance of Item Drop
21, 26, 30, 34	12	50% (Frost Shard)
48	12	90% (Power Tech)

Item Drops
None
Frost Shard
Power Tech
None
None
None

Elemental Attack Vulnerability			
Fire	Ice	Thunder	Aero
1.96	1.39	0.52	1.59

Status Attack Vulnerability			
Ignite	Freeze	Jolt	Air-Toss
Immune	Immune	0.15	0.15

Attack Information

Power Factor	Type	Element	Status Effect	Guard Type
1.05	Physical	—	—	Block
1.20	Physical	—	—	Block
1.87	Physical	—	—	None
1.40	Physical	—	—	None

LEECHGRAVE

94

A massive plant-like Heartless with a savage claw attack. The toxic pollen it spews from its head saps victims' HP for as long as they breathe it. Destroy all of the Tentaclaws to dizzy the main body before moving in. Note that defeating Tentaclaws or hitting them with magic will speed up the pollen bursts.

WORLDS

- *Twilight Town*

HP FACTOR	EXP FACTOR	DEF FACTOR	STUN	MUNNY
8.51	57.98	3.10	None	—

Mission(s)	LVL	Chance of Item Drop
66	40	—

Item Drops
None
None
None
None
None
None

Elemental Attack Vulnerability			
Fire	Ice	Thunder	Aero
Immune	Immune	Immune	Immune

Status Attack Vulnerability			
Ignite	Freeze	Jolt	Air-Toss
Immune	Immune	Immune	Immune

Attack Information

Power Factor	Type	Element	Status Effect	Guard Type
1.83	Physical	—	—	Block
0.09	Magical	—	—	None
0.02	Magical	—	—	Counter
0.03	Magical	—	—	None

LI'L CANNON

16

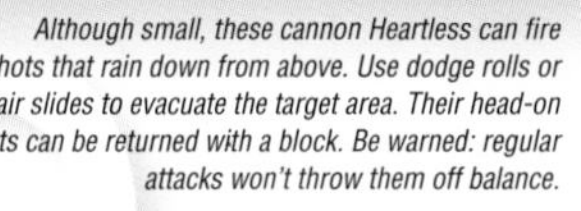

Although small, these cannon Heartless can fire shots that rain down from above. Use dodge rolls or air slides to evacuate the target area. Their head-on shots can be returned with a block. Be warned: regular attacks won't throw them off balance.

WORLDS

- *Olympus Coliseum*

HP FACTOR	EXP FACTOR	DEF FACTOR	STUN	MUNNY
3.59	2.43	1.30	None	11

Mission(s)	LVL	Chance of Item Drop
36, 41	13	50% (Gear Component A)
73	14	9% (Ankharite)

Item Drops
None
None
Gear Component A
None
None
Ankharite

Elemental Attack Vulnerability			
Fire	Ice	Thunder	Aero
Absorb	5.60	4.20	5.95

Status Attack Vulnerability			
Ignite	Freeze	Jolt	Air-Toss
0.30	0.50	1.50	1.00

Attack Information

Power Factor	Type	Element	Status Effect	Guard Type
1.43	Physical	Fire	Ignite (50%)	None
1.43	Physical	Fire	Ignite (50%)	Counter

LIVING POD

60

These mid-sized flying Heartless can spontaneously appear behind their targets and possess them. Although they behave similarly to Hover Ghosts, physical attacks won't stagger them. Remember, there's no shame in falling back to regroup.

WORLDS

- *Beast's Castle*

HP FACTOR	EXP FACTOR	DEF FACTOR	STUN	MUNNY
8.40	0	2.00	None	—

Mission(s)	LVL	Chance of Item Drop
80	51	—

Item Drops
None
None
None
None
None
None

Elemental Attack Vulnerability			
Fire	Ice	Thunder	Aero
1.05	1.20	0.45	1.29

Status Attack Vulnerability			
Ignite	Freeze	Jolt	Air-Toss
0.40	0.40	0.40	0.40

Attack Information

Power Factor	Type	Element	Status Effect	Guard Type
2.40	Physical	Light	Radar Zap (30%)	Block
0.23	Magical	—	—	None

LOCK, SHOCK AND BARREL

 —

LOCK

Despite being the trio's apparent leader, Lock lacks real combat skill. Instead, he'll run about wildly while throwing pumpkin bombs from afar. Hit them back with a block to send him sprawling.

SHOCK

Shock poses little threat in terms of strength, but will attack with a spinning charge. Stop that with a block, or hit her with one of Lock's pumpkin bombs to send her sprawling.

BARREL

Like Shock, Barrel poses little threat in terms of strength. Stop his rolling charge with a block and he will go flying. You can also hit him with one of Lock's pumpkin bombs to send him sprawling.

WORLDS

- *Halloween Town*

THREE OF A KIND

All of the following enemy statistics are identical for Lock, Shock and Barrel, but they are three unique enemies and do not share a common pool of HP. The only thing that distinguishes them in battle is their different attacks.

HP FACTOR	EXP FACTOR	DEF FACTOR	STUN	MUNNY
2.00	0	1.25	Normal atk.	—

Mission(s)	LVL	Chance of Item Drop
52	24	—

Item Drops
None
None
None
None
None
None

Elemental Attack Vulnerability			
Fire	Ice	Thunder	Aero
0.63	0.80	0.30	0.85

Status Attack Vulnerability			
Ignite	Freeze	Jolt	Air-Toss
0.10	0.10	0.10	0.10

Attack Information				
Power Factor	Type	Element	Status Effect	Guard Type
0.17	Physical	Fire	Ignite (3%)	None
0.20	Physical	—	—	Counter
0.15	Physical	—	—	Counter

LOUDMOUTH

12

These small Heartless cause the most trouble when they toot their horns to heal themselves and their cohorts. The wind missiles they shoot can be returned with a block. Wind-based attacks can air-toss your character. While airborne your character becomes an easy target and will take more damage if hit.

WORLDS

- *Agrabah*
- *Olympus Coliseum*

HP FACTOR	EXP FACTOR	DEF FACTOR	STUN	MUNNY
1.45	1.00	1.20	Normal Atk.	15

Mission(s)	LVL	Chance of Item Drop
15	4	15% (Hi-Potion)
18, 21, 24, 26, 30, 32, 34	8	15% (Hi-Potion)
46	17	—
48	17	25% (Shining Shard)
68	20	18% (Lightning Gem)
82	30	20% (Gear Component D)
90	20	20% (Gear Component D)

Item Drops
None
Hi-Potion
Shining Shard
None
Lightning Gem
Gear Component D

Elemental Attack Vulnerability			
Fire	Ice	Thunder	Aero
4.50	4.80	1.70	Absorb

Status Attack Vulnerability			
Ignite	Freeze	Jolt	Air-Toss
0.60	0.60	0.60	Immune

Attack Information				
Power Factor	Type	Element	Status Effect	Guard Type
0.73	Physical	Aero	Air-Toss (100%)	Counter

LURK LIZARD

70

Similar in form and behavior to the Veil Lizard, these foes attack prey with a tongue lash attack. Block it to dizzy the lizard, then strike back. Blizzard magic is also especially effective.

WORLDS

- *Wonderland*

HP FACTOR	EXP FACTOR	DEF FACTOR	STUN	MUNNY
6.80	11.05	1.60	None	36

Mission(s)	LVL	Chance of Item Drop
47	22	30% (Lightning Shard)
63	32	100% (Gear Component C)
85	52	80% (Mithril)

Item Drops
None
None
Lightning Shard
None
Gear Component C
Mithril

Elemental Attack Vulnerability			
Fire	Ice	Thunder	Aero
0.98	1.09	0.40	1.23

Status Attack Vulnerability			
Ignite	Freeze	Jolt	Air-Toss
Immune	0.16	Immune	Immune

Attack Information				
Power Factor	Type	Element	Status Effect	Guard Type
1.63	Physical	Space	Shoe-Glue (20%)	Block
0	Physical	—	—	Counter
1.70	Magical	Nil	Null Defense (100%)	None
1.63	Block	Light	Radar Zap (90%)	Block

MASSIVE POSSESSOR ♡ —

These living collectives are comprised of multiple Possessors and can drain life from anything they touch. When dealt lethal damage, the collective splits into individual creatures, so be prepared to face them.

WORLDS
- Beast's Castle
- Wonderland

HP FACTOR	EXP FACTOR	DEF FACTOR	STUN	MUNNY
1.20	2.03	1.00	Stun atk.	16

Mission(s)	LVL	Chance of Item Drop
35	12	30% (Panacea)
38, 43	12	35% (Gust Shard)
63	12	25% (Range Tech+)

Item Drops
None
Panacea
Gust Shard
None
Range Tech+
None

Elemental Attack Vulnerability

Fire	Ice	Thunder	Aero
4.40	4.80	1.80	5.10

Status Attack Vulnerability

Ignite	Freeze	Jolt	Air-Toss
0.60	0.60	Immune	0.60

Attack Information

Power Factor	Type	Element	Status Effect	Guard Type
0.23	Magical	Nil	Null Defense (100%)	None

MEGA-SHADOW ♡ —

These mid-sized Purebloods retain the attack patterns of their smaller cousins (Shadows), but also use a dangerous tackle. Block it and they're left wide open.

WORLDS
- Twilight Town
- Beast's Castle
- Halloween Town

HP FACTOR	EXP FACTOR	DEF FACTOR	STUN	MUNNY
1.20	2.33	1.25	Stun atk.	20

Mission(s)	LVL	Chance of Item Drop
06	1	10% (Blazing Shard)
31	10	30% (Combo Tech)
38, 43, 45	10	15% (Combo Tech)
44	21	15% (Combo Tech)
52, 59	15	50% (Dark Ingot)
62, 63	15	40% (Gust Gem)
75	20	25% (Range Tech+)

Item Drops
Blazing Shard
Combo Tech
Combo Tech
Dark Ingot
Gust Gem
Range Tech+

Elemental Attack Vulnerability

Fire	Ice	Thunder	Aero
2.20	2.67	1.00	2.83

Status Attack Vulnerability

Ignite	Freeze	Jolt	Air-Toss
0.60	0.60	0.60	0.60

Attack Information

Power Factor	Type	Element	Status Effect	Guard Type
0.63	Physical	—	—	Block
1.43	Physical	—	—	Block
1.63	Physical	—	—	Counter

MINUTE BOMB ♡ 13

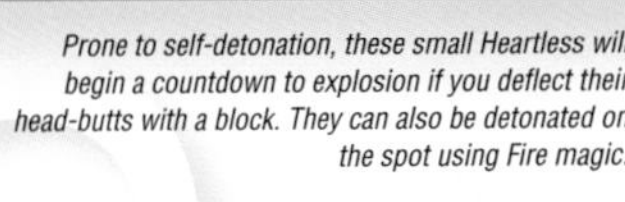

Prone to self-detonation, these small Heartless will begin a countdown to explosion if you deflect their head-butts with a block. They can also be detonated on the spot using Fire magic.

WORLDS
- Twilight Town

HP FACTOR	EXP FACTOR	DEF FACTOR	STUN	MUNNY
1.52	1.28	1.30	Normal atk.	10

Mission(s)	LVL	Chance of Item Drop
11, 12, 14	2	10% (Blazing Shard)
17	2	20% (Ether)
56	10	21% (Bronze)

Item Drops
Blazing Shard
Ether
None
Bronze
None
None

Elemental Attack Vulnerability

Fire	Ice	Thunder	Aero
Immune	4.80	1.10	4.80

Status Attack Vulnerability

Ignite	Freeze	Jolt	Air-Toss
Immune	1.30	1.00	1.00

Attack Information

Power Factor	Type	Element	Status Effect	Guard Type
1.30	Physical	—	—	Counter
2.02	Physical	Fire	Ignite (50%)	None
2.02	Physical	Fire	Ignite (50%)	None

MORNING STAR ♡ 44

Sharp spikes cover these large Heartless, a fact they exploit in a dangerous spin attack. Although they are impervious while spinning, you can slow their onslaught with a block, bringing them to an eventual halt. Alternatively, Aero magic will stop them with a single blast.

WORLDS
- Olympus Coliseum

HP FACTOR	EXP FACTOR	DEF FACTOR	STUN	MUNNY
6.39	4.95	2.80	None	27

Mission(s)	LVL	Chance of Item Drop
41	15	100% (Gear Component A)

Item Drops
None
None
Gear Component A
None
None
None

Elemental Attack Vulnerability

Fire	Ice	Thunder	Aero
1.23	1.14	0.43	2.55

Status Attack Vulnerability

Ignite	Freeze	Jolt	Air-Toss
0.10	0.10	0.12	0.20

Attack Information

Power Factor	Type	Element	Status Effect	Guard Type
0.27	Physical	—	—	Block
1.96	Physical	—	—	None

NEOSHADOW

♡ —

A pureblood Heartless that flows across the ground as a shadow, completely immune to attack. It may unleash a shockwave as it emerges, so stay on guard. Block when it charges to earn a few precious seconds during which you can deal double damage.

WORLDS

- Twilight Town
- Beast's Castle
- The Castle That Never Was

HP FACTOR	EXP FACTOR	DEF FACTOR	STUN	MUNNY
3.20	2.63	1.37	Stun atk.	21

Mission(s)	LVL	Chance of Item Drop
29	17	30% (Combo Tech)
38, 44	17	80% (Lightning Shard)
93	17	—

Item Drops
None
Combo Tech
Lightning Shard
None
None
None

Elemental Attack Vulnerability			
Fire	Ice	Thunder	Aero
1.35	1.60	0.60	1.70

Status Attack Vulnerability			
Ignite	Freeze	Jolt	Air-Toss
0.40	0.40	0.40	0.40

Attack Information

Power Factor	Type	Element	Status Effect	Guard Type
1.43	Physical	—	—	Block
1.54	Physical	—	—	Counter
1.70	Physical	Flower	Darkness (40%)	None

NOVASHADOW

The advanced form of the Pureblood Neoshadow can't be knocked off balance and it retains the ability to unleash a shockwave as it resurfaces from the ground. Block when it charges to earn a few precious seconds during which you can deal double damage.

WORLDS

- Wonderland

HP FACTOR	EXP FACTOR	DEF FACTOR	STUN	MUNNY
7.60	5.98	1.60	None	32

Mission(s)	LVL	Chance of Item Drop
65	40	40% (Shield Tech+)
85	50	18% (Shield Tech++)

Item Drops
None
None
None
None
Shield Tech+
Shield Tech++

Elemental Attack Vulnerability			
Fire	Ice	Thunder	Aero
1.24	1.40	0.53	1.59

Status Attack Vulnerability			
Ignite	Freeze	Jolt	Air-Toss
0.30	0.30	0.30	0.30

Attack Information

Power Factor	Type	Element	Status Effect	Guard Type
1.54	Physical	—	—	Block
1.76	Physical	Water	Damage Absorb (30%)	Counter
1.70	Physical	Illusion	Damage Drain (25%)	None

ORCUS

♡ —

Although faster and more powerful, these Heartless are otherwise the same as the Invisible. They attack with a fearsome shockwave. Time your combo finisher so it connects right after they catch their sword. This will cancel the shockwave and leave them open to a counter attack.

WORLDS

- Twilight Town
- Halloween Town

HP FACTOR	EXP FACTOR	DEF FACTOR	STUN	MUNNY
5.11	42.90	1.70	None	—

Mission(s)	LVL	Chance of Item Drop
88	54	80% (Gold)
89	50	80% (Gold)

Item Drops
None
None
None
None
None
Gold

Elemental Attack Vulnerability			
Fire	Ice	Thunder	Aero
0.59	0.68	Absorb	0.75

Status Attack Vulnerability			
Ignite	Freeze	Jolt	Air-Toss
Immune	Immune	Immune	0.20

Attack Information

Power Factor	Type	Element	Status Effect	Guard Type
1.35	Physical	—	—	Block
1.23	Physical	—	—	Block
1.06	Physical	—	—	Block
1.20	Magical	Nil	Null Defense (100%)	None
1.73	Physical	Thunder	Jolt (100%)	None
0.81	Physical	Time	Defense Lv. 1 (65%)	Block

PETE

♡ —

This shady character has been sighted in multiple worlds trying to amass an army of Heartless. His bowling-ball attack causes negative status effects at random. Though aggressive in combat, he'll flee the moment his HP runs out.

WORLDS

- Agrabah

HP FACTOR	EXP FACTOR	DEF FACTOR	STUN	MUNNY
6.80	11.58	1.50	None	—

Mission(s)	LVL	Chance of Item Drop
24	14	—

Item Drops
None
None
None
None
None
None

Elemental Attack Vulnerability			
Fire	Ice	Thunder	Aero
0.73	0.83	0.31	0.92

Status Attack Vulnerability			
Ignite	Freeze	Jolt	Air-Toss
Immune	Immune	Immune	Immune

Attack Information

Power Factor	Type	Element	Status Effect	Guard Type
1.17	Physical	—	—	Counter
1.30	Physical	—	—	Block
1.54	Physical	—	Random (100%)	Block

PHANTOMTAIL

70

These large aerial Heartless can't be harmed by blows to the head, instead warping to a remote location on impact. They won't warp, however, if you attack their wings or tail, so focus attacks there. Go in equipped for aerial combat.

WORLDS

- *Never Land*

HP FACTOR	EXP FACTOR	DEF FACTOR	STUN	MUNNY
6.40	8.90	1.50~1.90	None	28

Mission(s)	LVL	Chance of Item Drop
77	50	30% (Luck Tech)
86	58	30% (Luck Tech)

Item Drops
None
None
None
None
None
Luck Tech

Elemental Attack Vulnerability			
Fire	Ice	Thunder	Aero
1.04	1.15	0.43	1.30

Status Attack Vulnerability			
Ignite	Freeze	Jolt	Air-Toss
0.10	0.10	0.10	Immune

Attack Information

Power Factor	Type	Element	Status Effect	Guard Type
1.54	Physical	—	—	None
1.43	Physical	—	—	Block
1.92	Physical	—	—	Counter
1.30	Physical	Illusion	Flip-Foot (15%)	Block

PINK CONCERTO

16

A large flying Heartless. The toxic cloud it spits forth as it chases down targets will gradually drain the HP of anyone trapped within its bounds. Land a combo finisher to clear the cloud.

WORLDS

- *Wonderland*

HP FACTOR	EXP FACTOR	DEF FACTOR	STUN	MUNNY
7.60	2.73	1.40	Stun atk.	17

Mission(s)	LVL	Chance of Item Drop
51, 55, 57	26	40% (Range Tech)
65	26	45% (Aerial Tech+)

Item Drops
None
None
None
Range Tech
Aerial Tech+
None

Elemental Attack Vulnerability			
Fire	Ice	Thunder	Aero
2.93	1.05	0.40	1.28

Status Attack Vulnerability			
Ignite	Freeze	Jolt	Air-Toss
0.60	0.60	0.60	0.60

Attack Information

Power Factor	Type	Element	Status Effect	Guard Type
1.17	Physical	Flower	Darkness (10%)	Block
0.23	Magical	Flower	Darkness (30%)	Block

POISON PLANT

22

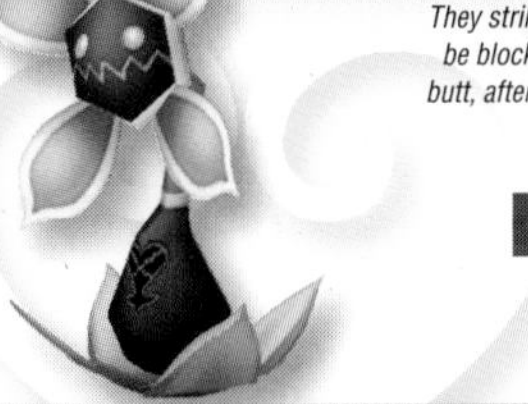

These large plant Heartless are rooted to the ground. They strike from afar with poison shots that cannot be blocked. At close range, they'll attempt a head-butt, after which they'll be wide open. They are also susceptible to Fire magic.

WORLDS

- *Twilight Town*

HP FACTOR	EXP FACTOR	DEF FACTOR	STUN	MUNNY
5.51	3.33	5.50	Stun atk.	26

Mission(s)	LVL	Chance of Item Drop
12	5	24% (Moonstone)
17, 23, 25	8	24% (Moonstone)
44	20	50% (Lightning Shard)
59	20	80% (Lightning Shard)
89	20	20% (Adamantite)

Item Drops
Moonstone
Moonstone
Lightning Shard
Lightning Shard
None
Adamantite

Elemental Attack Vulnerability			
Fire	Ice	Thunder	Aero
2.57	0.89	0.33	0.98

Status Attack Vulnerability			
Ignite	Freeze	Jolt	Air-Toss
1.60	0.50	0.50	Immune

Attack Information

Power Factor	Type	Element	Status Effect	Guard Type
0.77	Physical	Space	Shoe-Glue (10%)	Block
0.18	Physical	Flower	Darkness (30%)	None

POSSESSOR

—

These Pureblood Heartless are slow and generally weak, but can engulf targets and drain their life. Jump free to escape their capture.

WORLDS

- *Twilight Town*
- *Agrabah*
- *Beast's Castle*

HP FACTOR	EXP FACTOR	DEF FACTOR	STUN	MUNNY
0.71	1.00	1.00	Normal atk.	6

Mission(s)	LVL	Chance of Item Drop
05, 14	1	10% (Blazing Shard)
07	16	10% (Blazing Shard)
20, 21, 22, 26	8	10% (Potion)
43	14	20% (Hi-Potion)
63, 67	20	9% (Blazing Crystal)
77, 83, 89	30	10% (Lightning Crystal)

Item Drops
Blazing Shard
Potion
Hi-Potion
None
Blazing Crystal
Lightning Crystal

Elemental Attack Vulnerability			
Fire	Ice	Thunder	Aero
2.20	3.20	1.20	3.40

Status Attack Vulnerability			
Ignite	Freeze	Jolt	Air-Toss
1.00	1.00	Immune	1.00

Attack Information

Power Factor	Type	Element	Status Effect	Guard Type
0.20	Magical	Nil	Null Defense (100%)	None

POWERED ARMOR ♡ 97

This improved version of the Guard Armor still uses the same basic tactics. The powerful shockwave it produces causes it to drop its head. Strike when its head lowers and the body will eventually fall to pieces. Start with the limbs and take them all out.

WORLDS

- *Twilight Town*

HP FACTOR	EXP FACTOR	DEF FACTOR	STUN	MUNNY
3.12	65.63	1.60~1.85	None	—

Mission(s)	LVL	Chance of Item Drop
89	50	—

Item Drops
None
None
None
None
None
None

Elemental Attack Vulnerability			
Fire	Ice	Thunder	Aero
0.28	0.28	0.28	0.36

Status Attack Vulnerability			
Ignite	Freeze	Jolt	Air-Toss
Immune	Immune	0.20	Immune

Attack Information

Power Factor	Type	Element	Status Effect	Guard Type
1.14	Physical	—	—	Block
0.93	Physical	—	—	Block
1.22	Physical	—	—	Block
1.36	Physical	Earth	HP halved (20%)	None
1.39	Physical	—	—	Block

RARE VENDOR ♡ 0

Uncombative by nature, these large capsule Heartless will disappear after a short time. They hold rare and valuable prizes, however, and should be defeated when possible. They gain speed as they take damage, so don't let them get away!

WORLDS

- *N/A*

HP FACTOR	EXP FACTOR	DEF FACTOR	STUN	MUNNY
1.20	3.80	1.30	None	49

Mission(s)	LVL	Chance of Item Drop
54	24	100% (60%: Iron, 30%: Guard Tech, 10%: Elixir Recipe)
57	30	100% (60%: Iron, 30%: Guard Tech, 10%: Elixir Recipe)
59	30	100% (60%: Iron, 30%: Power Tech, 10%: Elixir Recipe)
61	31	100% (60%: Iron, 30%: Power Tech, 10%: Elixir Recipe)
72	41	100% (60%: Bronze, 30%: Frost Gem, 10%: Blazing Crystal)
74	42	100% (60%: Dark Ingot, 30%: Adamantite, 10%: Luck Tech)
76	43	100% (60%: Dark Ingot, 30%: Adamantite, 10%: Luck Tech)
81	49	100% (60%: Dark Ingot, 30%: Diamond, 10%: Luck Tech)

Item Drops
None
None
None
Elixir Recipe
Blazing Crystal
Luck Tech

Elemental Attack Vulnerability			
Fire	Ice	Thunder	Aero
0.98	1.60	0.60	1.70

Status Attack Vulnerability			
Ignite	Freeze	Jolt	Air-Toss
0.50	0.50	0.50	0.50

Attack Information

Power Factor	Type	Element	Status Effect	Guard Type
—	—	—	—	—

RIKU ♡ —

This warrior of the dark wears our Organization's coat. A master of combat, he combines combo attacks with a tight defense, a homing projectile, and a block-counter. His weapon grows in combat when the tides turn against him, increasing his attack range.

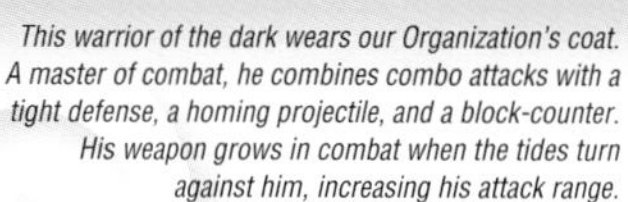

WORLDS

- *The Castle That Never Was*

HP FACTOR	EXP FACTOR	DEF FACTOR	STUN	MUNNY
8.56	118.05	1.20	Stun atk.	—

Mission(s)	LVL	Chance of Item Drop
93	61	—

Item Drops
None
None
None
None
None
None

Elemental Attack Vulnerability			
Fire	Ice	Thunder	Aero
0.33	0.33	0.14	0.41

Status Attack Vulnerability			
Ignite	Freeze	Jolt	Air-Toss
Immune	Immune	Immune	Immune

Attack Information

Power Factor	Type	Element	Status Effect	Guard Type
0.35 (1st attack); 0.40 (2nd attack); 0.70 (3rd attack)	Physical	—	—	Counter (before weapon is lit); Block (after weapon is lit)
1.67	Physical	—	—	None
1.40	Physical	—	—	Block
1.45	Physical	—	—	Block
1.40	Physical	—	—	Block
1.50	Physical	Flower	Darkness (40%)	Block
1.38	Physical	—	—	None
1.40	Physical	—	—	Block

RULER OF THE SKY ♡ 99

You need to destroy all the tail segments of this avian Heartless to reveal its core. After each segment is destroyed, the Ruler of the Sky will glow red and charge its foes. Wait too close to the water's surface and it will fire a salvo of water shots. Once the core is exposed, avoid the spray of coins and counter with Fire magic.

WORLDS

- *Never Land*

HP FACTOR	EXP FACTOR	DEF FACTOR	STUN	MUNNY
6.26	73.43	1.90~4.00	None	—

Mission(s)	LVL	Chance of Item Drop
78	49	—

Item Drops
None
None
None
None
None
None

Elemental Attack Vulnerability			
Fire	Ice	Thunder	Aero
0.43	Immune	Immune	Immune

Status Attack Vulnerability			
Ignite	Freeze	Jolt	Air-Toss
Immune	Immune	Immune	Immune

Attack Information

Power Factor	Type	Element	Status Effect	Guard Type
0.23	Physical	Water	Damage Drain (40%)	Block
1.00	Physical	Ice	Freeze (5%)	Block
0.50	Physical	—	—	Block
1.50	Physical	—	—	None
1.40	Physical	—	—	Block
1.95	Physical	—	—	Block

SAÏX

♡ —

The Organization's No. VII. Usually cool and calm, he turns into a berserker when he grips his giant blade in combat. Dodge his attacks as you watch for a rare opening. After taking damage, he will revert to his normal self, making him more susceptible to attack. Finish him quickly.

WORLDS

- *The Castle That Never Was*

HP FACTOR	EXP FACTOR	DEF FACTOR	STUN	MUNNY
5.44	99.83	1.28	None	—

Mission(s)	LVL	Chance of Item Drop
91	61	—

Item Drops
None
None
None
None
None
None

Elemental Attack Vulnerability			
Fire	Ice	Thunder	Aero
0.63	0.66	0.24	0.70

Status Attack Vulnerability			
Ignite	Freeze	Jolt	Air-Toss
Ignite	Ignite	Ignite	Ignite

Attack Information

Power Factor	Type	Element	Status Effect	Guard Type
0.30	Physical	Moon	Silence (100%)	Block
0.21	Physical	—	—	Block
0.19	Physical	—	—	Block
1.43 (creeping shock.); 1.30 (weapon shock.)	Physical	Moon	Silence (10%)	None
1.65	Physical	Moon	Silence (35%)	None
1.17	Physical	—	—	Block
0.13	Physical	—	—	Block
1.43	Physical	Moon	Silence (10%)	None

SAMURAI

♡ —

An advanced Nobody well-suited to combat in close quarters. It pairs naturally high attack power with a dual blade attack that brings targets into submission. These Nobodies serve under Roxas.

WORLDS

- *The Castle That Never Was*

HP FACTOR	EXP FACTOR	DEF FACTOR	STUN	MUNNY
11.60	5.03	1.25	Stun atk.	11

Mission(s)	LVL	Chance of Item Drop
33	12	—
71	41	—
91	14	—

Item Drops
None
None
None
None
None
None

Elemental Attack Vulnerability			
Fire	Ice	Thunder	Aero
0.99	1.12	0.41	1.25

Status Attack Vulnerability			
Ignite	Freeze	Jolt	Air-Toss
0.30	0.30	0.30	Immune

Attack Information

Power Factor	Type	Element	Status Effect	Guard Type
2.87	Physical	—	—	Block
1.95	Physical	—	—	Counter

SAPPHIRE ELEGY

♡ 23

These mid-sized flying Heartless can blink out when struck, avoiding damage and teleporting to a new location. Deflect their head-butts with a block to knock them out and leave them vulnerable to attack.

WORLDS

- *Wonderland*

HP FACTOR	EXP FACTOR	DEF FACTOR	STUN	MUNNY
2.80	3.63	1.25	Stun atk.	31

Mission(s)	LVL	Chance of Item Drop
47	7	70% (Rune Tech)
55	20	70% (Rune Tech)
65	20	40% (Rune Tech)
67	30	40% (Rune Tech+)
85	20	50% (Rune Tech++)

Item Drops
None
None
Rune Tech
Rune Tech
Rune Tech+
Rune Tech++

Elemental Attack Vulnerability			
Fire	Ice	Thunder	Aero
2.20	2.28	0.86	2.42

Status Attack Vulnerability			
Ignite	Freeze	Jolt	Air-Toss
Immune	Immune	Immune	Immune

Attack Information

Power Factor	Type	Element	Status Effect	Guard Type
1.30	Physical	Illusion	Flip-Foot (20%)	Counter

SCARLET TANGO

♡ 15

These small flying Heartless strike with fireballs that bounce around and you can't interrupt their magic by attacking. Fire-based attacks can ignite your character, which will gradually sap your HP for as long as it lasts.

WORLDS

- *Twilight Town*
- *Agrabah*

HP FACTOR	EXP FACTOR	DEF FACTOR	STUN	MUNNY
1.00	2.10	1.25	Stun atk.	16

Mission(s)	LVL	Chance of Item Drop
07	13	10% (Blazing Shard)
15	5	5% (Blazing Shard)
16, 18, 21, 24, 32, 34	8	5% (Blazing Shard)
74, 75, 89, 90	20	5% (Blazing Crystal)
82	30	5% (Blazing Crystal)

Item Drops
Blazing Shard
Blazing Shard
None
None
None
Blazing Crystal

Elemental Attack Vulnerability			
Fire	Ice	Thunder	Aero
Absorb	4.80	0.90	2.55

Status Attack Vulnerability			
Ignite	Freeze	Jolt	Air-Toss
None	1.50	1.00	1.00

Attack Information

Power Factor	Type	Element	Status Effect	Guard Type
0.98	Physical	Fire	Ignite (70%)	Block

SCORCHING SPHERE ♡ 46

Sharp spikes cover these large, fiery Heartless. Although they are impervious during their spin attack, you can slow their onslaught with a block, bringing them to an eventual halt. Alternatively, Blizzard magic will stop them with a single blast.

WORLDS

- Olympus Coliseum

HP FACTOR	EXP FACTOR	DEF FACTOR	STUN	MUNNY
3.60	5.63	2.90	None	32

Mission(s)	LVL	Chance of Item Drop
84	52	100% (Gear Component D)

Item Drops
None
None
None
None
None
Gear Component D

Elemental Attack Vulnerability			
Fire	Ice	Thunder	Aero
Absorb	0.73	Immune	Immune

Status Attack Vulnerability			
Ignite	Freeze	Jolt	Air-Toss
Immune	0.20	0.02	Immune

Attack Information				
Power Factor	Type	Element	Status Effect	Guard Type
0.40	Physical	Fire	Ignite (10%)	Block
2.02	Physical	Illusion	Flip-Foot (20%)	None

SERGEANT ♡ 21

Blocking works well against these mid-sized Heartless to stop their various kick attacks and create an opening. You can also nullify their attacks and trip them up by hitting them with a combo finisher when they start kicking.

WORLDS

- Beast's Castle
- Wonderland

HP FACTOR	EXP FACTOR	DEF FACTOR	STUN	MUNNY
4.79	3.10	1.35	Stun atk.	21

Mission(s)	LVL	Chance of Item Drop
22, 27, 28, 29, 31	11	30% (Shining Shard)
38, 49	11	50% (Shining Shard)
51	11	18% (Blazing Gem)
83	30	40% (Shield Tech+)

Item Drops
None
Shining Shard
Shining Shard
Blazing Gem
None
Shield Tech+

Elemental Attack Vulnerability			
Fire	Ice	Thunder	Aero
1.32	0.35	0.56	1.70

Status Attack Vulnerability			
Ignite	Freeze	Jolt	Air-Toss
0.60	0.60	0.60	0.60

Attack Information				
Power Factor	Type	Element	Status Effect	Guard Type
1.17	Physical	—	—	Block
1.70	Physical	—	—	Counter
1.17	Physical	—	—	Counter

SHADOW

♡ —

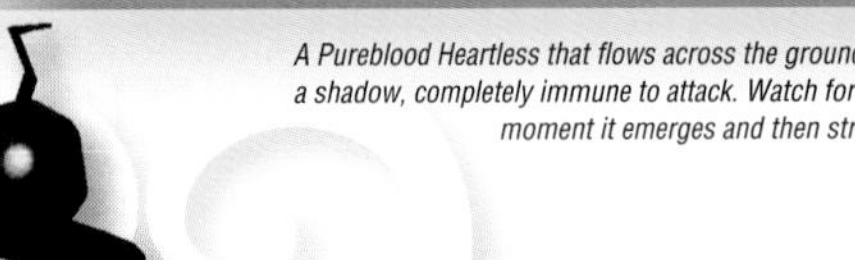

A Pureblood Heartless that flows across the ground as a shadow, completely immune to attack. Watch for the moment it emerges and then strike!

WORLDS

- Twilight Town
- Agrabah
- Beast's Castle

HP FACTOR	EXP FACTOR	DEF FACTOR	STUN	MUNNY
0.32	1.00	1.02	Normal atk.	5

Mission(s)	LVL	Chance of Item Drop
02, 05, 07, 08, 09	1	10% (Potion)
14	6	—
02, 21, 22, 23, 26, 27, 28, 29	8	10% (Potion)
35	12	10% (Potion)
42, 43[1]	12	25% (Ether)
59	25	15% (Moonstone)
61	25	—
74, 77, 83, 89	30	7% (Blazing Gem)

Item Drops
Potion
Potion
Ether
Moonstone
None
Blazing Gem

Elemental Attack Vulnerability			
Fire	Ice	Thunder	Aero
2.20	1.60	0.60	1.70

Status Attack Vulnerability			
Ignite	Freeze	Jolt	Air-Toss
1.00	1.00	1.00	1.00

Attack Information				
Power Factor	Type	Element	Status Effect	Guard Type
0.40	Physical	—	—	Block
1.17	Physical	—	—	Block

SHADOW GLOB

♡ —

These dark masses tend to attract Purebloods. Destroy them on sight.

WORLDS

- Twilight Town
- Agrabah
- Wonderland

HP FACTOR	EXP FACTOR	DEF FACTOR	STUN	MUNNY
0.66	1.00	1.00	None	6

Mission(s)	LVL	Chance of Item Drop
20	8	—
26	11	—
63	32	—
76	43	—

Item Drops
None
None
None
None
None
None

Elemental Attack Vulnerability			
Fire	Ice	Thunder	Aero
2.10	2.20	0.90	2.50

Status Attack Vulnerability			
Ignite	Freeze	Jolt	Air-Toss
Immune	Immune	Immune	Immune

Attack Information				
Power Factor	Type	Element	Status Effect	Guard Type
—	—	—	—	—

SKATER BOMB

♡ 17

These mid-sized Heartless begin a countdown to self-detonation if you deflect their head-butts with a block. Strike them during the countdown to send their payload hurtling into other enemies. Ice-based attacks like their explosion can freeze your character, hindering their ability to move.

WORLDS

- *Halloween Town*

HP FACTOR	EXP FACTOR	DEF FACTOR	STUN	MUNNY
2.39	2.95	1.32	Stun atk.	21

Mission(s)	LVL	Chance of Item Drop
42	16	30% (Frost Shard)
52, 54	16	50% (Frost Gem)

Item Drops
None
None
Frost Shard
Frost Gem
None
None

Elemental Attack Vulnerability			
Fire	Ice	Thunder	Aero
4.40	Absorb	1.50	4.25

Status Attack Vulnerability			
Ignite	Freeze	Jolt	Air-Toss
0.70	Immune	1.00	1.00

Attack Information				
Power Factor	Type	Element	Status Effect	Guard Type
1.54	Physical	—	—	Counter
2.13	Physical	Ice	Freeze (100%)	None
2.13	Physical	Ice	Freeze (100%)	None

SKY GRAPPLER

♡ 51

These mid-sized flying Heartless put the wind to expert use when attacking. They move swiftly, but are vulnerable just after kicking, so be ready to mount a counteroffensive. They also retain their kind's immunity to Aero magic.

WORLDS

- *Olympus Coliseum*

HP FACTOR	EXP FACTOR	DEF FACTOR	STUN	MUNNY
5.20	6.08	1.37	Normal atk.	—

Mission(s)	LVL	Chance of Item Drop
73	42	Premium Orb

Item Drops
None
None
None
None
None
Premium Orb

Elemental Attack Vulnerability			
Fire	Ice	Thunder	Aero
1.10	1.20	0.45	Absorb

Status Attack Vulnerability			
Ignite	Freeze	Jolt	Air-Toss
0.80	0.80	1.30	Immune

Attack Information				
Power Factor	Type	Element	Status Effect	Guard Type
1.76	Physical	Light	Null Movement (30%)	Block
1.41	Physical	—	—	Counter
1.30	Physical	—	—	Block
1.54	Physical	Aero	Air-Toss (100%)	Block

SNAPPER DOG

♡ 23

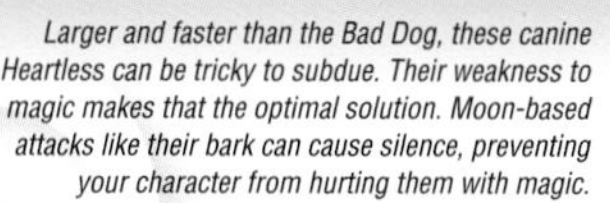

Larger and faster than the Bad Dog, these canine Heartless can be tricky to subdue. Their weakness to magic makes that the optimal solution. Moon-based attacks like their bark can cause silence, preventing your character from hurting them with magic.

WORLDS

- *Beast's Castle*

HP FACTOR	EXP FACTOR	DEF FACTOR	STUN	MUNNY
5.60	3.73	1.35	Stun atk.	26

Mission(s)	LVL	Chance of Item Drop
27, 28, 29, 31, 35	12	30% (Ether)
38, 49, 50	12	80% (Power Tech)

Item Drops
None
Ether
Power Tech
None
None
None

Elemental Attack Vulnerability			
Fire	Ice	Thunder	Aero
1.93	2.20	0.83	2.34

Status Attack Vulnerability			
Ignite	Freeze	Jolt	Air-Toss
1.20	1.20	1.20	1.20

Attack Information				
Power Factor	Type	Element	Status Effect	Guard Type
1.76	Physical	—	—	Counter
1.17	Physical	Moon	Silence (10%)	Block

SNOWY CRYSTAL

♡ 21

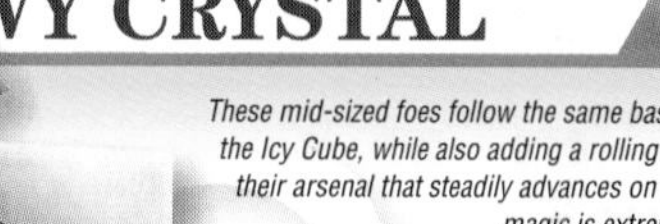

These mid-sized foes follow the same basic patterns as the Icy Cube, while also adding a rolling shockwave to their arsenal that steadily advances on its target. Fire magic is extremely effective.

WORLDS

- *Beast's Castle*
- *Olympus Coliseum*
- *Halloween Town*

HP FACTOR	EXP FACTOR	DEF FACTOR	STUN	MUNNY
5.20	3.20	1.70	Stun atk.	25

Mission(s)	LVL	Chance of Item Drop
35	12	50% (Ether)
45, 49, 52	22	30% (Frost Shard)
62	22	18% (Frost Gem)
73, 83	30	10% (Frost Crystal)
79	22	10% (Frost Crystal)

Item Drops
None
Ether
Frost Shard
Frost Shard
Frost Gem
Frost Crystal

Elemental Attack Vulnerability			
Fire	Ice	Thunder	Aero
6.60	Absorb	Immune	Immune

Status Attack Vulnerability			
Ignite	Freeze	Jolt	Air-Toss
1.50	Immune	Immune	Immune

Attack Information				
Power Factor	Type	Element	Status Effect	Guard Type
1.43	Physical	Ice	Freeze (15%)	Counter
0.98	Physical	Ice	Freeze (75%)	Block
0.48	Physical	Ice	Freeze (2%)	Block
1.17	Physical	Ice	Freeze (100%)	None

SOLDIER

16

These small Heartless primarily use their claws and a flurry of kicks to attack. The latter can be deflected with a block to trip them up.

WORLDS

- *Beast's Castle*
- *Olympus Coliseum*

HP FACTOR	EXP FACTOR	DEF FACTOR	STUN
1.60	2.28	1.20	Normal atk.

MUNNY **11**

Mission(s)	LVL	Chance of Item Drop
22, 27, 28	10	30% (Panacea)
40, 49	10	40% (Shield Tech)
50	22	—
39, 61	10	—
63	20	45% (Combo Tech++)

Item Drops
None
Panacea
Shield Tech
None
None
Combo Tech++

Elemental Attack Vulnerability			
Fire	Ice	Thunder	Aero
4.40	4.80	1.80	5.10

Status Attack Vulnerability			
Ignite	Freeze	Jolt	Air-Toss
1.00	1.00	1.00	1.00

Attack Information				
Power Factor	Type	Element	Status Effect	Guard Type
0.90	Physical	—	—	Block
1.43	Physical	—	—	Counter

SOLID ARMOR

45

Armor covers every inch of these large Heartless, allowing them to deflect blows from every direction. Instead, aim for the head and knock them down, rendering them vulnerable to further attack. Use Blizzard magic to keep them down longer.

WORLDS

- *Agrabah*

HP FACTOR	EXP FACTOR	DEF FACTOR	STUN
12.96	5.28	2.30	None

MUNNY **32**

Mission(s)	LVL	Chance of Item Drop
48	27	100% (Shield Tech)
68	35	18% (Lightning Gem)
82	51	90% (Orichalcum)

Item Drops
None
None
Shield Tech
None
Lightning Gem
Orichalcum

Elemental Attack Vulnerability			
Fire	Ice	Thunder	Aero
1.99	2.68	0.58	1.75

Status Attack Vulnerability			
Ignite	Freeze	Jolt	Air-Toss
Immune	Immune	Immune	Immune

Attack Information				
Power Factor	Type	Element	Status Effect	Guard Type
1.20	Physical	—	—	Block
1.30	Physical	—	—	Block
1.80	Physical	Moon	Silence (100%)	None
1.50	Physical	Moon	Silence (100%)	None

SPIKED CRAWLER

46

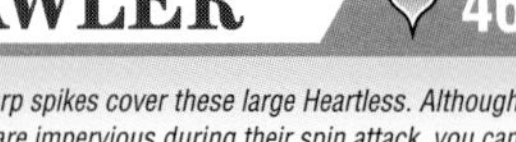

Sharp spikes cover these large Heartless. Although they are impervious during their spin attack, you can slow their onslaught with a block, bringing them to an eventual halt. Alternatively, Thunder magic will stop them with a single blast.

WORLDS

- *Agrabah*

HP FACTOR	EXP FACTOR	DEF FACTOR	STUN
4.40	5.73	3.00	None

MUNNY **21**

Mission(s)	LVL	Chance of Item Drop
82	51	—

Item Drops
None
None
None
None
None
None

Elemental Attack Vulnerability			
Fire	Ice	Thunder	Aero
0.44	0.49	0.32	0.54

Status Attack Vulnerability			
Ignite	Freeze	Jolt	Air-Toss
0.05	0.05	0.20	Immune

Attack Information				
Power Factor	Type	Element	Status Effect	Guard Type
0.73	Physical	Light	Null Movement (20%)	Block
2.02	Physical	Light	Null Movement (40%)	None

STALWART BLADE

71

This magic-resistant knight Heartless's skillful defense makes it tough to finish off. Although its focused slash can be stopped by a block, blasting the knight with Aeroga while it is storing up energy will stagger it, opening it up to extra damage, especially from magic.

WORLDS

- *Olympus Coliseum*
- *Twilight Town*

HP FACTOR	EXP FACTOR	DEF FACTOR	STUN
6.88	12.13	1.60	None

MUNNY **37**

Mission(s)	LVL	Chance of Item Drop
73, 89	50	50% (Adamantite)

Item Drops
None
None
None
None
None
Adamantite

Elemental Attack Vulnerability			
Fire	Ice	Thunder	Aero
Absorb	Absorb	Absorb	1.13

Status Attack Vulnerability			
Ignite	Freeze	Jolt	Air-Toss
Immune	Immune	Immune	Immune

Attack Information				
Power Factor	Type	Element	Status Effect	Guard Type
1.32	Physical	—	—	Block
0.57	Physical	—	—	Block
1.75	Physical	Earth	HP halved (70%)	Counter
1.52	Physical	Time	Defense Lv. 1 (30%)	None
1.34	Physical	Aero	Air-Toss (100%)	Block

STORM BOMB ♡ 17

These mid-sized Heartless begin a countdown to self-detonation if you deflect their head-butts with a block. Avoid being sucked in by the whirlwind they produce during the countdown by jumping or gliding away.

WORLDS

- *Twilight Town*

HP FACTOR	EXP FACTOR	DEF FACTOR	STUN
2.08	2.80	1.32	Stun atk.

MUNNY 17

Mission(s)	LVL	Chance of Item Drop
75, 89	20	30% (Combo Tech++)

Item Drops
None
None
None
None
None
Combo Tech++

Elemental Attack Vulnerability			
Fire	Ice	Thunder	Aero
1.06	2.13	0.80	Absorb

Status Attack Vulnerability			
Ignite	Freeze	Jolt	Air-Toss
Ignore	1.00	1.00	Ignore

Attack Information				
Power Factor	Type	Element	Status Effect	Guard Type
1.43	Physical	—	—	Counter
2.08	Physical	Aero	Air-Toss (100%)	None
2.08	Physical	Aero	Air-Toss (100%)	None

STRIPED ARIA

♡ 31

These small flying Heartless boast high defense and are resistant to physical attacks. Take them down with magic. Time-based attacks like their time missiles can rewind your defense to level 1, which causes your character to take more damage than normal.

WORLDS

- *Olympus Coliseum*
- *Wonderland*

HP FACTOR	EXP FACTOR	DEF FACTOR	STUN
5.60	4.63	2.00	Stun atk.

MUNNY 31

Mission(s)	LVL	Chance of Item Drop
47	20	40% (Gust Shard)
55, 61	20	21% (Bronze)
65	20	30% (Gear Component C)
85	20	9% (Luck Tech)

Item Drops
None
None
Gust Shard
Bronze
Gear Component C
Luck Tech

Elemental Attack Vulnerability			
Fire	Ice	Thunder	Aero
7.14	8.10	3.00	8.80

Status Attack Vulnerability			
Ignite	Freeze	Jolt	Air-Toss
1.50	1.50	1.50	1.50

Attack Information				
Power Factor	Type	Element	Status Effect	Guard Type
1.30	Physical	Time	Defense Lv. 1 (70%)	Block

SWITCH LAUNCHER

♡ 16

These mid-sized cannon Heartless fire shots that rain down from above. Use dodge rolls or air slides to evacuate the target area. Their head-on shots can't be blocked and will also warp victims into point-blank range. Regular attacks won't throw them off balance.

WORLDS

- *Olympus Coliseum*

HP FACTOR	EXP FACTOR	DEF FACTOR	STUN
3.60	2.58	1.70	None

MUNNY —

Mission(s)	LVL	Chance of Item Drop
73	40	50% (Shining Crystal)

Item Drops
None
None
None
None
None
Shining Crystal

Elemental Attack Vulnerability			
Fire	Ice	Thunder	Aero
1.47	1.87	0.90	1.98

Status Attack Vulnerability			
Ignite	Freeze	Jolt	Air-Toss
0.40	0.40	1.50	Immune

Attack Information				
Power Factor	Type	Element	Status Effect	Guard Type
1.43	Physical	—	—	None
1.43	Physical	Light	Null Movement (20%)	None

TAILBUNKER

♡ 42

These large aerial Heartless are hard to hit in mid-flight. Strike their wings and tail to force them to land, then target the head, which is susceptible to Blizzard magic.

WORLDS

- *Twilight Town*
- *Olympus Coliseum*

HP FACTOR	EXP FACTOR	DEF FACTOR	STUN
5.60	4.75	1.50~ 2.00	None

MUNNY 22

Mission(s)	LVL	Chance of Item Drop
17	14	100% (Aerial Tech)
59, 61	30	30% (Gear Component B)

Item Drops
None
Aerial Tech
None
Gear Component B
None
None

Elemental Attack Vulnerability			
Fire	Ice	Thunder	Aero
Absorb	1.60	0.45	1.38

Status Attack Vulnerability			
Ignite	Freeze	Jolt	Air-Toss
Immune	0.10	Immune	Immune

Attack Information				
Power Factor	Type	Element	Status Effect	Guard Type
1.30	Physical	—	—	None
1.30	Physical	—	—	Block
1.76	Physical	—	—	Block
1.63	Physical	—	—	Counter
1.43	Physical	—	—	Block
1.30	Physical	Fire	Ignite (20%)[1]	Block

TENTACLAW

♡ 0

This tentacle-shaped Heartless strikes with a savage bite. Block it or dodge roll out of the way, and then counterattack.

WORLDS

- *Halloween Town*

HP FACTOR	EXP FACTOR	DEF FACTOR	STUN	MUNNY
2.00	1.63	1.25	Normal atk.	—

Mission(s)	LVL	Chance of Item Drop
62	32	50% (Gear Component C)
66	40	50% (Gear Component C)

Item Drops
None
None
None
None
Gear Component C
None

Elemental Attack Vulnerability			
Fire	Ice	Thunder	Aero
1.40	1.40	1.10	1.10

Status Attack Vulnerability			
Ignite	Freeze	Jolt	Air-Toss
0.10	0.10	0.10	Immune

Attack Information

Power Factor	Type	Element	Status Effect	Guard Type
0.41	Physical	—	—	Block
0.41	Physical	—	—	Block
[1]	Magical	—	—	None

TRICKY MONKEY

♡ 22

Raw noise is the chief weapon of these large Heartless that lurk in treasure chests. Return their sound bullets and avoid getting flip-footed by blocking.

WORLDS

- *Twilight Town*
- *Agrabah*
- *Olympus Coliseum*

HP FACTOR	EXP FACTOR	DEF FACTOR	STUN	MUNNY
2.80	3.43	1.35	None	41

Mission(s)	LVL	Chance of Item Drop
55	24	30% (Gear Component B)
56	26	30% (Gear Component B)
66	40	50% (Shining Gem)
75	42	30% (Shining Crystal)
79	49	30% (Shining Crystal)
82	51	30% (Shining Crystal)
84	52	30% (Shining Crystal)
89	59	30% (Shining Crystal)

Item Drops
None
None
None
Gear Component B
Shining Gem
Shining Crystal

Elemental Attack Vulnerability			
Fire	Ice	Thunder	Aero
2.20	2.00	0.75	2.55

Status Attack Vulnerability			
Ignite	Freeze	Jolt	Air-Toss
0.60	0.60	0.60	0.60

Attack Information

Power Factor	Type	Element	Status Effect	Guard Type
1.17	Physical	Illusion	Flip-Foot (100%)	Counter

TURQUOISE MARCH

♡ 14

These small flying Heartless shoot water missiles. Attacking a Turquoise March during mid-cast won't interrupt its magic, so strike fast! Water-based attacks can damage-drain targets, awarding their HP to the attacker.

WORLDS

- *Never Land*

HP FACTOR	EXP FACTOR	DEF FACTOR	STUN	MUNNY
1.76	1.48	1.09	Stun atk.	25

Mission(s)	LVL	Chance of Item Drop
53, 58, 60	20	7% (Shining Gem)
64	20	20% (Shining Gem)
76	14	4% (Shining Crystal)
77, 86	20	4% (Shining Crystal)

Item Drops
None
None
None
Shining Gem
Shining Gem
Shining Crystal

Elemental Attack Vulnerability			
Fire	Ice	Thunder	Aero
1.46	1.60	1.80	2.55

Status Attack Vulnerability			
Ignite	Freeze	Jolt	Air-Toss
1.50	0.10	1.00	1.00

Attack Information

Power Factor	Type	Element	Status Effect	Guard Type
1.30	Physical	Water	Damage Drain (100%)	Counter

VEIL LIZARD

♡ 23

This camouflaged creature attacks prey with a tongue lash attack. Block it to dizzy the lizard, then strike back. You can nullify its camouflage with a solid hit. Light-based attacks like its glare will zap your radar, disabling the map.

WORLDS

- *Twilight Town*

HP FACTOR	EXP FACTOR	DEF FACTOR	STUN	MUNNY
10.16	3.85	2.35	None	31

Mission(s)	LVL	Chance of Item Drop
23	14	20% (Iron)
89	50	100% (Rune Tech++)

Item Drops
None
Iron
None
None
None
Rune Tech++

Elemental Attack Vulnerability			
Fire	Ice	Thunder	Aero
1.18	1.33	0.50	1.42

Status Attack Vulnerability			
Ignite	Freeze	Jolt	Air-Toss
Ignore	0.27	Ignore	Ignore

Attack Information

Power Factor	Type	Element	Status Effect	Guard Type
1.60	Physical	Flower	Darkness (20%)	Block
0	Physical	—	—	
1.70	Magical	Nil	Null Defense (100%)	None
1.43	Physical	Light	Radar Zap (80%)	Block

WATCHER — 12

These small, flying drone Heartles fire lasers that can be returned with a block, but they will respond with an even stronger power laser. Spaced-based attacks like this power laser can shoe-glue you, robbing you of the ability to jump.

WORLDS

- *Twilight Town*
- *Olympus Coliseum*

HP FACTOR	EXP FACTOR	DEF FACTOR	STUN	MUNNY
1.19	1.20	1.30	Stun atk.	15

Mission(s)	LVL	Chance of Item Drop
08, 11	3	10% (Potion)
20, 23	3	30% (Ether)
73	20	20% (Gust Gem)

Item Drops
Potion
Ether
None
None
None
Gust Gem

Elemental Attack Vulnerability			
Fire	Ice	Thunder	Aero
2.93	3.20	1.80	3.40

Status Attack Vulnerability			
Ignite	Freeze	Jolt	Air-Toss
1.00	1.00	1.00	1.00

Attack Information

Power Factor	Type	Element	Status Effect	Guard Type
0.40	Physical	—	—	Counter
1.63	Physical	Space	Shoe-Glue (15%)	None

WAVECREST — 64

These large aerial Heartless use their potent water breath to attack their prey. This strain cannot be forced to land, so face them well-equipped to do combat in midair.

WORLDS

- *Never Land*

HP FACTOR	EXP FACTOR	DEF FACTOR	STUN	MUNNY
4.40	7.78	1.50~2.05	None	28

Mission(s)	LVL	Chance of Item Drop
53	29	50% (Shining Gem)
76	24	20% (Gust Crystal)

Item Drops
None
None
None
Shining Gem
None
Gust Crystal

Elemental Attack Vulnerability			
Fire	Ice	Thunder	Aero
0.50	Immune	0.68	Immune

Status Attack Vulnerability			
Ignite	Freeze	Jolt	Air-Toss
0.10	Immune	Immune	Immune

Attack Information

Power Factor	Type	Element	Status Effect	Guard Type
1.54	Physical	—	—	None
1.43	Physical	—	—	Block
1.92	Physical	—	—	Counter
1.76	Physical	Water	Damage Drain (20%)	Block

WINDSTORM — 62

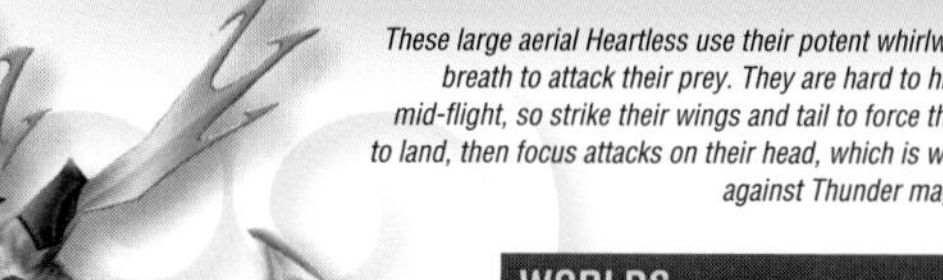

These large aerial Heartless use their potent whirlwind breath to attack their prey. They are hard to hit in mid-flight, so strike their wings and tail to force them to land, then focus attacks on their head, which is weak against Thunder magic.

WORLDS

- *Halloween Town*

HP FACTOR	EXP FACTOR	DEF FACTOR	STUN	MUNNY
6.80	7.48	1.85~2.08	None	28

Mission(s)	LVL	Chance of Item Drop
87	52	100% (Gust Crystal)

Item Drops
None
None
None
None
None
Gust Crystal

Elemental Attack Vulnerability			
Fire	Ice	Thunder	Aero
Immune	Immune	0.51	0.26

Status Attack Vulnerability			
Ignite	Freeze	Jolt	Air-Toss
Immune	0.02	0.30	Immune

Attack Information

Power Factor	Type	Element	Status Effect	Guard Type
1.54	Physical	—	—	None
1.43	Physical	—	—	Block
1.87	Physical	Aero	Air-Toss (80%)	Block
1.70	Physical	Aero	Air-Toss (100%)	Counter
1.43	Physical	—	—	Block
1.54	Physical	Aero	Air-Toss (100%)	Block

XIGBAR — —

The Organization's No. II, a master of the arrowgun and spatial manipulation. As a long-range fighter, he'll try to keep foes from closing in by warping away as he fires. The full salvo attack he uses in desperate situation is truly devastating.

WORLDS

- *Olympus Coliseum*

HP FACTOR	EXP FACTOR	DEF FACTOR	STUN	MUNNY
5.92	—	1.00	Stun atk.	—

Mission(s)	LVL	Chance of Item Drop
61	31	—

Item Drops
None
None
None
None
None
None

Elemental Attack Vulnerability			
Fire	Ice	Thunder	Aero
1.40	1.56	0.59	1.75

Status Attack Vulnerability			
Ignite	Freeze	Jolt	Air-Toss
Immune	0.02	0.02	Immune

Attack Information

Power Factor	Type	Element	Status Effect	Guard Type
0.16	Physical	—	—	Block
0.16	Physical	—	—	Block

XION: FIRST FORM

 —

Xion, transformed. Sora's memories from each world have multiplied her powers. Her barrier restores HP. Stop it by striking with your weapon before she can raise it. She'll counter if you block her sword combo, so dodge roll out of the way instead. She will always spread her wings to signal her Sonic Blade charge.

WORLDS

- *Twilight Town (map is Wonderland)*

HP FACTOR	EXP FACTOR	DEF FACTOR	STUN	MUNNY
2.80	0	1.80	None	—

Mission(s)	LVL	Chance of Item Drop
92	61	—

Item Drops
None
None
None
None
None
None

Elemental Attack Vulnerability			
Fire	Ice	Thunder	Aero
0.36	0.40	0.15	0.45

Status Attack Vulnerability			
Ignite	Freeze	Jolt	Air-Toss
Immune	Immune	Immune	Immune

Attack Information

Power Factor	Type	Element	Status Effect	Guard Type
0.35 (1st attack); 0.45 (2nd attack); 1.00 (3rd attack)	Physical	—	—	Counter
1.54	Physical	—	—	None
1.60	Physical	—	—	None
1.29	Physical	—	—	Block
1.85	Physical	—	—	Block

XION: SECOND FORM

 —

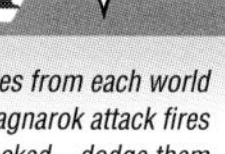

Xion, transformed. Sora's memories from each world have multiplied her powers. Her Ragnarok attack fires homing lasers that cannot be blocked—dodge them instead. However, play too hard to get and she'll fire repeatedly. Strike with your weapon if you see her trying to raise a barrier to prevent it from healing her.

WORLDS

- *Twilight Town (map is Halloween Town)*

HP FACTOR	EXP FACTOR	DEF FACTOR	STUN	MUNNY
5.60	0	1.80	None	—

Mission(s)	LVL	Chance of Item Drop
92	61	—

Item Drops
None
None
None
None
None
None

Elemental Attack Vulnerability			
Fire	Ice	Thunder	Aero
0.36	0.40	0.15	0.45

Status Attack Vulnerability			
Ignite	Freeze	Jolt	Air-Toss
Immune	Immune	Immune	Immune

Attack Information

Power Factor	Type	Element	Status Effect	Guard Type
0.54 (1st attack); 0.60 (2nd attack); 1.08 (3rd attack)	Physical	—	—	Counter
1.60	Physical	—	—	None
1.65	Physical	—	—	None
0.21	Magical	Nil	Null Defense (100%)	None
1.90	Physical	—	—	Block

XION: THIRD FORM

 —

Xion, transformed. Sora's memories from each world have multiplied her powers. Beware her Ars Arcanum attack, a fierce flurry of blows from her four arms. Most of her attacks cannot be blocked, so dodge roll out of the way, and then counter. Strike with your weapon if you see her trying to raise a barrier to prevent it from healing her.

WORLDS

- *Twilight Town (map is Agrabah)*

HP FACTOR	EXP FACTOR	DEF FACTOR	STUN	MUNNY
3.76	0	1.80	None	—

Mission(s)	LVL	Chance of Item Drop
92	61	—

Item Drops
None
None
None
None
None
None

Elemental Attack Vulnerability			
Fire	Ice	Thunder	Aero
0.31	0.35	0.13	0.40

Status Attack Vulnerability			
Ignite	Freeze	Jolt	Air-Toss
Immune	Immune	Immune	Immune

Attack Information

Power Factor	Type	Element	Status Effect	Guard Type
0.41 (1st attack); 0.42 (2nd attack); 1.03 (3rd attack)	Physical	—	—	Counter
1.60	Physical	—	—	None
1.52	Physical	—	—	None
1.33	Physical	—	—	None
1.30	Physical	—	—	Block
1.75	Physical	—	—	Block

XION: FINAL FORM

 —

Xion, transformed. Sora's memories from each world have multiplied her powers. This form packs a new arsenal of moves, including a powerful Final Limit once her HP dwindles. Glide up to her side and take shelter before it connects.

WORLDS

- *Twilight Town (map is Twilight Town)*

HP FACTOR	EXP FACTOR	DEF FACTOR	STUN	MUNNY
9.60	108.98	2.00	None	—

Mission(s)	LVL	Chance of Item Drop
92	61	—

Item Drops
None
None
None
None
None
None

Elemental Attack Vulnerability			
Fire	Ice	Thunder	Aero
0.12	0.20	0.05	0.17

Status Attack Vulnerability			
Ignite	Freeze	Jolt	Air-Toss
Immune	Immune	Immune	Immune

Attack Information

Power Factor	Type	Element	Status Effect	Guard Type
1.05	Physical	—	Random (100%)	Block
0.90	Physical	—	—	Block
1.69	Physical	—	—	Block
1.00	Physical	Earth	HP Drain (100%)	Block
1.34	Physical	—	—	None
0.06	Magical	Nil	Null Defense (100%)	None

YELLOW OPERA

13

These small flying Heartless strike with head-butts and Thunder magic that can't be interrupted by attacking. Lighting-based attacks can jolt your character. Coming into contact with something in that state will cost up to 10% of your character's max HP.

WORLDS

- Twilight Town
- Olympus Coliseum

HP FACTOR	EXP FACTOR	DEF FACTOR	STUN	MUNNY
0.32	1.38	1.00	Normal atk.	11

Mission(s)	LVL	Chance of Item Drop
02, 03, 04, 11	1	24% (Moonstone)
07	8	24% (Moonstone)
14	3	24% (Moonstone)
23, 25	10	24% (Moonstone)
61	20	24% (Moonstone)

Item Drops
Moonstone
Moonstone
None
Moonstone
None
None

Elemental Attack Vulnerability

Fire	Ice	Thunder	Aero
5.10	0.40	Absorb	1.70

Status Attack Vulnerability

Ignite	Freeze	Jolt	Air-Toss
1.00	1.00	Immune	1.00

Attack Information

Power Factor	Type	Element	Status Effect	Guard Type
0.85	Physical	Thunder	Jolt (10%)	Block
0.98	Physical	Thunder	Jolt (70%)	None

ZIP SLASHER

44

This sword-wielding Heartless's skillfull defense makes it tough to finish off. Its spinning slash has the added effect of damage-draining HP from victims. Watch for it, then evade or deflect it with a block.

WORLDS

- Twilight Town
- Agrabah
- Olympus Coliseum

HP FACTOR	EXP FACTOR	DEF FACTOR	STUN	MUNNY
14.40	5.13	0	None	27

Mission(s)	LVL	Chance of Item Drop
09	22[1]	100% (Moonstone)
23	48	100% (Combo Tech)
34	40	100% (Combo Tech)
41	43	100% (Elixir Recipe)

[1] In Mission Mode, level is 30.

Item Drops
Moonstone
Combo Tech
Elixir Recipe
None
None
None

Elemental Attack Vulnerability

Fire	Ice	Thunder	Aero
Immune	Immune	Immune	Immune

Status Attack Vulnerability

Ignite	Freeze	Jolt	Air-Toss
Immune	1.40	Immune	Immune

Attack Information

Power Factor	Type	Element	Status Effect	Guard Type
1.74	Physical	Water	Damage Drain (100%)	Block
0.75	Physical	—	—	Block

UNKNOWN

—

Little is known about this man, save that he wears the coat of our Organization. He has not been seen to engage members in combat, instead merely jumping and guarding while watching our movements. Do enough damage and he'll warp away.

WORLDS

- Twilight Town

HP FACTOR	EXP FACTOR	DEF FACTOR	STUN	MUNNY
—	—	—	Normal atk.	—

Mission(s)	LVL	Chance of Item Drop
74	42	—

Item Drops
None
None
None
None
None
None

Elemental Attack Vulnerability

Fire	Ice	Thunder	Aero
—	—	—	—

Status Attack Vulnerability

Ignite	Freeze	Jolt	Air-Toss
Immune	Immune	Immune	Immune

Attack Information

Power Factor	Type	Element	Status Effect	Guard Type
—	—	—	—	—

UNKNOWN

—

Reports on this figure have existed for some time now. It was assumed this was the man who defeated Xion, but the truth of the matter remains unclear.

WORLDS

- Twilight Town

HP FACTOR	EXP FACTOR	DEF FACTOR	STUN	MUNNY
—	—	—	Normal atk.	—

Mission(s)	LVL	Chance of Item Drop
75	42	—

Item Drops
None
None
None
None
None
None

Elemental Attack Vulnerability

Fire	Ice	Thunder	Aero
—	—	—	—

Status Attack Vulnerability

Ignite	Freeze	Jolt	Air-Toss
Immune	Immune	Immune	Immune

Attack Information

Power Factor	Type	Element	Status Effect	Guard Type
—	—	—	—	—

WRITTEN BY DAN BIRLEW & BRYAN STRATTON

BradyGAMES® is a registered trademark of Penguin Group (USA) Inc. All rights reserved, including the right of reproduction in whole or in part in any form.

DK/BradyGames, a division of Penguin Group (USA) Inc.
800 East 96th Street, 3rd Floor
Indianapolis, IN 46240

©Disney and developed by SQUARE ENIX/h.a.n.d. SQUARE ENIX and the SQUARE ENIX logo are registered trademarks of Square Enix Holdings Co., Ltd.

All Rights Reserved. SQUARE ENIX and the SQUARE ENIX logo are registered trademarks of Square Enix Holdings Co., Ltd. in the United States and/or other countries.

Please be advised that the ESRB ratings icons, "EC", "E", "E10+", "T", "M", "AO", and "RP" are trademarks owned by the Entertainment Software Association, and may only be used with their permission and authority. For information regarding whether a product has been rated by the ESRB, please visit www.esrb.org. For permission to use the ratings icons, please contact the ESA at esrblicenseinfo@theesa.com.

ISBN: 978-0-7440-1148-7

Printing Code: The rightmost double-digit number is the year of the book's printing; the rightmost single-digit number is the number of the book's printing. For example, 09-1 shows that the first printing of the book occurred in 2009.

12 11 10 09 4 3 2 1

Printed in the USA.

BRADY GAMES STAFF

Publisher
David Waybright

Editor-In-Chief
H. Leigh Davis

Licensing Director
Mike Degler

Marketing Director
Debby Neubauer

International Translations
Brian Saliba

CREDITS

Title Manager
Tim Cox

Screenshot Editor
Michael Owen

Book Designer
Keith Lowe

Production Designer
Tracy Wehmeyer

Copy Editor
Angie Blau

Translations
Jeremy Blaustein, Zpang Inc.